Digital Forensics Cookbook

Field-Tested Recipes for Real-World Investigations Across Windows, macOS, Linux, iOS, and Android

Cody Bounds

<packt>

Digital Forensics Cookbook

Portfolio Director: Vijin Boricha
Relationship Lead: Prachi Sawant
Project Manager: Gandhali Raut
Content Engineer: Akanksha Gupta, Rebecca Youé, Kinnari Chohan, Swathi Ajayakumar
Technical Editor: Nithik Cheruvakodan
Copy Editor: Akanksha Gupta
Indexer: Hemangini Bari
Proofreader: Akanksha Gupta, Shubhra Mayuri, Tazeen Shaikh
Production Designer: Ponraj Dhandapani
Growth Lead: Ankita Thakur

First published: March 2026

Production reference: 1300326

Published by Packt Publishing Ltd.
Grosvenor House
11 St Paul's Square
Birmingham
B3 1RB, UK.

ISBN 978-1-80512-755-0
`www.packtpub.com`

To my children, who are my reason for everything I do – and a constant reminder of why the pursuit of truth and justice matters.

"For nothing is hidden that will not be disclosed, and nothing concealed that will not be known or brought out into the open." – Luke 8:17

– Cody Bounds

Foreword

Real investigations do not happen in a vacuum, and they certainly do not happen under perfect conditions. Whether you are walking into a chaotic on-scene seizure, spinning up remote triage across thousands of enterprise endpoints, or staring down a sophisticated anti-forensics attempt, the margin for error is razor-thin. Evidence is volatile, devices are encrypted, and the sheer volume of data we are expected to analyze grows exponentially every year.

We live in an era of incredible automated tools, and there is a dangerous temptation in our industry to rely entirely on them. But automation does not replace the human examiner. A parser will inevitably fail. Timestamps will conflict. When that happens, you cannot simply throw your hands up. You have to know how the operating system actually works. You must be able to step outside predefined modules, query SQLite databases, and interpret raw data yourself.

Cody Bounds lives this reality, and that is exactly what makes the Digital Forensics Cookbook such a valuable resource.

Cody cuts through abstract theory to deliver the operational realities of the job. He starts where you do: on the front lines. From the first steps of targeted on-scene triage to scalable network incident response, he outlines a structured, defensible methodology for securing data before it disappears.

Cody distills the exact *recipes* needed to decode the evidence. Breaking down the core artifacts across Microsoft Windows, Apple macOS, Linux, iOS, and Android, this book equips you to reconstruct user behavior across any platform. He strikes a balance between using automation to accelerate your workflow and applying manual techniques to validate your findings. He also tackles the hurdles of anti-forensics, outlining the steps needed to recover what the suspect believed was destroyed.

Being a digital forensic examiner requires a commitment to continuous learning and a strict refusal to be a mere "push-button" operator. You have to understand what the system did so you can prove what the user did.

Cody has delivered the hands-on guidance needed to do exactly that. Keep this book close, practice these techniques, and use them to build accurate, defensible cases.

William Oettinger

Author, Learn Computer Forensics & Learn Mobile Forensics

Adjunct Associate Professor, Digital Forensics

Contributors

About the author

Cody Bounds is a digital forensics examiner and former detective with 15 years of law enforcement experience, specializing in digital forensics investigations. During his career, he has handled a wide range of cases, including complex criminal investigations involving digital evidence, with a focus on practical, defensible forensic methodologies.

Cody holds industry-recognized certifications, including those from IACIS and the SANS Institute, and has extensive experience in evidence acquisition, artifact analysis, and investigative workflows across multiple platforms. He now works in the private sector, continuing to specialize in digital forensics and investigative response, while also teaching and mentoring others in the field.

I would like to thank my family for their patience and support throughout the writing of this book. I am also grateful to the Packt team for their guidance during the publishing process, and to Steve Whalen of Sumuri for his valuable feedback and insight as a technical reviewer.

About the reviewer

Steve Whalen, CFCE, is a Co-Founder of SUMURI LLC, bringing digital forensics experience dating back to 1997 to his work. A former Delaware State Trooper of over 15 years, he served as the agency's first full-time forensic examiner for digital evidence and helped develop their first High Technology Crimes Unit in 2001. Steve is the creator behind successful forensic solutions like PALADIN, RECON, and TALINO Forensic Workstations. He regularly shares his expertise as a technical editor for cybersecurity and forensics publications. A lifelong Delaware resident, Steve is passionate about giving back to the community and leaving the world a little better than he found it. Combining his tech expertise with his humanitarian focus, he developed his own project and product, Catch-A-Predator, to actively help make the world a safer place.

Table of Contents

Preface

Digital evidence is now present in nearly every type of investigation. From computers and mobile devices to cloud services and network infrastructure, modern cases often involve multiple systems operating across different platforms. For investigators and digital forensic practitioners, this presents a fundamental challenge: understanding how to locate, collect, and analyze evidence across an increasingly complex and evolving technological landscape.

Many digital forensics resources focus on specific tools, operating systems, or artifact types in isolation. While these topics are important, real investigations rarely unfold in such a segmented way. A single case may involve a Windows system, a mobile device, cloud-hosted data, and multiple user accounts—each contributing different pieces of the overall picture. Despite these differences, the underlying investigative methodology remains consistent.

Operating systems change. Software evolves. New technologies emerge. What remains constant is the process used to identify, preserve, analyze, and interpret digital evidence.

This book was written with that philosophy in mind.

Rather than presenting digital forensics as a collection of isolated techniques, this book follows the investigative workflow from beginning to end. It starts with triage and evidence acquisition, moves through platform-based analysis across Windows, macOS, Linux, iOS, and Android, and concludes with practical investigative techniques such as artifact analysis, automation, anti-forensics detection, and memory analysis. Each section is designed to reflect how real investigations progress, rather than presenting tools, artifacts, or platforms as isolated topics.

To support this approach, the book incorporates real-world-style datasets that allow you to follow along with each recipe and apply the techniques in a practical context. These datasets are designed to reinforce investigative thinking by demonstrating how artifacts relate to one another across systems rather than in isolation.

My own experience in digital investigations heavily influenced this structure. Before becoming a digital forensics instructor, I spent over fifteen years in law enforcement as both a deputy sheriff and detective. During that time, I worked a wide range of cases, including Internet Crimes Against Children (ICAC) investigations, as well as homicide and other violent crimes. Across these investigations, it became clear that success did not depend on mastering a single tool or platform, but on the ability to think like an investigator and follow digital evidence wherever it appeared.

Digital forensics is not simply about artifacts, tools, or operating systems. It is about investigative thinking.

This book is intended for students, investigators, and digital forensic professionals who want to better understand how digital evidence fits into the broader investigative process. For those new to the field, it provides a structured introduction to how real investigations unfold. For experienced practitioners, it offers practical techniques, cross-platform insights, and investigative perspectives that can be applied in real-world cases.

The goal of this book is simple: to help you develop the mindset and methodology required to conduct thorough, defensible digital forensic investigations.

Who this book is for

This book is intended for digital forensic investigators, incident responders, and security professionals who want to develop practical investigation skills using real-world workflows and realistic datasets. It is also well suited for students and analysts entering the field who want hands-on experience recovering evidence, analyzing artifacts, and thinking like an investigator.

The content is designed to be accessible to those with a basic understanding of operating systems and computer concepts, while still providing meaningful depth for more experienced practitioners. Rather than focusing on any single tool or platform, this book emphasizes investigative methodology and cross-platform analysis, making it applicable across a wide range of environments and technologies.

Readers looking for step-by-step instruction tied to a specific forensic tool or highly specialized niche workflows may find this approach different from traditional resources. Instead, this book is best suited for those who want to understand how digital forensic investigations unfold in practice and how to apply core principles across systems, tools, and scenarios.

What this book covers

Chapter 1, Targeted On-Scene Triage, introduces techniques for quickly assessing systems in the field, identifying relevant data, and prioritizing evidence during initial investigations.

Chapter 2, Network Intrusion Response and Remote Triage, explores remote triage and incident response workflows, focusing on identifying compromised systems and collecting targeted evidence across a network.

Chapter 3, Physical and Cloud-Based Evidence Acquisition, covers the process of acquiring digital evidence from physical devices and cloud-based sources while maintaining forensic integrity and defensibility.

Chapter 4, Microsoft Windows, examines common Windows artifacts and investigative techniques used to reconstruct user activity and system behavior.

Chapter 5, Apple macOS and Linux, explores forensic analysis across macOS and Linux systems, highlighting key artifacts and platform-specific investigative approaches.

Chapter 6, Apple iOS and Android, focuses on mobile device forensics, examining key artifacts and demonstrating how to interpret user activity and system behavior.

Chapter 7, Analysis Automation, introduces automation techniques and tools that help streamline forensic workflows and scale analysis across larger datasets.

Chapter 8, User Artifacts, dives deeper into user-generated artifacts, demonstrating how to interpret activity across applications, files, and system interactions.

Chapter 9, Manual Analysis and Techniques, emphasizes manual verification and analysis methods used to validate findings and uncover additional evidence beyond automated tools.

Chapter 10, Overcoming Anti-Forensics, addresses techniques used to evade detection and demonstrates how investigators can identify and respond to anti-forensic activity.

Chapter 11, Memory Analysis, introduces memory forensics and shows how volatile data can provide critical insights into system activity and ongoing processes.

Appendix A, Digital Forensic Fundamentals, introduces the foundational concepts, terminology, and investigative methodologies used throughout the book.

Appendix B, Digital Forensic Analysis Field Guide, serves as a practical reference for locating and interpreting common artifacts across multiple platforms, helping investigators quickly identify relevant data during examinations.

To get the most out of this book

This book is designed to be both practical and hands-on. To get the most value from it, you should have a basic understanding of operating systems, file systems, and general computer usage. Prior experience with digital forensics tools is helpful but not required.

Each chapter is structured as a series of recipes that demonstrate specific investigative techniques. While individual recipes can be followed independently, the book is designed to be read progressively, as later chapters build on concepts introduced earlier.

Where possible, you are encouraged to work through the examples using the provided datasets. These datasets are intended to simulate real-world scenarios and allow you to apply the techniques in a practical context. Actively working through the data will significantly improve your understanding of how artifacts relate to one another across systems and investigations.

The tools used throughout the book are intended to support the investigative process, not define it. Many of the techniques demonstrated can be applied using alternative tools or manual methods. Focus on understanding the underlying concepts and workflows rather than relying on any one tool.

When working with forensic images and extracted datasets, you will need a tool capable of browsing and extracting data from these sources. Throughout the book, tools such as FTK Imager are commonly used due to their widespread adoption in digital forensics and their ability to access forensic image formats in a read-only manner. However, alternative tools may also be used depending on your environment and availability.

You can also use 7-Zip (`https://www.7-zip.org/download.html`) in combination with the Forensic7z plugin (`https://www.tc4shell.com/en/7zip/forensic7z/`) to browse and extract files from certain forensic image formats for learning purposes. However, dedicated forensic tools such as those referenced throughout this book are generally better suited to real-world examinations, particularly when forensic soundness, validation, and defensibility are required.

Download the example code files

This book includes a complete downloadable code bundle containing all the example projects and files used throughout the chapters. We recommend downloading the bundle so you can follow along smoothly and experiment with the examples.

Use the bundle as a practical starting point. Modify it, extend it, and apply what you learn by creating your own variations as you progress through the chapters.

Get the code bundle

If you bought the book directly from Packt:

1. Go to **packtpub.com**
2. Click your **profile picture** and select **Your Orders**
3. Find this book and click **Download Code**

If you bought this book from Amazon or any other channel partner:

1. Go to `packtpub.com/unlock` or scan the following QR code:

2. Search for this book
3. Sign up or log in to your free Packt account
4. Upload your proof of purchase and download the code bundle locally

Usage note: You're free to use and modify this code for personal learning and non-commercial projects.

Download the color images

Your purchase includes a color, DRM-free PDF copy of this book, ideal for viewing color images, screenshots, and diagrams. Refer to *Free benefits with your book section* at the end of the *Preface* to unlock your PDF copy.

Conventions used

There are a number of text conventions used throughout this book.

`CodeInText`: Indicates code words in text, database table names, folder names, filenames, file extensions, and pathnames. For example: "Application databases are often located under `/data/data/<application_id>/databases/` on Android devices."

A block of code is set as follows:

```
SELECT url, title
FROM urls
ORDER BY last_visit_time DESC;
```

Any command-line input or output is written as follows:

```
fsutil behavior query DisableDeleteNotify
```

Bold: Indicates a new term, an important word, or words that you see on the screen. For example: " Many forensic platforms recover deleted files using **data carving**, which typically relies on identifying a file's header and, when available, its footer (signature) within raw disk space."

> Note
>
> Warnings or important notes appear like this and highlight critical considerations that may impact evidence integrity or analysis results.

Tip

Tips and tricks appear like this and provide practical guidance to improve efficiency during forensic investigations.

Get in touch

Feedback from our readers is always welcome.

General feedback: If you have questions about any aspect of this book or have any general feedback, please email us at `customercare@packt.com` and mention the book's title in the subject of your message.

Errata: Although we have taken every care to ensure the accuracy of our content, mistakes do happen. If you have found a mistake in this book, we would be grateful if you reported this to us. Please visit `http://www.packt.com/submit-errata`, click **Submit Errata**, and fill in the form.

Piracy: If you come across any illegal copies of our works in any form on the internet, we would be grateful if you would provide us with the location address or website name. Please contact us at `copyright@packt.com` with a link to the material.

If you are interested in becoming an author: If there is a topic that you have expertise in and you are interested in either writing or contributing to a book, please visit `http://authors.packt.com/`.

Free benefits with your book

This book includes free benefits designed to support your learning and help you apply what you learn effectively. Activate them now for instant access (see the *How to unlock* section for instructions).

Here's a quick overview of what you can instantly unlock with your purchase:

Complete Code Bundle

Download the full source code for this book's examples and projects.

DRM-Free PDF Version

Download DRM-free PDF and ePub copies of this book.

7-Day Packt Library Access

Get 7-day unlimited access to 8,000+ books and videos. No credit card required.

Available for first-time Packt+ trial users only.

Next-Gen Reader Access

Read this book on Packt Reader with progress sync, dark mode and note-taking.

How to unlock

Scan the QR code (or go to `packtpub.com/unlock`). Search for this book by name, confirm the edition, and then follow the steps on the page.

UNLOCK NOW

Note: Have your invoice handy. Purchases made directly from the Packt website don't require an invoice.

Share your thoughts

Once you've read *Digital Forensics Cookbook*, we'd love to hear your thoughts! Scan the QR code below to go straight to the Amazon review page for this book and share your feedback.

https://packt.link/r/1805127551

Your review is important to us and the tech community and will help us make sure we're delivering excellent quality content.

Part 1

Triage and Evidence Acquisition

In this part of the book, you will learn how to approach digital forensic investigations from the earliest stages, focusing on identifying, prioritizing, and acquiring relevant data. You will explore how to quickly assess systems, perform targeted on-scene triage, and conduct remote triage during network intrusion response scenarios.

You will also learn how to acquire digital evidence in a forensically sound manner, including both physical devices and cloud-based data sources. Emphasis is placed on maintaining evidence integrity, preserving data in a defensible manner, and preparing collected data for further analysis.

This part is organized into the following chapters:

- *Chapter 1, Targeted On-Scene Triage*
- *Chapter 2, Network Intrusion Response and Remote Triage*
- *Chapter 3, Physical and Cloud-Based Evidence Acquisition*

1

Targeted On-Scene Triage

When you're the first on-scene, the clock has already started. From this moment forward, every move carries weight. What you collect, preserve, or overlook can alter the entire course of an investigation and mean the difference between success and failure.

This chapter begins at the front line of digital forensics: identification and collection, where we first interact with systems that may later become the evidence sources we collect for further analysis.

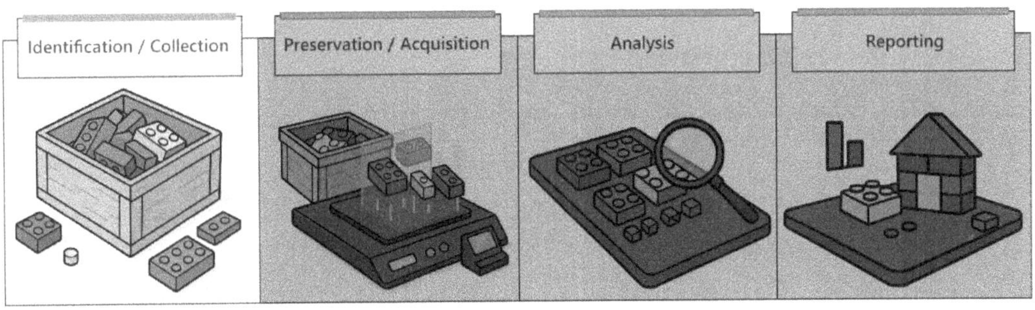

Figure 1.1 – Step one of the digital forensic methodologies: Identification and Collection

Here, evidence isn't neatly contained in a lab; it's alive in unpredictable environments, including powered-on systems, volatile memory, encrypted containers, and unfamiliar networks. The examiner's role is to bring order to chaos by identifying and collecting what matters most. Your level of preparedness may determine whether you can later gain access to encrypted data, recover key artifacts, and ultimately reveal the truth hidden within the system.

Through a targeted triage approach, you'll learn how to prepare your tools, capture critical data efficiently, and maintain evidentiary integrity throughout the process.

In this chapter we're going to cover the following recipes:

- Sanitizing a storage drive
- Preparing a triage USB drive
- Capturing Random-Access Memory (RAM)
- Powered-on systems
- Powered-off systems
- Router interrogation

If you're unfamiliar with the foundational concepts of the digital forensic process, you can learn more in *Appendix A – Digital Forensic Methodologies*.

Note

Your purchase includes a free PDF copy + exclusive extras

Your purchase includes a DRM-free PDF copy of this book, 7-day trial to the Packt+ library (no credit card required), and additional exclusive extras. See the *Free benefits with your book* section in the *Preface* to unlock them instantly and maximize your learning.

Technical requirements

To successfully complete the recipes in this chapter, you will need:

- Two USB drives: One to boot powered-off systems into an alternate operating system and another to serve as a triage or acquisition tool for live systems.
- A computer running Microsoft Windows: Required for preparing media, executing acquisition utilities, and performing basic validation tasks. The latest version of Microsoft Windows 11 is recommended.
- Access to a wireless router: The last recipe in this chapter demonstrates evidence collection from a wireless router.
- A secondary computer or test system (optional): Useful for simulating both powered-on and powered-off target machines during practice scenarios.

Because digital evidence exists across many device types, practicing on diverse hardware will better prepare you for real-world environments.

Sanitizing a storage drive

Just as an investigator avoids contaminating a biological sample with their own DNA, a digital forensic examiner must prevent contaminating evidence with unrelated data. **Sanitization** (sometimes referred to as **sterilization** or *wiping*) is the process of permanently deleting data by overwriting every bit on a storage device, typically with a known pattern such as `0x00`. This ensures that previous data cannot be recovered through standard or forensic methods.

If evidentiary data is unintentionally sanitized, it is permanently lost. In contrast, pre-sanitizing collection media ensures that no residual data contaminates your evidence.

Getting ready

Before you begin sanitizing, insert the storage drive into your computer. ***Verify that the drive does not contain any important data***, as all contents will be permanently erased during this process. Because full sanitization can take significant time depending on drive size and interface speed, it's recommended to start with a smaller-capacity drive (for example, 8 GB or less) while practicing. Before proceeding, download and install the following software tools:

- **Active@ KillDisk** by LSoft Technologies Inc. is free for personal use and capable of securely sanitizing storage devices by overwriting all data. Commercial licenses include advanced features such as parallel drive wiping and automated logging: `https://www.killdisk.com/killdisk-freeware.htm`
- **HxD** is a freeware hex and disk editor developed by Maël Hörz. This application is free for both personal and commercial use and is extremely powerful, offering a read-only mode, hashing, and file comparison capabilities useful to digital forensics: `https://mh-nexus.de/en/hxd/`

How to do it...

1. Install **Active@ KillDisk** and **HxD** on your computer and accept the default installation options during setup.
2. Insert a USB storage drive into your computer. Ensure this drive does not contain any data you wish to keep, as this process will permanently erase all information.
3. Run **Active@ KillDisk**. The software will automatically detect all available storage devices, including both internal and attached drives:

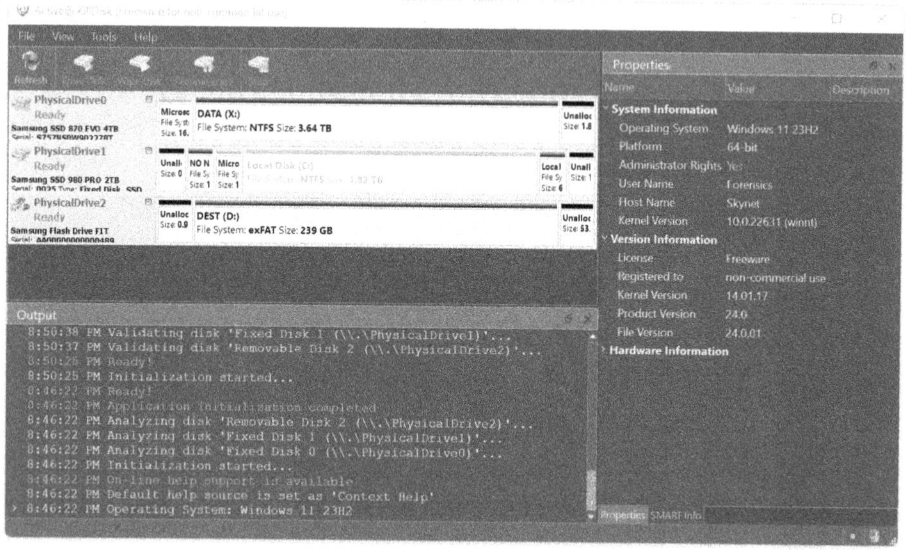

Figure 1.2 – Active@ KillDisk software

4. Select individual partitions or click on the **drive icon** on the left side to select an entire disk. The selected drive or partition will be highlighted in yellow. In this example, a **Samsung Flash Drive FIT** is selected:

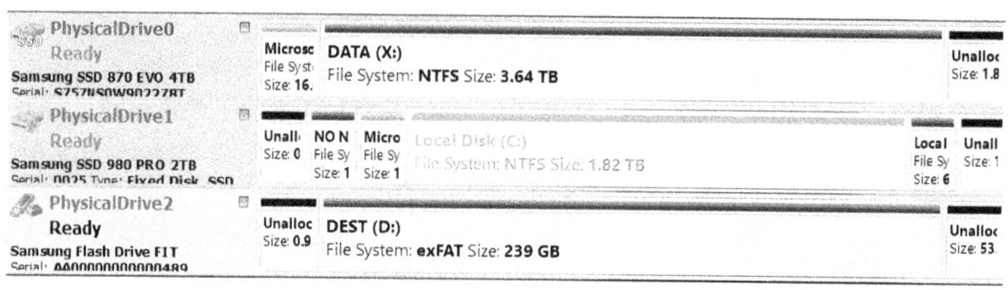

Figure 1.3 – Selected storage drives or partitions will be highlighted in yellow

5. Review the drive details in the right-side **Properties** panel. Double-check the selection before proceeding. Once sanitization begins, all data will be unrecoverable.

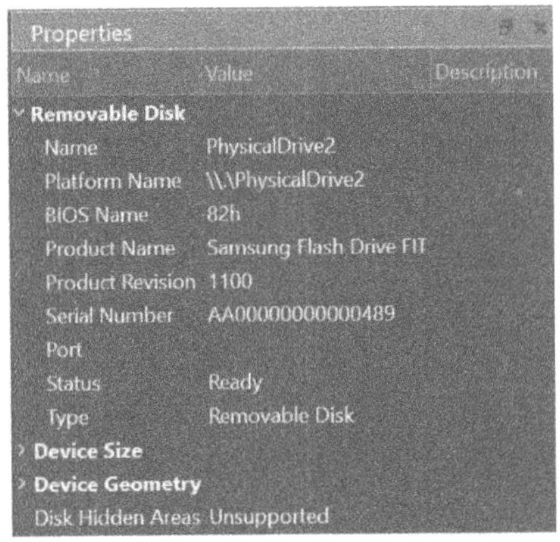

Figure 1.4 – Selected storage drive properties panel

6. After confirming the correct device, select **Erase Disk** from the top menu bar, or use *F10* for shortcut:

Figure 1.5 – Selected Erase Disk or press F10 on the keyboard

7. In the **Erase Disk** window, choose **Select all disk space**, then select **One Pass Zeroes** from the **Erase method** dropdown list. Leave other options unselected. When ready, click **Start**:

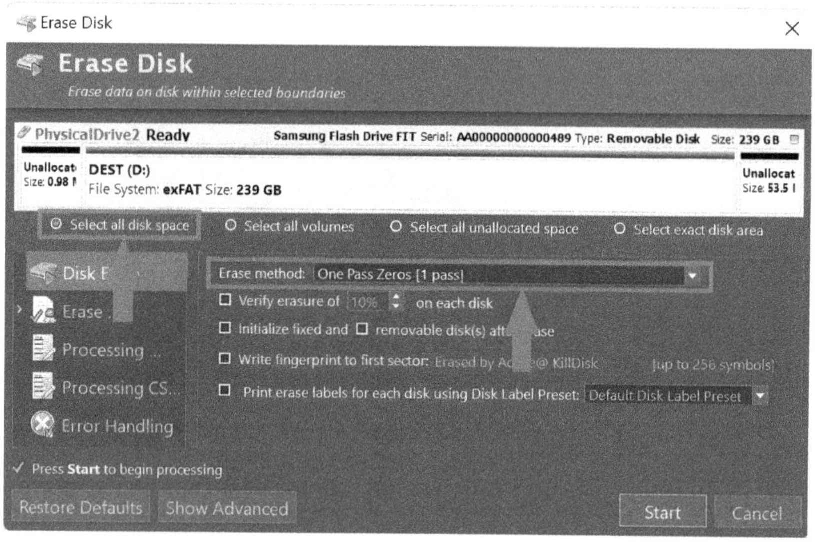

Figure 1.6 – Active@ KillDisk sanitization options

8. A confirmation prompt will appear. Type **ERASE-ALL-DATA** in the field and select **OK** to confirm:

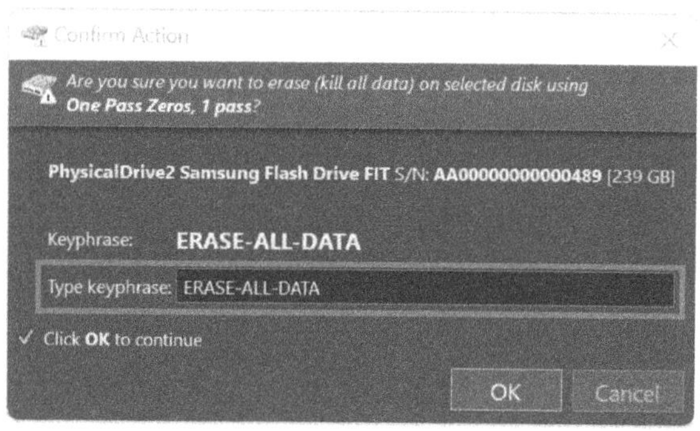

Figure 1.7 – Storage drive sanitization confirmation prompt

During sanitization, Active@ KillDisk displays a progress bar showing the status of the operation:

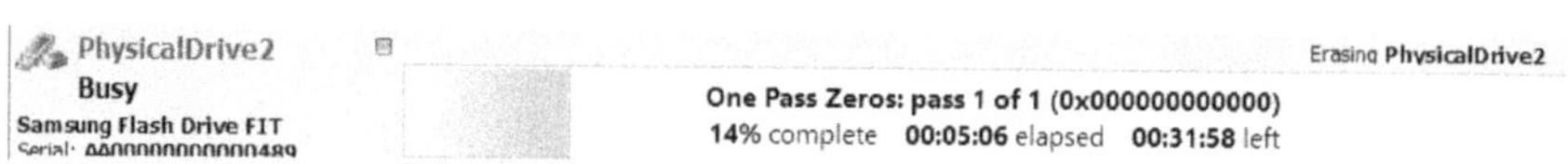

Figure 1.8 – Drive sanitization progress

9. Once the process is complete, a results window appears with options to view logs or generate an erase certificate. Click **OK** to close the prompt:

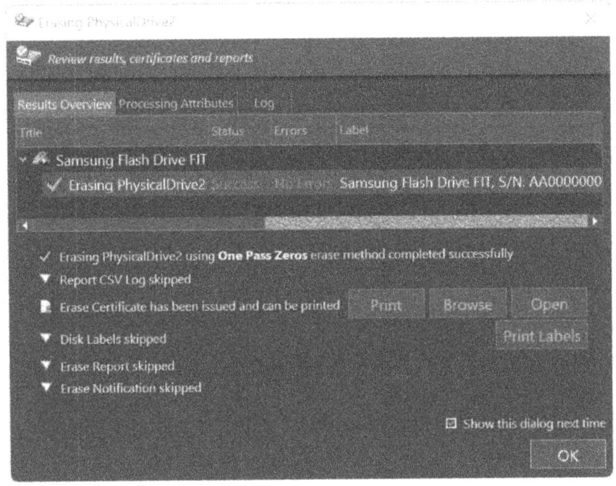

Figure 1.9 – Active@ KillDisk completion prompt

10. The drive's **Status** field will display **SUCCESS**, confirming sanitization is successfully completed. Close **Active@ KillDisk**:

Figure 1.10 – Status bar completion indicator

In *Step 7*, we skipped the **Verify erasure every x percent** option because we'll now perform manual verification.

11. Launch HxD (installed in step 1) **as Administrator** by right-clicking the application and selecting **Run as administrator**:

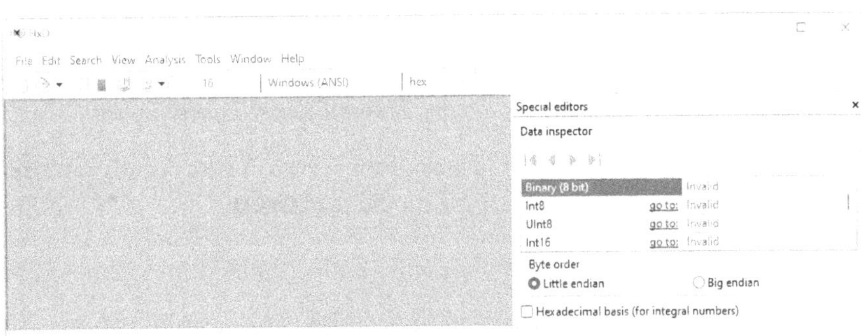

Figure 1.11 – Running the HxD software application

12. From the **Tools** menu, choose **Open disk...** or use the keyboard shortcut *Shift + Ctrl + D*:

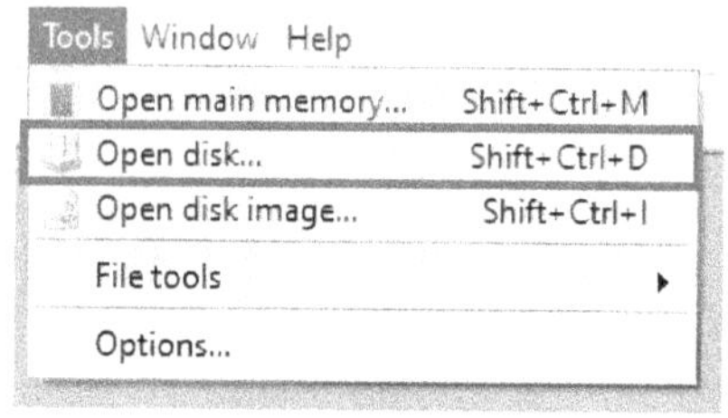

Figure 1.12 – Select the option to open an attached storage drive

Because the sanitized drive no longer contains a file system, Windows will not assign it a drive letter or show it as user-accessible. HxD, however, lists all physical disks directly.

13. In the lower-left corner, select **Open as read-only** to prevent changes, which is highly recommended in forensic workflows. Locate and select the sanitized drive (for example, **Removable disk 2**) and click **OK**:

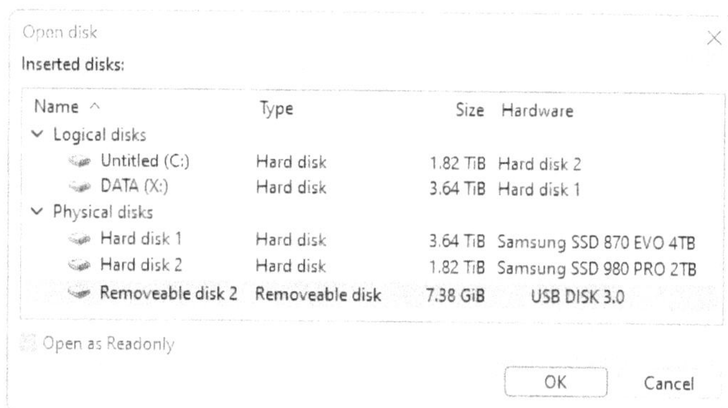

Figure 1.13 – Storage drive locations recognized by HxD

The drive contents will appear in hexadecimal view. A successfully sanitized drive will display no residual data—each byte should read **0x00**:

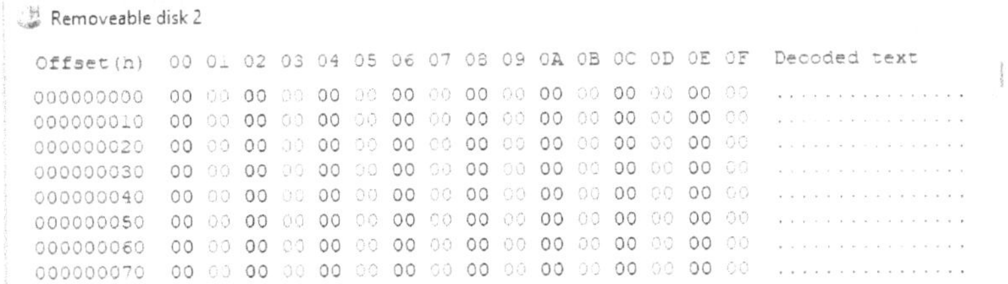

Figure 1.14 – Sanitized storage drive loaded into HxD

14. To confirm sanitization, navigate to the **Analysis** menu and select **Checksums...**:

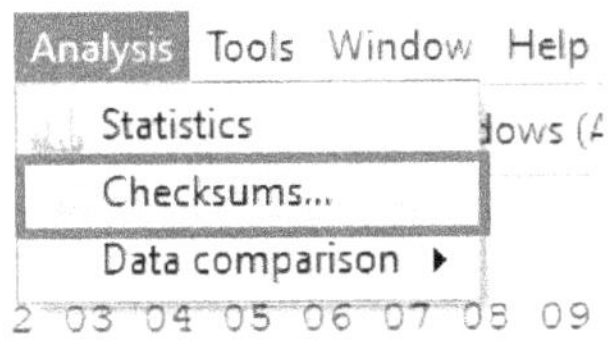

Figure 1.15 – HxD hashing menu

15. Choose **Checksum-64** from the available algorithms. The `Checksum-64` function calculates a sum of all bytes present on the device. Because every byte is `0x00`, the resulting sum should equal zero if sanitization was successful. Then, click **OK**:

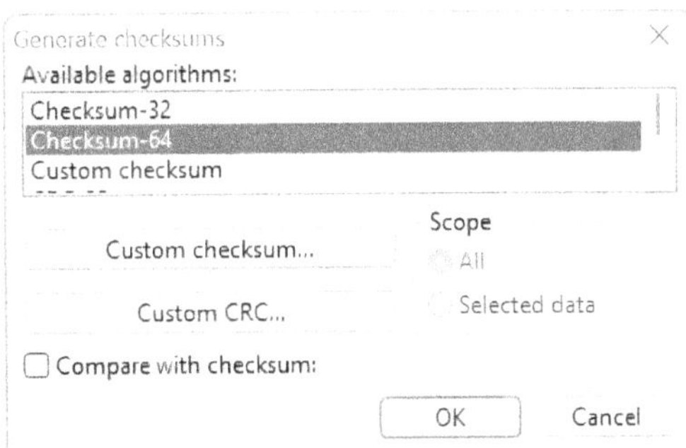

Figure 1.16 – Selecting the checksum64 hashing algorithm in HxD

HxD displays a progress bar while the checksum is calculated:

Figure 1.17 – HxD hashing algorithm progress

Upon completion, HxD presents the calculated value. A result of **0000000000000000** confirms that every byte is successfully overwritten with 0x00:

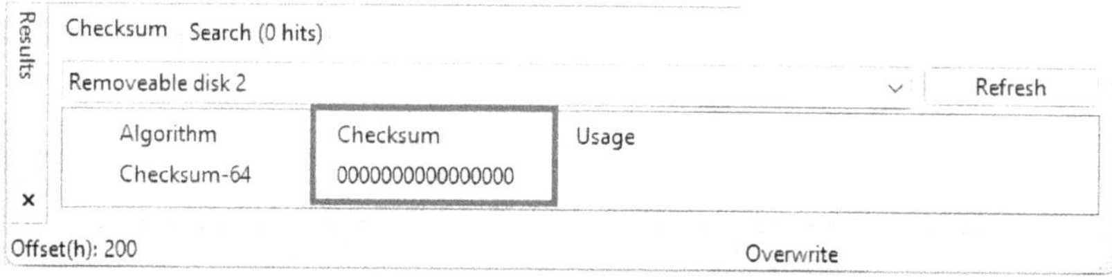

Figure 1.18 – Checksum64 value of 0000000000000000

Because the drive no longer has a file system, it must be formatted before it is reused.

16. Open **Disk Management** by right-clicking the **Start** button and selecting **Disk Management**, or press *Windows + R*, type `diskmgmt.msc`, and click **OK**:

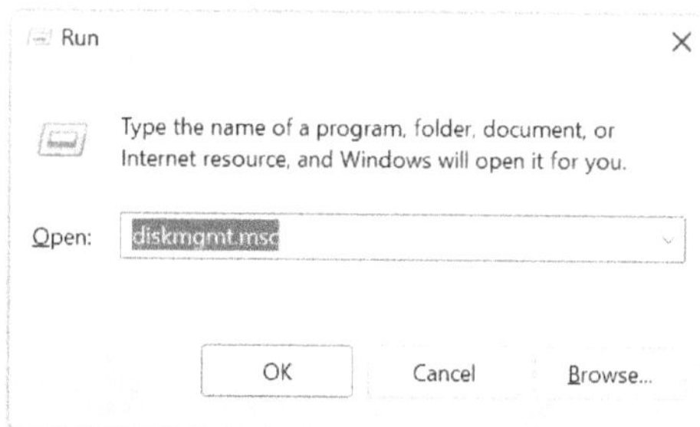

Figure 1.19 – Running Microsoft Windows Disk Management

17. Locate the sanitized drive—it will appear with a **RAW** file system and no assigned volume label:

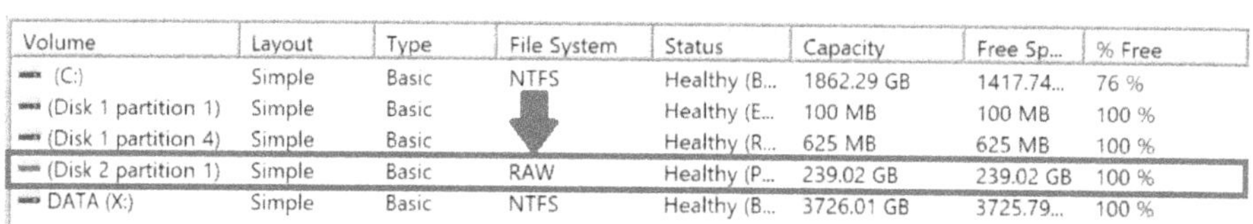

Figure 1.20 – Selecting the sanitized drive in Disk Management

18. Right-click the drive and select **Format.** Assign a volume label, choose a desired file system, and click **OK.** The drive will now be available within Windows Explorer:

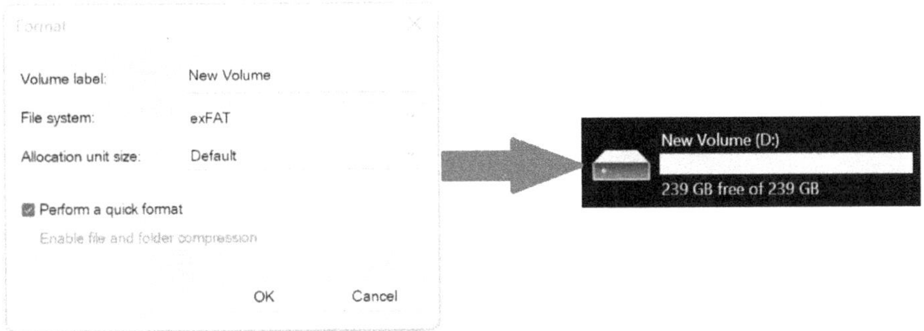

Figure 1.21 – Formatting the sanitized storage drive with a file system

19. If the drive does not appear in Windows after formatting, assign it a drive letter manually. Right-click the drive again, select **Change Drive Letter and Paths**, click **Add...**, choose a letter from the dropdown list, and select **OK**:

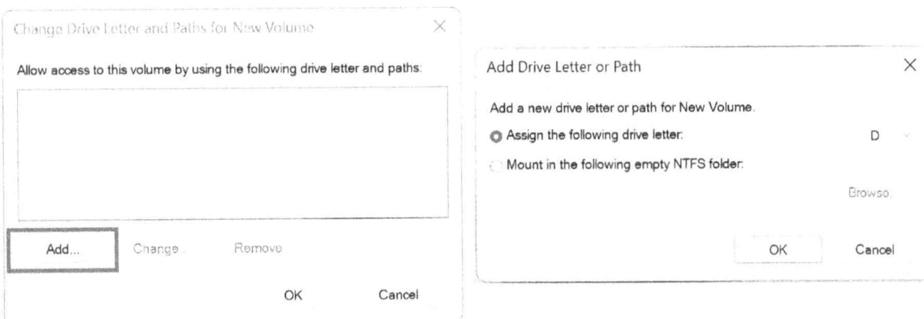

Figure 1.22 – Assign a path to the storage drive if it remains unrecognized by Windows

There's more...

As an alternative, the **DiskPart** utility in Windows can also sanitize a drive. Open **Command Prompt as Administrator** and enter the following commands:

```
diskpart        // Launches DiskPart utility
list disk       // Lists available storage drives
select disk #   // Selects the desired disk (replace # with the
                   appropriate disk number as determined from list disk
                   command)
detail disk     // Displays drive properties to confirm correct selection
clean all       // Writes zeroes to each sector, sanitizing the drive
```

Note

While this method performs a full zero-fill, Windows may write minimal data to physical sector 0 during initialization, which can result in unexpected checksum verification results, despite the content being adequately overwritten.

How it works...

When files are deleted or a quick format is performed, the data itself remains on the drive until it's overwritten by new data. This means that even a freshly formatted drive can still contain recoverable information, including remnants from previous cases, personal data, or even illicit material. Using a non-sanitized drive during evidence collection risks contaminating your findings or, worse, unintentionally exposing protected or criminal content to stakeholders.

Proper sanitization eliminates this risk entirely. By overwriting every byte with 0x00, we ensure that all bits are set to zero and that no original data remains. Verifying this process with the Checksum-64 algorithm provides mathematical confirmation: a sum of zero confirms a successful wipe and a truly sterile medium.

Once verified, the drive can safely be used for triage, acquisition, or evidentiary storage with full confidence that it is free from contamination.

With a sanitized drive ready for deployment, we can now move on to the next critical step – preparing a USB drive for use during on-scene evidence collection and triage.

Preparing a triage USB drive

A well-prepared examiner maintains multiple USB drives preloaded with trusted forensic and triage tools for on-scene use. Each drive should be sanitized prior to deployment and dedicated to a single target system to prevent cross-contamination of data between devices.

For field operations, it is recommended to keep several triage USB drives ready, with each containing preinstalled utilities for data acquisition and previewing. Drives with a minimum capacity of 256 GB are ideal, providing sufficient space for large memory captures or targeted acquisitions of critical artifacts.

In addition, it is wise to maintain several sterilized high-capacity drives that are multiple terabytes in size for full or partial acquisitions performed on scene. These larger drives are invaluable when dealing with encrypted systems that are actively logged in, data from servers that cannot be physically removed, or any environment requiring rapid, comprehensive data capture before shutdown.

In this recipe, you'll prepare two USB drives preloaded with software tools used throughout the triage and collection process.

Getting ready

Some of the tools listed below require account registration or submission of contact information before downloading. This is common for many free forensic utilities. Consider creating a dedicated email address for this purpose while practicing your forensic skills. This simplifies future downloads and often provides access to product updates, white papers, and community resources.

All demonstrations in this book use freely available or tool-agnostic solutions, ensuring each process can be completed without paid software. However, many of these vendors also offer professional or enhanced versions for those wishing to expand their toolkit.

To follow along with this recipe, download the following tools:

- **Sumuri Paladin LTS ISO** – Paladin is a bootable forensic operating system built on the Linux kernel, offering a complete suite of tools for previewing, searching, and acquiring data from target systems. It allows you to boot into an alternate environment without modifying the original evidence. To download Paladin LTS, complete the checkout process on Sumuri's website. A donation is optional for individual/personal use, and you can simply enter $0 if you wish to obtain the software for free: `https://sumuri.com/product/paladin-lts/`
- **Rufus** – Used to create a bootable USB device from ISO files. We'll use Rufus to prepare our Paladin LTS USB, though it can also be used for other Linux distributions and Windows installation media: `https://rufus.ie/en/`
- **Exterro/AccessData FTK Imager** – A long-standing forensic tool used for previewing and acquiring data from live Windows systems. FTK Imager supports forensic image creation, evidence previewing, and mounting of existing image files for examination: `https://go.exterro.com/l/43312/2023-05-03/fc4b78`
- **Belkasoft Live RAM Capturer** – A specialized tool for acquiring volatile memory (RAM) from live Windows systems. Download requires completing a short registration form to request a user account. Approval typically takes about one business day: `https://belkasoft.com/trial`
- **Magnet Encrypted Disk Detector** – A lightweight utility that automatically checks for encrypted storage volumes on Windows systems – ideal for identifying BitLocker, TrueCrypt, or other encrypted drives during triage: `https://www.magnetforensics.com/resources/encrypted-disk-detector/`

How to do it...

To create a bootable USB to preview and acquire powered-off systems, follow these steps:

1. Insert a sanitized USB storage drive into your computer.
2. Run Rufus and select the sanitized drive from the **Device** dropdown menu. Under **Boot selection**, click **SELECT** and choose the `PALADIN LTS.iso` file downloaded from Sumuri (you must first extract the contents of the downloaded archive file).
3. Adjust all other settings as follows:
    - **Persistence partition size** – adjust accordingly based on the capacity of your USB drive, for example, choose an 8 GB persistence size if using a 16 GB USB drive (this allocates 8 GB for Paladin LTS and 8 GB for storing Paladin settings, configurations, and other non-evidentiary data).
    - **Partition scheme** – select **GPT**
    - **File system** – select **NTFS**

    All remaining options can be left at their default values as shown in *Figure 1.23*.

    When ready, click **START** and select **OK** for any prompts that may appear:

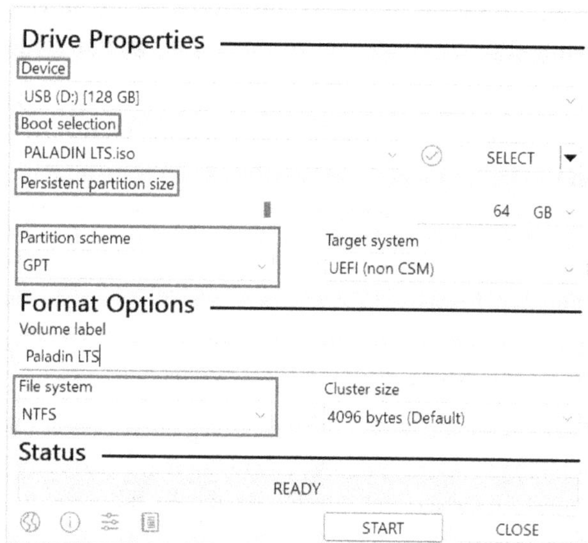

Figure 1.23 – Rufus settings for creating a bootable Paladin USB

4. Once complete, the **Status** bar will display **READY**. You can now close Rufus and safely remove the USB drive:

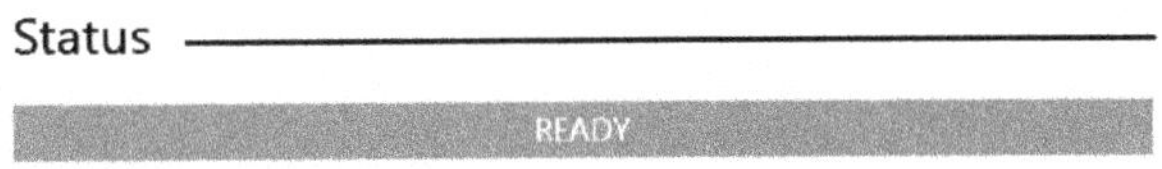

Figure 1.24 – Rufus status indicating the process is complete

Prepare a USB drive to triage live Microsoft Windows systems by following these steps:

5. Install FTK Imager on your host computer. The default installation options are acceptable but ***note the installation directory*** for later use.
6. Once setup is completed, uncheck the option to **Launch AccessData FTK Imager** and click **Finish**:

Figure 1.25 – FTK Imager installed to host computer

7. Insert another sanitized USB drive. Format this drive using the `exFAT` file system and assign it the volume label **TRIAGE.** The exFAT format is ideal because it supports very large files and is readable and writable across multiple operating systems. Labeling the drive helps quickly identify it during live collection and later during analysis, where it may appear within certain artifacts.
8. Copy FTK Imager to the TRIAGE drive. Navigate to the installation directory (the default is `C:\Program Files\AccessData\FTK Imager`) and copy the entire folder and its contents to the root of the TRIAGE USB drive:

Figure 1.26 – Directory on host computer containing FTK Imager installation files

FTK Imager can then be launched directly from the USB drive without installation by running `FTK Imager.exe`.

9. Download **Magnet Encrypted Disk Detector**. Extract the downloaded archive and copy the executable to your TRIAGE USB drive. The file is typically named `EDD` followed by a version number. You can rename it to **Encrypted Disk Detector** for clarity.
10. Download Belkasoft Live RAM Capturer. Extract the contents of the downloaded file and copy them to your TRIAGE USB drive. At this point, the TRIAGE USB should contain three key applications, as shown below:

Figure 1.27 – Final contents of our TRIAGE USB drive

11. Test the applications on your host system. Run each directly from the TRIAGE drive to verify they launch successfully and do not attempt to install themselves onto the host computer. This confirms the tools can be executed in a portable manner without installation.

How it works...

The USB drives created in this exercise allow us to preview and acquire evidence from different types of systems. We can boot a powered-off computer into the controlled forensic environment of a Sumuri Paladin LTS USB or use our TRIAGE USB drive to collect data from a live Windows system without altering its contents. Additional tools will be introduced later in the chapter, but you are free to add or remove tools from your TRIAGE USB as needed to support your investigative workflow.

> **Tip**
>
> It is good practice to maintain a dedicated directory on your examiner workstation for storing all downloaded forensic tools. This simplifies the process of rebuilding or updating multiple TRIAGE drives for field deployment. Remember, every USB drive used in evidence collection must first be sanitized and then dedicated to a single target system. Never reuse the same drive across multiple systems. This strict separation prevents cross-contamination and ensures the integrity of all collected evidence.

During on-scene triage, our goal is to collect critical evidence efficiently, focusing first on volatile data while minimizing any changes to the original system. To accomplish this, we rely on purpose-built forensic utilities that enable data acquisition and preview while reducing or preventing the alteration of timestamps, metadata, or other evidentiary attributes.

It is essential that **no software is ever installed directly onto the target device.** All tools should be executed from the prepared USB drives, ensuring a forensically sound workflow. Depending on the situation, this may involve launching triage utilities on an active, logged-in system or booting the target device into an alternate operating system using the Paladin media. In either case, the guiding principle remains the same: gather what is needed, preserve what matters, and limit the trace of your own activity.

Capturing random access memory (RAM)

Now that we've prepared USB drives preinstalled with essential forensic tools, it's time to put them to use. Following the order of volatility (see *Appendix A*), our first collection target is system memory (RAM). In this recipe, you'll capture RAM from your own computer using Belkasoft Live RAM Capturer or a similar tool.

As this chapter focuses on evidence collection, the objective of this recipe is to perform RAM acquisition. Analysis and interpretation of memory artifacts will be covered later in *Chapter 11, Memory Forensics*.

Getting ready

We are already prepared for this process, as our TRIAGE USB drive includes Belkasoft Live RAM Capturer (downloaded and installed in the previous recipe). This lightweight application has a small memory footprint, making it suitable for live systems where minimizing impact on RAM is critical.

Some investigators include additional RAM acquisition tools, such as Magnet RAM Capture, to provide fallback options in case of compatibility issues. Having multiple options ensures reliability in diverse environments. This utility can be added to the TRIAGE USB we created in the previous recipe if desired, and is downloadable from the following web address:

`https://www.magnetforensics.com/resources/magnet-ram-capture/`

FTK Imager is also capable of acquiring RAM, but it is a significantly larger application and will introduce a greater degree of memory alteration when launched. For that reason, smaller, dedicated utilities like those offered by Belkasoft or Magnet are preferred when working with volatile data.

How to do it...

1. Insert your TRIAGE USB drive into the target computer.

2. Navigate to the **RamCapturer** folder within the **LIVE TRIAGE** directory of your TRIAGE USB drive. Inside are two subdirectories for **Belkasoft Live RAM Capturer**:
    - x64 – for 64-bit Windows systems (modern versions)
    - x86 – for legacy 32-bit systems
3. Launch the appropriate version for the target system:

Figure 1.28 – Belkasoft Live RAM Capturer application stored to our TRIAGE USB

4. The application's default output path should match the directory from which it was launched (your TRIAGE USB drive). Always verify this path before starting, as you should never save the memory acquisition to the evidentiary computer itself. When ready, click **Capture!**:

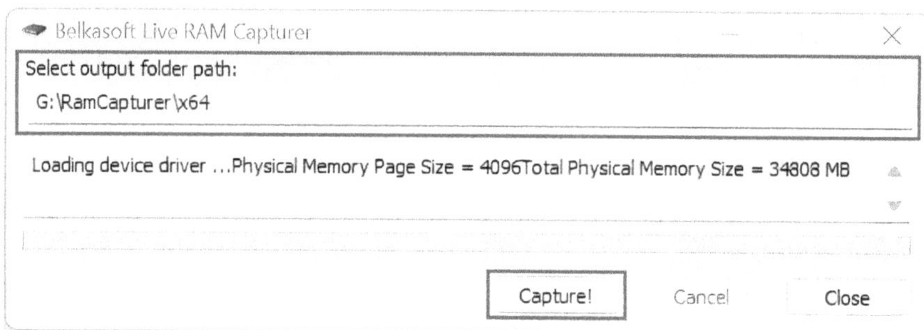

Figure 1.29 – Belkasoft Live RAM Capturer running on target computer

5. A progress bar will indicate capture status. When complete, a dialog box will display **"Memory dump completed."** Click **Close** to exit:

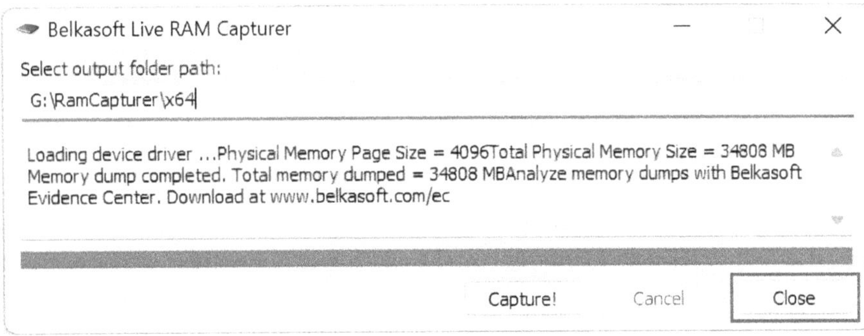

Figure 1.30 – RAM acquisition completed with Belkasoft Live RAM Capturer

6. Within the output directory, you'll find the captured memory image saved as a `.mem file`, named according to the date and time of acquisition. This file is now ready for analysis using your preferred memory forensics tools:

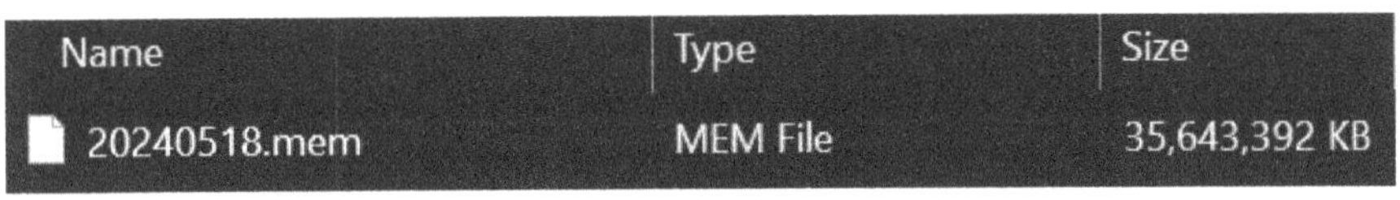

Figure 1.31 – RAM acquisition file stored to our TRIAGE USB

How it works...

This recipe represents what you might encounter in the field when discovering a powered-on computer that is actively logged into a Windows account. In such cases, insert the TRIAGE USB drive you prepared in the previous recipe and begin the proper evidence collection workflow.

When working with original evidentiary media, you would normally protect the original system or drive using a write-blocker. Because the TRIAGE USB drive is being used to acquire data, you cannot employ a write-blocking bridge, as doing so would prevent the acquisition process entirely. Running this and similar tools within a live Windows environment inevitably creates some forensic artifacts: logs indicating USB connection, execution of an application, and changes within the very memory we are capturing.

A RAM acquisition captures the most volatile and often the most forensically valuable data from a live system. The capture is written as an uncompressed memory image (commonly .mem, .raw, or similar), so the resulting file size will be roughly equal to the amount of physical RAM installed on the target machine (e.g., a system with 64 GB of RAM will produce a ≈64 GB image). Plan storage and transfer media accordingly.

While these changes are unavoidable, the key principle is to minimize the scope of modifications, understand what artifacts our actions generate, and justify why those actions were necessary for a forensically sound triage and collection process. By adhering to these principles, you can preserve evidentiary integrity while ensuring the most critical (and volatile) data is collected before it disappears.

There's more...

Memory can contain artifacts that do not exist anywhere else on disk, including: cleartext credentials, encryption keys, active network connections, running processes, in-memory-only configuration, unsaved documents, and malware. In some investigations, a successful RAM capture has enabled decryption of protected volumes, recovery of ephemeral user activity, and rapid identification of live compromises. Because of this, timing is critical and RAM should be acquired as early as possible in accordance with the order of volatility.

A few platform and tooling notes:

- Many Windows tools (Belkasoft Live RAM Capturer, Magnet RAM Capture, FTK Imager) produce raw, uncompressed memory images that are straightforward to analyze in memory forensics suites.
- Linux systems may be captured using tools such as LiME or Magnet's Linux utilities (e.g., DumpIt variants), depending on kernel and distro.
- Modern Apple platforms that include hardware memory encryption (T2 chip and Apple Silicon) make meaningful RAM acquisition impractical, because RAM is encrypted at the hardware level and cannot be trivially decrypted offline.

By understanding what a RAM capture contains, how large it will be, and the platform-specific limitations, an examiner can prioritize volatile collection appropriately and preserve the maximum investigatory value while maintaining evidentiary integrity.

Powered-on systems

When a user interacts with a computer (opening files, browsing directories, or running applications) these actions inherently modify data and update various system logs. To minimize additional changes, we will continue using the forensic tools stored on our TRIAGE USB drive. This ensures all activity remains as controlled and isolated as possible. This recipe will enable you to perform a brief on-scene preview or selectively collect specific data after capturing RAM from a target system.

Getting ready

We will continue using the TRIAGE USB drive that was employed to acquire RAM in the previous recipe, since we are still working with the same target system. If you're moving on to a different machine, you must use a separate, sanitized TRIAGE USB drive to prevent cross-contamination and ensure the evidentiary integrity of all collected data.

How to do it...

Follow these steps to check for encryption:

1. Launch Magnet Encrypted Disk Detector (EDD).
2. Run the EDD executable from your TRIAGE USB drive. This utility scans for numerous encryption methods including BitLocker, TrueCrypt, VeraCrypt, and others. If any detected drives are encrypted with BitLocker or similar tools, they will appear in red:

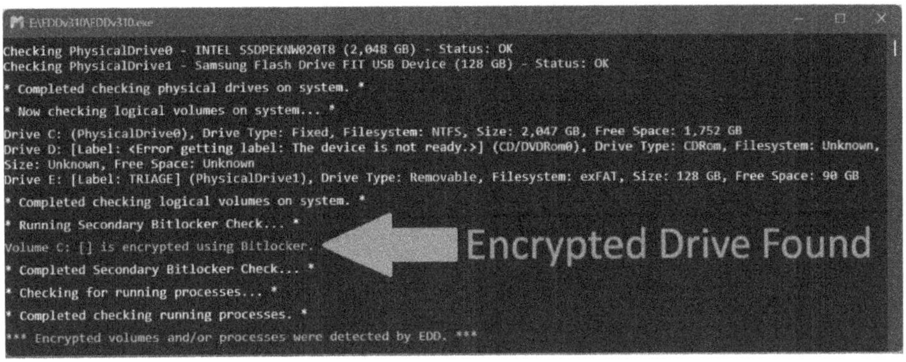

Figure 1.32 – Magnet EDD identifying encrypted volumes

3. To manually verify encryption software, open **Windows Settings** | **Apps** (or **Programs and Features**) to review installed applications.
   Because automated tools do not identify every encryption signature, you should always perform a manual check for related software.

   In **Windows Explorer**, encrypted BitLocker drives display a **padlock icon**:

Figure 1.33 – Active BitLocker as seen using Windows Explorer

If encryption is detected, perform two actions:

- Attempt to **obtain or back up the recovery key** if possible.
- Perform a **logical acquisition** of any data that is currently *unencrypted or accessible.*

Note

When an encrypted volume is unlocked and available, acquiring the data immediately is critical. Do not rely solely on recovering or decrypting the drive later, as the risk of key loss or corruption is too high.

4. If BitLocker is active, export the BitLocker recovery key. Here, Magnet Encrypted Disk Detector identified BitLocker protection on the system drive. Use the native Windows search to locate **Manage BitLocker**, then choose **Back up your recovery key.** Save the recovery key to your **TRIAGE USB** drive:

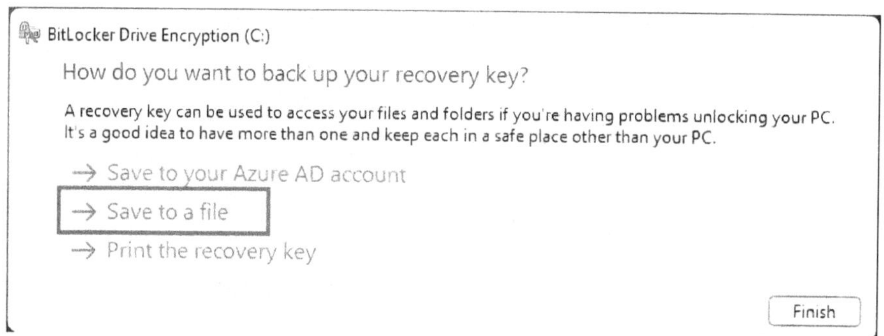

Figure 1.34 – Saving a Windows BitLocker recovery key

The recovery key will then be saved within a text file:

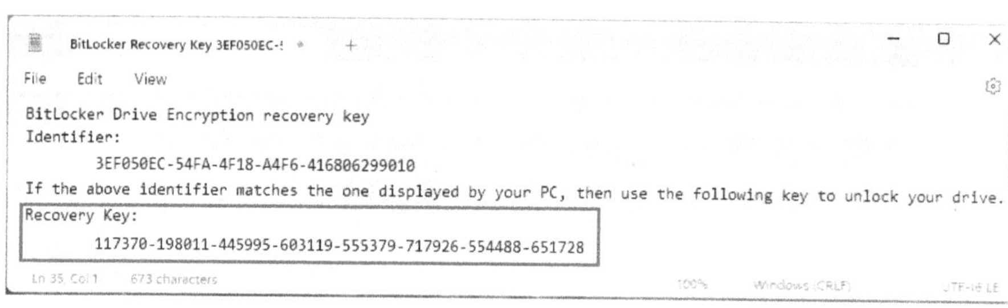

Figure 1.35 – Windows BitLocker recovery key stored to text file

5. Now, to preview a live Windows system with FTK Imager, launch FTK Imager directly from your TRIAGE USB drive:

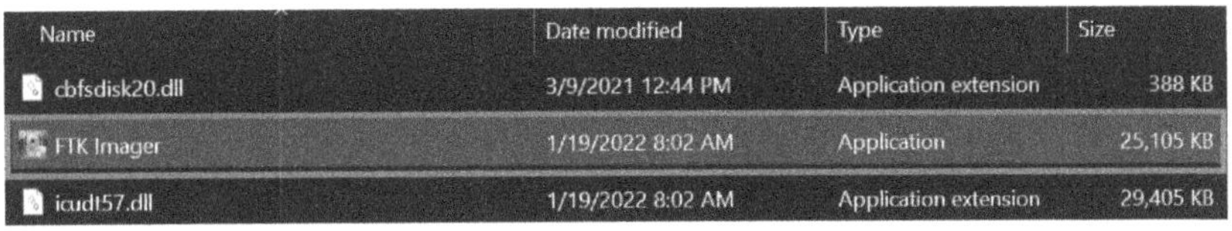

Figure 1.36 – FTK Imager application file

6. Run FTK Imager as a portable application. FTK Imager operates without installation, allowing you to preview data while limiting changes to the target system.

> **Note**
>
> Some changes will occur to the target system, as minimal artifacts such as logs of USB connection and program execution are unavoidable:

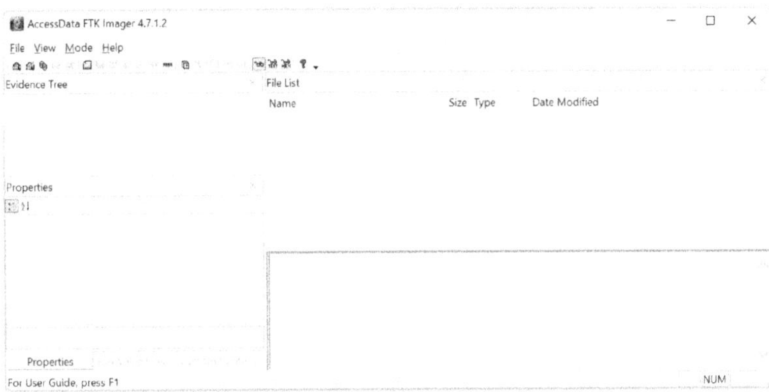

Figure 1.37 – FTK Imager application running on target machine

7. From the **File** menu, select **Add Evidence Item** to add evidence for preview.:

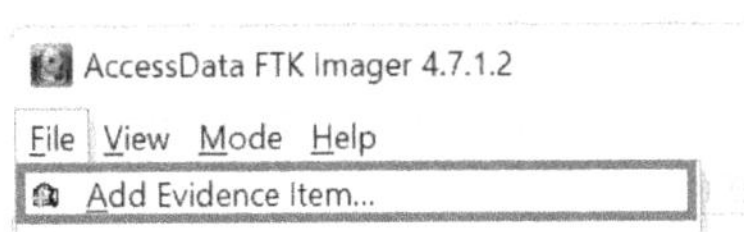

Figure 1.38 – Adding an evidence item to view in FTK Imager

8. Select **Physical Drive** and click **Next** to choose the evidence type:

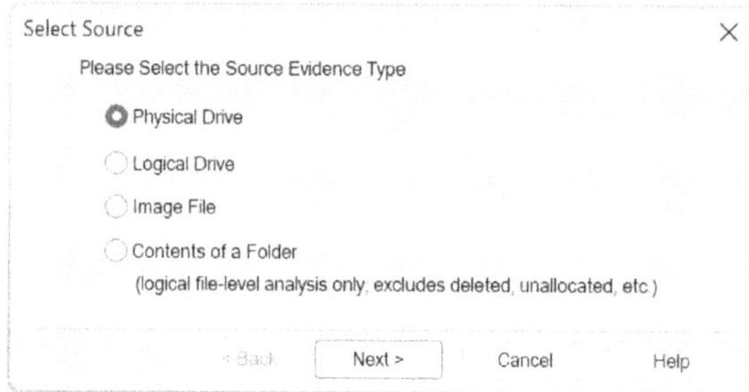

Figure 1.39 – Choosing to view the content of a physical drive with FTK Imager

9. The dropdown list displays all attached drives from which you can select the correct drive:
   - Identify your **TRIAGE USB** (often listed as `PHYSICALDRIVE 3` or higher).
   - Focus on the system's **primary storage**, typically `PHYSICALDRIVE 0`.
10. Highlight it and click **Finish**:

Figure 1.40 – Selecting to preview PHYSICALDRIVE0 in FTK Imager

11. FTK Imager presents a hierarchical **Evidence Tree**, a **File List** for each directory, and **Properties** and **Preview** panes. Browse the target system's file structure:

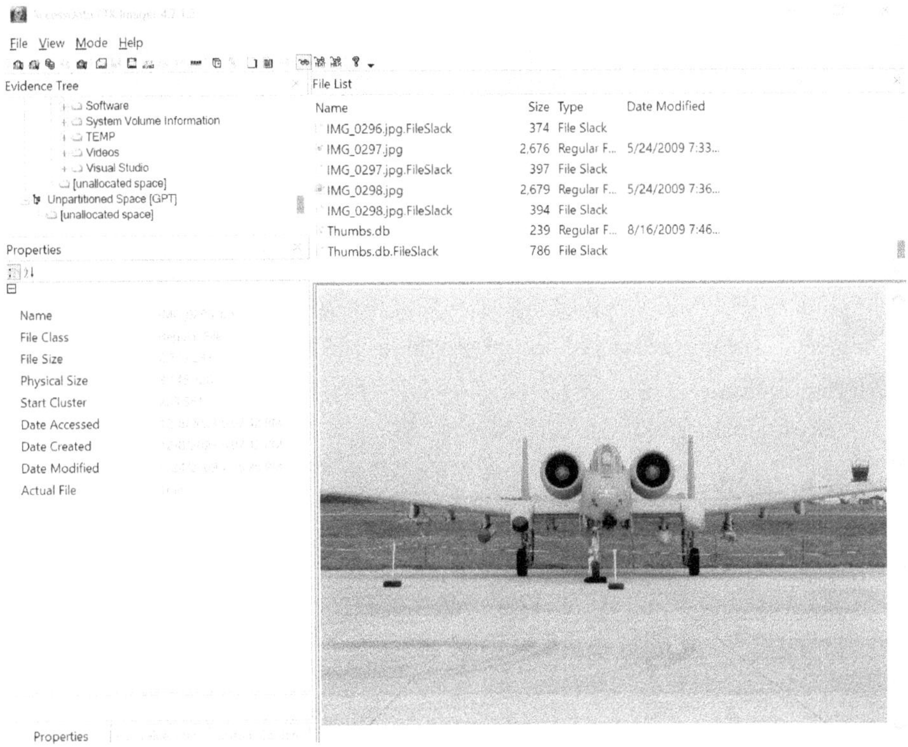

Figure 1.41 – Previewing content using FTK Imager

12. Mark files for acquisition by right-clicking any file or directory and selecting **Add to Custom Content Image (AD1)**:

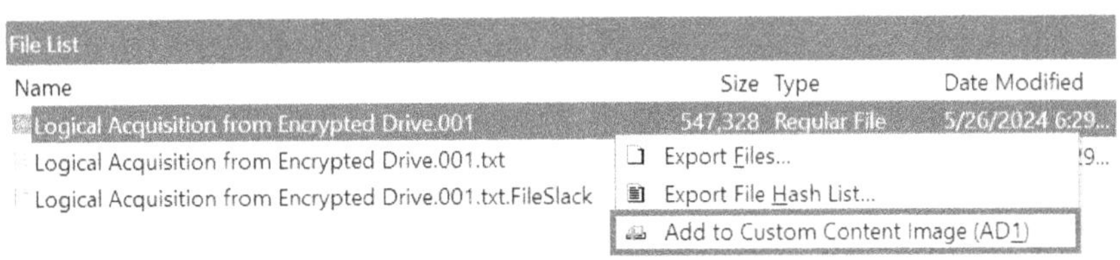

Figure 1.42 – Targeting specific files for acquisition in FTK Imager

13. Continue adding desired files or folders to the **Custom Content** list. Each selection appears under **Custom Content Sources**. When ready, choose **Create Image** from the toolbar or **File** | **Create Image**:

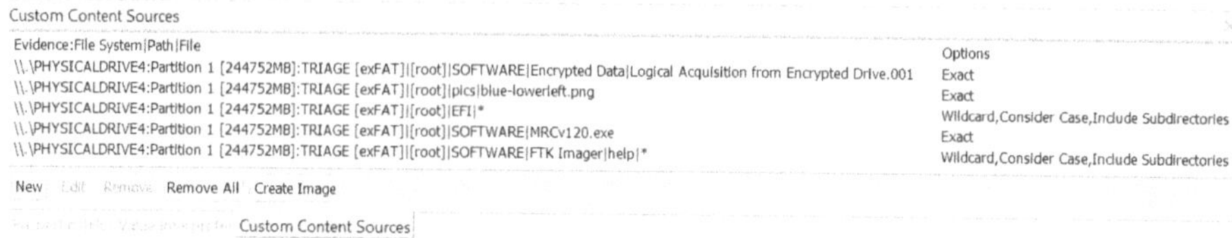

Figure 1.43 – Files and directories added to Custom Content Image in FTK Imager

14. Follow the image-creation prompts to generate an AD1 forensic container comprising your selected files. Detailed image-creation options are covered in *Chapter 3, Physical and Cloud-Based Evidence Acquisition*, where we further review evidence acquisition.
15. The resulting AD1 file can later be opened in FTK Imager or any compatible analysis suite for further review.

How it works...

At this stage, we have completed the essential live-response steps for a powered-on system: capturing volatile memory, checking for active encryption, and performing controlled preview or limited data acquisition. Each of these actions are executed using standalone, trusted applications launched from a sanitized USB drive to preserve evidence integrity and maintain a verifiable chain of custody.

The purpose of previewing a live target varies across investigations. In some cases, the examiner may need to confirm system relevance or identify potential artifacts before imaging; in others, the objective may simply be to secure volatile or decrypted data before shutdown. Regardless of the scenario, the priorities remain the same:

- Preserve volatile evidence first.
- Identify and address any active encryption.
- Minimize changes to the live environment.

By following this sequence, we ensure that every action taken on a powered-on system is defensible, intentional, and forensically sound.

It's important to remember that an on-scene preview is not always necessary. In many cases, it may be preferable to complete the RAM acquisition, verify that no actively encrypted drives or critical volatile data remain, and then proceed to collect the entire system for later analysis in a controlled lab environment.

There's more...

Encryption is increasingly common. Windows Pro editions ship with BitLocker, and Apple macOS includes **FileVault**. To check FileVault status on a macOS system, open **System Settings** and search for `FileVault`; if active, macOS displays which volume is protected:

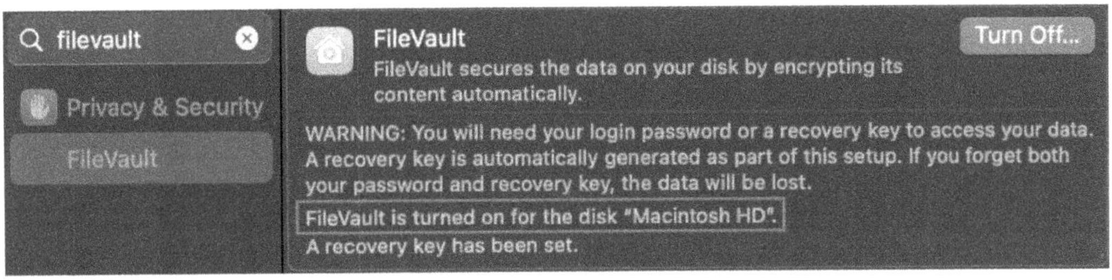

Figure 1.44 – FileVault encryption enabled in Apple macOS

While our TRIAGE USB drive lacks macOS-specific forensic utilities due to limited freeware options, its exFAT formatting allows macOS read/write access. You can manually copy files of interest to the drive if no better method is available. This should be considered a *last-resort* option. Commercial tools such as Sumuri Recon and Cellebrite Collector provide far more forensically sound acquisition methods for Apple systems.

Powered-off systems

When encountering electronic evidence in a powered-off state, it is best to leave it powered off whenever possible. However, there are situations where a limited preview may be necessary, and this can be done safely using forensically sound methods that avoid altering the original evidence.

The first option is to physically remove the storage drive, connect it to a hardware write-blocker, and access its contents from a controlled workstation. This ensures the evidence remains unmodified during review. However, some modern systems use non-removable storage, such as solid-state chips soldered directly onto the motherboard. In those cases, physical removal is not feasible.

The alternative approach is to boot the target computer using an external forensic operating system rather than its native OS. This allows examiners to preview and acquire data without writing to the original drive. A sanitized USB boot device containing Sumuri Paladin LTS works exceptionally well for this purpose, providing a stable and trusted Linux-based forensic environment.

In this recipe, we will use a bootable USB drive containing Sumuri Paladin LTS (created earlier in the *Preparing a triage USB drive* section of this chapter) to boot and preview a target system.

Getting ready

For this recipe, you will use the USB drive containing your bootable instance of Sumuri Paladin LTS, which can interface with Windows, Linux, and Intel-based Apple systems. Before you can boot into Paladin, you must ensure that **external device booting is allowed** on the target computer and that any firmware-level restrictions are disabled.

Accessing BIOS/UEFI on PCs: On most systems, you'll need to access the Basic Input/Output System (BIOS) or Unified Extensible Firmware Interface (UEFI) settings before the native operating system begins to load. This is done by pressing a specific key during startup. commonly *DEL*, *F1*, *F2*, or *ESC*, depending on the manufacturer.

While many users rapidly press these keys (*button mashing*) immediately upon startup, a more reliable approach is to consult the manufacturer's documentation to identify the correct key sequence for that system.

Once in the BIOS/UEFI interface:

1. Locate and **disable Secure Boot** (typically under a "Security" or "Boot Configuration" menu).
2. Review any other **boot restriction settings** that might prevent external device booting.
3. Save your changes before exiting:

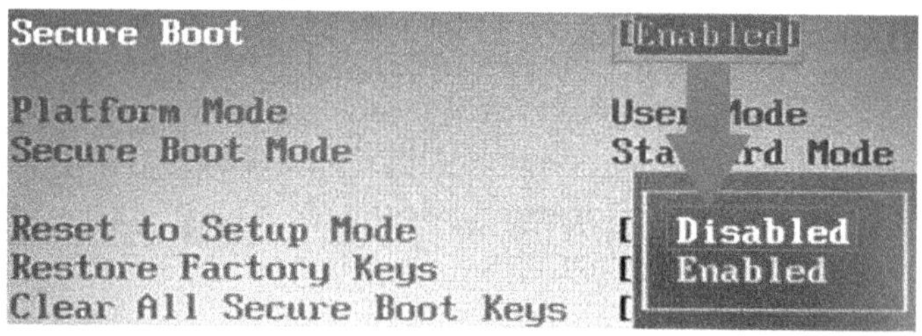

Figure 1.45 – Disabling Secure Boot in BIOS/UEFI settings on a PC

4. Next, either adjust the boot order in BIOS/UEFI so that USB devices have priority over the internal system drive or Windows Boot Manager, or "Catch" the boot menu during startup (often accessed with *F8*, *F11*, or *F12*) and manually select your USB drive as the boot device:

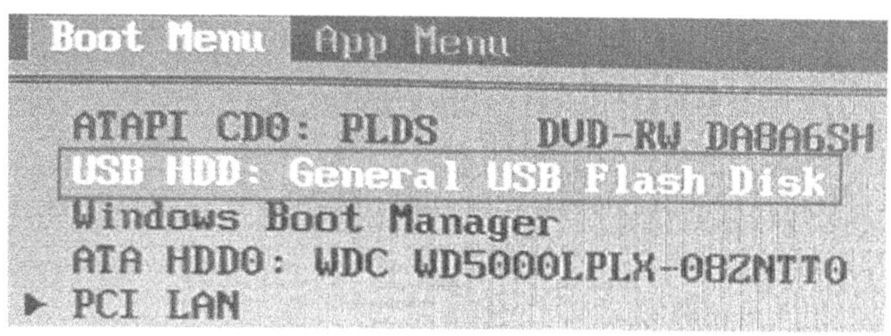

Figure 1.46 – Choosing an alternate boot device on a PC

For Intel-based Apple systems, access the Apple Startup Manager by holding the **Option** / **Alt** key during startup. From there, you can select your Paladin USB drive as the boot device:

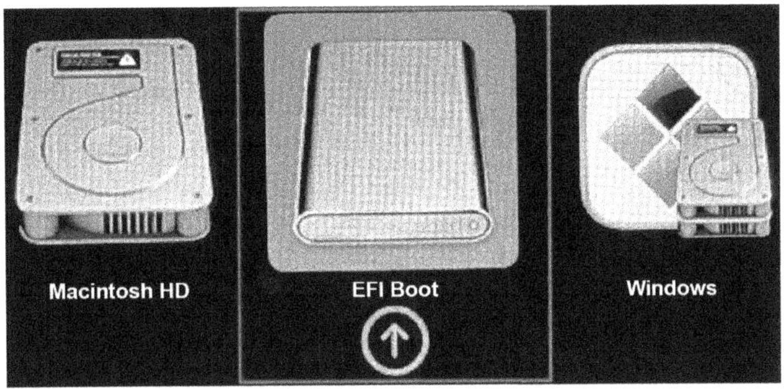

Figure 1.47 – Choosing an alternate boot device on an Apple system

5. For Apple Silicon (M1/M2 and later) systems, access the Startup Manager by pressing and holding the power button until startup options appear. While the Startup Security Utility allows reducing the default security policy to permit external booting, Paladin LTS and most other Linux-based forensic environments are not currently compatible with Apple Silicon hardware. At present, forensic examiners cannot rely on Paladin LTS or similar Linux distributions for booting Apple Silicon systems. Rather, you will need to know the correct password to unlock the computer and use tools such as Sumuri Recon ITR or Cellebrite Collector.

> Note
>
> Apple laptops manufactured after 2016 are automatically powered on when the lid is opened or when a power source is connected with the lid open. Be prepared for this behavior when handling those systems to avoid unintended boot sequences.

How to do it...

1. Insert the Paladin USB drive into a powered-off computer. Power on the system and select the Paladin USB drive as the boot device. From the boot options menu, choose **SUMURI PALADIN Live Session – Forensics Mode**.

   If you created a persistence partition and want Paladin LTS to retain configuration and settings between sessions, you can instead choose **SUMURI PALADIN Live Session – Forensics Mode (persistent)**:

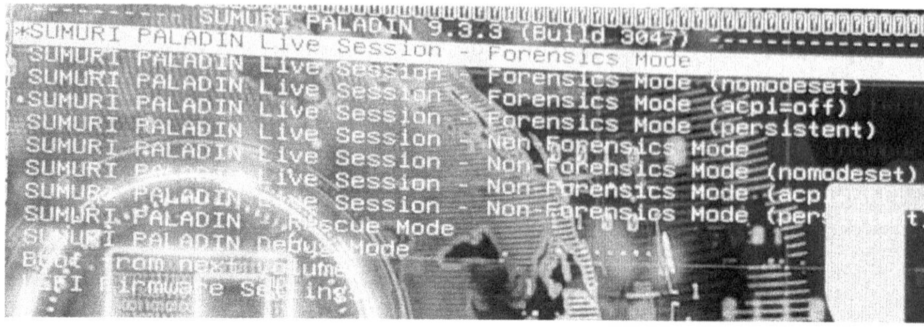

Figure 1.48 – Booting a system to Paladin

Be patient, as booting Paladin may take a few minutes. Once the system has fully booted, you will be presented with the **Paladin desktop environment**:

Figure 1.49 – Paladin desktop screen

2. Insert a second sanitized USB drive into the computer. This will serve as the output device for collected data. It is recommended that this drive be formatted using a file system that supports large file sizes, such as NTFS or exFAT. Assigning the drive a distinctive volume label (such as DEST or TRIAGE) will make it easier to identify in subsequent steps.
3. From the toolbar on the left side of the desktop, open the **Paladin Toolbox** and select **Disk Manager**.

Disk Manager allows you to mount evidence drives in read-only mode to protect data integrity. By default, only the Paladin USB drive is mounted, displayed in red text as a read-write volume:

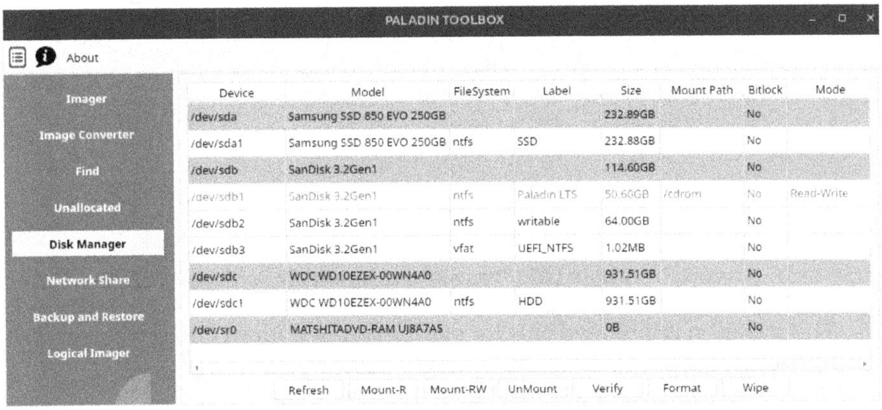

Figure 1.50 – Paladin Disk Manager utility

4. To mount the drives, select the target evidence drive and click **Mount-R** to mount it in read-only mode. This allows safe previewing of data without altering it. Then, select the secondary output USB drive (from *Step 2*) and click **Mount-RW** to mount it with write permissions.
   This allows you to safely examine the target system's storage while saving search results or collected data to the output USB drive:

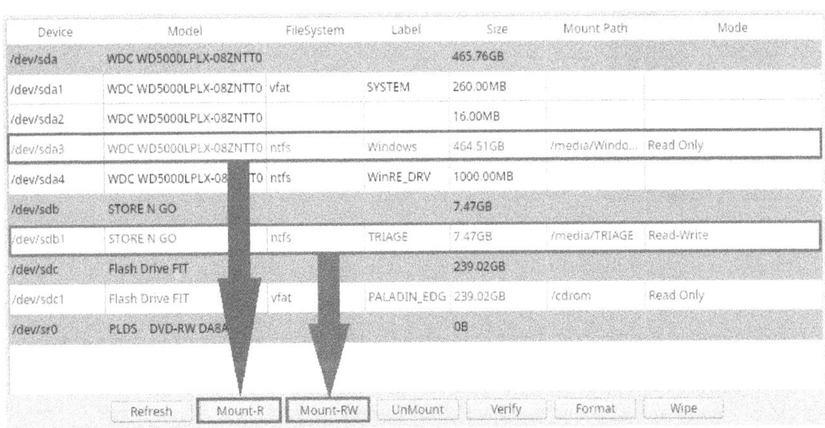

Figure 1.51 – Mounting drives using the Paladin Disk Manager utility

5. If you created a persistence partition on your Paladin LTS USB drive and booted into persistence mode, you can format it using **Disk Manager** by selecting the partition,

clicking **Format**, and setting the label to `writable` and the file system type to `ext4`. This allows configuration settings to persist across sessions:

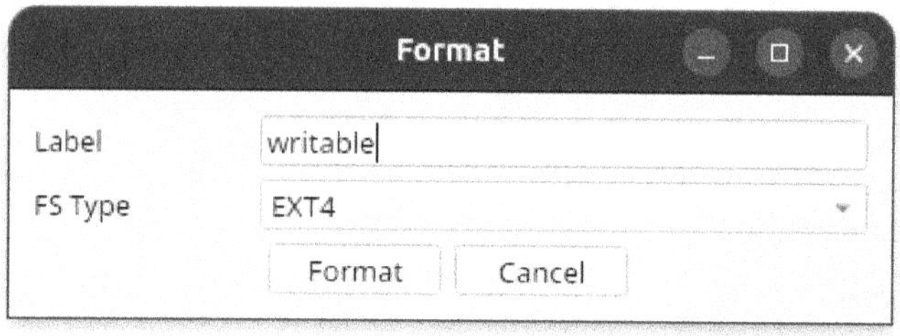

Figure 1.52 – Preparing the persistence partition in Paladin

This partition is intended only for storing configurations and settings and should not be used to store evidentiary data or search results.

6. After mounting the volumes, open the **Find** utility within the **Paladin Toolbox**. This tool allows you to search for artifacts by keyword or MIME type (for example, images, videos, documents, etc.):

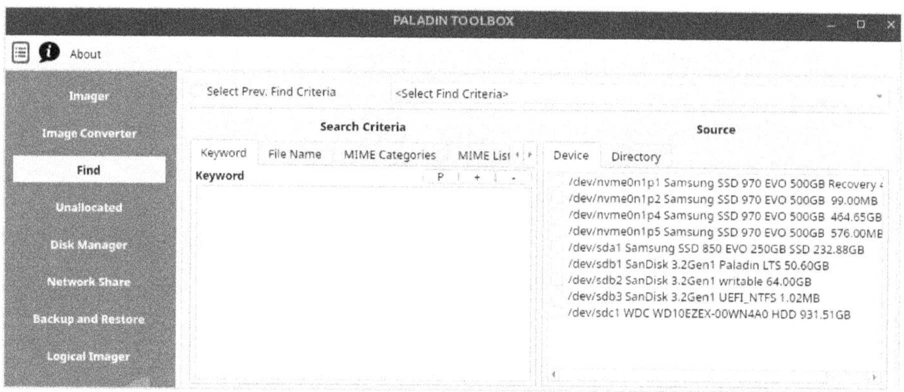

Figure 1.53 – Paladin Find utility

7. Under the **Keyword** tab in the **Search Criteria** section, click the **+** icon to add one or more general keywords. In this example, the keyword used is `suspect-email@gmail.com`:

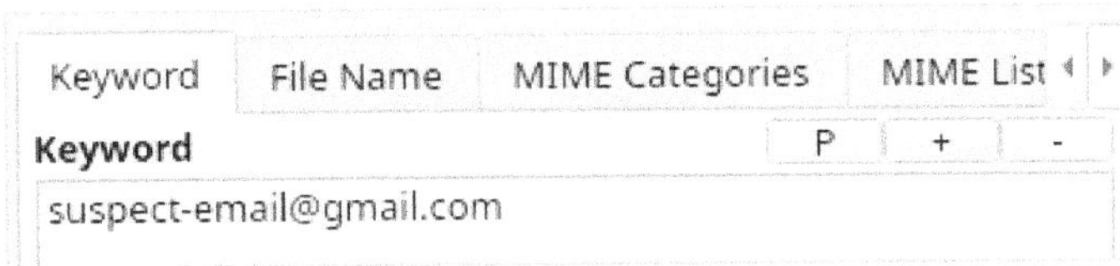

Figure 1.54 – Entering general keywords into the Paladin Find utility

8. Next, select the **File Name** tab under **Search Criteria** to add a specific filename keyword. In this example, the filename keyword is `ILLEGAL-KNOWN-FILENAME`:

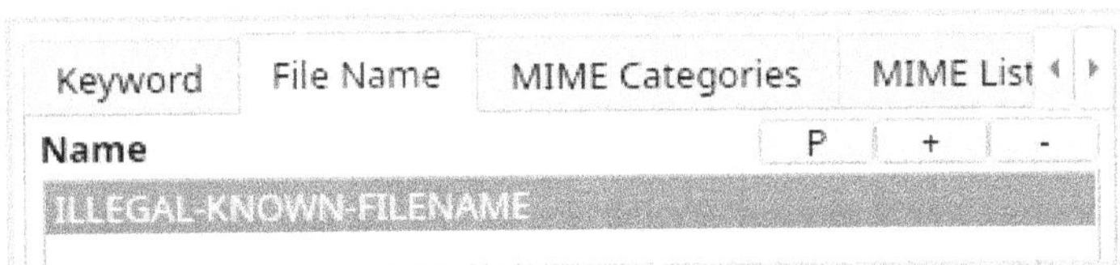

Figure 1.55 – Entering filename keywords into the Paladin Find utility

9. In the MIME Categories tab, select the file types you want to search for. In this example, the search is configured to locate `image` files:

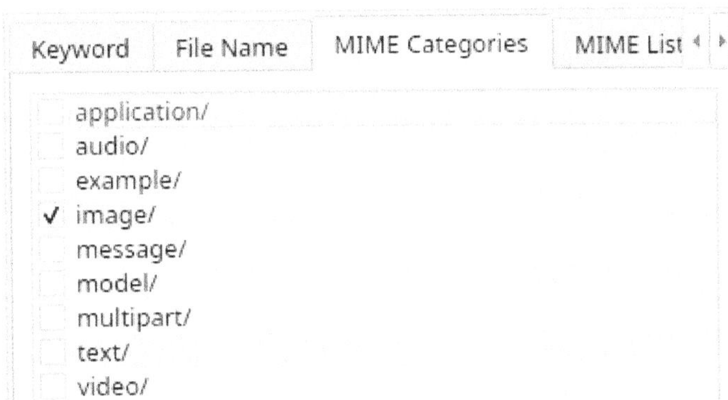

Figure 1.56 – Selecting MIME types in the Paladin Find utility

10. Under the **Device** tab in the **Source** section, select the evidence drive mounted in read-only mode. This specifies the drive to be searched:

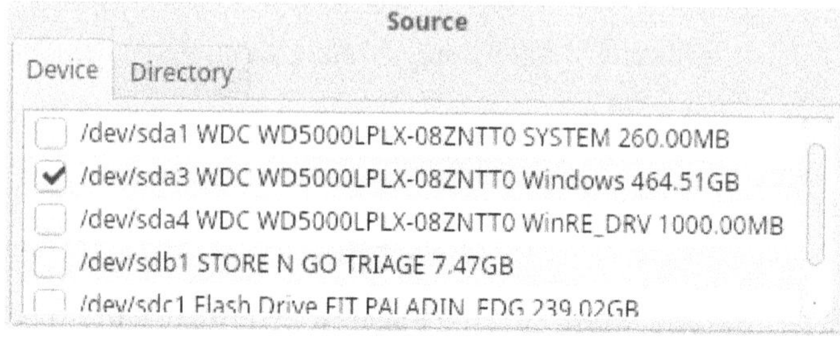

Figure 1.57 – Selecting an evidence source drive to search in Paladin

11. In the **Output Selection** section, choose the write-enabled USB drive as the destination device. Provide a descriptive label for the search in the **Label** field (for example, Keyword Search). Leave **Copy Original** set to **No** unless you want to automatically copy discovered files; many examiners prefer to review results first and copy selectively. Click **Search** to begin:

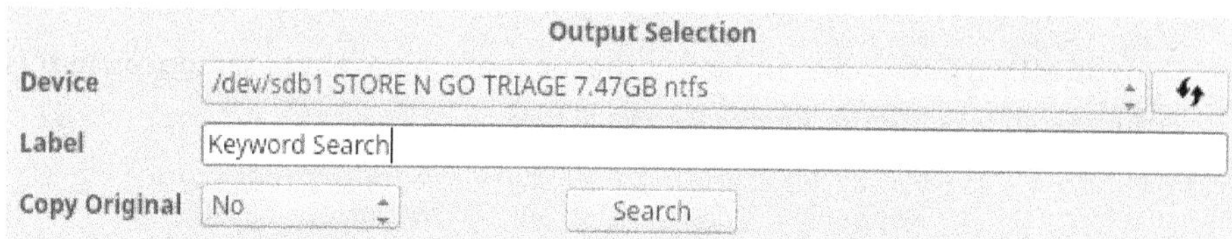

Figure 1.58 – Labelling and settings up output results Paladin

A status bar will display progress, including file counts and search metrics. Once complete, Paladin displays a summary dialog with the results:

Figure 1.59 – Keyword search completed in Paladin

Depending on the size of the volume and the amount of data present, this process may take considerable time.

12. The **search results** are saved to the **output USB drive** selected earlier:

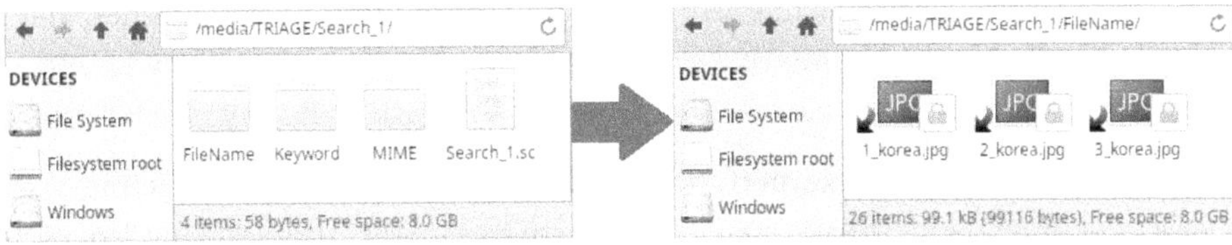

Figure 1.60 – Search results output in Paladin

How it works...

Booting a target machine from an alternate operating system on USB allows an examiner to access the target's storage volumes without launching the native OS. Many distributions can perform this role; we chose Paladin for its forensic toolset and built-in utilities. An alternative option is a bootable Windows Forensic Environment (WinFE), which works well for Windows targets but is limited to that platform.

When you boot externally and mount the evidence drive in read-only mode, you access the file system directly at the block level, bypassing local user accounts and operating system logins. This makes it possible to examine files even if you cannot authenticate into the installed OS. However, if the drive is encrypted (for example, BitLocker), the raw file content remains unreadable until the volume is unlocked or the decryption key is obtained.

While this recipe demonstrates a basic triage workflow using Paladin LTS, the platform also includes a broad set of forensic tools (such as Autopsy) for deeper analysis, which will be explored in Chapter 7 – Analysis Automation.

Router interrogation

Router interrogation is the process of examining a network router to identify evidence useful to an investigation. Routers are commonly present in both home and business environments and can provide valuable insight into connected devices, network activity, and configuration settings.

You should generally interrogate routers on scene, even if you do not plan to seize them, as they may contain active device lists, historical connection logs, configuration settings (including remote or administrative access), NAT/DHCP tables, and the current public IP address. This information can be critical in establishing device presence, user activity, and network relationships.

Router capabilities vary widely by manufacturer and model, and the depth of available data depends on the device's firmware, enabled logging, and any security controls in place. As a result, your approach will often be shaped by the specific router and its configuration.

Routers manage local devices while also connecting the network to the internet, making them a key point for distinguishing internal systems from externally assigned IP addresses during an investigation.

For this recipe, you will begin by performing a passive/active scan by connecting to the network to enumerate live hosts, open ports, hostnames, MAC addresses, and vendor fingerprints. You will then attempt to access the router's administrative interface (if available) to review logs and configuration data.

Getting ready

For this exercise you need a computer already connected to the target network and the **Fing Desktop** application installed and ready to use: `https://www.fing.com/fing-desktop/`

Fing Desktop will be used in this recipe to quickly identify active devices on the local network. Other tools such as Nmap or Wireshark can also be used, depending on your workflow and experience.

How to do it...

1. To connect to the network, check the router label first. Locate the physical router and inspect the label on the back or bottom. Many routers list the default **Service Set Identifier (SSID)** or 'network name', a default Wi-Fi password, and sometimes a QR code you can scan to join the network. Note that users may have changed these defaults:

Figure 1.61 – Example of a router label

2. Choose a wired connection when possible. If the SSID/password are unknown or the wireless credentials have been changed, plugging a laptop directly into an Ethernet port of the router will usually give immediate network access (no Wi-Fi password required) and bypass MAC-filtering.

3. If you have access to a device on scene that has previously connected to the network, you can often extract the cleartext password from that device:
    - Android and iOS – Accessing the network settings in an Android or iOS device will usually give you access to a cleartext password for any router the devices have previously connected to, though you may need the passcode for the device to access this information:

Figure 1.62 – Cleartext Wi-Fi router passwords stored to iOS and Android

    - Microsoft Windows – Open an instance of PowerShell with elevated administrative privileges and enter the following command, replacing SSID with the actual SSID of the network:

```
netsh wlan show profile name= "SSID" key=clear | FINDSTR Key
```

The command of `key=clear` will display the cleartext password and `FINDSTR Key` will limit the output to display only the password we are seeking.

Figure 1.63 – Cleartext Wi-Fi router password obtained from Microsoft Windows system

- Linux – Open an instance of terminal and enter the following command, which may need root privileges or slight adaptation to certain distros:

```
nmcli dev wifi show-password | grep 'Password'
```

Similar to the earlier `FINDSTR` command, `grep 'Password'` is used to limit the output to display only the password we need:

Figure 1.64 – Cleartext Wi-Fi router password obtained from Linux system

- Apple macOS – Open an instance of terminal and enter the following command, replacing SSID with the actual SSID of the network:

```
security find-generic-password -l "SSID" -w
```

This command retrieves the stored Wi-Fi password directly from the system keychain. You may be prompted to enter the administrator password to authorize access.

Figure 1.65 – Cleartext Wi-Fi router password obtained from Apple macOS system

While there are additional methods to obtain unknown login credentials to a router using more advanced tools popular to penetration testers, the methods shown above are almost always sufficient for our needs in digital forensic triage. After connecting to the network using a laptop computer or even a mobile device from our triage kit, we can then begin scanning the network.

4. To scan the network, install and run **Fing Desktop** (you'll be asked to create a free account). The application displays your **public IP** near the upper-right corner:

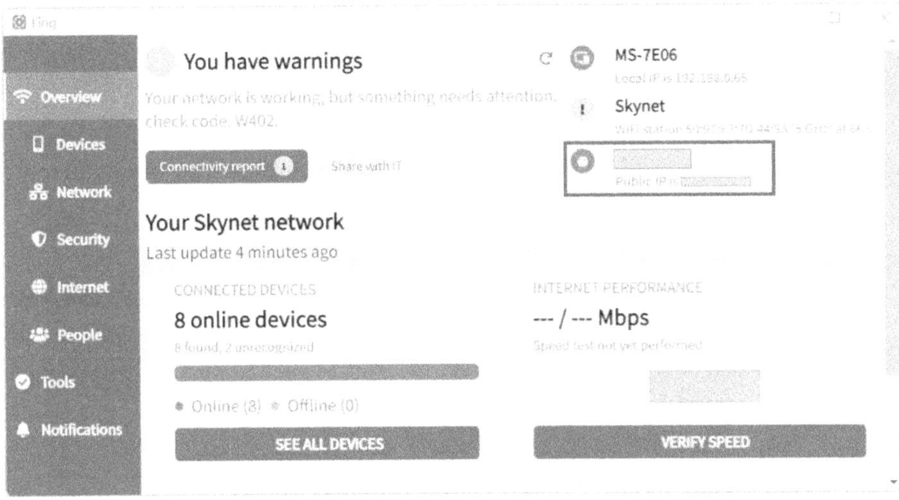

Figure 1.66 – Fing Desktop interface

5. Switch to **Devices** | **Technical view** (wrench icon) to get an expanded view of active hosts. Fing shows local IP, MAC, hostname (if available), open ports, and vendor fingerprinting based on MAC Organizationally Unique Identifier (OUI):

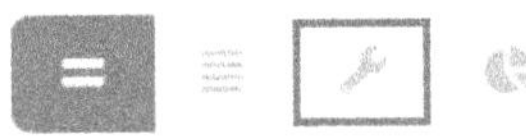

Figure 1.67 – Switching to Technical view in the Devices display of Fing

The Technical view helps identify active systems by displaying IP, vendor, and MAC information, which is useful for confirming all devices on the network during triage.

6. Select the devices individually to view further details:

Figure 1.68 – Technical view in of connected devices using Fing

Some devices may appear as "generic" in the Details column. This is common with IoT devices or systems that use outsourced network hardware. In some cases, modern mobile devices (such as iOS or Android) may also obscure their identity on the network by default.

Do not assume that "generic" entries are insignificant, as these may still represent important devices on the network. The two "generic" entries seen in Figure 1.68 actually consist of a Samsung Galaxy and Apple iPhone.

7. Now, choose **Network** from the left side pane menu, and then select **the Network Setup** tab. Note the Gateway IP Address. This is the local IP address for the router itself. This can also be found via command line utilities such as `ipconfig` in Windows, `nmcli` in Linux, or `route/netstat` in macOS:

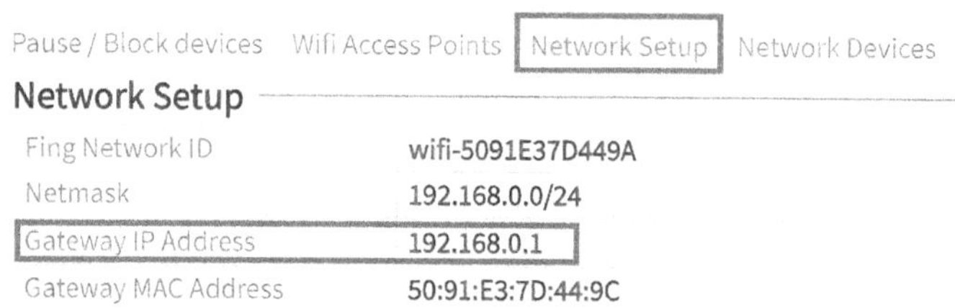

Figure 1.69 – Obtaining the default gateway address of a router using Fing

8. If the default credentials have not been changed for the router admin console, you can retrieve these by searching for the router documentation on the manufacturer's website or through `www.routerpasswords.com`.

> **Tip**
>
> Some routers do not contain a password at all for the admin console until the user attempts to access the console, at which time they are prompted to set a password. Otherwise, the most common default login credentials are a username of ***admin*** with a password of ***admin***.

9. Using the gateway IP address you obtained in the previous step, open a web browser and type the IP address into the search bar. This will take you to the router admin console login:

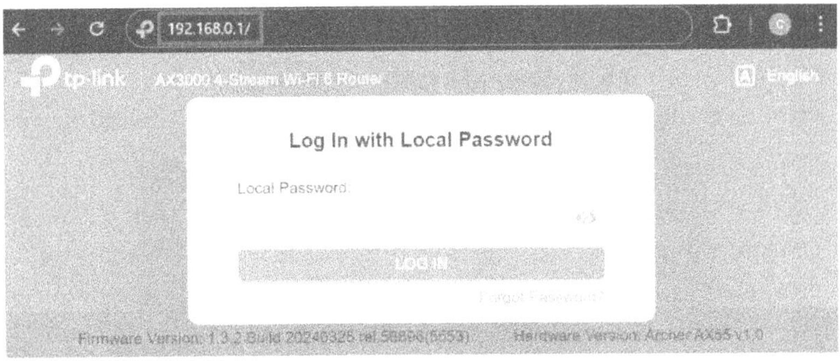

Figure 1.70 – Accessing a router admin console login screen

10. Enter the username and password to log in to the router admin console:

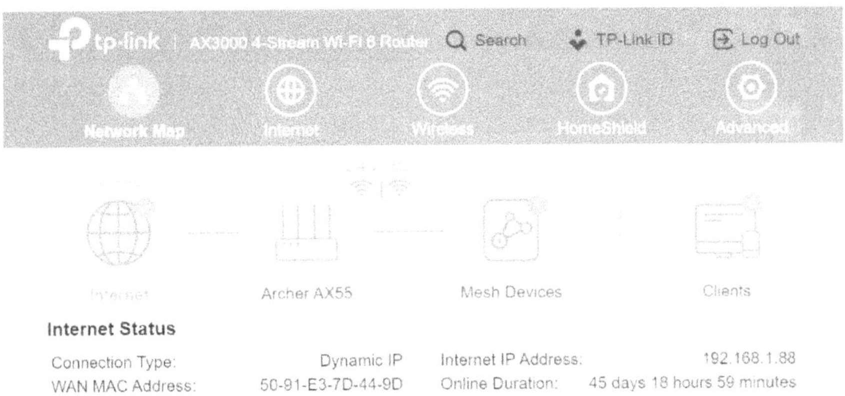

Figure 1.71 – Example router admin console

11. After logging in, review key artifacts such as SSIDs, DHCP leases, WAN/public IP settings, MAC information, security configuration, and any available logs (see *There's more...*)

How it works...

Router interrogation involves accessing the router's administrative interface or enumerating the network to identify connected devices, configuration settings, and available logs. This may include reviewing DHCP lease tables, SSID configurations, WAN/public IP settings, MAC address information, and any available monitoring or access logs. The exact data available depends on the router model, firmware, and enabled features.

There's more...

Router interrogation is often overlooked but should be included in every triage effort, as it can reveal unknown or hidden devices. Treat router data as evidence – avoid altering configuration settings, maintain proper documentation, and preserve chain of custody.

Router access may vary. ISP-provided devices may restrict direct admin access or require a mobile application for management. In some cases, the ISP may retain logs or configuration data that can be obtained through legal process.

> **Note**
>
> Alright, you got me...
>
> In one investigation, a suspect claimed that someone else had used his home network to share illicit files. Router logs told a different story: a complete history of connected devices showed no outside access, and every recently connected device could be accounted for within the residence. When confronted with this data, the suspect confessed.
>
> Router data has also been used to identify hidden devices and even externally connected storage concealed within a structure.

If default credentials have been changed, they were likely set from another device, and those credentials can often be recovered during triage. Users also frequently reuse passwords across systems. When appropriate, simply asking for the password may be effective.

Admin console interfaces vary widely by vendor and firmware, but most home router interfaces are designed to be straightforward to navigate. When examining a router, prioritize the following artifacts:

- **Additional SSIDs (guest or hidden networks)** – Hidden SSIDs do not appear in standard Wi-Fi scans and must be manually entered to connect. While this provides minimal security, the router console will display all configured SSIDs and their settings.
- **WAN / public IP (static vs. dynamic)** – Determine whether the ISP-assigned public IP is static or dynamic. Dynamic IPs may change periodically; if an observed external IP does not match the current value, the router may provide lease history or last change information.
- **Router MAC (and any MAC overrides)** – The router's MAC address can be used to correlate ISP records or device inventories. Be aware that MAC addresses may be

manually configured or spoofed; custom values are typically visible within the admin interface.

- **Historical DHCP client lists / lease tables** – DHCP records may identify devices that were previously connected but are no longer active. Retention varies by device and firmware, with higher-end consumer routers often maintaining longer histories.
- **Security configuration (SSID protection, encryption type)** - Review whether SSIDs are protected and which encryption standard is in use (WPA2, WPA3, and so on). Combined with DHCP and guest network data, this can help evaluate claims of unauthorized access.
- **Monitoring / parental-control / web-filter logs** - Some routers maintain web history, URL filtering logs, or parental-control records. These features are typically disabled by default but, when enabled, can provide direct insight into browsing activity.

Summary

Effective triage is not optional – it is often the foundation of a successful digital forensics investigation. Rapidly capturing volatile data, identifying and addressing encryption, and using sanitized, single-use collection media preserve the integrity and evidentiary value of what you gather on scene. These practices reduce uncertainty, protect chain of custody, and increase the likelihood you'll be able to recover critical artifacts during lab analysis. In this chapter, you applied multiple triage workflows across common on-scene scenarios.

At this point, you should be able to:

- **Sanitize and verify** a storage device so it can be safely reused for evidence collection without cross-contamination.
- **Build and test** a triage USB and a bootable forensic USB and understand when to use each on scene.
- **Capture RAM safely** from a live system while minimizing your own footprint and preserving volatile evidence first.
- **Handle powered-on vs powered-off systems** in a defensible way, including basic preview and targeted acquisition.
- **Interrogate a router** to identify connected devices, confirm network details, and collect configuration or log data that may support or refute user claims.

In the next chapter, we expand this methodology into incident response, applying the same priorities at scale to manage larger, distributed environments and higher volumes of evidence.

2

Network Intrusion Response and Remote Triage

When you move from a handful of systems to an entire estate, the rules change. Investigating a single computer allows an examiner to slow down, manually inspect artifacts, and build a careful timeline of activity. In an enterprise environment, investigators may be responsible for hundreds or even thousands of endpoints across servers, workstations, and cloud systems. The challenge shifts from deep inspection of a single system to rapidly identifying suspicious activity across many systems.

Single-system triage is deliberate and often manual. Incident response must be fast, repeatable, and scalable across a network. When responding to an intrusion, investigators are not just asking what happened on a single machine. The real questions become: Where else did the adversary go? What systems did they access? What evidence can we collect right now before it disappears?

In this chapter, we're going to cover the following main topics:

- Collecting evidence with KAPE
- Scaling evidence identification
- Building a Velociraptor server
- Initial malware investigation

By the end of the chapter, you'll be able to run broad hunts to narrow an incident to a prioritized host list, perform fast on-host triage to capture volatile evidence, and take the first safe triage steps when suspected malware is discovered.

Technical requirements

For this chapter, you will need the following:

- A host computer capable of running a Linux-based virtual machine (for example, VirtualBox or VMware) or acting as a dedicated Velociraptor lab server
- Two to three client systems connected to the same network environment, such as a home network or small lab environment
- Your Triage USB from *Chapter 1, Targeted On-Scene Triage*, to which we will add additional software

Collecting evidence with KAPE

When a potentially compromised machine is identified during incident response, investigators typically perform an initial triage before committing to full forensic imaging. This triage focuses on collecting a limited set of artifacts that help determine the system's relevance to the investigation and whether deeper analysis is required.

Artifacts related to system and user activity (such as program execution and process activity) are especially valuable during this stage. As with any interaction with a live system, investigators should still follow the order of volatility, beginning with the acquisition of RAM when possible. Because KAPE operates on a live system, it may introduce minor changes to the system state, which should be documented.

Getting ready

To improve efficiency during incident response, we will add another tool to the Triage USB created in *Chapter 1*.

Kroll Artifact Parser and Extractor (**KAPE**), created by Eric Zimmerman, is a standalone tool that enables rapid triage of Windows systems by collecting and parsing targeted forensic artifacts. It can run from a USB drive, mounted image, or remote source. KAPE can also parse data from mounted forensic images or collect and process artifacts from remote systems.

KAPE can be downloaded from the Kroll website here:

`https://www.kroll.com/en/services/cyber-risk/incident-response-litigation-support/kroll-artifact-parser-extractor-kape`

To download KAPE, ensure that your browser is not blocking popups and use a private or incognito browsing window. You will need to complete a short form with basic contact information, after which an automated email containing the download link will be sent. Failure to use private or incognito mode often results in a failed form submission.

How to do it...

1. After downloading KAPE, extract the contents of the zipped archive and copy the KAPE folder to the Triage USB drive that we created in *Chapter 1*. You should now have four tools available for triaging live Microsoft Windows systems:

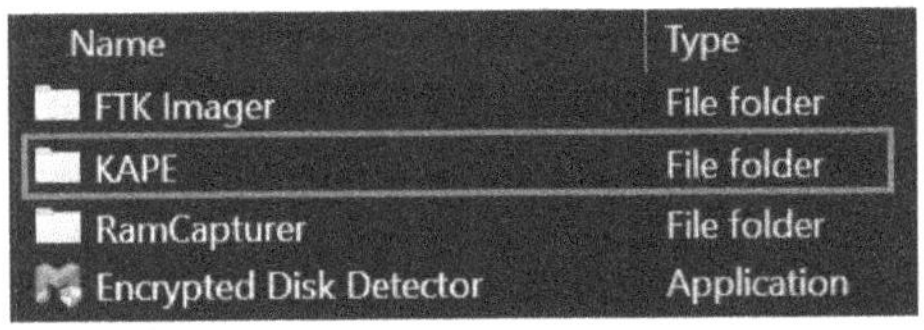

Figure 2.1 – Triage USB applications for live system response

2. Within the `KAPE` directory, locate the file titled `Get-KAPEUpdate.ps1`. This PowerShell script is used to update KAPE and can be executed by right-clicking the file and selecting **Run with PowerShell**:

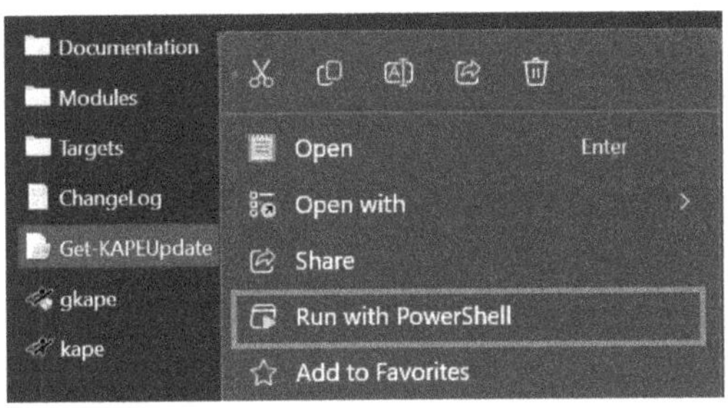

Figure 2.2 – PowerShell script used to update KAPE

> **Note**
>
> On some systems, Windows may prevent downloaded PowerShell scripts from running due to the system's execution policy. If the script does not run, open **PowerShell as an Administrator**, temporarily allow script execution for the current session, and then run the update script again:
>
> ```
> Set-ExecutionPolicy Bypass -Scope Process
> ```
>
> This setting only applies to the current PowerShell session and will revert once the window is closed.

3. Within the KAPE directory, you will see two applications: `kape` and `gkape`. For this exercise, double-click the **gkape** application to launch the graphical interface:

Figure 2.3 – CLI and GUI versions of KAPE

KAPE is primarily a **command-line interface** (**CLI**) tool that runs from the `kape` executable. The `gkape` application provides a **graphical user interface** (**GUI**) that helps generate the CLI commands automatically.

The GUI version is significantly larger than the CLI executable. Because of this larger memory footprint, investigators sometimes prefer the CLI version during live triage to minimize their impact on volatile data such as RAM. For this exercise, however, we will use the GUI version to simplify the workflow.

4. The KAPE graphical interface is divided into two primary sections. The left side is used for data collection, while the right side is for data parsing:

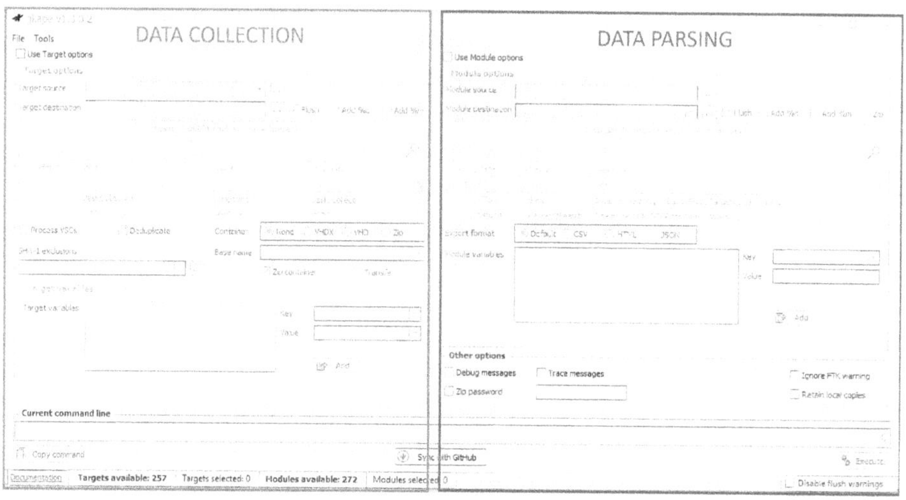

Figure 2.4 – GUI for KAPE

During incident response, these sections can be used together to rapidly collect artifacts from a system and immediately parse them for quick analysis. Investigators can collect data for later analysis or parse artifacts from previous acquisitions.

5. We will begin by configuring the data collection options on the left side of the KAPE interface. First, enable the collection settings by selecting the **Use Target options** checkbox.

Next, select the system or storage device you wish to collect artifacts from using the **Target source** field. In this example, the logical root directory of the system drive (`C:\`) is selected.

Then, choose where the collected data will be stored using the **Target destination** field. The destination should be a directory on the TRIAGE USB drive we prepared earlier. Collected data should never be stored on the target machine itself:

Figure 2.5 – Selecting the target source and storage destination in KAPE

The **Flush** option deletes the contents of the destination directory before the collection begins. Because the collection will be stored in a new directory, this option is left disabled.

Finally, enable **Add %d** and **Add %m**. These options append the collection date and the target machine name to the output directory. Although we will typically use a separate sanitized TRIAGE USB drive for each system, this information can help quickly identify which collection belongs to which system during later analysis.

6. Next, choose a collection module to run. In the **Targets** section of KAPE, select the **! SANS_Triage** module:

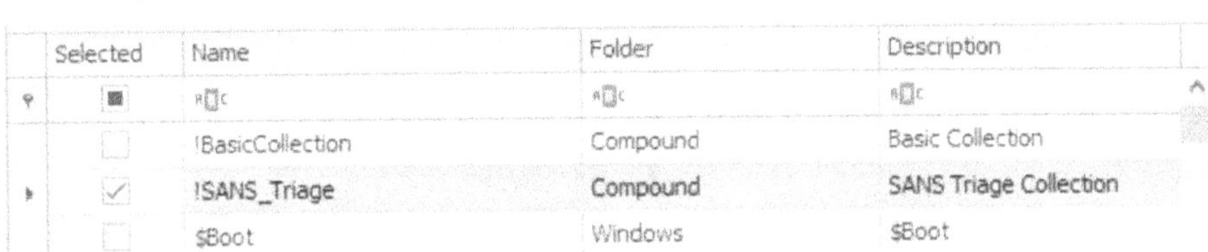

Figure 2.6 – Selecting a collection module to run in KAPE

KAPE uses collection modules to target specific categories of forensic artifacts. These modules allow investigators to quickly gather relevant evidence without manually locating each artifact across the system.

Modules can be designed to collect very specific data, such as web browser artifacts, or broader sets of activity-related evidence. At the time of writing, KAPE includes more than 250 collection modules and more than 260 parsing modules.

7. Below the **Targets** section are additional collection options.

Enable **Process VSCs (Volume Shadow Copies)** and **Deduplicate**. Then, select **Zip** under the **Container** options and set **Base name** to **Data Collection**. Storing the results in a zip container helps preserve the integrity of the collected artifacts by reducing the likelihood that files are modified during later handling or transfer:

Figure 2.7 – Configuring additional collection options in KAPE

Processing volume shadow copies allows KAPE to collect artifacts from Windows Volume Shadow Copy service. These shadow copies may contain older versions of files and logs that can be valuable if an adversary has attempted to hide activity by modifying or deleting artifacts on the live system.

The **Deduplicate** option reduces redundant data during collection, helping minimize duplicate artifacts stored in the output.

8. Now move to the right side of the KAPE interface to configure the parsing modules. Enable parsing by selecting the **Use Module options** checkbox.
   Next, choose a module destination to store the parsed results on your TRIAGE USB drive:

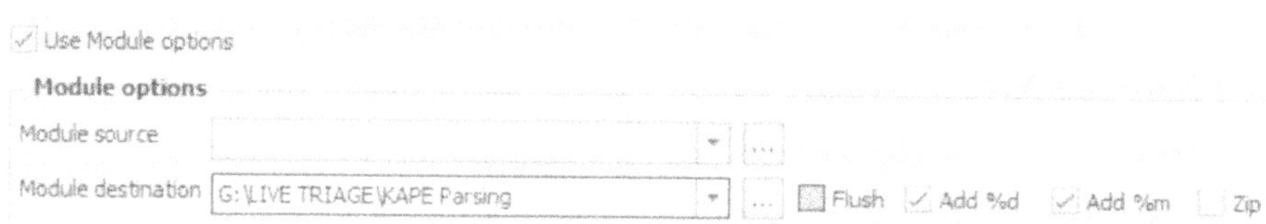

Figure 2.8 – Selecting the storage destination for data parsing in KAPE

As with the collection settings, leave the **Flush** option disabled and enable **Add %d** and **Add %m** so the output directory includes the collection date and target machine name.

The **Module source** option can be ignored in this scenario. It is used when parsing artifacts that were previously collected. Because we are collecting and parsing data simultaneously, KAPE automatically recognizes the collected artifacts from the target configuration on the left side of the interface.

9. Now choose the **parsing modules** to run. In the **Modules** section of KAPE, select the **! EZParser** module:

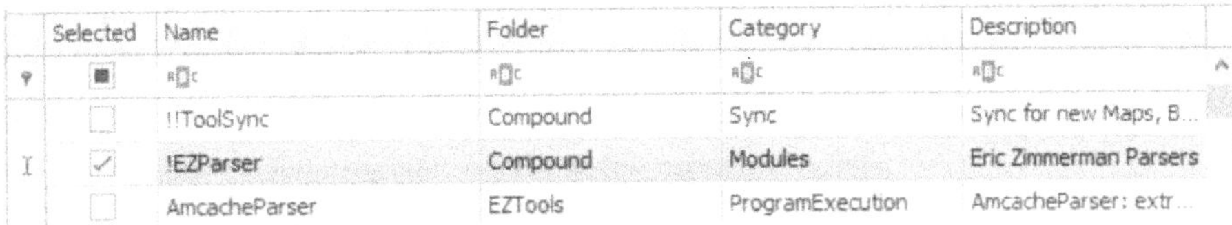

Figure 2.9 – Selecting a parsing module to run in KAPE

Parsing modules process collected artifacts and extract usable forensic data. The **!EZParser** module leverages **Eric Zimmerman's EZ Tools** to quickly parse common Windows system artifacts.

10. We are now ready to execute a basic data collection and parsing workflow with KAPE. The options we selected provide a good starting point during incident response for quickly determining the evidentiary relevance of a system suspected of compromise. Within the **Current command line** output at the bottom of the KAPE interface, you may have noticed a command being generated as options were selected or deselected. This represents the equivalent command used when running the CLI version of KAPE:

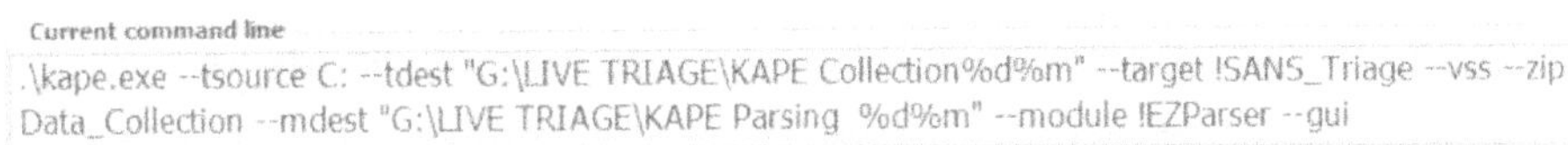

Figure 2.10 – CLI command to collect and parse data using KAPE

11. Select **Execute!** in the lower-left corner to run the command generated by KAPE:

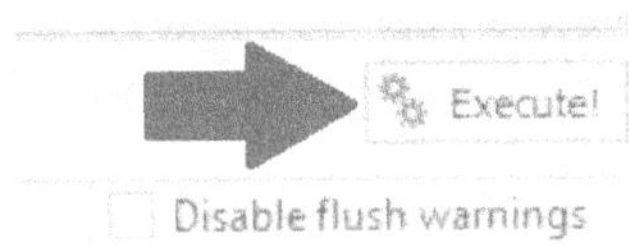

Figure 2.11 – Execute KAPE

12. Windows Command Prompt will open, and the command generated by KAPE will begin running. KAPE requires administrator access to the target computer, so if these commands were entered directly in the CLI version, the Command Prompt session would need to be launched with administrator privileges.
KAPE is a fast, efficient tool designed for rapid triage. The commands we selected will typically complete in a short period of time. Execution progress can be observed in the upper-right corner of Command Prompt:

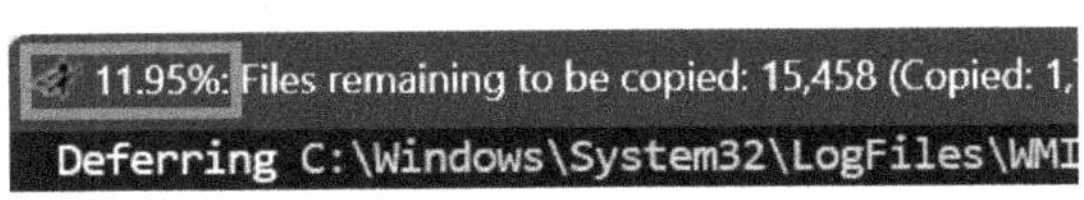

Figure 2.12 – Execution progress in KAPE

13. Once the process is complete, the Command Prompt window will display the total execution time and prompt you to press any key to exit KAPE. This indicates that the collection and parsing workflow has finished successfully:

Figure 2.13 – Execution progress completed in KAPE

14. If we browse to the directory on our **TRIAGE USB** where we stored the collection output and parsed results, we will see two output directories with the corresponding date, time, and target computer name appended to the folder names:

Figure 2.14 – Resulting output from KAPE

15. Within the directory we designated for data collection is the zipped container holding the artifacts acquired from the target computer using the **!SANS_Triage** module. Within the directory we designated for data parsing are the results generated by processing the collected artifacts using the **!EZParser** module, along with their respective log files:

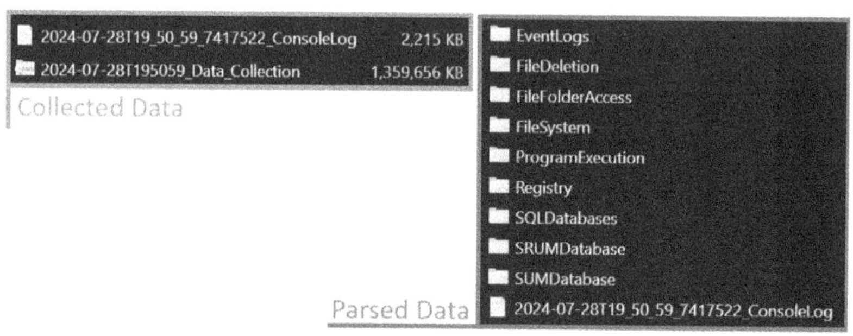

Figure 2.15 – Data collected and parsed using KAPE

By going through the data within the parsed output directories, we can quickly view items such as event logs or executed applications.

The following shows what example results from the `ProgramExecution` artifacts could look like, which record applications executed on the system:

82	C\Windows\prefetch\GKAPE.EXE-E9CCC071.pf	GKAPE.EXE	1
83	C\Windows\prefetch\ITUNES.EXE-C536C2B2.pf	ITUNES.EXE	2
84	C\Windows\prefetch\MSEDGE.EXE-37D25FAA.pf	MSEDGE.EXE	32
85	C\Windows\prefetch\SHELLEXPERIENCEHOST.EXE-BD8CF62B.pf	SHELLEXPERIENCEHOST.EXE	12
86	C\Windows\prefetch\SIHCLIENT.EXE-98C47F6C.pf	SIHCLIENT.EXE	6
87	C\Windows\prefetch\SIHOST.EXE-115B507F.pf	SIHOST.EXE	6
88	C\Windows\prefetch\SMARTSCREEN.EXE-EACC1250.pf	SMARTSCREEN.EXE	25
89	C\Windows\prefetch\SNIPPINGTOOL.EXE-914232B3.pf	SNIPPINGTOOL.EXE	14
90	C\Windows\prefetch\SPPSVC.EXE-96070FE0.pf	SPPSVC.EXE	50
91	C\Windows\prefetch\SRTASKS.EXE-3C9D2EEC.pf	SRTASKS.EXE	5
92	C\Windows\prefetch\SRUPDATEAPI.EXE-8F5AFB13.pf	SRUPDATEAPI.EXE	2
93	C\Windows\prefetch\STARTMENUEXPERIENCEHOST.EXE-4DCEE2F2.pf	STARTMENUEXPERIENCEHOST.EXE	16
94	C\Windows\prefetch\SVCHOST.EXE-012BA85C.pf	SVCHOST.EXE	1
95	C\Windows\prefetch\SVCHOST.EXE-0EC77F95.pf	SVCHOST.EXE	1
96	C\Windows\prefetch\SVCHOST.EXE-14758CE1.pf	SVCH0ST.EXE	21
97	C\Windows\prefetch\SVCHOST.EXE-1A7CA621.pf	SVCHOST.EXE	1
98	C\Windows\prefetch\SVCHOST.EXE-1C33C471.pf	SVCHOST.EXE	5
99	C\Windows\prefetch\SVCHOST.EXE-2186C203.pf	SVCHOST.EXE	13

Figure 2.16 – Program execution data parsed using KAPE

Look closely at line item **96** in *Figure 2.16*. While there are several executions of `SVCHOST.EXE` present (a normal Windows process), the entry shown on line item 96 substitutes the number `0` for the letter `O`. The `SVCHOST` is often abused by attackers in a Windows environment because it is a common process and there are many of them running at any given time, making it easy to blend in.

Additionally, this process has been run 21 times, which could indicate a persistence mechanism in place, meaning it is designed to help the attacker maintain access to the system by overcoming actions such as a system restart. This discovery would be worrisome enough to warrant additional triage or analysis of the system.

At this stage, we have not proven compromise, but we have identified enough evidence to justify deeper analysis and prioritize this system for further investigation.

How it works...

During incident response, investigators often identify multiple potentially affected systems across a network. Creating a full forensic image of every suspected machine immediately is rarely practical, so investigators must first determine which systems require the most urgent attention.

Tools such as KAPE allow investigators to rapidly preview a system by collecting and parsing targeted sets of artifacts. This allows responders to quickly assess a system's relevance and prioritize further analysis.

For example, if triage reveals dormant malware but no evidence of recent activity, the system may still require full forensic imaging but can be analyzed later while investigators continue identifying other affected systems. In contrast, if triage reveals active malware in memory or evidence of ongoing data exfiltration, that system immediately becomes a higher priority for deeper investigation.

This prioritization is one of the key advantages of using KAPE during incident response. Rather than performing time-consuming analysis on every machine, investigators can quickly identify the systems most likely to contain critical evidence. KAPE can be run directly on a target machine, and later in this chapter, we will also see how similar collection capabilities can be leveraged remotely using Velociraptor. While KAPE provides fast triage on individual systems, enterprise investigations require visibility across many systems simultaneously.

Scaling evidence identification

Quickly triaging a single machine is extremely useful, but it is still too slow for modern incidents. Ideally, we need the ability to search across thousands of systems simultaneously to track an adversary and rapidly identify which hosts are relevant to the investigation. That's where Velociraptor comes in.

Velociraptor is a free, open source platform for monitoring, querying, and collecting evidence across large networks, regardless of the endpoint operating system. It contains a large library of ready-made artifacts, and when something custom is required, investigators can write queries using **velociraptor query language** (**VQL**), which is similar to SQL but purpose-built for endpoint forensic collection.

Getting ready

We will start by performing a simple evaluation-style deployment to familiarize ourselves with the capabilities of Velociraptor. This local evaluation instance is intended to demonstrate workflow rather than a production deployment. It requires only a single local computer and a copy of the Velociraptor executable.

Velociraptor can be downloaded from the following GitHub repository:

`https://github.com/Velocidex/velociraptor/releases/`

Once there, click on a recent release of Velociraptor. Scroll to the bottom of the page to locate the version appropriate for the operating system you plan to install Velociraptor on. You will notice many versions available because Velociraptor can be installed on a variety of operating systems. We are running Microsoft Windows workstations, so in this case, we will locate and download the Windows executable `velociraptor-vX.Y.Z-windows-amd64.exe`, as shown:

Figure 2.17 – Downloading Velociraptor

How to do it...

1. To perform a local evaluation installation of Velociraptor, navigate to the directory where the Velociraptor executable was saved.
   Click in the Windows Explorer location bar, type **cmd**, and press *Enter*. This launches a Command Prompt instance directly within the same folder as the Velociraptor executable, allowing commands to be executed without manually changing directories.

   For full access to system artifacts during the evaluation, run Command Prompt with administrative privileges:

Figure 2.18 – Running Command Prompt from the appropriate directory

2. When Command Prompt opens, it will display the file path of the current directory. In this example, the Velociraptor executable is stored in the default `Downloads` folder, so Command Prompt opens in this location.
   From this directory, enter the Velociraptor executable filename followed by the `gui` argument to launch a local evaluation instance of Velociraptor:

```
velociraptor-v0.72.4-windows-amd64.exe gui
```

3. After executing the command, output will begin to display in the Command Prompt window, and the Velociraptor GUI will launch in your default web browser, as shown:

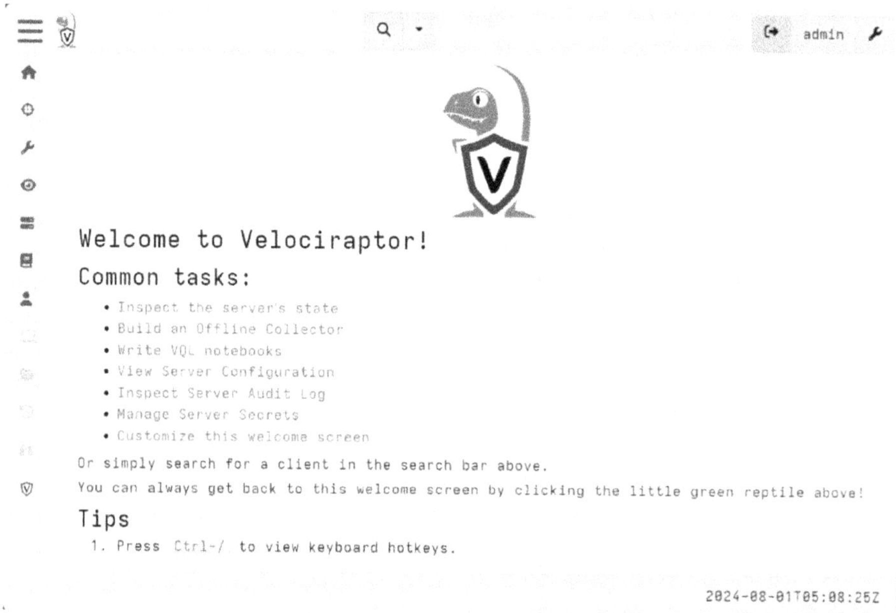

Figure 2.19 – Velociraptor admin GUI

The Velociraptor GUI provides a user-friendly interface for interacting with the platform. Key elements include configuration options in the upper-right corner, a search bar for locating connected endpoints or clients, and an expandable sidebar on the left containing available tools and functions.

> **Note**
>
> This local evaluation instance uses a self-signed certificate by default, so your browser may display a security warning. This warning is expected in a local evaluation environment and can be safely bypassed.
>
> The Command Prompt window can be minimized, but do not close it. Closing this window will terminate the local Velociraptor instance.

4. In the client search bar at the top, open the dropdown and select **Show All**, or enter `all` in the search field to display a list of all connected endpoints:

Figure 2.20 – Searching for connected endpoint clients in Velociraptor

5. Here, you will see a single client representing your local computer. This entry includes the computer name and details about the installed operating system.
   In a full deployment of Velociraptor, client software is installed on each endpoint within the network, and this list may contain hundreds or thousands of clients:

Figure 2.21 – Viewing connected endpoint clients in Velociraptor

6. Click the client ID for your local computer, highlighted in green in the **Client ID** column. This will open a screen displaying details for that endpoint.
   From this view, various options are available at the top of the interface that allow you to interact with the system, including accessing files, acquiring evidence, quarantining the endpoint to restrict user access, and running shell commands. The expandable sidebar on the left also becomes fully available, providing access to additional functions:

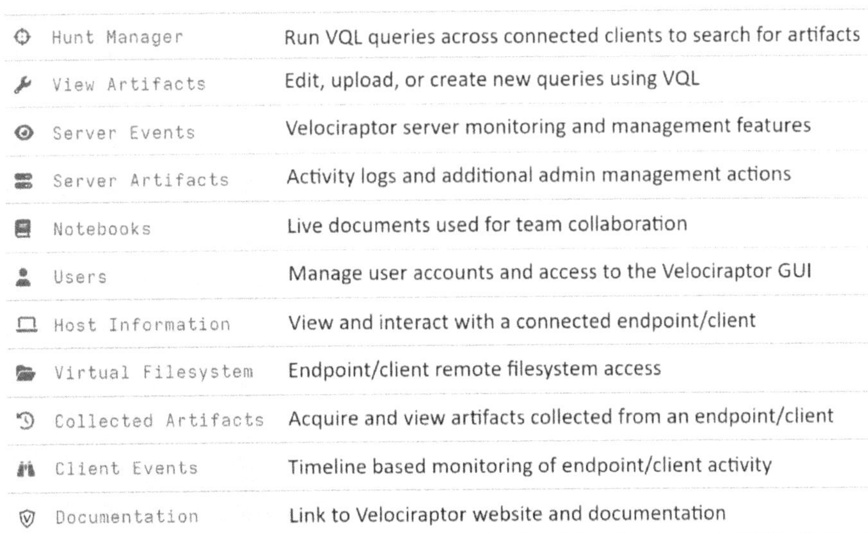

Figure 2.22 – Velociraptor menu options

7. Next, initiate a hunt in Velociraptor. Hunts allow investigators to run artifact-driven collection or analysis tasks across one or more clients.
   From the sidebar menu, select **Hunt Manager**, then click the plus (**+**) button to start a new hunt:

Figure 2.23 – Starting a new hunt in Velociraptor

8. In the pop-up window that appears, enter `Web Browser History` in the `Description` field.
   Additional configuration options are available, including setting how long the hunt will run and whether to search all clients, specific clients, or only certain operating systems within the environment.

   Since only a single client is connected (the local machine), the default settings can be used. Then, choose **Select Artifacts** from the options at the bottom:

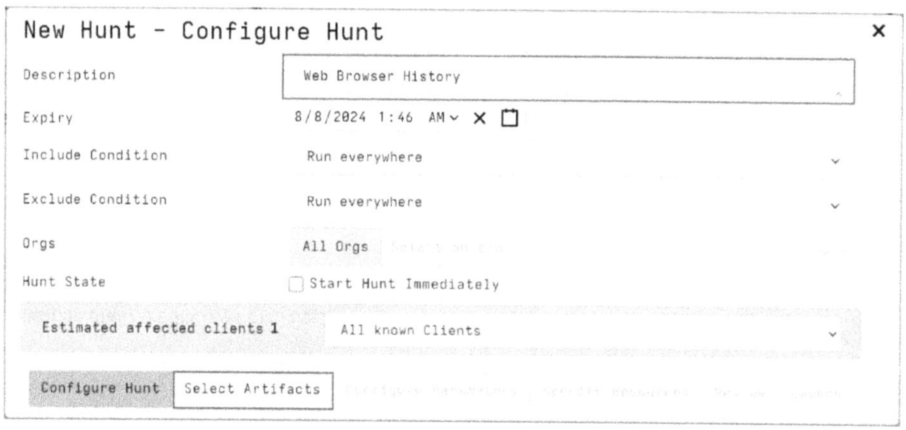

Figure 2.24 – Configuring a hunt in Velociraptor

9. Scroll down to the Windows artifact section and select the artifacts corresponding to the web browsers installed on your system.
   As artifacts are selected, additional information will appear to the right, including a description and the associated VQL query used for collection.

   In this example environment, Chrome, Edge, and Firefox artifacts are available and selected. Prepackaged artifacts may not exist for all applications (such as Opera). In such cases, a custom artifact may need to be created or an existing community artifact imported into Velociraptor.

   After selecting the desired browser artifacts, click **Configure Parameters**:

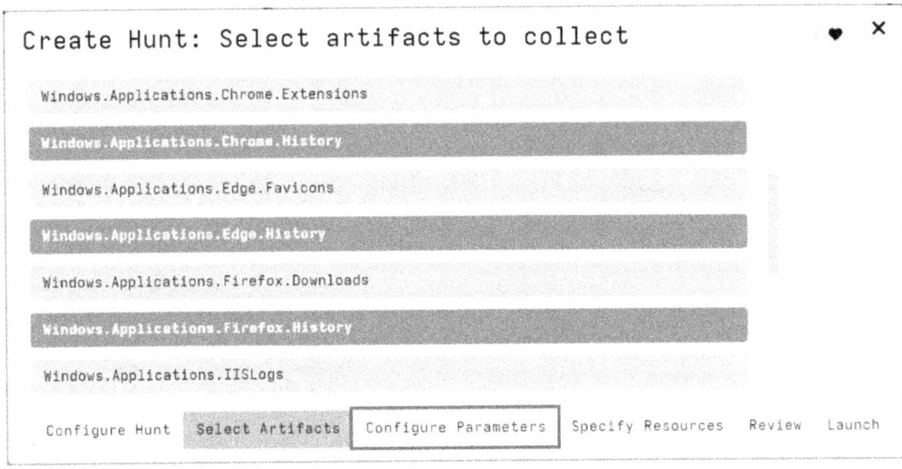

Figure 2.25 – Selecting hunt artifacts in Velociraptor

10. These options allow modification of the VQL associated with the selected artifacts. Additionally, **regular expressions** (**regex**) can be used to target specific data within the collected web browser history.
    Regex filtering can be used to target specific indicators, such as known malicious URLs, allowing investigators to quickly identify affected systems.

    For this example, the default settings can be used. Click **Specify Resources** to continue:

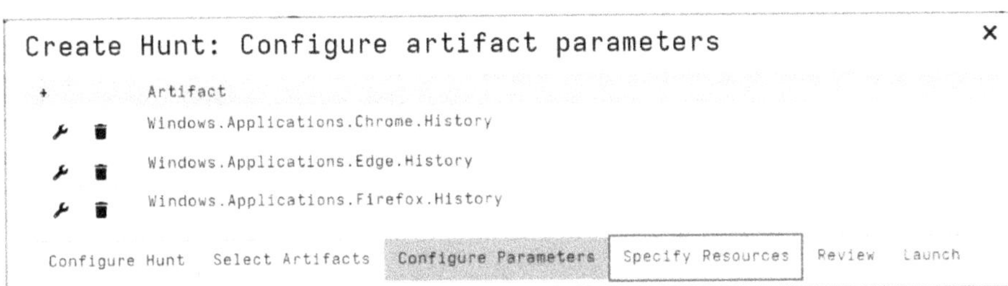

Figure 2.26 – Configuring hunt parameters in Velociraptor

11. These options allow limits to be placed on system resources used during a hunt, such as CPU utilization.
    These fields can be left blank to accept the default behavior of no resource limitations. In a production environment, however, it may be necessary to define these limits based on the expected data volume or duration of the hunt.

    Click **Review** to continue:

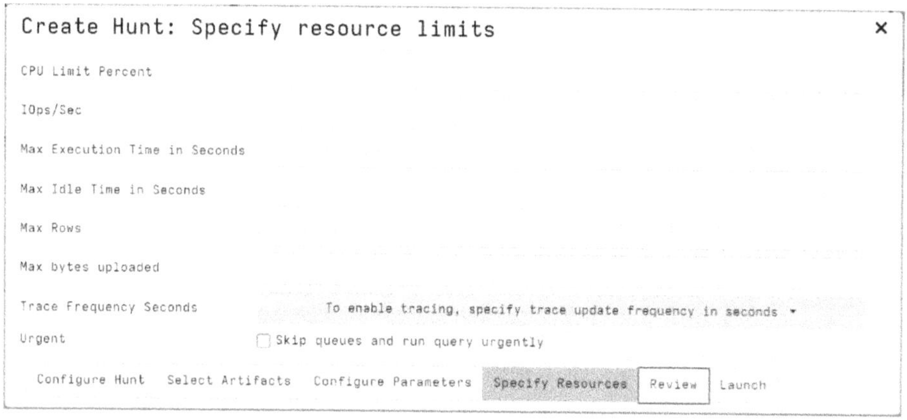

Figure 2.27 – Limiting physical resource usage during a hunt in Velociraptor

12. This screen provides a summary of the hunt configuration. Changes cannot be made directly from this view, but previous steps can be revisited using the menu options. Click **Launch** to begin the hunt:

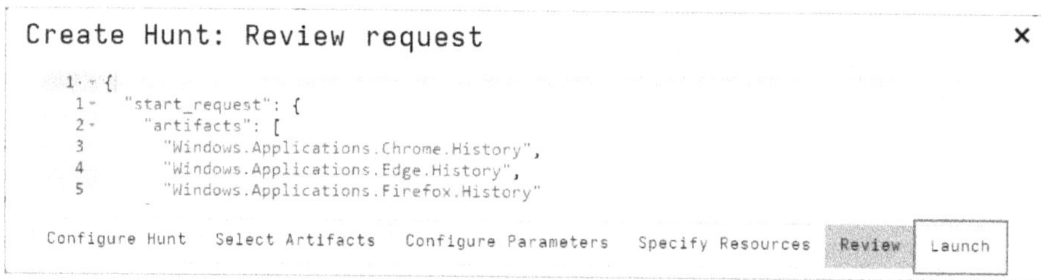

Figure 2.28 – Reviewing hunt configuration selections in Velociraptor

13. Select the hunt you created, then click the play button from the menu options:

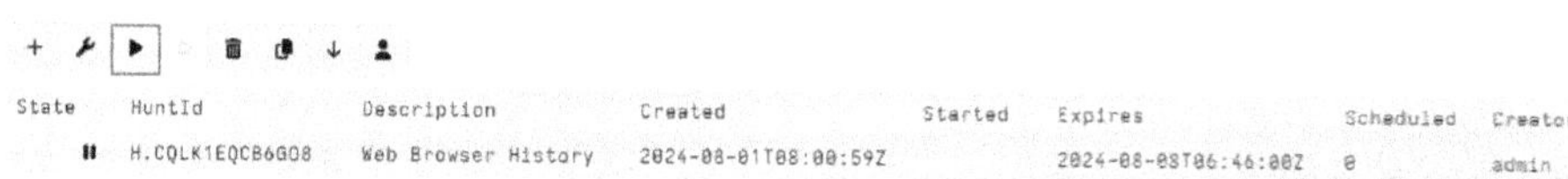

Figure 2.29 – Choosing a configured hunt to run in Velociraptor

14. When prompted to run the hunt, click **Run it!**.

Figure 2.30 – Running a hunt in Velociraptor

15. During the initial configuration, an expiry time was set to define how long the hunt will run. By default, this duration is approximately one week.

    For this example, allow the hunt to run for a few minutes, then click the stop button to end it:

Figure 2.31 – Ending a hunt in Velociraptor

16. In the **Results** summary in the lower-right corner of the screen, click the download results option, then select **Full Download**:

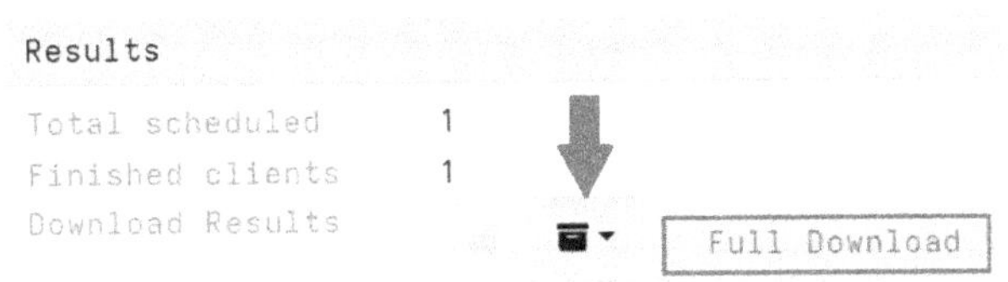

Figure 2.32 – Options to download hunt results in Velociraptor

17. A new section will appear displaying the downloaded results. Click the results filename shown to save the file to your computer:

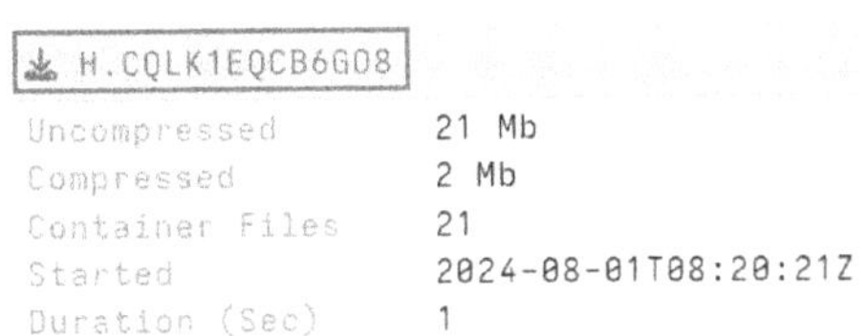

Figure 2.33 – Downloadable file containing hunt results from Velociraptor

18. The downloaded results will be contained in a compressed archive. Extract the archive and navigate to the `results` folder.

    The folder contains CSV and JSON files with web browser history data for each selected artifact. The CSV files can be opened using a spreadsheet application such as Microsoft Excel or LibreOffice Calc.

    In this example, the collected results contained nearly 10,000 combined entries spanning several months of browser activity, including software searches and installation-related activity:

1	User	visit_time	title	visit_count	last_visit_time	visit_duration
2	cboun	2023-12-04T01:44:41Z	Welcome to Microsoft Edge	1	2023-12-04T01:44:41Z	00:05.0
3	cboun	2023-12-04T01:45:32Z	asus tuf rtx 4060ti driver - Search	2	2023-12-04T01:45:34Z	18:11.4
4	cboun	2023-12-04T01:49:37Z	download msi afterburner - Search	2	2023-12-04T01:50:11Z	04:37.7
5	cboun	2023-12-04T01:49:44Z	download corsair rgb fan software - Search	1	2023-12-04T01:49:44Z	00:31.1
6	cboun	2023-12-04T01:49:54Z	download ccleaner - Search	2	2023-12-04T01:50:25Z	00:33.9
7	cboun	2023-12-04T01:50:00Z	download firefox - Search	2	2023-12-04T01:50:33Z	00:36.0
8	cboun	2023-12-04T01:50:04Z	download chrome - Search	2	2023-12-04T01:50:39Z	00:36.1

Figure 2.34 – Example results from web browser history hunt using Velociraptor

19. In the previous section, data was triaged and collected using KAPE. Velociraptor can perform similar collection tasks remotely and at scale.
    Using the same process, create another hunt. This time, instead of selecting web browser history artifacts, locate and select the `Windows.KapeFiles.Targets` artifact.

    Click **Configure Parameters** to continue:

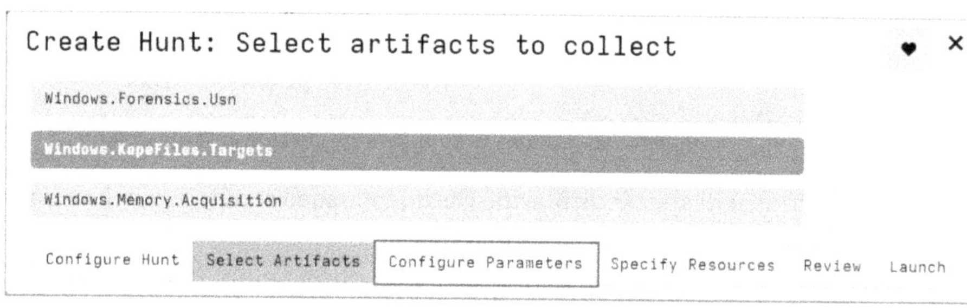

Figure 2.35 – Configuring a KAPE collection hunt using Velociraptor

20. Select the wrench-shaped icon next to the selected artifact:

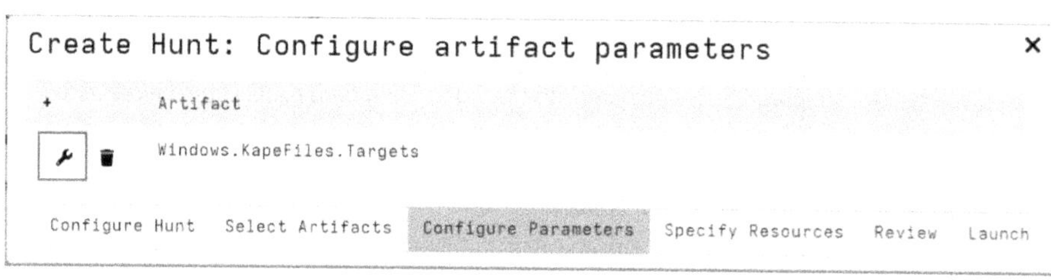

Figure 2.36 – KAPE artifact parameter configuration in Velociraptor

21. In the Device field, multiple drive letters may be listed depending on the system configuration. In this example, both C: and D: are present due to a secondary storage drive.

    Artifacts can be collected from each listed drive:

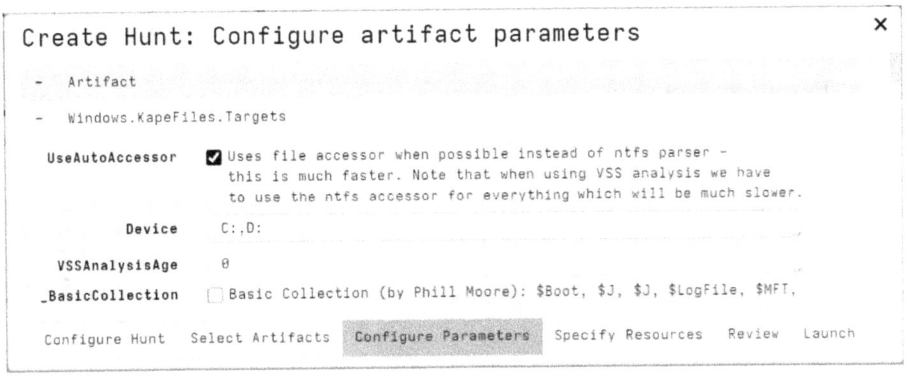

Figure 2.37 – KAPE settings in Velociraptor

22. Scroll down and select the **_SANS_Triage** option, then click **Launch**. Run the hunt using the same steps as before:

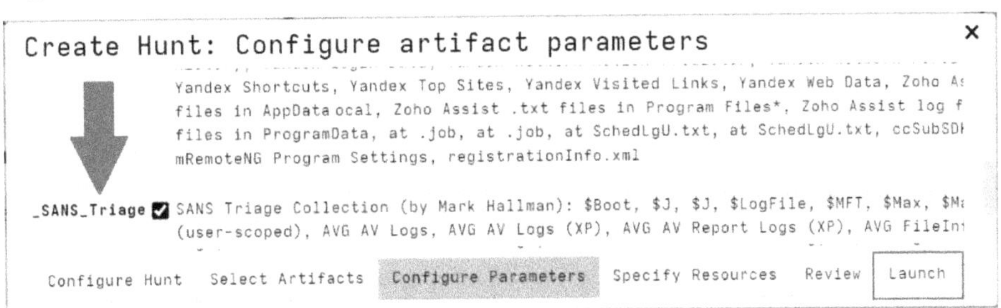

Figure 2.38 – Selecting a KAPE collection module in Velociraptor

23. After sufficient data has been collected, stop the hunt to review the results. In this example, the hunt was allowed to run for approximately 10 minutes and collected nearly 5 GB of data, though results will vary depending on the selected modules and the number of targeted hosts.

    Using the same methods as before, download and review the results. Both collected data and parsed results will be available, similar to when KAPE is executed locally.

    The collected data can be further processed using KAPE or analyzed with other forensic tools as part of a broader investigation workflow:

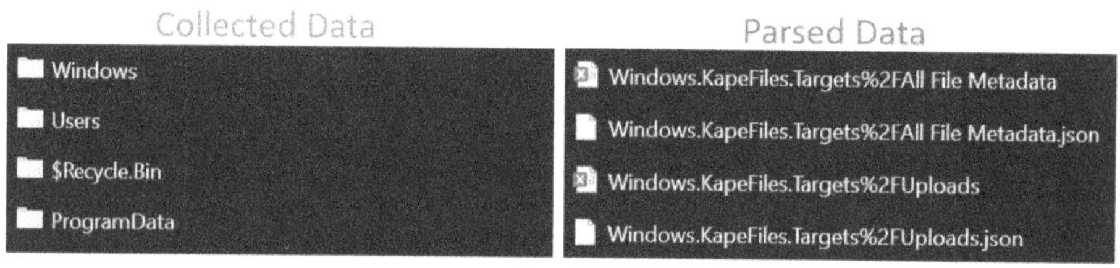

Figure 2.39 – Data acquired using a KAPE artifact hunt in Velociraptor

24. Click **Virtual Filesystem** from the expandable menu:

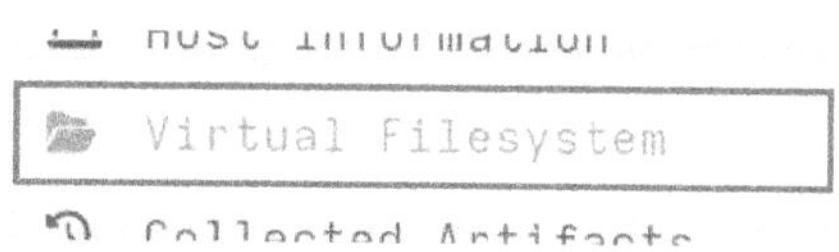

Figure 2.40 – Choosing the Virtual Filesystem option in Velociraptor

25. **Virtual Filesystem** allows you to browse and interact with files on a connected endpoint in real time.

    To begin, select the **auto** folder in the left pane. Then, click the refresh button in the upper-right menu to populate the directory contents.

    You can continue navigating through subdirectories by selecting folders and refreshing as needed:

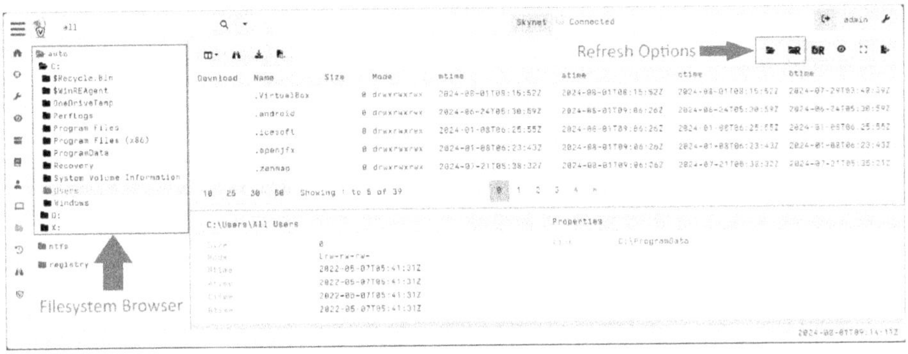

Figure 2.41 – Browsing endpoint filesystems with Velociraptor

> **Note**
>
> Note on evidence integrity
>
> Accessing files in a live environment can modify filesystem metadata such as access timestamps and system logs. Always document any interaction with the filesystem to preserve forensic integrity.

26. Click **Host Information** from the expandable menu:

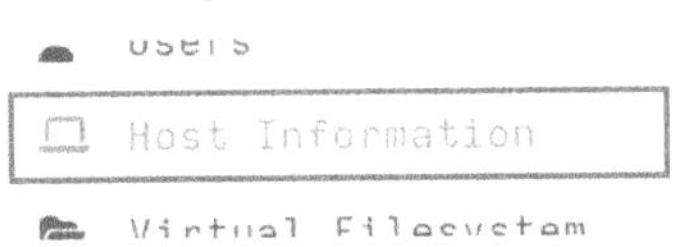

Figure 2.42 – Choosing the Host Information option in Velociraptor

27. Click **>_Shell** from the upper-right menu bar:

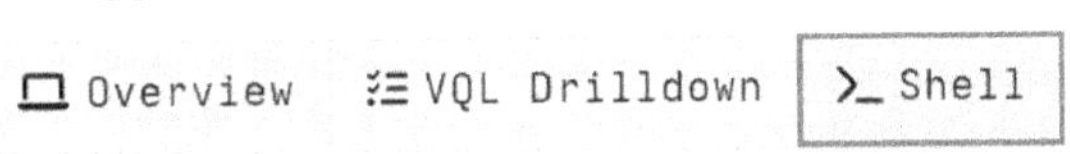

Figure 2.43 – Choosing the Shell access option for a connected client in Velociraptor

28. The command input field allows you to execute CLI commands on a connected client. By default, PowerShell is selected.
    Run the following command:

```
netstat -aon
```

This command displays all active network connections and listening ports on the system, along with their associated **process IDs** (**PIDs**).

This is useful when investigating potential unauthorized remote access, allowing you to identify suspicious connections and map them to running processes.

When ready, click **Launch** to execute the command:

Figure 2.44 – Running CLI input on a connected client via PowerShell in Velociraptor

29. Once the command has completed, click the load output option (the eye-shaped icon) near the left side of the `netstat -aon` results:

Figure 2.45 – Loading output from endpoint PowerShell commands in Velociraptor

30. The output is displayed directly within the Velociraptor GUI, as shown in the following figure.
    The netstat command provides a quick way to identify suspicious remote connections that may serve as **indicators of compromise** (**IoCs**). Additionally, PowerShell and shell access within Velociraptor can be leveraged to perform a wide range of incident response tasks.

    Correlating suspicious connections with PIDs can help identify unauthorized or malicious processes running on the system:

Figure 2.46 – Viewing output from endpoint PowerShell commands in Velociraptor

How it works...

Running an evaluation instance of Velociraptor provides a simple way to launch the platform and begin exploring its capabilities without requiring a full deployment. In this mode, all artifacts execute locally on the host system and return results directly to the GUI, rather than being distributed across multiple endpoints.

This local configuration is intended for evaluation and basic practice. It uses a self-signed certificate, is not configured as a production service, and terminates when the console window is closed.

Next, we will examine how to deploy Velociraptor in a more complete operational environment.

Building a Velociraptor server

In real investigations, centralized DFIR platforms enable investigators to coordinate response across multiple systems simultaneously, rather than operating on isolated machines. Deploying, securing, and operating a Velociraptor server for incident response is a complex undertaking that extends beyond the scope of this chapter. A practical way to develop familiarity is to build a small-scale deployment in a controlled environment and practice core tasks such as client enrollment, artifact collection, and hunt execution.

This section focuses on a lab-style deployment designed to teach the mechanics of setup and operation rather than provide a comprehensive production hardening guide. The following steps outline a minimal, defensible server deployment along with the controls needed to conduct safe, auditable hunts.

Getting ready

A real-world Velociraptor deployment requires installation on a server, with the Velociraptor frontend communicating with endpoint clients across the network and providing access through a web-based administrative GUI.

For a lab-style environment, you will deploy a single system as the server along with several client machines (Windows, macOS, and Linux). This setup allows you to practice client enrollment, run hunts, and perform targeted collections across multiple operating systems using systems available within your home network.

How to do it...

1. The Velociraptor server can be deployed on a physical system or within a **virtual machine** (**VM**). While Velociraptor supports Windows and macOS, it is optimized for Linux-based operating systems. A distribution such as Ubuntu is commonly used and can be downloaded from `https://ubuntu.com/download/desktop`.

   For a persistent lab environment, install Ubuntu on a dedicated system or within a VM. When using a virtualization platform such as **VirtualBox** or **VMware**, configure the network adapter in **bridged mode** so the server receives an IP address from your home network. This allows client systems to communicate with the server while preserving the environment across reboots.

   > Note
   >
   > Alternative approach: Bootable Ubuntu USB
   >
   > If networking issues are encountered in a VM, an alternative is to create a bootable Ubuntu USB drive using a tool such as Rufus and run Velociraptor from a separate system. Standard live USB environments do not persist changes across reboots, so this method is best suited for temporary lab use.

Once the system is prepared, open a terminal and download the latest version of Velociraptor from the GitHub repository. Here is an example:

```
wget https://github.com/Velocidex/velociraptor/releases/download/v0.72/
velociraptor-v0.72.4-linux-amd64
```

2. Now, make the Velociraptor binary executable:

```
chmod +x velociraptor-v0.72.4-linux-amd64
```

3. Run the executable to begin the Velociraptor configuration process:

```
./velociraptor-v0.72.4-linux-amd64 config generate -i
```

The configuration process prompts you with a series of questions based on how you plan to deploy the Velociraptor server:

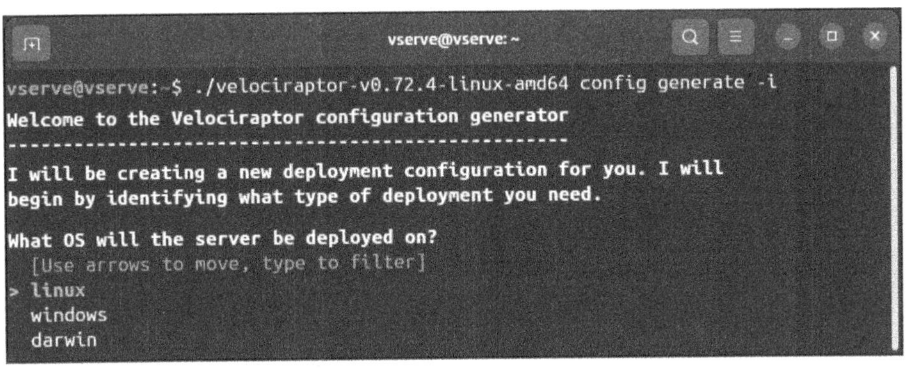

Figure 2.47 – Velociraptor server configuration generator

4. During the configuration process, you will be prompted to specify directories for storing data:

Figure 2.48 – Velociraptor server configuration storage directory options

When prompted for directory paths, you can specify custom locations or press *Enter* to accept the default values.

To avoid permission-related issues, you can create the directory manually and assign appropriate ownership before continuing. Run the following commands, replacing <username> with your own:

```
sudo mkdir /opt/velociraptor
sudo chown -R <username> /opt/velociraptor
```

The first command creates the default directory used by Velociraptor. The second assigns ownership to your user account to prevent access denials during the configuration process.

5. You will be prompted to select a certificate type. The **Self Signed SSL** option shown in the Velociraptor prompt is sufficient for a lab or practice deployment. For a production environment, consider using `Let's Encrypt` or **single sign-on** (**SSO**) for improved security:

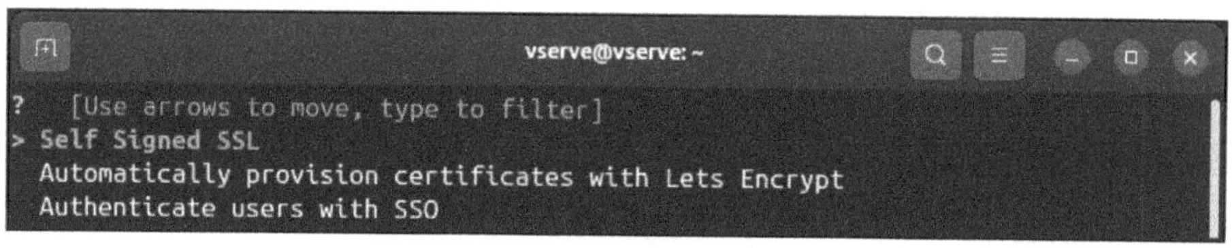

Figure 2.49 – Velociraptor certificate/authentication options

When prompted for the DNS name (`hostname`) of the master frontend, a real-world deployment would use a publicly accessible hostname. For a lab environment, you can specify the local IP address of the server. To determine the IP address, open a new terminal and run the following command:

```
hostname -I
```

Enter the returned IP address in place of the default localhost value so client systems on your network can communicate with the server.

6. Continue through the configuration process, accepting the default port settings. You will be prompted to create a GUI username and password, which will be used to log in to the Velociraptor interface.

   You can add multiple users if desired, or press *Enter* after creating the first user to continue.

   In this example, a single user named `admin` has been created:

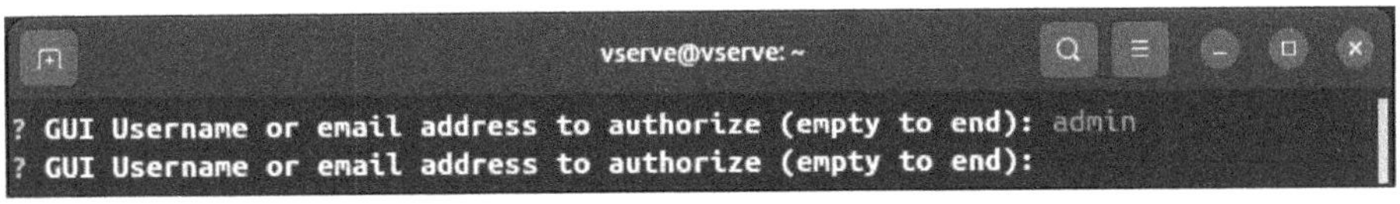

Figure 2.50 – Creating Velociraptor users during the configuration process

7. Complete the configuration process, accepting the default values for the server and client configuration files.
8. Next, create a Debian package to install Velociraptor using the generated `server.config.yaml` file. Since Ubuntu is a Debian-based distribution, a `.deb` package is used for installation.
   Run the following command:

```
./velociraptor-v0.72.4-linux-amd64 --config server.config.yaml debian
server --binary velociraptor-v0.72.4-linux-amd64
```

9. Install the Velociraptor Debian (`.deb`) package:

```
sudo dpkg -i velociraptor_server_0.72.4_amd64.deb
```

10. Verify that the Velociraptor service is running by executing the following command:

```
systemctl status velociraptor_server
```

11. If the service is running successfully, you should see output similar to the following. You are now ready to log in to the Velociraptor GUI:

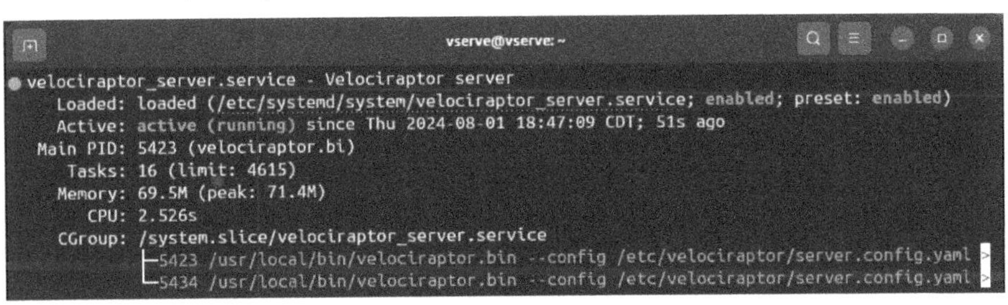

Figure 2.51 – Checking the Velociraptor server status

12. Open a web browser and enter the address `https://localhost:8889`:

Figure 2.52 – Accessing the Velociraptor GUI

13. Your browser will display a security warning when accessing the interface. This occurs because the **Self Signed SSL** option was selected during configuration.
For a lab environment, this warning can be safely bypassed by selecting **Advanced...** and then **Accept the Risk and Continue**:

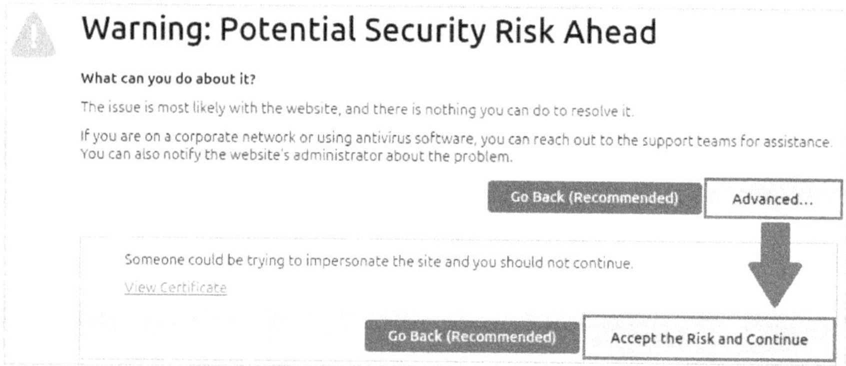

Figure 2.53 – Accessing the Velociraptor GUI (cont.)

14. You will be prompted to log in using the username and password created during configuration:

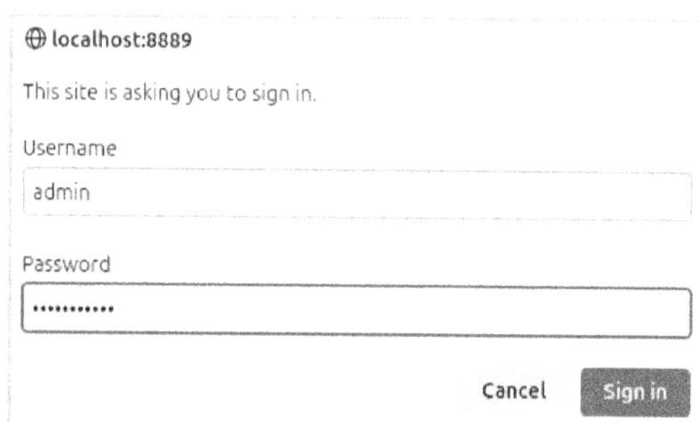

Figure 2.54 – Velociraptor GUI login

15. After logging in to the Velociraptor GUI, you will see that no clients are currently connected. The next step is to enroll client systems from other machines on your network:

Figure 2.55 – Empty client list in Velociraptor

16. **Adding a Linux client**: Since this system is already running Linux, the server can also be enrolled as a client. First, generate the client package:

```
./velociraptor-v0.72.4-linux-amd64 --config client.config.yaml debian
client
```

17. Next, install the generated package:

```
sudo dpkg -i velociraptor_client_0.72.4_amd64.deb
```

18. After installation, return to the Velociraptor GUI and refresh the client list. The system will appear as a connected client:

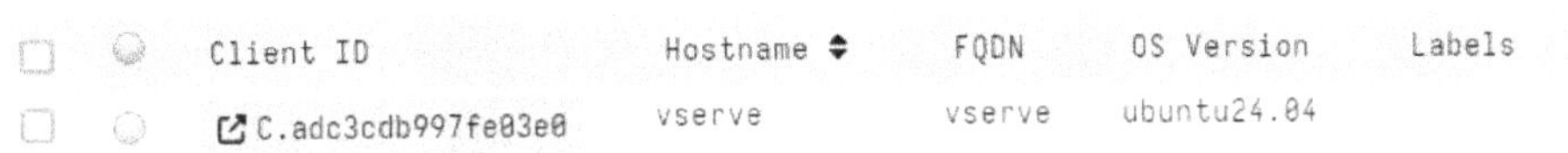

Figure 2.56 – Linux-based client added in Velociraptor

19. **Adding a Windows client**: To add a Windows client, begin by downloading the Velociraptor Windows MSI package from the GitHub repository. You can download it directly using the following command:

```
wget https://github.com/Velocidex/velociraptor/releases/download/v0.72/
velociraptor-v0.72.4-windows-amd64.msi
```

20. Next, repackage the MSI file to include your preconfigured `client.config.yaml` file created earlier. Run the following command, specifying a name for the output file (in this example, `windows_agent`):

```
./velociraptor-v0.72.4-linux-amd64 config repack --msi velociraptor-
v0.72.4-windows-amd64.msi client.config.yaml windows_agent
```

This generates a single installer file named `windows_agent` in the current directory. This file can be reused to enroll multiple Windows clients:

Figure 2.57 – MSI file to install on a Windows-based machine

21. Copy the generated file to a Windows system on your network. From the target system, open a Command Prompt in the directory containing the file and run the following command:

```
msiexec /i windows_agent
```

Adding a Darwin (macOS) client: Velociraptor provides macOS client binaries labeled as *Darwin*, which correspond to the Unix-based operating system underlying macOS.

22. Begin by copying your preconfigured `client.config.yaml` file from the Velociraptor server to the macOS system you wish to enroll.
23. Next, download the appropriate Velociraptor Darwin binary from the GitHub repository. Be sure to select the correct architecture:
    - Arm64 for Apple Silicon (M1/M2/M3 systems)
    - AMD64 for Intel-based Macs

The example file used for this exercise is `velociraptor-v0.72.4-darwin-arm64`.

Place both the Velociraptor binary and the `client.config.yaml` file in the same directory on the macOS system. Open a terminal and navigate to that directory.

Make the binary executable:

```
chmod +x velociraptor-v0.72.4-darwin-arm64
```

If macOS blocks execution due to security restrictions, remove the `quarantine` attribute with the following:

```
xattr -d com.apple.quarantine velociraptor-v0.72.4-darwin-arm64
```

Now install the client as a service using the preconfigured YAML file:

```
sudo ./velociraptor-v0.72.4-darwin-arm64 --config client.config.yaml
service install
```

At this point, you have a functioning Velociraptor deployment capable of monitoring and performing incident response across multiple systems on your network.

This lab environment allows you to practice real-world workflows such as client enrollment, artifact collection, remote triage, and live response across operating systems.

In this example, a laptop running Ubuntu has been configured as the Velociraptor server, with multiple connected clients including Linux, Windows, and macOS systems:

Client ID	Hostname	FQDN	OS Version
C.42737686a9471500	DESKTOP-7MP7E92	DESKTOP-7MP7E92	Microsoft Windows 11 Pro10.0.22631 Build 22631
C.62bf5aac71abac6e	ubuntu	ubuntu	ubuntu24.04
C.c86c745a8f14c75a	Codys-Mac-mini.local	localhost	darwin14.5
C.d21513f0565b9164	Skynet	Skynet	Microsoft Windows 11 Home10.0.22631 Build 22631

Figure 2.58 – Velociraptor clients connected across the home network

This approach scales from small home labs to enterprise environments with hundreds or thousands of endpoints.

If you encounter issues with connecting clients, you can run Velociraptor in verbose mode on the server to identify potential problems, such as directory permission issues or connection failures.

24. To do so, run the following command from a terminal on the Velociraptor server:

```
velociraptor --config server.config.yaml frontend -v
```

How it works...

We have achieved scalable incident response by deploying a centralized server capable of accessing, monitoring, quarantining, and acquiring evidence from systems across a network. Implementing a DFIR platform such as Velociraptor or commercial tools such as F-Response significantly expands and streamlines incident response and threat-hunting capabilities.

As systems of interest are identified, Velociraptor can be used to initiate targeted evidence collection to identify and validate potential IoCs. Once confirmed, affected systems can be isolated and further investigated through additional artifact collection or full forensic acquisition as needed.

In a production deployment, securing the Velociraptor server is critical. For example, instead of using self-signed certificates, a trusted certificate authority should be implemented. Because centralized DFIR platforms provide broad access across the network, they must be properly secured to prevent unauthorized use. If compromised, such a system could be leveraged by an attacker in the same way it is used by defenders.

Further documentation, including guidance on securing deployments, can be found at the Velociraptor website: `https://docs.velociraptor.app/docs/`.

Initial malware investigation

If an investigation yields a recovered malware sample, the next step is to assess its capabilities and potential impact. Understanding what the malware is designed to do helps identify attacker objectives, affected systems, and where additional artifacts may be found.

While in-depth analysis may ultimately be performed by a malware reverse-engineering specialist, digital forensic investigators can take several immediate steps to begin building an initial understanding of the sample.

One of the first steps is to conduct research to determine whether the malware has been previously identified. Many malware families are well documented, with publicly available reports, IoCs, and behavioral profiles.

In other cases, particularly when dealing with more advanced or custom malware, little or no external information may be available. In these situations, basic malware analysis techniques and tools can be used to begin identifying functionality and behavior.

Getting ready

To avoid accidental infection during analysis, this section does not use live malware samples. All examples are performed using a controlled dataset.

For additional practice, real malware samples can be obtained from sources such as MalwareBazaar, which maintains a repository of known malicious files: `https://bazaar.abuse.ch/browse/`.

If working with live malware, ensure analysis is conducted within an isolated and controlled environment.

For the exercises in this section, we will use the Microsoft Windows dataset available in this book's GitHub repository. To access the repository link, follow the steps in the *"Download the example code files section"* in the Preface.

How to do it...

In this section, we will use quick and effective techniques to identify executable files of interest and determine whether they may be malicious.

Scanning with Sigcheck

Sigcheck is a command-line utility developed by Mark Russinovich that provides detailed information about executable files on Microsoft Windows systems, including version data and digital signature details. It can also be used to scan a system for executables matching specific criteria, such as unsigned files, making it a useful tool for quickly identifying potential malware.

Sigcheck can be downloaded from the Microsoft Sysinternals collection:

`https://learn.microsoft.com/en-us/sysinternals/downloads/sigcheck`

Before scanning for suspicious executables, the forensic image must first be mounted so its contents can be examined:

1. In many investigations, Sigcheck is used against acquired forensic images. Begin by mounting the image using Arsenal Image Mounter, available at `https://arsenalrecon.com/downloads`.

   Mount the Microsoft Windows forensic image as read-only by selecting **Mount disk image**, choosing the `Lenovo ThinkPad.E01` image, and ensuring **Disk device, read only** is selected before clicking **OK**.

   Take note of the assigned drive letter. In the examples shown, the image is mounted as drive `G:`

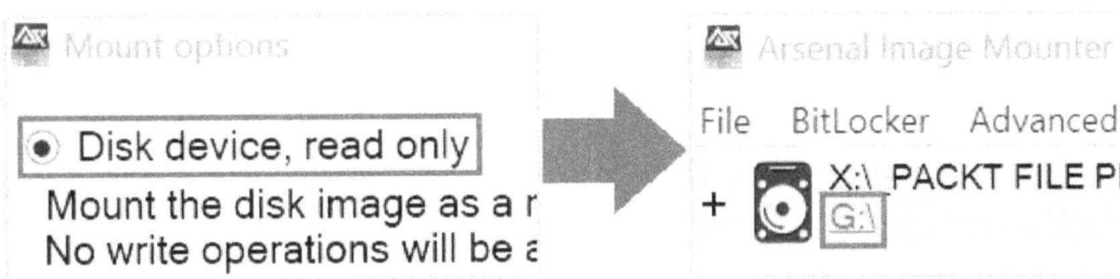

Figure 2.59 – Mounting image and noting path with Arsenal Image Mounter

> Note
>
> **WARNING**
>
> The dataset used in this exercise is safe and does not contain live malware.
>
> However, in real-world investigations involving unknown or potentially malicious files, precautions must be taken to protect the forensic environment. Perform analysis within an isolated system, such as a VM or a dedicated offline workstation. Ideally, the analysis environment should be disposable or capable of being forensically sanitized after use.

2. Once the forensic image is mounted, open a Command Prompt from the directory where Sigcheck has been downloaded and extracted.

This can be done by typing `cmd` into the address bar of the Windows File Explorer window and pressing *Enter*:

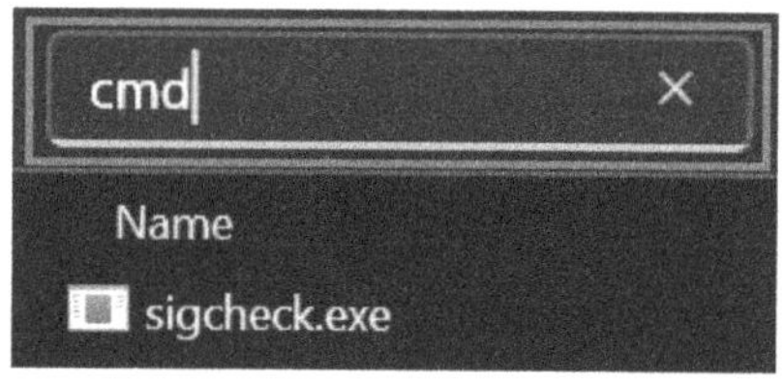

Figure 2.60 – Launching Command Prompt from the folder containing Sigcheck

3. Sigcheck supports many parameters, which can be viewed by running:

```
sigcheck -help
```

We will begin with a simple scan of the mounted forensic image to identify executable files within the `AppData\Local` directory for the `Leroy Jenkins` user account.

Run the following command, replacing `G:\` with the drive letter assigned to your mounted image:

```
sigcheck -e -s "G:\Users\Leroy Jenkins\AppData\Local"
```

This command may take one to two minutes to complete and will produce multiple results.

The `-e` parameter limits results to executable files, while the `-s` parameter recursively searches all subdirectories within the specified path.

Alternatively, you could scan the entire mounted image by specifying only the drive letter (for example, `G:`), though this will increase the processing time.

4. Reviewing the final result, we observe an executable file named `PCHealthCheck`. The output indicates that the file is digitally signed and verified, with Microsoft Corporation listed as the publisher.
Digitally signed files from trusted vendors are generally considered lower risk and are often part of legitimate system or application activity. In this case, the file appears consistent with known Microsoft software.

However, it is important to note that a valid digital signature alone does not guarantee that a file is safe. Attackers may abuse legitimate signed binaries or use compromised certificates. As such, file reputation, location, and behavior should also be considered when determining whether a file is suspicious:

```
g:\users\leroy jenkins\appdata\local\PCHealthCheck\zh-hant\PCHealthCheck.exe.mui:
        Verified:       Signed
        Signing date:   5:31 PM 2/14/2024
        Publisher:      Microsoft Corporation
        Company:        Microsoft Corporation
        Description:    PCHealthCheck.exe
        Product:        n/a
        Prod version:   3.9.240214001-s2
        File version:   3.9.2402.14001
        MachineType:    32-bit
```

Figure 2.61 – Result from an executable file search using Sigcheck

5. Many malicious files are unsigned, making unsigned executables a useful starting point for identifying potentially suspicious files.

   To reduce the number of results, we can limit our search to unsigned executables by adding the `-u` parameter. We will also include the `-h` parameter to generate hash values for each file.

   Run the following command:

   ```
   sigcheck -e -s -u -h "G:\Users\Leroy Jenkins\AppData\Local"
   ```

6. This command completes more quickly and returns a reduced set of results, identifying three executable files that were downloaded and cached by Microsoft Edge and Opera. We will focus on the final result, which is an unsigned executable associated with `UNetbootin`. Because the file is both unsigned and located within a browser cache directory, it represents a higher-priority candidate for further analysis.

   At this stage, the goal is to determine whether the file is legitimate or potentially malicious based on its origin, characteristics, and behavior:

```
g:\users\leroy jenkins\appdata\local\Opera Software\Opera Stable\Default\Cache\Cache_Data\f_000210:
        Verified:       Unsigned
        Link date:      6:00 PM 12/31/1969
        Publisher:      n/a
        Company:        Geza Kovacs
        Description:    UNetbootin - Universal Netboot Installer - http://unetbootin.sourceforge.net
        Product:        UNetbootin - Universal Netboot Installer
        MachineType:    32-bit
        MD5:    AC970460E91A32A128C813F9226ABE79
        SHA1:   DE3DCE853C08B385D43822AAAFC55D1E19F6055F
```

Figure 2.62 – Result from an unsigned executable file search using Sigcheck

Research with VirusTotal

VirusTotal is an online analysis platform available at `www.virustotal.com`.

It uses multiple antivirus engines to assess files, file hashes, and URLs for potential malicious activity.

Investigators can upload a file or submit a file hash to quickly determine whether the sample has been previously identified and analyzed. VirusTotal can also be used to evaluate website URLs for IoCs.

> **Note**
>
> VirusTotal can be used without creating an account and is free for basic use. Premium subscriptions provide additional capabilities, including access to previously submitted files and enhanced analysis features.
>
> However, investigators should be aware of potential **operational security** (**OPSEC**) concerns when uploading files. Submitting a previously unknown sample may expose it to the broader security community. In some cases, this could alert a threat actor that their malware has been discovered, potentially prompting them to alter their behavior, destroy evidence, or escalate their activity if they still have access to the environment.

Sigcheck can also be used to query files against VirusTotal by using the `-v` parameter.

1. To do this, run the following command, specifying the full path to the target file and using the appropriate drive letter for your mounted image:

```
sigcheck -v "G:\Users\Leroy Jenkins\AppData\Local\Opera Software\Opera Stable\Default\Cache_Data\f_000210"
```

The output includes a VirusTotal detection score (`VT detection`) and a link to the full analysis results (`VT link`).

In this example, the detection score indicates that 3 out of 77 security vendors have flagged the file as potentially malicious. A low detection count does not determine whether a file is safe or malicious. It may reflect emerging or low-prevalence malware, or it may represent false positives.

As with all findings, VirusTotal results should be considered alongside other factors, such as file origin, location, behavior, and supporting artifacts, before making a determination:

```
g:\users\leroy jenkins\appdata\local\opera software\opera stable\default\cache\cache_data\f_000210:
        Verified:       Unsigned
        Link date:      7:00 PM 12/31/1969
        Publisher:      n/a
        Company:        Geza Kovacs
        Description:    UNetbootin - Universal Netboot Installer - http://unetbootin.sourceforge.net
        Product:        UNetbootin - Universal Netboot Installer
        Prod version:
        File version:
        MachineType:    32-bit
        VT detection:   3/77
        VT link:        https://www.virustotal.com/gui/file/65ba5ff090be1cc96dec40509c9002582f4663634cb63
                        b311941321907701483/detection
```

Figure 2.63 – Result from using Sigcheck to scan the file against VirusTotal

> **Note**
>
> Air-gapped workstations
>
> The `-v` parameter requires an **active internet connection** to query the VirusTotal service. In forensic environments where analysis systems are **air-gapped or isolated from the internet**, this command will fail.
>
> In those cases, investigators can instead generate the file hash locally using Sigcheck:
>
> ```
> sigcheck -h <path_to_file>
> ```
>
> The resulting hash can then be copied to a separate connected system and searched manually on VirusTotal.

2. To further analyze the file, copy and paste the VT link provided by Sigcheck into a web browser.
   Review the **Security vendors' analysis** section to see which vendors have flagged the file as potentially malicious and which have not. It is common for results to vary across vendors, and a lack of consensus does not definitively indicate whether a file is safe or malicious.

   Use the available tabs to examine additional information, including file details, behavioral indicators, and relationships with other known samples. The **COMMUNITY** section may also provide valuable insight from other analysts who have encountered or investigated the file:

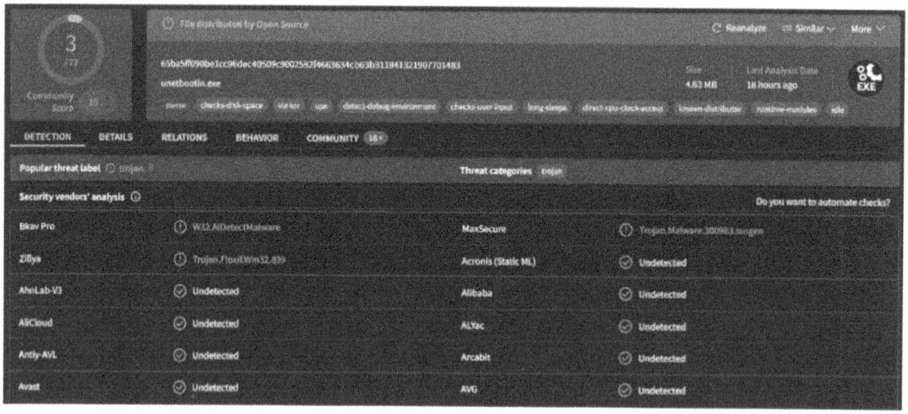

Figure 2.64 – VirusTotal scan results of target file

3. To better interpret these results, we will compare our previous sample to a known piece of malware using VirusTotal.

   Open a web browser and navigate to `www.virustotal.com`. Select the **SEARCH** feature and enter the following hash value:

   ```
   c0202cf6aeab8437c638533d14563d35
   ```

   Press *Enter* to view the results:

Figure 2.65 – Performing a hash value search with VirusTotal

   This comparison helps illustrate how detection patterns differ between low-confidence results and files that are widely recognized as malicious.

4. The hash value provided corresponds to the well-known Ryuk ransomware.

Notice the significantly higher number of detections across security vendors, with the majority identifying the file as malicious. This type of widespread agreement is more commonly observed in well-known and well-documented malware samples.

Comparing these results to the previous file helps illustrate the difference between low-confidence detections and strong consensus across multiple engines.

However, it is important not to assume that a file is safe simply because it is flagged by only a small number of vendors. Less-detected files may represent emerging threats, targeted malware, or false positives, and should be evaluated in the broader context of the investigation:

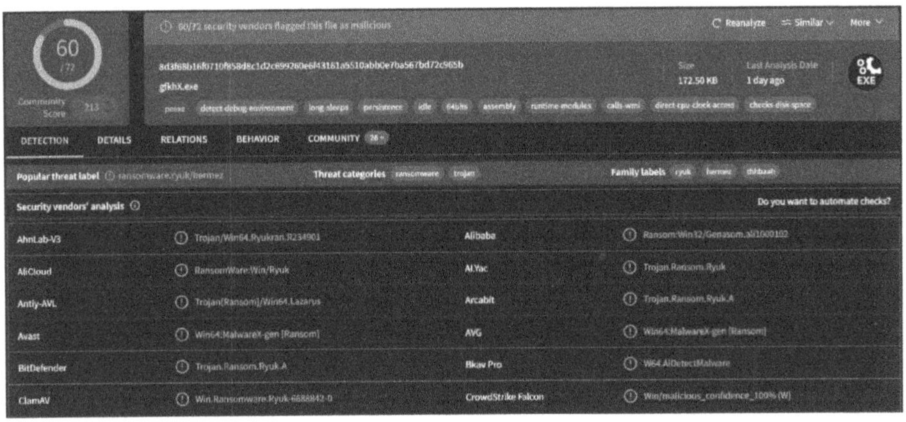

Figure 2.66 – VirusTotal scan results of hash value for Ryuk ransomware

How it works...

Initial malware triage identifies candidate executables, validates them using hashes and metadata, and performs external research before execution. This helps determine whether a file is known, suspicious, or requires deeper analysis.

Hash lookups allow investigators to check whether a sample is already known without exposing the file. If submission is required, be aware that public uploads may alert an adversary. Document your rationale and consider private platforms when OPSEC is a concern.

If research is inconclusive, proceed to controlled dynamic analysis in a fully isolated, disposable environment. Observe behaviors such as network activity, file creation, persistence, and system modifications. Never execute suspected malware on production or network-connected systems.

Automated sandbox services such as Joe Sandbox (`www.joesandbox.com`) can assist with behavioral analysis, but results should be treated as a single data point. The absence of detected malicious behavior does not guarantee that a file is safe.

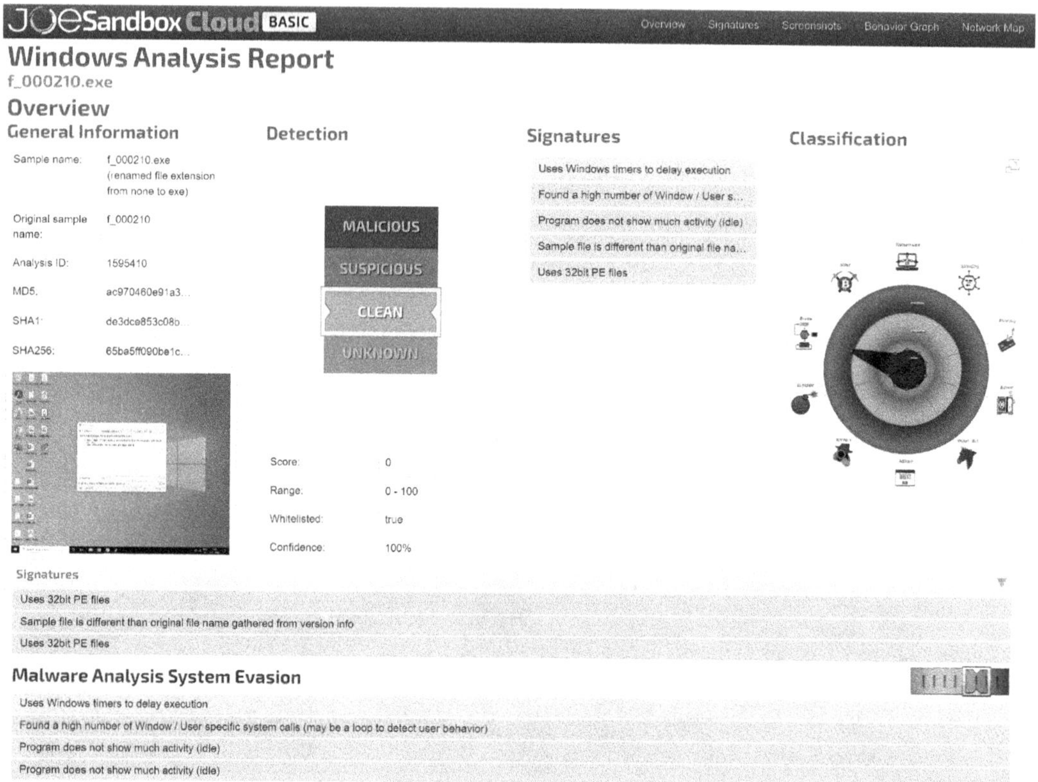

Figure 2.67 – Joe Sandbox analysis results of suspicious file

Finally, while quick triage and research techniques are often sufficient for case-level decision-making, complex or high-risk samples should be escalated to a malware reverse engineer for deeper static and behavioral analysis.

Summary

Effective network intrusion response depends on speed, scale, and disciplined prioritization. Broad hunts help investigators identify the systems most likely to matter, while targeted triage and cautious malware review preserve volatile evidence and support defensible decisions under pressure. By combining scalable remote collection with focused host-based triage, investigators can reduce uncertainty, prioritize the highest-risk systems, and move efficiently from detection to deeper forensic analysis. At this point, you should be able to do the following:

- **Use KAPE to perform rapid triage** of a suspected Microsoft Windows system and quickly identify artifacts relevant to incident response

- **Use Velociraptor** to perform basic remote hunting, targeted collection, and live-response actions across one or more systems
- **Build and test a small lab deployment of a Velociraptor server** and enroll client systems for practice
- **Use Sigcheck and VirusTotal** to identify suspicious executables, generate hashes, and perform safe initial malware research
- **Distinguish** between broad enterprise hunting, focused host triage, and the first investigative steps taken when malware is discovered

In the next chapter, we move from identifying and prioritizing systems of interest to acquiring larger volumes of data in preparation for deeper forensic analysis of systems, devices, and online accounts.

3

Physical and Cloud-Based Evidence Acquisition

When triage is complete, the next step is acquisition: preserving and extracting data from the identified items. Wherever possible, perform acquisitions in a forensic lab environment rather than on-scene so you minimize interaction with original evidence and reduce the risk of inadvertent changes.

The goal is straightforward: create defensible copies for analysis while preserving the original source. This chapter moves us from identification and collection into the preservation and acquisition phase of the digital forensic process.

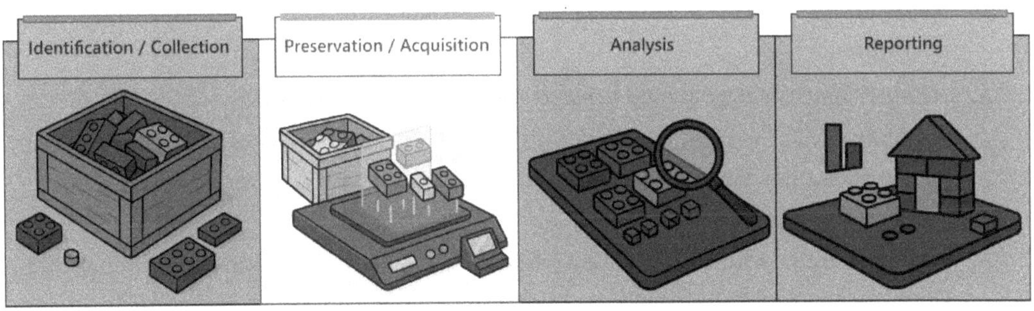

Figure 3.1 – Phase two of the digital forensic methodology: Preservation and Acquisition

Because more users store important data in online services, we'll cover acquiring evidence from common cloud accounts as well as traditional device-level acquisition. Finally, we'll review data-validation techniques you can use to demonstrate that what you acquired is complete, untampered, and court-ready.

In this chapter, we're going to cover the following main topics:

- Implementing write-blocking
- Protecting SSD evidence
- Storage drive acquisition
- Integrated storage acquisition
- Mobile device acquisition
- Online accounts and cloud data
- Data validation

By the end of this chapter, you'll be prepared to acquire data from physical evidence sources (computers, storage drives, and mobile devices) as well as online accounts, and to validate that data so it can withstand scrutiny.

Technical requirements

For this chapter, you will need:

- A computer running Microsoft Windows to act as your forensic workstation. This system will be used to prepare media, run acquisition utilities, and validate collected data. Windows 11 is recommended. Ensure the workstation has sufficient free disk space to store the practice acquisitions you create.
- Two USB drives: your TRIAGE USB configured as a bootable alternate OS (Paladin), and a second USB drive to serve as the evidentiary source from which we will perform data acquisition.
- A large-capacity external hard drive to store acquired evidence.
- A mobile device to serve as evidence, along with the appropriate cable to connect it to your workstation. For more in-depth practice, having both an Android device and an iOS-based device is preferred.
- An online account for testing cloud-based data acquisition. We will use Facebook and Google accounts for the examples shown.
- Because evidence can exist across many device types and service providers, you should practice using a variety of hardware and cloud accounts beyond the examples shown.

Implementing write-blocking

When a storage drive is attached to a computer, the operating system may read from, and sometimes even write to, the device. Because this can alter original data (for example, timestamps and system logs), it should be avoided when handling evidentiary media. To prevent inadvertent modification, we implement write-blocking, which allows a drive to be read while blocking any write requests from the host workstation.

Write-blocking solutions are available as hardware devices (physical bridges placed between the host and the evidence drive) or as software controls on the host. Hardware write-blockers are firmware-based appliances and are generally the most reliable option; they are specifically designed to refuse write commands.

Software write-blocking relies on the host operating system or drivers to prevent writes and is more prone to accidental failure or misconfiguration. Because some drive types and connection interfaces can behave unexpectedly, it's wise to have both approaches available for testing and fallback.

For this recipe, we will demonstrate a software-based blocking workflow for USB-connected media, but you should prefer and validate hardware write-blockers when handling evidentiary media.

Getting ready

For this exercise, you simply need your Windows-based computer and any type of storage drive that can be connected via USB. This storage drive will be considered evidence that we want to protect and prevent altering. You will also need to download the Windows executable (.exe) release of the software listed below.

USB Write Blocker by Digital Sleuth: `https://github.com/digitalsleuth/Registry-Write-Block/`

How to do it...

1. Connect the target storage drive to your computer via USB. Create or transfer a few files to the storage drive. For the example shown, I have simply created some empty files in Windows (**Right-click | New**):

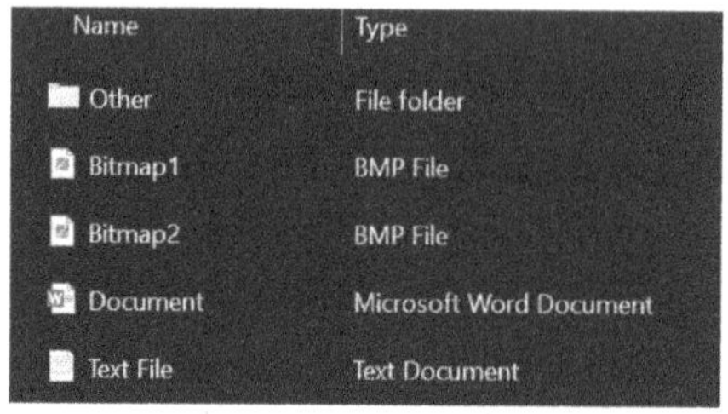

Figure 3.2 – Target USB drive containing several files

2. Eject and remove the USB drive from your computer. It is now "evidence".
3. Download and extract the USB Write Blocker utility (Digital Sleuth). This utility works by modifying Windows registry keys to block writes to mass-storage USB devices; it only affects USB ports and will not act as a full forensic write-blocker for other interfaces (such as built-in SD card readers or other drives which operate on the PCIe bus).

> **Note**
>
> It may be wise to create a system restore point or registry backup in Windows before running the tool, so you can easily revert any changes if needed.

4. Locate the Windows Command Script file named **USB-Write-Blocker**. Right-click the file and choose **Run as administrator**:

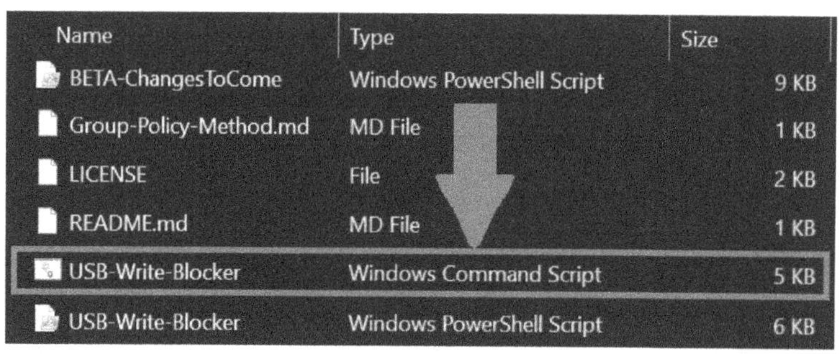

Figure 3.3 – Script file for USB Write-Blocker

5. The script will open in Command Prompt along with a short list of options. Enter the letter **E** into Command Prompt and press *Enter* to apply the changes to the Windows Registry:

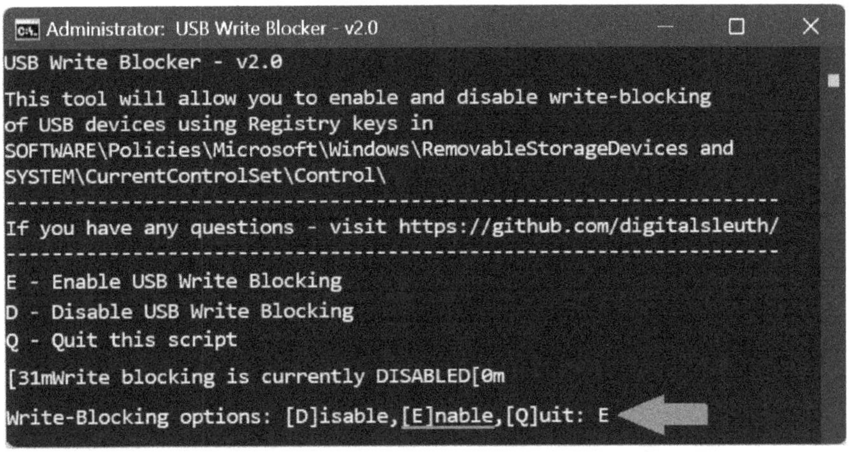

Figure 3.4 – Script file to alter the Windows registry and block USB write requests

6. Write requests via the host machine's USB ports should now be disabled. Command Prompt will display several status messages indicating that write-blocking is enabled. There may be some errors, as seen in the below example, due to certain registry keys being different from what the script expected based on your currently installed version of Windows. Leave Command Prompt open for now:

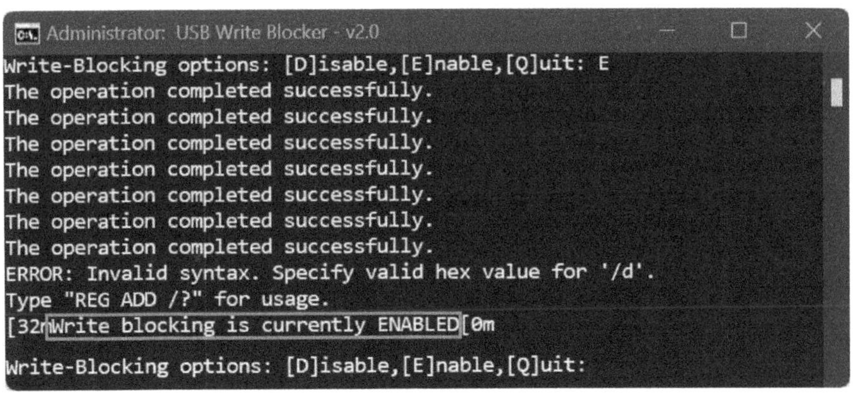

Figure 3.5 – Output showing that write blocking is now enabled

7. Insert your "evidence" storage drive and attempt to open, edit, delete, and copy files. You should be able to browse and read the contents but not modify or remove existing data. You may receive error messages like the one shown below when attempting to make changes to the "evidence" drive. This indicates the device is now write-protected, allowing data acquisition while preserving the original evidence:

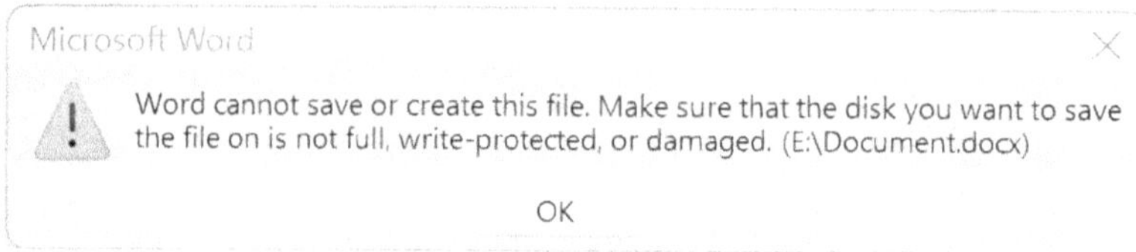

Figure 3.6 – Error message from attempting to save changes to a document

8. Eject and remove the "evidence" drive from your computer.
9. Return to Command Prompt. Enter *D*, then press *Enter* to restore the Windows Registry keys to their original values and disable write blocking:

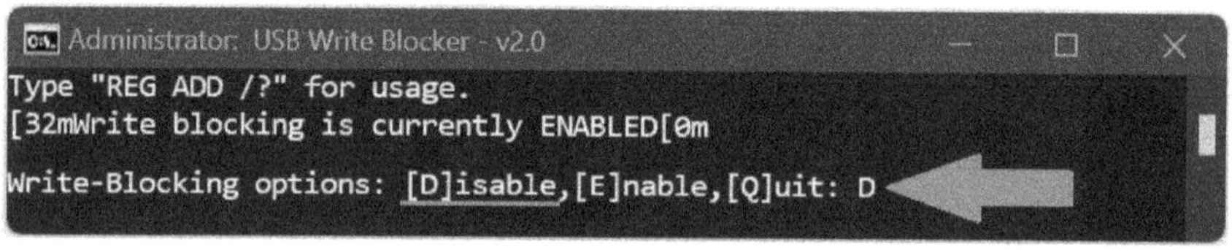

Figure 3.7 – Option to restore the original Windows Registry values

10. Command Prompt will display several status messages indicating that write blocking is disabled:

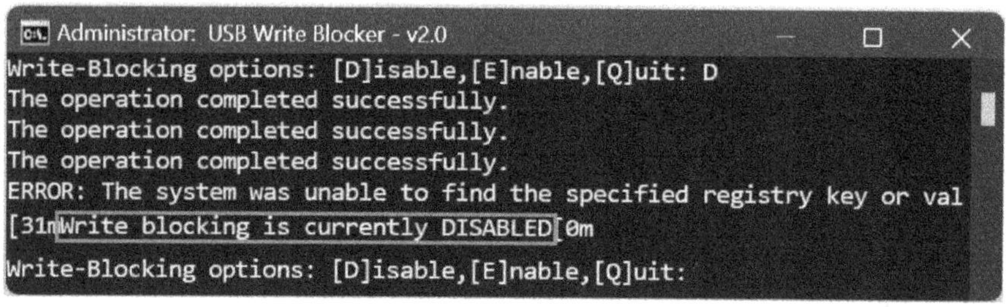

Figure 3.8 – Output showing that write blocking is now disabled

11. Close Command Prompt and reinsert your "evidence" drive into the computer. Attempt to change or delete the files on the drive to confirm that write blocking is now disabled and the USB ports are functioning as expected.

How it works...

Microsoft Windows is commonly used as the operating system of choice for many host workstations, as it has a rich ecosystem of forensic tools; but it does not provide a native, foolproof mechanism to prevent the host from modifying connected media. When you attach a storage device to a Windows host, the operating system may read from and sometimes write to the device, so write-blocking must be implemented to protect original evidence.

Firmware-based (hardware) write-blockers are the preferred option. Common examples include dedicated forensic write-blocking devices from vendors such as Tableau and similar platforms, though the underlying principle remains the same regardless of the tool used. Software methods (including registry-based approaches on Windows like the one we just used) are fallbacks that can be useful in constrained situations but must be validated before use.

By contrast, many Linux-based forensic environments provide simple, reliable software write-blocking by mounting devices read-only. Sumuri Paladin (used in *Chapter 1*) is a good example: drives attached within Paladin are mounted read-only by default, which makes it a much more trustworthy software-based option than modifying Windows registry keys. Regardless of the method used, always verify the write-blocker's effectiveness on non-evidentiary media and document the verification before handling case evidence.

Protecting SSD evidence

Even when implementing write-blocking, a target **solid-state drive (SSD)** can exhibit changes because their internal controllers perform housekeeping to extend drive life and improve performance. Garbage collection and wear-leveling are managed in firmware; so, simply applying power can allow the SSD to relocate valid data within pages so entire blocks can be erased and reused. Because individual pages cannot be erased directly, the controller must erase whole blocks, and wear-leveling moves data between blocks to spread writes across the device. These controller behaviors can change on-disk content independently of host writes.

TRIM is a host-originated command that tells the SSD which logical blocks are no longer in use so the controller can reclaim them during garbage collection. Because the operating system issues TRIM, it can be controlled at the host level by the operating system. Disabling the TRIM command on a host prevents the OS from telling the SSD to free those blocks while you are handling evidence. That said, disabling TRIM does **not** stop the SSD's internal garbage collection (the controller may still perform internal maintenance on its own), nor does it eliminate all risk of evidence loss. It only reduces one vector of change (host-initiated block reclamation).

Be aware that SSD controller activity can permanently change or erase data and will affect hash-based verification. The hash of a live SSD may differ from that of a later forensic image, and disabling TRIM is not a guaranteed preservation method. It serves as an additional mitigation to help preserve data long enough to perform acquisition of the target SSD.

In this recipe, we will demonstrate how to reduce SSD-driven data modification by disabling TRIM on a Windows system prior to acquisition.

Getting ready

For this exercise, we only need an elevated (administrator) Command Prompt on a Windows host workstation to alter how the system handles connected SSDs. Because TRIM is a host-side behavior, we will run these commands on the acquisition workstation (the machine connected to the evidentiary SSD), not on the evidence device itself.

How to do it...

1. Open an instance of Command Prompt (as administrator) and enter the following command:

```
fsutil behavior query DisableDeleteNotify
```

2. A returned value of `0` for `DisableDeleteNotify` indicates that TRIM is enabled for the listed file systems (NTFS and ReFS). A value of 1 indicates that TRIM is disabled. Ensure these steps are completed before connecting the evidentiary SSD to the system.
3. To disable TRIM, enter the following commands:

```
fsutil behavior set DisableDeleteNotify NTFS 1
fsutil behavior set DisableDeleteNotify ReFS 1
```

4. Once acquisition is complete, re-enable TRIM to preserve SSD health and longevity on the host system. While TRIM can hinder data recovery on target media, it is beneficial for normal system operation.
5. To re-enable TRIM, undo the previous commands by entering the following:

```
fsutil behavior set DisableDeleteNotify NTFS 0
fsutil behavior set DisableDeleteNotify ReFS 0
```

The output should appear similar to the following:

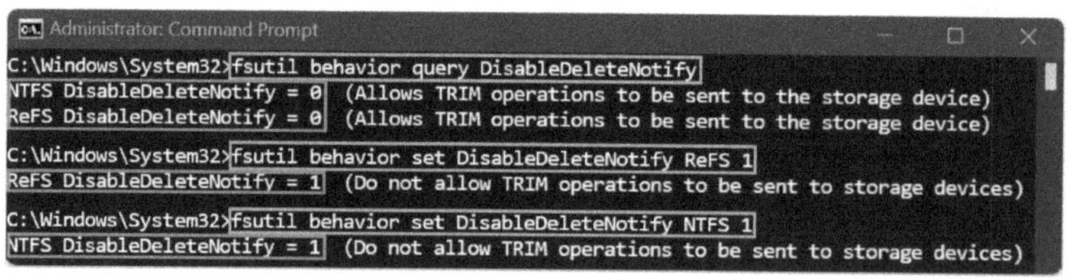

Figure 3.9 – Disabling TRIM in Microsoft Windows

How it works...

SSDs do a lot of work behind the scenes. The controller maps logical block addresses (LBAs), which are used by the operating system to reference data, to physical flash locations. It also performs garbage collection and wear-leveling to maximize performance and longevity. Garbage collection consolidates valid data so entire blocks can be erased and wear-leveling moves data around to avoid over-using the same physical cells. Because these processes happen inside the drive firmware, they can alter physical storage even when the host does nothing more than apply power.

TRIM is a host-issued command that marks blocks as unused so the controller can reclaim them sooner. Disabling TRIM on your host workstation prevents Windows from sending those discard commands, reducing the chance of host-initiated block reclamation during acquisition. However, disabling TRIM does **not** stop the controller's autonomous garbage collection or wear-leveling, so the SSD may still relocate or erase data independently. That means the physical contents of an SSD can change between the moment you seize it and the moment you image it, and those changes will likely cause device-level hashes to differ from the resultant hash of the image we create.

Treat TRIM-disable as an additional, host-side mitigation when working with SSD evidence and using software write-blocking. The preferred protection remains a hardware write-blocking bridge, and many forensic-grade units are also designed to block TRIM/discard commands from the host operating system. Always understand and verify the behavior of your exact write-blocking tools of choice.

Storage drive acquisition

Acquiring data from a storage drive is a simple and straightforward process, provided that the target evidence is functioning properly. This method is effective for obtaining a physical forensic image from a variety of storage media, including hard disk drives removed from a system, external storage drives, SD cards, and other solid-state storage devices. The forensic image we create will include allocated files, deleted files, data within unallocated space, file slack space, and even non-partitioned space.

In this recipe, we will acquire a bit-for-bit forensic image from a storage device using a standard acquisition workflow.

Getting ready

For this exercise, you will acquire data from a storage device that you can properly connect to your forensic workstation using the appropriate hardware interface. Ensure that your destination storage location has sufficient capacity to store the acquired image and exceeds the size of the target evidence.

Write-blocking should be implemented whenever possible and is essential when working with real evidence.

We will use FTK Imager, which was introduced in *Chapter 1*.

How to do it...

1. Connect the storage device you will be acquiring data from to your forensic workstation using an appropriate write-blocking method (hardware or validated software) to protect the source evidence.
2. Launch FTK Imager.
3. From the **File** menu, select **Create Disk Image...**:

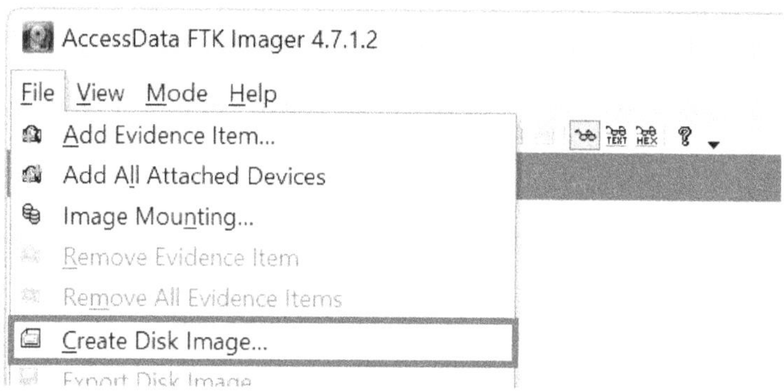

Figure 3.10 – Choosing to create a disk image in FTK Imager

4. The **Select Source** window will appear, and we will ensure the radio button next to **Physical Drive** is selected, as we will be acquiring evidence from a physical storage device connected to the forensic workstation. This will create a physical forensic image of the target storage device, resulting in a bit-for-bit copy of the device. This includes unallocated space and file slack, which increases the likelihood of recovering deleted content.
For this reason, a physical acquisition is almost always preferred. However, FTK Imager also supports logical acquisition, which consists of only allocated files, or a targeted acquisition to collect content from specific directories. Select **Next >**:

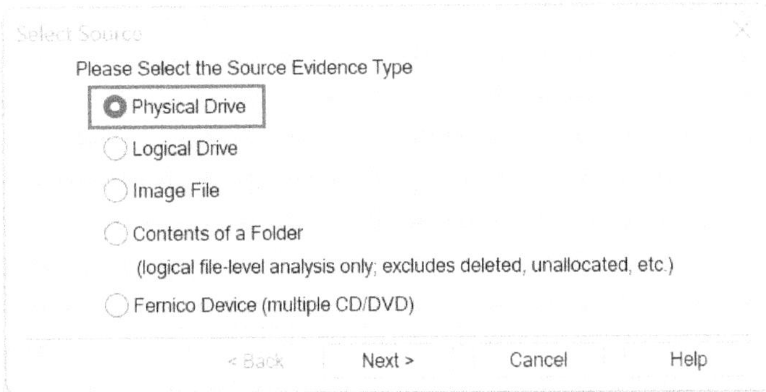

Figure 3.11 – Selecting the source type for acquisition in FTK Imager

Note

Getting Logical

Although physical imaging is typically preferred for its ability to capture unallocated and slack space, logical acquisition has a critical role when you encounter an encrypted volume that is currently in an unencrypted (mounted) state. In that scenario, a logical acquisition lets you preserve actively decrypted files and artifacts that would otherwise be lost once the system is powered down or the encryption context is removed. Use logical collection only when necessary and document the rationale and steps taken.

5. The **Select Drive** window will now appear. This is where we select the target storage device (the write-blocked evidence source).
   Remember, write-blocking prevents changes to the source device but does not prevent data acquisition.

   Locate the target storage device from the drop-down list and select it.

   In the example shown, the evidence source is a Verbatim STORE N GO USB device. This device can be acquired quickly due to its small size (8 GB). Larger storage devices will take much longer.

6. Select **Finish**:

Figure 3.12 – Selecting a source drive for acquisition in FTK Imager

7. The **Create Image** window will appear. Select the checkbox for **Verify images after they are created**, which uses hashing to verify the integrity of the acquisition. This is important to demonstrate that the forensic image is an accurate representation of the evidence source.
   Optionally, you can select **Precalculate Progress Statistics** to estimate the remaining acquisition time.

8. Finally, select **Add...:**

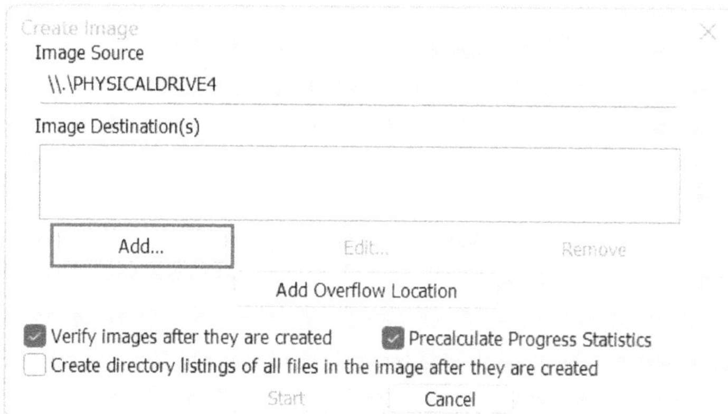

Figure 3.13 – Selecting forensic image creation options in FTK Imager

9. This is where we select the forensic image type we wish to create. A *Raw (dd)* forensic image acquires the data as-is, which will result in the forensic image being the same size as the evidence source being acquired. An **E01** forensic image will give us the ability to compress the acquisition and save storage space.
   The **E01** forensic image type will also allow us to add a header to the forensic image file detailing information about its creation, though the evidentiary data itself remains

unaltered. These are the two most popular forensic image types, though **SMART** and **AFF** will also allow for compression. Click the radio button to choose the **E01** forensic image type and then select **Next >**:

Figure 3.14 – Selecting a forensic image type in FTK Imager

10. Now we can enter details about the evidence source item we are acquiring. Information entered will be included as part of our **E01** forensic image. Entering this information is optional, and the fields presented can be left blank if desired. Select **Next >**:

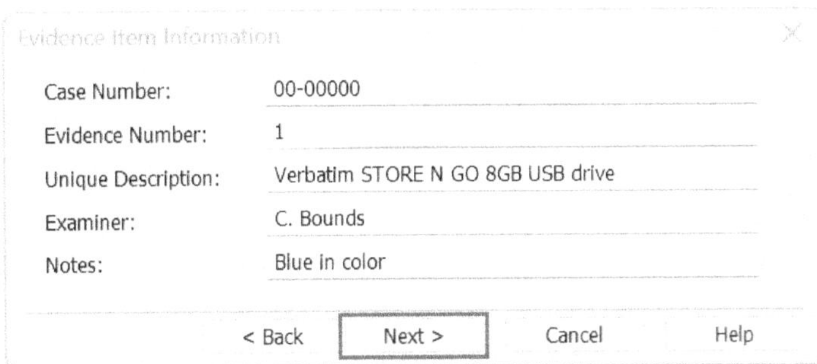

Figure 3.15 – Evidence Item Information fields in FTK Imager

11. This final window is where we select an *Imager Destination Folder*, or storage location, for the forensic image we will acquire. Be sure that the destination you select has adequate space to store the forensic image. In the example below, I have chosen to store my forensic image in a case directory on a large disk drive dedicated for evidence storage. Next, choose a name for the forensic image under *Image Filename*, ideally one signifying the type of storage drive being acquired.
12. Finally, you can select the *Image Fragment Size* and *Compression* level. For the example shown, I have entered an *Image Fragment Size* of 0. This will create a single forensic image file. Alternatively, you can fragment the forensic image into multiple smaller files if desired. I have also entered a *Compression* level of 9, which will compress the forensic image as much as possible to save storage space, though this will increase acquisition

time. Optionally, you can check the box to *Use AD Encryption* if you wish to encrypt the forensic image. This feature can be useful if the acquisition contains protected or illicit files. Select **Finish** and then select **Start** when the option appears:

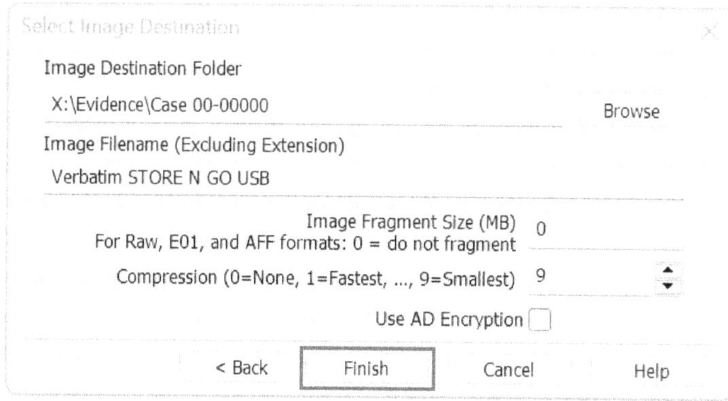

Figure 3.16 – Selecting a forensic image storage location in FTK Imager

13. The data acquisition process will begin, followed by a verification process due to previously selecting the option to *Verify images after they are created*. In the example, you can see the computed MD5 hash values match and no bad blocks were encountered, as the acquisition completed without error. Had bad blocks been encountered, FTK Imager will write these to the forensic image as 0x00 and the previous data stored to the bad blocks would not be acquired.

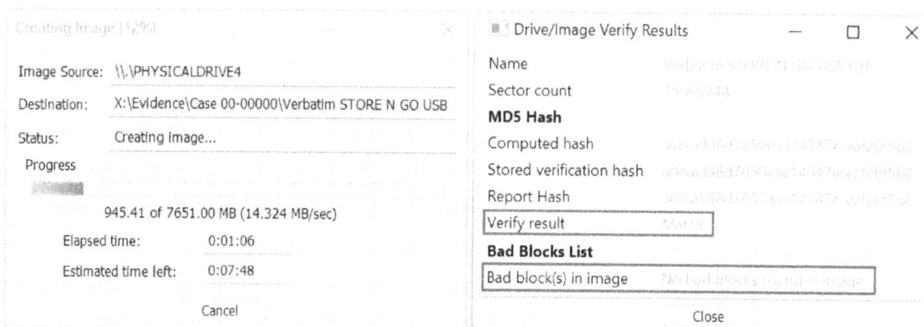

Figure 3.17 – Forensic image creation and verification result in FTK Imager

14. Once complete, we are left with a forensic image of an `E01` file type (or multiple forensic image files segmented as `E01`, `E02`, `E03`, etc., if you chose to fragment the acquisition) and a text file detailing the acquisition results. This text file can be used to gain further information if an error was encountered and serves as good documentation to show hash verification results:

Figure 3.18 – Forensic image and associated text file detailing the acquisition results

How it works...

A physical acquisition, or bit-for-bit forensic copy, is the gold standard for forensic data imaging. We can then perform analysis upon the forensic image instead of working directly with an evidence source. This acquisition method must always be used in conjunction with the implementation of write-blocking to protect the target evidence source. A forensic image can be acquired this way from a wide variety of physical evidence sources, so long as we are able to connect the evidence source to our computer and gain the appropriate level of access needed.

In some cases, we may not be able to gain the level of access needed to perform a physical acquisition. If this occurs, we can always attempt a logical acquisition, though this method will not collect certain areas of storage needed for most data recovery efforts. In other cases, we may encounter physical evidence sources with non-removable storage drives or evidence sources which cannot be directly connected to our host computer for successful acquisition. This is a very common scenario for computers that contain integrated storage.

There's more...

While FTK Imager is a recognized and defensible method for forensic acquisition, other reliable tools should be part of your toolkit. These include:

- **Magnet ACQUIRE** – used in the upcoming *Mobile device acquisition* recipe
- **Sumuri Paladin LTS** – used in the upcoming *Integrated storage drive acquisition* recipe and is also capable of imaging attached storage
- **Guymager** – a GUI-based forensic imaging tool for Linux
- **dc3dd** – a command-line imaging utility with integrated hashing and logging

For example, in a Linux environment, `dc3dd` can be used to acquire a forensic image after identifying connected drives with `lsblk`:

```
dc3dd if=/dev/sdX of=/mnt/dest/evidence.dd hash=md5 hashlog=/mnt/dest/hash.txt
log=/mnt/dest/image.log
```

In this command, `if` specifies the source device, `of` defines the output image location, and the `hashlog` and `log` options provide verification and documentation of the acquisition process.

Regardless of the tool used, the underlying process remains the same: acquire a bit-for-bit copy, verify integrity with hashing, and document the acquisition. Having multiple tools available allows you to adapt when a particular method is not suitable for a given evidence source.

Integrated storage acquisition

Many modern laptops and small form-factor computers use integrated solid-state storage chips soldered directly to the motherboard, instead of a removable drive. Powering on those systems and performing a live logical acquisition is possible, but it changes the original evidence and risks missing lower-level artifacts; for that reason, it should be avoided.

A more practical approach is to boot the system into a trusted, external forensic operating system from sanitized media and acquire data that way, where we interact with the integrated target storage through a controlled environment rather than the native operating system of our target evidence.

In this recipe, we will acquire a forensic image from a system that uses integrated storage by booting into a trusted external environment. You will use the Paladin USB drive prepared earlier to access the target system in a forensically sound manner and create a verified forensic image for analysis.

Getting ready

You will need the Paladin USB drive you previously prepared in *Chapter 1*, a computer (powered off) to act as a target "evidence" source, and an external destination drive with capacity larger than the target "evidence" computer storage. This destination drive will hold the forensic image and should be formatted as exFAT to accommodate large file sizes (see Chapter 1 – Targeted On-Scene Triage, for instructions on preparing external storage media).

How to do it...

1. Beginning with the "evidence" computer in a powered-off state, insert the Sumuri Paladin LTS USB drive and boot to Paladin. The steps for booting to Paladin are detailed in the *Powered-off computers* section of *Chapter 1* if you need a refresher on how to do this.

   Once booted, open the **Paladin Toolbox** and select **Disk Manager** from the options in the left side pane. This should be very familiar, as this is the same utility we used in *Chapter 1*. In Paladin the target media will normally be mounted read-only, providing a software write-blocking protection while you prepare the image. This should always be confirmed before proceeding.

2. Connect the external "destination" storage drive to the "evidence" system. We will use this drive to store our forensic image. You may need to select **Refresh** for the drive to appear in **Disk Manager**. Mount the drive using the **Mount-RW** option to allow the forensic image to be written to the drive. In the example below, you will see the "destination drive" shows as a large capacity Western Digital Elements device labeled **TRIAGE** and formatted using the exFAT file system:

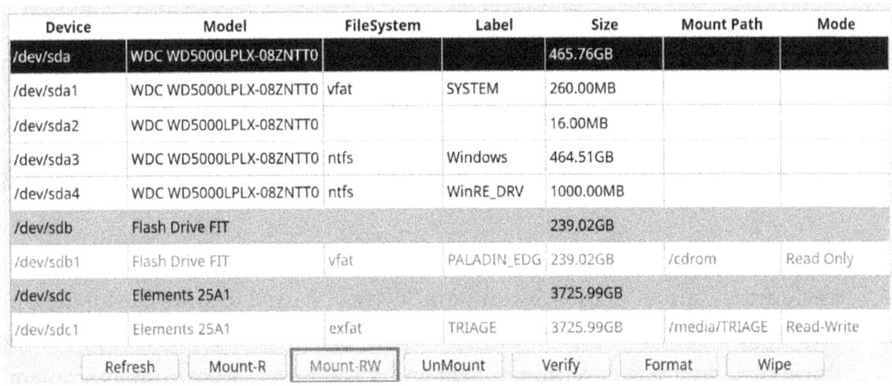

Device	Model	FileSystem	Label	Size	Mount Path	Mode
/dev/sda	WDC WD5000LPLX-08ZNTT0			465.76GB		
/dev/sda1	WDC WD5000LPLX-08ZNTT0	vfat	SYSTEM	260.00MB		
/dev/sda2	WDC WD5000LPLX-08ZNTT0			16.00MB		
/dev/sda3	WDC WD5000LPLX-08ZNTT0	ntfs	Windows	464.51GB		
/dev/sda4	WDC WD5000LPLX-08ZNTT0	ntfs	WinRE_DRV	1000.00MB		
/dev/sdb	Flash Drive FIT			239.02GB		
/dev/sdb1	Flash Drive FIT	vfat	PALADIN_EDG	239.02GB	/cdrom	Read Only
/dev/sdc	Elements 25A1			3725.99GB		
/dev/sdc1	Elements 25A1	exfat	TRIAGE	3725.99GB	/media/TRIAGE	Read-Write

Figure 3.19 – Available drives shown in Disk Manager utility of Sumuri Paladin

3. Now select the **Imager** utility (left side menu). From the **Source** dropdown menu, select the evidence source (this is the integrated storage drive of our "evidence" computer) then choose the desired forensic image file type from the **Image Type** dropdown menu. In the example, I have again chosen a forensic image type of E01.
4. Assign a label to serve as the name of the `E01` file and select the **Verify after creation** checkbox to verify the hash value of the forensic image once it is acquired. Just like in FTK Imager, you also have the option to segment the forensic image if needed, though I have left this option unchecked in order to create a single forensic image file. When ready, select **Start**:

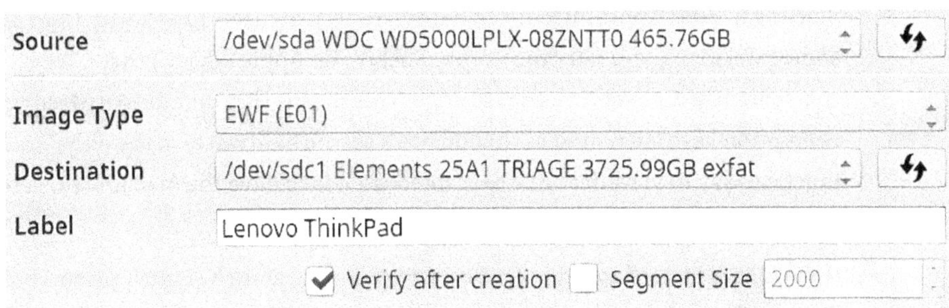

Figure 3.20 – Preparing the Imager utility in Sumuri Paladin

5. A status window will begin displaying progress information for the forensic acquisition before finally performing verification of the forensic image. As you can see, this acquisition consists of a source that is several hundred gigabytes in size and will therefore take several hours to complete (the estimated time shown for the example ~500 GB drive is approximately 4 hours). Once this has finished, you can shut down the computer and remove the destination drive:

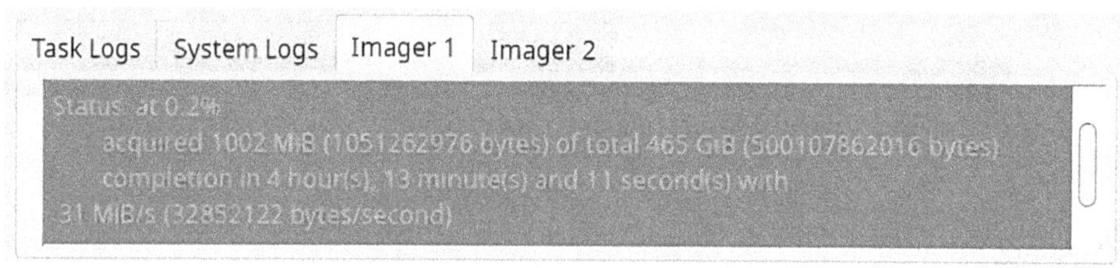

Figure 3.21 – Forensic acquisition progress in Sumuri Paladin

6. Review the content of the "destination" drive you used to store the forensic image. You will notice Paladin automatically created a directory using the label previously input during imaging setup. Within this directory is the E01 forensic image we acquired, along with files detailing the acquisition process:

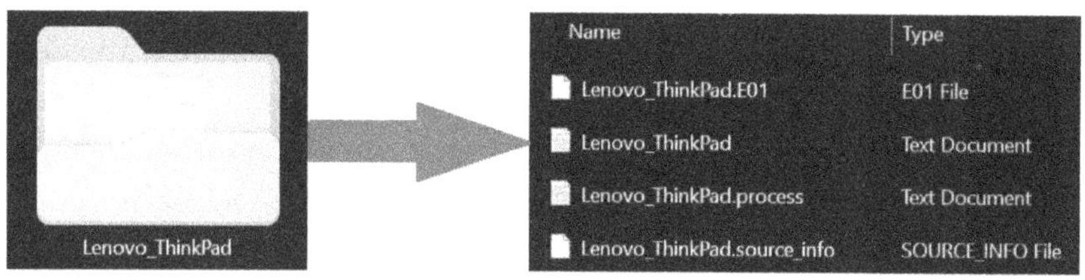

Figure 3.22 – Forensic image files obtained using Sumuri Paladin

> **Note**
>
> Macs pain
>
> Starting in 2018 Apple introduced hardware security (the T2 Security Chip on some Intel Macs, and later the Secure Enclave on Apple Silicon) that transparently encrypts internal storage. This means that on modern Macs the encryption keys are bound to that device's secure hardware, so the only practical way to view data in a decrypted state is to have the machine powered on and unlocked with the appropriate credentials.
>
> If the Mac is located in a powered on and unlocked state, we must preserve decrypted data by performing a live logical capture. Consider the following

> workflows for the different types of newer (approximately post 2018) Macs you may encounter:
>
> • Intel Macs: Physically connect the target Mac to another Mac designated for digital forensic purposes using a high-speed data cable (such as a Thunderbolt or USB 3.x cable), then use **Target Disk Mode** (hold **T** at boot) to expose the target Mac's drive to the "forensic" Mac. This can allow a logical copy if the target volume can be unlocked.
>
> • Apple Silicon Macs: Again, physically connect the target Mac to a "forensic" Mac. Boot the target Mac into Recovery (hold the power button down during startup) and choose **Options | Share Disk**. You will usually need the account password (or appropriate keys) to unlock encrypted volumes.
>
> Commercial forensic tools (for example, Sumuri Recon ITR and Cellebrite Collector) provide guided workflows for Mac collection and can simplify these steps and allow for easier logical acquisition of Macs found in an unlocked state. When a logical copy is appropriate and possible, packaging acquired files into an Apple Disk Image (.dmg) is a portable, forensically-acceptable option that forensic tools can ingest for later analysis.

How it works...

Booting the evidentiary computer to a trusted alternate operating system lets us interact with integrated or removable storage without running the native operating system, thereby preventing unwanted alterations to the source data. This approach enables safe previewing and imaging on many devices and can bypass local account passwords because it accesses the file system directly, provided the target volume is not encrypted. Of course, for this method to work, the target system itself must be operable and able to be powered on.

Mobile device acquisition

Acquiring data from modern mobile devices is one of the most challenging parts of digital forensic work today. Phones and tablets ship with strong, hardware-backed File Based Encryption (FBE) enabled by default; so, even with a passcode in hand there are instances in which you may only be able to perform a logical acquisition.

Commercial vendors invest heavily in developing exploits to gain privileged access to protected areas of device storage, and though such capabilities are often expensive, they allow us to obtain full file system-level acquisitions. That said, investigators with limited budgets can still collect valuable, admissible evidence using free tools, but expect the dataset to be narrower and often to exclude much third-party app data.

What we can expect to get from a simple logical acquisition are active artifacts related to native SMS/iMessage content, call logs, user contacts, and files such as photographs and videos saved by the user. The level of data that can be acquired can vary widely and depends on the OS versions, device models, and whether or not the device may be rooted (Android) or jailbroken (iOS). Rooting or jailbreaking a device introduces significant risk to evidence integrity and should be avoided.

In this recipe, we will perform a logical acquisition of mobile devices. This process demonstrates how to collect available user data from both Android and iOS devices when full file system access is either not needed, or not possible.

Getting ready

Sometimes we only need a more targeted logical acquisition to obtain the data we are seeking. This can be accomplished without paid commercial tools. Unlike a full file system acquisition, our logical acquisitions will contain only a limited amount of user data by comparison. Even so, logical acquisition can still acquire data which may not be easily accessible to the device user and if the device contains removable storage such as a microSD card, a physical acquisition of the removable storage media can be performed separately.

When performing data acquisition from a mobile device, you will find we must interact with the device and often make several changes within device settings to be successful. This may feel like we are abandoning forensic best practices at times, but we are not, as this is often the only means of data acquisition. Even so, we should still avoid making unnecessary changes as much as possible and use the right tools to minimize our impact on the evidentiary device. We may face an unfavorable outcome during litigation if we tainted or missed important evidence simply because we could not afford the software to conduct a proper acquisition. If we are attempting to add such capabilities to our lab, then we need to be sure we can implement those capabilities correctly, which may at times cost a significant amount of money.

To perform our logical acquisition, you will need at least one mobile device – though it is desirable to have both an Android and an Apple iOS device if possible. You will also need to download the software listed below.

- Magnet ACQUIRE by Magnet Forensics to acquire data from mobile devices: `https://www.magnetforensics.com/resources/magnet-acquire/`
- Apple iTunes to enable the acquisition iOS-based devices: `https://www.apple.com/itunes/`

Note

Note: Magnet ACQUIRE typically requires registration and a business email address to download. If access is restricted, consider alternative acquisition methods such as device backups (iTunes/Finder for iOS or native Android backup methods for Android).

How to do it...

1. Place your mobile device into **Airplane Mode** and connect the device to your computer. This device needs to be in an unlocked state, and you will need to select any prompts that appear on the mobile device asking to establish a connection with or trust the computer. Unlike the other acquisition methods we have completed so far, we will not implement write-blocking, as mobile device acquisition requires the ability to communicate with the source device and sometimes even install a software client to our source evidence.
2. To help establish and maintain a connection, there are some settings you will want to change on the mobile device.
    - **iOS**: Ensure the device will not become locked during acquisition by going to **Settings**, **Display & Brightness**, **Auto-Lock**, and select **Never**.
    - **Android**: There are many variations of Android devices, so the settings for these devices can vary, but our goal is to enable developer options. For most devices, you will need to go to Settings, About Device, and look for an option titled Build Number, which is sometimes within another menu related to software information. Once located, tap on Build Number seven times, and you will receive a notification that developer options are enabled. Locate the Developer Options menu within settings, which for most devices will be located near the bottom of the main Settings options. Select the Developer Options menu, toggle on Stay Awake, toggle on USB Debugging, and toggle off Verify Apps over USB. Again, the location of these menus varies widely among Android versions, but their titles are relatively similar.
3. Install Apple iTunes. Ensure that you do not install the Apple iTunes application from within the Microsoft Store, and instead download and install the Apple iTunes installation file itself from the web address provided earlier. This is essential, as the Apple iTunes application from the Microsoft Store will not install certain services that we rely upon to acquire data from an iOS device.

4. Run Magnet ACQUIRE. You will notice Acquire recognizes all the storage drives connected to your computer, as it is also capable of acquiring data from these drives like we did using FTK Imager. You should further notice that the mobile device connected to your computer is also recognized. I have attached both an Android-based Samsung cellular telephone and an Apple iPhone to my computer in the example shown, both of which are recognized. Select **NEXT**:

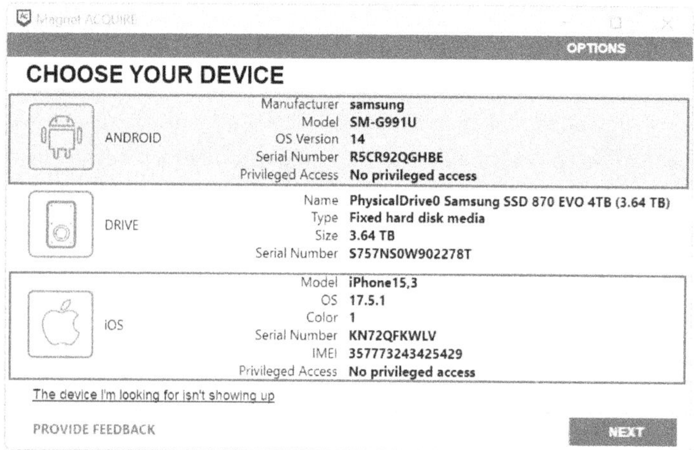

Figure 3.23 – Magnet ACQUIRE showing both Android and iOS devices recognized

5. If for any reason your mobile device source is not populating within Acquire, first attempt to physically disconnect the device from your computer, check all settings as described previously in *step 2*, and then reconnect the mobile device. You may also need to troubleshoot Acquire by selecting **The device I'm looking for isn't showing up**, located near the lower left corner, to gain assistance in ensuring the underlying software and drivers needed for acquisition are installed:

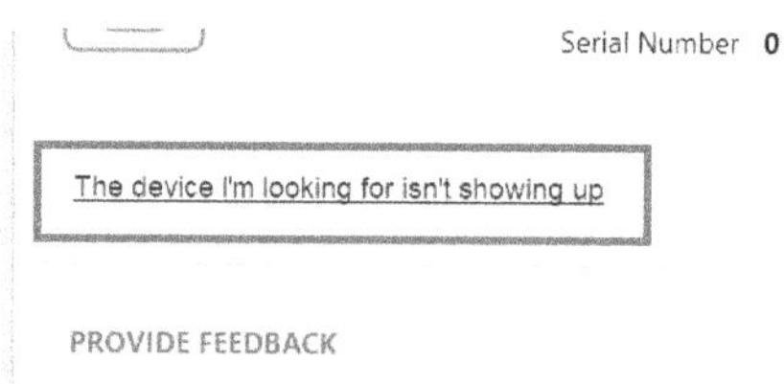

Figure 3.24 – Enabling Magnet ACQUIRE to recognize a connected mobile device

6. For an Android device, the next screen presents only a single option for a *Quick* acquisition, as we do not have access to protected storage areas. This is a logical acquisition of data and will unfortunately fail to obtain many valuable artifacts such as third-party applications data and web browser activity. Paid tools such as Cellebrite

and GrayKey/VeraKey can often overcome these restrictions and obtain a rich dataset from the protected areas of the operating system and applications. Alternatively, an Android device can be *rooted* to gain privileged access, though doing so carries inherent risks such as further altering data or even *bricking* the device, rendering it inoperable. Select **NEXT**:

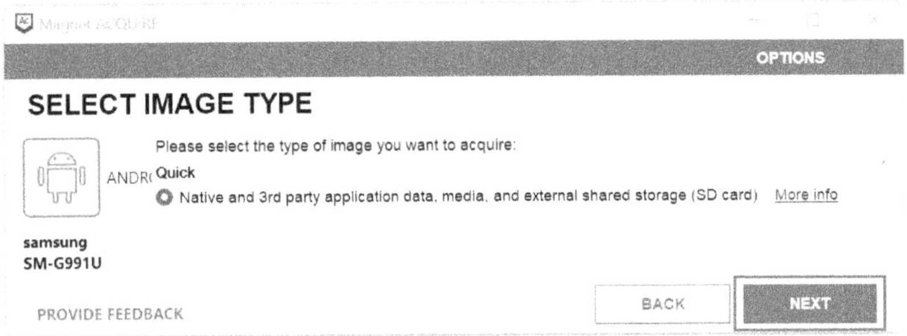

Figure 3.25 – Selecting an acquisition type for Android

7. Now you will select a destination storage drive to store the results and can optionally enter and change information regarding the acquisition details. Ensure you have chosen a storage destination large enough to accommodate the acquisition and select **ACQUIRE**:

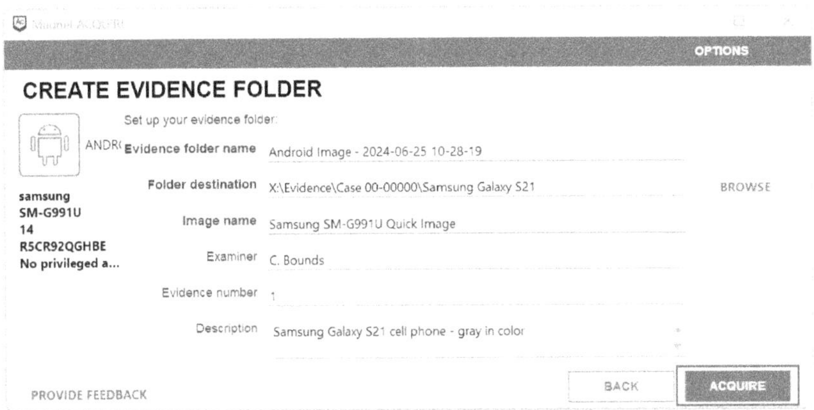

Figure 3.26 – Choosing a storage location and details for Android acquisition

8. The acquisition process will begin. For Android, you may notice certain activity occurring on the source mobile device, such as creating a backup. Absent the need to correct potential connection errors, there is no need to interact with the source mobile device, as Acquire will select the options needed:

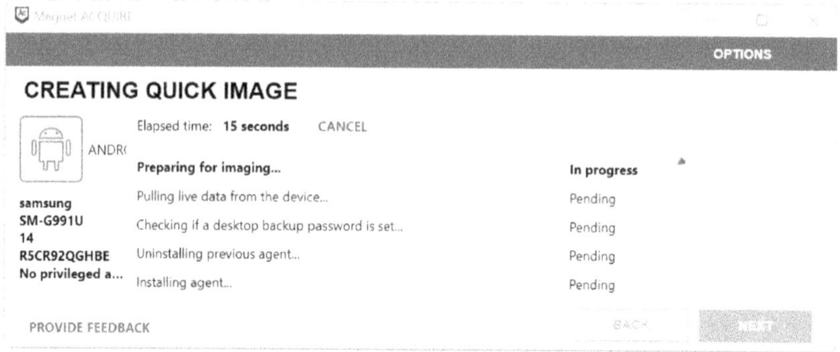

Figure 3.27 – Magnet ACQUIRE acquisition process for Android

9. As the acquisition process proceeds, pay attention to Magnet ACQUIRE, as it may require some minimal interaction during certain steps. When this occurs, follow the onscreen directions and then select **NEXT**. Additionally, there may be certain processes that the Microsoft Windows firewall attempts to block. When this occurs, be sure to **Allow** the blocked processes:

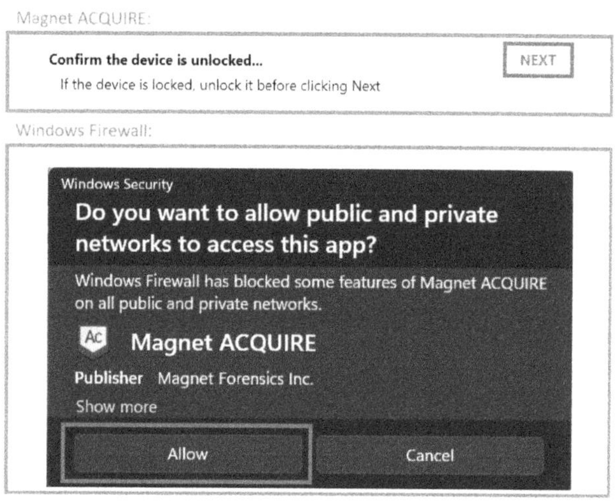

Figure 3.28 – Selecting potential prompts to ensure successful acquisition

10. Once the acquisition and hash verification has completed, a final screen will be presented depicting the elapsed time and total size of the acquired evidence image file. The acquisition is completed, and you can now select **EXIT**:

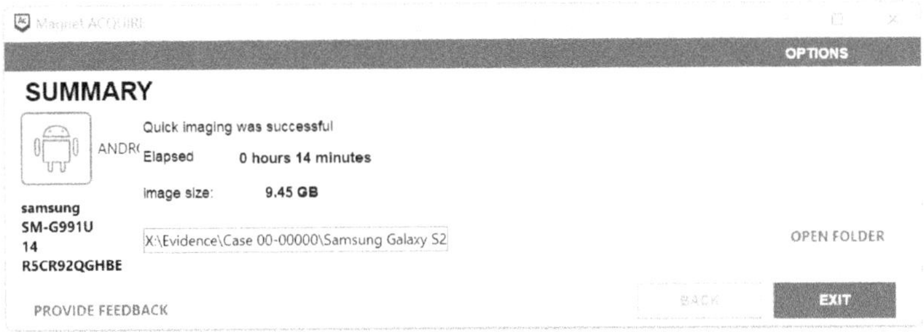

Figure 3.29 – Android mobile device acquisition complete

11. The acquisition of an iOS device is nearly identical to the Android acquisition shown above, except for some minor variations and the underlying processes for iOS acquisition which will rely upon our installation of Apple iTunes. As an example, I will now select to acquire data from my attached Apple iPhone and select **NEXT**:

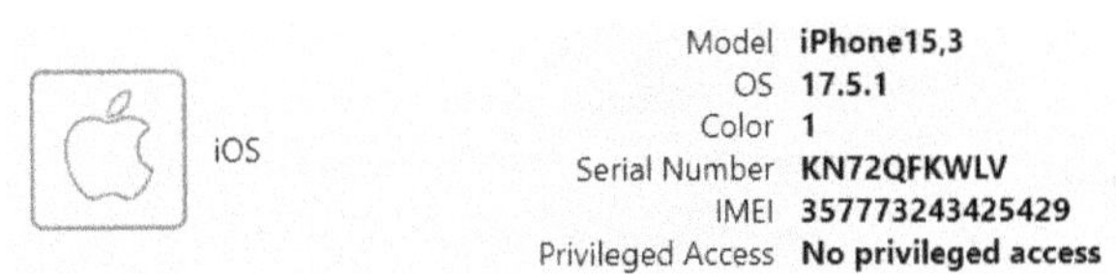

Figure 3.30 – Selecting an iOS device for acquisition

12. One difference between the Android and iOS acquisitions can be seen when selecting the image type. You will notice in the example below that we have options for a *Quick* or a *Full* acquisition, though the *Full* acquisition is grayed out and cannot be selected as we do not have privileged access to protected data areas of the connected device. Similar to the Android acquisition we performed, this means we are obtaining a logical acquisition of a limited dataset which will not include certain third-party application data. This again can often be overcome through the use of paid solutions such as Cellebrite and GrayKey/VeraKey or by manually escalating our privileges and *jail breaking* the iPhone. Jail breaking an iPhone will gain similar results and carries similar risks to *rooting* an Android device. We will select the option for a *Quick* image type and then select **NEXT:**

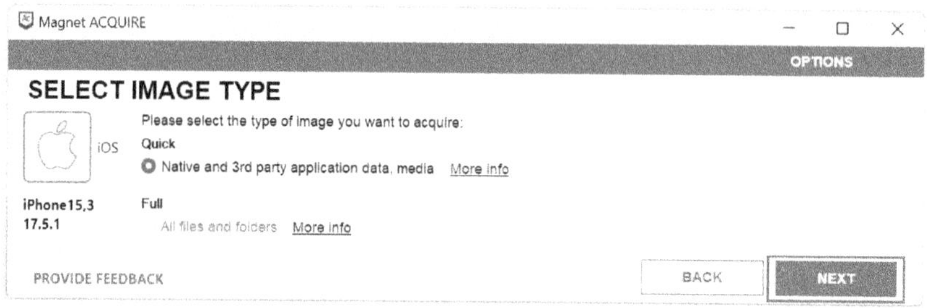

Figure 3.31 – Selecting an acquisition type of iOS

13. Again, choose a destination storage drive, enter details of the acquisition, and select **ACQUIRE**:

Figure 3.32 – Choosing a storage location and details for iOS acquisition

14. The acquisition process will begin. For iOS, if a passcode is set then the target mobile device may prompt you to reenter the passcode again during the acquisition process. Wait for the acquisition to complete.

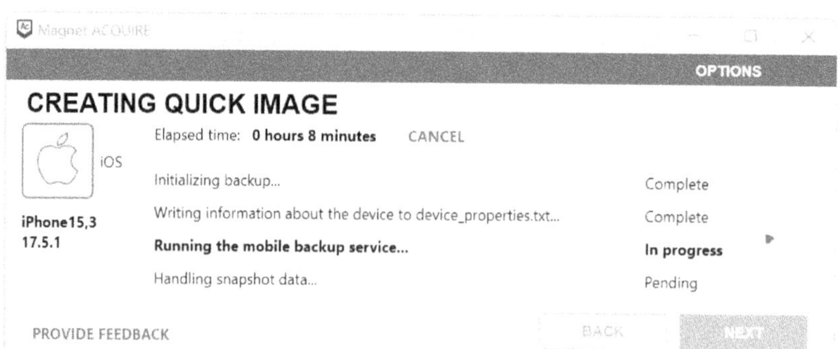

Figure 3.33 – Magnet ACQUIRE acquisition process for iOS

15. Once the acquisition and hash verification has completed, we can select **EXIT**:

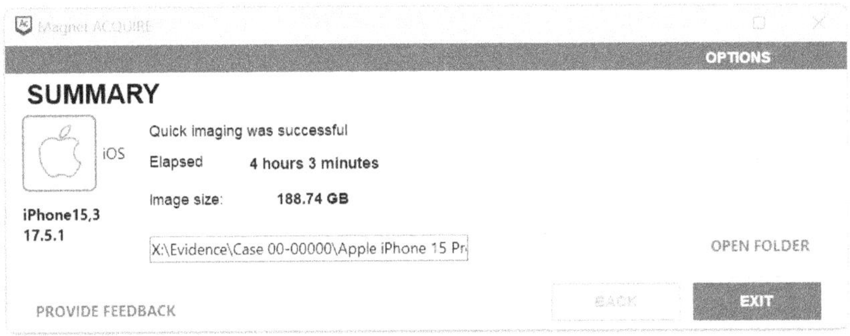

Figure 3.34 – iOS mobile device acquisition complete

16. In the directories we chose to store our acquisitions, you will see compressed folders containing the acquired data and text files detailing the acquisition. These compressed folders can later be processed using analysis software:

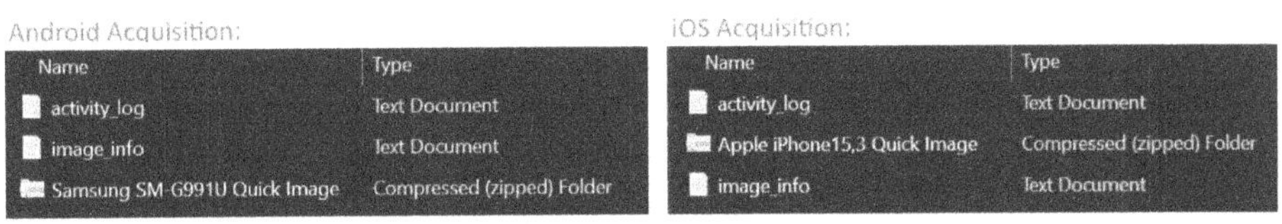

Figure 3.35 – Android and iOS acquisition files

> **Note**
>
> Don't stand by waiting for the trash truck
>
> Many "deleted" items on phones aren't immediately gone - photos, notes, messages, and other user-deleted content often sit in a "Recently Deleted" folder (typically 30 days) or in app trash bins where they remain recoverable. That window can close quickly. If you let a seized device sit powered and unlocked, those recoverable items (and other transient interaction records) can become permanently removed. For mobile evidence, speed matters: acquire as soon as practicable and use isolation methods so the device can't sync or be remotely wiped before you capture the data.

How it works...

Not using a hardware write-blocker during mobile acquisition departs from our usual lab procedures, but it is often the only practical way to get data from a locked or unlocked phone, as communication must be established with the device to acquire the data. That does not mean we abandon forensic discipline. We limit interaction to what's required, record every action, and create verifiable forensic outputs so later analysis can be performed without repeatedly touching the original device. Always be prepared to explain and justify why a mobile acquisition required host interaction, what changes were likely made, and which tools and commands were used.

Mobile acquisitions commonly require troubleshooting and one-off workarounds, so preserve acquisition logs, tool versions, screenshots, and hashes. If simple logical methods fail, alternatives include using other software-based acquisition techniques (e.g., device backups via iTunes on Windows or Finder on modern macOS), targeted file export, or (as a last resort) manual scroll analysis while photographing the user interface. Because logical images omit protected areas of modern devices, budget-conscious teams should strongly consider investing in a commercial device-acquisition tool if mobile evidence is mission-critical; otherwise, plan to document limitations and preserve opportunities for future deeper collection.

Alternative open-source approaches to mobile device acquisition include Android Debug Bridge (ADB)–based collection and tools such as UFADE (for iOS), though these methods vary in complexity, device support, and data coverage.

Online accounts and cloud data

Cloud accounts and online services now hold large amounts of user data. File-storage providers (Google Drive, iCloud, OneDrive, Dropbox, MEGA, etc.) are obvious examples, but many social media, messaging, and productivity platforms also persist user content to servers so it can be accessed from any device. Because some content never syncs or is later purged from a local device, relying solely on a seized phone or laptop can miss important historical material that lives only in the cloud.

When possible, obtain cloud data via a legal-service request to the provider (preservation notice, subpoena, MLAT, court order, etc.). Legal requests often yield the most complete and defensible datasets and avoid the need to handle account credentials yourself. If you do have lawful access to credentials (owner consent or appropriate legal authority), downloading data directly can be faster or necessary when a provider won't comply or when you must preserve volatile content immediately. Always document authority, consent, and every action you take.

In this recipe, we will acquire user data from online accounts using built-in data export features. You will learn how to download account data from common platforms (such as Facebook and Google) in a forensically sound manner for later analysis.

Getting ready

You will need a desktop or laptop with a web browser and lawful access to the target account. For practice, use a test or personal account. The examples in this recipe demonstrate data collection workflows for common providers (Facebook/Instagram and Google).

Be aware that logging into an account from a new device or IP address may trigger multi-factor authentication (MFA) or generate security alerts (such as "New Login Detected" notifications). You may need access to the user's trusted device to approve the login request. This activity may also create account artifacts or alert the account holder. When possible, first perform these actions on a test account to understand how the environment will respond.

Interface layouts may vary slightly between providers or as platforms update over time, but the overall process remains consistent.

How to do it...

1. Run your web browser of choice. At a minimum, open a new private/incognito window. Using private/incognito mode will ensure the credentials for other accounts do not attempt to sync or cross-contaminate one another. This helps prevent cross-contamination between accounts and protects the integrity of the target account data. To add an extra layer of protection when attaining real evidence, it would be wise to use a new virtual machine (for example, using platforms such as VMware or VirtualBox) each time you acquire account data.
2. Go to `www.facebook.com` and log into an existing account:

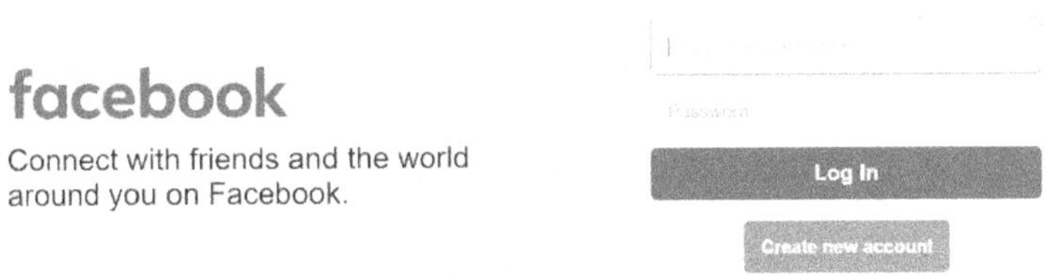

Figure 3.36 – Facebook login screen

In the upper right corner of the screen, select the profile to access the dropdown menu for the account. Select **Settings & privacy**, then select **Settings**:

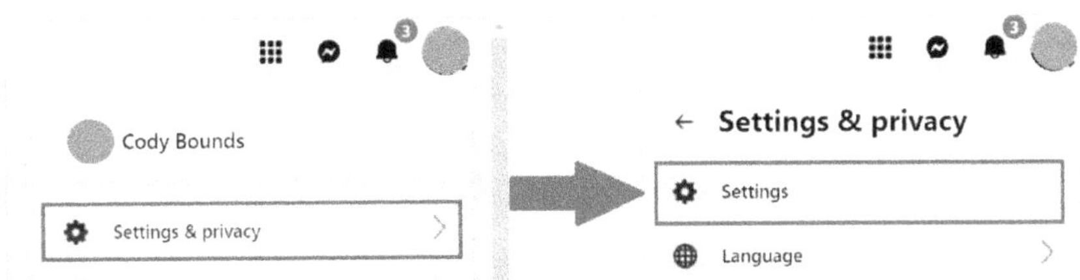

Figure 3.37 – Facebook settings

3. A webpage will load with a menu on the left side. Scroll down this menu until you find the **Your information** section, then select **Download your information**:

Figure 3.38 – Facebook Download your information option

4. An option will appear to begin the process of downloading the account data. Select **Continue**:

Figure 3.39 – Facebook process to download account data

5. A menu will appear to begin selecting options for the download. Ensure **Current Activity** is underlined and then select **Download or transfer information**:

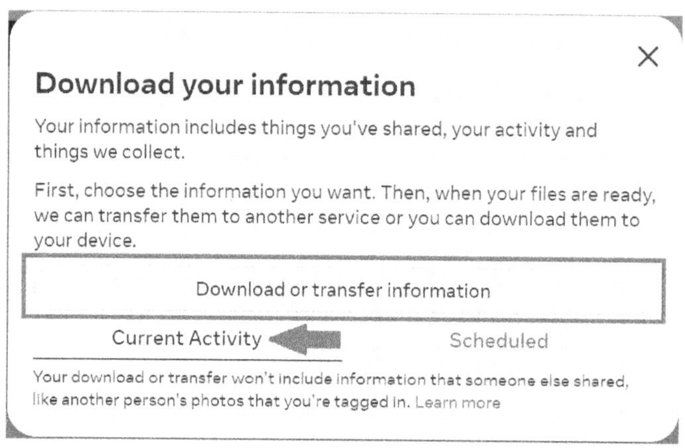

Figure 3.40 – Facebook Download your information menu

6. The next options will allow you to choose which account you wish to download. It is common for there to be multiple accounts, as Meta owns both Facebook and Instagram, and a user can also manage multiple other accounts from a single profile. Select the target account and choose **Next**:

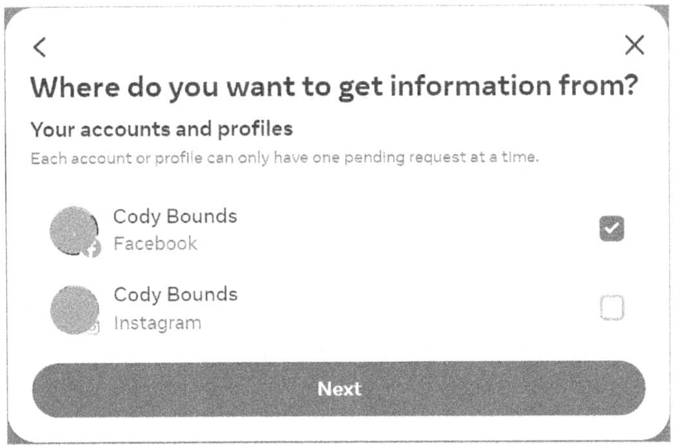

Figure 3.41 – Facebook account selection options

7. Now we can choose from the data we want to download from the account. You have the option to select **Specific types of information** to target only a limited amount of data that may be important, otherwise you can acquire a complete download of all available information for the account by selecting **Available information**:

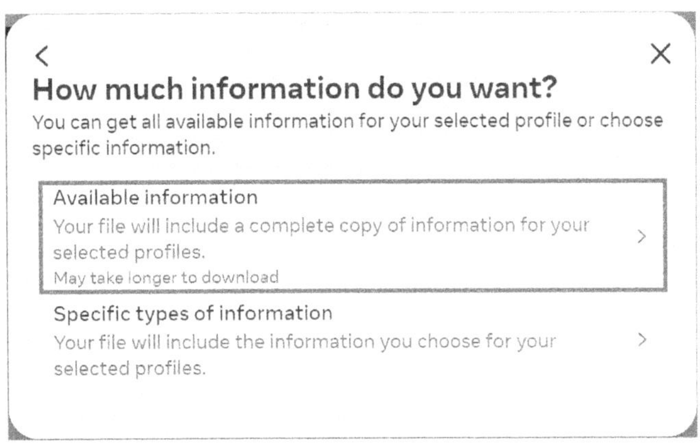

Figure 3.42 – Facebook options to target specific data or acquire complete data

8. Here we can either download the data directly or transfer the data to another online service. We will choose to **Download to device** and select **Next:**

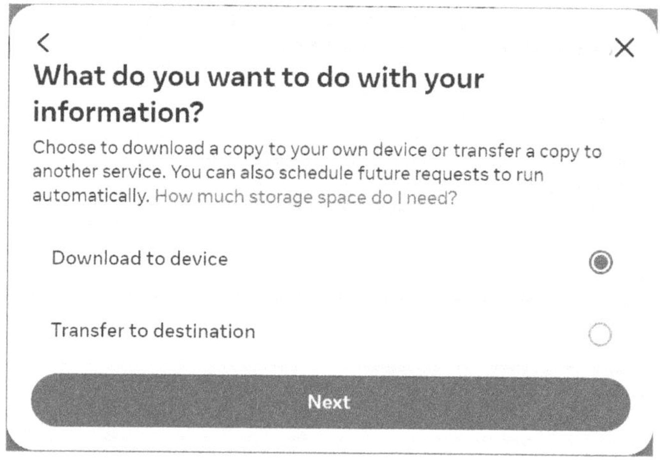

Figure 3.43 – Facebook option to download data directly to our computer

9. Now we can choose a date range for the data we wish to download. You can opt to download data for the entire life of the account, though if the user created their account when Facebook was in its infancy this could be more than 15 years of content and could take a considerable amount of time!
   Alternatively, we can limit the date range as desired. You will also choose which e-mail address you would like a notification sent to when the download has completed, the format to receive the data in (HTML or JSON), and the media quality.

   A higher media quality can also prolong the amount of time the download will take but could be worth increasing if media files are an important part of your investigation. After choosing the desired options, select **Create files**:

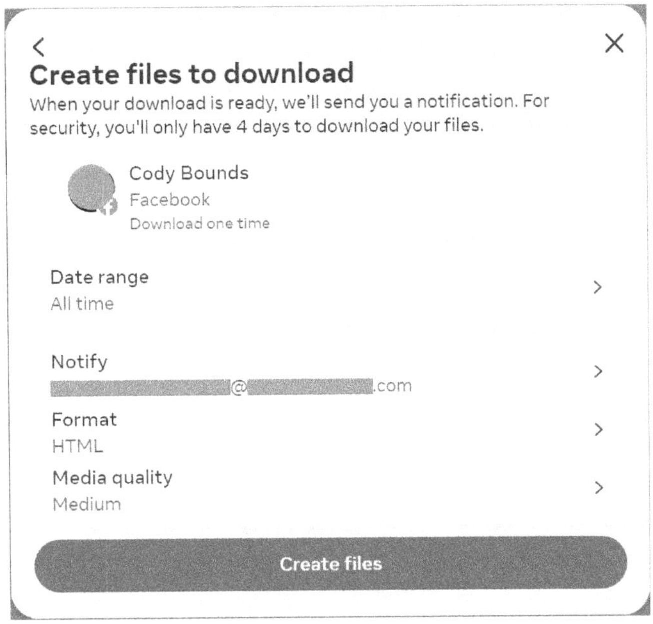

Figure 3.44 – Facebook option for date range, download format, and media quality

10. Lastly, you will see a summary display for the download, showing **In progress**. The menu can now be closed while you await notification to the e-mail address previously chosen once the download is complete:

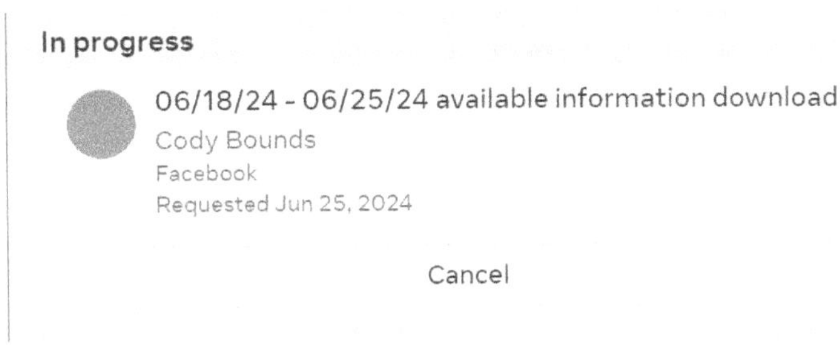

Figure 3.45 – Facebook download In progress summary

11. Once e-mail notification is received, follow the **download your information** link:

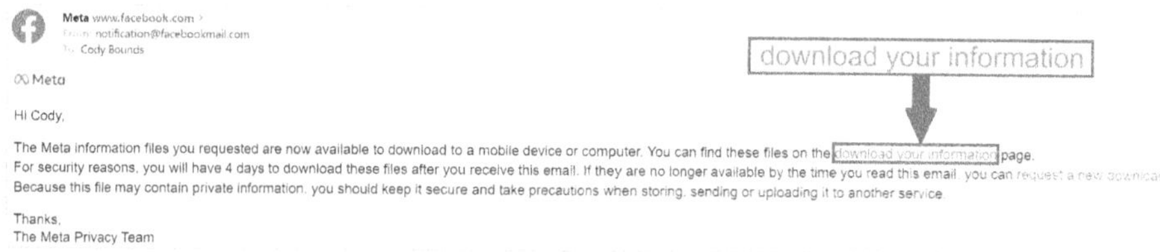

Figure 3.46 – Facebook download In progress summary

12. The link provided via e-mail will redirect you to the appropriate web address, where you will select **Download**, at which time you may be prompted to reenter the target account password and the download will begin:

Figure 3.47 – Facebook download link

13. Once downloaded, you will have a zipped file containing the target account data. This download should be secured and treated as the original evidence. We will only perform further actions on a copy of the original downloaded data:

Figure 3.48 – Facebook downloaded data

> **Note**
>
> Working with and storing acquired evidence
>
> You may be noticing that much of our acquired data is stored within zipped containers or forensic image file types. This helps to ensure the data is not at high risk of contamination or alteration. We should always hash these original archives and only perform analysis on working copies. Treat the original archive as the evidence source.

14. Most accounts allow for a download of user data as shown above, though obviously the locations to acquire the user data will vary per platform. Downloading user data from

Google is slightly different, as they use a specific Google service to perform the download, called Google Takeout.

We will begin this process by using a private/incognito browser window to go to `www.google.com` and log into an existing Google account:

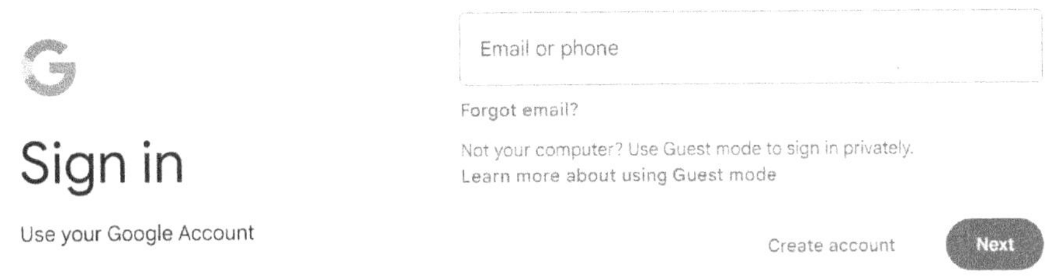

Figure 3.49 – Google login screen

15. In your web browser, go to `www.takeout.google.com` to access the Google Takeout service. From here, we can target specific data stored by Google or we can select all the data available for a complete download. In the example, I have chosen to select all 50 options available to perform a complete download:

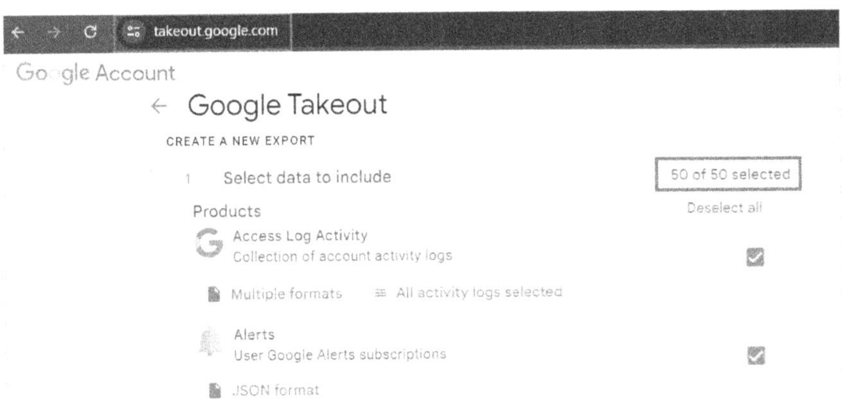

Figure 3.50 – Google Takeout data selections

16. Upon scrolling to the end of the available download options, choose **Next step**:

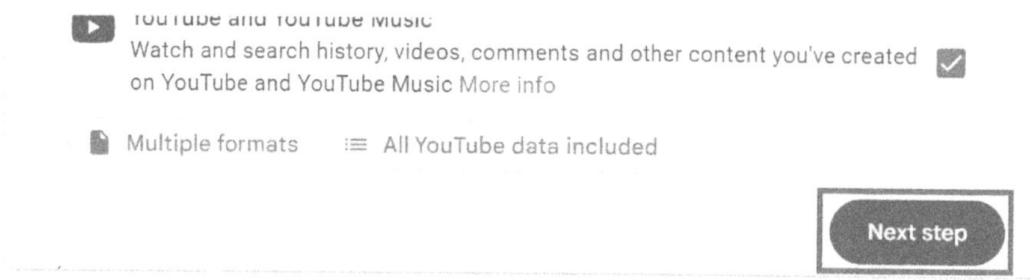

Figure 3.51 – Google Takeout continuation to Next step

17. The next options will allow you to choose how to create the download. The *Destination* dropdown contains several options on where the download will eventually be set. Most of these options require you to sync another account to the target account, which we **do not** want to do. The best option available is to **Send download link via email** so we can avoid adding a synced account. This will result in an e-mail being sent to the target Google account when the download is ready, and unfortunately, does not allow us to choose an alternate e-mail account. We will then select a download **Frequency** of **Export once**, to prevent scheduled exports of the account data and a **File Type** of **.zip** so the download will be contained as a zipped file to offer better protection against unintentional changes to the data later. For the **File size**, I have selected the largest available option of **50 GB** to prevent, or at least minimize, possible segmentation of the file. When ready, select **Create export**:

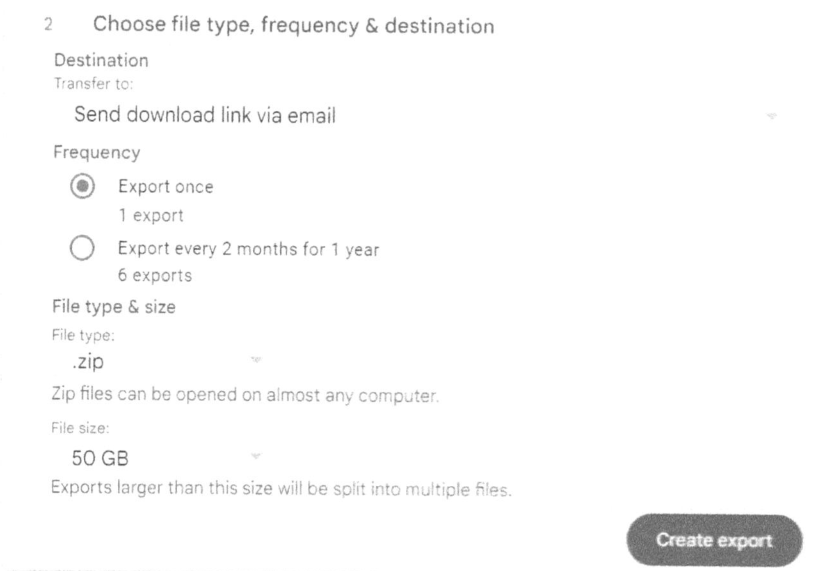

Figure 3.52 – Google Takeout export creation options

18. A minimal summary of the account data export will show under **Export progress**. We can now await notification to the target account e-mail address once the download is complete:

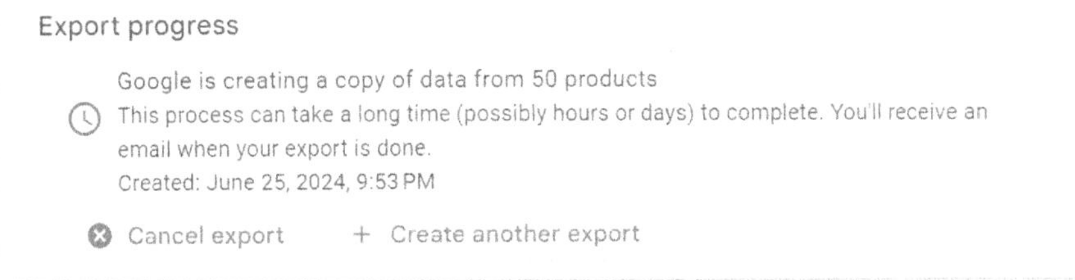

Figure 3.53 – Google Takeout export summary

19. An e-mail will be received from **Google Takeout** once the data is ready for download. Select the **Download your files** link provided in this e-mail, at which time you will be prompted to reenter the login credentials of the target account:

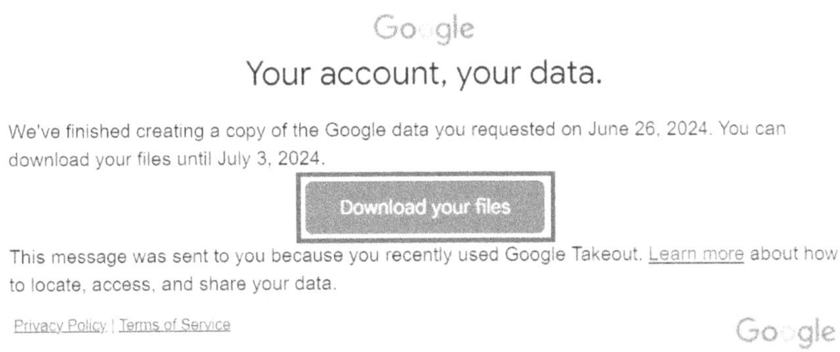

Figure 3.54 – Google Takeout e-mail notification

20. After verifying login credentials, you will be directed to the Google Takeout export management webpage. Select the **Download** link and the account contents will begin downloading to your computer:

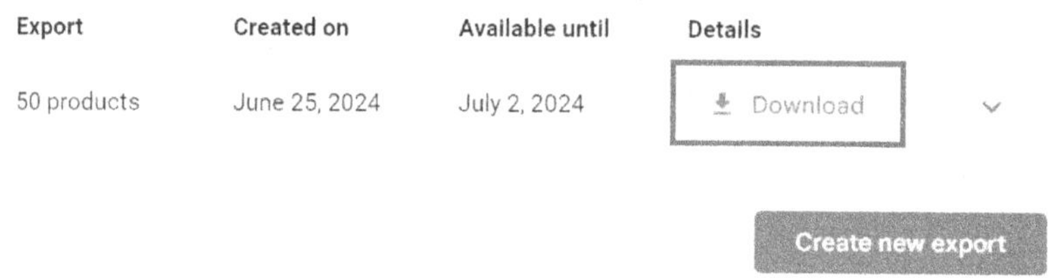

Figure 3.55 – Google Takeout download link

21. Once downloaded, you will have a zipped file or multiple zipped files containing the target account data on which we can later perform analysis. Like with any account download, this file should be treated as the original evidence:

Figure 3.56 – Google account downloaded data

How it works...

When you have valid login credentials for an online account, downloading the account data yourself is often the fastest option, but it isn't instantaneous. Exports can take hours or days to prepare, so target only what you need if time is critical. Maintain access to the account during the export and, when appropriate and lawful, temporarily secure the account (revoke other sessions, update recovery options, or change credentials) to reduce the chance the user or synced devices alter data. Use an isolated acquisition environment (private browser or disposable VM), capture screenshots of account settings and export confirmations, and treat the original downloaded archive as the evidentiary source: compute cryptographic hashes, log timestamps, and perform all analysis against only working copies you create.

Data validation

As we acquire data, we must validate it so we can prove the evidence stayed bit-for-bit identical during handling, transfer, or analysis. A cryptographic hash acts as a digital fingerprint for a file or image. Compute it immediately after acquisition, record the hash value generated, then recompute whenever the file is copied or moved to show the data is unchanged. If even one binary bit has changed, the resultant hash value will not match. This provides reproducible, mathematical proof to validate that our data has remained unaltered. Many acquisition tools (for example FTK Imager) compute hashes automatically; you can also compute them independently with other software utilities when needed.

In this recipe, we will validate acquired data by computing and comparing cryptographic hash values. You will use a hashing utility to demonstrate how identical files produce matching hashes and how even minor changes result in different values, confirming data integrity.

Getting ready

For this section, we will use Eric Zimmerman's Hasher utility. This free software is developed with digital forensics in mind and allows us to choose from numerous hashing algorithms and also hash bulk files if needed.

The Hasher software can be downloaded from Eric Zimmerman's website: `https://ericzimmerman.github.io/#!index.md`

How to do it...

1. Run **Hasher**. From the File menu choose **Select File** and browse to the file or forensic image you want to hash. You can also drag and drop files into the window. By default, Hasher produces MD5 and SHA-1 values; you can change algorithms via **Tools | Options**:

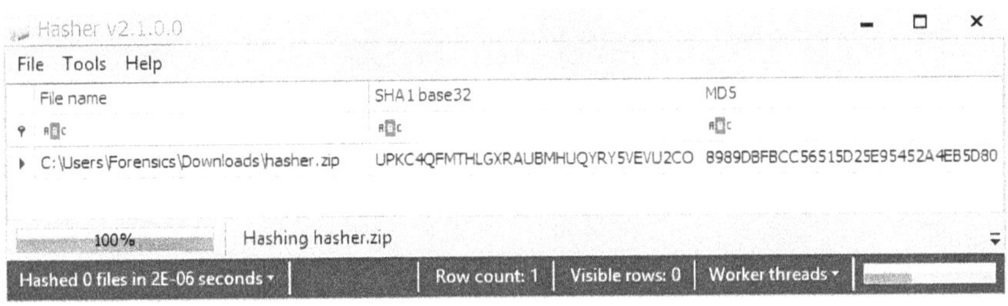

Figure 3.57 – MD5 and SHA1 values calculated using Hasher

2. Grab a photograph as a test file and make a copy so you have two identical files. Hash both files. The computed values should match even if you rename one of the copies, because filenames are not part of the file's binary data:

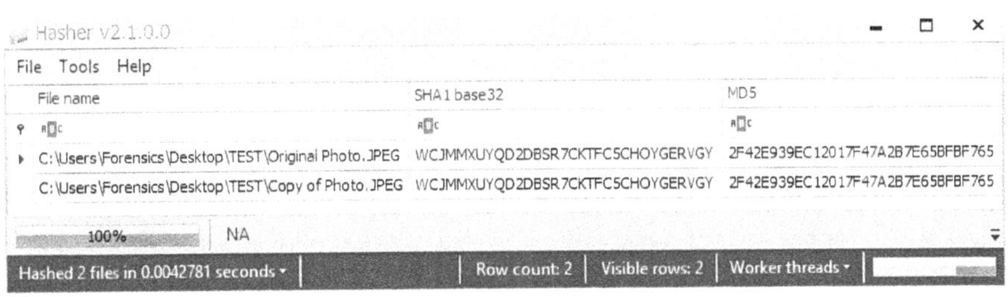

Figure 3.58 – Hash values calculated for two identical files using Hasher

3. Right-click one of the copies and open it in Microsoft Paint. Make a tiny, obvious edit (for example, add a single pixel/dot) and then save:

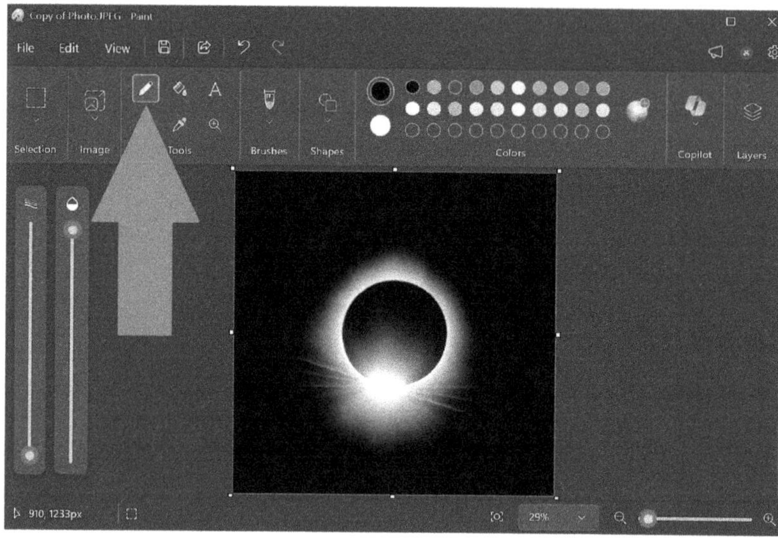

Figure 3.59 – Altering a file copy using Microsoft Paint

4. Hash both files again. Even a single-pixel change will result in completely different hash values. This demonstrates that hashing detects any bit-level change to a file – exactly why we use it to validate forensic evidence:

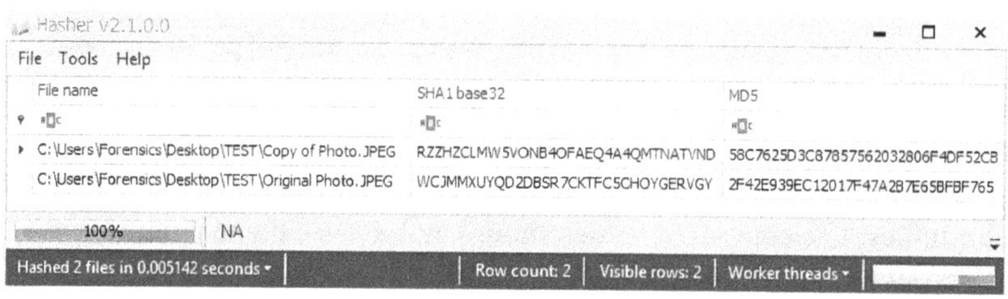

Figure 3.60 – Hash values comparing an altered file using Hasher

How it works...

By computing a cryptographic hash, you create a mathematical fingerprint of a file or forensic image. The hash is calculated from the file's binary contents, so even a single-bit change produces a different resultant hash value. Compute and record the hash immediately after acquisition (note the algorithm, tool, and timestamp), then recompute the same hash whenever the file is copied or transferred – matching values prove the copy is bit-for-bit identical.

Summary

Data acquisition can involve both physical media and cloud-based accounts, and it is the gateway to everything that follows in a digital forensic investigation. The method you choose (physical, logical, or targeted) directly impacts the completeness of your dataset and your ability to recover artifacts such as deleted data. Because acquisition requires interaction with original evidence, it is critical to follow defensible procedures, minimize unnecessary changes, and document every action taken.

Throughout this chapter, you implemented write-blocking, accounted for SSD-specific behavior, acquired data from storage devices and systems with integrated storage, performed logical acquisition of mobile devices, collected data from online accounts, and learned how to use cryptographic hashing for validating acquired data. These processes ensure that acquired evidence is reliable, reproducible, and suitable for further forensic analysis.

At this point, you should be able to:

- Implement and verify write-blocking techniques to protect evidentiary media.
- Recognize SSD-specific behaviors (such as TRIM and garbage collection) and apply mitigation strategies.
- Acquire forensic images from physical storage devices using standard workflows.
- Perform acquisitions from systems with integrated storage using external forensic environments.
- Conduct logical acquisitions of mobile devices while understanding their limitations.
- Collect user data from cloud-based accounts using built-in export features.
- Validate acquired data using cryptographic hashing to ensure integrity.

In the next chapter, we move from acquisition to analysis, focusing on examining Microsoft Windows systems to identify user activity, artifacts, and evidence of system and user behavior.

Get this book's PDF version and more

Scan the QR code (or go to `packtpub.com/unlock`). Search for this book by name, confirm the edition, and then follow the steps on the page.

UNLOCK NOW

Note: Keep your invoice handy. Purchases made directly from Packt don't require an invoice.

Part 2

Platform-Based Analysis

In this part of the book, you will focus on analyzing digital evidence across major operating systems and platforms. Each chapter explores the structure, artifacts, and investigative techniques relevant to major operating systems encountered in modern digital forensics, helping you understand how user activity and system behavior are recorded.

You will examine common artifacts, learn how to interpret them, and understand their investigative significance in real-world cases. By the end of this part, you will be able to navigate and analyze evidence from Windows, macOS, Linux, iOS, and Android operating systems with confidence.

This part is organized into the following chapters:

- *Chapter 4, Microsoft Windows*
- *Chapter 5, Apple macOS and Linux*
- *Chapter 6, Apple iOS and Android*

4

Microsoft Windows

Following acquisition in *Chapter 3*, we now move into analysis – the phase where we parse and examine acquired data. Think of evidence collection as gathering boxes of toy building blocks: acquisition gave us the raw, unordered pieces. Analysis is where we sort those pieces, figure out how they fit together, and build the picture that answers our investigative questions.

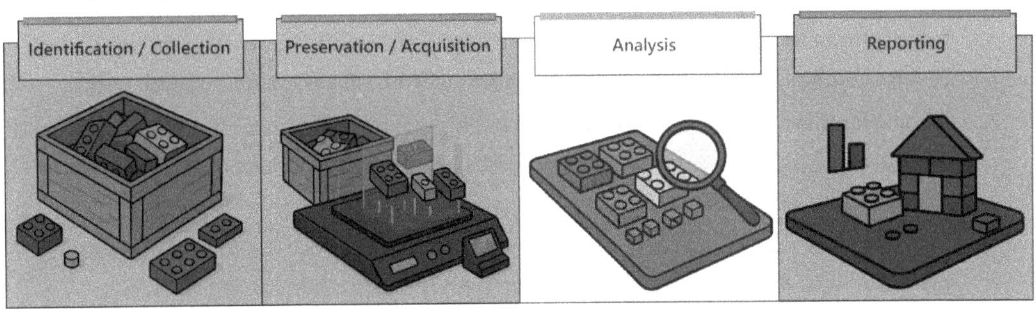

Figure 4.1 – Step three of the digital forensic methodology: analysis

At this stage, the goal is not just to find data but to interpret it in a way that answers specific investigative questions.

To be accurate and thorough, you must understand how the operating system you're examining actually works so you can correctly interpret user activity and system behavior. The three most common desktop operating systems are Microsoft Windows, Apple macOS, and various Linux distributions. This chapter is a crash course on the artifacts and structures most useful for analyzing Microsoft Windows systems.

Windows, the most widely used operating system today, remains a primary target for adversaries. It is also quite unique among operating systems, using the NT kernel, a distinct shell and syntax, and storing system and user data in formats not found on platforms like Apple macOS or Linux.

In this chapter, we're going to cover the following main topics:

- Windows registry
- Recycle bin
- Link files
- Shellbags
- Jump lists
- Prefetch
- Event logs
- Thumbcache
- Volume Shadow Copy Service (VSS)

Technical requirements

For this chapter, you will need:

1. A computer running Microsoft Windows to act as your forensic workstation—required for installing analysis utilities and running the exercises. Windows 11 is recommended. Ensure you have ample disk space for any forensic images you plan to work with.
2. A basic familiarity with concepts related to data parsing, file systems, OS behavior, and the Microsoft Windows directory structure is required. If you need a refresher, consult the appendix in this book.
3. Microsoft Windows data for analysis is required. You may use the forensic image provided with the examples or create your own image for hands-on practice.
4. An instance of FTK Imager (as used in previous chapters) or an alternative tool capable of browsing forensic images. For example, 7-Zip may be used with additional support (such as the Forensic7z plugin) to access E01 image contents, as introduced earlier in this book.

Windows registry

The Windows registry is a central source of system and user activity artifacts and plays a critical role in forensic analysis. It stores configuration data for the operating system, applications, and user activity, making it one of the most valuable sources of evidence on a Windows system. In this recipe, we will examine the structure of the registry, identify key hives, and explore high-value locations commonly used during an investigation.

Getting ready

The sample **Microsoft Windows** forensic image dataset containing the artifacts used for examples in this recipe can be downloaded from the Packt Publishing GitHub repository for this book. To access the repository link, follow the steps in the *"Download the example code files"* section in the *Preface*.

If you use the sample dataset, the easiest way to pull the individual files needed for each example is with FTK Imager or another tool capable of browsing forensic images (installed in earlier chapters).

Load the forensic image into your chosen tool and navigate the evidence tree to the file(s) you need, right-click, and choose **Export Files...**

To export multiple files at once, hold `Ctrl` to select each file before exporting. *Figure 4.2* shows selecting and exporting multiple Windows Registry files, which we'll discuss in the upcoming recipe steps.

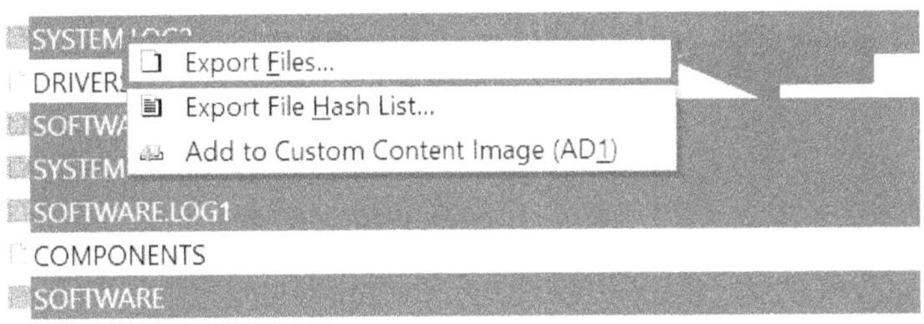

Figure 4.2 – Using FTK Imager to export multiple registry files

Also, you will need to download, extract, and install **Registry Explorer** from Eric Zimmerman's website:

`https://ericzimmerman.github.io/#!index.md`

If prompted during installation, opt to download and install Microsoft Windows Desktop Runtime, which is required to run Registry Explorer.

How to do it...

1. Sometimes the best way to understand what we are viewing forensically is to start by viewing how the concept works on your own system. Press *Windows + R*, type **regedit**, and `Enter` to open the **Windows Registry Editor**.

   You'll see your registry presented as a hierarchical tree, made up of *hives* (think of a hive as a top-level container), each containing *keys* (like parent folders), *subkeys* (subfolders), and finally *values* (the data types and entries stored at the leaf nodes). In Regedit, this looks very much like a file-system directory tree and is a useful way to explore configurations, installed software, device settings, and many user-activity artifacts:

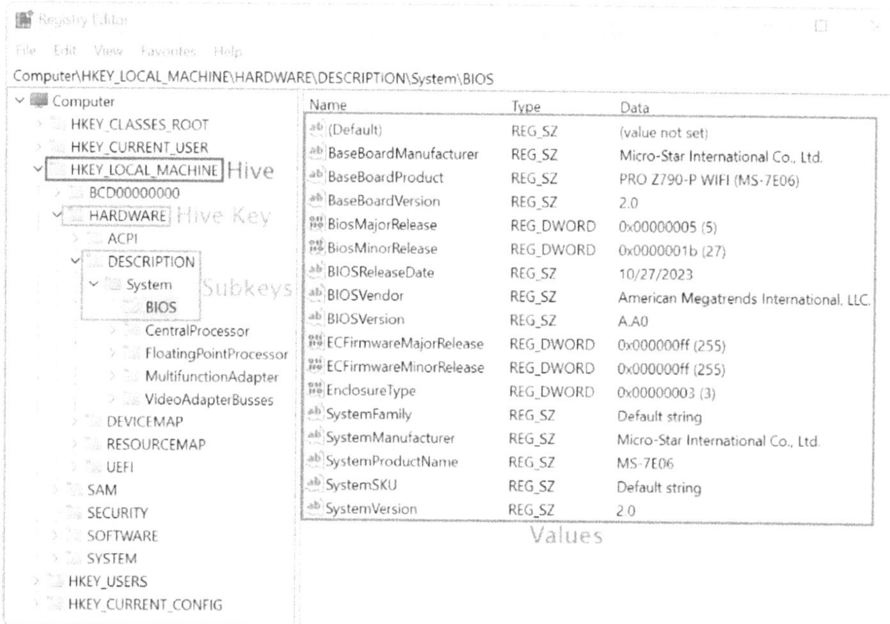

Figure 4.3 – Windows registry viewed with Registry Editor

Note

Some people casually call large top-level keys "hives," and the terms are sometimes used interchangeably in conversation; for example, you might see the `HARDWARE` key under `HKEY_LOCAL_MACHINE` referred to as a "hive," even though it lives inside the `HKEY_LOCAL_MACHINE` hive file.

2. While Windows includes Registry Editor (regedit) for viewing and editing the live registry on your own system, forensic analysis should be performed using a read-only viewer, which allows you to safely examine externally collected registry hive files without modifying the source system.
3. Launch **Registry Explorer**:

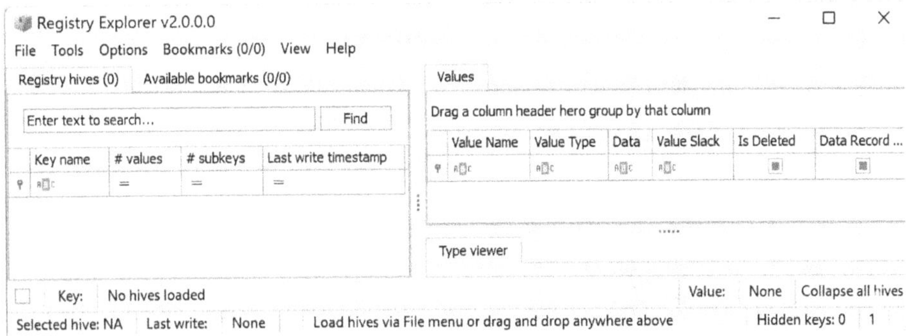

Figure 4.4 – Registry Explorer

4. Some hives live under the system `config` folder and others live in each user profile. Collect the following files (work from copies extracted from your image):
   `HKEY_LOCAL_MACHINE` hive files from `{root}\Windows\System32\Config\`

   - **Security Account Manager** (**SAM**): For local account information and references to account password hashes.
   - **SECURITY**: Stores local security information such as audit policies.
   - **SOFTWARE**: Holds information about the operating system and installed application configurations.
   - **SYSTEM**: Contains information pertaining to the installed operating system in addition to previously attached storage drives.
     `HKEY_USERS` hive files from `{root}\Users\UserProfile\`
   - **NTUSER.DAT**: Stores configuration information specific to the associated user account. NTUSER.DAT exists for each individual user account on the system, so you must go to each user profile to obtain all NTUSER.DAT files.
     Additional user-specific hive files may be found at:

     `{root}\Users\UserProfile\AppData\Local\Microsoft\Windows`
   - **UsrClass.dat**: Exists for each user profile and works with `NTUSER.DAT` to store user configurations, including the majority of shellbag artifacts (we will cover shellbags later in this section)
5. Export the registry files shown above, along with any corresponding transaction logs (e.g., `.LOG1`, `.LOG2` files)
6. Load the registry files into Registry Explorer by dragging or dropping each hive into the interface, selecting **File | Load hive**, or using the shortcut keys of *Ctrl* + *O*:

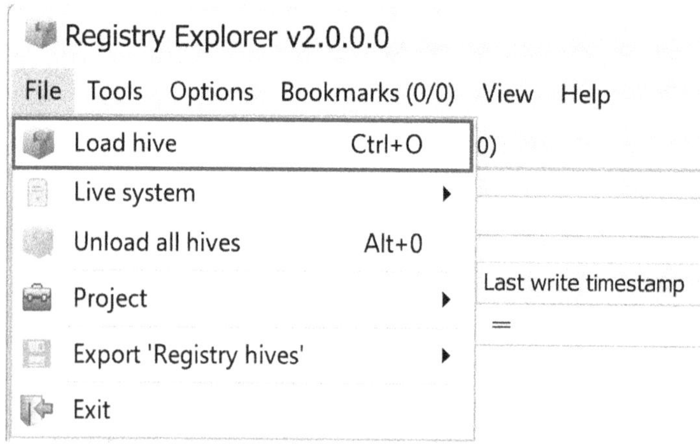

Figure 4.5 – Loading registry hives into Registry Explorer

7. When you load the hive copies, Registry Explorer will often prompt you to "replay" the associated transaction logs. Accept this prompt and point the tool to the matching `.LOG1` / `.LOG2` (or other transaction log) files that sit next to the hive.

> Note
>
> Note:
>
> Windows hides these files by default. Enable **Show hidden files** and *uncheck* **Hide protected operating system files** in Explorer's Folder Options so that you can see them on your workstation.

8. Save the replayed (reconstructed) hive to a new location so you never overwrite your original copies and click **Yes** when prompted to load the updated or "dirty" hive.
9. Once complete, Registry Explorer will show the original (dirty) hive alongside the cleaned or replayed hive so you can compare them.

> Note
>
> Registry data is not always written to the primary hive files in real time. Instead, changes are often recorded in transaction log files (`.LOG1`/`.LOG2`) and committed later, such as during system shutdown or user logoff.
>
> As a result, the log files may contain more up-to-date registry values than the primary hive. Registry Explorer detects this condition when sequence numbers do not match and allows reconstruction of a clean hive by replaying these logs.

By saving the reconstructed hive and loading the original ("dirty") hive, we can compare both versions to identify differences and ensure that no relevant artifacts are missed.

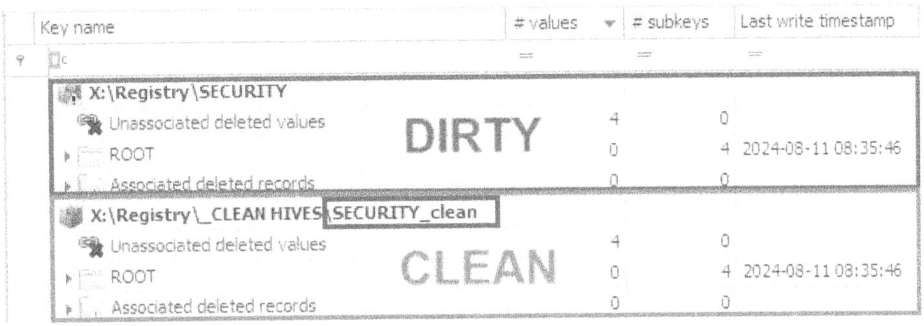

Figure 4.6 – Clean vs. dirty hives displayed in Registry Explorer

Because the Registry is hierarchical, keys and subkeys can be read like a file path:

Figure 4.7 – Registry keys and subkeys shown similarly to a file path

10. In **Registry Explorer**, browse through each hive using the left side of the interface. When selecting a subkey, you will see the stored values on the right. Browse to `SYSTEM\ControlSet001\Control\TimeZoneInformation` and select the **TimeZoneInformation** tab above the panel on the right side of the screen:

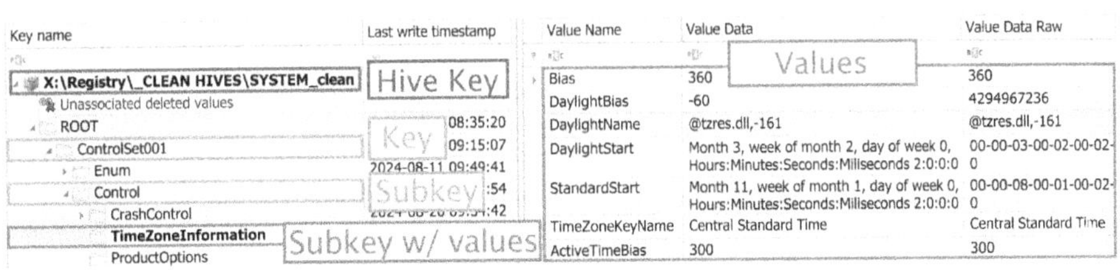

Figure 4.8 – Keys, subkeys, and values displayed in Registry Explorer

Here, you can see the values show the system clock is currently set to **Central Standard Time**. This also shows a **DayLightBias** of **-60**, which means the system is also accounting for daylight saving time, the parameters of which are shown in the values for **DaylightStart** and **StandardStart**.

This demonstrates how the Windows Registry can be used to determine system time, a critical factor when establishing accurate timelines during an investigation.

> **Note**
>
> Can you tell me what time it is?
>
> Some artifacts record times in UTC, while others are stored in the system's local time. That distinction is critical; getting it wrong can invalidate an entire timeline.
>
> In one case I testified in, differing timestamp conventions were central to the investigation. The opposing expert failed to distinguish between local and UTC times and was forced to concede the error under cross-examination. That mistake became a key factor in the outcome of the case.
>
> Always confirm the system time zone and clearly document any time conversions before presenting a timeline.

Now let's look at when the system was last shut down.

11. Information about when the system was last shut down is stored at `SYSTEM\ControlSet001\Control\Windows` and can be seen within **ShutdownTime.** Here, the value is **2C-28-75-47-90-E1-DA-01**:

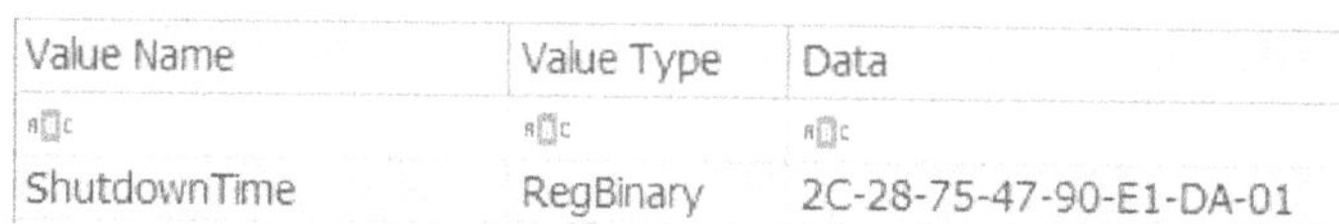

Value Name	Value Type	Data
ShutdownTime	RegBinary	2C-28-75-47-90-E1-DA-01

Figure 4.9 – Last ShutdownTime value displayed using Registry Explorer

12. Data is not always presented in a way that is easily readable. In this case, the last shutdown time value is displayed in hexadecimal and must be converted. To do this, right-click on the value and choose **Data Interpreter**:

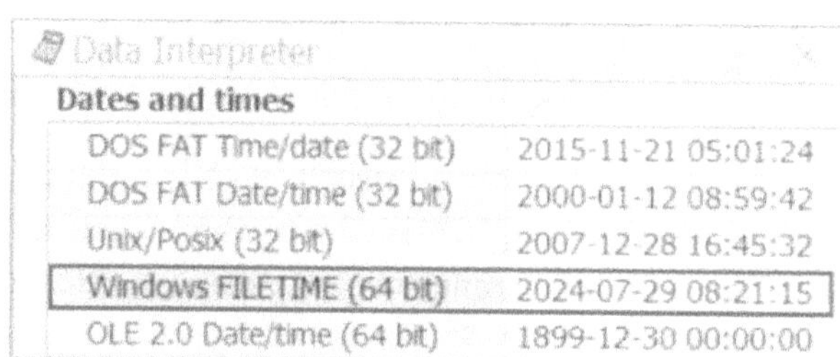

Data Interpreter

Dates and times	
DOS FAT Time/date (32 bit)	2015-11-21 05:01:24
DOS FAT Date/time (32 bit)	2000-01-12 08:59:42
Unix/Posix (32 bit)	2007-12-28 16:45:32
Windows FILETIME (64 bit)	2024-07-29 08:21:15
OLE 2.0 Date/time (64 bit)	1899-12-30 00:00:00

Figure 4.10 – Last ShutdownTime value converted using Registry Explorer

When converted to a 64-bit **Windows FILETIME** value, the date and time show as **2024-07-29** at **08:21:15**, which is in UTC. Be careful here not only regarding time zones, but also to recognize that different factors can affect the reliability of some artifacts. For example, perhaps the last true shutdown time was not recorded due to an improper shutdown caused by power loss.

> **Note**
>
> Registry values often require interpretation. Many fields are booleans (`0 = false`, `1 = true`), others are raw binary or hexadecimal that represent `FILETIME` timestamps, and some are ASCII or use other encodings.

Gaining insight into certain registry artifacts will require you to piece information together from numerous hives and subkeys.

13. Browse to `SOFTWARE\Microsoft\Windows NT\CurrentVersion\ProfileList` and select the **ProfileList** tab above the panel on the right side of the screen. Here you will find a list of the local user accounts present on the system:

Key Name	Profile Image Path
S-1-5-21-3063303759-3547812523-4161226937-1001	C:\Users\Leroy Jenkins
S-1-5-21-3063303759-3547812523-4161226937-1002	C:\Users\Chief
S-1-5-21-3063303759-3547812523-4161226937-1004	C:\Users\Nessy

Figure 4.11 – Viewing local user accounts using Registry Explorer

The **Key Name** column shows us the SID for each account, followed by the **Profile Image Path**, which tells us the name of each user. You may notice a discrepancy here; that is, the RIDs jump from **1002** to **1004**, skipping RID 1003. This occurs when a user account has been removed.

14. Now browse to `SAM\Domains\Account\Users\Names` and select the subkey for **John**:

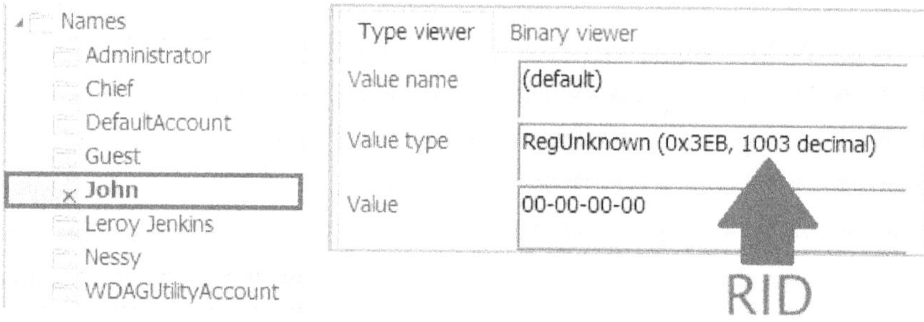

Figure 4.12 – Identifying a deleted user account with Registry Explorer

You will see an account that was not present in the previous registry subkeys. This account is for user **John**, and Registry Explorer recognizes this as a previously deleted subkey and has signified that by using red text.

15. Click on the field and you can also see a RID of **1003** within the Value type, which confirms that it is our missing account.
    A value of **0x3EB** is also present, representing the RID associated with this user account. Browse to `SAM\Domains\Account\Users` to locate the corresponding user record:

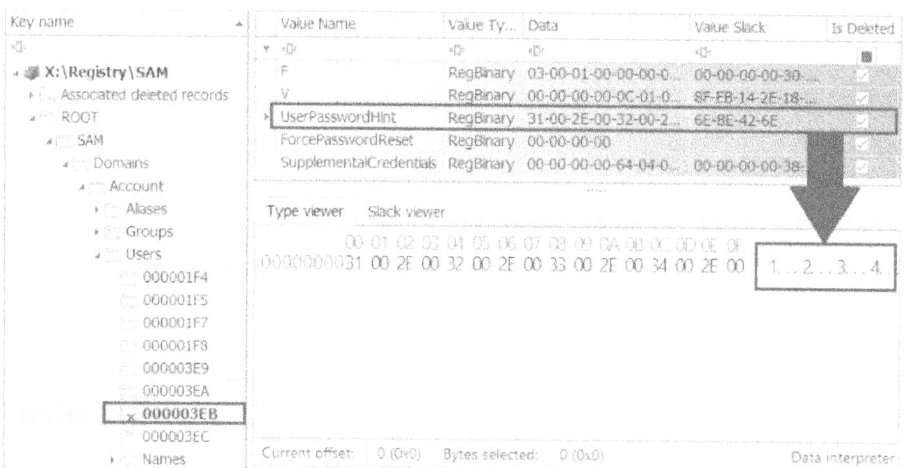

Figure 4.13 – Identifying additional account information with Registry Explorer

By mapping user **John** to RID value 0x3EB, we can identify the matching SAM entry and examine additional account details such as password hints, login metadata, and account attributes. This entry shows that the account was previously password-protected and had a password hint of "1...2...3...4...".

16. Select the **Users** subkey at `SAM\Domains\Account\` and view the **User accounts** tab. Registry Explorer presents a concise summary for local and built-in accounts on the system:

User Id	Total Log...	User Name	Full Name	Password ...	Groups	Internet User Name
500	0	Administrator			Administrators	
501	0	Guest			Guests	
503	0	DefaultAccount			System Managed Accounts Group	
504	0	WDAGUtilityAccount				
1001	35	Leroy Jenkins	Leroy	GOAT	Administrators	
1002	2	Chief			Users	master.chiefjohn117@outlook.com
1003	3	John		1.2.3.4.		
1004	9	Nessy			Users	

Figure 4.14 – User account summary displayed in Registry Explorer

The view shows the RID (displayed as User ID) and key columns such as **User Name**, **Full Name**, **Password Hint**, **Groups**, and **Internet User Name**. The **Internet User Name** appears only when an account is tied to a Microsoft online account. This can affect how Windows counts interactive logins, so treat the Login Count field with caution when the account is a synced Microsoft account.

> **Note**
>
> Back to the basics
>
> Understanding the Microsoft Windows OS structure and its use of SIDs/RIDs for account identification is covered in *Appendix A* of this book.

17. To access the powerful search feature of Registry Explorer, navigate to **Tools** | **Find**, or use the shortcut keys *Ctrl+F*. Launch this feature, and in the **Search for** box, enter the values **John**, **0003EB**, and **6937-1003** on separate lines, then select **Search**:

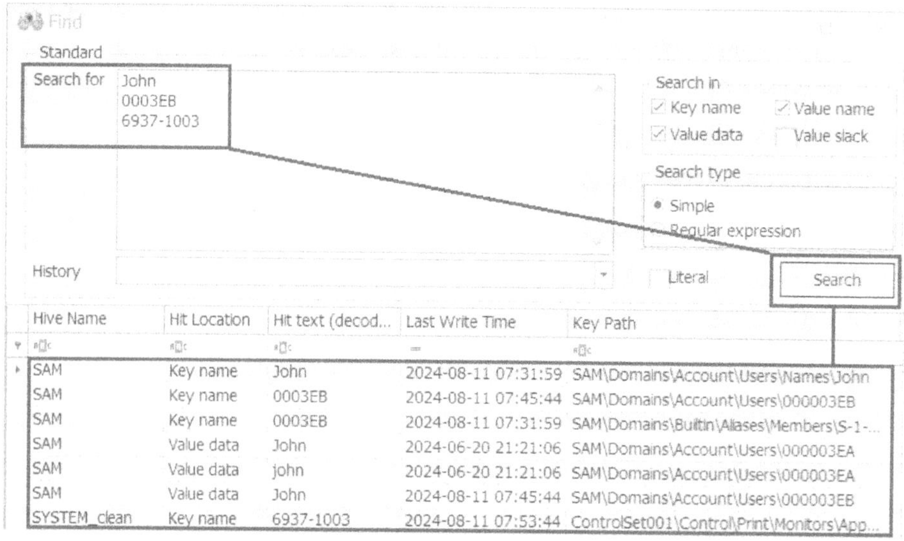

Figure 4.15 – Searching across the registry with Registry Explorer

This search located dozens of additional registry values and keys associated with the missing user account, **John**.

This is a quick way to locate additional artifacts that may provide further insight into how the account was used.

There's more...

The Registry contains a huge amount of forensic value. Below is a concise set of commonly useful locations (examples shown are typical on modern Windows up through Windows 11). Also, prefer `CurrentControlSet` when you want the active configuration (it maps to the appropriate ControlSet00x):

- User account information
  - `SAM\Domains\Builtin\Aliases`
  - `SAM\Domains\Account\Users`
  - `SOFTWARE\Microsoft\Windows NT\CurrentVersion\ProfileList`
  - `Machine and installed operating system information`
  - `SOFTWARE\Microsoft\Windows NT\CurrentVersion`
  - `SYSTEM\Setup\Source OS`
  - `SYSTEM\ControlSet001\Control\ComputerName\ComputerName`

  - `SYSTEM\ControlSet001\Control\Session Manager\Environment`
  - `SYSTEM\ControlSet001\Control\TimeZoneInformation`
- Recently accessed files and folders
  - `NTUSER.DAT\SOFTWARE\Microsoft\Windows\CurrentVersion\Explorer\Recent Docs`
  - `NTUSER.DAT\SOFTWARE\Microsoft\Windows\CurrentVersion\Explorer\ComDlg 32\OpenSavePidlMRU`
- Network history and usage
  - `SOFTWARE\Microsoft\Windows NT\CurrentVersion\NetworkCards`
  - `SOFTWARE\Microsoft\Windows NT\CurrentVersion\NetworkList`
  - `Previously connected USB devices`
  - `SYSTEM\CurrentControlSet\Enum\USBSTOR`
  - `SYSTEM\CurrentControlSet\Enum\USB`
  - `SYSTEM\MountedDevices`
  - `SOFTWARE\Microsoft\Windows Portable Devices`
  - `SOFTWARE\Microsoft\Windows Search\VolumeInfoCache`

Exploring these locations helps build familiarity with commonly encountered registry artifacts and their investigative significance. Registry Explorer also provides plugins that simplify access to high-value artifact views. To use this feature, select **Bookmarks** | **Common**. The available options vary depending on the hive currently loaded.

How it works...

The steps in this recipe focus on examining Windows Registry data in a forensically sound manner by working with offline hive files instead of interacting with a live system.

The Windows Registry is a hierarchical database stored in discrete hive files (`SAM`, `SYSTEM`, `SOFTWARE`, and user-specific hives such as `NTUSER.DAT` and `UsrClass.dat`). These files record system configuration, installed software, device state, and a wide range of user activity artifacts as keys and values.

By opening these hive files in a read-only tool such as Registry Explorer, we avoid modifying the original system while gaining the ability to efficiently search, recover, and analyze registry data. Unlike regedit, which interacts with the live registry, Registry Explorer allows us to safely work with extracted hives and provides enhanced visibility into protected keys and deleted or recovered data.

Additionally, associated transaction log files (`.LOG1`/`.LOG2`) can be replayed to recover uncommitted changes, helping to reconstruct a more complete and consistent view of registry activity at the time of acquisition.

Registry keys also store `LastWrite` timestamps, which are useful for building timelines of system and user activity. However, these timestamps must be interpreted carefully, particularly when considering time zones (local time versus UTC) and how updates to keys are recorded.

The user account view displays key attributes such as User ID (RID), User Name, Full Name, Password Hint, Groups, and Internet User Name. The Internet User Name field appears only when an account is associated with a Microsoft online account, which can affect how Windows tracks and reports interactive logons.

Registry values should be interpreted with caution, as they may be incomplete or transient. System shutdowns, crashes, or delayed writes can result in missing or stale data. Where possible, corroborate registry-derived findings with other sources, such as Windows event logs.

By combining offline analysis, transaction log replay, and artifact interpretation, the registry becomes a powerful source of evidence for reconstructing user behavior and system changes during an investigation.

Additionally, Registry Explorer can handle numerous registry files from multiple systems simultaneously, making the Find feature an excellent way to add scalability when performing analysis on the Windows Registry if an investigation spans multiple systems.

Recycle bin

The Recycle Bin is a common location for recovering recently deleted files and associated metadata on a Windows system. Because it retains information such as original file paths and deletion timestamps, it can provide valuable insight into user activity. In this recipe, we will examine the structure of the Recycle Bin and identify artifacts that can be used to recover and interpret deleted data.

Getting ready

Though each user has their own Recycle Bin space available to them from the *Desktop*, the Recycle Bin itself is stored at the root of the system drive within a hidden system directory named `$Recycle.Bin` (or `Recycler` for older versions of Windows). This content can be easily viewed with FTK Imager or another tool capable of browsing forensic images:

Figure 4.16 – Viewing Recycle Bin contents in FTK Imager

For this recipe, also download and install **Dcode** by Digital Detective, which will be used to decode timestamp values encountered during analysis:`https://www.digital-detective.net/dcode/`

How to do it...

1. Navigate to the Recycle Bin directory on the volume (for example, \$Recycle.Bin). Observe that each subfolder is named with a user SID, which can be used to attribute deleted files to specific user accounts. Within these folders, locate files beginning with `$R` (file content) and their corresponding `$I` files (metadata containing the original name, path, and deletion timestamp).
2. Using FTK Imager (or a similar tool capable of viewing file contents), view the file `$RXT2LC3.jpg` and its associated `$I` file. You will see the original file name of `56713.jpg` and an original file path of `C:\Users\Leroy Jenkins\Downloads`:

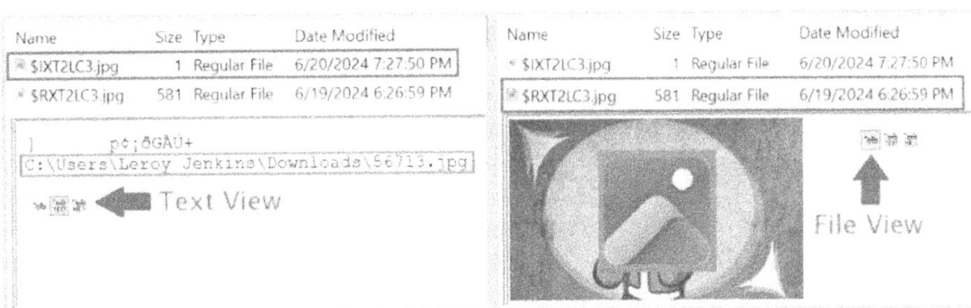

Figure 4.17 – Recycle Bin $I file (left) and its associated $R file (right)

3. Observe the timestamps associated with the `$R` and corresponding `$I` files. Note that the file system timestamps on the `$R` file reflect the original file activity (for example, when the file was created or downloaded), while the `$I` file records the deletion event when the file was placed into the Recycle Bin. Locate the deletion timestamp within the `$I` file (at offset 0x10, length 8 bytes) to determine when the user removed the file.

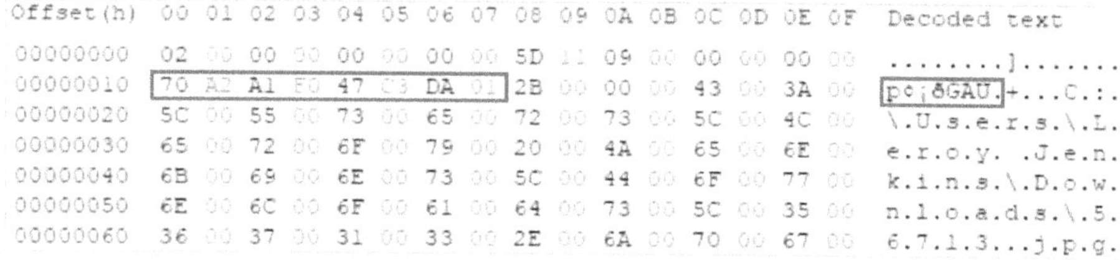

Figure 4.18 – "Deleted" date for file sent to Recycle Bin

4. Copy the hexadecimal timestamp value from the `$I` file and paste it into DCode. Select the format as **Hexadecimal (Little Endian)** and choose **No Time Zone Adjustment** to keep all times consistent in UTC, then decode the value to obtain the deletion timestamp:

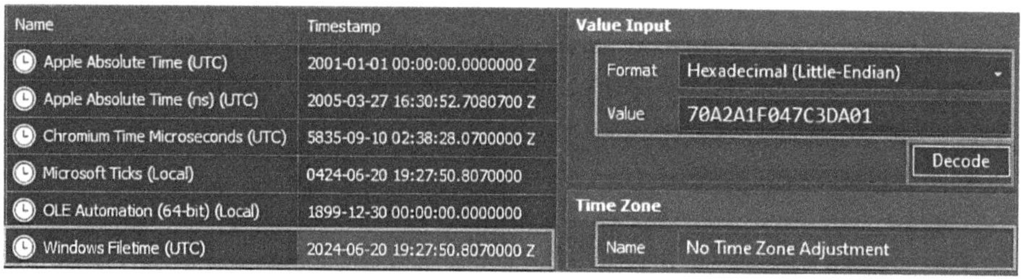

Figure 4.19 – Recycle Bin file "Deleted" date converted using DCode

How it works...

When a user "deletes" a file in Windows, it is typically not destroyed. Instead, it is moved into a per-user Recycle Bin folder (located at `$Recycle.Bin` on the volume) and renamed. The file contents are stored as an $R file, while a corresponding $I file contains metadata, such as the original file path and deletion timestamp.

Because the Recycle Bin relocates files rather than wiping them, recovering $R/$I file pairs often yields both the original content and the time the user attempted to remove it. This makes recovery straightforward and provides valuable timeline evidence of user activity, including potential cleanup attempts.

Adversaries may also use the Recycle Bin to hide payloads. For this reason, any suspicious $R files should be collected, hashed, and analyzed in a controlled environment.

Link files

Shell link files, also known as shortcuts or LNK files due to the .lnk file extension, contain a pointer that redirects to a file or application stored elsewhere on a system. LNK files can be created by the operating system, an application, or intentionally by the user. Common examples include application shortcuts created for easier access or user-created shortcuts to frequently accessed files or programs:

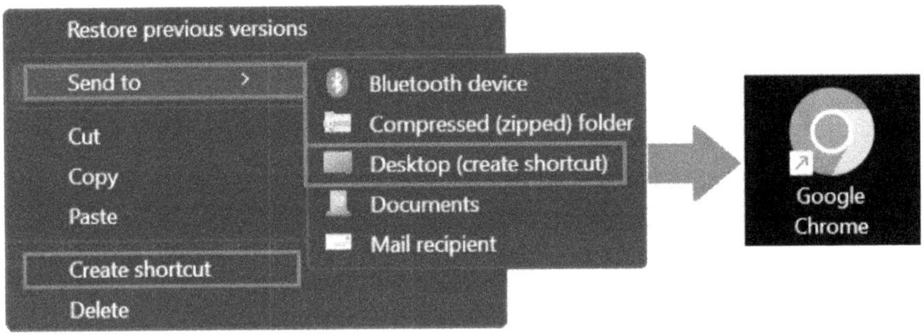

Figure 4.20 – Desktop shortcut created by the user for Google Chrome

LNK files can provide valuable information about user interactions with files and applications on a system. When a file is opened, Windows will often automatically create an associated LNK file. This behavior also occurs when files are accessed from external storage devices or network shares. For example, if a user connects an encrypted USB drive and opens a file, Windows may generate a LNK file on the local system that can later be examined to identify that interaction.

In this recipe, we will examine LNK file structure and identify key artifacts that can be used to reconstruct user activity.

Getting ready

Windows stores LNK files at the following locations on the system:

- `{root}\Users\UserProfile\AppData\Roaming\Microsoft\Windows\Recent`
- `{root}\Users\UserProfile\AppData\Roaming\Microsoft\Office\Recent`

Export LNK files from the described locations within the sample data set provided, or from your own system for additional practice. Place the exported LNK files into an empty folder on your workstation for further analysis discussed in the following section.

Also, you will need to download and extract **LECmd** by Eric Zimmerman:

`https://ericzimmerman.github.io/#!index.md`

How to do it...

1. From the extracted folder containing **LECmd**, launch an instance of Command Prompt by typing **CMD** into the address bar. Then, press **Enter**:

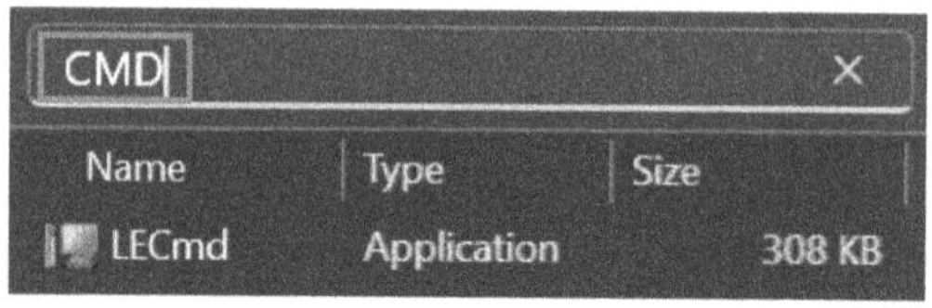

Figure 4.21 – Launching Command Prompt from the folder containing LECmd

2. Enter the following command:

```
LECmd.exe -d "location of LNK files"
```

3. Here, `-d` will recursively process all LNK files within a directory, and "*location of LNK files*" is the file path where you have stored the provided LNK files.
   For example,

```
LECmd.exe -d "C:\Users\Forensics\Desktop\LNK"
```

> **Note**
>
> You can also simply enter `LECmd.exe` as a command to see a full list of options for parsing LNK files with this tool.

4. The following is a reduced sample output highlighting key artifacts from one of the provided LNK files, titled **ILLEGAL_FILE-9874565.lnk**:

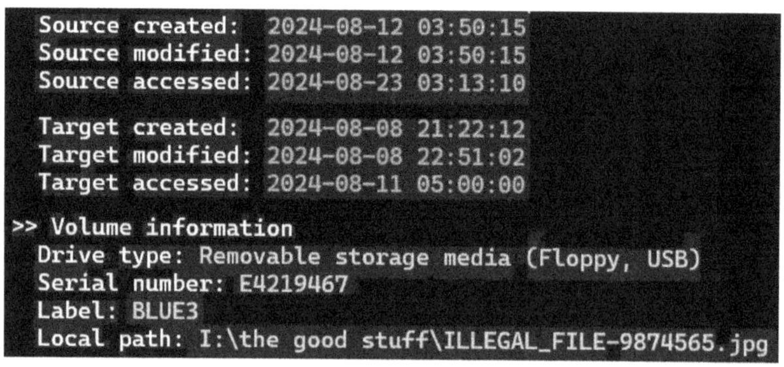

Figure 4.22 – Reduced sample output of an LNK file parsed with LECmd

Examine the parsed LNK file output shown in *Figure 4.22*.

Observe the Source MAC (Modified, Accessed, Created) timestamps for the LNK file. These values relate to the LNK file itself. The Source created time reflects when the shortcut was first created, which typically corresponds to the first time the target file was opened on the system. The Source modified time reflects the last time the target file was accessed, as opening the file updates the LNK. The Source accessed time can generally be ignored, as it may be updated during analysis.

> **Note**
>
> It Was You, Not the Suspect
>
> Parsing a LNK file with tools such as LECmd does not modify the internal metadata of the LNK artifact itself. However, the Last Accessed timestamp of the exported file on the analyst's workstation may be updated when the file is processed by the tool. This reflects interaction with the local copy during analysis, not user activity on the original system.

Note that these Source timestamps are recorded in UTC and should be interpreted accordingly when building timelines.

Examine the Target MAC timestamps. These values are derived from the file system on which the target file resided and may not represent the true creation time of the file. For example, file system events such as copying a file can update these values.

Observe the Target accessed time (05:00:00). This is an artifact of the FAT32 file system, which stores only the last accessed date and not the time. When interpreted alongside NTFS-based systems, this can result in inherited or misleading time values. Always validate timestamps against the underlying file system behavior.

Review the Volume Information section. Identify the drive type, volume serial number, volume label, and local path. In this example, the data indicate a removable device (likely FAT-formatted) with the label BLUE3 and serial number E4219467.

Analyze the local path (`I:\the good stuff\ILLEGAL_FILE-9874565.jpg`) to determine where the file was stored on the external device.

Correlate the timestamps and volume data to reconstruct activity. Based on this information, the file was likely created or copied to the removable device on August 8, 2024, accessed on the system on August 12, 2024, and opened once (as indicated by matching modification times).

From this single LNK file, we can determine that a removable storage device was connected, a file was accessed from it, and user interaction occurred with that file.

How it works...

When Windows creates a shortcut (`.lnk`), it writes a binary shell-link structure that records both metadata about the shortcut itself and details about the target (path, volume serial/label, and target file timestamps). Parsing tools extract the embedded fields, so we can easily attribute a user action on the local system to a specific file on a particular volume. Because the target timestamps come from the target filesystem and the LNK times are shown in the parser's time zone, always note the filesystem type and time zone when interpreting those values.

Shellbags

Windows File Explorer remembers how users view and interact with folders (window size, view mode, column order, and more) and stores those preferences as shellbag artifacts in a user's registry hive. Shellbags persist long after a folder is deleted, and they can record folders that live on local volumes, removable media, network shares, cloud-synced volumes, and (since Windows 11 22H2) opened ZIP containers. Because shellbags record paths, view settings, and timestamps, they are invaluable for showing that a user opened or inspected particular folders (including directories on external or encrypted media) even when the original files are gone.

In this recipe, we will examine shellbag artifacts and identify how they can be used to reconstruct user interactions with folders.

Getting ready

The `UsrClass.dat` registry file stores shellbag data at the following locations:

- `Local Settings\Software\Microsoft\Windows\Shell\Bags`
- `Local Settings\Software\Microsoft\Windows\Shell\BagMRU`

Some shellbag remnants for folders accessed from the *Desktop* or a shared location on a network may also be present within the `NTUSER.DAT` Registry file:

- `SOFTWARE\Microsoft\Windows\Shell\Bags`
- `SOFTWARE\Microsoft\Windows\Shell\BagMRU`

For this recipe, use the exported `UsrClass.dat` file you prepared earlier when examining the Registry.

Also, you will need to download and extract ShellBags Explorer from Eric Zimmerman's website:

`https://ericzimmerman.github.io/#!index.md`

How to do it...

1. Launch **ShellBags Explorer** (you will need to input an e-mail address the first time this software is run):

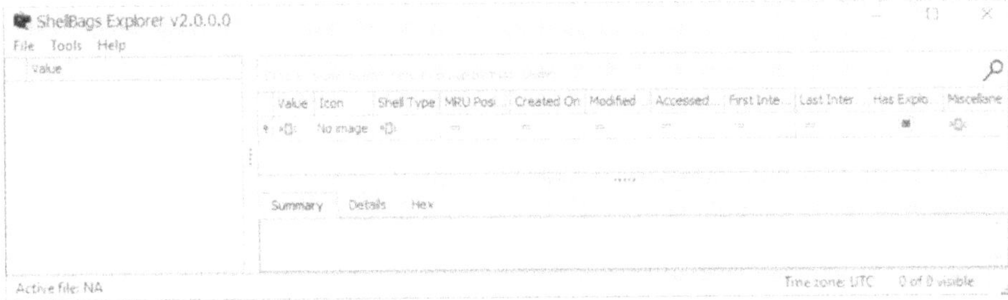

Figure 4.23 – ShellBags Explorer

2. From the **File** menu, choose **Load offline hive** or use the shortcut keys *Ctrl+O* to select and load the `UsrClass.dat` file.

3. Expand **This PC** in the left pane menu and select **Pictures** (alternatively, you can browse the Shellbag artifacts of your own system by choosing **Load active registry** or *Alt+1*):

Value	Created On	Accessed On	First Interacted	Last Interacted
photography	2024-08-11 06:46:48	2024-08-11 06:48:20	2024-08-11 06:54:26	2024-08-12 03:34:40
other	2024-08-11 06:48:36	2024-08-11 06:49:28	2024-08-11 07:11:11	
airshow	2024-08-11 06:48:28	2024-08-11 06:49:20	2024-08-11 07:15:51	
trips	2024-08-11 06:41:22	2024-08-11 06:46:42	2024-08-11 09:53:55	

Figure 4.24 – Viewing data for directories using Shellbags Explorer

Here we can see Shellbag information for each child folder within the default Windows **Pictures** folder.

a. Observe the Last Interacted timestamps for each folder. Note that only the parent folder (for example, photography) contains a Last Interacted value. This is because a single registry key stores this information, and it reflects the most recent interaction with the parent folder or any of its child folders.

b. Review the timestamps for patterns. If multiple folders show timestamps that are very close together, this may indicate grouped user activity.

c. Compare these values to the system's last update time. If they align, the timestamps may have been altered during a major operating system update rather than reflect actual user activity.

d. To validate this, examine the InstallTime value located at `SOFTWARE\Microsoft\Windows NT\CurrentVersion`, which records when the last major system update occurred.

How it works...

Boot-time and UI actions in File Explorer leave small registry footprints called Shellbags. BagMRU records the tree-like order of folders a user browses, while Bags stores per-folder metadata (view settings, last-interacted timestamps, and often volume/serial info and the original path). Because these entries are written to the user's registry hive, they survive simple deletions and can show access to folders on removable, network, or compressed volumes even after the source is gone. Treat Shellbag timestamps as indicators of browsing activity (not proof of a specific file action), and always corroborate them with other artifacts, since OS updates or system events can cluster or alter their times.

Jump lists

Much like shortcut or LNK files, jump lists act as links that redirect the user to an application, file, or directory. These jump lists may be created automatically when a user interacts with certain files and applications or can be created when a user chooses to 'pin' something to a menu within Windows for easier access. In either event, the jump list metadata will store useful information about these interactions that can be used to help determine how and when a user interacted with specific applications and files.

In this recipe, we will examine jump list artifacts and identify how they can be used to reconstruct user interactions with applications and files.

Getting ready

Jump list files are stored in the following locations within each Windows user profile:

- `AppData\Roaming\Microsoft\Windows\Recent\AutomaticDestinations`
- `AppData\Roaming\Microsoft\Windows\Recent\CustomDestinations`

Jump list files within `AutomaticDestinations` are those created by the system when a user opens a file or software program, whereas the jump list files within `CustomDestinations` are those created intentionally by the user when adding or *pinning* a destination to the Windows Start Menu or Taskbar.

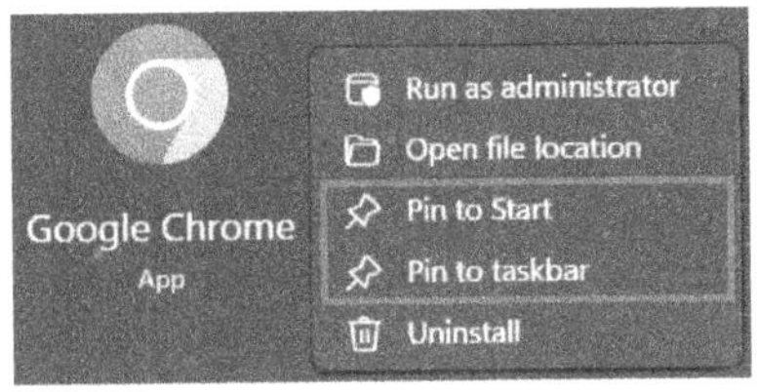

Figure 4.25 – Pinning Google Chrome to the Start menu or Taskbar in Windows 11

Export all files from these directories within the **Microsoft Windows** dataset, and place them in a working folder on your workstation for analysis.

Also, you will need to download and extract **JumpList Explorer** from Eric Zimmerman's website:

`https://ericzimmerman.github.io/#!index.md`

How to do it...

1. Launch **JumpList Explorer**:

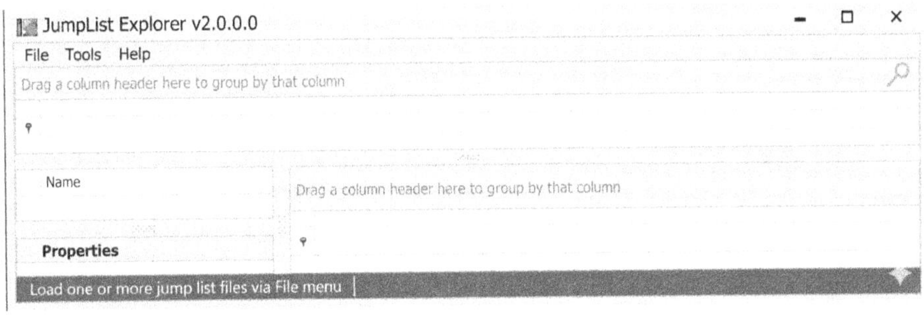

Figure 4.26 – Jump List Explorer

2. Choose **File | Load jump lists** (or press *CTRL+O*), and point the tool to the folder where you exported the jump list files.
3. Use *CTRL+A* to select and load all the files you exported from both `AutomaticDestinations` and `CustomDestinations`:

Jump List Type	App ID	App ID Description	Lnk File Count	File Size
Automatic	de1b2111ec8aaada		0	2,560
Automatic	ecd1a5e2c3af9c46	LibreOffice 5.1.0.3 Press	1	3,584
Automatic	f01b4d95cf55d32a	Windows Explorer Windows 8.1	21	27,136
Automatic	f18460fded109990	Windows Connected Devices	1	3,072
Automatic	fb3b0dbfee58fac8	Microsoft Word 2016 64-bit	1	3,072
Custom	fb3b0dbfee58fac8	Microsoft Word 2016 64-bit	2	1,292

Figure 4.27 – Viewing data for jump lists using Jump List Explorer

Here you can see whether the jump list item was automatically generated by the system or manually pinned by the user, along with the **App ID** and **App ID Description** if it can be resolved. You can also see a **Lnk File Count**, which provides insight into how often the jump list destination was accessed.

> **Note**
>
> Keep in mind, the *Lnk File Count* pertains to the number of times the destination was accessed using the jump list, so each destination may have been interacted with more if the user chose to access the application in another way.

4. Select any of the rows to gain more information about interactions with each destination. Here, I have selected the **Windows Explorer Windows 8.1** row:

Target Created On	Target Modified On	Target Accessed On	Absolute Path	Interaction Count
2024-08-08 21:18:52	2024-08-08 22:54:54	2024-08-08 05:00:00	I:\\the good stuff	4
2024-06-19 04:07:30	2024-08-11 10:24:48	2024-08-12 03:51:26	My Computer\Documents	28

Figure 4.28 – Viewing additional data for jump lists using Jump List Explorer

Since the sample shown is for Windows File Explorer, we can see additional information about directories that were accessed, including those accessed from a previously attached USB drive (as seen in the **Absolute Path** column).

How it works...

Jump lists are compound files (`.automaticDestinations-ms` and `.customDestinations-ms`) stored in the user's *Recent* folder. Metadata stored for these files carry target paths, volume information (label and serial number), and file MAC timestamps. So, a single jump list can reveal that a removable or network volume was accessed and when that access occurred. Because jump lists are written under the user profile area, they often survive simple file deletion and are a high-value source for timeline and attribution. As with any other data points we gather from various artifacts, always remember to corroborate jump list data with other artifacts (LNK files, Registry data, etc.) for a defensible timeline.

Prefetch

Prefetch is a Windows feature that preloads pieces of application data to speed up subsequent launches—it literally "*pre-fetches*" files that an application commonly uses so the program will load faster if it is launched later. Prefetch is enabled by default on client versions of Windows (it is commonly disabled or configured differently on many server versions). The metadata retained by prefetch files can help us determine when an executable was launched and how often it ran.

In this recipe, we will examine prefetch artifacts to identify program execution, frequency of use, and associated execution details.

Getting ready

Prefetch files have a `.pf` file extension and are stored in the following location:

`{root}\Windows\Prefetch`

Export all files from these directories within the **Microsoft Windows** dataset and place them in a working folder on your workstation for analysis.

Also, you will need to download and extract **VSCMount** from Eric Zimmerman's website:

`https://ericzimmerman.github.io/#!index.md`

How to do it...

1. From the extracted folder containing **VSCMount**, launch an instance of Command Prompt by typing **CMD** into the address bar, then press **Enter**.
2. Enter the following command, where `-f` will process a single prefetch file we have selected, and `"location of prefetch files"` is the file path (we are only processing one prefetch file, as processing all of them can be overwhelming):

   ```
   PECmd.exe -f "location of prefetch file"
   ```

   For example:

   ```
   PECmd.exe -f "C:\Users\Forensics\Desktop\Prefetch\CHROME.EXE-AED7BA44.pf"
   ```

3. Examine the artifact to identify key details including a **Run count**. This shows the number of times the application was run, along with various dates and times when the application was previously run:

Figure 4.29 – Application Run Count and Run Times in PECmd

4. Analyze the file system timestamps of the prefetch file to help determine the first and last times the application was run:

Figure 4.30 – File system timestamps for prefetch file

1. This appears consistent with the run times we see stored in the prefetch file itself, with the **Date Created** representing the first time the application was run and the prefetch file was created, and the **Date Modified** representing the last run time (that is, the most recent update to the prefetch file).
2. Be sure to account for minor timing differences. You will notice the **Date Modified** seems to be off by a few seconds compared to the last run time. This is because it takes time for the prefetch file to update, usually about 10 seconds.

> **Note**
>
> If You're Not First, You're Last
>
> In this example, the earliest timestamp observed in the prefetch file is June 20, 2024; however, this does not necessarily indicate the first time the application was executed on the system. Windows maintains a limited number of prefetch files (up to 1,024 on modern systems), and older entries may be deleted over time. If the original prefetch file was removed and later recreated, it can appear as though this was the first execution when, in reality, earlier activity may no longer be present.

3. Identify and compare any prefetch files associated with the same application. Examine the executable name and hash value in each filename (for example, **CHROME.EXE-AED7BA44.pf**). Differences in hash values may indicate the application was executed

from different locations (such as a USB device) or that different versions of the application were run:

Figure 4.31 – Prefetch file name components

4. Alternatively, you can process all prefetch files simultaneously in `PECmd` and output them into a CSV file for easier review using the following command:

```
PECmd.exe -r "location of prefetch files" --csv "location to save CSV
output file"
```

How it works...

When an executable runs, Windows records information that lists the files and DLLs accessed and stores run timestamps and a run count. The prefetch file is basically an indexed snapshot of the runtime footprint that the OS can use to speed future application launches. This allows us to infer execution frequency and approximate run times. Because the OS updates or removes prefetch files as systems age or as executables change, we need to substantiate these data points with other information (like event logs) to determine whether additional launches may have occurred or whether the program successfully executed. Prefetch files are an excellent way to further establish user interactions with a system or track down previously executed malware.

Event logs

Windows event logs keep a detailed record of operating system, application, and hardware activity and are commonly used by computer repair technicians to diagnose system problems. They are also invaluable in investigations because they timestamp events such as logons/logoffs, failed logons, system restarts and shutdowns, time changes, audit clears, and many other security-relevant actions. Event Viewer (the native Windows application for viewing event logs) lets you view these logs interactively, but as analysts we will use specialized viewers that make searching, filtering, and timeline analysis easier when working with exported logs from one or multiple systems simultaneously.

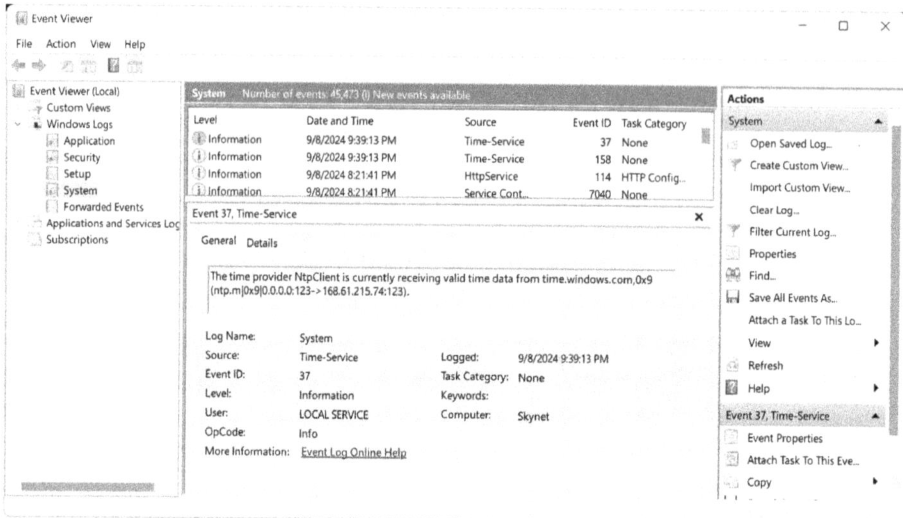

Figure 4.32 – Microsoft Windows native Event Viewer

There are three primary event log categories in all recent versions of Windows:

- Application: Events pertaining to installed software applications
- Security: Access control and auditing, such as user logins
- System: Operating system events such as restarts and time changes

Beginning with Windows Vista, Microsoft introduced many additional event log categories to track more granular system activity. As of Windows 11, systems may contain hundreds of event log categories, though not all are populated on every system.

In this recipe, we will examine Windows event logs to identify system activity, user authentication events, and other security-relevant actions during an investigation.

Getting ready

Windows event logs use the `.evtx` file extension and are stored at:

```
{root}\Windows\System32\winevt\Logs
```

In older systems prior to Windows Vista, event logs use the `.evt` file extension and are stored at the following location:

```
{root}\System32\config
```

Export the event logs from the **Microsoft Windows** dataset and place them in a working folder on your workstation for analysis.

Also, you will need to download and extract **EvtxECmd and Timeline Explorer** by Eric Zimmerman:

`https://ericzimmerman.github.io/#!index.md`

How to do it...

1. From the extracted folder containing **EvtxECmd**, launch an instance of Command Prompt by typing **CMD** into the address bar, then press *Enter*.
2. Enter the following command, where `-d` will process all event logs exported to the path entered for `"path to exported logs"` and `--csv` will produce a CSV file containing the event log information at the specified `"output directory"`:

```
EvtxECmd.exe -d "path to exported logs" --csv "output directory"
```

   This will process all `.evtx` files and produce a structured dataset for analysis.

   For example:

```
EvtxECmd.exe -d "C:\Users\Forensics\Desktop\Event_Logs" --csv "C:
\Users\Forensics\Desktop\Event_Logs\Output"
```

3. Launch Timeline Explorer and load the generated CSV file (*CTRL+O*). This will display parsed event logs in a tabular format for analysis:

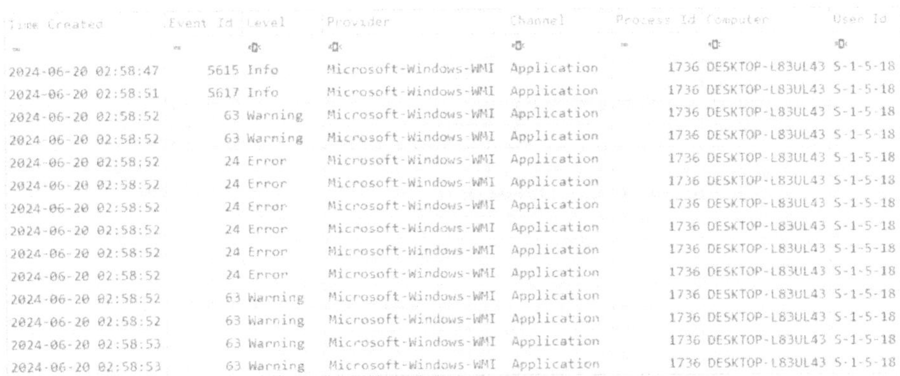

Time Created	Event Id	Level	Provider	Channel	Process Id	Computer	User Id
2024-06-20 02:58:47	5615	Info	Microsoft-Windows-WMI	Application	1736	DESKTOP-L83UL43	S-1-5-18
2024-06-20 02:58:51	5617	Info	Microsoft-Windows-WMI	Application	1736	DESKTOP-L83UL43	S-1-5-18
2024-06-20 02:58:52	63	Warning	Microsoft-Windows-WMI	Application	1736	DESKTOP-L83UL43	S-1-5-18
2024-06-20 02:58:52	63	Warning	Microsoft-Windows-WMI	Application	1736	DESKTOP-L83UL43	S-1-5-18
2024-06-20 02:58:52	24	Error	Microsoft-Windows-WMI	Application	1736	DESKTOP-L83UL43	S-1-5-18
2024-06-20 02:58:52	24	Error	Microsoft-Windows-WMI	Application	1736	DESKTOP-L83UL43	S-1-5-18
2024-06-20 02:58:52	24	Error	Microsoft-Windows-WMI	Application	1736	DESKTOP-L83UL43	S-1-5-18
2024-06-20 02:58:52	24	Error	Microsoft-Windows-WMI	Application	1736	DESKTOP-L83UL43	S-1-5-18
2024-06-20 02:58:52	24	Error	Microsoft-Windows-WMI	Application	1736	DESKTOP-L83UL43	S-1-5-18
2024-06-20 02:58:52	24	Error	Microsoft-Windows-WMI	Application	1736	DESKTOP-L83UL43	S-1-5-18
2024-06-20 02:58:52	63	Warning	Microsoft-Windows-WMI	Application	1736	DESKTOP-L83UL43	S-1-5-18
2024-06-20 02:58:52	63	Warning	Microsoft-Windows-WMI	Application	1736	DESKTOP-L83UL43	S-1-5-18
2024-06-20 02:58:53	63	Warning	Microsoft-Windows-WMI	Application	1736	DESKTOP-L83UL43	S-1-5-18
2024-06-20 02:58:53	63	Warning	Microsoft-Windows-WMI	Application	1736	DESKTOP-L83UL43	S-1-5-18

Figure 4.33 – Parsed event logs loaded into Timeline Explorer

4. It is not feasible to view each log file individually. Instead, we must filter for event logs that are likely to be of interest to our investigation.
   For example, we may be interested in seeing all the failed login attempts on the system, which are kept in the **Security** event log.

We will isolate those events:

- Locate the **Channel** field
- Set the operator (left portion of the column filter) to **Equals**
- Enter: **Security**

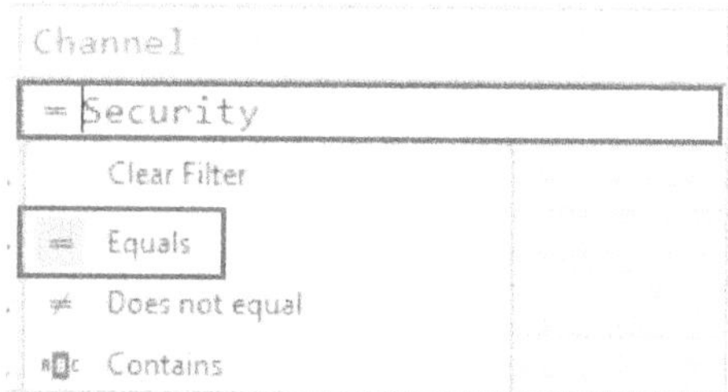

Figure 4.34 – Filtering Security event logs in Timeline Explorer

This reduces the dataset to the events most relevant to user activity and authentication.

5. Now, filter for the failed logon attempts by entering **4625** into the **Event Id** field:

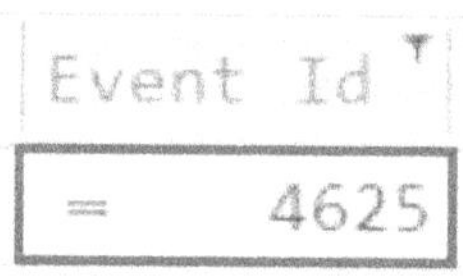

Figure 4.35 – Filtering Event ID 4625 in Timeline Explorer

This reduces the dataset to only failed logon events, allowing us to focus on authentication-related activity. We could also apply additional filters pertaining to a specific time frame, user, or other criteria to reduce the data further if needed.

6. Review the filtered results and examine additional event fields by scrolling through the dataset:

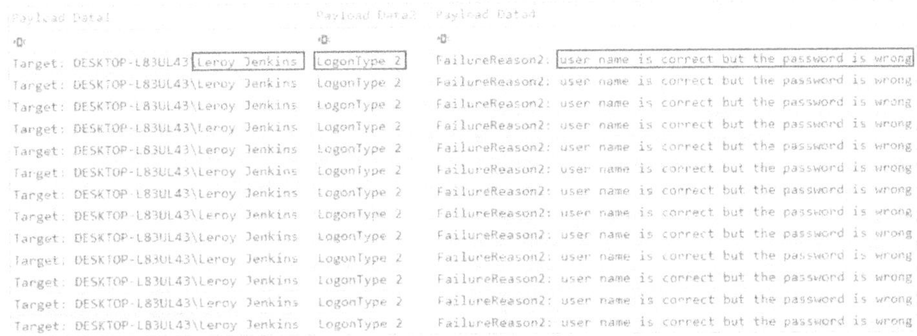

Figure 4.36 – Viewing parsed event data in Timeline Explorer

Notice that several **Payload Data** fields are present. In Timeline Explorer, these fields represent the parsed contents of the event's XML <EventData> and <UserData> sections. This is structured data recorded by Windows for that event ID.

From this data, we can determine that the failed logon attempts correspond to the **Leroy Jenkins** account. A **LogonType 2** indicates an interactive (local) logon attempt, while other values (such as 3 or 10) indicate network or remote access attempts.

The failure reason indicates the username was valid, but the password entered was incorrect, suggesting either user error or repeated unsuccessful access attempts. This should be evaluated within the broader investigative context.

Note

From Failure to Intrusion

This type of event log filtering is commonly used to identify potential unauthorized access attempts. For example, multiple Event ID **4625** entries for the same account with a **LogonType 10** (remote access) in a short time period may indicate a brute-force or remote login attack.

There's more...

Windows event logs are widely used in system administration and are therefore well documented. As such, the event IDs, error codes, and other descriptive information you encounter during analysis can often be found online, and you will begin to easily recognize much of this information yourself for some of the most commonly encountered and useful event logs.

The best way to build familiarity is to explore additional event logs and try to determine what information they hold. The following is a short list of event IDs that are often very useful during digital forensic analysis:

Event ID	Purpose
4624	Successful account logon
4625	Failed account logon
4634, 4647	Successful account logoff (4634) or user-initiated logoff (4647)
4720, 4726	An account was created (4720) or deleted (4726).
4723	Account password changes
1074	System shutdown or restart
6013	System uptimes (recorded in seconds)
4616	System time change
8001, 8003	Successful network connection (8001) or disconnection (8003)
4778, 4779	Successful remote connection (4778) or disconnection (4779)
1102, 104	Event log cleared from Security (1102) or System (104).

Table 4.1: Event IDs

There are hundreds of event IDs available to track system, application, and user-related events. A detailed list of event IDs can be found on the Microsoft Learn website at `https://learn.microsoft.com/en-us/windows-server/identity/ad-ds/plan/appendix-l--events-to-monitor`.

How it works...

Windows stores modern event logs as `.evtx` files in `\Windows\System32\winevt\Logs`. Each EVTX file is a binary container of individual event records. Each record includes a provider, an Event ID, a level, a timestamp (stored in UTC), and structured event data. Event logs are highly detailed and serve as one of the most valuable sources for reconstructing system and user activity. This makes them one of the most valuable sources of information for establishing timelines and confirming other data points in Windows.

Some event logs may roll over for frequent events (e.g., older logs can be overwritten by the system to make room for newer ones).

EvtxECmd parses event logs without modifying the original evidence files. Always perform analysis on exported copies to maintain forensic integrity. Using a tool such as Timeline Explorer allows efficient searching, filtering, and correlation of event log data across large datasets.

Thumbcache

When a user views files in File Explorer, they may choose to present those files as small icons or thumbnails, which provide a preview of the file content. These thumbnails are stored on the system within thumbcache databases.

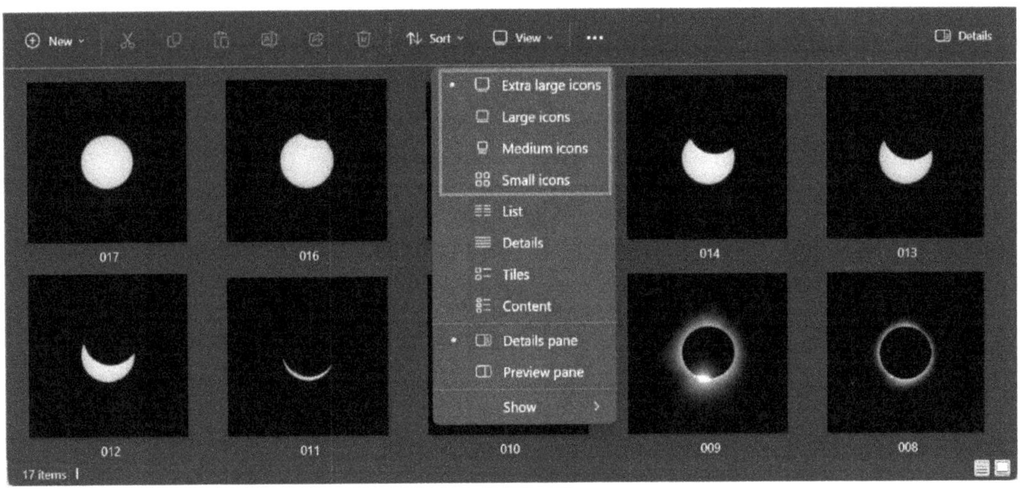

Figure 4.37 – Thumbnail icons presented in Microsoft Windows 11

The system saves a thumbnail representation of file content so previews can be quickly loaded the next time the user views their saved media content.

Windows thumbcache databases are stored for each individual account, making it easy to determine which user viewed the files. Moreover, thumbnails are retained for files that were viewed from an external source, such as an external storage drive, and they persist even if the original file is moved or deleted, making these databases a rich source of information to help determine what media files may have been stored or viewed by a user.

In this recipe, we will examine thumbcache artifacts to identify previously viewed images and determine user interaction with media files, even when the original files are no longer present.

Getting ready

The Windows thumbcache databases exist individually per size option. If the user chooses to view files as small icons, they are stored in `Thumbcache_32.db`, whereas medium icons are stored in `Thumbcache_96.db`, large icons in `Thumbcache_256.db`, and extra-large icons in `Thumbcache_1024.db`. Additional databases may be present on modern versions of Windows (beginning with Windows 8) to store intermittent icon sizing options.

Windows thumbcache databases are stored for each individual account at:

```
{root}\Users\User Account\AppData\Local\Microsoft\Windows\Explorer
```

You will also notice many `iconcache` databases at this location. These were implemented beginning with Windows 8 and are used to store application icons.

Though Microsoft Windows XP systems are rarely encountered today, note that thumbnails on these older systems are not as centralized and are instead stored in the individual folders where the original files were located. This means there may be a large number of thumbnail databases present on older systems, stored as `thumbs.db` files.

Export the various thumbcache databases from the described locations within the **Microsoft Windows** dataset. Prior to exporting, you may wish to sort these databases by size to more easily determine which ones are in use or are likely to contain the most data.

Also, you will need to download and extract **Thumbcache Viewer** from Eric Kutcher:

```
https://thumbcacheviewer.github.io/
```

How to do it...

1. After launching **Thumbcache Viewer**, click on **Open...** from the **File** menu (or use the shortcut keys **CTRL+O**) to import the thumbcache databases you exported:

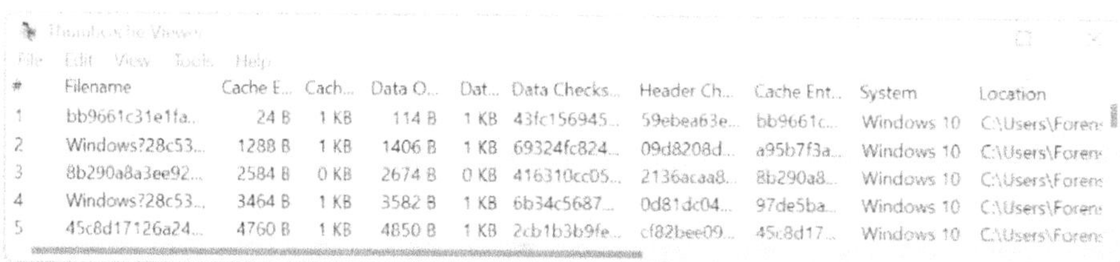

Figure 4.38 – Thumbcache databases loaded into Thumbcache Viewer

2. From here, click the **Data Size** column heading once to sort the individual thumbnail files by their respective sizes in descending order. This will allow you to prioritize the largest and highest quality thumbnails first:

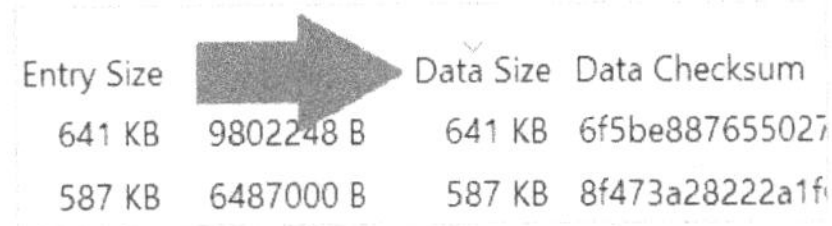

Figure 4.39 – Sorting thumbnails in Thumbcache Viewer

3. When selecting a row, you will see the stored thumbnail:

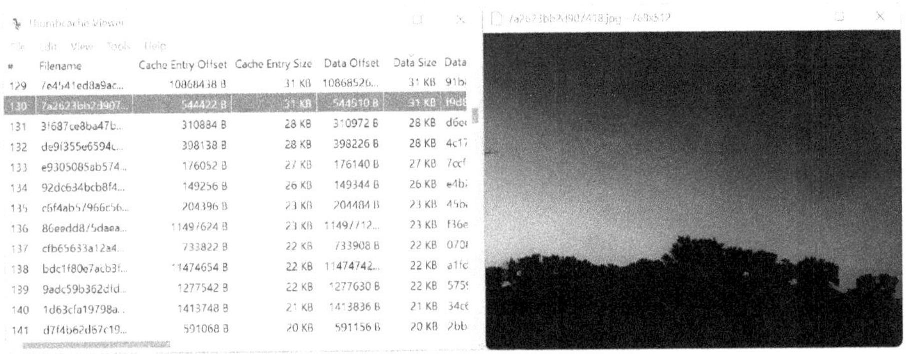

Figure 4.40 – Viewing thumbnail content using Thumbcache Viewer

While the thumbcache database is useful for identifying media that was present on a system and viewed by the user, it does not provide file paths, timestamps, or additional metadata associated with those files.

To build a more complete picture, we can correlate these findings with the Windows Search database, which stores indexed file metadata and can help associate thumbnail entries with their original file locations and activity. This database is stored as **Windows.edb** (or **Windows.db** in Windows 11 version 22H2 and later) and can be found at the following location:

```
{root}\ProgramData\Microsoft\Search\Data\Applications\Windows
```

To ingest this database to map its data to our thumbcache databases in **Thumbcache Viewer**, navigate to **Tools** | **Map File Paths...** (or shortcut **CTRL+M)**.

4. Once the options window for this feature opens, select the **Load Windows Search Database** tab, browse out to the `Windows.edb` database (this database will first need to be exported if using the provided dataset), and check the option to **Retrieve Extended Information**:

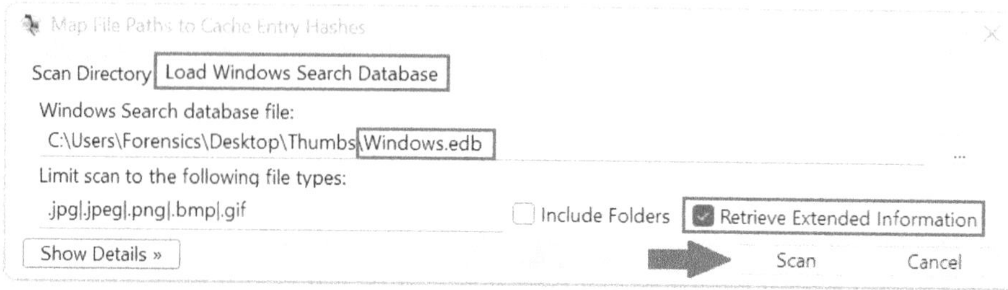

Figure 4.41 – Importing the Windows.edb database into Thumbcache Viewer

5. After hitting **Scan**, you may receive a message stating that no files were mapped, followed by an error indicating the database was not shut down cleanly and needs to be repaired. This can occur with certain databases and can typically be repaired by launching an instance of Command Prompt from the folder where you exported the database and then running the following command:

```
esentutl /p Windows.edb
```

> **Note**
>
> The esentutl utility is intended for extensible storage engine (ESE) databases (for example, `Windows.edb`). Systems using the newer `Windows.db` SQLite database (Windows 11 22H2+) are not compatible with this tool, and attempts to run esentutl will result in an error; parsing or recovery must be performed using SQLite-aware tools.

6. Once the repair is complete, import the database again, and click **Scan**.
7. Once successful, you will see that many of the thumbnails present have now been mapped to a file path showing the location of the associated files from which the thumbnails were generated. Each file path will be colored green:

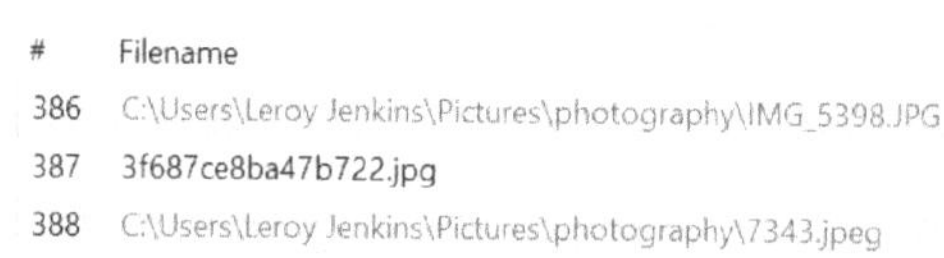

#	Filename
386	C:\Users\Leroy Jenkins\Pictures\photography\IMG_5398.JPG
387	3f687ce8ba47b722.jpg
388	C:\Users\Leroy Jenkins\Pictures\photography\7343.jpeg

Figure 4.42 – Thumbnails mapped in Thumbcache Viewer

> **Note**
>
> Wiped Off the Face of the Map
>
> You may notice that many of the thumbnails remain unmapped. This is because if the original file information cannot be found in the `Windows.edb` database, there is no data to map to it. This is a great way to easily determine which thumbnails may no longer be present on the system due to having been moved, deleted, or viewed from an external storage drive. It should be noted, however, that some thumbnails associated with moved or deleted files may still be mapped if the action was recent and the data still remains in the `Windows.edb` database.

8. Double-click on a mapped thumbnail to view extended information about the original file, including timestamps and available EXIF data:

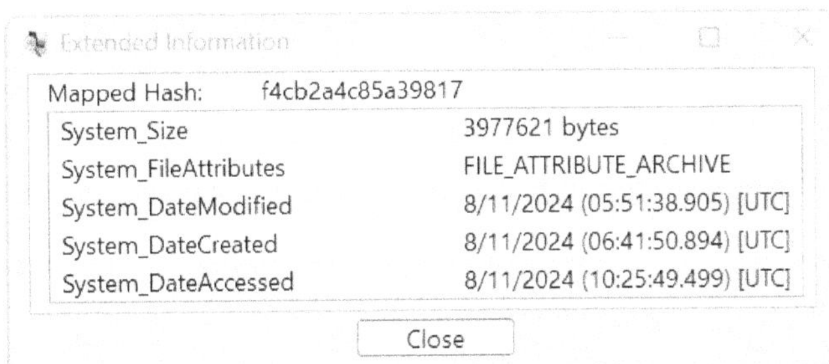

Figure 4.43 – Extended information sample viewed with Thumbcache Viewer

How it works...

When Windows generates thumbnails, it stores the image previews in per-size thumbcache databases so the system can render folder contents quickly. Those databases hold the thumbnail image data but little or no file path or timestamp metadata, so mapping a thumbnail back to its original filename and location typically requires correlating the cache with the Windows Search index (`Windows.edb`). Because thumbnails are just representations of the original image stored, they can persist even after the original file is moved or deleted, making them a useful source for recovering visual evidence that was once saved or viewed by the user.

Volume Shadow Copy Service (VSS)

Volume Shadow Copies (VSC) are not always available on a system, but when present, they can be a valuable source of data. The **Volume Shadow Copy Service (VSS)** is how Windows creates VSC snapshots, or restore points, to back up almost the entirety of a system volume. A user can manually create restore points or, if enabled, the system may automate their creation during certain events like installing Windows updates. VSC files allow the system to be restored to an earlier point if needed.

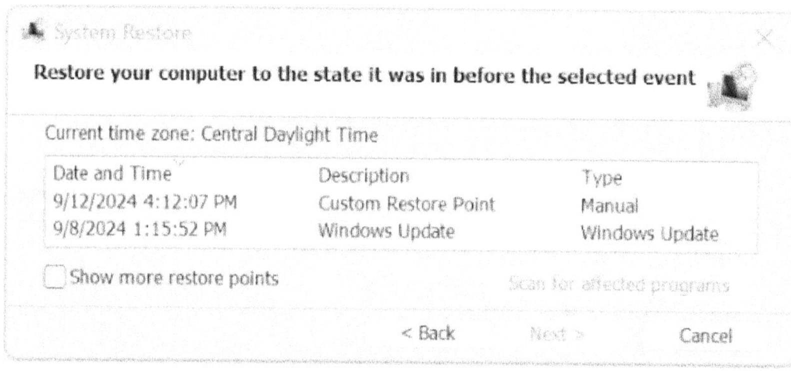

Figure 4.44 – System restore points created manually and during updates

VSC files are like a time capsule of the system's previous state and often contain data that has since been deleted or changed by the user.

In this recipe, we will examine Volume Shadow Copies to recover historical versions of data and to identify previously deleted or modified artifacts.

Getting ready

If present, VSC files are stored in the hidden **System Volume Information** folder at the root of the volume and are named using a **Globally Unique Identifier (GUID)**:

Figure 4.45 – Location of VSC within a Windows forensic image

Rather than exporting individual files as we have done in previous sections, we will instead mount the **Microsoft Windows** forensic image and then mount the VSC snapshots to view their contents.

Also, you will need to download and extract the following software

- **Arsenal Image Mounter** by Arsenal Recon (to mount forensic image files): `https://arsenalrecon.com/downloads`
- **PECmd** by Eric Zimmerman (to mount VSC files): `https://ericzimmerman.github.io/#!index.md`

How to do it...

1. After installing **Image Mounter,** launch the software and select **Mount disk image**:

Figure 4.46 – Mounting forensic image with Arsenal Image Mounter

2. A new window will appear with mount options.
When mounting a forensic image, the default option is typically **Disk device, read only**. However, here, you need to be able to further interact with the image file, so choose **Disk device, write temporary** to allow interaction without modifying the original evidence.

> **Note**
>
> Arsenal Image Mounter does not modify the original forensic image when using write-temporary mode. Instead, it uses a temporary overlay file to capture any changes, preserving the integrity of the original evidence.

3. Choose the option to **Store differencing data in host RAM only (not in a file)**, as this will preclude you from having to temporarily store an actual differencing file to your disk. Then, select **OK**:

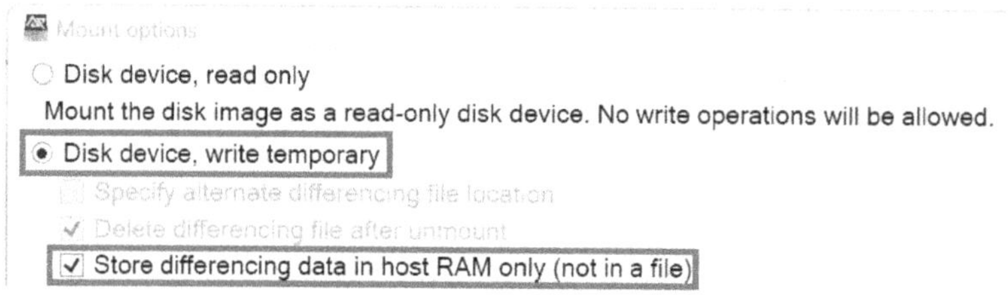

Figure 4.47 – Options to store differencing data in Arsenal Image Mounter

Note that this option relies entirely on available system RAM. Insufficient memory may cause the mount to fail or become unstable.

4. The forensic image will now be mounted and accessible using Windows File Explorer. Note the assigned drive letter that the mounted image has been mapped to (here, the forensic image was mapped as drive `G:\`):

Figure 4.48 – Forensic image mounted and accessible

5. Now, to mount the VSC file, use **VSCMount** by launching an instance of Command Prompt (using administrator privileges) within the folder where you extracted VSCMount.
6. Run the following command, where `--dl #` is used to specify the mapped drive letter to the mounted forensic image, `--mp filepath` specifies where we will map the VSC files to access them, and `--ud` appends a timestamp to the VSC files so we will know when they were originally created:

```
VSCMount.exe --dl # --mp "filepath" --ud
```

As an example, since my mounted forensic image was mapped to drive letter *G*, I entered the following: `VSCMount.exe --dl G --mp "G:\VSCMount" --ud`

7. When ready, press *Enter*:

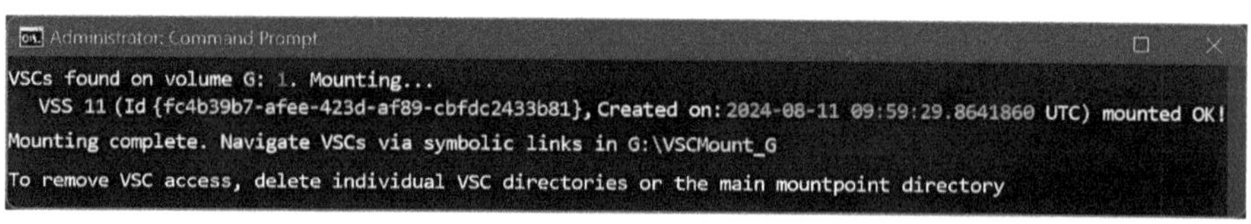

Figure 4.49 – VSC file mounted using VSCMount

If successful, you will receive output similar to the example above, showing the number of VSC files that were located and mounted. If more than one VSC file is present, `VSCMount` will mount each one and provide a list describing each available shadow copy.

8. Now, navigate to the mounted forensic image using Windows File Explorer. You will see a new file path that provides access to the mounted VSC files. Since we specified the name **VSCMount** for this file path when entering our command, that is the name of the folder created for the mount point.
   Note that this is not a real folder; it is a virtual mount point that allows us to expose and view the snapshot contents. This distinction is important, as actions performed within the mount point do not modify the underlying shadow copy data itself. Within the mount point are folders for each VSC, which in our case is just one:

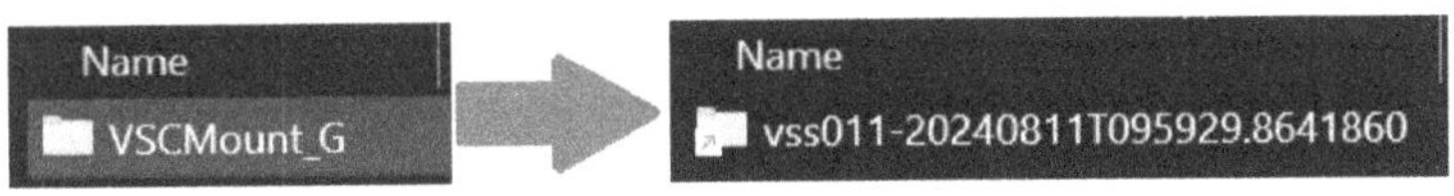

Figure 4.50 – Symbolic link to mounted VSC folder

You can explore this VSC file in its entirety now or acquire it using a utility like FTK Imager to create a logical forensic image of the mounted VSC.

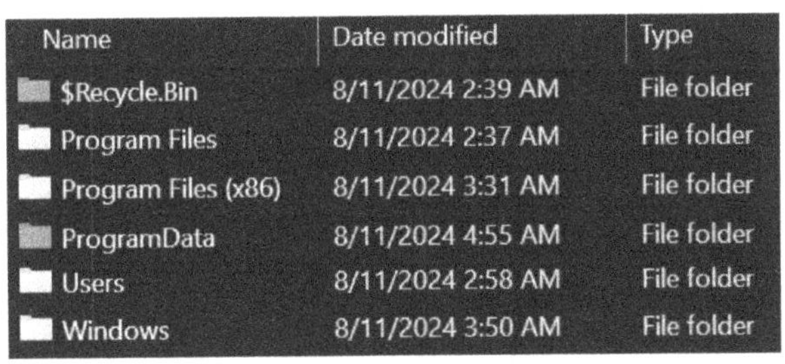

Figure 4.51 – Accessing contents of a VSC mounted using VSCMount

How it works...

Volume Shadow Copies (VSC) are point-in-time snapshots that the Windows Volume Shadow Copy Service (VSS) creates to preserve previous states of a volume. Because snapshots capture a prior logical view of files and folders, they frequently contain deleted or overwritten data that no longer exists in the live filesystem, making them a rich source for recovery and timeline reconstruction. VSCs live in the protected System Volume Information folder and are managed by the OS (they may be created automatically during updates or by user restore-point actions and can be pruned when disk space is low), so don't assume they'll always be present.

Summary

Effective Windows forensic analysis depends on understanding how operating system artifacts capture user activity, system behavior, and application interactions. By examining artifacts such as the Registry, Recycle Bin, LNK files, Shellbags, jump lists, prefetch data, event logs, thumbnail caches, and volume shadow copies, investigators can reconstruct timelines, identify user intent, and uncover evidence that may no longer exist in the live file system.

No single artifact tells the full story. Strong analysis comes from correlating multiple data sources. Each artifact provides a partial view of system activity, but when combined, they allow investigators to validate findings, identify inconsistencies, and build defensible conclusions about what occurred on the system.

At this point, you should be able to do the following:

- Identify and extract key Windows artifacts from forensic images using appropriate tools and workflows
- Interpret Registry data to determine system configuration, user accounts, and historical activity
- Analyze Recycle Bin artifacts to recover deleted files and identify deletion events
- Analyze LNK files, Shellbags, and jump lists to reconstruct user interaction with files, folders, and external devices
- Examine prefetch files to determine program execution, frequency, and approximate run times
- Parse and filter Windows event logs to identify authentication activity, system events, and potential security concerns
- Correlate thumbcache data with Windows Search databases to identify previously viewed media and associated file locations
- Leverage Volume Shadow Copies to recover historical system states and previously deleted or modified data.
- Correlate multiple artifacts to validate findings and build accurate, defensible timelines.

In the next chapter, we extend these investigative principles beyond Microsoft Windows to macOS and Linux, applying the same artifact-driven approach to identify and interpret key evidence across these platforms.

Get this book's PDF copy, code bundle, and more

Scan the QR code (or go to `packtpub.com/unlock`). Search for this book by name, confirm the edition, and then follow the steps on the page.

UNLOCK NOW

Note: Have your invoice handy. Purchases made directly from the Packt website don't require an invoice.

5

Apple macOS and Linux

Leaving Windows behind, we move analysis to two Unix-like platforms: the proprietary Apple macOS and the open-source Linux. These operating systems share many command-line and filesystem conventions and produce similar classes of artifacts that are quite different from Microsoft Windows.

Apple macOS runs on Apple's hybrid XNU kernel and exposes a BSD-style userland and shell. Unlike Windows, macOS does not use a central hierarchical registry; instead, it relies on Property List (`.plist`) files, SQLite databases, unified logging, and other file-based sources for configuration and usage data. Many low-level Darwin components are open source, but the full macOS platform and GUI frameworks are proprietary and tied to Apple hardware.

Linux, on the other hand, uses the Linux kernel and a GNU-style userland. Linux distributions vary widely, but they share core Unix behaviors like text configuration files, shell histories, standard filesystem layouts, and common CLI tools. Originally developed by Linus Torvalds in the early 1990's, Linux has evolved into numerous different distributions, or "flavors", and continues to be developed by the open-source community. Because Linux is modular and open, artifact locations and formats can differ between distributions, but the same forensic analysis concepts apply.

In this chapter, we're going to cover the following main topics:

- Property Lists (macOS)
- SQLite Databases (macOS)
- .DS_Store Records (macOS)
- ZSH/Bash History (macOS)
- FSEvents (macOS)
- Configuration Files (Linux)

- Trash Bin (Linux)
- Recently Used Files (Linux)
- Bash History (Linux)
- Thumbnails (Linux)
- Additional macOS and Linux Artifacts

Technical requirements

For this chapter, you will need:

1. A computer running Microsoft Windows to act as your forensic workstation – required for installing tools and running the exercises. Windows 11 is recommended. Ensure you have ample disk space for any forensic images you plan to work with.
2. A basic familiarity with concepts related to data parsing, file systems, operating system behavior, and the Apple macOS and Linux directory structure. If you need a refresher, consult the appendix in this book.
3. Apple macOS and Linux datasets for analysis. You may use the forensic images provided with the examples or create your own images for additional hands-on practice.
4. FTK Imager (as used in previous chapters) or an alternative tool capable of browsing forensic images. For example, 7-Zip can be used with additional support (such as the Forensic7z plugin) to access forensic image contents, as introduced earlier in this book.

Property lists (macOS)

Apple macOS does not use a centralized hierarchical registry. Instead, it stores settings and configurations in numerous property list files (commonly referred to as plist files due to their `.plist` extension). Plists may be stored as readable XML or as a binary (bplist) format. These files are distributed throughout the system rather than being centrally located, although many of the most useful system-level plists reside in the `/Library/Preferences` directory (and per-user plists under `~/Library/Preferences` directory).

The most useful property lists often include the following (note that paths preceded by ~ indicate user-specific, non-global artifact locations per user):

Operating system artifacts:

- `/System/Library/CoreServices/SystemVersion.plist`
- `/Library/Preferences/SystemConfiguration/preferences.plist`

- /Library/Preferences/.GlobalPreferences.plist
- /Library/Preferences/SystemConfiguration/com.apple.storage.plist

User accounts and activity:

- /Library/Preferences/com.apple.preferences.accounts.plist
- /Library/Preferences/com.apple.loginwindow.plist
- ~/Library/Preferences/com.apple.recentitems.plist
- ~/Library/Preferences/com.apple.loginitems.plist
- ~/Library/Preferences/com.apple.sidebarlists.plist

Software application data:

- /System/Library/LaunchDaemons/<app>.plist
- ~/Library/Containers/<app>/Data/Library/Preferences/*.plist
- ~/Library/Preferences/<app>.plist

Wireless network and Bluetooth connections:

- /Library/Preferences/SystemConfiguration/NetworkInterfaces.plist
- /Library/Preferences/SystemConfiguration/com.apple.airport.preferences.plist
- /Library/Preferences/com.apple.Bluetooth.plist
- /Library/Preferences/com.apple.MobileBluetooth.devices.plist

Previously attached or mounted devices:

- ~/Library/Preferences/com.apple.iPod.plist
- ~/Library/Preferences/com.apple.finder.plist

In this recipe, we will examine selected property list files to demonstrate how plist data can be interpreted to identify system details, user activity, and configuration artifacts.

Getting ready

For this recipe, we will use the **Apple macOS** forensic image.

Export the following files from their respective locations:

- /System/Library/CoreServices/SystemVersion.plist
- /Library/Preferences/.GlobalPreferences.plist
- /Library/Preferences/SystemConfiguration/preferences.plist

This will allow us to explore several property list files to determine basic information about the system we are examining.

Although macOS can read and display property lists natively, our Microsoft Windows workstations cannot, so we will use a third-party viewer. The Xplist project provides a Windows utility for this (Xplist-Win64.zip), which can be downloaded from:

`https://github.com/ic005k/Xplist/releases`

Download and unzip the utility, then run Xplist.exe to view both XML (plist) and binary (bplist) files.

How to do it...

1. Using `Xplist`, click **Open** from the **File** menu (shortcut key *Ctrl+O*), then select all three property list files to load them into the application. Each file will open in a separate tab:

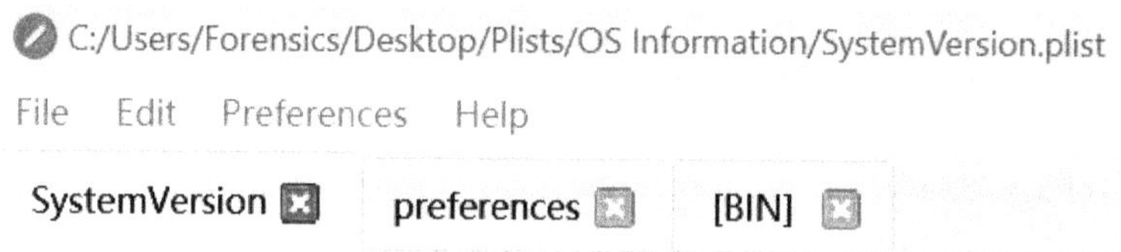

Figure 5.1 – Plist file tabs opened in Xplist

2. Inspect the `SystemVersion.plist` file to determine operating system information:

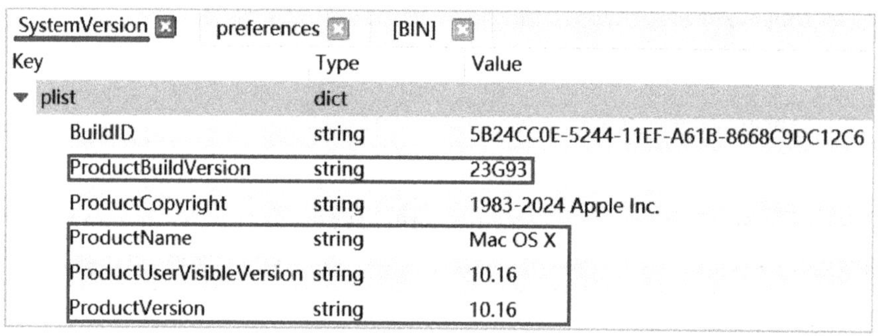

Figure 5.2 – SystemVersion.plist viewed with Xplist

Be careful here, as **ProductVersion** can sometimes be misleading (older compatibility shims may show 10.16 or similar, as in the preceding screenshot). Instead, use **ProductBuildVersion** to map the build to a marketing release.

For example, a build starting with 23 indicates a 2023 release; build **23G93** corresponds to macOS Sonoma 14.6.1.

3. Expand the `preferences.plist` to view system metadata such as the computer model and name:

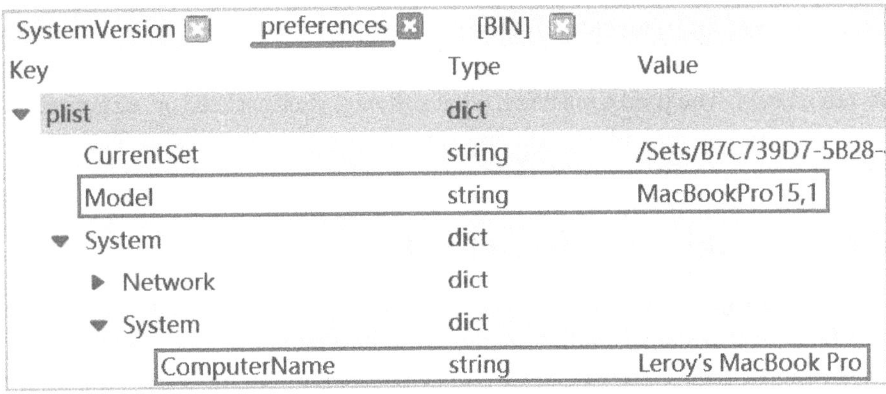

Figure 5.3 – preferences.plist viewed with Xplist

4. In `.GlobalPreferences.plist` (**[BIN]**), inspect the `com.apple.TimeZonePref.Last_Selected_City` key (or an equivalent key) to determine the user-selected time zone and city:

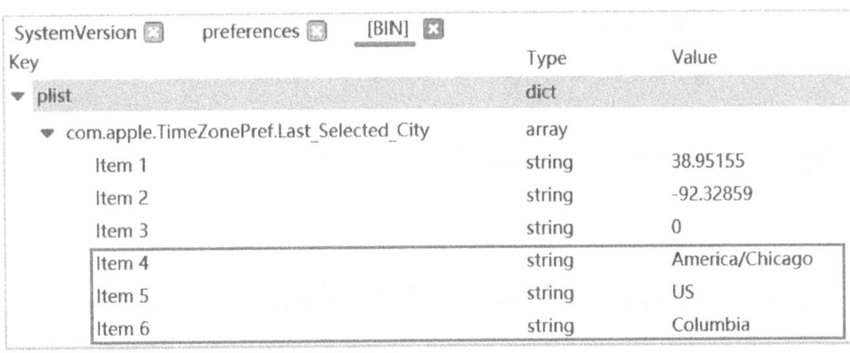

Figure 5.4 – .GlobalPreferences.plist viewed with Xplist

From these property list files, we can determine that the system is an Apple MacBook Pro named **Leroy's MacBook Pro**, installed with macOS Sonoma version 14.6.1 and set to the Central Standard time zone. This provides a strong starting point for understanding the system under investigation.

Notice that some plist files appear simply as **[BIN]** when opened in Xplist. This occurs when the file is of the binary plist (bplist) variety.

How it works...

Property lists are the file-based equivalent of a configuration database, storing structured key/value settings and usage metadata for the OS and installed applications within the system. Applications and the system will update plist keys as settings change or as events occur, so plists often reveal who used a machine, what software was installed or configured, network and device metadata, and other useful information. Understanding plist files allows us to uncover these important details.

SQLite databases (macOS)

Property lists are great for small configuration items. When larger, relational storage is needed, macOS (and many installed applications) use SQLite databases. SQLite is a lightweight, open-source relational engine that can quickly and efficiently access and write data. SQLite files found in macOS commonly use extensions like `.sqlite`, `.db`, `.sqlitedb`, `.storedata`, `.abcddb`, or no extension at all.

These databases are normally accompanied by `-shm` (shared-memory) and `-wal` (write-ahead log) files; the WAL is especially important because it often contains recent, uncommitted user data that can be recovered. Common macOS artifacts kept in SQLite databases include Safari history, iMessage data, and Photos metadata. Because SQLite is also heavily used on mobile platforms, learning to parse it pays off across both desktop and mobile forensics.

The following are common per-user locations for databases associated with default macOS applications:

- Photos: `~/Pictures/Photos Library.photoslibrary/database/Photos.sqlite`
- Notes: `~/Library/Group Containers/group.com.apple.notes/NoteStore.sqlite`
- Contacts: `~/Library/ApplicationSupport/AddressBook/Sources/<GUID>/AddressBookv-v*.abcddb`
- Messages: `~/Library/Messages/chat.db`
- Call History: `~/Library/Application Support/CallHistory.storedata`

Depending on system usage, some of these databases may not exist until the associated application has been opened or used.

In this recipe, we will examine a SQLite database to demonstrate how application data can be analyzed and interpreted during forensic analysis.

Getting ready

For this recipe, we will use the **Apple macOS** forensic image and examine the Apple Photos database.

You will need **DB Browser for SQLite** to view and query the database:

`https://sqlitebrowser.org/dl/`.

Export the Photos database and its associated files from the user's Photos library bundle. The database is located at the following path (where `leroyjenkins` is the username in our dataset):

```
/Users/leroyjenkins/Pictures/Photos Library.photoslibrary/database/Photos.sqlite
```

Also export the associated `Photos.sqlite-wal` (write-ahead log) and `Photos.sqlite-shm` files from the same directory and place them in a working folder on your workstation.

How to do it...

1. Load the exported database into DB Browser for SQLite by selecting **Open Database Read Only...** (or shortcut the key *Ctrl+Shift+O*). **DB Browser for SQLite** is capable of editing databases, so opening the database as read only prevents inadvertent changes. The software will also automatically incorporate the `-wal` and `-shm` files if they are in the same directory as the exported database:

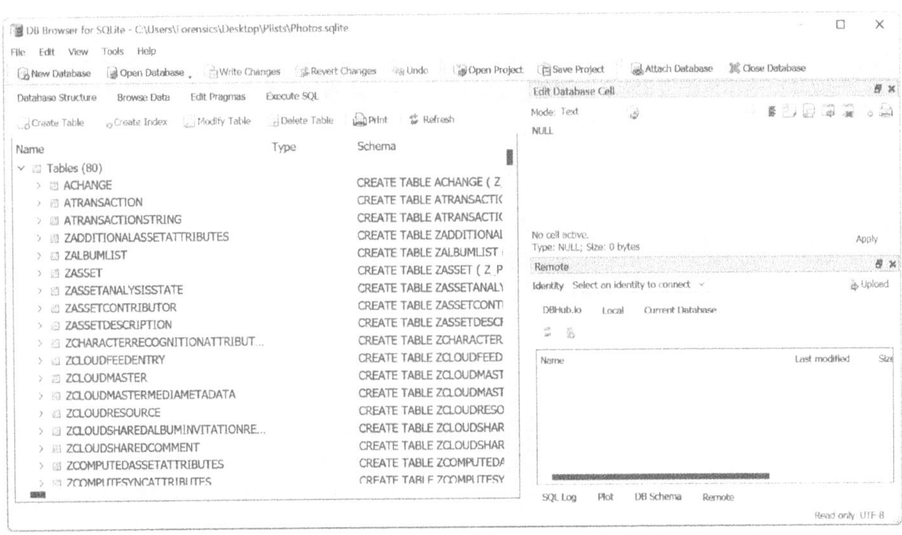

Figure 5.5 – Photos.sqlite opened in DB Browser for SQLite

2. Select the **Browse Data** tab near the top of the left side pane. This allows us to select which tables we want to view from a dropdown menu:

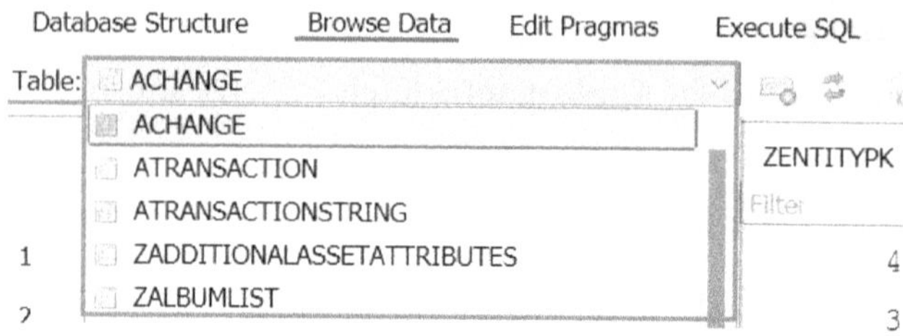

Figure 5.6 – Selecting database tables in DB Browser for SQLite

3. Select the `ZADDITIONALASSETATTRIBUTES` table from the **Table** dropdown menu. This table contains information about media files that have been imported into the Photos application:

ZORIGINALFILENAME	ZEXIFTIMESTAMPSTRING	ZIMPORTEDBYDISPLAYNAME
Filter	Filter	Filter
IMG_0028.HEIC	2024:07:09 14:40:04	NULL
IMG_0021.MOV	2024:07:06 21:00:36	NULL
IMG_0003.JPG	NULL	Safari
IMG_0015.MOV	2024:07:06 15:44:22	NULL

Figure 5.7 – ZADDITIONALASSETATTRIBUTES table data

Some of the more relevant data from this table can be seen in *Figure 5.8*. `ZORIGINALFILENAME` records the name of the media file at the time it was imported into the Photos application, which can be useful if the filename is later changed by the user. `ZEXIFTIMESTAMPSTRING` provides an EXIF timestamp associated with the file, and `ZIMPORTEDBYDISPLAYNAME` identifies the application used to import it.

In this example, IMG_0003.JPG was downloaded from the Internet using the Safari web browser, as reflected by the import source information.

4. Select the `ZASSET` table from the dropdown menu:

ZUUID	ZLATITUDE	ZLONGITUDE	ZMODIFICATIONDATE	ZDATECREATED
Filter	Filter	Filter	Filter	Filter
F41DF93F-D355-4E08-87E7-E09788616D0A	-180.0	-180.0	742890953.832116	589389480
8BFFEB00-2A7E-4D64-AC26-F67616803A28	39.1733783333333	-92.356155	745174110.697887	742246804.657
BCB02816-37B7-44D3-B59D-43779B9B5FAD	-180.0	-180.0	745174110.698594	742012010
BEEBEDD9-2114-4042-B54F-B3727557C931	38.9474716666667	-92.3014966666667	741980308.803445	741980307.112
0B4C95F6-E88E-4391-85FB-F3EA2D3D8F67	-180.0	-180.0	741926693.173065	741926692
A0CB645F-BCDA-4A19-9BF0-590C347272E6	-180.0	-180.0	742181032.465403	741994165.727
DD862E74-2DE0-45FA-A9E1-0CF71050A057	-180.0	-180.0	745174110.697121	742011948.79

Figure 5.8 – ZASSET table data

`ZASSET` contains a lot of valuable information, some of which is shown in *Figure 5.9* and is relatively self-explanatory based on field names such as `ZALTITUDE/ZLONGITUDE` for location information, or items pertaining to associated dates. `ZUUID` is less clear – this reflects the current filename assigned after import.

To match files between the `ZASSET` table and the previous `ZADDITIONALATTRIBUTES` table we reviewed, you can match the value in the `ZADDITIONALATTRIBUTES` field (not shown in the preceding figure) and find the corresponding number within the `ZADDITIONALATTRIBUTES` table, where the associated number will be shown by `Z_PK`.

You will notice the created and modified dates (ZDATECREATED and ZMODIFICATIONDATE) in the sample in `Figure 5.8` are not immediately clear, as they are stored in Mac Absolute time format. These values can be converted using tools such as DCode to convert these times into a readable format, however, **DB Browser for SQLite** can also generate the appropriate SQL command to do this more efficiently. Simply right-click the heading and choose **Edit display format** from the options, then select **Apple NSDate to date** from the available dropdown menu before clicking **OK:**

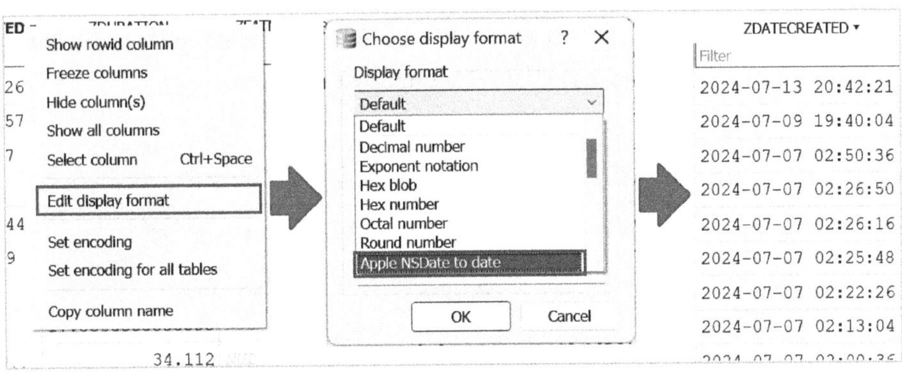

Figure 5.9 – Converting time formats in DB Browser for SQLite

Note

Running Out of Time

When did time begin? For computers, it depends.

Computers need to track time to function. To do this, they count time – and to count time, you need a starting point. Developers define an arbitrary reference point and measure time from that moment, typically in seconds, milliseconds, or nanoseconds. This reference point is known as an **epoch**.

> In many cases, you will encounter Unix time, which begins at 00:00:00 UTC on January 1, 1970. However, the example we just reviewed uses Mac Absolute time, which begins at 00:00:00 UTC on January 1, 2001.
>
> Other common epoch formats you may encounter include:
>
> - *- Windows FILETIME (January 1, 1601, UTC)*
> - *- FAT time (January 1, 1980, local time)*
> - *- Chrome/WebKit time (January 1, 1601, UTC)*
>
> It is important to identify the correct epoch format before converting timestamps. In practice, this can often be inferred from the value itself. For example, Unix timestamps are currently in the ~1.7 billion range, while Mac Absolute timestamps are significantly smaller due to their later starting point. Recognizing these patterns helps quickly identify the correct format during analysis.

5. Lastly, examine the `ZEXTENDEDATTRIBUTES` table. This table contains the majority of useful EXIF information available for imported media files:

ZCAMERAMAKE ▾	ZCAMERAMODEL	ZLENSMODEL
Filter	Filter	Filter
SONY	ILCE-7M3	FE 55mm F1.8 ZA
Canon	Canon EOS 80D	EF24-70mm f/4L IS USM
Apple	iPhone 12	iPhone 12 back camera 4.2mm...
Apple	iPhone 12	iPhone 12 back camera 4.2mm...

Figure 5.10 – ZEXTENDEDATTRIBUTES table data

6. Many additional tables exist within the Photos application, some of which may not contain data depending on user activity. For example, the Photos application in macOS has face detection features and allows users to assign names to individuals, making it easier to locate photos containing specific people. If this feature was used, this information can be found in the `ZDETECTEDFACE` and `ZPERSON` tables.

   As part of your analysis, explore additional tables to identify other potential artifacts or related data. This same concept applies across many forensic sources, where high-value data such as messages, web history, and third-party application activity are often stored in SQLite databases – making them one of the richest sources of forensic artifacts.

How it works...

SQLite databases are becoming the pillar for storing richer, relational data across macOS applications (and many apps on other systems, especially mobile devices). `Photos.sqlite` serves as a practical, real-world example of patterns you will encounter repeatedly. When you open any macOS SQLite database, look for consistent patterns: tables that store entities (assets, messages, history), and related tables you can join by a primary key or UUID.

> **Tip**
>
> SQLite databases are widely used across many systems, especially mobile platforms. We revisit SQLite analysis in *Chapter 6, Apple iOS and Android, Chapter 8, User Artifacts*, and *Chapter 9, Manual Analysis*, where we begin writing our own SQLite queries.

.DS_Store records (macOS)

`.DS_Store` files are Finder (macOS file explorer) per-folder metadata files. They're hidden by default and appear in directories the user has opened with Finder (including folders on external drives and some network shares). Each `.DS_Store` holds entries for the items in that folder plus small preference values (icon positions, view mode, window size/position, etc.).

Because they are written locally for each directory, `.DS_Store` files can help identify which folders a user viewed and may preserve filenames that are otherwise deleted or moved, making them a useful, lightweight forensic artifact.

In this recipe, we will examine `.DS_Store` files to demonstrate how folder metadata can reveal user activity and previously present files.

Getting ready

For this section, we will use the **Apple macOS** forensic image.

There is no need to export any files, as we will explore the filesystem directly using a forensic image viewer (for example, FTK Imager or an equivalent tool).

How to do it...

1. After loading the **Apple macOS** forensic image into FTK Imager, browse out to the following location:
   `/Users/leroyjenkins/Documents/Transfer from my USB drive/airshow/`

While doing this, you will likely notice many of these directories contain a hidden `.DS_Store` file:

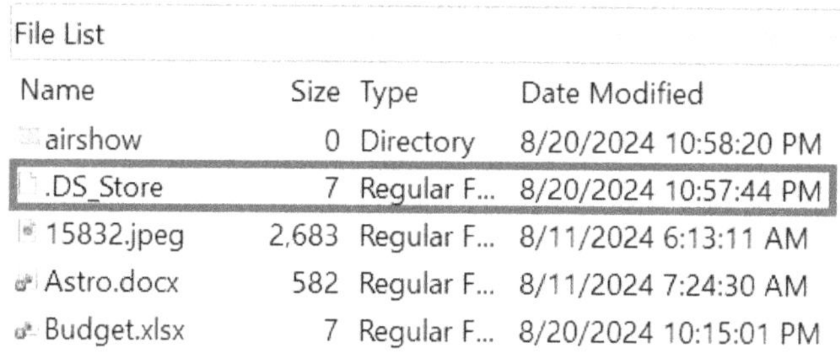

Figure 5.11 – Example of a .DS_Store file viewed using FTK Imager

2. The data stored within `.DS_Store` files is minimal and rather easy to interpret using a hex viewer. In the following screenshot, the `.DS_Store` file has been selected within the airshow folder. We can see the file listed in the ASCII interpreter (each file within a folder will be listed here).
   Data within these files may persist until Finder rewrites the `.DS_Store` file, which can give us potential insight into files that once existed in the directory but have since been removed:

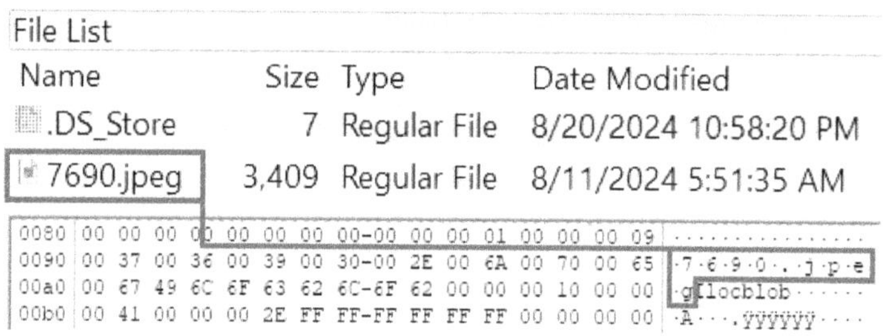

Figure 5.12 – .DS_Store file content viewed using FTK Imager

3. While filenames displayed in the ASCII view may reflect files currently present in the directory, additional data stored in the `.DS_Store` file primarily consists of layout and view preferences (such as icon positions, window bounds, and label colors), which are generally of limited evidentiary value but may provide useful context in some cases.

How it works...

When a folder is opened in Finder, macOS creates or updates a `.DS_Store` binary file in that directory to store view preferences and per-item attributes. Each record in the file associates a filename with certain attributes (for example, icon location or display flags). Although the .DS_Store format is binary, filenames are stored in plain text within the file, so a hex/ASCII view will often reveal file names quickly.

In short: .DS_Store files are a per-folder snapshot of Finder metadata for that directory at the time it was written and can provide useful indicators of folder access and prior file presence.

ZSH/Bash history (macOS)

If a user runs commands in Terminal, those commands are often recorded in a hidden per-user file (.zsh_history) in the user's home directory. Historic terminal commands are an excellent source of user activity (and skill level) because many average macOS users never open the Terminal.

> Note
>
> In older versions of macOS (prior to Catalina) this will be shown as a .bash_history file and you may sometimes find either or both – users may use either shell, and the older bash shell can also appear as a legacy item due to updates from an older operating system.

In this recipe, we will examine shell history files to demonstrate how command-line activity can be used to reconstruct user actions during an investigation.

Getting ready

For this section we will use the **Apple macOS** forensic image.

You do not need to export files; user shell history files (such as ~/.zsh_history or ~/.bash_history) can be viewed directly using a forensic image viewer (for example, FTK Imager or an equivalent tool) or any text editor after extraction.

Check both history files (and the root account), as macOS systems may use different shells for different users. In the examples for this section, the referenced files can be found at /Users/leroyjenkins/.

How to do it...

1. Navigate to the home folder for the *Leroy Jenkins* account and select the .zsh_history file. Each line within the .zsh_history file represents a separate command entered by the user:

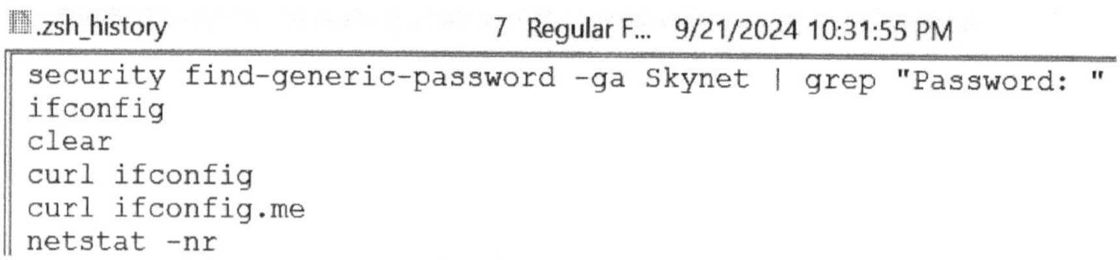

Figure 5.13 – Example data from .zsh_history viewed with FTK Imager

Also within the home folder of each user is a folder named `.zsh_sessions`, which retains additional information about Terminal commands entered by the user.

Each Terminal session creates two files named using a GUID: `<GUID>.history` lists the commands entered during the Terminal session and each matching `<GUID>.session` shows a timestamp relating to the session.

View these files from the home folder of the *Leroy Jenkins* account:

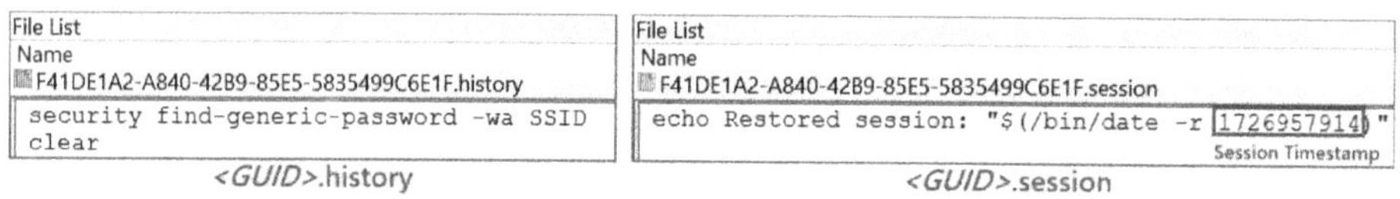

Figure 5.14 – <GUID>.history and <GUID>.session viewed with FTK Imager

The timestamp is recorded in UTC and uses Unix seconds.

Earlier, when reviewing Microsoft Windows in *Chapter 4*, we used DCode to convert timestamps. We can do the same here, entering the timestamp from `<GUID>.session` as a numeric value into DCode, and then referencing the **Unix Seconds** conversion:

Figure 5.15 – Converting timestamp from <GUID>.session using DCode

How it works...

When a user executes commands in Terminal, the shell records the commands to a disk-backed history file (for zsh, `~/.zsh_history`; for bash, `~/.bash_history`). These can include embedded epoch timestamps for each session, which helps us build a timeline of command activity. This evidence can be extremely useful when dealing with more advanced users, common in intrusion response cases, as it can reveal precise actions taken by the user.

FSEvents (macOS)

FSEvents are macOS's file system change logging mechanism. Each mounted volume maintains an `.fseventsd` directory that records file system change events (creates, deletes, renames, and modifications) along with associated timestamps. These records provide a valuable source for identifying items that once existed, tracking directory changes, and building timelines of file system activity.

In short, FSEvents can quickly show when files and folders were modified and help identify altered or deleted data even when the original files are unrecoverable.

In this recipe, we will examine FSEvents to demonstrate how filesystem change activity can be analyzed to identify file and directory activity and construct a timeline of system activity.

Getting ready

For this recipe we will use the **Apple macOS** forensic image.

Download the latest release of `mac_apt` (by ydkhatri) from GitHub and use the Windows-compatible binary (`mac_apt.exe`) for running the application on your workstation:

`https://github.com/ydkhatri/mac_apt/releases`.

To review results, we will also need the *DB Browser for SQLite* software we used earlier.

How to do it...

1. FSEvents are located in macOS at `/private/var/db/fseventsd` (and as a `.fseventsd` directory at the root of each volume). Rather than export these logs, we will run `mac_apt` directly against our **Apple macOS** image. This allows us to parse FSEvents without manually extracting and interpreting the raw binary log files and provides a structured dataset for analysis.
2. From the browser window where you stored the `mac_apt` executable file, run an instance of Windows Command Prompt by entering **CMD** in the File Explorer address bar and press **Enter**. In Command Prompt, we can view available options offered by `mac_apt` by entering the name of the executable file followed by `-h`, as follows (this also helps us to ensure `mac_apt` is running as expected):

```
mac_apt.exe -h
```

> **Tip**
>
> You may need to run `mac_apt` as an admin (elevated Windows privileges) if you encounter errors.

3. Create a folder to store your results and name the folder DEST. Note the location of the folder you created, as you will need to know its file path.
4. Since we are targeting FSEvents, we will enter the command shown below. The `-o` parameter specifies the output directory where results will be saved, followed by the forensic image type (DMG in this case), the path to the **Apple macOS** image, and finally the `FSEVENTS` plugin to indicate which artifact to parse:

```
mac_apt.exe -o "output_path" TYPE "image_source_path" FSEVENTS
```

For example, I have saved my **Apple macOS** image to a drive designated in Windows as **D:**, and have also created my `DEST` folder to store the results on this same drive, so the command I will enter is as follows:

```
mac_apt.exe -o "D:\DEST" DMG "D:\Apple macOS.dmg" FSEVENTS
```

5. The `mac_apt` application will take a few minutes to process the logs.

Once completed, you will see the results appear in the **DEST** folder we created, along with `mac_apt` logs and an export of the macOS FSEvents that were parsed. The results we are interested in are stored in the `mac_apt.db` file:

Figure 5.16 – mac_apt processing results stored to mac_apt.db file

6. The mac_apt.db file stores the parsed results in a SQLite database. Using **DB Browser for SQLite**, open the `mac_apt.db` file (**File | Open Database**), then select the **Browse Data** tab and choose the **FsEvents** table:

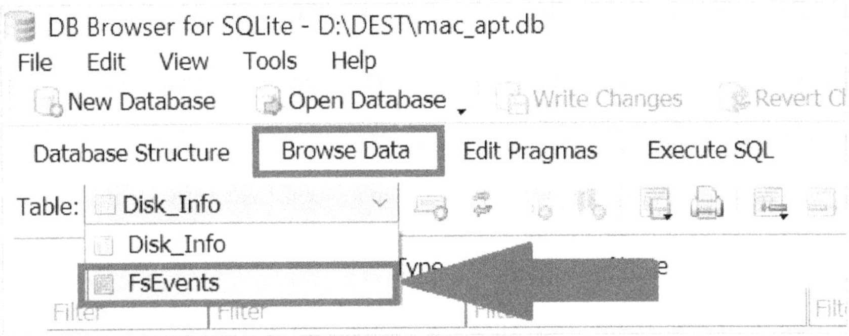

Figure 5.17 – Using DB Browser for SQLite to open mac_apt results

7. The parsed results contain numerous file system records related to files, folders, and volumes.

   In the results below, we can see where a volume was mounted, files were modified, and folders were created and removed. In this dataset, records appear to persist for approximately two months; however, there is no fixed retention period. Persistence depends on system activity, OS version, and available disk space:

EventType	EventFlags	Filepath	SourceModDatenown
	Mount	/System/Volumes/Data/home	2025-11-25 22:33:44
File	InodeMetaMod|Modified	/System/Volumes/Update/…	2025-11-25 22:33:44
File	Created|RenamedOrMoved	/System/Volumes/…	2025-11-25 22:33:44
Folder	Removed|FolderCreated	/System/Volumes/…	2025-11-25 22:33:44
File	Removed	/System/Volumes/Update/db/…	2025-11-25 22:33:44

Figure 5.18 – FSEvents parsed with mac_apt and view with DB Browser

   This allows investigators to reconstruct sequences of file system activity even when the original files are no longer present on the system.

How it works...

Each volume maintains its own FSEvents data store at `/private/var/db/fseventsd` (and a small per-volume copy at the root), so investigators must parse every relevant store to build a complete picture. FSEvents function as a rolling, append-style change log – that is, old records roll off as the system records new records.

This makes FSEvents a strong source for reconstructing *what* happened and *when*, but not for recovering file contents. A tool like `mac_apt` makes parsing these binary files into a readable format easy, allowing us to incorporate another artifact source as we build a timeline of system and user activity. Additionally, `mac_apt` can be used to parse more macOS data by using the plugin *ALL* in place of the *FSEVENTS* plugin we used.

> **Note**
>
> There's a parser for that
>
> Artifact formats and application data structures evolve frequently across operating system versions and updates. As a result, parsing tools may occasionally produce incomplete or misleading output.
>
> Always verify parser results by reviewing tool logs, documentation, and by manually inspecting the raw data when you find an artifact of evidentiary value. If something looks incomplete or inconsistent, assume the tool may not fully support that artifact version and validate your findings accordingly.

Configuration files (Linux)

Linux relies upon numerous plain-text files to store system settings and related data. These files are spread throughout the filesystem rather than in a single directory or database and provide a straightforward way to quickly gain insight into the system and its users.

In this recipe we will examine several common configuration files to demonstrate how system and user information can be identified during analysis.

Getting ready

In this section we will use the **Linux** forensic image.

Since Linux stores this information as plain-text files, we can view these artifacts directly using a forensic image viewer (such as FTK Imager or an equivalent tool).

How to do it...

1. Load the Linux forensic image into a forensic image viewer and browse to the `os-release` file located at `{root}/usr/lib` (note that on some systems this file is often located at `{root}/etc/os-release`).
   Review the file content:

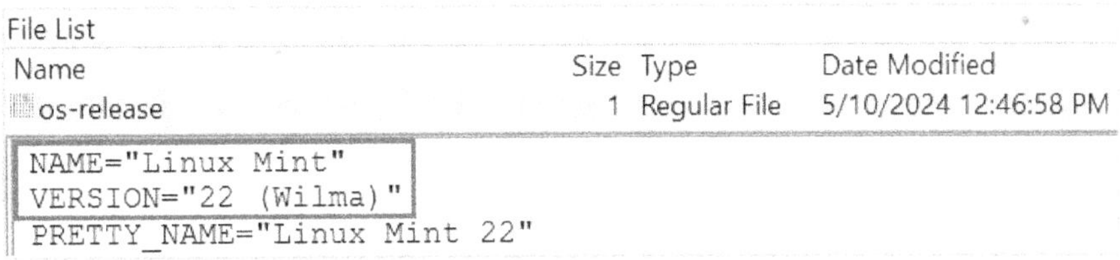

Figure 5.19 – Linux version in os-release file

As you can see, this file shows the operating system to be Linux Mint (Wilma) version 22.

> **Note**
>
> Location, Location, Location
>
> On Linux systems, many files may exist in multiple locations or appear duplicated due to the use of symbolic links (`symlinks`). A file such as `/etc/os-release` may simply reference another file (for example, `/usr/lib/os-release`) that contains the actual data.
>
> Depending on how a forensic image was acquired or mounted, symbolic links may not be fully resolved, which can cause one path to appear empty, minimal, or incomplete while the linked file contains the full content. When expected data is missing, always check for alternate paths or `symlink` targets elsewhere in the filesystem.

2. Now browse to the `hostname` file located at `{root}/etc`:

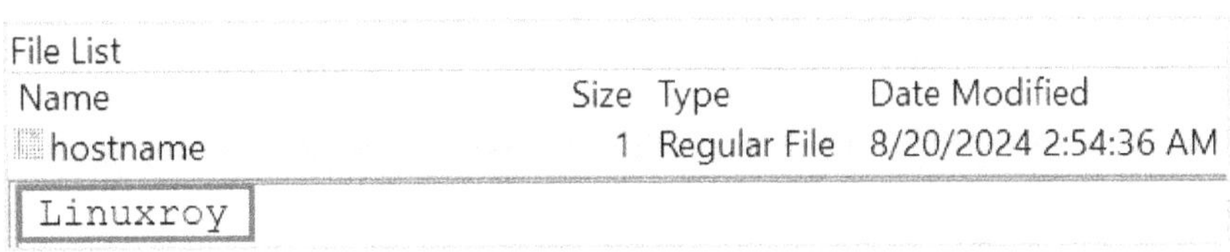

Figure 5.20 – System name in hostname file

This tells us the system hostname, **Linuxroy** in this case.

3. Browse to the `timezone` file, also located at `{root}/etc`:

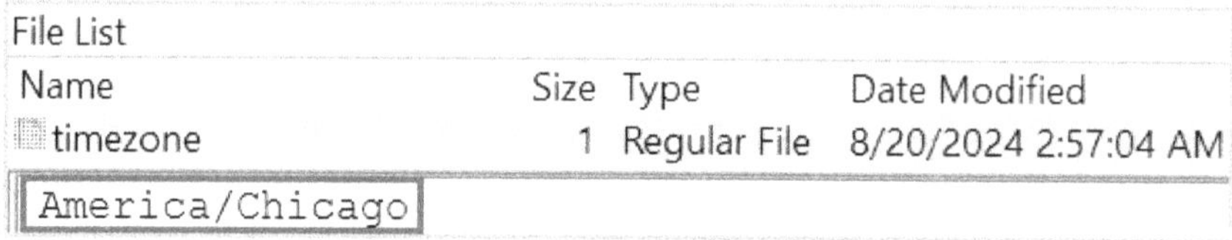

Figure 5.21 – System time zone in timezone file

This file shows us the system is configured with the **America/Chicago**, or **Central Standard Time (CST)** time zone.

4. Next, let's look at the user accounts present within the **home** directory. Here we see subdirectories for accounts named `chief`, `george`, `leroy`, and `nessy`:

Figure 5.22 – Linux active user account subdirectories

While this information is helpful, it fails to provide us with details regarding each user, such as the complete usernames.

5. Browse to the `passwd` configuration file located at `{root}/etc`, and scroll to the bottom of the file.

```
leroy:x:1000:1000:Leroy Jenkins,,,:/home/leroy:/bin/bash
chief:x:1001:1001:Master Chief,,,:/home/chief:/bin/bash
nessy:x:1002:1002:Loch Ness,,,:/home/nessy:/bin/bash
george:x:1004:1004:George Washington,,,:/home/george:/bin/bash
```

Figure 5.23 – User account details in passwd file

This provides more detailed information, including the full names of each user account. You will also notice unique numbers for each user, beginning with 1000. These are the **User Identifiers (UIDs)** assigned to each user when an account is created and are similar to a Microsoft Windows RID. From the example, we can see UID 1003 appears to be missing. This is the result of a user account being deleted in Linux.

6. Browse to the passwd- file, also located within the `{root}/etc` directory:

```
leroy:x:1000:1000:Leroy Jenkins,,,:/home/leroy:/bin/bash
chief:x:1001:1001:Master Chief,,,:/home/chief:/bin/bash
nessy:x:1002:1002:Loch Ness,,,:/home/nessy:/bin/bash
john:x:1003:1003:John,,,:/home/john:/bin/bash
george:x:1004:1004:George Washington,,,:/home/george:/bin/bash
```

Figure 5.24 – Deleted user account identified in passwd- file

This backup file reflects the previous state of the `passwd` file. In this case, it includes an additional entry for a user account that has since been removed. We can see this account was named *John* and shows our missing UID of 1003.

7. Finally, browse to the **shadow** file at `{root}/etc`. At the bottom of this file, we see our usernames again, along with additional values:

```
leroy:$y$j9T$3aDAOu6LZ8s9xidw4pQ9zvEE02N75Mgevi0:19955:0:99999:7:::
chief::19955:0:99999:7:::
nessy::19955:0:99999:7:::
george::19956:0:99999:7:::
```

Figure 5.25 – Identifying password protected accounts in shadow file

This file is used to store account password hashes. We can see the account for `leroy` has a much longer value, and that is because this is the only account on the system that is password protected.

8. Now, examine the `shadow-` file (located at `{root}/etc`), which represents a backup of the primary **shadow** file and may retain entries for previously deleted accounts (such as `john`) if those entries were not fully removed:

```
leroy:$y$j9T$3aDAOu6LZ8s9xidw4pQnml$pJH6uVsa7
chief::19955:0:99999:7:::
nessy::19955:0:99999:7:::
john::19956:0:99999:7:::
george::19956:0:99999:7:::
```

Figure 5.26 – Removed account still present in corresponding shadow- file

Note

A Remnant of the Past

Files ending in - (such as passwd- and shadow-) often contain previous system states and should always be reviewed for evidence of deleted or modified accounts.

These backup files are overwritten as changes occur, so they may reflect only the most recent prior state rather than a complete historical record.

How it works...

System and user settings are stored in configuration files throughout the Linux environment. These files typically have no extension, as Linux does not rely on file extensions to determine how files are handled. Most configuration files are plain text, allowing them to be easily viewed and interpreted using standard tools (such as a text editor).

From an analysis standpoint, this makes it relatively straightforward to determine system state and configuration once relevant files are identified. While exact locations and formats may vary between distributions, the underlying analysis concepts remain consistent. When differences are encountered, system documentation or direct examination of the file system can be used to identify relevant artifacts.

Trash bin (Linux)

The Linux Trash bin functions similarly to the Recycle Bin in Microsoft Windows, and files will persist here until the Trash is emptied by the user, at which point the files are permanently deleted from the system. Until then, these files remain easily accessible and restorable to their original locations by the user.

The Trash bin folder does not exist until the user places an item into the Trash. Once this occurs, a `Trash` folder is created for the user. Within the Trash folder are two subdirectories:

- `files` stores the actual files that were removed by the user
- `info` stores related metadata for those files

In this recipe, we will examine the Linux Trash bin to identify deleted files that may still be recoverable, along with associated metadata that can help reconstruct when and how those files were deleted.

Getting ready

For this section, we will use the Linux forensic image.

Using FTK Imager or another tool capable of reviewing forensic images, the per-user Trash folder can be found at the following location:

```
{root}/home/username/.local/share/Trash
```

How to do it...

1. Browse to the **files** directory of the Trash folder for the `leroy` account (`/home/leroy/.local/share/Trash/files`). Here you will see a file titled `Budget.xlsx`. This file has been moved to the Trash by the user but has not yet been emptied so the file remains easily accessible at this location:

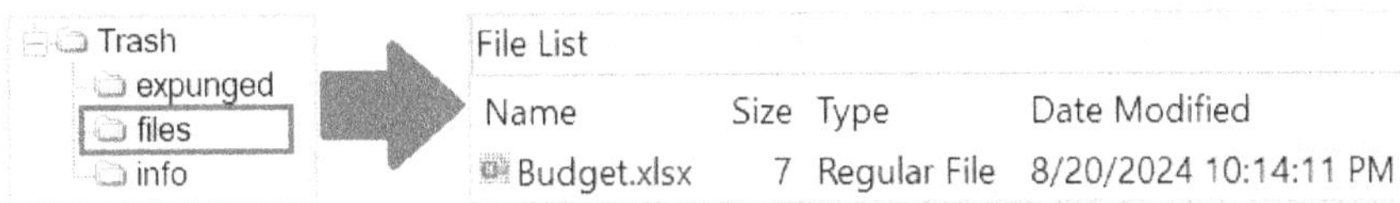

Figure 5.27 – Restorable files located in Trash folder

2. Now browse to the `info` folder (`/home/leroy/.local/share/Trash/info`) and select the file titled `Budget.xlsx.trashinfo`. When a file is placed into the Trash, a plain-text file for the item ending with a `.trashinfo` extension is generated. The contents of the `.trashinfo` file show the original directory from which the file was stored and the date and time (in local system time) that the file was moved to the Trash bin by the user:

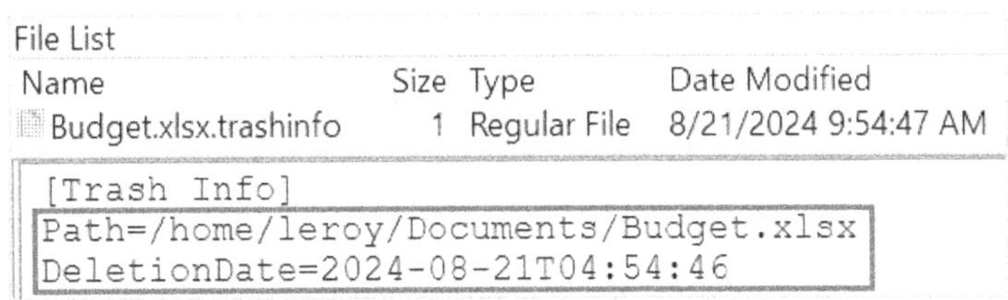

Figure 5.28 – Metadata from .trashinfo file

The remaining expunged subdirectory of the Trash folder is unique to some Linux distros, including the one used for our data set. It acts as a temporary file space when the Trash bin is emptied. Artifacts of value are unlikely to be recovered from this directory, though its existence shows that the Trash has been previously emptied, as the expunged directory does not exist until this occurs.

How it works...

When a user "deletes" a file in a Linux desktop, the desktop environment usually moves the file into the per-user Trash and writes a small metadata file describing the original path and the deletion timestamp. Until the user empties the Trash, those file bodies and metadata remain intact and restorable.

Remember to also check removable volumes as well, which can create a similar hidden artifact at the root of the volume, typically named `.Trash-<UID>`, with the UID identifying the user account. You may encounter artifacts of this type on removable storage drives that a Linux user has attempted to remove data from.

Recently used files (Linux)

When a Linux user opens or interacts with a file, information about that activity is stored in a per-user XML file called `recently-used.xbel`. This data describes the file location of what the user opened, the application used to open the file, visit counts, and a series of related timestamps.

In this recipe, we will examine `recently-used.xbel` to identify files a user has interacted with, along with associated applications and timestamps that can help reconstruct user activity.

Getting ready

For this section we will use the **Linux** forensic image.

Using FTK Imager or another tool capable of reviewing forensic images, the per-user `recently-used.xbel` file can be found at the following location:

```
{root}/home/username/.local/share/recently-used.xbel
```

How to do it...

1. Browse to the `recently-used.xbel` file for the `leroy` account of our data set (`/home/leroy/.local/share`).
2. Because this file is created per-user account, it allows us to determine recent file interactions for a specific account. As file interactions occur, they are immediately written to the `recently-used.xbel` file, with the most recent entries being written at the end of the file:

```
</bookmark>
<bookmark href="file:///home/leroy/Documents/Budget.xlsx" added="2024-08-20T22:04:40.350316Z"
 modified="2024-08-20T22:14:11.413311Z" visited="2024-08-20T22:04:40.350318Z">
  <info>
    <metadata owner="http://freedesktop.org">
      <mime:mime-type type="application/vnd.openxmlformats-officedocument.spreadsheetml.sheet" />
      <bookmark:applications>
        <bookmark:application name="nemo" exec="&apos;libreoffice --calc %U&apos;" modified="2024-08-20T22:04:40.350321Z" count="1"/>
        <bookmark:application name="LibreOffice 24.2" exec="&apos;soffice %u&apos;" modified="2024-08-20T22:14:11.413310Z" count="4" />
      </bookmark:applications>
    </metadata>
  </info>
</bookmark>
```


Figure 5.29 – Sample data from recently-used.xbel file

3. From the sample data, we can observe several key elements of user interaction with the `Budget.xlsx` file:

   - **File path (bookmark href):** The `href` value shows the full path to the file (`/home/leroy/Documents/Budget.xlsx`), indicating where the file was located when accessed.
   - **Timestamps:** The modified timestamps are updated each time the file is interacted with. These reflect the date and time of the most recent interaction and are recorded in UTC, while other timestamps (such as added and visited) remain unchanged.
   - **Associated application (**`exec`**):** The application entries identify the program used to open the file. In this case, the file was opened using LibreOffice Calc.
   - **Interactions (**`count`**):** The count value tracks how many times the file has been accessed from this path. In this example, the count indicates a single recorded interaction for this entry.

   If the file is moved or opened from a new location, a separate entry is created for that path. Subsequent interactions at the same location update the existing entry, increase the interaction count, and update the modified timestamp.

   The interaction count associated with an application may not directly correspond to the exact number of times the application was launched. In this example, LibreOffice Calc shows a count of 4, although it was only launched twice in the dataset. This value can reflect multiple internal events, so it should be treated as an indicator of repeated access rather than a precise execution count.

How it works...

The `recently-used.xbel` file is a per-user XML (XBEL) file that Linux desktop environments use to record file access activity. It contains multiple records, with each entry storing a file path (`href`), the application that opened it, timestamps, and a visit/count value. The file is updated as interactions occur, with new record entries being appended to the end of the file. Like many files within the Linux environment, `recently-used.xbel` is just a writable file that is easily human-readable, making it easy to review once we understand how it records file access.

This makes `recently-used.xbel` a valuable artifact for identifying user file access patterns, even when the files themselves are no longer present.

Bash history (Linux)

Like Apple macOS, many Linux distributions keep a per-user shell history file that records commands entered in a terminal. These are stored as hidden plain-text files (named `.bash_history`) for each user on the system. By default, bash only stores the command lines themselves, with no associated timestamps indicating when they were executed. However, in some cases administrators or advanced users may enable additional configuration (such as the `HISTTIMEFORMAT` setting), which results in Unix timestamps being recorded alongside commands.

> **Note**
>
> Note that systems and users sometimes use other shells (for example zsh), which use different history files and may include timestamps if configured.

In this recipe, we will examine `.bash_history` files to identify command-line activity and demonstrate how shell history can be used to reconstruct user actions during an investigation.

Getting ready

For this section we will use the **Linux** forensic image.

Using FTK Imager or another tool capable of reviewing forensic images, the per-user `.bash_history` files can be found at the following location:

```
{root}/home/username/.bash_history
```

How to do it...

1. Browse to the `leroy` home folder (`/home/leroy`) and open the `.bash_history` file to review recorded commands:

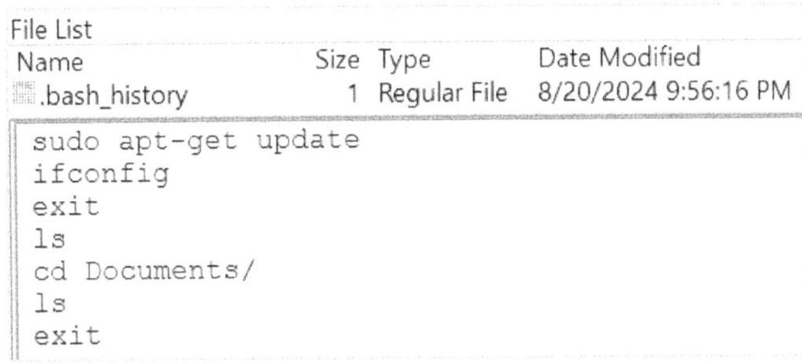

Figure 5.30 – Content stored to .bash_history file

Each command is recorded as a new line in the file but contains no timestamps to indicate when commands were executed. In most cases, investigators must rely on the file's modified timestamp or correlate with other artifacts; however, the modified timestamp typically reflects when the history file was last written (often when the shell session closed), not when individual commands were executed.

This makes shell history useful for identifying user actions, but less reliable for establishing precise timelines without supporting artifacts.

How it works...

Linux bash typically writes commands to the hidden plain-text `.bash_history` file when a shell session exits, and the contents reflect commands entered during previous sessions. Commands here are typically written when a session is closed (or periodically if configured). Some users enable timestamping or switch to shells that embed time information by default, so investigators should also check for related session logs.

Thumbnails (Linux)

Thumbnails in Linux function much the same as they do within the Microsoft Windows environment; that is, they are generated when the user views icon representations of the file content stored to the system or another volume (such as an attached USB storage drive) and persist even if the original file is moved or deleted. In Linux, however, there are no thumbnail databases and there is no need for third-party tools to view the thumbnail content. Instead, thumbnails are cached as easily viewable .PNG files in a hidden directory for each user account, making it easy to identify the user who viewed the files.

In this recipe, we will examine Linux thumbnail cache files to identify files a user has viewed, including files that may no longer exist on the system.

Getting ready

For this section we will use the **Linux** forensic image.

Linux per-user thumbnail files can be found at the following location:

`{root}/home/username/.cache/thumbnails/`

How to do it...

1. Browse to the `thumbnail` directory of the `leroy` user account, located at: `/home/leroy/.cache/thumbnails/`

   You will see three subdirectories:

   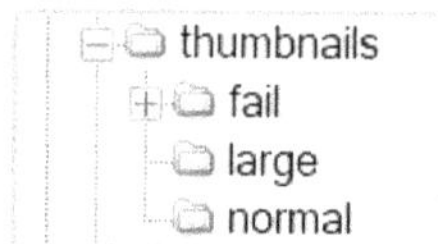

   Figure 5.31 – Linux thumbnail directories

   The `fail` directory stores the names of thumbnails for which a preview failed to generate. These are stored within a subdirectory titled using the name of the utility that attempted to generate the thumbnail previews, although the files themselves do not contain viewable media content.

   The normal and `large` directories are where you will find the viewable thumbnails that did successfully generate content previews, with the `normal` directory containing standard size thumbnails and the `large` directory storing thumbnails that were viewed using increased sizing preferences.

2. Select from either the `normal` or `large` folder, and view the content stored:

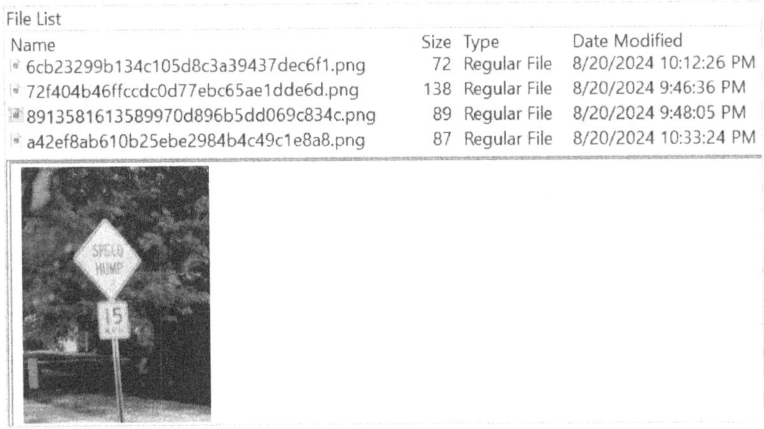

Figure 5.32 – Linux thumbnail file from large folder of leroy account

Each thumbnail filename is an MD5 hash of the original file's full path (including filename) at the time the thumbnail was generated. While this hash is not salted, it is not intended to be reversed to recover the original path.

However, if a likely original path is known, the MD5 value can be recomputed to verify whether a given thumbnail corresponds to that file.

3. Figure 5.32 shows a thumbnail image named 8913581613589970d896b5dd069c834c. You will find the same apparent image, titled 15832.jpeg, within the default `Pictures` folder of the `leroy` account.
   Using a web browser, go to the website `https://10015.io/tools/md5-encrypt-decrypt`. In the text box, enter the file path `file:///home/leroy/Pictures/15832.jpeg` and select `Encrypt >`:

Figure 5.33 – Linux thumbnail hash validation

If entered correctly, you will receive a resultant hash value matching that of the thumbnail name. A possible scenario where this technique may be useful is when you need to show that the user viewed a known file, but the thumbnail failed to generate, leaving only an unviewable file within the fail thumbnail directory.

4. While entering file paths into online tools may seem low risk, it can expose sensitive case information. Avoid using external services when working with real evidence. An alternative method is opening an instance of Windows PowerShell and running the following command (placing the file path in the `$string` variable)

```
$string = "text string to hash"
$bytes = [System.Text.Encoding]::UTF8.GetBytes($string)
$hash = [System.Security.Cryptography.MD5]::Create().ComputeHash($bytes)
[BitConverter]::ToString($hash) -replace "-", ""
```

This is an effective method of hashing any text string and will produce the resultant hash as shown:

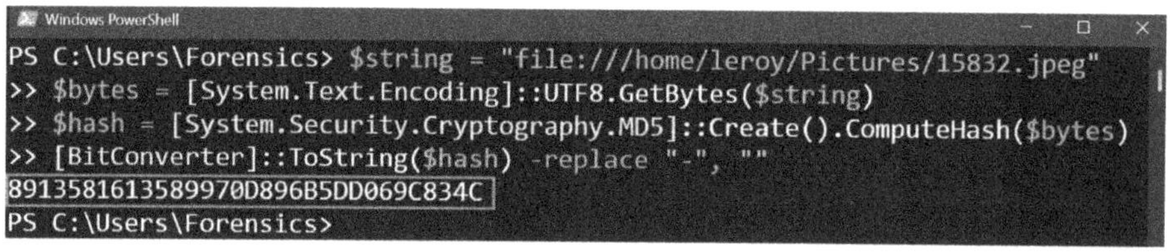

Figure 5.34 – Text string hash produced using Windows PowerShell

How it works...

When a user views files in a folder (such as in icon view), Linux generates and caches thumbnail images within the per-user directory (`~/.cache/thumbnails/`). Usable previews are stored in the normal and large directories, while the fail directory contains thumbnails that the system could not render.

This artifact is an excellent way to show which media files a user has viewed and can even provide visual evidence of files that were stored on removable media or were later deleted.

Thumbnail filenames are not random; they are MD5 hashes of the file's URI (for local files, the file:/// URI representing the absolute path). If you can propose a candidate original path, reproducing the MD5 hash (for example, "`file:///full/path/to/file`") allows you to verify whether a thumbnail corresponds to that file.

Additional macOS and Linux artifacts

> **Tip**
>
> In addition to the artifacts examined in the preceding recipes, the following macOS artifacts are commonly encountered during investigations and may provide valuable context to support the investigation.

Trash

Like the Recycle Bin on Windows systems, the Trash folder temporarily stores files deleted by the user until they are permanently removed. On macOS, each user account maintains a hidden `.Trash` directory within the user's home folder. Files in this location may provide evidence of recently deleted content and can often be restored by the user unless the Trash has been emptied or automatic deletion settings are enabled.

In modern macOS systems, access to the contents of the .Trash directory may be restricted during forensic acquisition, particularly when user data is protected by encryption and privacy controls. When relevant, investigators may need to acquire this data through alternative methods, such as accessing the Trash from a logged-in user context.

Time Machine backups

Users can create backups of their system and files using the macOS Time Machine application. If this feature has been used, you will find a property list file at `/Library/Preferences/com.apple.TimeMachine.plist` detailing the snapshots that were created, including dates of creation, whether the backups were encrypted, information pertaining to the storage drive used to store the backups, and the backup frequency if automatic backups are turned on. If unencrypted macOS backups are located, their contents can be analyzed directly.

Mobile Backups

Users may back up Apple iPhone content with macOS. Backups are stored at `~/Library/Application Support/MobileSync/Backup`. The user is given an option to encrypt these backups during the process. If you are able to obtain readable mobile backup content, mobile device analysis techniques (such as examining application data, message databases, call history, or media files) can be performed on the iOS data.

Synced Data

You are likely to encounter data that has been synced from accounts during analysis of any operating system, however, this is often more prevalent with macOS. Many macOS users sync data across a variety of Apple devices via their iCloud account and associated Apple ID, including call logs, iMessages, etc. The data related to these artifacts is often stored in SQLite databases, making analysis straightforward.

For this reason, be aware of the possibility that some artifacts in the macOS environment may not have been generated using the system you are examining – as this data may have originated from other devices such as an iPhone or iPad.

Keychains

Keychains are used to store keys, certificates, and passwords. The system keychain can be found at `/Library/Keychains/System.keychain` and access is protected by another file located at `/private/var/db/SystemKey` (protected system file). The content of this keychain can be accessed using an administrator account, but unfortunately recent macOS versions have taken further measures to protect the `SystemKey` file, which prevent it from being copied out.

The creation of a user account also generates a keychain which is stored for each account at `~/Library/Keychains/login.keychain-db` and is protected by the user login password by default, though this password can be changed by a user. This keychain is often used to store a variety of online account passwords, as well as passwords to encrypted backups and secure notes.

KnowledgeC and Biomes

KnowledgeC is an often-underutilized SQLite database in macOS forensics but can be extremely valuable for some investigations, as it captures granular details of various system, application, and user activity. This database is located in each user account at `~/Library/Application Support/Knowledge/knowledge.db`, and much of its useful data is stored in the `ZOBJECT` table. That said, Apple has begun migrating the data from KnowledgeC into Biomes. These artifacts will be covered more in the next chapter when we examine iOS.

Unified Logs

Apple unified logs retain a significant amount of detailed data related to system usage and processes. These logs have a `.tracev3` file extension and are stored at `/private/var/db/diagnostics` and `/private/var/db/uuidtext`. Unified logs are stored in binary format, so software must be used to make them readable, but they can be of significant value when investigating a compromised system. The volume of log data present on a system can reach millions of entries when parsed and the retention period can vary.

Tip

Following the macOS artifacts discussed previously, the following Linux artifacts are also commonly encountered during investigations and may provide valuable context or supporting evidence.

System Logging

Linux maintains log files that record system details. Located at `{root}/var/log` in Debian-based systems, the file `syslog` records global system activity, and the file `auth.log` records user events similar to Windows Security event logs.

The most recent events are appended to the end of each log file, with associated timestamps for each event recorded using the system time zone.

Cron

The Cron CLI utility in Linux can be used for scheduling automated tasks. If this has been used, you will find Cron jobs at `{root}/etc` within subdirectories starting with `cron` and titled based on task frequency (i.e. `cron.hourly`, `cron.daily`, `cron.weekly`, `cron.monthly`, and `cron.yearly`). Cron related messages may also be found within `{root}/var/log/syslog` or `{root}/var/log/cron.log`.

Snapshots

Just as a user can create system snapshots or backups in Microsoft Windows with VSS or Apple macOS with Time Machine, Linux also has such a utility. In Linux, snapshots may be created using tools such as **Timeshift**. If this service has been used, you will find the snapshots at the volume root, within `{root}/timeshift` (though users may also choose to store these on a separate or even removable volume), where there are various subdirectories containing log files based on the backup frequency. The snapshots subdirectory contains the actual data backups, which are maintained within folders titled with timestamps from when the snapshots were created.

Summary

Effective forensic analysis of macOS and Linux systems requires a clear understanding of how operating systems store and record user activity, system behavior, and application interactions. By examining key artifacts such as configuration files, shell history, cached thumbnails, and system logs, investigators can reconstruct user actions, identify system usage patterns, and validate investigative hypotheses. While artifact locations and implementations may vary between systems, the underlying analysis concepts remain consistent and allow investigators to adapt their approach across different environments.

At this point, you should be able to do the following:

- **Identify and examine common macOS and Linux artifacts** that record user activity, system configuration, and application usage.
- **Locate and interpret configuration files**, shell history, and other text-based artifacts to determine system state and user behavior.
- **Analyze cached thumbnail data** and validate file access through hash-based correlation techniques.
- **Understand the structure and limitations of artifacts** such as bash history and recognize when additional context (for example, timestamps) may or may not be available.
- **Recognize the value of system logging artifacts** and how they can support investigations involving user activity, system events, and potential compromise.
- **Apply consistent investigative techniques** across different operating systems, even when artifact locations and formats differ.

In the next chapter, we move from host-based artifact analysis to examining data from mobile devices, focusing on how user activity, application data, and system artifacts are stored and analyzed within iOS and Android environments.

Get this book's PDF copy, code bundle, and more

Note: Have your invoice handy. Purchases made directly from the Packt website don't require an invoice.

6

Apple iOS and Android

Digital evidence is increasingly concentrated on mobile devices, making smartphones one of the most valuable sources of forensic data available. This chapter turns our attention to the two dominant mobile platforms – Apple's proprietary iOS and the Linux-based Android, developed by Google as part of the AOSP (Android Open-Source Project). The patterns we learned in the previous chapter as we examined other Unix-like systems map directly to phones and tablets, but often with heavier emphasis on communications, location data, and synced artifacts. It is increasingly common to find the same data both locally on a device, synced across other mobile devices, and mirrored in online accounts or backups. Because of that, effective mobile work requires attention to where these artifacts come from so we can ensure we capture all meaningful evidence and accurately attribute each artifact.

iOS is tightly controlled and derived from the same Darwin foundations as macOS; modern versions use an APFS file system and favor file-based stores such as property lists and SQLite databases. iOS uses only two partitions, and analysis is focused on only the user partition where all user-related data lives, as opposed to the read-only system partition, which carries the OS framework. In iOS, we can enjoy consistency among each device we examine, which tends to change only minimally between most OS releases, with Apple restricting where third-party application developers can store data.

Android, by contrast, is an open, vendor-modified ecosystem built on a Linux kernel and gives developers much more freedom. That diversity can complicate exact file locations during analysis due to the sheer number of different Android implementations, but many core concepts are still shared: we will find a large number of plain-text configuration files and heavy use of SQLite databases, in addition to XML and JSON-formatted files. Android can use several different file systems and has numerous partitions, though analysis here is concentrated primarily on the data partition (and sometimes the sdcard partition) where the majority of user data is stored.

Because mobile evidence is so similar across mobile platforms, each recipe in this chapter follows the same pattern for both iOS and Android. We will examine device information, installed applications, user data and interactions, and then outline other important OS-specific artifacts.

In this chapter, we're going to cover the following main topics:

- Device information (iOS)
- Application data (iOS)
- User files (iOS)
- User interactions (iOS)
- Device information (Android)
- Application data (Android)
- User files (Android)
- User interactions (Android)

Technical requirements

For this chapter, you will need:

- A computer running Microsoft Windows to act as your forensic workstation – required for installing tools and running the exercises. Windows 11 is recommended. Ensure you have ample disk space for any forensic images you plan to work with.
- A basic familiarity with concepts related to data parsing, file systems, operating system behavior, and Apple iOS and Android filesystem structures. If you need a refresher, consult *Appendix A* of this book.
- Apple iOS and Android datasets for analysis. You may use the forensic images provided with the examples or create your own images for additional hands-on practice.
- FTK Imager (as used in previous chapters) or an alternative tool capable of browsing forensic images. For example, 7-Zip can be used with additional support (such as the Forensic7z plugin) to access forensic image contents, as introduced earlier in this book.
- DB Browser for SQLite and Xplist (as used in *Chapter 5*) for examining exported files and databases.

Device information (iOS)

Since iOS shares the same Darwin foundation as macOS, it also utilizes property list files to store configuration-related artifacts and system information. These plist files are often either XML or binary (bplist) format and are distributed throughout the system.

Though property list files can be found throughout iOS, many property lists related to device settings and information are stored within **Preferences** directories. Specifically, the following directory contains many high-value property lists:

`/private/var/mobile/Library/Preferences/`

For this recipe, we will use these property lists to find device and user identifiers, device setup details, and previously connected networks.

Getting ready

We will use the **Apple iOS** forensic image.

Just as we did when examining other forensic images, we will use FTK Imager (or another tool capable of browsing forensic images) to navigate and export items from our iOS acquisition.

We will then use `Xplist` to view the content of each property list file we export:

`https://github.com/ic005k/Xplist/releases`

How to do it...

1. Export the `com.apple.Preferences.plist` file located at **private | var | mobile | Library | Preferences** and open the file with `XPlist`. We can determine certain device preferences here, including a potential owner name:

Key	Type	Value
▼ plist	dict	
VSIdentityProviderAvailabilityStatus	integer	1
cachediCloudTitle	string	Leroy Jenkins

Figure 6.1 – Apple iOS preferences with potential device owner name

2. Repeat this process to view the `data_ark.plist` file located at `/private/var/root/Library/Lockdown/`. This file shows us additional device information, including the device name and time zone settings:

Key	Type	Value
▼ plist	dict	
-UseRaptorCerts	bool	true
-DeviceName	string	Leroy Jenkins's iPhone
com.apple.mobile.wireless_lockd(	bool	false
-ProtocolVersion	string	2
-TimeZone	string	America/Chicago

Figure 6.2 – Apple iOS device name and time zone settings

3. Export and view the `com.apple.homesharing.plist` file located at `/private/var/mobile/Library/Preferences/`. This file will tell us the associated Apple ID account:

Key	Type	Value
▼ plist	dict	
homeSharingDidSetDefaultAp...	bool	true
homeSharingAppleID	string	leroy.jenkins92@icloud.com

Figure 6.3 – Apple iOS associated Apple ID account

4. You will find the associated device phone number throughout various property list files and databases. One such property list file is `com.apple.commcenter.plist` located at `/private/var/wireless/Library/Preferences/`:

Key	Type	Value
▼ plist	dict	
▶ PersonalWallet	dict	
WaitingForActivationFlag	bool	false
EnhancedLQMDataTransferTimeRegistration	bool	false
PhoneNumber	string	15735902982

Figure 6.4 – Apple iOS associated device phone number

Although not shown in *Figure 6.4*, this same property list will also contain the last known ICCID for the device within the `LastKnownICCID` key if needed.

Note

Note that we can further corroborate this data and view previously inserted SIM information in the `subscriber_info` table of the `CellularUsage.db` database. This SQLite database can be found at `/private/var/wireless/`

> `Library/Databases/`, then exported and viewed using DB Browser for SQLite, as demonstrated in the previous chapter.

5. Turning to `com.apple.commcenter.device_specific_nobackup.plist`, also located at `/private/var/wireless/Library/Preferences/`, we will find the device's MEID and IMEI information:

Key	Type	Value
▾ plist	dict	
meid	string	35304111480805
kOperatorRoamingInfo_Subscriber_Mnc	string	480
▾ imeis	array	
▾ Item 1	dict	
second	string	353041114808055

Figure 6.5 – Apple iOS associated device MEID and IMEI

IMEI (**International Mobile Equipment Identity**) and **MEID** (**Mobile Equipment Identifier**) are unique device identifiers assigned to mobile devices. These values can be used to identify a specific device and correlate it with records from carriers, logs, or other data sources.

6. Some device information can also be found within log files, which can be easily exported and viewed in any text editor or directly using tools such as FTK Imager. As an example, export the file `general.log` from `private/var/logs/AppleSupport`.
7. Once exported, open the file using a text editor such as Notepad. You will see this log file provides several useful items, including the device serial number, operating system version, device model, and dates pertaining to when the device was first set up and last updated:

general.log

```
{"report":"Device Software Diagnostic Log",
"serial":"F17DJ0V50DY0",
"os_build":"iPhone OS 17.5.1 (21F90)",
"updated":"2024-06-13 19:28:36 -0500",
"model":"iPhone13,2","version":4,
"installed":"2024-06-13 19:28:36 -0500"}
```

Figure 6.6 – Apple iPhone device information

8. Further information to help corroborate the date and time of when the device was initially set up can be found by examining Purple Buddy, which is Apple's setup assistant application used when a device is first configured or reset. This data is stored in the `com.apple.purplebuddy.plist` file at `/private/var/mobile/Library/Preferences/` and shows the region that was selected during setup to help verify the device's time zone configuration in the `GuessedCountry` key. We can also see how the device was set up (for example, if it was restored from an iCloud backup) by looking at the `SetupState` key. In this case, we see a value showing that it was an iTunes setup, indicating the device was set up using the standard setup assistant and not restored from an iCloud backup:

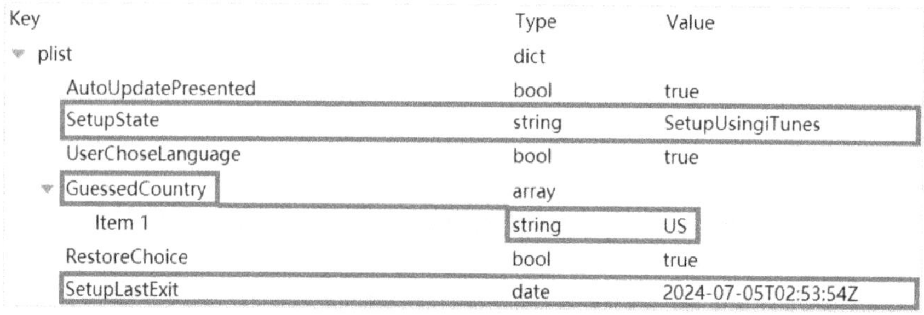

Key	Type	Value
plist	dict	
AutoUpdatePresented	bool	true
SetupState	string	SetupUsingiTunes
UserChoseLanguage	bool	true
GuessedCountry	array	
Item 1	string	US
RestoreChoice	bool	true
SetupLastExit	date	2024-07-05T02:53:54Z

Figure 6.7 – Apple iPhone Purple Buddy setup information

Note that the key for `SetupLastExit` also contains a date and time value; however, this value can change if the user chose to skip certain setup features until later.

9. When an iOS device connects to a wireless network, information about known wireless networks is stored in the `com.apple.wifi.known-networks.plist` file located at `/private/var/preferences/`. Export and view this file to see these networks:

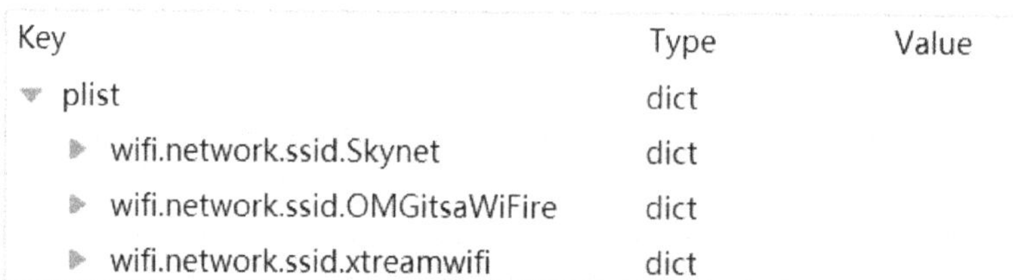

Key	Type	Value
plist	dict	
wifi.network.ssid.Skynet	dict	
wifi.network.ssid.OMGitsaWiFire	dict	
wifi.network.ssid.xtreamwifi	dict	

Figure 6.8 – Apple iOS connected wireless networks

From *Figure 6.8*, we can see this device has had previous connections to networks with SSIDs such as **Skynet**, **OMGitsaWiFire**, and **xtreamwifi**. Each one of these connections can be expanded to determine further information about the network to which it was connected.

How it works...

iOS keeps device-level metadata scattered across many small files rather than a single database. Property lists and a few compact SQLite databases are the primary stores: Property list (`plist`) files capture configuration and account settings (owner name, time zone, Apple ID), other logs often preserve physical device descriptors (serial number and model), and telephony-related files record certain usage details (IMEI/MEID, ICCID, phone number).

Remember that acquisition type and device protections will affect what files we are able to obtain and read—if something's missing, consider whether you need a more complete or advanced data acquisition method (such as full filesystem) before concluding the data doesn't exist.

Application data (iOS)

There are many preinstalled native applications common in iOS that you should be familiar with. User data for many iOS applications is commonly stored in databases at the following locations on modern iOS releases (though Apple has been known to make slight changes to the database names over time):

- **Contacts:** `/private/var/mobile/Library/AddressBook/AddressBook.sqlitedb`
- **Calendar:** `/private/var/mobile/Library/Calendar/Calendar.sqlitedb`
- **Call Logs:** `/private/var/mobile/Library/CallHistoryDB/CallHistory.storedata`
- **Voicemails:** `/private/var/mobile/Library/Voicemail/voicemail.db`
- **SMS/MMS and iMessages:** `/private/var/mobile/Library/SMS/sms.db`
- **Notes:** `/private/var/mobile/Library/Notes/notes.sqlite`
- **Photos metadata:** `/private/var/mobile/Media/PhotoData/Photos.sqlite`

Each of these databases is easily viewable using *DB Browser for SQLite*. As these databases are present on every iOS device, they are well researched and understood, making them easily parsed using various software tools as we will see in the next chapter of this book, which addresses analysis automation. Even so, it is important to know the location of these databases, as automated tools will not always parse all the data present within a database, and we should always manually review artifacts of evidentiary value to extrapolate additional data and verify findings.

In addition to these databases, applications will also have associated plist files, which are typically used to store application settings. Furthermore, user files and cached data are typically stored in directories referenced by these databases. This typically leaves three key areas to examine:

- App databases
- Associated configuration files
- File storage directories (user and cached)

When a third-party application is installed, three directories are created to act as containers and are named using a **UUID** (**Universally Unique Identifier**):

- **Bundle:** `/private/var/containers/Bundle/Application/<UUID>`
- **Data:** `/private/var/mobile/Containers/Data/Application/<UUID>`
- **Shared:** `/private/var/mobile/Containers/Shared/AppGroup/<UUID>`

The UUID is different for each container even though it is for the same application. This is all done to sandbox the application's data and help protect access. This means the UUID is also different for the same application installed on another device, and you cannot rely on the UUID to identify a specific app.

For this recipe, we will explore how application data is stored across these locations and why it may sometimes be absent.

Getting ready

We will use the **Apple iOS** forensic image and continue browsing the file system while exporting relevant files.

This recipe will involve property list (plist) files and SQLite databases, so ensure both Xplist and DB Browser for SQLite (`https://sqlitebrowser.org/dl/`) are available to view the exported data.

How to do it...

1. First, let's examine what applications are installed on the device. We'll look at `applicationState.db`, located at `/private/var/mobile/Library/FrontBoard/` to do this. This database records certain data about applications that have been launched. Export the database (including the associated `-shm` and `-wal` files), then open it in read-only mode using DB Browser for SQLite (*Ctrl* + *Shift* + *O*). Once opened, select the **Browse Data** tab and view the `application_identifier_tab` table:

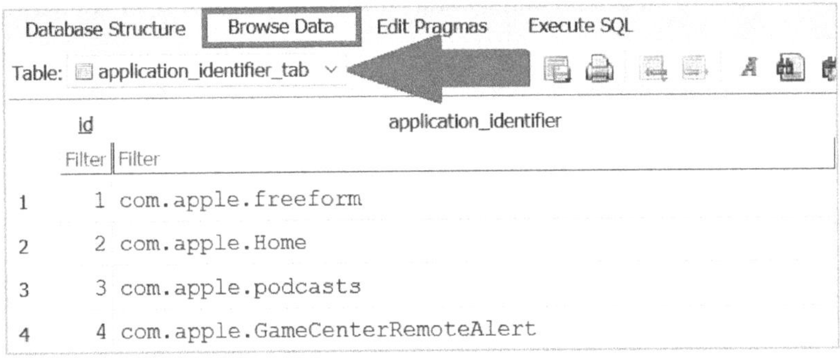

Figure 6.9 – Apple iOS apps shown in applicationState.db

2. The `application_identifier` column shows the Bundle ID of each application. Note that iOS native applications begin with `com.apple`. Knowing this, we can filter for third-party applications that are present on the device. Right-click the **Filter** field and choose **Set Filter Expression** > **Not containing...**, then type `com.apple` to filter out all native Bundle IDs, leaving us with just the third-party applications present:

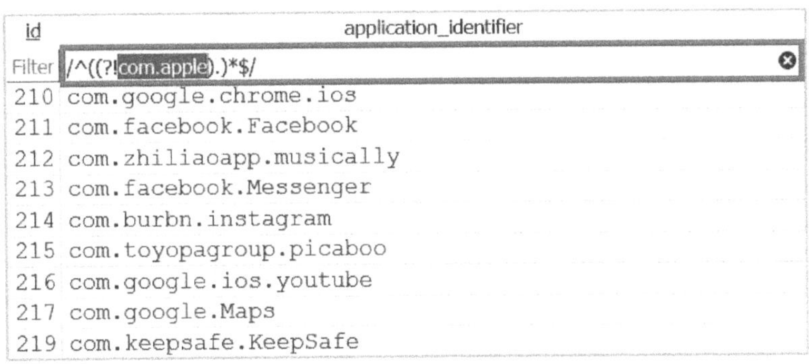

Figure 6.10 – Filtering for third-party apps in applicationState.db

> **Note**
>
> Note that while some of these Bundle IDs are rather obvious (com.google.chrome.ios, com.facebook.Facebook), not all are. This is because many applications undergo name changes by the developer if they choose to rebrand their app, but the original Bundle ID is maintained because changing it would break application dependencies and provide no user-facing benefit. In *Figure 6.10*, we can see this with `com.zhiliaoapp.musically` (TikTok) and `com.toyopagroup.picaboo` (Snapchat).

3. Now that we know what applications we can expect to find in our dataset, let's see how the data is stored. The first container we will look at stores the application binary and is located at `/private/var/containers/Bundle/Application/<UUID>`. Inside each container is a subdirectory that helps identify the application.
   Examine the container for `2D388564-5356-4E59-A38B-05DE82911E81` and you will see that it is associated with the Snapchat application:

Figure 6.11 – Apple iOS application directory for Snapchat bundle container

> **Tip**
>
> Within each of these more 'friendly named' subdirectories, you will find a property list titled `Info.plist`. Examining this plist file will give you more information about the application, such as the installed version as shown within the `CFBundleVersion` key.

4. If the app was third-party installed, there will be an `iTunesMetadata.plist` file in the main container. Export this file from the current Snapchat container and view it using `Xplist`. This file provides the date and time the application was originally downloaded (or *purchased*—even if the app was free) from the iTunes store (in UTC) and the account associated with that download:

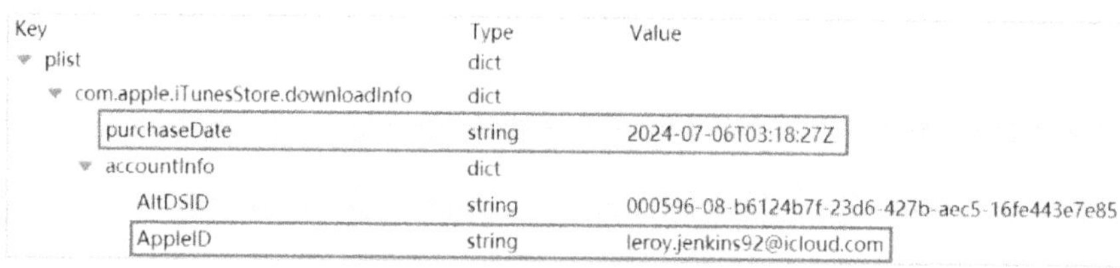

Figure 6.12 – Apple iOS application purchase date and account

5. The next container we will examine is located at `/private/var/mobile/Containers/Data/Application/<UUID>`. This container is where a significant amount of forensically relevant data is stored for an installed application, including databases for third-party apps. This is a sandboxed environment, so other applications cannot access

the data stored here. This is also where you will notice less consistency in how and where items are stored, as that is left up to each app's developers.

Within the `<UUID>` folder, locate UUID `E465FD6D-49E9-4E21-90BE-E53A389FBFD6`, which is associated with the Snapchat application (we can confirm this by examining the `.com.apple.mobile_container_manager.metadata.plist`). Notice that this container has a different UUID than the one in the previous location:

Figure 6.13 – Apple iOS application for Snapchat data container

Within this container, examine common application data locations such as the **Documents**, **Library**, and **tmp** directories. These locations often contain user-generated content, cached data, and application databases, depending on how the application stores its data.

6. The final container we will examine is located (with its own unique UUID) at `/private/var/mobile/Containers/Shared/AppGroup/<UUID>`. This container is unique because it exists outside the sandbox, making it less restricted for developers and allowing them to share data across other apps. User data may also be found here, though how it is stored is determined by the developer.

   Locate the container with UUID `599588E9-F80E-4178-BB6C-F942795021F4`, which is also associated with the Snapchat application and can be confirmed by examining the related `.com.apple.mobile_container_manager.metadata.plist` file:

Figure 6.14 – Apple iOS application for Snapchat Shared container

In exploring the last two application locations, you may have noticed there is little data present, where we would typically expect to find user data. This is often indicative of an application that has been installed but minimally used or never actively interacted with.

From an investigative standpoint, the absence of expected data can itself be meaningful, helping differentiate between installed applications and those actively used by the user.

7. When an application is used in the iOS environment, especially when used for the first time, the user will receive prompts requesting that they allow certain permissions, such as access to the device photo gallery, user contacts, microphone, and more. These settings are stored in the **Transparency, Consent, and Control** (**TCC**) database located at `/private/var/mobile/Library/TCC/`.

   Export `TCC.db` (along with its associated `-shm` and `-wal` files) and open it as read-only with **DB Browser for SQLite**. Navigate to the `access` table:

client	client_type	auth_value	auth_reason
Filter	Filter	Filter	Filter
com.google.chrome.ios	0	2	5
com.facebook.Facebook	0	2	4
com.facebook.Messenger	0	2	4
com.burbn.instagram	0	2	4
com.apple.Music	0	2	4
com.google.Maps	0	2	2
com.apple.news	0	2	5
com.keepsafe.KeepSafe	0	2	4

Figure 6.15 – Apple iOS access table from the TCC database

   For each application client in this table, you will notice an `auth_value` field that represents the permission state for each application. In the example above, all values are set to 2, which in modern iOS indicates that these applications have full access to the requested permissions. A value of `0` indicates access was denied, whereas a value of 3 indicates limited access.

   The `auth_reason` indicates how the permissions were authorized. Common values include 2 for user-granted consent authorizations, 4 for permissions granted by the system, and 5 for permissions granted as part of a system service policy.

How it works...

iOS installs applications within a sandboxed structure consisting of three container types: the *Bundle* container (contains the app binary needed for installation), the *Data* container (used to store application data such as databases, preferences, and caches) and optionally a *Shared* container (used for cross-app sharing). Each container directory is named with a UUID generated at install time, so the folder name alone is not sufficient to identify the application; you must examine the related metadata to determine which container is associated with a specific application (e.g., `applicationState.db` for Bundle IDs, `Info.plist` in the Bundle container, or `com.apple.mobile_container_manager.metadata.plist` in the Data container). As we saw with Snapchat, an app can be present but unused, resulting in a lack of user artifacts within these containers.

Application artifacts are primarily stored in property lists and SQLite databases, and while Apple enforces this sandboxed structure, developers decide what each app stores inside its containers. Be aware that some files are protected by iOS data protection, which is tied to the device passcode, and may be inaccessible without the appropriate keys. We can learn what permissions each application has been granted by examining the TCC database.

In practice, investigators rarely rely solely on manual navigation of these containers, but understanding their structure is critical for validating automated results or investigating less common scenarios.

User files (iOS)

User files reside in several locations under `/private/var/mobile/` and within each application's sandbox. These are the actual photos, videos, documents, downloads, and app files users create and access on the device. Because many users sync content (via iCloud Photos, iCloud Drive, app sync, backups, etc.), we often need to determine whether an item is stored locally, exists only in the cloud, or has been synced.

In this recipe, we will explore how to follow these artifacts and determine this information when needed.

Getting ready

We will use the **Apple iOS** forensic image and continue to browse the filesystem, exporting files of interest for examination using *DB Browser for SQLite*.

How to do it...

In the last recipe, we discussed the locations of several native iOS application databases, including `Photos.sqlite`. This database stores metadata about each media asset in iOS but does not contain the media files themselves. Rather, the actual media files are stored at /private/var/mobile/Media/DCIM/.

1. Navigate to this directory, where you will observe multiple subdirectories. These subdirectories are named using a numeric prefix starting at `100`, followed by `APPLE`, in the format of `100APPLE`, `101APPLE`, `102APPLE`, etc.

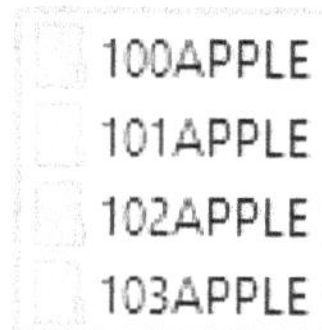

Figure 6.16 – Apple iOS media file storage directories

> **Note**
>
> Once the original `100APPLE` directory reaches 1,000 media files, the `101APPLE` directory is created to store the next 1,000 media files, regardless of whether these files are photographs or videos.

2. Examine the `###APPLE` directories and you will find the individual media files stored by the user, each filename beginning with `IMG_` and followed by a four-digit number starting at `0100`. This results in a sequential naming format of `IMG_0001`, `IMG_0002`, `IMG_0003`, etc. (There is no differentiation between photographs and videos with this naming convention; file type must instead be determined by examining file extensions, signatures, or associated metadata):

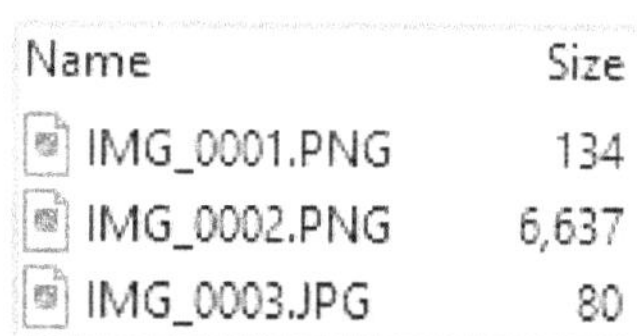

Figure 6.17 – Apple iOS stored media files

You will often find a variety of files within these storage locations, including photographs that were created using the integrated camera of the device, screenshots, downloaded media files, and files shared via Airdrop, etc.

Note

Where did this file come from?

If media files from numerous sources are all stored in the same directories, you might be wondering how to differentiate them. Remember, we are just looking at the storage directories right now. Don't forget about the `Photos.sqlite` database—this database contains metadata that will provide the information needed to determine the origin of the media files present on a device. Automated forensic analysis tools will often coordinate all this data into a single view to make navigation much easier.

3. Review the ordering numbers of these files and notice that `IMG_0039` is missing. This occurs because iOS does not reuse file names once files are deleted, resulting in gaps in the numbering sequence. As a result, directories may contain fewer files than their maximum capacity suggests.

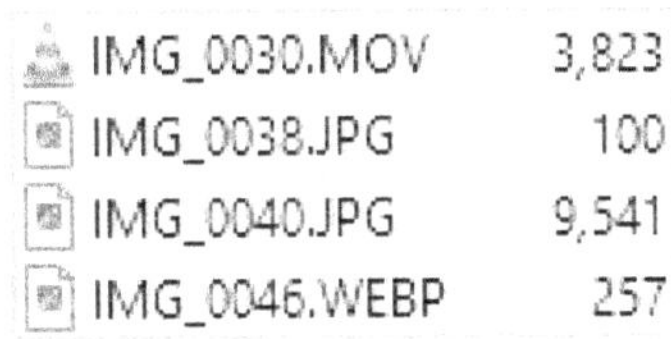

Figure 6.18 – Apple iOS missing media files

Note

It should be noted that once the four-digit filename limit is reached in iOS, the last file will be named `IMG_9999` and will be stored to the `109APPLE` directory. Once this occurs, the directory naming convention continues with `110APPLE` and the files stored in this directory restart at `IMG_0001`, `IMG_0002`, `IMG_0003`, etc.

4. As with many other operating systems, thumbnails are also created for each stored media file in iOS. Thumbnails are stored within directories located at `/private/var/mobile/Media/PhotoData/Thumbnails/V2`. Navigate to this location, where you can view thumbnail representations of each file. Each thumbnail is saved as a JPEG file titled `5005.jpg`:

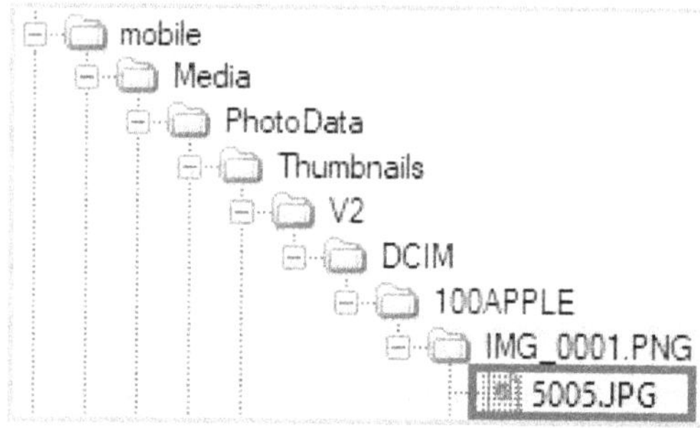

Figure 6.19 – Apple iOS thumbnail file

Note

Similarly, you will also find cached video frame thumbnails stored as JPEG files titled `LocalVideoKeyFrame` within subdirectories named for each file at `/private/var/mobile/Media/PhotoData/Thumbnails/VideoKeyFrames/DCIM`.

Additional cached thumbnails may also be present within the `PhotoData` directory depending on device usage, such as subdirectory `CPL`, which is used for media files that were synced from an associated iCloud account, or at `/private/var/mobile/Library/SMS/Attachments` if media was sent using the native Messages application.

5. When a user deletes a media file in iOS, the file is sent to the trash and remains recoverable for approximately 30 days by default. After this, both the original file and the associated thumbnail are permanently deleted. From a user perspective, these trashed files can be accessed from the **Recently Deleted** album in the native iOS Photos application. From a forensic perspective, however, these files are not actually moved to a new location as we might expect. Instead, they are instead marked for deletion within the `Photos.sqlite` database.

   Navigate to `/private/var/mobile/Media/PhotoData/` and export `Photos.sqlite` along with its associated `-shm` and `-wal` files. Open this database using **DB Browser for SQLite** and go to the **ZASSET** (or **ZGENERICASSET** in some iOS versions) table. If a file is marked for deletion, the `ZTRASHEDSTATE` field will contain a value of `1`, whereas files that are not marked for deletion will contain a value of `0`:

ZTRASHEDREASON	ZTRASHEDSTATE	ZVIDEOCPDURATIONVALUE	ZVIDEOCPVISIBILITYSTATE
Filter	Filter	Filter	Filter
0	0	0	0
0	0	2753333333	0
0	0	2651666667	0
0	0	0	0
1	1	0	0

Figure 6.20 – Determining whether a media file has been marked for deletion in iOS

This allows investigators to identify media the user intended to delete before it is permanently removed from the device.

> **Note**
>
> Photos.sqlite is an extremely comprehensive database. In the next chapter, we will use automated tools (iLEAPP) to parse this database and extract relevant artifacts.

6. For management of other user files, iOS uses the **Files** app, which allows documents and files to be saved and navigated via a folder structure. The **Files** app can be used for both locally stored content and content located in iCloud or other third-party cloud services such as Dropbox and Google Drive. While the **Files** app presents a familiar file system view similar to a traditional computer, it is still an application, and its data is stored like any other application (within the containers discussed earlier).
   We will look specifically at iCloud items, which may include files that have been synced to the device. Navigate to `/private/var/mobile/Library/MobileDocuments/`, where you will see several subdirectories for items that can be stored in iCloud:

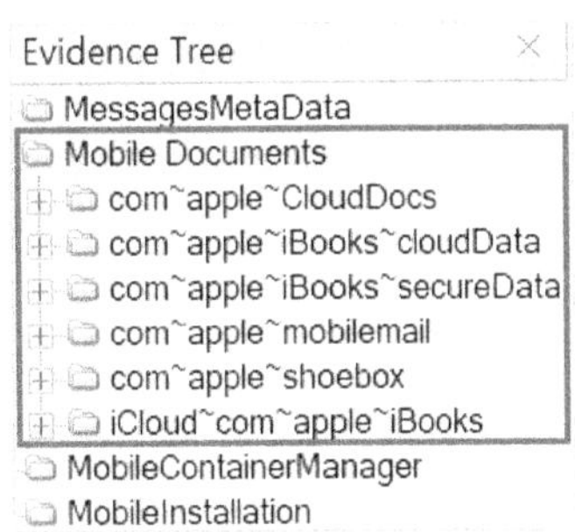

Figure 6.21 – Storage location of iCloud files

If a file is stored in iCloud and synced to the device, you will find it within these subdirectories. Since the **Files** app has its own version of **Trash**, you may also find a **Trash** folder, whereas the absence of a **Trash** folder typically indicates the user has not deleted any iCloud items from the device. Metadata for items that have not been synced may still be present, though the actual file content will not be available—these metadata files are named after the original file but use the .icloud extension.

This can indicate the presence of cloud-based evidence even when the full file content is not available on the device.

7. To help determine what files may exist locally versus those stored in iCloud, there are two databases we can reference, both stored at the same location. Navigate to `/private/var/mobile/Library/ApplicationSupport/CloudDocs/session/db/` and export the `server.db` and `client.db` databases (along with their associated `-shm` and `-wal` files).

   Open the `client.db` database using **DB Browser for SQLite** and go to the `client_items` table, where we can see each filename along with associate epoch dates. While there are several system folders present here, the only user file we see is `pexels-egos68-1906658.jpg`. Since we are exploring the `client.db` database, this file is present on the device and available locally:

item_filename	item_birthtime	item_lastusedtime
Downloads	1720234004	0
pexels-egos68-1906658.jpg	1720234004	1724194456
Documents	1720235907	0
Documents	1720235909	0

Figure 6.22 – Locally stored items detailed in the client.db database

8. Now open the **server.db** database using *DB Browser for SQLite* and go to the `server_items` table. Here you will see the same `pexels-egos68-1906658.jpg` file as before. `Server.db` details items stored in iCloud, and this item is cross-referenced between both databases because it exists both locally on the device and within iCloud:

item_filename	item_birthtime	item_lastusedtime
UbiquitousCards	1720148045	0
Downloads	1720234004	0
pexels-egos68-1906658.jpg	1720234004	1724194456

Figure 6.23 – iCloud stored items detailed in the server.db database

9. Now go to the `devices` table of the `server.db` database, where you will find the only item listed has a name of `iPhone`. There will typically be at least one item here (the items you are examining), though multiple items may also appear if the user has other devices synced with the same iCloud account. Given that we see none, we can be less concerned with the possibility of synced data from other devices appearing in what we examine:

key	name
Filter	Filter
1	iPhone

Figure 6.24 – Devices shown by server.db as synced with iCloud

How it works...

iOS stores user media (photos, videos, screenshots) in the familiar DCIM folder under `/private/var/mobile/Media/DCIM/` using the `###APPLE` directories and `IMG_####` filename pattern, with extensive metadata maintained within the `Photos.sqlite` database. Thumbnails for these files are cached separately under `/private/var/mobile/Media/PhotoData/Thumbnails/V2` for quick previewing, though iOS has become more aggressive with cleaning thumbnails out when the original file is deleted, so persistence of these cached files is less reliable in more recent OS releases.

The Files app and iCloud adds another layer: iCloud items are represented by metadata and sync databases (`client.db` and `server.db`) and by `.icloud` placeholder files in `MobileDocuments` when the item is not locally stored to the device. Correlating `client.db` (locally available items) with `server.db` (iCloud data) lets you determine whether an item is local, synced, or cloud-only.

User interactions (iOS)

iOS retains extremely detailed device logging that captures a wide range of user interactions. These artifacts allow investigators to reconstruct detailed timelines of device usage, including when the device was active, what actions occurred, and which applications were in use.

The availability of this data is highly time-dependent, as many of these logs are volatile and persist only for a limited period. In practice, investigators should expect PowerLog artifacts to typically persist for several days up to approximately one week, KnowledgeC and Biomes data for up to around 30 days, and certain cached system data for roughly one week.

Because these artifacts require full filesystem access, they are typically only available through advanced acquisition methods, often performed using commercial forensic tools (such as Cellebrite Premium or Magnet GrayKey/Verakey) capable of obtaining full filesystem extractions.

In this recipe, we will examine these key sources of user activity.

Getting ready

We will use the **Apple iOS** forensic image and continue browsing the filesystem while exporting files of interest to examine using **DB Browser for SQLite**.

How to do it...

1. PowerLog information is designed to track data related to device power consumption and can be found in the CurrentPowerlog.PLSQL database, located at:

   /private/var/containers/Shared/SystemGroup/<UUID>/Library/BatteryLife

   Using the example acquisition data, the UUID needed to locate this database is B9083441-B0E3-4FCE-A0C9-6ECE1D272BFB.

   Navigate to this location and export the database (along with its associated -shm and -wal files), then open the database with DB Browser for SQLite. Note that you will need to change your selection to *All files* to see the appropriate database when attempting to open it, as the .PLSQL extension is not automatically recognized by DB Browser for SQLite:

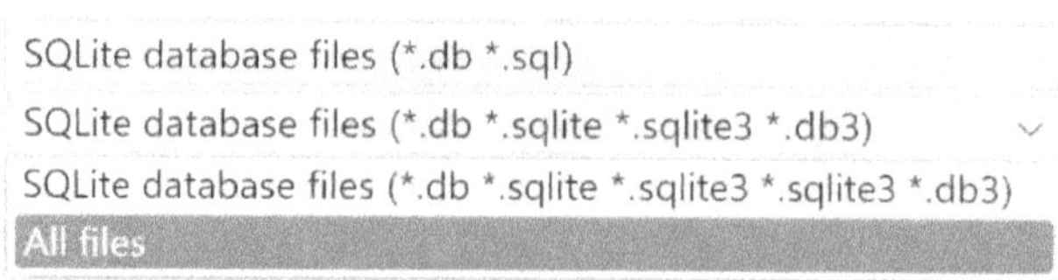

Figure 6.25 – Selecting All files to recognize the database in DB Browser for SQLite

2. Navigate to the `BatteryMetrics_Battery_1_2` table. Here you will find the various battery percentages for any given date and time, along with a field titled `IsCharging`, where a value of `0` indicates the device is not attached to a charger and a value of `1` indicates it is actively charging. The timestamp shown uses an epoch time – SQLite can easily convert this timestamp into a readable format by simply right-clicking the timestamp field, choosing **Edit display format**, and choosing the correct conversion from the drop-down menu (which in this case is Unix):

ID ▾	timestamp	IsCharging	Level
Filter	Filter	Filter	Filter
18046	2024-09-09 23:24:52	1	85
18045	2024-09-09 23:24:32	1	84
18044	2024-09-09 23:24:12	1	84

Figure 6.26 – Apple iOS Powerlog database showing battery charging

In the example above we can see the device was being actively charged and went from a battery level of 84 percent to 85 percent on the date shown.

> **Note**
>
> My phone died
>
> During a homicide investigation I worked, call detail records obtained from the mobile service provider showed the suspect's cell phone appeared to have been turned off during the time of the murder. When being interviewed, the suspect claimed his phone battery had simply run out of power. A quick check of the battery metrics showed otherwise, and additional logs proved he had powered off the device prior to committing the murder.

3. Additional tables within this database can also provide insight into other device activity related to battery consumption (such as camera activations, app usage, etc.). Though we will see much of this same information in other databases, PowerLog can be used to validate multiple sources for the same event. It also contains additional records beyond battery usage statistics.
   As an example, go to the table titled `PLCameraAgent_EventForward_Torch`. (The **Torch** in iOS refers to the device camera flash when it is used as a flashlight.) Here you can determine dates and times showing when the device's flash was activated:

timestamp	BundleId	Level
2024-07-14 22:56:47	[illegible]	0
2024-09-09 23:07:09	[illegible]	1
2024-09-09 23:07:16	[illegible]	0

Figure 6.27 – Apple iOS Powerlog database showing flash usage

In this context, the `Level` value follows boolean logic, where a value of `1` indicates that the flash was active and `0` indicates that it was not.

Note that some applications may also activate the flash. When this occurs, the associated `BundleId` field will typically identify the responsible application, meaning this does not always indicate that the user manually enabled Torch.

4. If we do not need as detailed information as battery usage statistics, then power event logs are a good and quick place to check. Unlike the previous power log database, power event information can also persist longer. The first set of logs is at `/private/var/mobile/Library/Logs/mobileactivationd/` and titled `mobileactivationd.log`. This can be read in plain text, though interpreting it can be confusing at first. Navigate to this file and scroll down through the log until you see a section that reads **Mobile Activation Startup**. This signifies an event where the device was powered on, and the date and time in UTC can be seen on the corresponding line item. There will likely be numerous entries like this, each showing the date of power on events:

```
Thu Jul 4 21:53:59 2024 [145] MA: -[Mob:Daemon issueClientCertificateWithRefere::c
Fri Jul 5 21:08:44 2024 [147] MA: main: ________ Mobile Activation Startup ________
Fri Jul 5 21:08:47 2024 [147] MA: main: build_version: 21F90
Fri Jul 5 21:08:47 2024 [147] MA: main: internal_build: false
Fri Jul 5 21:08:47 2024 [147] MA: main: uid: 0
Fri Jul 5 21:08:47 2024 [147] MA: main: user_name: root
```

Figure 6.28 – Apple iOS device power-on event

5. To determine events where the device was powered off, we can look for the `logd.0.log` file at `/private/var/db/diagnostics/`. Like the previous log, this log file can be read in plain text. Each time the device is powered-off, an entry reading **No userlevel firehose clients left** is generated, along with the corresponding date and time. You can easily search for each one of these events to determine dates and times in which the device has been powered off:

```
2024-07-04 21:55:50-0500 logd[32]:Error connecting to logd_helper: Connection invalid
2024-07-04 21:55:50-0500 logd[32]:Error connecting to logd_helper: Connection invalid
2024-07-04 21:55:52-0500 logd[32]:No userlevel firehose clients left
2024-07-05 21:08:38-0500 logd[32]:libtrace_kic=0
2024-07-05 21:08:38-0500 logd[32]:_read_kernel_uuid calling _logd_uuiddb_harvest_kernel
2024-07-05 21:08:38-0500 logd[32]:assertion failed: 21F90: logd + 102064 [5674513D-7522
```

Figure 6.29 – Apple iOS device power-off event

6. Now, let's look at `KnowledgeC`. This database tracks a huge number of user interactions. Navigate to `/private/var/mobile/Library/CoreDuet/knowledge/` and export the `knowledgeC.db` database. Open this database using **DB Browser for SQLite** and navigate to the `ZOBJECT` table. Within the `ZSTREAMNAME` field of this table you will see listings for various activities including certain app usage events, when the screen turns on or is backlit, when the device becomes locked and requires a passcode to regain access again, and more:

ZVALUEINTEGER	ZCREATIONDATE	ZSTREAMNAME	ZVALUESTRING
Filter	Filter	Filter	Filter
0	2024-08-20 23:22:30	/display/isBacklit	
1	2024-08-20 23:22:33	/device/isLocked	
-4957155955735585612	2024-08-20 23:22:36	/app/usage	com.apple.Preferences
2957788248955960870	2024-08-20 23:23:02	/app/usage	com.apple.camera
1	2024-08-20 23:23:02	/display/isBacklit	
0	2024-08-20 23:23:02	/device/isLocked	
0	2024-08-20 23:23:03	/display/isBacklit	

Figure 6.30 – Events from Apple iOS KnowledgeC database

You will notice in the `ZSTREAMNAME` field from the example above there are entries for `/display/isBacklit` and `/device/isLocked`.

Pay special attention here, as these fields need to be compared to the `ZVALUEINTEGER` field to determine the correct status. The `ZSTREAMNAME` value identifies the type of event being recorded (for example, whether the system is tracking screen backlight or lock status), while the actual state (true or false) is determined by the corresponding `ZVALUEINTEGER` value.

So, from the example above, we can see the first entry shows that the device `isBacklit` with a value of `0` for false, signifying that the screen was not illuminated during this time. The second entry shows `isLocked` with a value of `1` for true, meaning that the device was in a locked state at that time. Moving down the list, we can see an entry where the device shows `isLocked` with a value of `0` (false) at `23:23:02` hours, showing a successful unlock and user access to the device.

This information can be used to construct a timeline showing when a device was used, including periods where the device was unlocked and accessible to the user. Combined with app usage data, we can show when a device was accessed and precisely what apps were used.

With more recent releases of iOS, you will notice KnowledgeC data is tracking fewer interactions. This is because Apple has started moving this information into a new format, known as Biomes. This data is located at `/private/var/mobile/Library/Biome/streams/restricted/`, where each activity type is retained within an appropriately named subdirectory. Apple stores Biomes within a proprietary format (SEGB, or SEGB version 2 in modern iOS), and the only way to read this data is by parsing protobuf data from the SEGB binaries. Modern forensic automation tools will do this work for us, as we will see in the next chapter.

> **Note**
>
> Thanks for the criminal activity timeline you created for me!
>
> Between Apple iOS power logs, KnowledgeC, and Biomes, pretty much everything a user does with an Apple iPhone is recorded in extreme detail. During an investigation I worked on, an iPhone was provided for analysis where the device user was suspected of stealing a car. Piecing together user activity:
>
> Location data showed that he traveled to the victim's residence on the date and time when the car was stolen.
>
> Biomes showed he placed his phone into **Airplane Mode** in an apparent attempt to prevent location tracking (side note: that doesn't work!)
>
> Power logs showed he used the device flashlight during the time the car was being stolen.
>
> Connection logs showed he synced the device via **Bluetooth** to the stolen car as he drove it away.
>
> Further location data showed where he took the car and when he turned **Airplane Mode** back off. Thanks for documenting all of that!

7. Lastly, iOS retains a significant amount of location information. When attempting to determine whether a device was at a location during a specific time, it is important to first understand where the location information is being recorded to ensure accurate interpretation of the data.

For example, if a user receives a photograph that contains location data, we may see these coordinates during analysis, but this does not necessarily mean the examined device was ever physically present at that location.

GPS data detailing iOS device locations is stored in the `cache.db` database located at `/private/var/mobile/Library/Caches/com.apple.routined/`, which is a highly reliable location source. Export this database and open it with **DB Browser for SQLite**. Navigate to the table titled `ZRTCLLOCATIONMO`:

ZALTITUDE	ZLATITUDE	ZLONGITUDE	ZSPEED	ZTIMESTAMP
Filter	Filter	Filter	Filter	Filter
235.403625488281	38.9523496153196	-92.329794075426	0.0	746492979.356357
240.877563476563	38.9523314265897	-92.3297933210547	0.0	746492981.269606
239.348999023438	38.9523442928111	-92.3298163712885	0.0	746492980.271127
239.576843261719	38.9523425745209	-92.3297907226648	0.0	746492982.270665
239.576843261719	38.9523425745209	-92.3297907226647	-1.0	746493985.319964
239.569885253906	38.9067253237952	-92.2923750803734	36.5900001525879	746494912.301116
169.08154296875	38.9083780255531	-92.2932370752956	-1.0	746494907.400766
234.97119140625	38.9070218755295	-92.2925717198218	36.6300010681152	746494911.302831

Figure 6.31 – Apple iOS location information from cache.db

Here you will find extremely detailed location data, including latitude, longitude, altitude, perceived accuracies (measured in meters), associated timestamps, and even the speed (measured in meters per second) at which the device was traveling when the coordinates were recorded. *The example shown is a partial view and does not include all available columns.*

How it works...

iOS records user interactions across several logging methods. Power and hardware-related events (battery levels, charger state, torch on/off, camera usage, etc.) are captured in PowerLog databases and related plain-text power logs, which are optimized for troubleshooting and thus have relatively short retention (days).

Richer behavioral events (app focus, screen on/backlight, lock/unlock) are stored in KnowledgeC, which is gradually being migrated into Biomes with more recent iOS releases. These records tend to persist for around one month.

The primary iOS location cache (cache.db) supplies authoritative geolocation data that tends to get recorded multiple times per minute but only persists for approximately one week.

Because these artifacts span different formats and retention windows, reliable timelines require expedient acquisition and validation.

Device information (android)

Jumping into Android, you will notice the same pattern—much like the similarities seen between macOS and iOS, similarities will emerge between Linux and Android. One of those consistencies is Android's use of plain-text and XML configuration files scattered throughout the filesystem. Modern versions of Android will also often use Android Binary XML (AXML/ABX) format.

In this recipe, we will look at some of the most common configuration files often seen in Android to help determine information about the device, including user attribution. Unlike iOS, however, there are a huge number of Android variations between many manufacturers, so the artifacts we see are not always in the same location on all devices. Additionally, an artifact recorded on one Android device may not be present on other Android devices.

Getting ready

We will use the Android forensic image and continue to browse and export items from our Android acquisition as needed to view them using **DB Browser for SQLite**.

How to do it...

1. Navigate to the `/system/` directory. We can quickly identify basic device information by examining the `build.prop` file, including the device manufacturer, model, Android version, and indicators of biometric protection (such as fingerprint access):

```
# begin common build properties
ro.system.build.date=Wed Sep 29 00:08:46 KST 2021
ro.system.build.date.utc=1632841726
ro.system.build.fingerprint=samsung/o1qsqw/o1q:11/RP1A.200720.012/G991USQS4AUIN
ro.system.build.id=RP1A.200720.012
ro.system.build.version.release=11
ro.system.build.version.release_or_codename=11
ro.system.build.version.sdk=30
ro.product.system.manufacturer=samsung
ro.product.system.model=SM-G991U
```

Figure 6.32 – Basic device information found in build.prop file

2. Now go to `/data/user_de/0/com.samsung.android.fmm/shared_prefs`. Within the file titled `com.sec.pcw.device.xml`, we can see the device IMEI, the ICCID of the inserted SIM, and an associated e-mail address for the device user:

```
<?xml version="1.0" encoding="utf-8" standalone="yes" ?>
<map>
  <string name="pref_acc_info">{"accessToken":"aDcPjYNonooIOZ4","authServerUrl":"us-
   auth2.samsungosp.com","cntCode":"USA","deviceId":"IMEI:350336264458286","email":"leroyjinks87@gmail.com",
   "mcc":"313","remoteControl":true,"serverUrl":"www.ospserver.net","userId":"10h97iwgdb"}
   </string>
  <string name="offline_noti">Y</string>
  <string name="SIM_SLOT_1">89011004300056709265</string>
  <string name="IS_FMM_LITE">N</string>
</map>
```


Figure 6.33 – Additional device information stored in XML file

The `com.sec.pcw.device.xml` artifact is specific to Samsung devices, though other manufacturers often have similar artifacts.

The device phone number can also be found in the `SimCard.dat` file located at `/data/system/`, labeled as `CurrentSimPhoneNumber=`:


```
00000330  6C 0A 43 75 72 72 65 6E 74 53 69 6D 43 6F 75 6E  l.CurrentSimCoun
00000340  74 72 79 49 73 6F 3D 75 73 0A 43 75 72 72 65 6E  tryIso=us.Curren
00000350  74 53 69 6D 4F 70 65 72 61 74 6F 72 3D 33 31 33  tSimOperator=313
00000360  31 30 30 0A 43 75 72 72 65 6E 74 53 69 6D 4F 70  100.CurrentSimOp
00000370  65 72 61 74 6F 72 4E 61 6D 65 3D 0A 43 75 72 72  eratorName=.Curr
00000380  65 6E 74 53 69 6D 53 65 72 69 61 6C 4E 75 6D 62  entSimSerialNumb
00000390  65 72 3D 38 39 30 31 31 30 30 34 33 30 30 30 35  er=8901100430005
000003A0  36 37 30 39 32 36 35 0A 43 75 72 72 65 6E 74 53  6709265.CurrentS
000003B0  69 6D 50 68 6F 6E 65 4E 75 6D 62 65 72 3D 31 35  imPhoneNumber=15
000003C0  37 33 32 32 38 34 30 35 36 0A 53 69 6D 43 68 61  732284056.SimCha
000003D0  6E 67 65 54 69 6D 65 3D 31 37 32 35 35 36 39 36  ngeTime=17255696
000003E0  38 36 38 36 31 0A 53 69 6D 43 68 61 6E 67 65 4F  86861.SimChangeO
000003F0  70 65 72 61 74 69 6F 6E 3D 33 0A                 peration=3.
```


Figure 6.34 – Android device current phone number

In addition to the device phone number, the SIM ICCID (a unique identifier assigned to the SIM card) is labeled as `CurrentSimSerialNumber=`, and an epoch timestamp indicating when the SIM was inserted is labeled as `SimChangeTime=`.

3. Another more consistent place to check for SIM related information in Android is the `telephony.db` database. This can be found in the filesystem at `/data/user_de/0/com.android.providers.telephony/databases/`. Export this database and open it using DB Browser for SQLite, then browse to the `siminfo` table, where you will find the carrier information, ICCID and other identifiers:

icc_id	imsi	display_name	iso_country_code
89011004300056709265	313100005670926	FirstNet	us

Figure 6.35 – SIM information from telephony.db database

4. Android supports multiple user profiles, with the primary profile always being user 0, and additional profiles being named 10, 11, and 12 (if present). Additionally, even more profiles can be created for certain features (such as Samsung Secure Folder, which is assigned user 150 if enabled by the user).
5. Navigate to `/data/system/users/`. Here you will see the primary user profile of `0`, user `150` indicating usage of the encrypted Samsung Secure Folder, and a system user (user `1000`).
6. Select the `users` directory to view its content and examine the file titled `0.xml`:

```
<?xml version="1.0" encoding="utf-8" standalone="yes" ?>
<user id="0" serialNumber="0" flags="3091" attributes="0" type="android.os.usertype.full.SYSTEM" created="0"
  lastLoggedIn="1725569684638"
  lastLoggedInFingerprint="samsung/o1qsqw/o1q:11/RP1A.200720.012/G991USQS4AUIN:user/release-keys"
  icon="/data/system/users/0/photo.png" profileGroupId="0" profileBadge="0">
  <name>Leroy Jenkins</name>
  <restrictions />
  <device_policy_local_restrictions />
</user>
```

Figure 6.36 – User data pertaining to Android user profile 0

Each user profile in Android generates this XML file to store data about the profile, including the assigned username and an epoch timestamp indicating when the profile was last accessed (we can also examine the Secure Folder profile this way by looking at `150.xml`, or additional user profiles with each related XML file corresponding to the assigned profile identifier).

7. From here, access the subdirectory `0` for user profile `0`, and you will find several files related to various profile settings, the profile photo (if set by the user), and the wallpaper set by the user, as seen in the example:

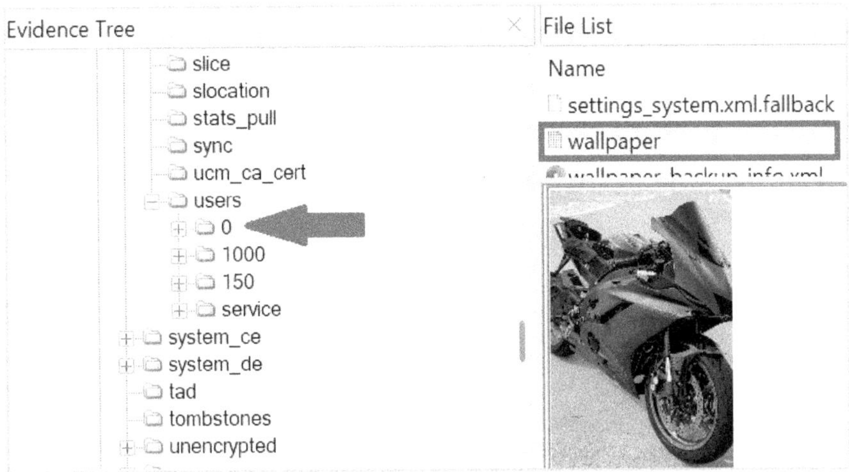

Figure 6.37 – Device wallpaper set for Android user profile 0

This same data can be found for any other user profile on the device.

8. To find more user-related attribution information, navigate to `/data/data/com.google.android.apps.photos/shared_prefs/` and examine the `accounts.xml` file. This will show us the Google account name and ID:

```
<string name="0.gaia_id">102253364416799402873</string>
<boolean name="0.add_skinny_page_boolean" value="true" />
<string name="0.account_name">leroyjinks87@gmail.com</string>
<string name="0.family_name">Jenkins</string>
<boolean name="0.created" value="true" />
```

Figure 6.38 – Google account name and ID from accounts.xml

This artifact is application-specific and reflects account data used by Google Photos. Depending on the device, apps installed, and user activity, this file may not always be present. However, similar account-related artifacts can often be found in other application directories.

9. Wi-Fi connection artifacts can be found in the `WifiConfigStore.xml` file, located at `/data/misc/apexdata/com.android.wifi/`.

   Examine this file and you will see Wi-Fi network information, including an SSID (network name) and sometimes stored network credentials:

```
<NetworkList>
- <Network>
  - <WifiConfiguration>
      <string name="ConfigKey">"CressyMeado 139"WPA_PSK</string>
      <string name="SSID">"CressyMeado 139"</string>
      <string name="PreSharedKey">"cctf4966"</string>
      <null name="WEPKeys" />
```

Figure 6.39 – Android Wi-Fi connections from WifiConfigStore.xml

10. Bluetooth connection artifacts can be found within the plain text `bt_config.conf` and `bt_config.bak` files located at `/data/misc/bluedroid/`.
11. Examine these files to see the device name, MAC address, and UTC timestamps (in Unix seconds) for previously connected devices:

```
[54:d1:7d:b0:97:68]
Timestamp = 1721367423
Name = SKM34U7-BT
DevClass = 5898764
```

Figure 6.40 – Android Bluetooth connection from bt_config.conf

How it works...

Android devices expose basic device and user metadata via a mix of plain-text and XML files (and sometimes binary XML) scattered across the file system, with artifact locations often varying by manufacturer.

Android also supports multiple user profiles and special profiles (user 0 is primary; some features, such as Samsung Secure Folder, use dedicated user profiles), so always check `/data/system/users/` to determine what profiles may exist on the device (especially since secure spaces like Samsung Secure Folder or Google Private Space may be encrypted and contain restricted data).

Application data (Android)

Though not all Android devices are the same and the location of artifacts can vary, native applications and their related databases within the Android environment can often be found in the following locations:

- **Contacts:** `/data/data/com.android.providers.contacts/databases/contacts2.db`
- **Calendar:** `/data/data/com.android.providers.calendar/databases/calendar.db`
- **Call Logs:** `/data/data/com.android.providers.contacts/databases/calllog.db`

- **SMS:** /data/data/com.android.providers.telephony/databases/mmssms.db
- **Email:** /data/data/com.google.android.gm/databases/bigTopDataDB.<######>

Note that some Android devices store call logs and contacts together within the contacts2.db database, rather than using a separate calllog.db database for call logs.

These locations can also be device manufacturer dependent. For example, in our Android dataset created from a Samsung device, many of these databases exist in the Samsung-specific equivalents of these directories (such as com.samsung instead of com.android), with database names sometimes differing from standard Android implementations.

This same basic sandboxed storage location continues for any third-party apps installed in the Android environment, typically following the naming pattern:

/data/data/<Application ID>/

Within the directory based on the Application ID, developers have a lot more freedom than seen with iOS to store their data how and where they want, though many do choose to use some of the Android standard subdirectories such as /databases/ (for app databases), /cache/ (for cached files), and /files/ (for general file storage). Applications will also often store data within /data/media/<user>/Android/data/, usually for user-related file storage (though this is not always the case, and they may choose to store databases and other files here as well).

In this recipe, we will explore how application data is generally stored in an Android-based device.

Getting ready

We will use the Android forensic image and continue to view and export items from our Android acquisition as needed to view them using DB Browser for SQLite.

How to do it...

1. Navigate to the /data/data/ directory, where you'll find individual subdirectories named using each Application ID (which looks similar to the Bundle IDs we are familiar with from iOS). Unlike iOS though, app directories are more plainly named rather than using a UUID naming convention, making it much easier to identify the application storage locations. Note that we can gain quick information here about what is installed on Android by simply looking at the folder names.
   Also notice how they are named, where standard Android apps begin with com.android, Google apps often begin with com.google, manufacturer related apps

with `com.samsung` (since we are looking at a Samsung device), and third-party apps use their own naming, usually beginning with `com.<developer name>`:

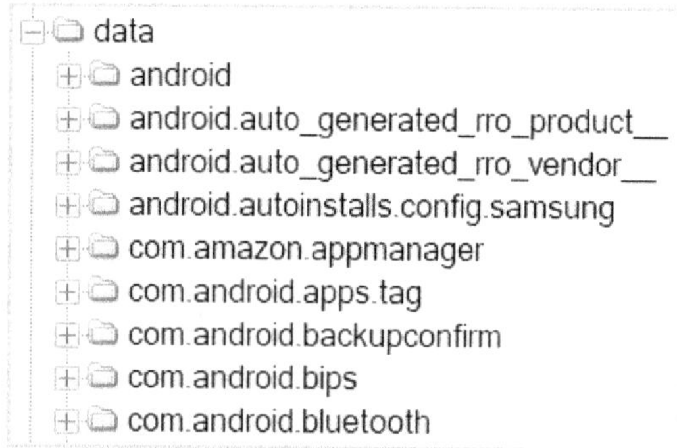

Figure 6.41 – Android application directories

2. Beyond this is where Android analysis can begin getting slightly more cumbersome than Apple iOS; unlike Apple, Android developers have significantly more flexibility in how they store application data. As such, the subdirectories you will find within the Application ID folders will vary.
   Nonetheless, you will often find associated account data by browsing through the subdirectories for each app. As an example, navigate to the Application ID for the Tinder dating application (`/data/data/com.tinder/`) where you will see several more subdirectories that are given fairly obvious names. Based on these names, the subdirectories of `/files/datastore/` would seem to be an interesting place to start – at this location we will find several files for user data, including a file titled `account`. Examine this file and you will find the user's account information for the Tinder application:

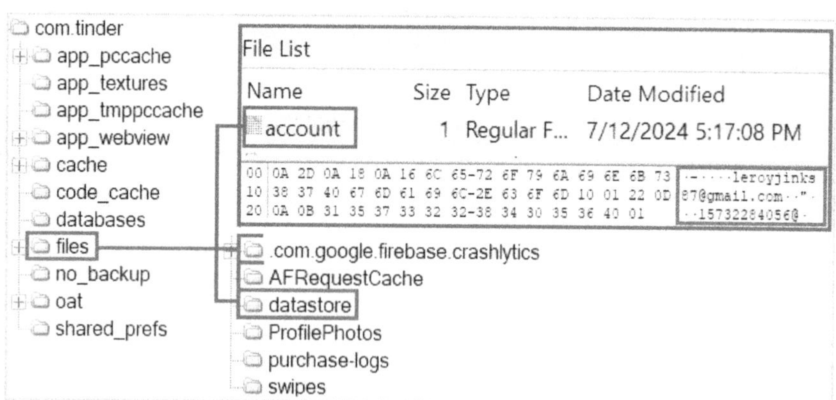

Figure 6.42 – Exploring Android application directory content for the Tinder app

3. Now navigate to `/data/system/` and locate `packages.xml`. This file can be overwhelming at first glance, as it stores metadata about installed applications – but we can target searches to find what we need. For example, if we want to find applications the user installed via Google Play, we only need to know that that installation method invokes the `com.android.vending` service.

   With the `packages.xml` file selected in FTK Imager or opened within a text editor, press *Ctrl+F* on your keyboard and enter the search term `installer="com.android.vending"`. Moving through these results we will see several applications fitting this criteria, which are identifiable by the associated `package name`. For example:

```
<package name="com.snapchat.android"
  codePath="/data/app/~~3SRhgaYtDErrww8q8oBVhg==/com.snapchat.a
  nativeLibraryPath="/data/app/~~3SRhgaYtDErrww8q8oBVhg==/com.sn
  primaryCpuAbi="arm64-v8a" publicFlags="811187780" privateFlags="-13925
  version="103873" userId="10310" installer="com.android.vending" installIn
- <sigs count="1" schemeVersion="3">
```

Figure 6.43 – Locating Android applications installed via Google Play

4. We can also determine certain permissions that were granted to an app using the `packages.xml` file. Perform another search for `com.tinder.permission` and you will see an entry indicating Tinder is set to allow location services:

```
  <item name="android.permission.VIBRATE" granted="true" flags="0" />
  <item name="android.permission.ACCESS_WIFI_STATE" granted="true" flags="0" />
  <item name="android.permission.USE_BIOMETRIC" granted="true" flags="0" />
  <item name="com.google.android.gms.permission.AD_ID" granted="true" flags="0" />
  <item name="android.permission.WAKE_LOCK" granted="true" flags="0" />
  <item name="com.tinder.permission.MAPS_RECEIVE" granted="true" flags="0" />
</perms>
```

Figure 6.44 – Android application permission settings

5. To confirm the Google Play account used to install an app, navigate to `/data/data/com.android.vending/databases/` and export the `localappstate.db` database.
6. Open this database with DB Browser for SQLite, and inspect the `appstate` table:

package_name ▾	auto_update	account
police.scanner.radio.broadcastify.ci...	1	leroyjinks87@gmail.com
org.torproject.torbrowser	1	leroyjinks87@gmail.com
org.thoughtcrime.securesms	1	leroyjinks87@gmail.com
com.tinder	1	leroyjinks87@gmail.com

Figure 6.45 – Android application information from localappstate.db

Here you will see a large amount of information pertaining to each app, including the following which can be useful to many investigations:

- **Account** – The Google Play account name used to download the app.
- **auto_update** – Indicates whether the application will automatically receive updates (1 = enabled, 0 = disabled)
- **Timestamps** – These may record original download dates and subsequent update activity (not shown in the example).

How it works...

Android stores each application's private data inside a sandboxed directory located at /data/data/<Application ID>/. First-party (native) apps such as Contacts, SMS, Call Logs, and Calendar use consistent directory structures, typically storing their SQLite databases inside a /databases/ subfolder, whereas third-party apps follow the same base location but often deviate in what directories they choose to implement and how (often adding a host of custom subdirectories). Many applications will also store user-visible data within user-accessible storage at /data/media/<user>/Android/data/<Application ID>/.

Beyond app-specific storage, Android maintains global metadata files that provide context about installation sources, permissions, and app ownership (such as packages.xml and localappstate.db). Together, these artifacts allow us to identify installed applications, locate their stored data, determine where the apps came from, and attribute them to a specific Google account.

In Android, you will also often find certain application databases duplicated across the following locations:

- /data/data/<Application ID>/databases/
- /data/user/<user>/<Application ID>/databases/
- /data/user_de/<user>/<Application ID>/databases/

Note

Note that `/data/data/` typically maps to `/data/user/0/` for the primary user.

While the number of duplicative artifacts can sometimes be frustrating during analysis, this also gives investigators a greater opportunity to recover deleted data, as artifacts like text messages may persist longer within one of the available databases if multiple copies exist. This redundancy can also be used to validate findings across multiple sources, strengthening the reliability of recovered evidence.

User files (Android)

User files in Android are generally stored at `/data/media/<user>,` where Android provides standard directories for items such as Documents, Download, Music, Pictures, Videos, etc. We can easily browse these files in the same way we can in most other systems that use this type of storage (similar to traditional desktop operating systems like Windows) by simply looking in each directory to see what the user stored.

For this recipe, we will examine these user directories.

Getting ready

We will use the Android forensic image and our preferred forensic image browsing tools (such as FTK Imager) to navigate and view items of interest.

How to do it...

Android takes a much different approach to storing media files than seen with iOS, choosing to separate files that were created using the integrated camera of a device from files that are screenshots or downloads.

1. Navigate to `/data/media/0/DCIM/` for the default user profile, where you will see different subdirectories exemplifying how Android separates its media file storage into photographs generated using the device camera (Camera), screenshots taken using the device (Screenshots), and media files saved from within an application (in this case, Facebook):

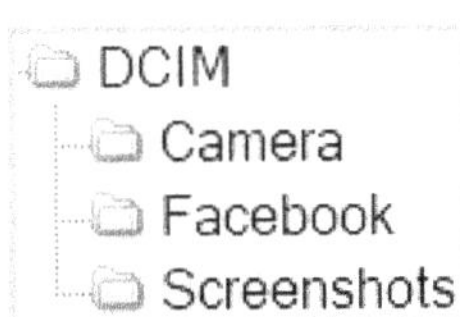

Figure 6.46 – Subdirectories for media file storage in Android

2. Look in the **Camera** subdirectory, where you will find photographs and videos that were created using the integrated camera of the device. The naming convention used by Android for these files is `date_time`, typically in the format of `YYYYMMDD_HHMMSS`. The date and time used are typically based on the local system time of the device rather than UTC and are based on a 24-hour clock:

Figure 6.47 – Media files stored in the Camera directory in Android

3. Now look in the **Screenshots** subdirectory, which is created when the user takes a screenshot using the device. Files here have an interesting and unique naming convention often in the format of `Screenshot_YYYYMMDD-HHMMSS_Application`. This format tells us the file is a screenshot, the date and time the screenshot was created based on the local device time zone, and the name of the application that was open when the screenshot was created:

Figure 6.48 – User screenshots stored in Android

4. Like other operating systems, Android will generate and cache thumbnails of media file content. Thumbnails in Android will usually persist if the original files are deleted and can be found as JPEG files at `/data/media/0/Pictures/.thumbnails/`, or at `/data/data/com.sec.android.gallery3d/cache/`, where they are stored to various numerically titled subdirectories, and individual files are numerically titled and followed by a `.0` file extension. Follow the `/data/data/com.sec.android.gallery3d/cache/` path and select a subfolder to explore:

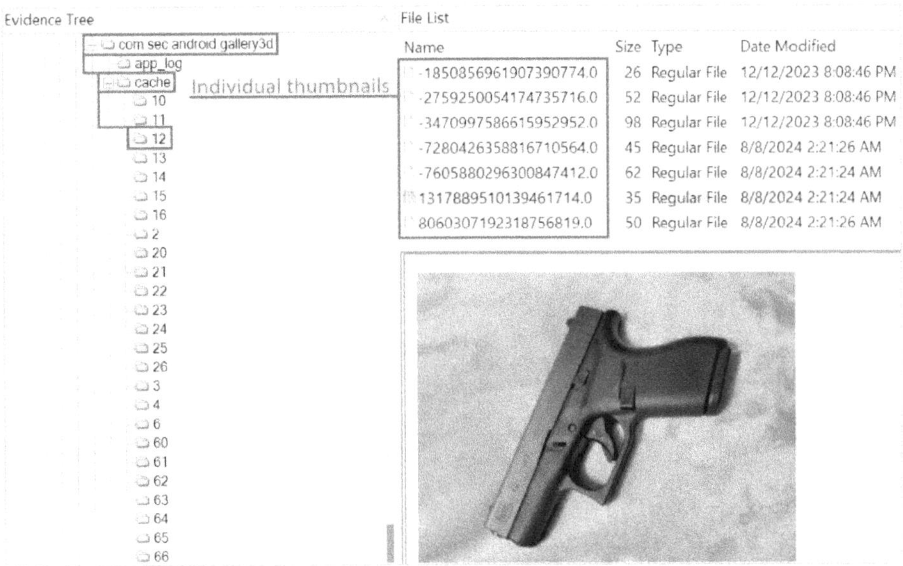

Figure 6.49 – Android media files cached to com.sec.android.gallery3d

> **Note**
>
> Many individual applications will also cache media file thumbnails via the Glide image-loading library used by many Android applications. Glide is used to help the Android applications with smoother scrolling of content, and to do so it caches photographs for faster load times. When this occurs, the cached thumbnails are stored per application location, with the individual files titled using a long alphanumeric name and an extension of `.0`. Each file is placed in the `image_manager_disk_cache` subdirectory for the specific application. The complete file path is `/data/data/<App ID>/cache/image_manager_disk_cache/<filename>.0`.

5. We can view other user files stored in similar directories by merely browsing their locations. As an example, navigate to `/data/media/0/Download/` where you will find files downloaded to the device by the user:

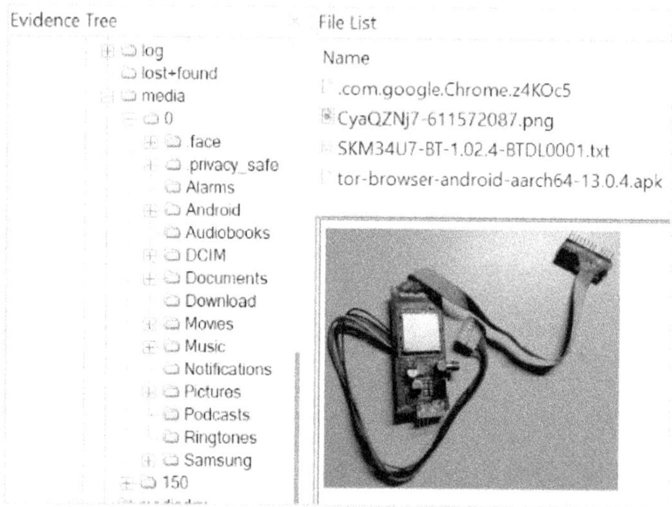

Figure 6.50 – Android Download folder contents for user profile 0

How it works...

Android stores user files in a predictable structure under `/data/media/<user>/`. Here, the system maintains standard folders (such as DCIM, Pictures, Videos, and Download), each containing files generated or saved by the user. Camera photos follow a timestamp-based naming convention (e.g., 20240205_134812.jpg), while screenshots include both timestamps and the active application name.

Android also generates and caches thumbnails for quick preview; these remain recoverable even after the original images are deleted. Common thumbnail cache stores include both Android system directories (such as `.thumbnails` within the `Pictures` directory) and sometimes manufacturer-specific stores (such as the `cache` directory at `com.sec.android.gallery3d`). Applications also often cache images, as seen with the Glide cache feature.

User interactions (Android)

Unfortunately, Android does not provide the same level of unified, system-wide interaction logging found in iOS with features such as PowerLog, KnowledgeC, and Biomes. However, there are some methods we can use to gain similar (though less detailed) user interaction information surrounding events such as application usage. The types of user interaction logging you find in Android are largely system-dependent and vary widely, as many manufacturers tend to implement their own logging features.

Getting ready

We will use the Android forensic image and continue to view and export items from our Android acquisition as needed to view them using DB Browser for SQLite.

How to do it...

1. Modern versions of Android contain a feature to provide usage statistics and interaction data to help users become more cognizant of how often they use their mobile devices and which applications they spend the most time on. This feature, called Digital Wellbeing, retains information on user interactions with a device and is similar to the KnowledgeC and Biomes artifacts in Apple iOS – though not quite as detailed, unfortunately. This application is stored at `/data/data/com.google.android.apps.wellbeing/databases/` and is often titled `app_usage` in most Android devices.
   Samsung devices (like in our dataset), use a manufacturer specific version, often called `dwbCommon.db`.
2. Navigate to `/data/data/com.samsung.android.forest/databases/` and export this database. Then open it using **DB Browser for SQLite**.
3. Browse to the `usageEvents` table:

timeStamp	eventType	className
Filter	Filter	Filter
1723101744100	2	com.privatephotovault.screens.MainActivity
1723101744106	1	com.android.launcher3.uioverrides.QuickstepLauncher
1723101744650	23	com.privatephotovault.screens.MainActivity
1723101752489	2	com.android.launcher3.uioverrides.QuickstepLauncher
1723101752507	1	com.keepsafe.app.frontdoor.FrontDoorActivity
1723101752744	2	com.keepsafe.app.frontdoor.FrontDoorActivity
1723101752790	1	com.keepsafe.app.accountentry.WelcomeActivity

Figure 6.51 – Android Digital Wellbeing data (Samsung version)

Here you will see applications listed along with timestamps of when activity occurred. The `eventType` field details the specific events using a numbering system that correlates to certain activities, such as applications being paused and sent to the background, resumed and brought to the foreground, stopped, etc. We can determine which activity each entry corresponds to by using a test device to document and review our activity. Additionally, automated tools like aLEAPP, which parse the Digital

Wellbeing database, will automatically assign a friendly name to each activity that better describes what has occurred.

How it works...

Android provides far less unified user-interaction logging than iOS, and the available artifacts vary by manufacturer. One primary source of interaction and app-usage metadata on modern devices is Digital Wellbeing, which stores timestamps and event types indicating when specific app-related events occurred. The Digital Wellbeing database helps us to form a basic usage timeline surrounding application activity.

Summary

Effective forensic analysis of mobile devices requires understanding how Apple iOS and Android store device information, application data, user-generated content, and interaction artifacts. While both platforms share common concepts such as SQLite databases, configuration files, and sandboxed application storage, they differ significantly in implementation. iOS provides highly structured and consistent artifact locations, whereas Android introduces greater variability due to manufacturer customization and developer flexibility.

By examining key artifacts such as property lists, application databases, filesystem storage locations, and usage metadata, investigators can reconstruct user activity, identify installed applications, attribute actions to specific accounts, and validate investigative findings across both platforms.

The level of insight gained from mobile devices is highly dependent on acquisition type, with full file system extractions providing significantly greater visibility than logical or targeted acquisitions.

At this point, you should be able to:

- **Identify and examine key iOS and Android artifacts** used to determine device information, user attribution, and system configuration.
- **Locate and interpret common mobile application data stores**, including SQLite databases and configuration files, across both mobile platforms.
- **Understand application sandboxing** and how it differs between iOS (UUID-based containers) and Android (Application ID–based directories).
- **Navigate user file storage locations** and differentiate between locally stored, cached, and cloud-synced data.
- **Analyze cached mobile artifacts** such as thumbnails and determine their persistence and investigative value

- **Recognize how user interaction data is recorded** in iOS (PowerLog, KnowledgeC, Biomes) and Android (Digital Wellbeing and manufacturer-specific artifacts), including their limitations and retention differences.
- **Apply consistent investigative techniques** to reconstruct user activity and validate findings across mobile operating systems despite differences in structure and implementation

In the next chapter, we begin implementing automated forensic tools, focusing on how platforms such as Autopsy, iLEAPP, and aLEAPP can be used to efficiently parse, correlate, and present data across the operating systems we have covered throughout the last chapters.

Get this book's PDF copy, code bundle, and more

Scan the QR code (or go to `packtpub.com/unlock`). Search for this book by name, confirm the edition, and then follow the steps on the page.

UNLOCK NOW

Note: Have your invoice handy. Purchases made directly from the Packt website don't require an invoice.

Part 3

Practical Analysis and Investigative Techniques

As your skills develop, you will build on foundational analysis techniques by applying practical workflows used in real-world digital forensic investigations. You will learn how to automate analysis, extract and interpret user artifacts, and apply manual techniques to validate findings and uncover additional evidence.

This part also addresses common challenges investigators face, including anti-forensic techniques, deleted data recovery, encryption, and memory analysis. By the end of this part, you will be equipped with the tools and methodologies needed to conduct deeper and more comprehensive forensic examinations.

This part is organized into the following chapters:

- *Chapter 7, Analysis Automation*
- *Chapter 8, User Artifacts*
- *Chapter 9, Manual Analysis and Techniques*
- *Chapter 10, Overcoming Anti-Forensics*
- *Chapter 11, Memory Analysis*

7

Analysis Automation

In the previous chapters, we examined operating systems by manually reviewing key forensic artifacts. While this manual approach is valuable for understanding artifact structure and behavior, it becomes highly inefficient when applied to full examinations. Parsing a system one directory at a time (exporting and inspecting every database, configuration file, and piece of user-generated content) would take an extraordinary amount of time for even a single system.

In real-world investigations, the challenge becomes clear: how can we efficiently analyze large volumes of data without missing critical evidence?

To address this, examiners rely on automated analysis tools. These tools enable rapid searching, filtering, and organization of data, allowing investigators to quickly surface relevant artifacts and reduce overall analysis time.

However, automation does not replace the examiner. Automated tools can misinterpret data, miss artifacts, or fail under certain conditions. Results must always be validated.

A wide range of automation platforms exist, and tool selection often depends on evidence types, workflow requirements, and examiner preference. Commercial suites such as Magnet, Sumuri, Exterro, Belkasoft, X-Ways, Cellebrite, and others provide extensive capabilities and frequent updates. In this chapter, we will use free and open-source tools (Autopsy, iLEAPP, and aLEAPP) to demonstrate how automated analysis is applied in practice.

In this chapter, we're going to cover the following main topics:

- Creating a case with Autopsy
- Adding modules and evidence in Autopsy
- Forensic analysis with Autopsy
- Applying Intelligence in Autopsy
- Parsing mobile devices with iLEAPP and aLEAPP

Technical requirements

For this chapter, you will need:

- A 64-bit Windows 11 system with an Intel i7 (or equivalent) and a minimum of 16 GB of RAM is recommended. This system will be used to install and run Autopsy, iLEAPP, and aLEAPP, as well as to store and process forensic images.
- Ensure sufficient disk space is available, as the datasets used in this chapter total approximately 50 GB. If possible, use separate storage drives for evidence and processing to improve performance.
- Datasets for analysis: many of these we have already worked with in previous chapters. They are available from the Packt Publishing GitHub repository. To access the repository link, follow the steps in the *Download the example code files* section in the *Preface*.

Creating a case with Autopsy

Autopsy, developed by Sleuth Kit Labs, is a completely open-source yet highly capable forensic analysis suite. While many examiners choose to invest in commercial solutions, Autopsy remains an essential tool to learn—not just because it is free, but because its features and capabilities closely mirror those found in commercial platforms. It also serves as an effective secondary tool for validating findings produced by primary forensic solutions. In some environments, it may even serve as the primary analysis platform.

Getting ready

Autopsy for Windows can be downloaded from the following website, where you will also see options to download Autopsy installation packages for Apple macOS and Linux, as it can be installed to run on all three systems: `www.autopsy.com/download/`

Download and install the latest available version before proceeding.

You will also need the **Microsoft Windows** dataset introduced in *Chapter 4*. This dataset will be used to create an initial case and demonstrate Autopsy's workflow in a practical context.

How to do it...

1. Run Autopsy with administrator privileges (right-click, **Run as administrator**). When processing forensic evidence, ensure your tools are not interfered with by security software. Antivirus scanning can interfere with ingest modules and may prevent artifacts from being parsed correctly, so it is recommended to whitelist the Autopsy installation directory.

2. Once Autopsy is launched, click **New Case** to begin creating your first case:

Figure 7.1 – Creating a new case in Autopsy

3. Enter a name for your case in the **Case Name** field. This can be any descriptive label, although examiners typically use a case number or another unique identifier to ensure consistency and traceability across investigations.
4. In the **Base Directory** field, click **Browse** and select the folder where Autopsy should store all case-related data. It is best practice to store case data on a separate internal drive rather than the operating system disk. This improves performance and helps protect case data in the event of a system failure.
   In the example below, the Base Directory contains subfolders for the specific case number and for Autopsy processing, supporting consistent organization across cases.

   The **Case Type** option enables multi-user collaboration via shared network resources, but this requires additional configuration. While useful in larger lab environments, many examiners prefer offline or air-gapped systems to reduce risk during analysis.
5. Once the required fields are set, click **Next**:

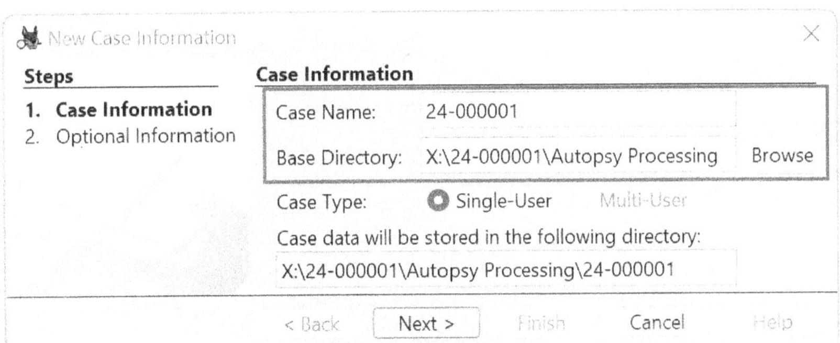

Figure 7.2 – Entering case information in Autopsy

This screen allows you to enter optional case details. While optional, it is best practice to complete these fields, as this information becomes part of the case record and is included in generated reports. This provides stakeholders with key information such as a case number and examiner contact details, which support documentation, reporting, and chain-of-custody clarity.

The `Organization` field is especially useful if you conduct examinations for multiple agencies or companies, as it allows you to clearly associate the case with the appropriate entity.

6. When finished, click **Finish**:

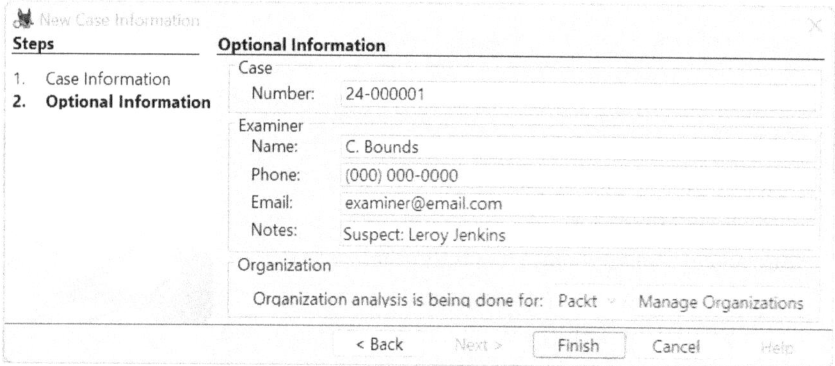

Figure 7.3 – Entering optional case information in Autopsy

7. After the case is created, navigate to the folder you selected earlier as your **Base Directory**. Autopsy will have generated several subdirectories and files, which collectively store all case-related data. This includes evidence processing output, log files documenting each ingest action, and default locations for file exports and report generation throughout your analysis:

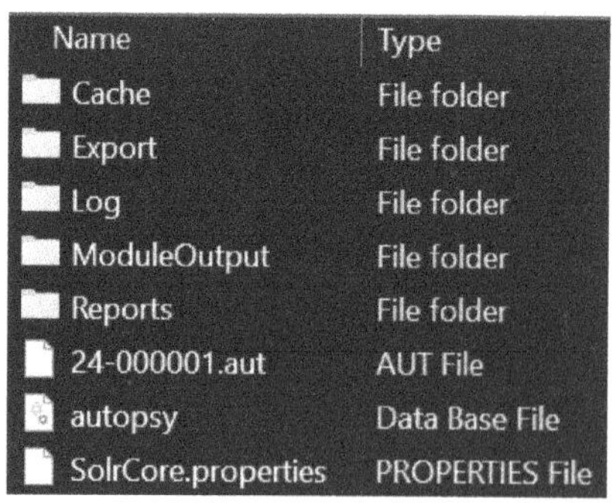

Figure 7.4 – Base directory content created by Autopsy

8. Upon creating the case, Autopsy will display the **Add Data Source** window. Begin by selecting a **host**, which represents the evidence item you are adding. Autopsy provides a default name, but choose **Specify new host name** so you can enter a clearer, more descriptive label. Using consistent, descriptive naming helps maintain organization, especially when you are working with multiple evidence sources.
   In this example, the Microsoft Windows acquisition is named `Item01 - Lenovo ThinkPad`. Once the host name is set, click **Next**:

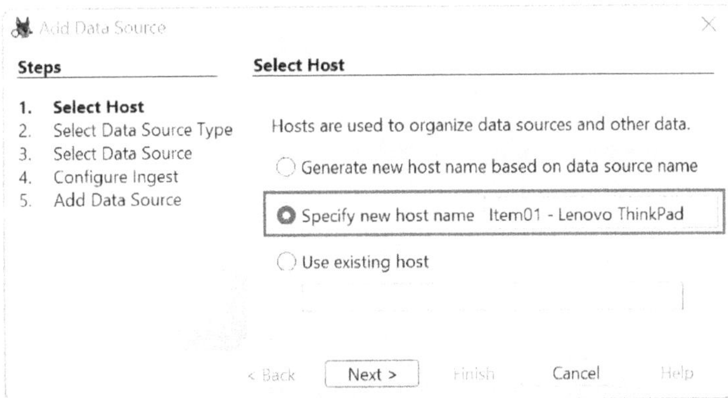

Figure 7.5 – Specifying an evidence source name in Autopsy

9. In the **Select Data Source Type** window, keep the default option **Disk Image or VM File** selected, since our Microsoft Windows acquisition is stored as a forensic image. This is also the most common evidence type added in routine examinations. Autopsy supports additional data source types, such as analyzing a locally attached storage device (*Local Disk*) or processing exported files (*Logical Files*), but for this scenario, the default selection is appropriate.

10. Click **Next**:

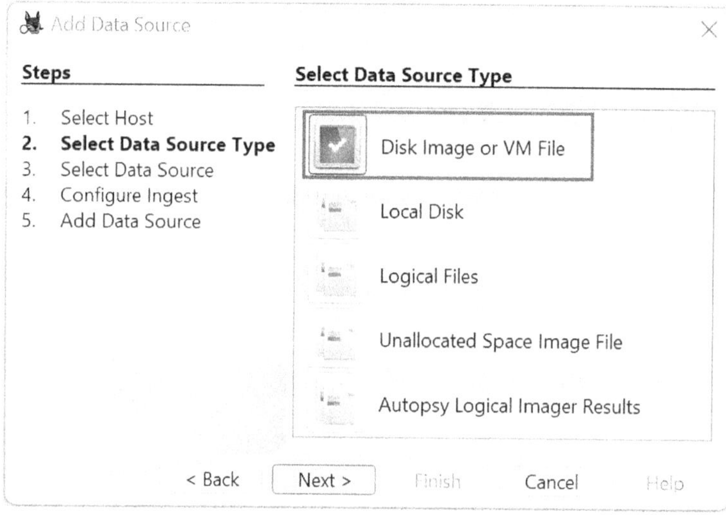

Figure 7.6 – Selecting a data source type in Autopsy

11. In the **Select Data Source** window, browse to the location where your forensic image is stored. In this example, the Microsoft Windows acquisition is stored in the same directory as the Autopsy case, though many practitioners store forensic images on a separate internal drive dedicated to evidence storage.
    Set the **Time zone** to **UTC** (or the time zone that matches the source system, if known). Accurate time zone configuration is critical, as it directly affects timeline analysis and event correlation. All other settings can remain at their default values.

    You will also see options for **Hash Values**, which allow you to enter the original hash verification from the acquisition process. Hash validation is a key step in confirming evidence integrity and should be performed during real examinations.

    Autopsy can validate these hashes during ingest and include the results in the final case report. For this example, we will skip validation to reduce processing time, as the provided dataset has been modified for size.

12. When ready, click **Next**:

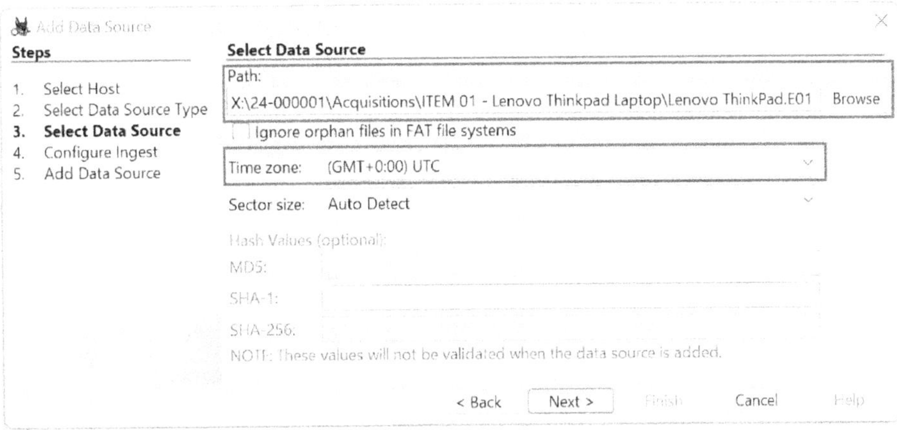

Figure 7.7 – Selecting a data source type in Autopsy

The **Configure Ingest** window allows you to choose which processing modules Autopsy will run against the evidence. Selecting any module displays a brief description and configuration options in the right-hand pane. A dropdown menu also lets you control which portions of the acquisition are processed (for example, excluding unallocated space).

It is best practice to enable only the modules you actually need, as each additional module increases processing time. Any module can be run again later if needed.

13. Click **Deselect All**, then enable the modules shown in *Figure 7.8*.
    Leave all other options at their default values. These selected modules provide a balanced baseline for identifying user activity, file types, and potential indicators of interest without significantly increasing processing time.

14. When ready, click **Next** to begin ingest. The ingest process is where Autopsy parses the evidence, extracts artifacts, and builds searchable indexes used throughout your analysis:

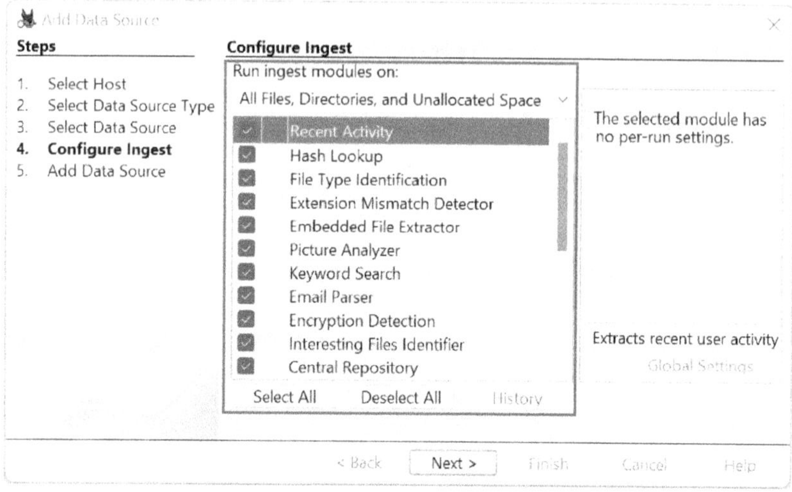

Figure 7.8 – Selecting modules to use during evidence processing in Autopsy

15. Once the evidence source has been added, you may receive a notification that errors were encountered. Click **View Log** to see a summary of these messages. Reviewing ingest logs is an important step, as warnings or errors may indicate missed artifacts, unsupported formats, or encrypted content that requires further investigation. In the example shown, we can see that possible encrypted files were detected.

16. Click **Finish** to close this window:

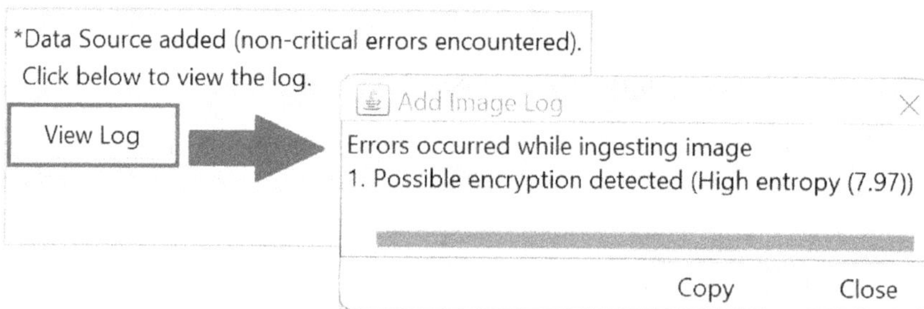

Figure 7.9 – Viewing log file after evidence is added in Autopsy

17. Autopsy will continue processing the evidence source, and you can monitor progress in the lower-right corner of the interface. Processing times can vary widely depending on your workstation's hardware, the size and number of evidence sources, and the ingest modules selected. Clicking the red circular icon next to the progress bar will display additional details, including any errors encountered and modules that were skipped:

Figure 7.10 – Evidence source processing status bar in Autopsy

> **Note**
>
> No time off
>
> Love digital forensics? Good – because your evidence doesn't care about business hours.
>
> Don't worry... I'm not saying *you* should work 24/7. But your tools can. One of the easiest workflow hacks is to kick off long processing jobs right before you leave at the end of the day or week. Queue it, close the lid, walk away. If everything behaves, you'll come back to a fully processed case and a big head start on your analysis... without sacrificing a single minute of your free time.

As processing completes, Autopsy will begin populating the interface with parsed artifacts. The top toolbar provides the primary analysis functions, including keyword searching, additional ingest options, report generation, and specialized viewers for items such as media files and chat data artifacts.

The left pane is the **Tree Viewer**, which displays a traditional file-system view (similar to what we used in FTK Imager) along with several artifact categories created by the modules selected during ingest. Within this pane, you can browse **Data Sources** (for raw file-system directories), **File Views** (for filtering files by characteristics), **Data Artifacts** (for parsed results), and **Analysis Results** (for items grouped by analytical characteristics, such as detected encryption).

18. When you select a directory or artifact category, the **Result Viewer** (upper right pane) displays the contents in a spreadsheet-style layout. This view allows you to quickly sort, filter, and identify items of interest across large datasets.
    Clicking any individual file or artifact shows its detailed view in the **Content Viewer** located in the lower-right pane. The Content Viewer provides the underlying details of the selected item, which is essential for verifying findings and understanding artifact context:

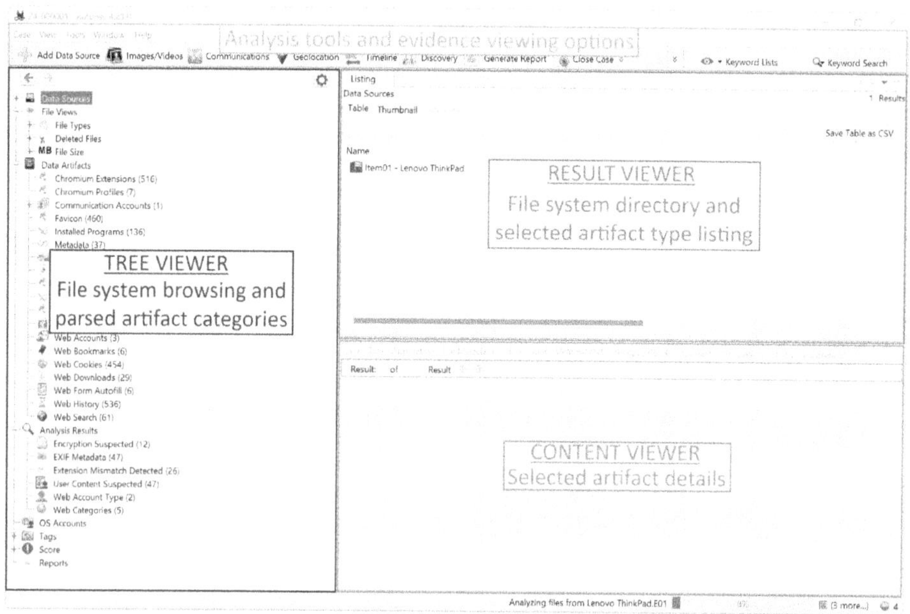

Figure 7.11 – Basic overview of the Autopsy interface

> **Note**
>
> Out of memory
>
> If Autopsy runs out of memory during ingest, increase the **JVM memory allocation** under **Tools | Options | Application**. Setting this to at least 8GB (or ~50% of system RAM) can significantly improve performance on large datasets.

How it works...

When you create a case in Autopsy, the program sets up a structured workspace that stores evidence, logs, and processing output. The case name and base directory determine where all generated data is stored throughout the analysis. Adding a host allows you to label each evidence item clearly, which is especially important when you are working with multiple acquisitions.

Once a forensic image is selected, Autopsy records its metadata, optional hash values, and time zone settings before beginning ingest. The ingest process runs various modules that automatically parse relevant artifacts. Each module extracts specific types of data (such as user activity, communications, or file metadata) and contributes structured results to the case database. As ingest completes, the Autopsy interface becomes populated with these results.

Investigators can then pivot between raw data and parsed artifacts to validate findings and build an accurate understanding of system activity.

Adding modules and evidence in Autopsy

Autopsy comes preinstalled with several modules (or plug-ins) used to add evidence sources, parse operating system and application artifacts, generate content views, and produce reports. These modules automate the extraction and organization of forensic artifacts, allowing investigators to focus on analysis rather than manual data parsing. Additional modules can also be integrated into Autopsy, many of which are developed by the digital forensics community and later adopted or supported by Sleuth Kit Labs to extend the platform's capabilities. These third-party add-on modules, distributed as `.nbm` files, can be downloaded from: `www.github.com/sleuthkit/autopsy_addon_modules`

A key strength of modern forensic analysis platforms is the ability to process and correlate multiple evidence sources within a single case. This allows examiners to connect artifacts across devices or datasets and build more complete, well-supported conclusions about user activity and system behavior.

In this section, we will walk through adding modules and incorporating additional evidence sources into an existing Autopsy case.

Getting ready

We will begin by adding enhanced artifact-viewing capabilities to Autopsy to improve parsing of Microsoft Windows Event Logs. Extending tool capabilities through modules allows investigators to extract additional artifacts that may not be parsed by default configurations. Download the **Event Log Viewer** `.nbm` module:

`https://github.com/sleuthkit/autopsy_addon_modules/raw/refs/heads/master/ContentViewerModules/Event_Log_viewer/Event_Log_Viewer.nbm`

In this section, we will also add the remaining evidence datasets introduced in *Chapter 5* and *Chapter 6*. Since the Microsoft Windows dataset has already been processed, you will now need the **Apple macOS**, **Linux**, **Apple iOS**, and **Android** datasets to complete the full evidence set.

How to do it...

1. From the **Tools** menu in Autopsy, select **Plugins**. In the window that opens, go to the **Downloaded** tab and click **Add Plugins...** then browse to the `Event_Log_Viewer.nbm` file you downloaded and select it:

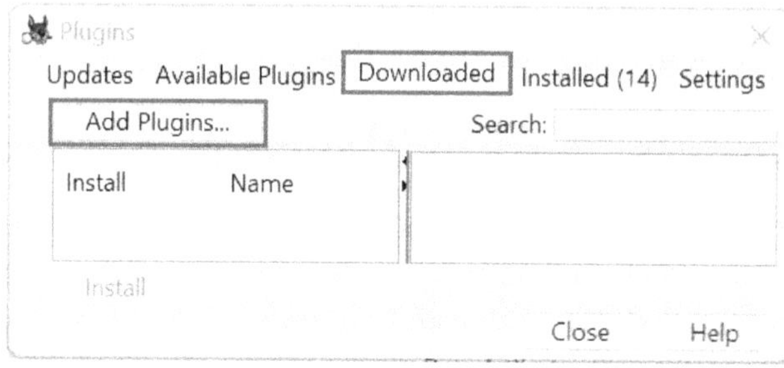

Figure 7.12 – Adding a new module in Autopsy

2. Once the `Event_Log_Viewer.nbm` file loads into Autopsy, click **Install** and follow the installation prompts. After the module installs, Autopsy will ask you to restart the program. As long as no evidence is currently being processed, choose **Restart Now**, then click **Finish**:

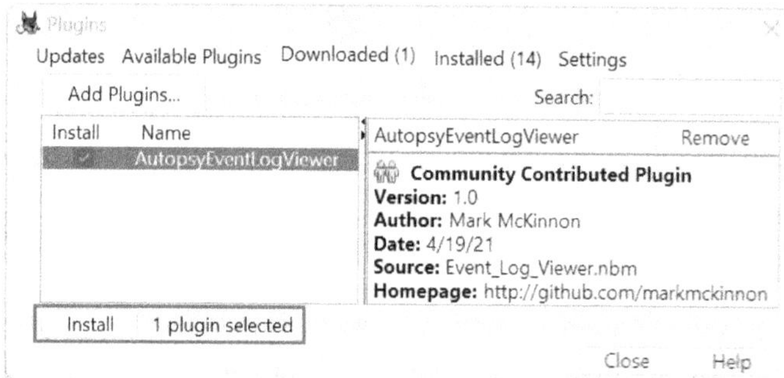

Figure 7.13 – Installing a new module in Autopsy

3. After Autopsy restarts, select **Reopen Recent Case** to reload the case you were working on. Then return to **Tools | Plugins** and open the **Installed** tab. You should now see the Event Log Viewer listed as an installed module:

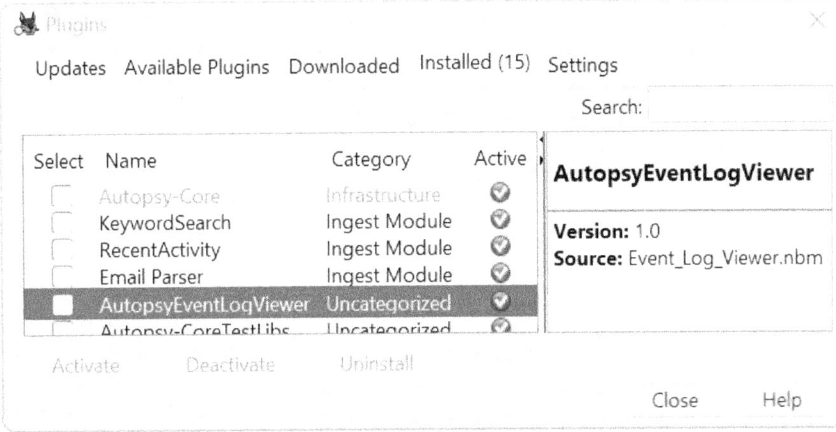

Figure 7.14 – New module installed in Autopsy

4. In the left-side pane, navigate to **Windows Event Logs** under **vol6** within the **Data Sources** for `Item 01 - Lenovo ThinkPad`. Windows Event Logs are stored at `/Windows/System32/winevt/logs`.
5. Select `Security.evtx` to view its entries in the **Event Viewer** tab in the lower-right pane. This tab is provided by the Event Log Viewer module, allowing you to review Windows Event Logs directly within Autopsy:

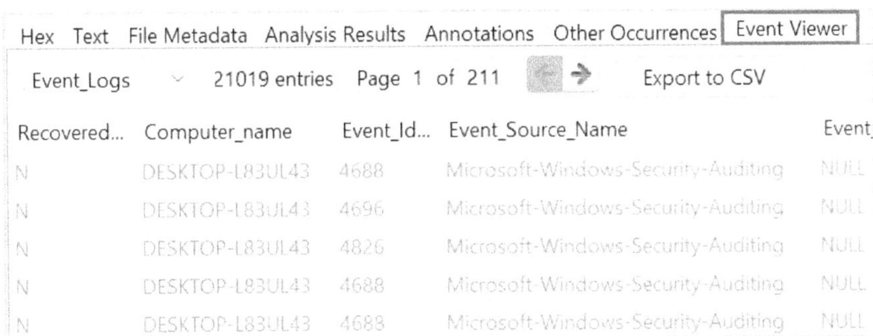

Figure 7.15 – Event Viewer tab as a content viewer option in Autopsy

What we installed is a *content viewer module*, which expands Autopsy's ability to display certain artifacts—in this case, Windows Event Logs. Content viewer modules only require a restart for the new features to become available.

If this had been an *ingest module* (one that parses artifacts during processing), we would need to run that module after installation. Newly added ingest modules can be executed on an existing case at any time by selecting **Run Ingest Modules** from the **Tools** menu.

6. Now, add the remaining evidence sources to the case, starting with the Apple iOS dataset used in *Chapter 6*. Click **Add Data Source** in the upper-left corner of Autopsy or select **Case** | **Add Data Source** from the menu:

Figure 7.16 – Adding evidence sources in Autopsy

7. The same **Add Data Source** window used earlier will appear. In the **Specify new host name** field, enter a descriptive label for this acquisition (for example, `Item 04 - Apple iPhone`). Once named, click **Next**:

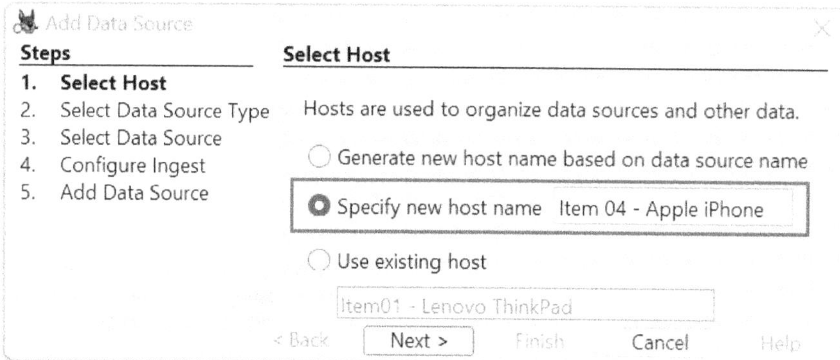

Figure 7.17 – Adding a new evidence source host name in Autopsy

8. The Apple iOS sample data was acquired using a method that stores the extraction inside a zipped archive rather than a traditional forensic image format such as an E01. Because of this, add the `Apple iPhone` dataset as a `Logical Files` data source. Select **Logical Files**, then click **Next**:

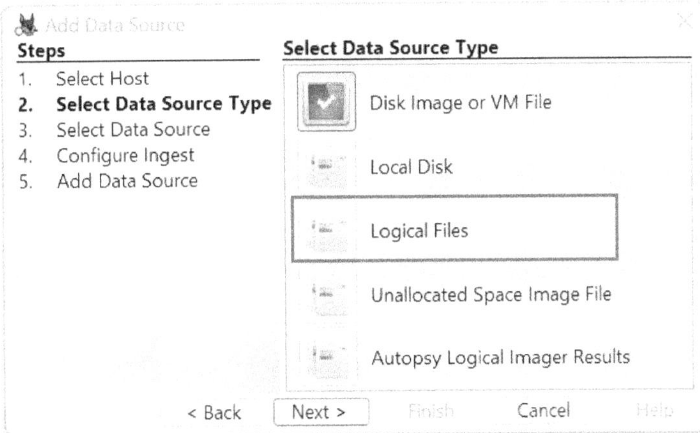

Figure 7.18 – Adding a logical data source type in Autopsy

9. To add the zipped archive containing the Apple iOS sample data, ensure **Local files and folders** is selected in the dropdown menu, then click **Add** to browse to and select the archive. Next, click **Change** under `Logical File Set Display Name` and replace the default text with a more descriptive label such as `Apple iPhone`.
10. Make sure all checkboxes in the **Timestamps to Include** section are selected, then click **Next**:

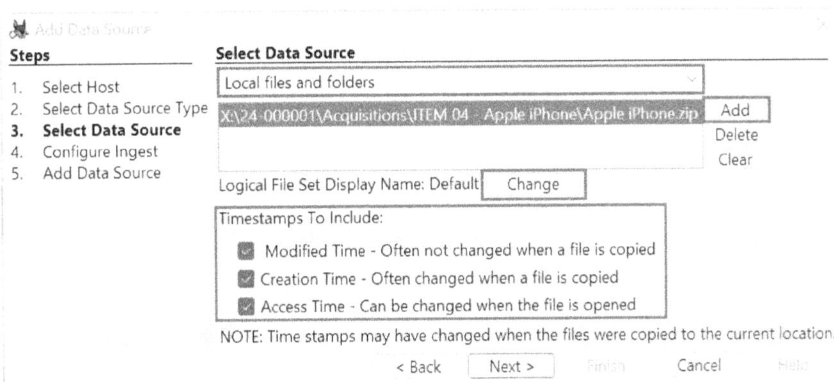

Figure 7.19 – Selecting a data source and options in Autopsy

11. In the **Configure Ingest** window, keep the same module selections used for the `Microsoft Windows` dataset. This time, also enable the **iOS Analyzer (iLEAPP)** module to process Apple iOS artifacts. Click **Next** to begin processing:

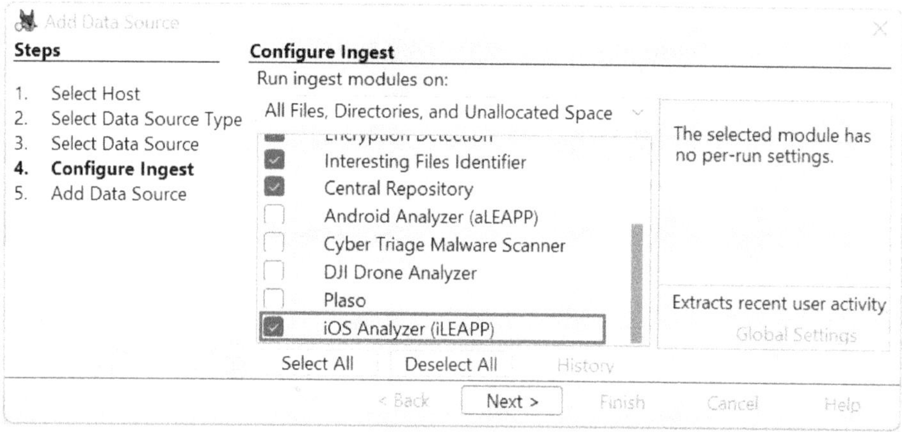

Figure 7.20 – Selecting the additional iOS Analyzer module in Autopsy

After processing is complete, Autopsy will populate the artifact tree with the newly parsed iOS artifacts, and the evidence source will appear in both the tree and the artifact list in the upper-right pane. These results were generated using the iLEAPP module, which we will examine in more detail later in the chapter.

12. If your case involves multiple individuals, you can also associate each evidence source with a specific owner/user by right-clicking the source and selecting **Associate with Person**, then entering the appropriate name:

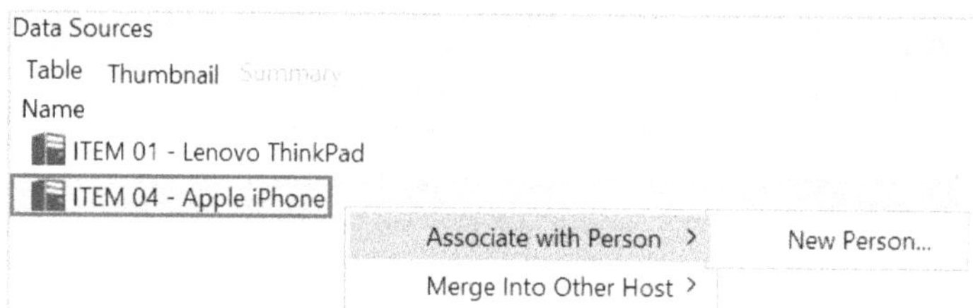

Figure 7.21 – Evidence source listing with association options in Autopsy

13. Continue practicing by adding the remaining sample datasets (**Apple macOS**, **Linux**, and **Android**) from *Chapter 5* and *Chapter 6* using the same method demonstrated in this section. Be sure to enable the appropriate ingest modules for each dataset so Autopsy can parse artifacts specific to each OS.

How it works...

Autopsy's modular design allows you to tailor processing to each case. Content viewer modules control how artifacts are displayed, while ingest modules parse data during processing. Installing a module requires loading its `.nbm` file and restarting Autopsy; ingest modules can then be run immediately or applied later to existing evidence.

Autopsy also supports adding multiple datasets from various source types into a single case. Each evidence source can be clearly labeled and even associated with an individual user/owner, enabling cleaner organization and easier cross-device correlation.

This provides a flexible means of efficiently analyzing diverse evidence types within one unified case.

Forensic analysis with Autopsy

During analysis, most data will be irrelevant to your investigation. The examiner's task is to efficiently filter through it and identify artifacts that matter. When relevant items are located, they must be preserved and organized for reporting. In Autopsy, this is accomplished through bookmarking and tagging.

In this recipe, we will briefly cover how to bookmark artifacts, then focus on improving efficiency through sorting and filtering within the interface.

Getting ready

For this section, we will use the existing Autopsy case that was already created to explore how to begin searching and navigating across processed datasets.

How to do it...

1. To create a bookmark, right-click any artifact of interest and select **Bookmark** from the **Add Result Tag** submenu (or press *Ctrl+B*). A yellow indicator will appear in the `S` column, showing that the item has been bookmarked.
   You may also classify the artifact as `Notable` or mark it for `Follow Up` if its relevance is uncertain. In the example below, an interesting web search referencing credit card skimmers has been bookmarked:

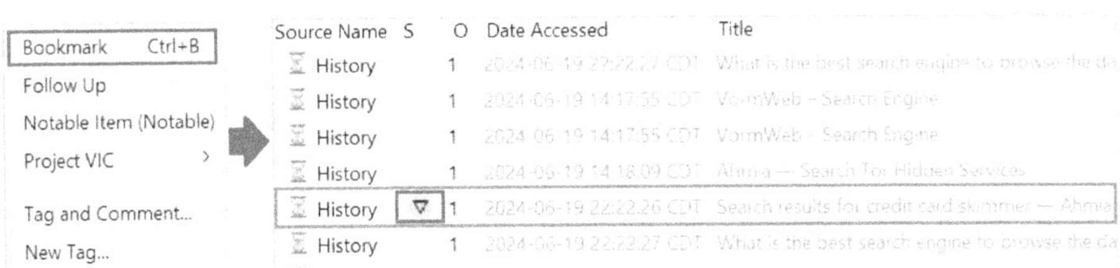

Figure 7.22 – Bookmarking an artifact of interest in Autopsy

2. Within the same submenu, you can create custom tags by selecting **New Tag** and entering a descriptor of your choice. Once created, each tag will appear under the **Add Result Tag** menu for future use:

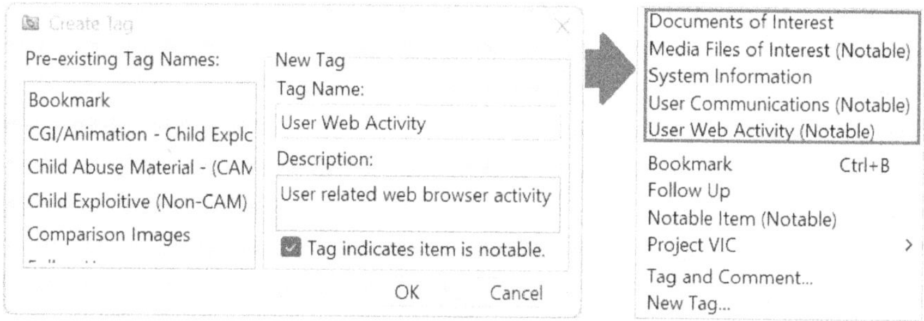

Figure 7.23 – Creating custom tags in Autopsy

3. As we bookmark artifacts during analysis, they will appear in the left-side artifact tree under the **Tags** category. This provides a centralized location to quickly access and review bookmarked items:

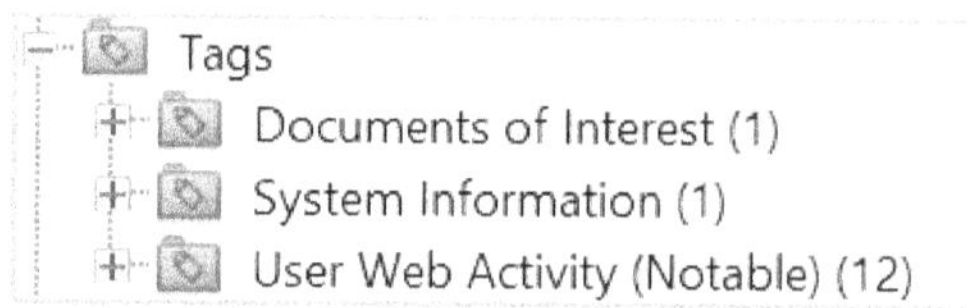

Figure 7.24 – Tagged items list in Autopsy

Tags can be edited or deleted through **Tools | Options**, under the **Custom Tags** tab.

Autopsy frequently displays parsed artifacts in a table format consisting of rows and columns. You can control which columns are visible.

4. Begin by selecting an artifact type from the Tree Viewer. In the example below, **Recent Documents** is selected, displaying files that were recently accessed as recorded in the Microsoft Windows **NTUSER.DAT** registry hive.
5. Right-click any column header to open a list of available fields. From here, you can toggle individual columns on or off to simplify the view. In this example, the display has been reduced to three columns for clarity:

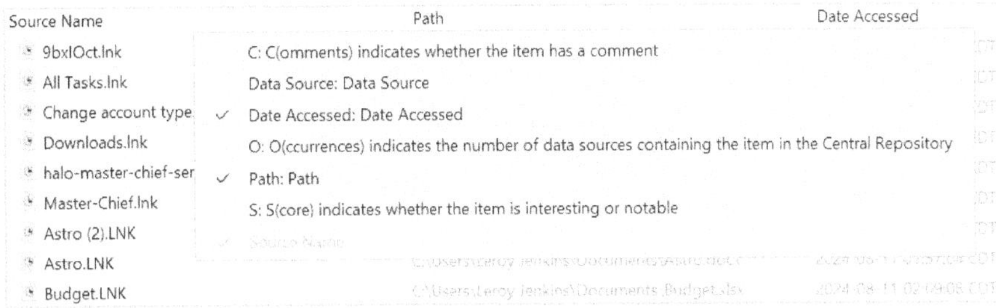

Figure 7.25 – Choosing which columns to display in Autopsy

6. Left-clicking a column header will sort the data in ascending order. Clicking the same column again sorts in descending order, and a third click returns it to the default view. This technique allows you to quickly group and identify items based on dates, file names, or file paths.
   In the example below, artifacts are sorted alphabetically by file name, indicated by bold text and an upward-facing arrow in the selected column header:

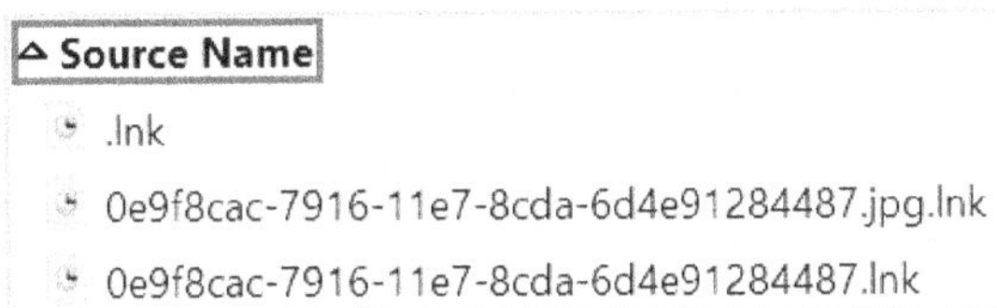

Figure 7.26 – Sorting by columns in Autopsy

   This is a foundational technique for quickly organizing results. Many commercial platforms provide more advanced capabilities, including column-specific keyword searching, filtering, and compound filtering, which combines multiple criteria to better refine results.

7. To further explore and analyze results, open the **Discovery** interface from the top toolbar:

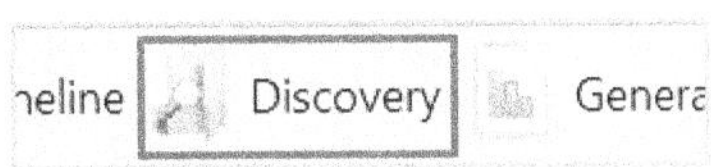

Figure 7.27 – Discovery Content Viewer button in Autopsy

8. The **Discovery** tool provides basic filtering options for Images, Videos, Documents, and web activity (Domains). To begin, run a document filter using the default settings, which identify documents larger than 1 MB. This initial search should return several dozen results.

9. To execute the search, click **Documents** at the top of the Discovery window, then select **Search**:

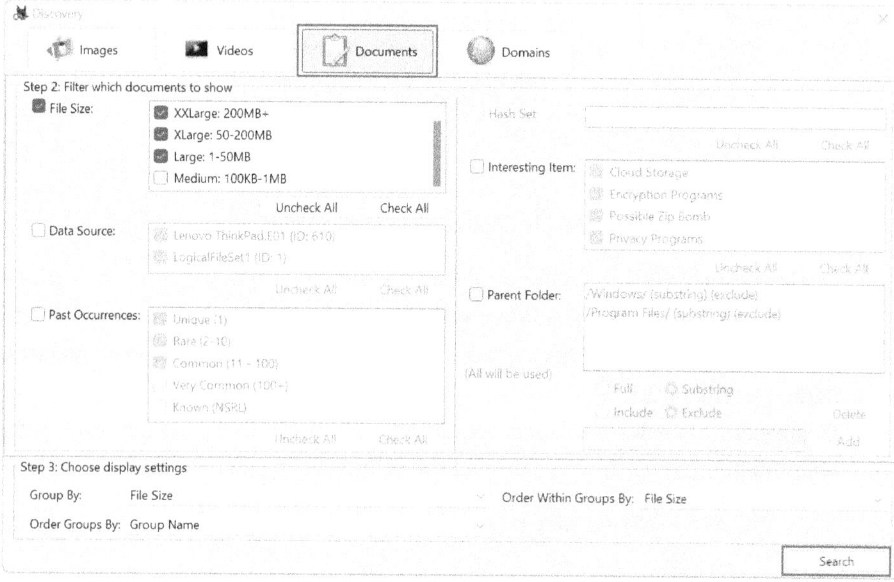

Figure 7.28 – Discovery content viewer window in Autopsy

10. To refine the results, return to the **Discovery** window and select the **Parent Folder** filter. Ensure **Substring** and **Exclude** are selected. The goal is to reduce system-related documents and focus on files more likely created by the user. In the field next to **Add**, type `/ProgramData/` then click **Add**. Repeat this process for `/AppData/` and `/Program Files (x86)/`.

11. These exclusions remove common system directories from the results. Once applied, run the search again:

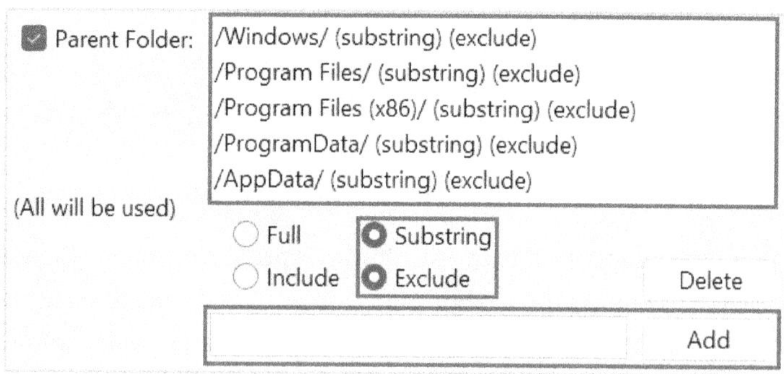

Figure 7.29 – Using Discovery tool to search for documents in autopsy

Depending on how many evidence sources are loaded, this refined search should produce a small number of results. In this example, a single file titled `Airshow` appears within the default Microsoft Windows **Documents** directory:

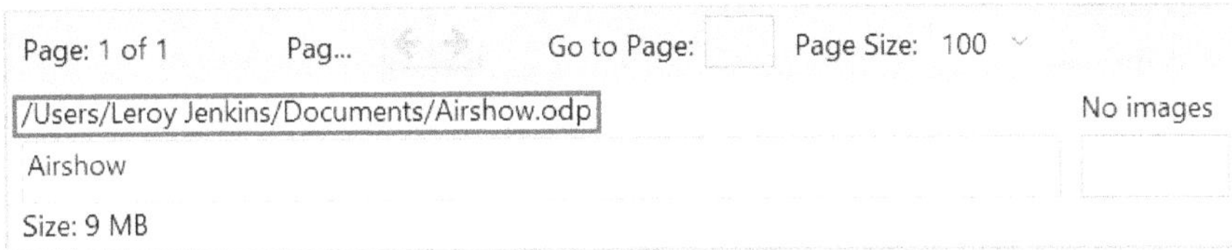

Figure 7.30 – Document file search results using the Discovery tool in Autopsy

Files can exist in many locations within an operating system, making manual directory-by-directory review impractical. Instead, filter by file type using the **Tree Viewer** pane.

12. Expand **File Views**, then select **File Types**. From here, filter files by extension under **By Extension** or by content classification using **By MIME Type**:

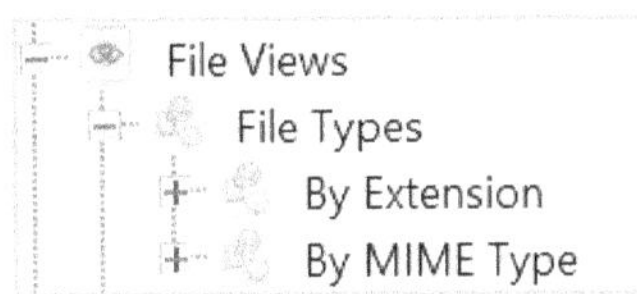

Figure 7.31 – Filtering by file extension or MIME type in Autopsy

13. Expand **By Extension** and select **Images**. In the **Result Viewer**, switch to the **Thumbnail** tab. This displays image thumbnails in a gallery view, allowing rapid review of visual content without navigating individual directories. The same approach can be used to review other file types, including video, audio, archives, and documents:

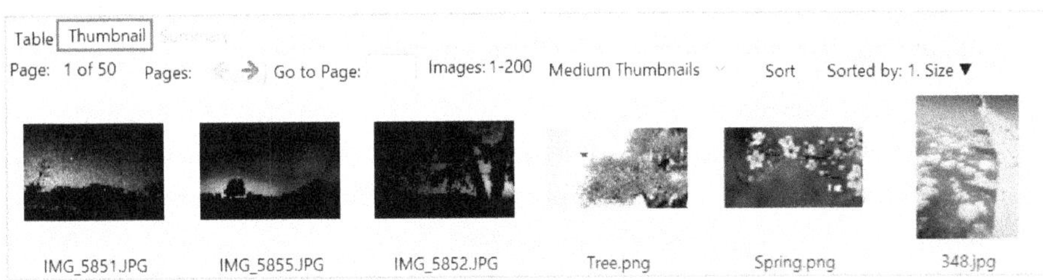

Figure 7.32 – Filtering and displaying images as thumbnails in Autopsy

Within the **Thumbnail** view, the left and right arrows labeled **Pages** navigate between thumbnail pages. A dropdown menu adjusts the thumbnail size, and the **Sort** option organizes the results.

14. Open the **Sort** options to organize results. You can sort thumbnails in ascending or descending order based on criteria such as name, date, file size, hash value, extension, or MIME type. You can also apply multiple sorting criteria by selecting **Add Sort Criteria**.
    When reviewing media content (or most file types) sorting by file size (descending) is often effective. Larger files are more likely to represent user-created content, while system files are often smaller to conserve space:

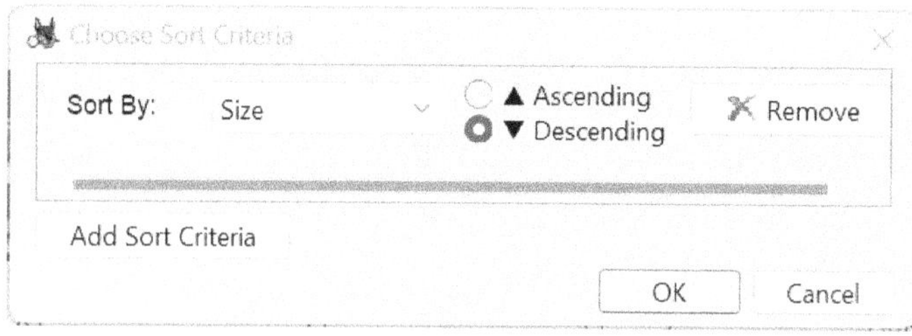

Figure 7.33 – Sorting by file size in Autopsy

15. We can also apply media-specific filtering options. Open the **Images/Videos** viewer from the top toolbar. If prompted, select **OK** to display media files from all added evidence sources:

Figure 7.34 – Images/Videos Content Viewer button in Autopsy

The **Images/Videos** content viewer provides filtering and sorting options for media files, making large datasets more manageable. Without these capabilities, thoroughly reviewing all media content would be impractical.

This viewer also allows examiners to categorize media files, which can be particularly useful in CSAM investigations that often use categorization schemas. Even outside those cases, you may find it helpful to mark files as **Non-Pertinent** to track reviewed items while bookmarking relevant evidence:

Figure 7.35 – Images/Videos content viewer window in Autopsy

16. Use the **Group By** dropdown to apply grouping and filtering options, including **Camera Make** and **Camera Model**. Select **Camera Make**, then choose **Samsung**:

Figure 7.36 – Filtering media files by camera make in Autopsy

Once **Samsung** is selected, results are filtered to display media files containing EXIF metadata indicating they were created using a Samsung device. Filtering by device make or model is an effective way to quickly identify content likely created by the user.

17. You can perform compound filtering based on file attributes using **File Search by Attributes** within the **Tools** menu. This allows filtering by name, size, MIME type, hash value, and date. You can also limit results to a specific data source, apply hash set matching, or restrict results to recovered deleted files.

18. Configure the search as shown to locate JPEG files within the **Lenovo ThinkPad** data source that are larger than 3 MB and have created dates between October 10 and October 12, 2024. Once configured, click **Search**:

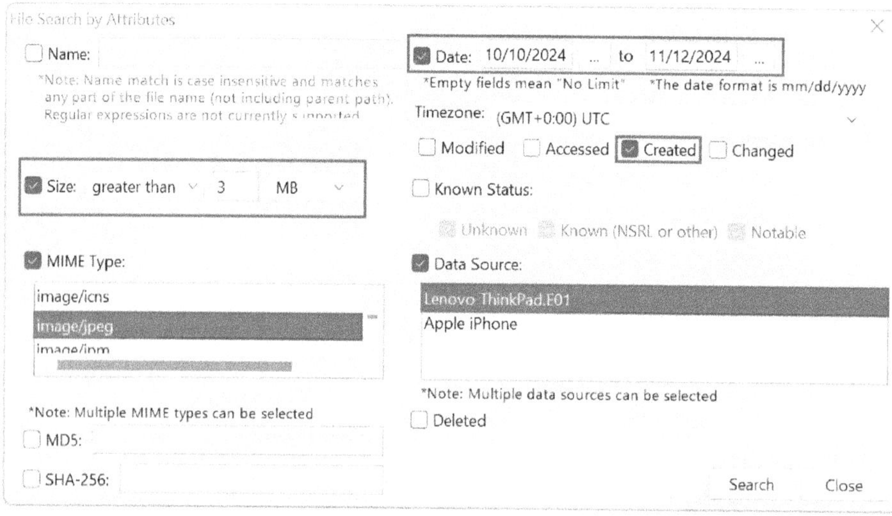

Figure 7.37 – Filtering based on file attributes in Autopsy

Based on the criteria applied, this compound filter should return only two results from the sample dataset:

Figure 7.38 – Filtered results based on file attributes in Autopsy

19. Do you notice anything about these results? Comparing the two entries reveals they are the same file, despite having different filenames, as they share identical hash values. The created dates match; however, the created time for `IMG_9147.jpg` is approximately one hour later than that of `348.jpg`. Expand the `Location` column to review the full file paths:

Figure 7.39 – Comparing file paths in Autopsy

Based on the paths, `348.jpg` appears to be cached within the `/AppData/` directory of the `Leroy Jenkins` user account by Google Drive, as indicated by the `/Google/DriveFS/` folder structure. In contrast, `IMG_9147.jpg` is stored in a user-created directory titled `other` within the default Windows `Pictures` folder.

Also note that the file is identified as an .HEIC image format, commonly associated with Apple devices. This suggests the file was likely created on an Apple device, synchronized to the Windows system via Google Drive, and then saved locally within the user's Pictures directory.

> **Note**
>
> Autopilot on... let's play Nintendo
>
> With automated tools like Autopsy, why spend so much time learning to parse individual artifacts throughout this book? The short answer: just because your aircraft has autopilot doesn't mean you don't need qualified pilots.
>
> Unfortunately, some examiners rely almost entirely on automation during analysis. This mindset is sometimes referred to as "Nintendo forensics" - simply pushing buttons and accepting whatever the tool produces. That approach is dangerous and, I would argue, ethically irresponsible. Even the most respected and expensive commercial suites can fail to parse evidence correctly or misinterpret it entirely. As examiners, we must understand what our tools are doing and be able to independently validate our findings.
>
> If you find yourself becoming overly dependent on automation, take a step back. Complacency in this profession leads to missed evidence, and missed evidence can mean the difference between stopping a follow-up attack, securing justice for a victim, or contributing to the wrongful accusation of an innocent person.

How it works...

Autopsy organizes parsed artifacts into searchable tables that can be sorted, filtered, and categorized to quickly isolate relevant evidence. Rather than manually browsing every directory, you can use tools such as File Views, Discovery, media grouping, and attribute-based searches to narrow large datasets to manageable results.

Bookmarking and tagging preserve items of evidentiary value and centralize them under the **Tags** category for reporting. Column sorting, file-type filtering, metadata grouping, and compound searches (by size, date, MIME type, hash, or data source) allow you to refine results with precision.

Effective analysis is not about viewing everything; it is about intelligently filtering data while retaining the ability to validate and explain your findings.

Applying intelligence in autopsy

In many investigations, examiners are provided with known intelligence that must be located within collected evidence. This may include malware identifiers, usernames, specific text phrases, documents, or known files. Rather than manually searching through datasets, targeted techniques can be used to quickly determine whether these indicators exist within the evidence.

In this section, we will apply keyword searching, pattern matching, and known file hash values to identify intelligence within the case data.

Getting ready

We will continue using the Autopsy case previously created to search for known intelligence, tagging artifacts of evidentiary value as they are located. At this stage, we are applying digital forensic techniques as we would in a real-world investigation.

As we move into deeper filesystem searching, you will also need the **HxD** software introduced in *Chapter 1*, which can be downloaded from `https://mh-nexus.de/en/hxd/`.

How to do it...

Keyword Searching: Keyword searching generally involves three primary search types:

- **Exact** searches locate a precise word or phrase. For example, searching for `light` returns only results containing the exact term **light**.
- **Substring** searches identify occurrences where the keyword appears within other words. Searching for `light` may also return results such as **lights**, **lightly**, **lighting**, **lightning**, **slight**, **flight**, **flashlight**, **floodlight**, **highlight**, **daylight**, **sunlight**, and **moonlight**.
- **Fuzzy** searches attempt to locate similar terms and are useful when accounting for possible misspellings. For example, searching for `light` may also return **ligth**.

Exact matches run faster and reduce false positives but may miss relevant variations. Substring and fuzzy searches require more processing time and often return more results, including additional false positives.

Autopsy and other forensic suites provide a **global search** feature that spans all parsed artifacts within a case. Even in cases involving large volumes of data, these searches run quickly because the software builds an index during ingest. This indexed structure allows searches to execute efficiently without repeatedly scanning raw files. Refer to the following steps:

1. The global search box is located in the upper-right corner of Autopsy. Click **Keyword Search** to access the available options:

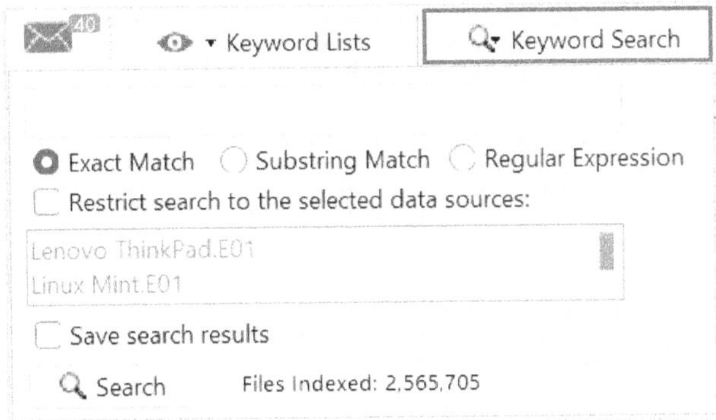

Figure 7.40 – Global keyword search options in Autopsy

The search dialog supports exact and substring matches, along with options for regular expressions, which we will cover later in this section.

The **Restrict search to the selected data sources** checkbox limits the query to specific evidence sources. If left unchecked, the search spans all ingested evidence in the case.

The **Save search results** option stores the results under **Keyword Hits** in the left-side tree viewer, allowing you to revisit them without rerunning the search.

2. Using the **Keyword Search** box, run an **Exact Match** search for `leroy jenkins`. Enable **Restrict search to the Lenovo ThinkPad** evidence source and **Save search results**. The search should be completed within a few seconds and populate the **Result Viewer** with the matching entries. The total number of keyword hits is displayed in the upper-right corner of the pane:

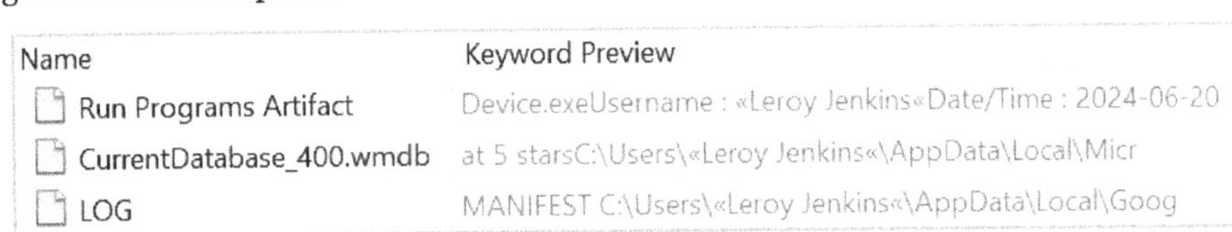

Figure 7.41 – Sample search results for keyword leroy.jenkins

Scroll through the results, which include columns for file name and a **Keyword Preview** showing a snippet of the surrounding text. You may notice that the same file appears multiple times if the keyword occurs more than once within that artifact.

Also note that the results span multiple artifact types, including user files, databases, and system artifacts, such as the Windows registry.

3. Global keyword searches operate only on content that has been parsed and indexed during ingest. To compare this with a raw-level search, load the `Lenovo ThinkPad.E01` image into HxD and perform a text-string search (*Ctrl* + *F*) for `leroy jenkins`. Set the search direction to **All**, then run the search:

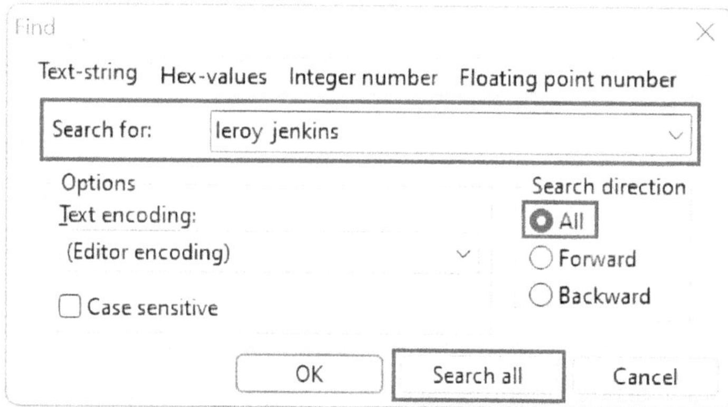

Figure 7.42 – Searching across a file system using HxD

4. This search will run significantly slower (often taking several minutes) because it scans the entire image rather than only indexed artifacts. As a result, it may return thousands of keyword hits.

   While less efficient, this deeper search can be valuable when artifact-level searches produce limited results. It may reveal relevant content within unparsed or unsupported artifacts that were not indexed during ingest:

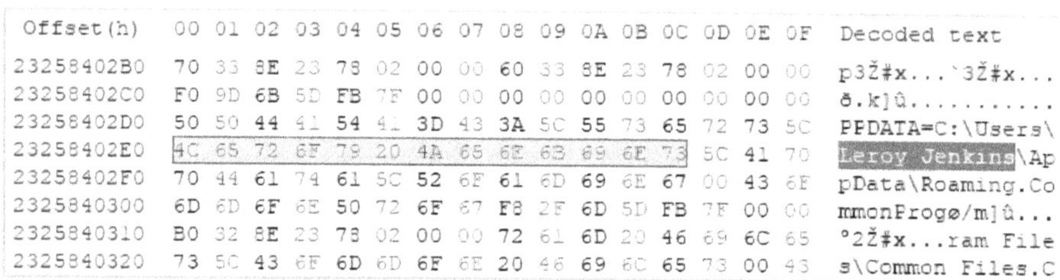

Figure 7.43 – Sample keyword search match in HxD

5. Forensic analysis suites also allow you to search multiple terms simultaneously using a **keyword list**. These lists can typically be added during initial ingest or after processing is complete.

6. In Autopsy, keyword lists can be configured within the **Keyword Search** module settings during case setup or added later. To add a list after processing, open **Tools | Options**, then select **Keyword Search**:

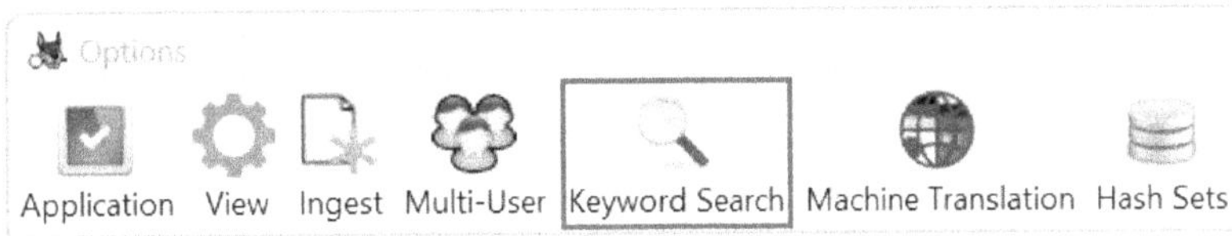

Figure 7.44 – Keyword Search options button in Autopsy

7. In the left section of the **Keyword Search** options window, click **New List** and create a keyword list named **Case Keywords**:

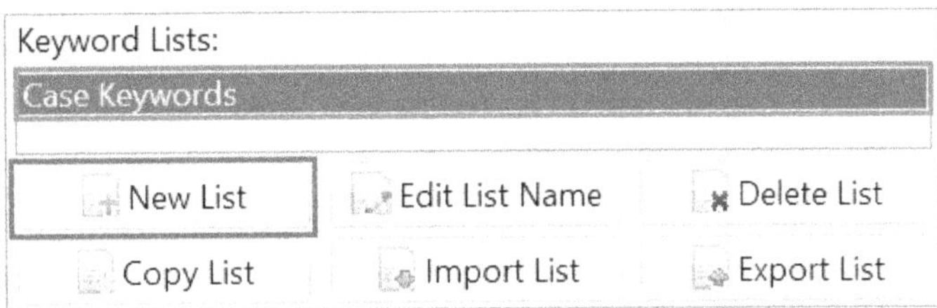

Figure 7.45 – Keyword list created in Autopsy

8. With the **Case Keywords** list selected, click **New Keywords** and add the following terms: `solar eclipse`, `apple iphone`, `samsung galaxy`, and `mow the lawn`. Leave **Exact Match** selected, then click **OK**.
9. Back in the main **Keyword Search** window, click **Apply** to save the list. You should now see the keywords associated with the **Case Keywords** list. Click **OK** to close the window:

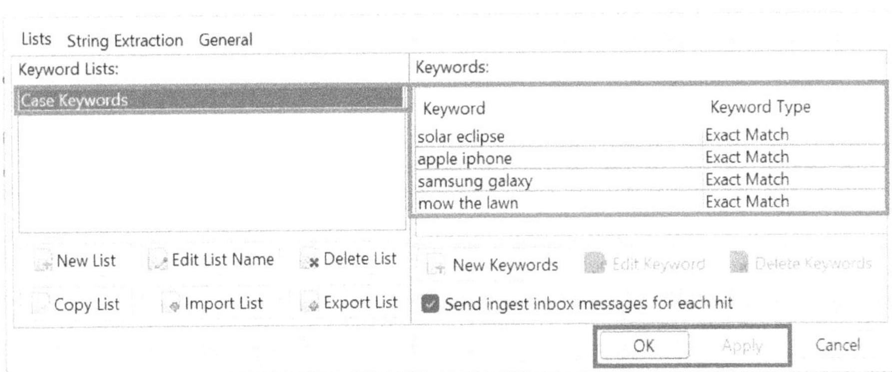

Figure 7.46 – Keywords added to keyword list

10. In the upper-right corner, open **Keyword Lists**, select the **Case Keywords** list, restrict the search to the **Lenovo ThinkPad** evidence source, and run the search.
    This will execute a query for all keywords contained in the list. Once the search is completed, review the results:

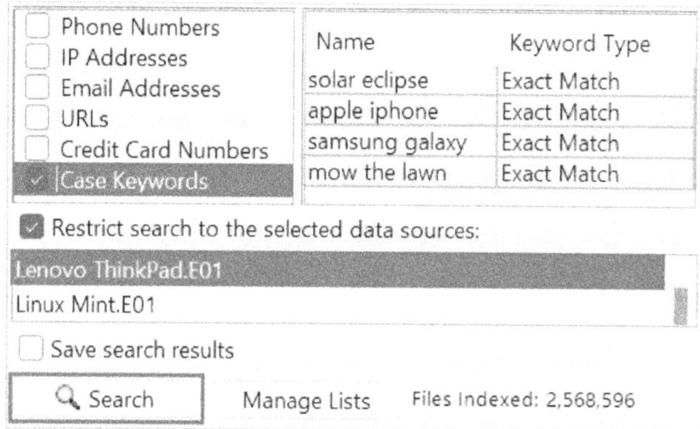

Figure 7.47 – Running a search against a keyword list in Autopsy

11. Do you notice anything missing from the results? In most cases, the keyword phrase `mow the lawn` will not appear. Although the phrase exists within the dataset, it is embedded in an image rather than stored as plain text.
    Many forensic analysis suites (including Autopsy) can extract and index text from images and PDFs using **optical character recognition (OCR)**.

12. To enable this capability, navigate to **Tools | Run Ingest Modules**, select the `Lenovo ThinkPad.E01` evidence source, and configure the modules as shown below. Enable the **Keyword Search** module and select the option to **Enable Optical Character Recognition (OCR)**. When finished, click **Finish**:

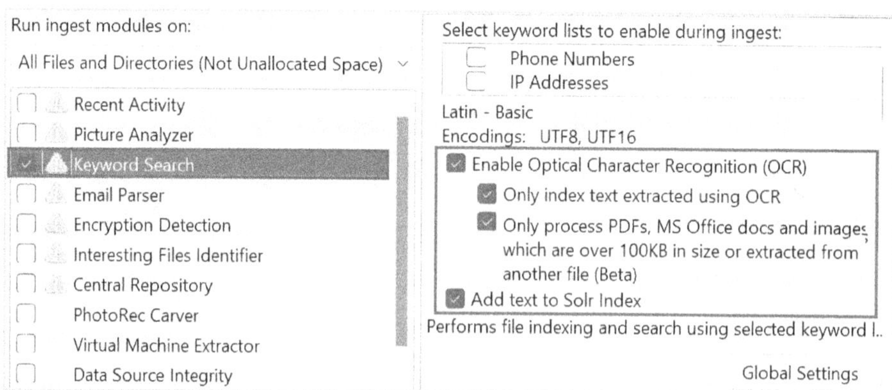

Figure 7.48 – Running Keyword Search Module with OCR in Autopsy

13. Run another **Exact Match** keyword search for the phrase `mow the lawn` and review the results. This time, the search should return a hit. You will see that OCR has extracted the text from an image file titled `6.2.jpg`:

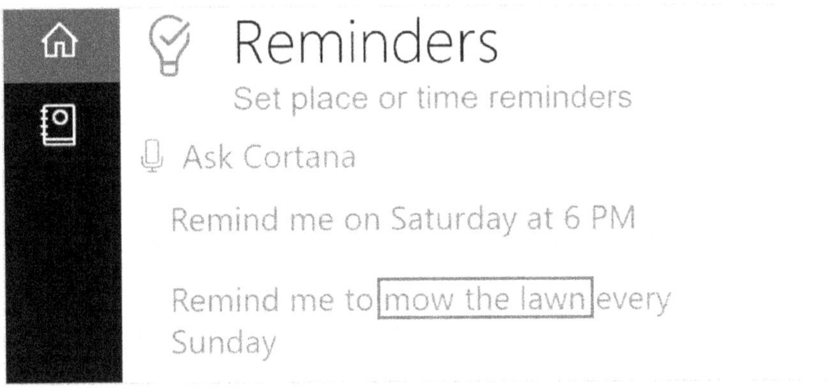

Figure 7.49 – Sample image file text found using OCR in Autopsy

14. **Regular Expressions:** Unlike keywords, which search for exact terms, regular expressions (regex) are used to search for patterns in text. For example, if we had a known credit card number, we could search for that exact number using a keyword. However, if we wanted to locate all credit card numbers in our case, we would use regex to find strings that match the general pattern of a credit card number.
To build on this example, consider how credit card numbers are commonly formatted. Typically, they consist of 16 digits. These digits may appear consecutively (`1234567890987654`), separated by spaces after every fourth digit (`1234 5678 9098 7654`), or separated by hyphens (`1234-5678-9098-7654`). A regex pattern matching this structure could look like: `^(\d{4}[-\s]?){3}\d{4}$`

    Breaking this down:

    - `^` marks the beginning of the string
    - `\d` represents any digit from 0–9
    - `{4}` limits the match to exactly four digits

    After each four-digit group, the pattern allows an optional hyphen (`-`) or space (`\s`). This portion is enclosed in brackets `[-\s]`, and the `?` indicates that the hyphen or space may or may not be present. The entire first section is grouped using parentheses: `(\d{4}[-\s]?)`

    This captures the first four digits optionally followed by a space or hyphen, producing matches like `xxxx-`, `xxxx`, or `xxxx`.

The `{3}` repeats this grouped pattern three times, producing matches such as `xxxx-xxxx-xxxx-`, `xxxx xxxx xxxx`, or `xxxxxxxxxxxx`.

We still need the final four digits. We cannot repeat the grouped pattern a fourth time because it would allow the string to end with a space or hyphen. Instead, we add: `\d{4}`

This matches the final four digits with no trailing separator. The `$` symbol marks the end of the string.

Of course, this pattern only matches 16-digit credit cards. Some cards, such as American Express, use 15 digits. You can see how patterns can quickly become more complex. The complexity increases further with formats like phone numbers, which vary by region and may include country codes, parentheses, hyphens, or other separators.

Regex includes many additional symbols and operators. The goal here is not to make you an expert, but to provide a foundation for recognizing and applying pattern-based searches during an investigation. If you would like to learn more about writing regex strings, there are many free tutorials available online, including practical guides from websites such as `freeCodeCamp`.

> **Note**
>
> Thanks! I hate it.
>
> Some digital forensic examiners love writing regex. Most, however, approach it with the same enthusiasm as scheduling a root canal. Depending on the pattern, regex can become surprisingly complex—entire books are dedicated to it. Fortunately, the level of regex we typically use in digital forensics is minimal, and I have two *local e*-administered anesthetics to help ease the pain a little—yeah, I know that was a painfully nerdy "dad joke"... moving on.

The first way to avoid manually writing regex is to leverage the built-in capabilities of your forensic software when available. Many forensic tools include prebuilt regex patterns for commonly encountered data.

Autopsy, for example, provides predefined regex patterns for phone numbers, IP addresses, credit card numbers, email addresses, and Social Security numbers. These can be accessed through the **Keyword Lists** option near the upper-right corner of Autopsy.

Running a regex search for e-mail address patterns will return numerous results across parsed artifacts. Be aware, however, that regex searches generally take longer to complete than simple exact-match keyword searches:

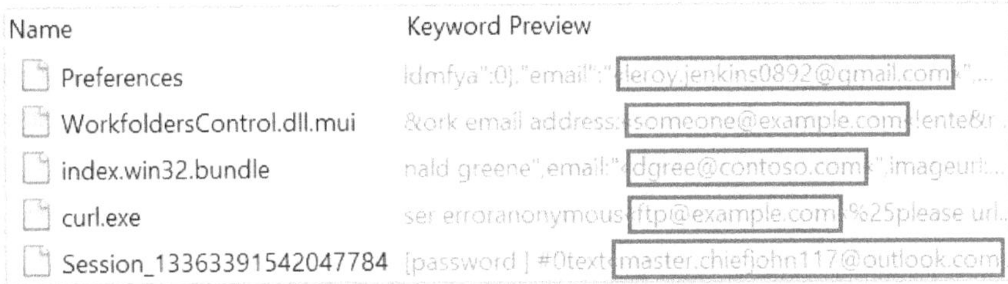

Figure 7.50 – Regex search results for e-mail address patterns in Autopsy

15. Unfortunately, not all digital forensic suites provide prewritten regex patterns, and we may encounter more unique or uncommon formats that require custom expressions. A practical alternative is to leverage tools that can generate regex for you, such as artificial intelligence.
AI tools are remarkably effective at generating regex with little to no modification required. For example, tools such as ChatGPT can produce patterns quickly.

Perhaps a driver's license begins with a letter and is followed by ten digits. We could ask AI to "write a regular expression for text that starts with a letter (a-z), followed by ten digits (0-9)," which will produce results like those shown:

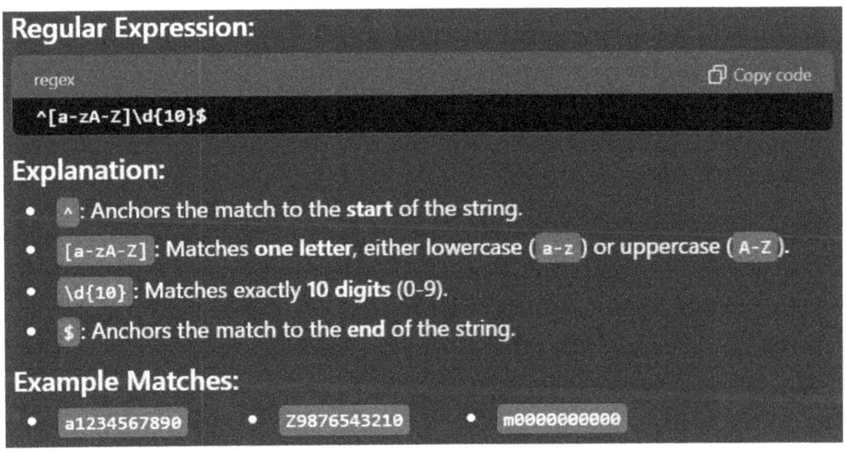

Figure 7.51 – Using AI to write regex

As you can see, ChatGPT also provides explanations and example matches. This makes it easier to validate the pattern and refine it before use in an investigation. As with any automated output, always validate the generated regex before relying on it in a forensic examination.

Hash Sets (Known Relevant Files): Another form of potential intelligence we may gather consists of hash values, which are alphanumeric strings produced by applying a mathematical algorithm to a file. Hashes are widely used in computer science to verify data integrity. For example, when data is transmitted over a network, hash values can be used to confirm that packets were not corrupted or tampered with by comparing the received hash values to expected values. This makes hashing an important concept in fields such as network engineering and cybersecurity.

In essence, a hash value functions like a digital fingerprint, uniquely representing the contents of a file or data.

In digital forensics, hash values are used to validate and verify acquired data. Common hashing algorithms in forensic practice include Message-Digest Algorithm 5 (MD5) and Secure Hash Algorithm (SHA) variants, such as SHA-1, SHA-256, and SHA-512. We have already used hashing algorithms in previous chapters to validate acquisitions and verify sanitized drives.

Because hashing can be applied to entire drives or individual files, hash values can also help locate known files. Examples include identifying malware executables or locating specific evidentiary files discovered during an investigation, such as illicit material previously reported online.

File names and extensions do not affect a file's hash value, as these attributes are stored by the file system rather than within the file itself. Conversely, even a minor change to a file's contents (such as modifying a single pixel in a photograph or a single character in a document) will produce a completely different hash value. This means we can identify files with absolute certainty, even if they have been renamed or moved.

16. Since we enabled the **Hash Lookup** module during initial processing, Autopsy has calculated hash values for parsed files within our case. This allows us to search for known hash values. From the **Tools** menu, use **File Search by Attributes**, enable the **MD5** checkbox, and enter the MD5 hash value `201151d33a835f4eda334942a7b21565`. When ready, click the **Search** button:

Figure 7.52 – Searching for a hash value in Autopsy

17. This search should return a single result: a video file titled `7919.mp4`, depicting a Northrop B-2 Spirit stealth bomber flying overhead.

Figure 7.53 – Results of hash value search in Autopsy

18. If you have multiple hash values, you can import them as a hash set. Hash sets allow us to quickly identify known files across large datasets, whether they are known good, known malicious, or otherwise relevant to a case.
    Download the `Hash Sets` dataset from the book's GitHub repository. To access the repository link, follow the steps in the *Download the example code files* section in the *Preface*.

    This list contains several dozen hash values corresponding to files in the **Lenovo ThinkPad** evidence source. Once downloaded, extract the contents and locate the file titled `Evidence Files`. These represent known evidence files we want to identify on the system.

    From **Tools** | **Options**, select **Hash Sets** and click **Import Hash Set**:

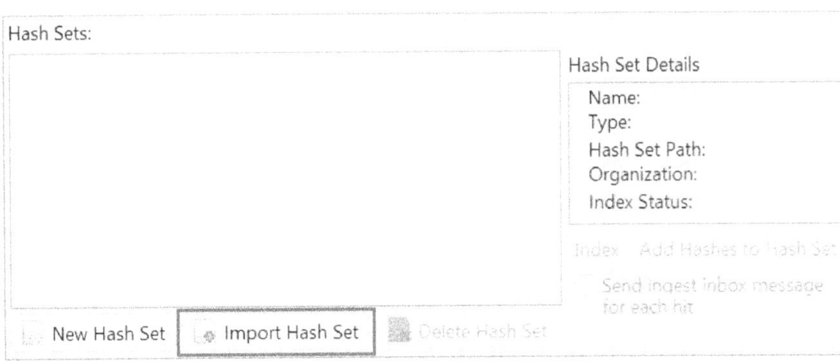

Figure 7.54 – Hash set options in Autopsy

19. For **Hash Set Path**, browse to the downloaded `Evidence Files` hash list. Ensure the following settings are configured:
    - **Destination**: **Local**
    - **Type of hash set**: **Notable**
    - **Send ingest inbox message for each hit**: Selected

    Click **OK** to complete the import:

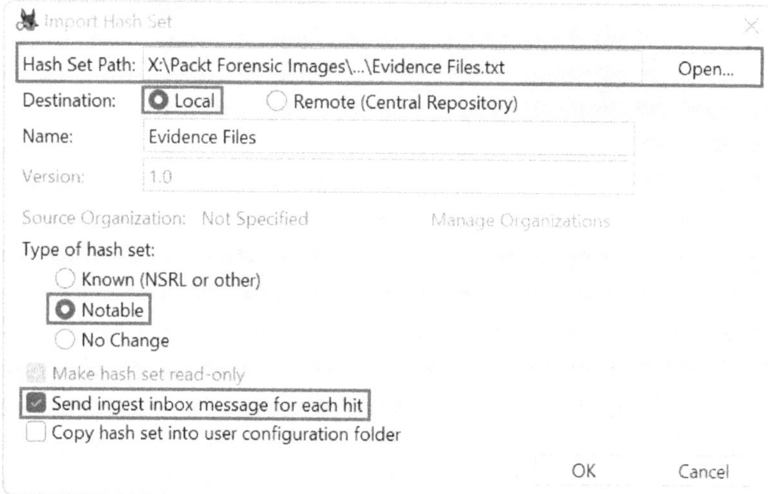

Figure 7.55 – Importing a hash set in Autopsy

20. The hash set details will appear in the list. Click **Index**, then **Apply**:

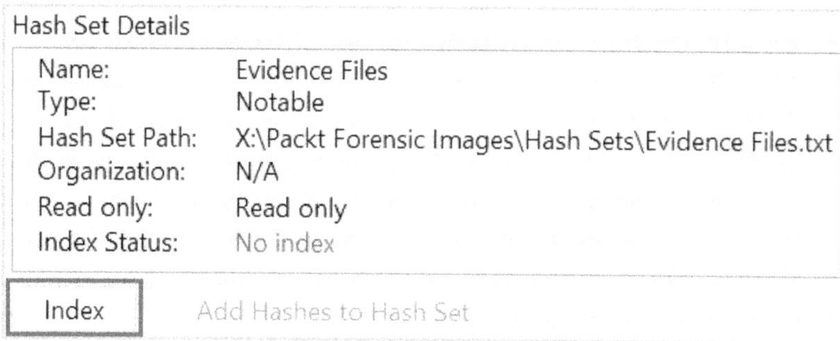

Figure 7.56 – Indexing a hash set in Autopsy

21. We now need to rerun the **Hash Lookup** module to incorporate the newly imported hash set.

Rerun ingest on the `Lenovo ThinkPad.E01` evidence source with only the **Hash Lookup** module enabled.

Ensure the **Evidence Files (Notable)** hash set is selected, then click **Finish**:

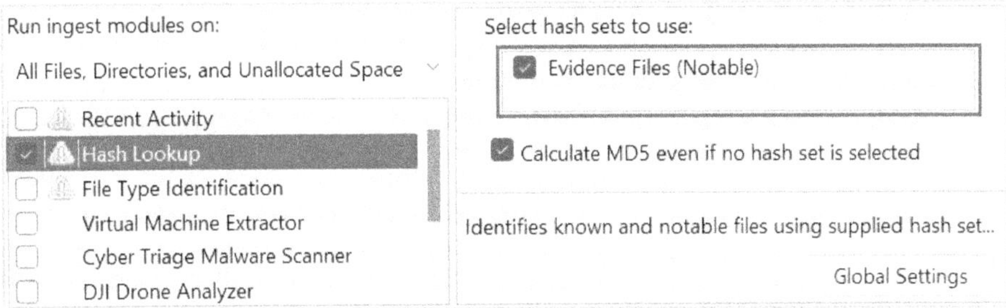

Figure 7.57 – Rerunning the Hash Lookup module in Autopsy

22. If any values from the imported hash set are present in the parsed artifacts, results will appear in the **Tree Viewer** pane of Autopsy. Expand **Hashset Hits**, then select the relevant hash set name to review matching results in the **Result Viewer** pane. While different forensic suites may display hash set matches differently, all major platforms provide a method for performing bulk hash comparisons. This capability is especially useful when quickly identifying known files across large datasets, such as malware, contraband, or previously identified evidence:

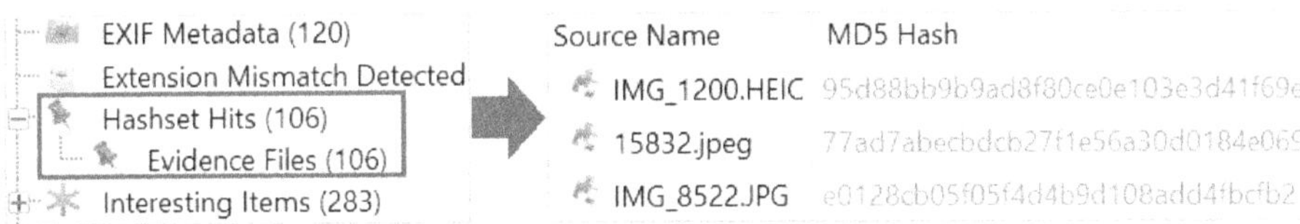

Figure 7.58 – Notable hash set results in Autopsy

> **Note**
>
> Known file databases
>
> Certain investigations rely on established databases of known files. These may include known malware, illicit material, or other evidentiary content. For investigations involving child sexual abuse material (CSAM), databases such as **Project VIC** in the United States and the **Child Abuse Image Database (CAID)** in the UK are commonly used. These systems maintain hash values for files previously identified and cataloged by law enforcement. Leveraging these databases allows examiners to rapidly identify known material by automatically matching file hash values against known entries.

Hash Sets (Non-Pertinent Files): In addition to locating known evidence, hash values can also be used to filter out non-pertinent files. This technique improves efficiency by reducing the number of files that must be reviewed. On most systems, the majority of files will have no evidentiary value. These commonly include operating system files, application components, icons, and other standard software artifacts.

NIST maintains a large reference database of known files for common operating systems. This dataset, known as the **National Software Reference Library (NSRL)**, can be downloaded from: `https://www.nist.gov/itl/ssd/software-quality-group/national-software-reference-library-nsrl/nsrl-download/current-rds`

From this page, you will see multiple download options. The **Full SQL Downloads** contain the complete dataset, while **Delta SQL Downloads** provide incremental updates with newly cataloged files.

NIST now distributes NSRL primarily in SQLite format. Some forensic tools support this format directly, while others require conversion to a text-based hash set. The NIST download page includes documentation explaining how to export hash values from the SQL database if needed. Because the NSRL dataset is large, downloading and ingesting it into forensic software can take considerable time. In practice, it is common to allow hash set ingestion to run overnight.

Breakpoint Forensics provides an **NSRL RDSv3 Hash Converter** tool to reduce these datasets to essential hash values and prepare them for import into most forensic tools: `https://breakpointforensics.com/tools/`

To keep this exercise manageable, a sample `Known System Files` hash set is included in the `Hash Sets` dataset downloaded earlier from the book's GitHub repository.

23. As before, open **Tools** | **Options**, select the **Hash Sets** tab, and **Import Hash Set**. For **Hash Set Path**, browse to the downloaded **Known System Files** hash set. This time, select **Known (NSRL or other)** so these files are treated as nonpertinent instead of being flagged as notable hits.
24. Click **OK**, then **Index**, followed by **Apply** as before:

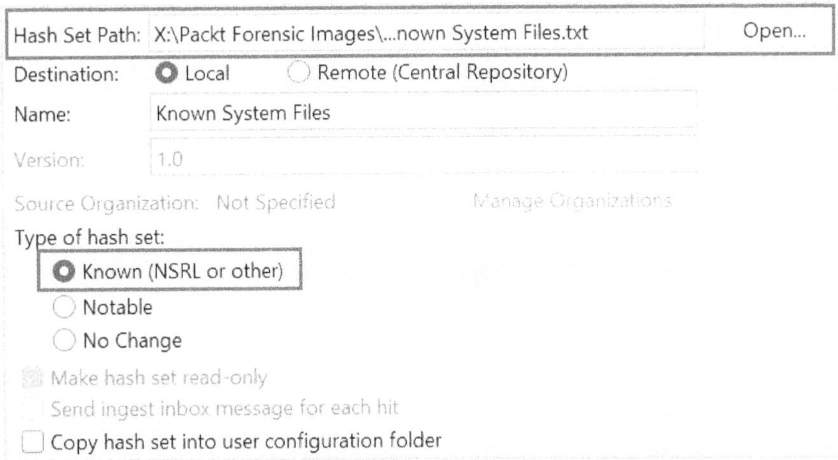

Figure 7.59 – Adding a known file hash set for ignorable files in Autopsy

25. In the **Tree Viewer** pane, navigate to **File Views** | **File Types** | **By Extension**, then select **Images**. The **Result Viewer** will populate with image files. Note the total page count displayed in this view (each page contains 10,000 files by default).
26. Next, rerun the **Hash Lookup** module by navigating to **Tools** | **Run Ingest Modules** and selecting the `Lenovo ThinkPad.E01` evidence source. In the module configuration window, ensure the **Known System Files (Known)** hash set is selected, then click **Finish**:

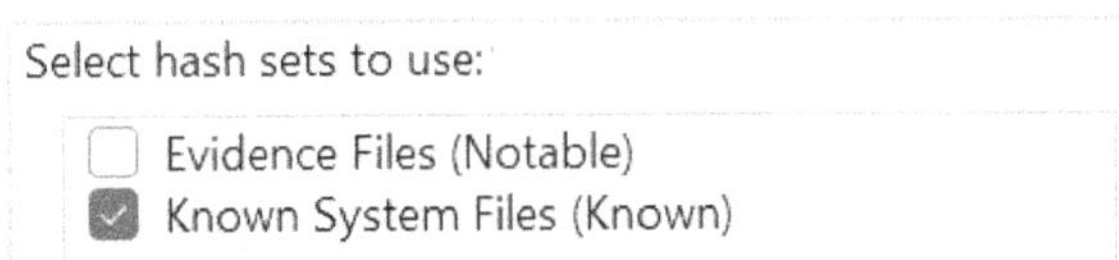

Figure 7.60 – Rerunning the Hash Lookup module in Autopsy

Once processing completes, return to the **Tree Viewer** and review the page count for the parsed images. You should see one fewer page of results than before, reflecting the 10,000 files that were identified as known and filtered from view.

27. Note that these files have not been removed from the case – they are simply hidden from the current view. If needed, they can be displayed again by clicking the **Cog Wheel** icon in the **Tree Viewer** pane to open **Global Settings**, then unchecking the option to hide known files:

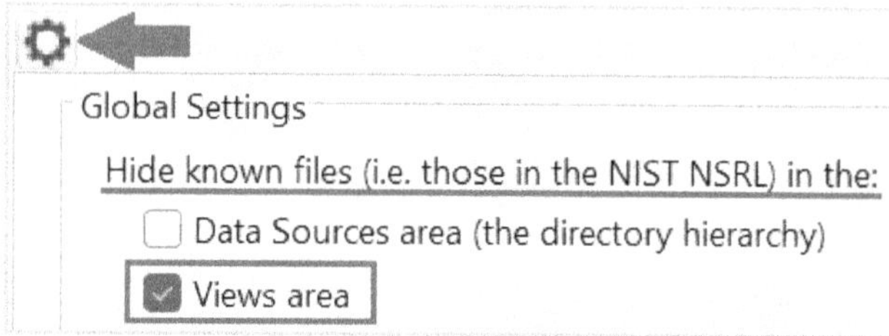

Figure 7.61 – Global Settings options to hide known files in Autopsy

How it works...

Applying intelligence in Autopsy shifts analysis from broad exploration to targeted identification. Instead of manually reviewing artifacts, we use indexed keyword searches, pattern matching, and hash comparisons to quickly locate known indicators across large datasets.

Keyword searches operate against indexed content, allowing fast global queries. OCR extends this capability by extracting searchable text from images and PDFs. Regular expressions further enhance searching by identifying structured patterns (such as credit card numbers or email addresses) rather than fixed strings. Prebuilt regex and AI-assisted generation can simplify this process, provided the results are validated.

Hash values offer another powerful technique. Because hashes uniquely represent file contents, they allow us to instantly identify known files regardless of name or location. Hash sets can be used both to locate known evidentiary files and to filter out nonpertinent system files, reducing investigative noise without removing evidence.

Together, these techniques enable intelligence-driven analysis—focusing on what is known, isolating what is relevant, and increasing efficiency without sacrificing accuracy.

Parsing mobile devices with iLEAPP and aLEAPP

Throughout this chapter, we have focused on leveraging automation to increase efficiency while maintaining analytical rigor. The same philosophy applies when examining mobile devices. Rather than manually locating and parsing each artifact within an acquisition, we can use specialized tools to automatically extract and interpret commonly relevant mobile artifacts.

Commercial forensic suites such as Magnet Axiom and Cellebrite provide powerful mobile parsing capabilities, but they require licensing and ongoing costs. Fortunately, the digital forensic community also benefits from a robust open-source alternative developed by FBI Special Agent Alexis Brignoni.

This project, collectively known as **xLEAPP**, consists of multiple tools designed to parse artifacts from mobile devices, vehicle infotainment systems, and other digital evidence sources. In this section, we will focus specifically on **iLEAPP** (for Apple iOS) and **aLEAPP** (for Android), which automate artifact parsing from mobile device acquisitions and generate structured, review-ready results.

Getting ready

The **xLEAPP** applications are available on Alexis Brignoni's GitHub page: `https://github.com/abrignoni`

Previously, installing **iLEAPP** and **aLEAPP** required manually installing Python and several dependencies. This process was simplified with the release of standalone Windows GUI executables.

For **iLEAPP**, download the latest `ileappGUI-<version>-Windows.zip` file from: `https://github.com/abrignoni/iLEAPP/releases/`

For **aLEAPP**, download the latest `aleappGU-<version>-Windows.exe` file from: `https://github.com/abrignoni/aLEAPP/releases/`

How to do it...

1. After downloading the **iLEAPP** executable, extract the contents and double-click the file to launch the application. When running it for the first time, Windows may display a security warning indicating that the application is from an unknown publisher. If this occurs, select **More info | Run anyway** to proceed.
   A Command Prompt window may briefly appear as the application initializes. After a few moments, the **iLEAPP** interface will load:

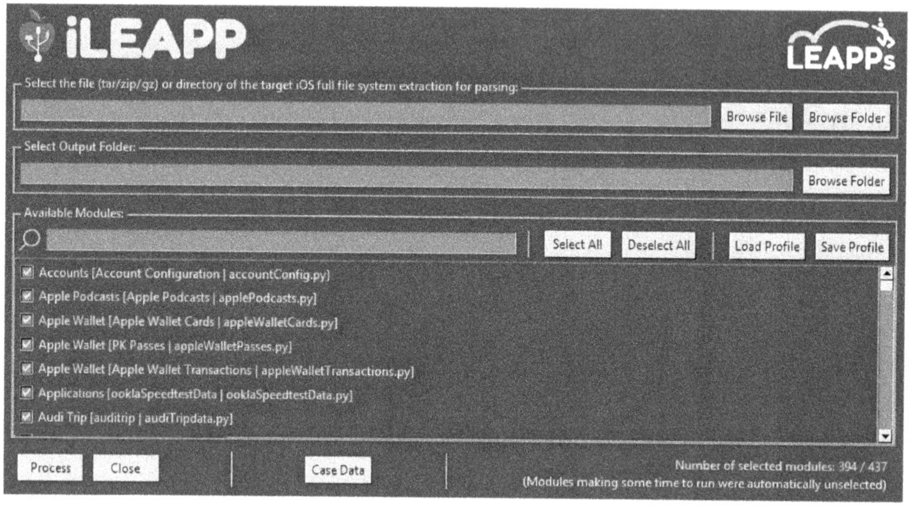

Figure 7.62 – Running iLEAPP

2. Click **Browse File** in the first file path field and navigate to the sample Apple iOS acquisition, or select your own iOS acquisition.
3. In the second field labeled **Select Output Folder**, click **Browse Folder** to choose a destination where iLEAPP will store the parsed results:

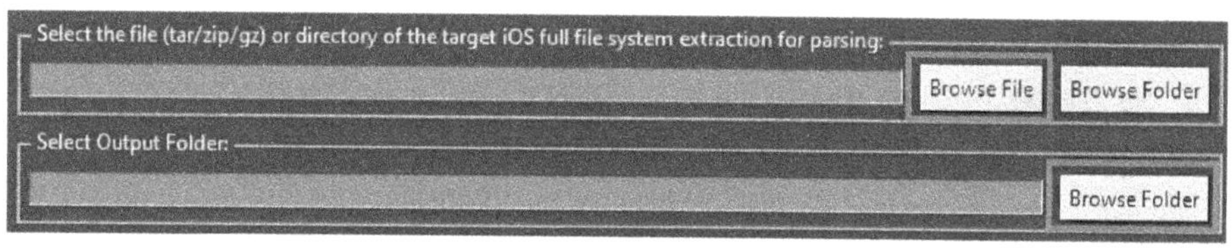

Figure 7.63 – Selecting input and output options in iLEAPP

4. The next section allows you to select which artifacts to parse. Click **Select All** to process all available iLEAPP artifacts.
5. If you routinely perform specific types of analysis (such as rapid triage) you can select only the desired artifacts and click **Save Profile** to preserve that selection for future cases. Selecting all artifacts is useful for full analysis, while targeted selections can significantly reduce processing time during triage:

Figure 7.64 – Saving and loading profiles in iLEAPP

6. The **Available Modules** section lists individual artifacts that can be selected or deselected. Since we chose **Select All**, we can click **Process** to begin parsing all the selected modules:

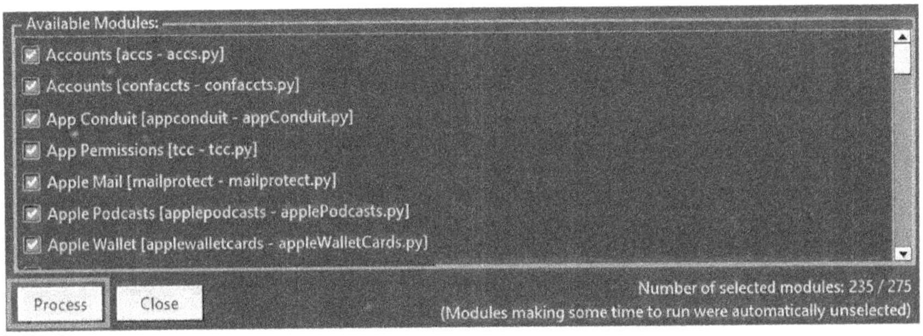

Figure 7.65 – Module list in iLEAPP

As artifacts are processed, a detailed log and progress bar are displayed, allowing you to monitor activity in real time:

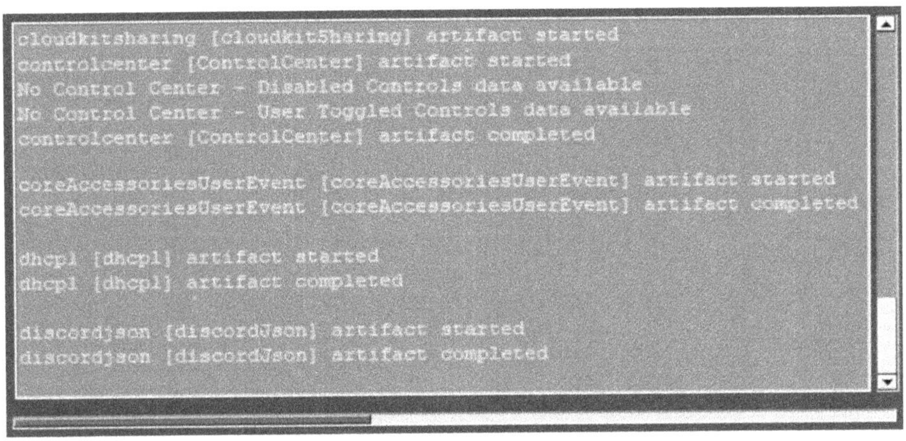

Figure 7.66 – Processing progress in iLEAPP

Once processing completes, iLEAPP provides the option to open the results, which are generated as HTML files viewable in any web browser. The main report page, **index.html**, is located in the output folder you selected earlier:

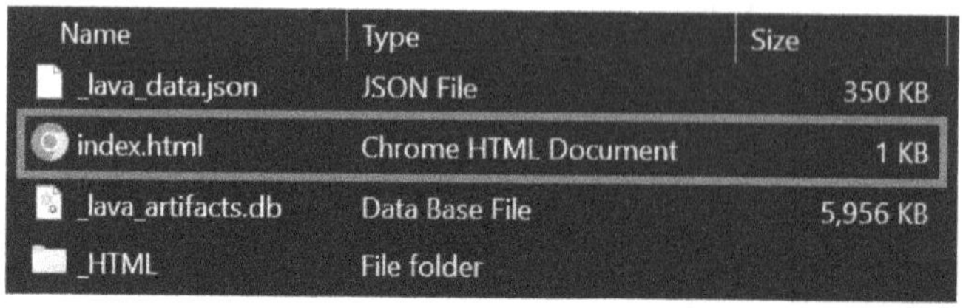

Figure 7.67 – Parsed results stored from iLEAPP

Opening **index.html** loads the home page of the parsed artifact report. Case information is displayed in the main pane, while the navigation panel on the left provides access to individual artifact categories and detailed results:

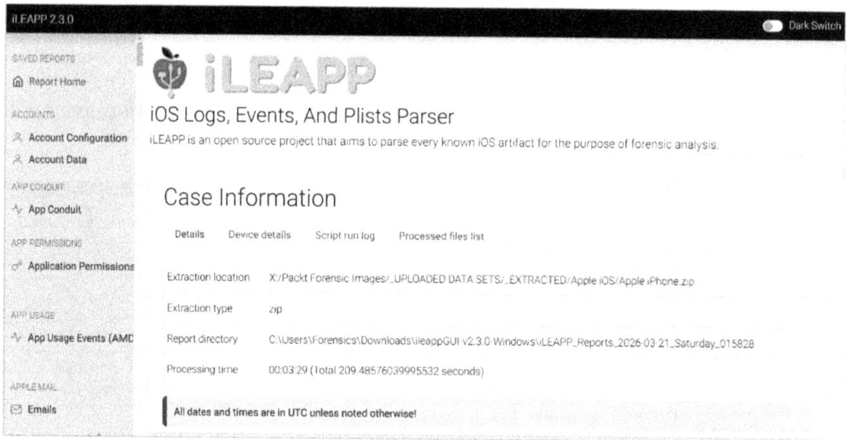

Figure 7.68 – Parsed results stored from iLEAPP

Within the case information section, several tabs provide quick access to device details and parsing logs. The example below shows sample device data:

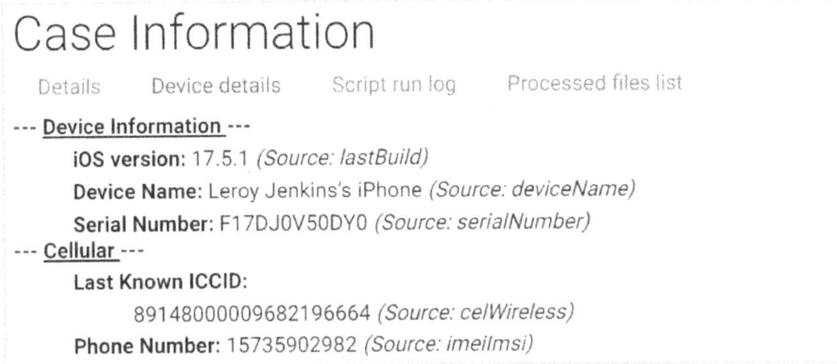

Figure 7.69 – Device details presented in iLEAPP

7. Selecting a category in the left-side navigation pane displays details for that artifact. Each category corresponds to a module selected during processing. The example here shows media files on the iPhone marked as hidden by the user, which can indicate an attempt to conceal content:

zAsset-Modification Date-0	zAsset-Hidden-1	zAsset-Directory-Path-2	zAsset-Filename-3	zAsset-zPK-8	zAsset-UUID = store.cloudphotodb-10
2024-07-17 06:28:54	1-Asset Hidden-1	DCIM/100APPLE	IMG_0011.JPG	11	2D757F3C-E614-4042-AD69-134D0A44274F
2024-07-17 06:28:54	1-Asset Hidden-1	DCIM/100APPLE	IMG_0009.WEBP	9	026109CA-E58D-436D-93C1-1CE81A0861A6
2024-07-17 06:28:54	1-Asset Hidden-1	DCIM/100APPLE	IMG_0010.JPG	10	810AE914-20C0-462D-AE14-6150B6A9ED9F
2024-07-17 06:28:54	1-Asset Hidden-1	DCIM/100APPLE	IMG_0012.JPG	12	4F8784E2-421D-48A5-ABBE-13F06DE9B797
2024-07-17 06:28:54	1-Asset Hidden-1	DCIM/100APPLE	IMG_0013.WEBP	13	E5CE845D-2A5E-4C2A-AD18-451BE41DE865
2024-07-17 06:28:54	1-Asset Hidden-1	DCIM/100APPLE	IMG_0008.JPG	3	849C1AD0-DC8A-49B4-8DE6-82FC53925EFB

Figure 7.70 – Files marked as hidden within the Photos.sqlite database

In the previous chapter, we reviewed iOS artifacts such as KnowledgeC and SEGB data. SEGB artifacts are extremely difficult to manually parse, as they require carving numerous protobuf entries from binary files.

Within the iLEAPP report, locate the section labeled `Biome Keybag`. Here, iLEAPP parses these protobuf entries and presents them in a readable format showing device state transitions, including timestamps for when the device was locked and unlocked by the user. These records can help establish user activity timelines, such as when a device was actively in use versus idle or locked:

SEGB Timestamp	Start Time	End Time	isLocked
2024-08-13 02:50:18.861060+00:00	2024-08-12 16:33:24+00:00	2024-08-13 02:50:16+00:00	1 - Locked
2024-08-13 02:53:07.825370+00:00	2024-08-13 02:50:16+00:00	2024-08-13 02:53:04+00:00	0 - Unlocked
2024-08-13 02:54:59.135857+00:00	2024-08-13 02:53:04+00:00	2024-08-13 02:54:56+00:00	1 - Locked
2024-08-13 02:55:46.697029+00:00	2024-08-13 02:54:56+00:00	2024-08-13 02:55:44+00:00	0 - Unlocked
2024-08-13 03:17:05.456339+00:00	2024-08-13 02:55:44+00:00	2024-08-13 03:17:04+00:00	1 - Locked
2024-08-13 03:18:16.609081+00:00	2024-08-13 03:17:04+00:00	2024-08-13 03:18:16+00:00	0 - Unlocked
2024-08-13 03:18:22.447756+00:00	2024-08-13 03:18:16+00:00	2024-08-13 03:18:20+00:00	1 - Locked

Figure 7.71 – Parsed SEGB data showing device lock/unlock states

There are too many artifacts that iLEAPP and aLEAPP can parse, especially from a full filesystem acquisition like our practice dataset, to realistically review each one manually. Rather than attempting to catalog every available artifact, the focus here is on understanding how parsed results can be used to answer investigative questions. In practice, examiners prioritize artifacts based on case context, using tools like iLEAPP and aLEAPP to rapidly surface relevant data rather than exhaustively reviewing every artifact category.

Processing an Android device follows the same steps outlined above, using aLEAPP instead of iLEAPP.

How it works...

iLEAPP and aLEAPP parse artifacts from Apple iOS and Android acquisitions by reading known databases, configuration files, and structured data (such as SQLite databases, property lists, and binary files) and converting them into organized, human-readable reports. Rather than manually carving and interpreting raw data, these tools parse known artifact types and present them in a structured format.

However, as with any automated solution, the results are limited to what the tool is programmed to recognize and parse. Newly introduced artifacts, corrupted data, or edge-case structures may not be interpreted correctly – or at all. For this reason, automated parsing should be viewed as an accelerator, not a replacement for examiner validation.

Even so, automation dramatically improves efficiency. Tools like iLEAPP and aLEAPP allow us to quickly surface high-value artifacts, establish timelines, and triage mobile device evidence, making them an excellent starting point for analysis.

Summary

Efficient digital forensic analysis depends on the ability to move from broad data exploration to targeted, intelligence-driven investigation. In this chapter, we introduced automated analysis techniques that allow examiners to scale their workflows while maintaining analytical rigor.

By leveraging tools such as Autopsy, iLEAPP, and aLEAPP, we demonstrated how structured parsing, indexing, and filtering can rapidly surface relevant artifacts across large data sets.

We applied investigative intelligence through keyword searches, pattern matching, OCR processing, and hash analysis, showing how known indicators can be identified quickly and used to guide deeper analysis. We also explored the strategic use of hash sets to identify known evidence and reduce investigative noise by filtering non-pertinent system files.

While automation significantly improves efficiency, it does not replace examiner judgment. Instead, it serves as an accelerator, enabling investigators to prioritize effort, validate findings, and focus on the artifacts that matter most.

At this point, you should be able to:

- **Create and configure a forensic case** in Autopsy, including ingest module selection and evidence source management
- **Use keyword searching and pattern searching** to locate relevant data across parsed artifacts
- **Apply hash analysis to identify known files** and reduce non-pertinent data during review
- **Leverage iLEAPP and aLEAPP to parse mobile device acquisitions** and review structured artifact output
- **Distinguish between automated results and validated findings**, recognizing the need for examiner verification

In the next chapter, we move from tool-driven parsing to behavior-driven interpretation, focusing on user activity, intent, and the digital footprints left behind in forensic artifacts.

Get this book's PDF copy, code bundle, and more

Scan the QR code (or go to `packtpub.com/unlock`). Search for this book by name, confirm the edition, and then follow the steps on the page.

UNLOCK NOW

Note: Have your invoice handy. Purchases made directly from the Packt website don't require an invoice.

8

User Artifacts

Up to this point, we've focused on understanding operating systems, parsing their artifacts, and using automation to accelerate analysis. These skills allow us to interpret *what the system did,* but a complete forensic examination requires something deeper: understanding *what the user did.*

Every investigation ultimately hinges on user behavior. People search the web, create documents, save images, send communications, sync data across accounts, move files between devices, and leave behind thousands of subtle digital traces. Some are intentional; many are accidental. Some are obvious; others are buried inside application data, cloud sync artifacts, or remnants left behind after deletion.

This chapter focuses on those user-driven artifacts. Understanding common user artifacts moves us from tool operation to true investigation, allowing us to more accurately reconstruct behavior, sequence events, and answer the questions that matter most in real-world cases.

In this chapter, we're going to cover the following main topics:

- Web usage
- User files and metadata
- Cloud storage and online accounts
- Mass storage devices

Technical requirements

For this chapter, you will need:

- A computer running Microsoft Windows as your forensic workstation. 64-bit Windows 11 with an Intel i7 quad-core processor or better, and a minimum of 16 gigabytes of

RAM is recommended. This workstation will be used to examine user-generated artifacts and apply the tools and techniques introduced in earlier chapters.

- Datasets for analysis: Many of these were introduced in previous chapters. All required sample datasets (along with additional artifacts referenced throughout this chapter) are available on the Packt Publishing GitHub repository and will be referenced throughout each section.
- FTK Imager (as used in previous chapters) or an alternative tool capable of browsing forensic images. For example, 7-Zip can be used with additional support (such as the Forensic7z plugin) to access forensic image contents, as introduced earlier in this book.
- DB Browser for SQLite (as used in previous chapters) for examining SQLite databases.
- Your existing Autopsy case, created during *Chapter 7*.

Web usage

Web browser activity is often one of the most revealing categories of user artifacts. Search terms, visited websites, downloaded files, and synced account activity can expose what a user was thinking, planning, or attempting to accomplish at a specific moment in time. This type of evidence is also easy for juries and stakeholders to understand, since searching for something is usually interpreted as *intentional* behavior.

For example, a suspect might claim an illicit download was accidental, but that narrative collapses quickly if browser history shows they explicitly searched for the contraband beforehand. Beyond intent, browser artifacts help us identify who was likely using a system, trace the origins of files found elsewhere on the device, and, in some cases, even recover saved passwords.

There are numerous web browsers available. Some users prefer the defaults (like Microsoft Edge on Windows or Safari on macOS and iOS), while others prefer third-party options such as Google Chrome or Mozilla Firefox. Privacy-minded users may gravitate toward DuckDuckGo or Brave, and advanced users may rely on the Tor Browser bundle, which stores minimal local artifacts by default and enables access to .onion domains.

Many browsers are built on the Chromium engine, but even non-Chromium browsers still generate comparable classes of artifacts. In general, browser evidence falls into a few core categories:

- **History** records keep track of website visits, user search terms, text entered into online web forms, and lists of downloaded files

- **Cached data** can also include evidence of user activity, such as images retained by the browser to improve performance during future visits
- **Cookies** are used by websites to track user activity and to perform tasks like targeted advertising and storage of certain user-specific website preferences

Additional artifacts may include bookmarks, autofill entries, browser extensions, and profile-based sync data. Browser profiles, in particular, add another complication: activity seen on a local system may have originated on a different device if the user was logged into a synced account. Recognizing these nuances is essential for accurate interpretation.

For this recipe, we will examine common web browser artifacts across multiple platforms, using the provided sample datasets to locate, interpret, and correlate user activity. By working through browser history, cache, cookies, and related artifacts, you will learn how to reconstruct user behavior and apply these findings in real-world investigations.

Getting ready

Web browser artifacts are stored in predictable locations across operating systems. Below are the common paths you'll encounter when examining browser data:

- **Microsoft Windows**: Browser data is stored within each user account at `\Users\<user>\AppData\Local\` (or `\Users\<user>\AppData\Roaming\`), inside the folder corresponding to the specific browser (e.g., Chrome, Edge, Firefox).
- **Apple macOS**: Safari artifacts are stored in `/Library/Safari` within each user account. Third-party browsers store their data under `/Library/Application Support/<BrowserName>/`.
- **Linux**: Many Linux distributions use Mozilla Firefox, which stores data under `~/.mozilla/firefox/`. Third-party browsers typically store their profiles in `~/.config/<BrowserName>/`.
- **Apple iOS**: Safari data is stored in /private/var/mobile/Library/Safari/. Third-party browser data is stored under /private/var/mobile/Containers/Data/Application/<AppID>/.
- **Google Android**: Browser artifacts (such as those from Chrome) are located under `/data/data/com.android.chrome/` or the corresponding package directory for other browsers.

For this chapter, the browser data extracted from the forensic acquisitions used in previous chapters is provided as a standalone `Web Browser Data` dataset. You can download it from the Packt Publishing GitHub repository for this book. To access the repository link, follow the steps in the *Download the example code files* section in the *Preface*.

How to do it...

1. We'll begin with the Chromium-based browser Google Chrome, one of the most widely used browsers. Within the `/Chrome/User Data/` directory, you will typically find a **Default** profile folder containing the primary history and user-data artifacts. If the user has created additional profiles, Chrome will generate subdirectories such as `Profile 1`, `Profile 2`, and so on. These profiles allow either multiple users to share the same system account or a single user to maintain separate browsing contexts (e.g., personal vs. work activity):

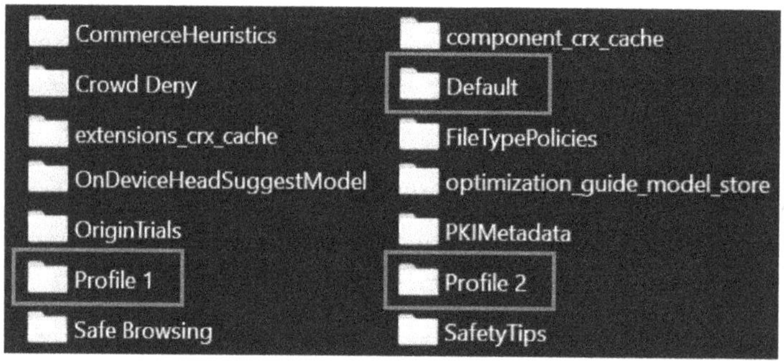

Figure 8.1 – Contents of the /Chrome/User Data/ directory

From the user's perspective, these profiles appear as selectable options when launching Chrome. The `Default` profile often shows the user's full name because it is tied to a synced **Google** account, while additional profiles (`Profile 1`, `Profile 2`, etc.) typically exist only locally:

Figure 8.2 – User perspective of profiles in Google Chrome

Each Chrome profile subdirectory contains its own independent set of activity records and data, similar to how an operating system user account maintains separate artifacts for each individual user. Because of this, you should analyze each profile directory to fully assess overall Google Chrome activity on the system.

2. Using a database viewer (such as **DB Browser for SQLite**), open the `History` SQLite database located inside the `Profile 1` directory. Chrome's History database does not use a file extension, so when selecting it, you may need to change the file filter to **All Files** for it to appear:

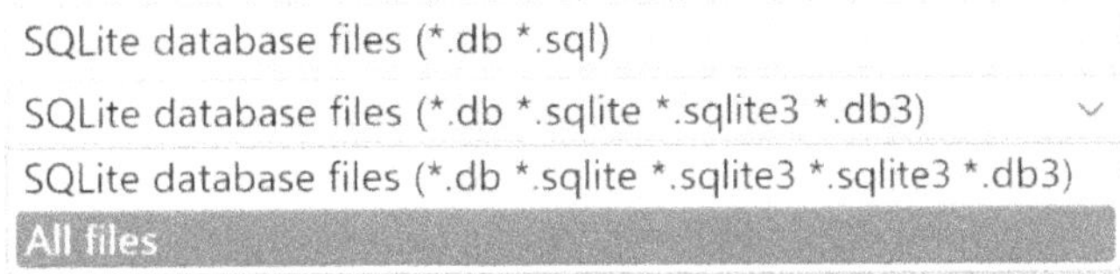

Figure 8.3 – Opening Google Chrome History database in DB Browser for SQLite

The `History` database is one of the most valuable artifacts produced by Google Chrome, especially since Chrome typically retains browsing history for a period of time (often around 90 days), unless it is manually cleared, modified by the user, or private browsing (incognito) mode is used.

Within this database, several tables are particularly important: `urls`, `visits`, `downloads`, and `keyword_search_terms`.

Begin by examining the `urls` and `visits` tables. These tables work together to reconstruct browser activity:

- The `urls` table lists every visited webpage, along with visit counts and metadata.
- The `visits` table records each individual visit event, including timestamps (stored in `WebKit/Chromium` epoch time), visit duration, and navigation type.

The two tables are correlated by matching the `id` field in the `urls` table with the **url** field in the `visits` table, allowing you to build a clearer picture of when (and how often) specific websites were accessed:

***urls* Table**

id	url	title	visit_count	last_visit_time
1	https://www.google.com/..	best free vpn - Google Searc	3	13363303655856488
2	https://www.techradar.cc	The best free VPN in 2024 |	1	13363303404256281
3	https://www.tomsguide.cc	The best free VPN in 2024 |	1	13363303434568034

***visits* Table**

id	url	visit_time	from_visit	external_referrer_url	transition	segment_id	visit_duration
1	1	13363303391354559	0		838860805	0	12907367
2	2	13363303404256281	1		805306368	0	25478326
3	1	13363303429730324	0		855638021	0	4845372
4	3	13363303434568034	3		805306368	0	221293011

Figure 8.4 – Cross referencing the urls and visits tables in Google Chrome history

3. Next, review the `downloads` table within the `History` database. This table provides detailed records for every file downloaded through Google Chrome, including the original file name, the system path where each file was initially saved, timestamps, total download size, and much more.
   These entries can often establish whether a user intentionally obtained certain files, trace where those files originated, and correlate downloads with other browsing events:

target_path ▲	start_time	referrer
C:\Users\Leroy Jenkins\Downloads\GoogleDriveS	13367831286116682	
C:\Users\Leroy Jenkins\Downloads\UrbanVPN.exe	13363303741709958	https://www.urban-vpn.com/
C:\Users\Leroy ...	13363329686170496	https://www.virtualbox.org/

Figure 8.5 – The downloads table in Google Chrome history

4. Finally, review the `keyword_search_terms` table within the `History` database. This table contains the actual search terms the user typed into Google Chrome's search bar. Each entry includes a `url_id` field that maps back to the id field in the `urls` table, allowing you to determine when the search occurred and which page the browser navigated to afterward.
   You'll notice that this table includes far fewer entries than the total number of URLs stored in the `History` database. That's normal, as most visited pages are the result of clicking links from previous searches, visiting bookmarked pages, or manually typing URLs, rather than entering a new search term. As a result, the keyword table becomes especially useful because it isolates the moments when the user explicitly typed something into the browser, making it one of the most direct indicators of user intent:

url_id	term	normalized_term
1	best free vpn	best free vpn
4	best free vpn	best free vpn
8	best free vm to run linux	best free vm to run linux
14	download vmware player	download vmware player
16	download free version of vmware	download free version of vmware
41	download free version of virtualbox	download free version of virtualbox

Figure 8.6 – The keyword_search_terms table in Google Chrome History

Beyond the `History` database, each Chrome profile subdirectory contains several additional databases that store valuable artifacts about user activity:

- **Login Data** records usernames and encrypted passwords for websites where the user has logged in. It also stores associated URLs and timestamps, making it extremely helpful for identifying account access patterns.
- **Top Sites** maintains Chrome's ranked list of the user's most frequently visited websites. When you're dealing with a large volume of web activity, this database provides a quick way to identify the sites that mattered most to the user.
- **Web Data** is often the richest source of user-driven artifacts. Within it, the `autofill` table stores text strings typed into website form fields and search boxes (the same data Chrome uses to autocomplete previously entered text).

This means you can often recover usernames, email addresses, phone numbers, search queries typed directly into website search bars, and other information entered into web forms. In some cases, investigators can even recover credit card numbers or cleartext passwords stored within this database, depending on how the user configured their browser.

If you want to see firsthand how much activity Chrome records, try examining these databases on your own system. Because the data reflects your own input, reviewing your autofill and login data can be an eye-opening way to understand just how much a web browser quietly retains about its user.

Note

Message in a Bottle... or Web Browser...

I have used autofill data in more investigations than I can count. Since the data stored here can be largely dependent upon what certain website forms ask for, you never know for sure what you might find. In one case, a suspect completed an online form seeking legal advice through a website after being accused of committing a criminal offense.

> This website had a freeform box asking for a summary description of what the user needed help with. Within this freeform box, the user described what they were being accused of and made multiple admissions, complete with additional information such as their full name, address, phone number, and e-mail.

Aside from the SQLite databases used by Chromium-based browsers, Chrome also stores several standalone files that can reveal additional user activity.

1. Browse to the `Default` profile within the Google Chrome sample data and open the `Bookmarks` file. Despite its importance, this file is simply a text-based JSON structure that can be viewed in a basic text editor (such as Notepad) or a forensic tool like FTK Imager.

   Within this file, you will see Chrome's default bookmark folders (`Bookmarks bar`, `Other bookmarks`, and `Mobile bookmarks`) along with any bookmarks the user manually created. Each entry contains the URL, bookmark name, and a Chromium/WebKit epoch timestamp, allowing you to determine when the bookmark was added or modified.

Figure 8.7 – Website bookmarked using Google Chrome

Web browsers also cache a significant amount of data. For Google Chrome, this data is stored within the `/Cache/Cache_Data/` subdirectory of each Chrome profile. Within that directory, you will typically see three primary cache components:

- `data_#` – Block-based storage segments containing smaller cached items
- `f_######` – Individual cached files that are too large to fit into the `data_#` blocks
- `index` – A data table linking cached content to the original URLs

Most cached content consists of images, icons, JavaScript files, CSS, and other resources loaded during normal web browsing. These files improve page load times on subsequent visits, often without the user ever knowing they exist. Forensically, cached images are especially valuable, as they may reveal content that the user viewed but did not intentionally save. Autopsy can preview many of these cached files automatically, making initial triage straightforward.

For deeper analysis, however, tools like **ChromeCacheView** by NirSoft consolidate the cache structure and metadata, allowing you to view cached entries in a clean table instead of manually navigating the raw cache folder. ChromeCacheView supports numerous Chromium-based browsers, including Google Chrome, Microsoft Edge, Opera, Yandex, and Brave.

Tools such as ChromeCacheView (by NirSoft) can be used to parse Chrome's cache structure. You can download this utility from NirSoft: `https://www.nirsoft.net/utils/chrome_cache_view.html`

2. By default, the tool will parse the cache from the local system. To examine a specific dataset, use the tool's option to load an alternate cache folder (available in the **File** menu) and point it to the `Cache_Data` folder for `Profile 1` in the sample dataset. Once loaded, the tool presents cached entries in a structured format, including URL, content type, size, fetch timestamp, and expiration.
This can reveal webpages the user visited, even if entries were later removed from browser history:

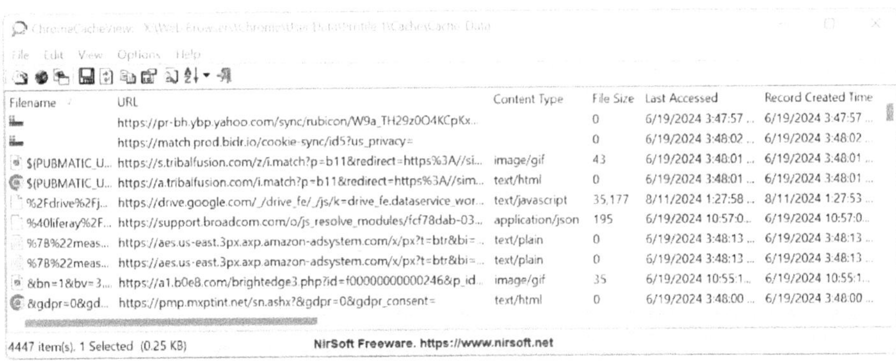

Figure 8.8 – Viewing Chromium cache folder with ChromeCacheView

3. When other artifacts are limited, web browser cookies can provide valuable insight, as they often survive long after the user has cleared their browsing history. Many users selectively delete history but avoid clearing cookies because doing so logs users out of

websites and is often inconvenient. As a result, cookies can remain intact even when more direct artifacts are gone.

Cookies vary widely because their structure depends on the website that created them. Some store simple preference data; others contain identifiers tied to login sessions or activity patterns. Modern browsers (including Google Chrome) also encrypt certain cookie values, so not all fields will be readable.

In Chrome, cookies are located in the `Network` folder within each profile, stored in a SQLite database named `Cookies`.

4. Locate the `Cookies` database in the sample dataset for `Profile 1`, open the database in **read-only** mode, and examine the **cookies** table.

   You'll see entries containing domain information and timestamps that can help reconstruct activity when history, cache, and searches are missing:

creation_utc	host_key	name	encrypted_value
Filter	Filter	Filter	Filter
13363303740943566	.urban-vpn.com	_uetvid	BLOB
13363303740972684	.bing.com	MSPTC	BLOB
13363303845703426	.urban-vpn.com	_ga_0NQ2DPN8JC	BLOB
13363329070951248	.reddit.com	csv	BLOB
13363329107723227	.linux.org	FCNEC	BLOB

Figure 8.9 – Sample of cookie data from Google Chrome

   From this table, fields such as `host_key` and `top_frame_site_key` can help identify which websites were visited or interacted with, while `creation_utc` and `last_access_utc` timestamps provide insight into when those interactions occurred. While cookies rarely tell the whole story, they can be invaluable when other artifacts are sparse, overwritten, or intentionally deleted.

5. We can also examine `web-browser settings` for each Chrome profile, which are stored in a JSON file named `Preferences` within each profile subdirectory. JSON files are best viewed with a tool that formats and color-codes their structure, and **Notepad++** (created by *Don Ho*) is a lightweight, free option that works perfectly for this purpose (`https://notepad-plus-plus.org/downloads/`).

6. After installing Notepad++, open the program and go to **Plugins** | **Plugins Admin...**. Scroll through the list, check the box for **JSON Viewer**, and click **Install**. Notepad++ will restart automatically once the plugin is added:

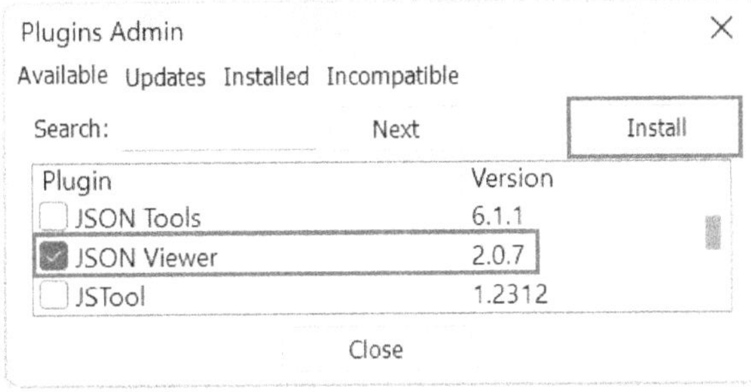

Figure 8.10 – Installing Notepad++ JSON Viewer plugin

7. Open the `Preferences` file from the Google Chrome `Profile 1` sample data folder.
8. Press *Ctrl + Alt + Shift + J* to launch the JSON viewer in Notepad++, or access it through **Plugins | JSON Viewer | Show JSON Viewer**. This formats the `Preferences` file into an expandable tree structure, making it easier to browse Chrome's configuration settings. The `Preferences` file contains a wide range of user-specific data, including profile identifiers, sync-related settings, and account metadata. Expand the `account_info` section to view key details such as the profile name, Google account ID, and the email address associated with the Chrome profile:

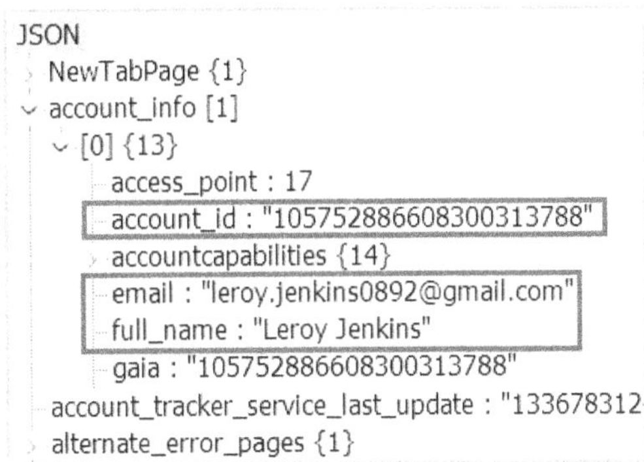

Figure 8.11 – Sample data from the Google Chrome Preferences file

Two of the most widely used non-Chromium browsers are **Mozilla Firefox** and **Apple Safari**. Like Chrome, both are available on desktop and mobile platforms, though Safari is now supported only on **macOS** and **iOS**, as it was discontinued on Windows years ago.

For this section, we'll examine **Mozilla Firefox** from our Linux sample dataset. Unlike Chromium-based browsers, Firefox uses its own storage architecture and maintains a very different directory structure, which is important to be familiar with during forensic analysis. Inside the Firefox folder, you'll find one or more profile directories, each containing separate user data, history, cookies, and session artifacts:

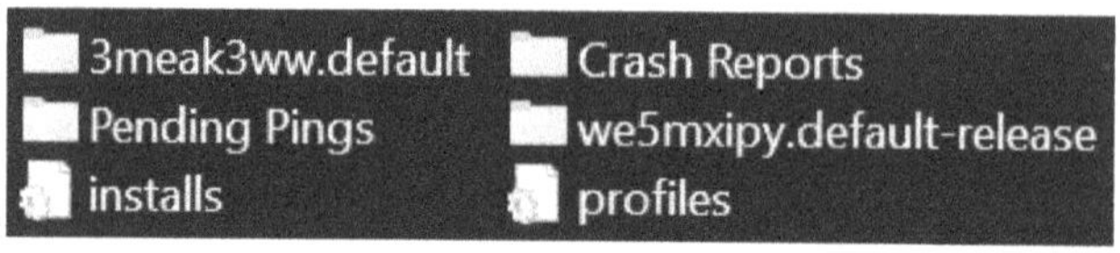

Figure 8.12 – Contents of Mozilla Firefox directory

Even though Mozilla Firefox uses a very different directory structure compared to Chromium-based browsers, the core forensic artifacts remain the same: browser history, bookmarks, cached files, cookies, and site-specific databases containing user activity. Firefox also supports multiple browser profiles, each stored in its own directory. These profile folders typically begin with a randomized alphanumeric string followed by the profile name.

In the example shown, you can see a default profile alongside two additional user-created profiles (`Cody Bounds` and `Leroy Jenkins` – used here for illustration only, not included in the sample dataset):

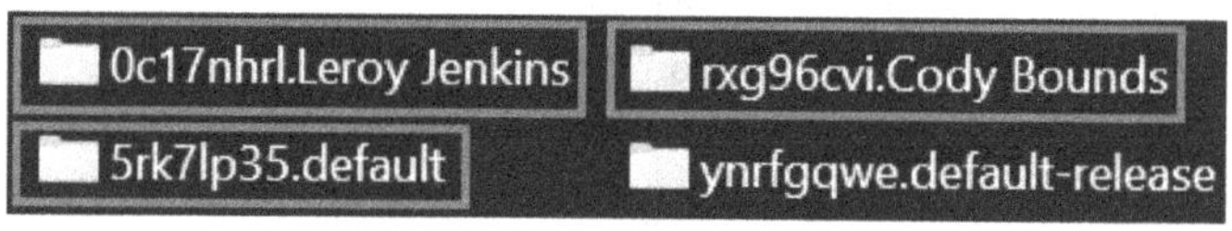

Figure 8.13 – Multiple user profiles in Mozilla Firefox

Firefox profiles are less commonly encountered in real-world cases because creating additional profiles requires a more deliberate process than in Chrome. However, advanced or privacy-conscious users may take advantage of this, and Firefox even allows a profile to be stored in a custom directory of the user's choosing – making it easier for a suspect to hide browser activity outside the standard paths.

9. Locate the main Mozilla Firefox profile directory where browser artifacts are stored. In the provided sample dataset, this directory is named `we5mxipy.default-release`. This is where Firefox keeps its core history and related browser data (much like the `Default`, `Profile 1`, and `Profile 2` folders you saw in Google Chrome). On real systems, these artifacts might appear in either a `default` or `default-release` directory depending on the Firefox version and installation method.
   Inside this folder, you'll notice that Firefox's structure becomes more reminiscent of Chromium-based browsers: a collection of SQLite databases, JSON configuration files, and cache subdirectories.

10. Open `places.sqlite` with your SQLite database viewer. The `moz_places` table stores Firefox's browser history, working similarly to the `urls` table in Google Chrome's History database (though Firefox timestamps are kept in **Unix epoch time measured in microseconds**, not Chromium epoch).

11. These records can be correlated with the `moz_historyvisits` table, which logs each visit event. Matching `place_id` from `moz_historyvisits` to `id` in `moz_places` allows you to reconstruct user browsing activity, including visit timings, frequency, and navigation paths:

url	title	last_visit_date
https://www.google.com/search?cl	cats - Google Search	1724192497996806
https://www.scientificamerican.c	The 6 Most Intriguing Things We Learn	1724192654362369
https://www.forbes.com/advisor/p	How Much Does A Cat Or Kitten Cost? -	1724192784076999
https://thumbor.forbes.com/thumb	how-much-does-a-cat-cost.jpeg.webp	1724192836238000
https://www.google.com/search?cl	pixles free images - Google Search	1724192944208916
https://www.pexels.com/	Free Stock Photos, Royalty Free Stock	1724192977614781

Figure 8.14 – Sample data from place.sqlite database in Mozilla Firefox

12. Unlike Google Chrome, Firefox does *not* store user-created bookmarks in a standalone JSON or CSV-style file. Instead, all bookmark data is kept directly inside `places.sqlite`, specifically in the `moz_bookmarks` table. Deleted bookmarks can also be reviewed using the `moz_deletedbookmarks` table, which often provides valuable context when examining whether a user attempted to conceal activity:

parent	position	title	dateAdded	lastModified
2	0	Mozilla Firefox	1724190294230000	1724190294230000
7	0	Get Help	1724190294230000	1724190294230000
7	1	Customize Firefox	1724190294230000	1724190294230000
7	2	Get Involved	1724190294230000	1724190294230000
7	3	About Us	1724190294230000	1724190294230000
3	0	Getting Started	1724190368443000	1724190368443000

Figure 8.15 – Sample data from place.sqlite bookmarks in Mozilla Firefox

13. Download activity is stored within the `moz_annos` table inside `places.sqlite`. These entries reference individual websites through the `place_id` field, which allows you to correlate each downloaded file to its originating URL by matching `place_id` with the corresponding **id** value in the `moz_places` table.

This linkage helps establish not only *what* was downloaded but also *where it came from*, which is a key detail in many investigations:

place_id	content	dateAdded
25	file:///home/leroy/Downloads/npp.8.6.7.Installer.arm64.exe	1724191535059000
26	file:///home/leroy/Downloads/npp.8.6.7.Installer.arm64(1).exe	1724192308843000
38	file:///home/leroy/Downloads/how-much-does-a-cat-cost.jpeg.webp	1724192861079000
42	file:///home/leroy/Downloads/pexels-haohd-22602397(1).jpg	1724193177977000

Figure 8.16 – Downloaded files shown by places.sqlite in Mozilla Firefox

14. Next, open the `formhistory.sqlite` database from the `we5mxipy.default-release` profile. Locate the `moz_formhistory` table. This is where Mozilla Firefox records text the user has typed into website search bars and form fields. These entries often reveal search queries, login identifiers, names, and other user-entered strings that may not appear anywhere else:

fieldname	value	timesUsed	firstUsed	lastUsed
searchbar-history	download opera for linux	1	1724190650731000	1724190650731000
searchbar-history	download notepad++	1	1724191001499000	1724191001499000
searchbar-history	download hex viewer for linux	1	1724191137745000	1724191137745000
searchbar-history	cats	1	1724192497920000	1724192497920000
searchbar-history	pixles free images	1	1724192944125000	1724192944125000

Figure 8.17 – User search terms from formhistory.sqlite in Mozilla Firefox

15. Cached files for Mozilla Firefox are often stored in a different location than the rest of the browser artifacts. In our Linux sample dataset, the cache resides under `/.cache/mozilla/firefox/<profile>/cache2/` rather than within the main `.mozilla` directory. On a Windows system, Firefox history artifacts typically reside under `/AppData/Roaming/`, while cached files are found under `/AppData/Local/`.
    Much like with Google Chrome, we can use a NirSoft utility to simplify cache review. Download MZCacheView: `https://www.nirsoft.net/utils/mozilla_cache_viewer.html`

    After launching it, point the program to the `cache2` folder from our Mozilla Firefox dataset. The tool will automatically load and display cached items (including images, scripts, and other web resources), making it far easier to analyze them than reviewing raw cache files manually:

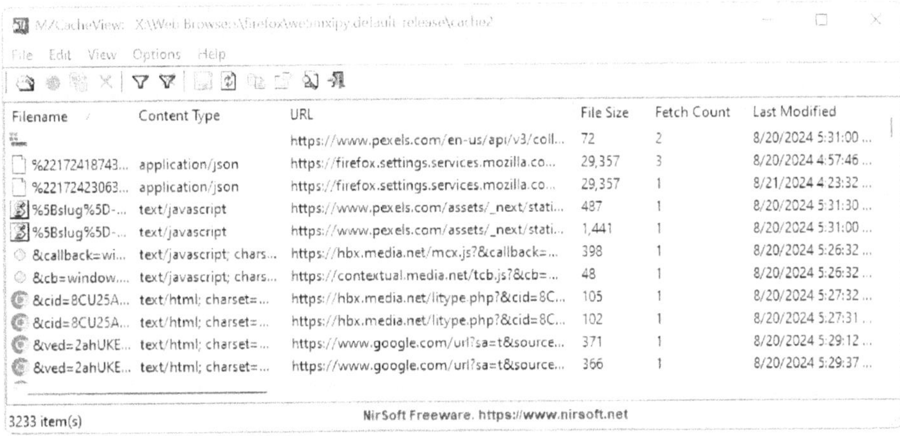

Figure 8.18 – Viewing Mozilla Firefox cache folder with MZCacheView

16. Finally, Mozilla Firefox stores cookies in the `cookies.sqlite` database, located in the same profile directory as `places.sqlite`. Open and examine `cookies.sqlite` and you'll see a structure very similar to the Chrome `Cookies` database: host keys, cookie names, values (encrypted when applicable), creation timestamps, and last-access timestamps.

    This database is especially useful when other browser artifacts (such as history or form data) have been deleted, since many users forget or choose not to delete cookies, which can still reveal website activity and login-related metadata:

name	value	host	creationTime
AEC	AVYB7crfx88_qaDozvlfa9FsG47Z3_zjsXaoQQI	.google.com	1724190650911768
_gcl_gs	2.1.k1$i1724190740	.opera.com	1724190793315038
__cflb	0H28vsnweR1JffJftktw7nLubZgqkwnQFkoWFm	linuxconfig.or	1724191192873986
_ga_4D4TX2QCXR	GS1.1.1724191192.1.0.1724191192.0.0.0	.tecmint.com	1724191192911392
_ga	GA1.1.324965621.1724191193	.tecmint.com	1724191192912932
_ga_06CVYXZPHS	GS1.1.1724191082.1.1.1724191192.60.0.7:	.notepad-plus-	1724191082307901

Figure 8.19 – Sample of cookies data from Mozilla Firefox

Most modern web browsers offer a private browsing mode (such as **Incognito** in Google Chrome), which limits or disables the retention of web history, cookies, cached files, and other traces of user activity. These modes must be intentionally launched, and because they leave behind so little data, they can significantly reduce the artifacts available to examiners.

Privacy-focused browsers like Brave and the DuckDuckGo browser promote enhanced anti-tracking features; however, they still retain a meaningful amount of local artifacts unless the user explicitly switches to their private windows. One major exception is **Tor Browser**, designed specifically for anonymity. Tor leaves behind almost no usable data by default.

Tor also differs from conventional browsers in how it installs. It does not embed itself into standard OS directories. Instead, it installs as a self-contained folder wherever the user chooses. In our Microsoft Windows sample acquisition, this folder appears on the Desktop within the `Leroy Jenkins` profile, named `Tor Browser`. With the exception of the application files themselves, the folder contains virtually nothing of evidentiary value.

17. Browse to `Tor Browser/Browser/TorBrowser/Data/Browser` of the Window dataset. Inside you'll find the `profile.default` directory. The structure should look familiar, as Tor is built on the same underlying codebase as Mozilla Firefox:

Figure 8.20 – Web activity data directories for Tor Browser

18. Open and examine the `places.sqlite` database from the `profile.default` directory in Tor Browser. As you browse through the available tables, you'll notice that almost all of them contain no usable data; Tor simply does not retain history, downloads, form entries, or most other artifacts by default. There are only two meaningful exceptions:
    - `moz_places` – contains a few internal, program-related entries (not user activity)
    - `moz_bookmarks` – contains the default Tor bookmarks *plus* any bookmarks manually created by the user
19. Open `moz_bookmarks` and scroll through the entries. The first group you see will be Tor's default bookmarks (e.g., Tor Project links). The final four entries, however, were created by the user and represent some of the only persistent user-generated artifacts Tor leaves behind:

title	dateAdded
anonymous marketplace with Escrow System. - Anonymous Marketplace	1718825154686000
Buy bank logs and carding tools 2023 | Cashoutcarders	1718825205041000
RedBull Market - #1 Darkweb Escrow Marketplace	1718825212553000
HowTo - Carding - tutorial, manual	1718825259059000

Figure 8.21 – Bookmarks shown in places.sqlite for Tor Browser

> **Note**
>
> Onions and a Leaky Ship
>
> The Tor Project sometimes gets a bad reputation due to its ability to access the "dark web", where users can browse websites that support criminal activity such as narcotics sales, CSAM distribution, fraud, and human trafficking. Criminal elements utilize the websites accessible through Tor because it achieves true anonymity by utilizing thousands of Internet traffic relays, making it nearly impossible to trace an accurate IP address to a physical location. This concept is known as **onion routing** due to its many layers of encryption and was originally developed by the United States Navy to secure the transmission of protected government intelligence. This form of decentralized networking cannot utilize the URL types we have grown accustomed to, such as "www.google.com", and instead uses very long unique identifiers for each website, followed by `.onion`. This sometimes creates a 'leak' in user activity; remembering the unique identifier for such a website is impractical, so users must bookmark the websites they like to visit. In my experience, if you are unable to find such websites bookmarked in Tor, you will find them stored in a note or document.

You can continue examining other Tor artifacts (such as cookies or cached files), but you'll quickly notice they contain no meaningful user data. Private browsing modes are designed to minimize footprint, and Tor takes this even further by intentionally avoiding long-term storage of user activity.

Even so, "private" doesn't mean invisible. A few categories of artifacts can still leak valuable information:

- **Downloaded files** must be saved somewhere, and those file-system traces remain fully recoverable.
- **Operating system usage artifacts** (like recent file lists, prefetch data, or application execution records) can reveal that Tor was used, when it was opened, and how often.
- **External applications** such as messaging apps, cloud sync tools, or screenshot utilities may also intersect with Tor usage and leave behind correlating metadata.

While private browsing strips away most of the browser-level evidence, the *system* itself often tells enough of the story to establish context, usage patterns, and intent.

How it works...

Web browsers (regardless of platform or brand) leave behind a remarkably consistent trail of artifacts. Whether the user is on Windows, macOS, Linux, iOS, or Android, browsers must retain certain data to function: history entries, cached content, form inputs, download records, and cookies. Much of this information is stored in SQLite databases, which makes cross-platform analysis relatively straightforward once you know where to look.

Tools like Autopsy simplify this process even further. Instead of manually examining each SQLite table, Autopsy parses the common browser artifacts, organizes them into clear categories (history, downloads, search terms, cookies, cache), and converts many raw timestamps into human-readable values. This lets you quickly identify user intent, account usage, downloaded files, and behavioral patterns.

However, as with all automated tools, parser coverage varies. Some artifacts may be unsupported, partially parsed, or missed entirely – especially across non-Chromium browsers or privacy-focused platforms. That's why a complete examination still requires manually reviewing the underlying databases when something does not align with expectations.

Browser artifacts give you one of the closest views into user behavior, but only if you understand how they're structured and what your tools are (and aren't) parsing for you.

User files and metadata

Computers and mobile devices aren't just platforms for web browsing – they are storage hubs for documents, spreadsheets, PDFs, audio recordings, photographs, videos, emails, and countless other user-generated files. While the visible content of these files often matters most to the end user, the metadata embedded within them is just as important in a forensic investigation.

Unlike basic file system metadata (such as created, modified, and accessed dates), embedded metadata can reveal details such as associated device make and model, GPS coordinates, software version, author information, edit history, and timestamps generated directly by the application that created the file. These details can help establish origin, authorship, timeline, and user intent.

In this recipe, we will walk through several of the most common user file types and show how to locate and interpret the metadata they contain – an essential skill for reconstructing user behavior and building a reliable forensic narrative.

Getting ready

Download the **User File Analysis** dataset from the Packt Publishing GitHub repository for this book. To access the repository link, follow the steps in the *Download the example code files* section in the *Preface*.

Create a new case in Autopsy and add the downloaded archive as a logical evidence source. When configuring ingest, enable the following modules: `Recent Activity`, `File Type Identification`, `Embedded File Extractor`, `Picture Analyzer`, and `Email Parser`.

How to do it...

1. Locate `Budget.xlsx` in the `User File Analysis` dataset and select it. In the **Content Viewer**, switch to the **Text** tab. Autopsy will display a plain-text rendering of the spreadsheet contents, including the user's budget entries. Note the `Sheet1` label in the upper-left corner (this is the default worksheet name embedded in the Office XML structure):

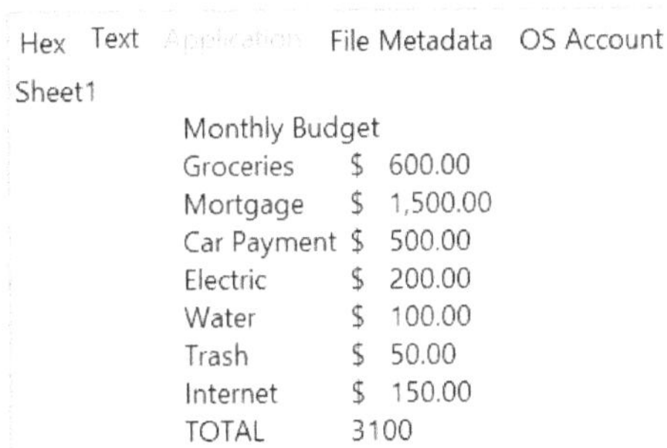

Figure 8.22 – Viewing Budget.xlsx file in Autopsy content viewer

2. Although Autopsy's **Content Viewer** displays the spreadsheet in a simplified text view, the `.xlsx` extension confirms this is a Microsoft Excel spreadsheet. Opening the file in an actual spreadsheet application (such as Microsoft Excel or LibreOffice Calc) reveals its proper formatting and structure under the worksheet `Sheet1`.

   Commercial forensic suites like Magnet Axiom often provide richer in-tool rendering for Office documents, but best practice is to export and open significant files natively to confirm formatting, content, and embedded metadata:

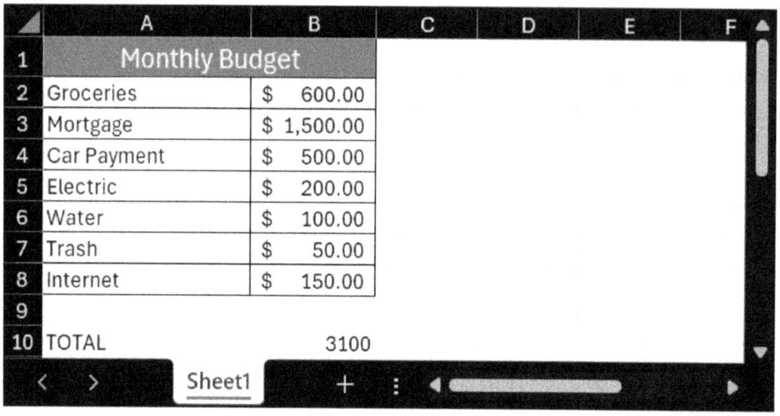

Figure 8.23 – Viewing Budget.xlsx file in a spreadsheet application

3. Switch to the **File Metadata** tab in Autopsy's **Content Viewer**. This panel shows the *file system metadata* (such as created, modified, accessed times, file size, and related attributes). While these timestamps can be useful, they are also not inherently trustworthy.
   Actions such as downloading a file from the Internet, copying it between drives, or moving it across different file systems will often overwrite these values, replacing the original creation time with the time of transfer. As a result, file system metadata should always be treated as *contextual*, not definitive:

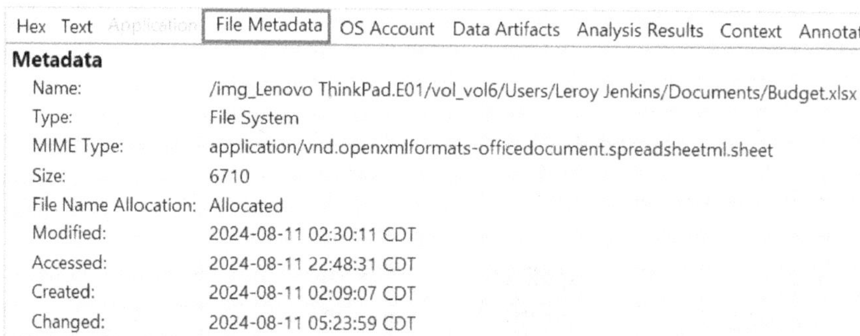

Figure 8.24 – File system metadata for Budget.xlsx file

4. Return to the **Text** tab in Autopsy's **Content Viewer** and scroll until you locate the **METADATA** section. Unlike the file system metadata we just reviewed, this is **embedded metadata**, or information written *inside* the `Budget.xlsx` file itself.
   Embedded metadata typically includes details such as the document author ("*Leroy*"),

creation and modification timestamps, the application used ("*LibreOffice Calc*"), and other internal properties.

Because embedded metadata travels *with* the file, it doesn't change when the file is downloaded, copied, or moved between systems, making it far more reliable than file system timestamps (assuming the system clock on the machine where it was created was accurate). However, it is important to note that some platforms (such as social media services, messaging applications, and cloud-sharing tools) may strip or modify embedded metadata for privacy or security reasons.

Note also that the `Author` name simply reflects whatever the user entered when configuring their office software:

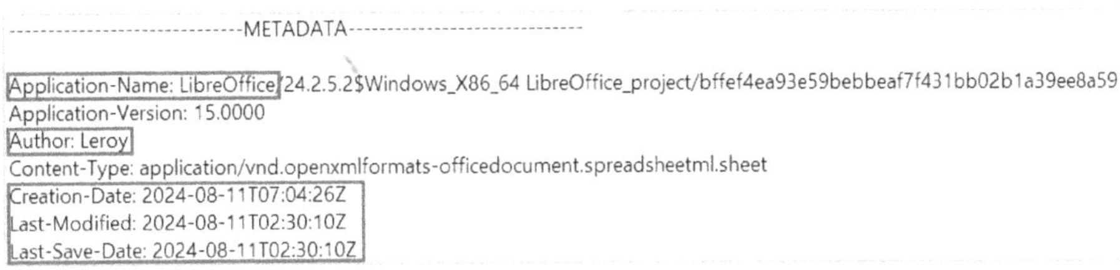

Figure 8.25 – Embedded file metadata for Budget.xlsx file

5. Embedded file metadata can also be validated using a native spreadsheet application. Open the file in Microsoft Excel, for example, allows you to view the document properties exactly as the application recorded them. Here you'll see additional fields (such as `Last Printed`), which would contain a timestamp if the document had ever been printed. Most document formats also store both the *original author* and the *last modifying user*, giving us another way to verify authorship and editing history across systems:

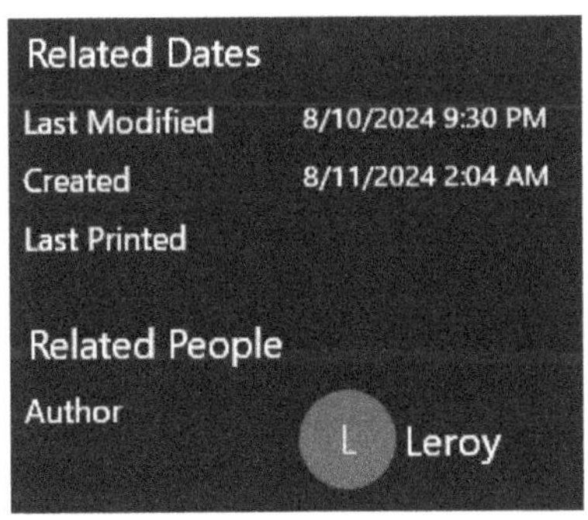

Figure 8.26 – Embedded file metadata viewed using Microsoft Excel

Note

Some Killer Metadata

From the mid-1970's and into the early 1990's, there were several murders at the hands of an unidentified serial killer that came to be known as *BTK*, due to his tendency to bind, torture, and then kill his victims. Beginning in 2004, BTK began communicating with the media and law enforcement in an apparent attempt to regain notoriety. As part of these communications, BTK provided a floppy disk, which contained a deleted document that digital forensics was able to recover. The metadata of this document showed a file author of *Christ Lutheran Church* with a last edited author of *Dennis*. Further investigation identified a member of the Christ Lutheran Church to be that of Dennis Rader, and DNA evidence confirmed Rader to be BTK. In the end, it was mere metadata from a deleted document that caught a serial killer after 30 years.

6. Locate the files `Photos.pptx` and `Astro.docx`. Viewing the embedded metadata for `Photos.pptx` shows the same type of internal information we saw in the spreadsheet example: the listed author (`Leroy`), creation and modification timestamps, and the application used (Microsoft PowerPoint).
   However, when you open `Astro.docx`, you'll notice something different: the embedded metadata is *not* visible. Only the file system metadata is shown. This is because the document is encrypted, and encryption protects not just the file contents but the embedded metadata as well. Without the correct password, the internal metadata fields cannot be read or parsed:

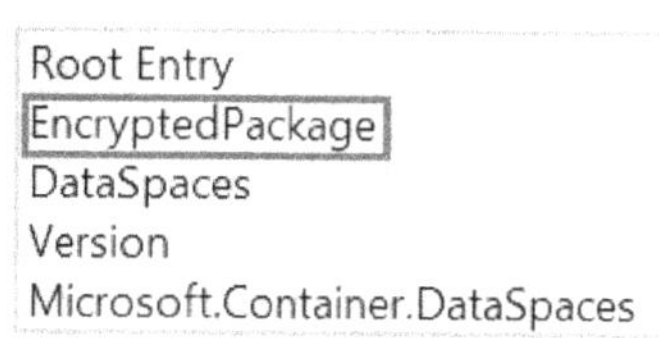

Figure 8.27 – Embedded file metadata not viewable for encrypted document

7. Next, let's look at the kinds of insights we can extract from **media files** – specifically photographs. Image files often contain **Exchangeable Image File Format (EXIF)** metadata, which records detailed information about the camera and settings used when the photo was taken. Photographers use EXIF for creative troubleshooting, but in forensic work, its value is far more investigative.

In a forensic context, some of the most relevant EXIF fields typically include timestamps (the true time of capture, independent of file system metadata), camera make and model, camera serial number, and GPS coordinates (commonly embedded by mobile devices).

8. Locate `IMG_5881.JPG`, a photograph taken during the tail end of a solar eclipse.
9. Open it in Autopsy and select the **Text** tab within the **Content Viewer**. You'll see a large amount of EXIF metadata – including the device used, the fact that the photo was later edited on macOS using Adobe Lightroom, and additional camera details such as the serial number:

```
Digital Time Created: 15:07:53
Exif IFD0:Date/Time: 2024:05:16 22:32:53
Exif IFD0:Make: NIKON CORPORATION
Exif IFD0:Model: NIKON D5300
Exif IFD0:Resolution Unit: Inch
Exif IFD0:Software: Adobe Lightroom 7.2 (Macintosh)
```

Figure 8.28 – Sample EXIF data from IMG_5881.JPG

10. Now locate **IMG_5869.JPG**, another photograph of the near-total solar eclipse. Open it in Autopsy and select the **Text** tab to view the EXIF metadata. This time you'll notice something important: Autopsy wasn't able to parse most of the EXIF fields accurately. This happens occasionally depending on how the metadata is structured or compressed within the file.
    To validate what EXIF data is actually present, we will use an external viewer.
11. Download **IrfanView** (`https://www.irfanview.com/main_download_engl.htm`)
12. Once installed, launch `IrfanView` and open `IMG_5869.JPG`; either manually or by right-clicking the file in Autopsy and selecting **Open in External Viewer**, then choosing **IrfanView**.
13. Inside IrfanView, click **Image** | **Information** (or press *I*), then select the **EXIF info** button in the pop-up window.
    You'll see that IrfanView successfully extracts a far more complete set of EXIF metadata, including detailed camera information that Autopsy couldn't parse:

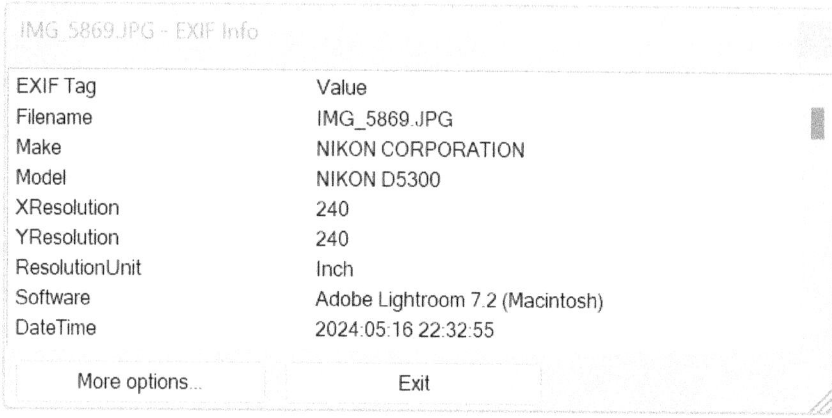

Figure 8.29 – EXIF data from IMG_5881.JPG viewed with IrfanView

14. Next, locate `IMG_2442.HEIC`. As a reminder, **HEIC** is the default photo format used by modern Apple iOS devices. When you attempt to open this file in Autopsy, you'll notice it cannot properly render the image or extract most of the associated EXIF metadata. This is common with HEIC files, as they rely on codecs not always supported by forensic tools.
15. Open the same file in IrfanView, and you'll see that the image loads correctly – revealing a photograph of a mountain bike. By clicking **Image** | **Information** | **EXIF info**, you'll also be able to view the underlying metadata. Here you can see that the image was captured using an **Apple iPhone 14 Pro Max** on **July 7, 2023**, along with additional camera and exposure details:

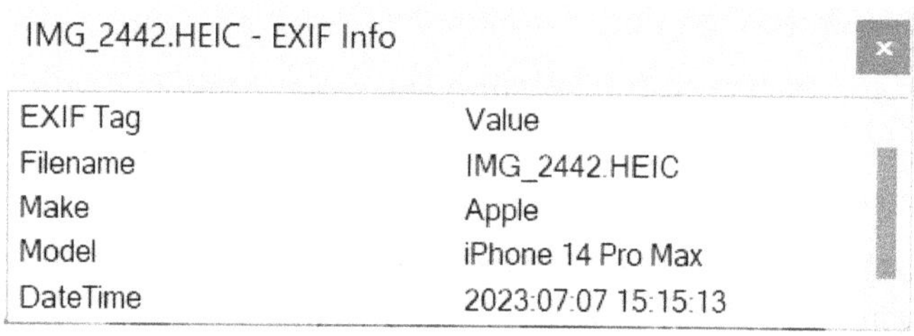

Figure 8.30 – EXIF data from IMG_2442.HEIC viewed with IrfanView

16. Scroll to the bottom of the EXIF information window in IrfanView, and you'll see that GPS coordinates are embedded within this photograph. These coordinates were captured automatically by the iPhone at the time the photo was taken.

17. Click **Show in Google Maps** to open the exact location in your default browser. This is an excellent example of how powerful EXIF geolocation can be in reconstructing a user's movements and identifying where key events occurred:

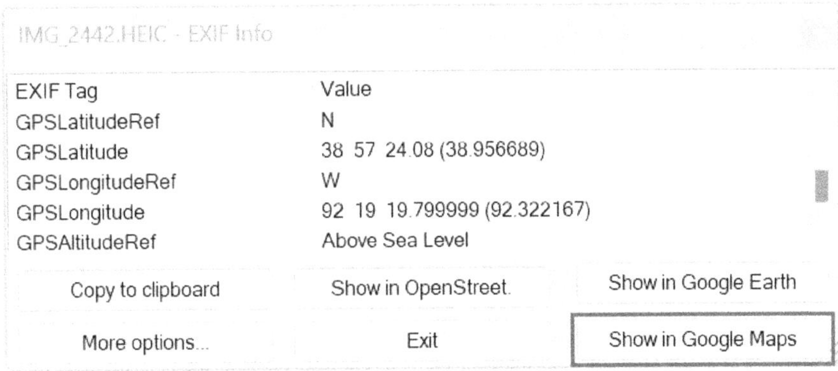

Figure 8.31 – GPS coordinates embedded within IMG_2442.HEIC

When Google Maps opens, the embedded coordinates are automatically plotted, allowing you to see the approximate location where the photo was taken. In this case, the GPS data places the image at or near *Walts Bicycle and Wilderness* in Columbia, Missouri:

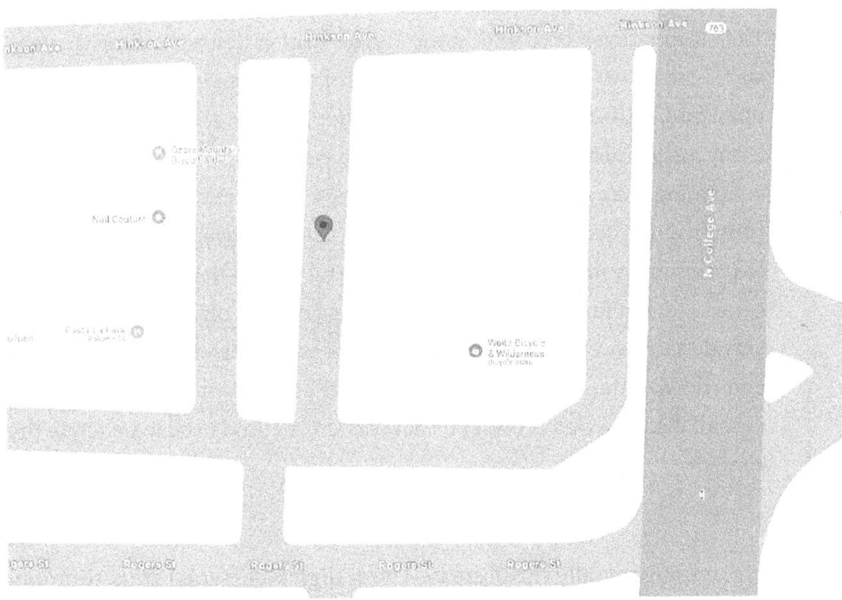

Figure 8.32 – Plotting GPS coordinates embedded within IMG_2442.HEIC

18. Now locate the video file `5800.mp4`, which shows a deer walking through a wooded area. Open the file in IrfanView and review the available metadata. You'll notice it is *very* limited. This is common, as video files often contain far fewer embedded metadata fields than still photographs. The exact amount of metadata depends heavily on how the video was recorded, but it's always worth checking in case useful details (such as creation timestamps or device information) are present:

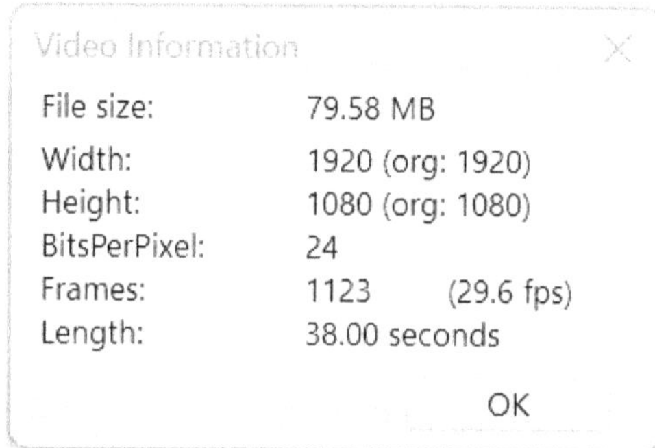

Figure 8.33 – Metadata for video file 5800.mp4

> **Note**
>
> Artificially Flavored
>
> The information stored within the metadata of various user files can vary significantly, with EXIF data being some of the most detailed metadata we will often find. EXIF data is not only present in the photographs we take though, as many images generated using AI will also embed EXIF information. Rather than containing metadata about camera settings, AI-generated images sometimes contain data about the software that was used and even the text the user typed to generate the image. Not only is this useful to help determine if a file was AI generated, but for investigations involving criminal offenses, it can provide very descriptive evidence of user actions. If such user-entered prompts are not embedded within the metadata of a file, we can still often find them in the autofill data of a web browser if that was the method used to generate the content.

19. Some images (especially those created with digital cameras) store thumbnail previews directly inside the EXIF metadata. If you've ever scrolled through photos on a camera and seen tiny preview images, that's what you're looking at. These thumbnails are embedded *inside the file itself*, not generated by the camera's storage system.

From a forensic standpoint, this matters because the embedded thumbnail often survives edits applied to the main photograph. Even if a user alters or obscures content, the thumbnail may still reveal the original, unedited version.

20. Open the file `DSC_0046.jpg`, which has been intentionally edited to obscure part of the image:

Figure 8.34 – Photograph DSC_0046.jpg edited to obscure content

If a photograph contains an EXIF-embedded thumbnail, we can carve the thumbnail directly from the parent image file and save it as its own JPEG. This can be extremely valuable when the main image has been edited or partially obscured, as thumbnails are often left untouched.

21. Open the `User File Analysis` dataset (shown in the following steps using FTK Imager) and browse to `DSC_0046.jpg`.
22. Select the file and choose **hex viewer**. Near the beginning you'll see the JPEG file signature `FF D8 FF E0` (the standard magic number identifying a JPEG file):

```
000000 FF D8 FF E0 00 10 4A 46-49 46 00 01 01 01 01 2C  ÿØÿà··JFIF·····,
000010 01 2C 00 00 FF E1 4D A2-45 78 69 66 00 00 4D 4D  ·,··ÿáM¢Exif··MM
```

Figure 8.35 – File signature of DSC_0046.jpg file

23. Press *Ctrl* + *F* in the hex viewer and run a binary search for the JPEG/EXIF header signature `FF D8 FF E0`. The next matching instance you see inside the file is **not** the main image – it marks the beginning of the EXIF-embedded thumbnail stored inside the photograph's metadata:

Figure 8.36 – File signature of DSC_0046.jpg embedded EXIF thumbnail

The offset is the starting point you'll carve from in the next steps.

24. Right-click on the first byte of this embedded thumbnail (the `FF` in the `FF D8 FF E0` signature) and select **Set Selection Length...**
25. Enter a decimal value of `835,925` bytes, which represents the size of the thumbnail data block (the process of determining carving lengths is covered in *Chapter 10* during *Deleted Data Recovery*).
26. Click **OK** to highlight the full thumbnail region:

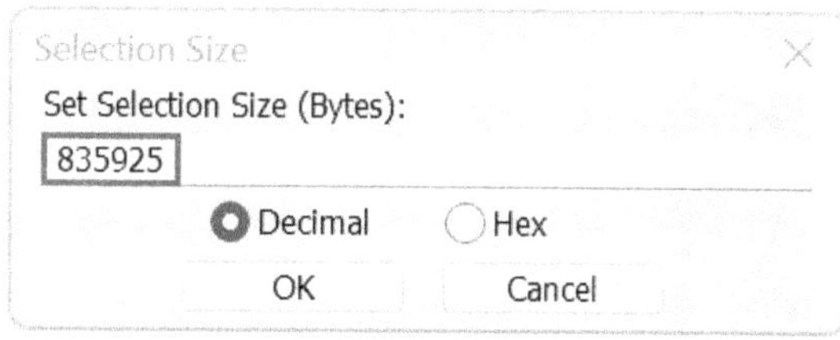

Figure 8.37 – Setting a data block selection size in FTK Imager

27. With the full thumbnail region still selected, right-click the highlighted block and choose **Save Selection...**, then export the carved data as `CarvedEXIF.jpg`.

    Even though EXIF thumbnails are lower resolution than the original photograph, they often preserve the unedited version of the image. In cases where a photo has been altered, blurred, or otherwise modified (as in this example) the embedded thumbnail may reveal content from **before** the edit took place:

Figure 8.38 – Recovered EXIF thumbnail

Recovering EXIF thumbnails is also especially helpful when dealing with partially recovered photographs. Even if the main image data is incomplete or corrupted, the EXIF thumbnail is often intact and provides a crucial look at the photo's original appearance.

Email files are another major category of user-created content and often provide both **content evidence** (what was communicated) and **routing metadata** (how it was delivered). This can often play a critical role in investigations – especially incident response and business-email-compromise (BEC) cases, where attackers frequently rely on phishing emails to gain initial access. Entire courses exist on BEC, but we will focus on the two core components relevant to digital forensics:

- **The email body and attachments**, which may contain malicious content, social-engineering elements, or files of evidentiary value.
- **Email headers (metadata)**, which reveal routing paths, sender servers, timestamps, and authentication results that help determine whether the email is legitimate or spoofed.

Two sample emails are included in the dataset for this section: `Hello!.eml` and `The Apple Store Shopping Event is here.eml`.

Most forensic analysis suites provide dedicated email parsing capabilities. In Autopsy, these messages are automatically parsed when the **Email Parser** ingest module is enabled, and they can then be viewed under the **E-Mail Messages** artifact category:

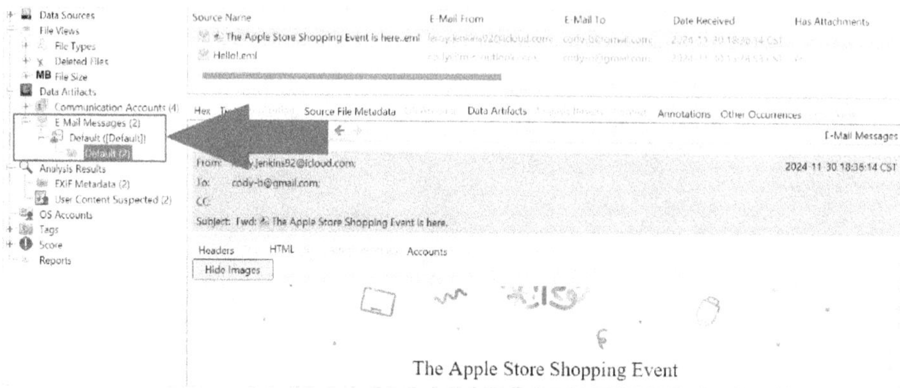

Figure 8.39 – Viewing emails using Autopsy

Email files can also be viewed using a third-party email viewer, which is especially useful when we want to inspect message content and metadata without loading an entire dataset into a forensic analysis suite. Many email viewers support a wide range of formats (such as `.OST`, `.PST`, `.NST`, `.DBX`, `.OLM`, `.MSG`, `.MBOX`, `.OFT`, `.EML`, and `.EMLX`), allowing us to handle artifacts created by the various email clients a user may have installed.

Some users, however, never rely on a traditional email client at all and instead read all their email through a web browser. In those situations, there may be no local email files present on the device you're examining. If you have lawful access to the account itself, you can typically download any individual message directly from the web interface. Most providers include a menu option (often labeled `Download message`, `Save as .eml`, or similar) that allows you to export the email and analyze it offline:

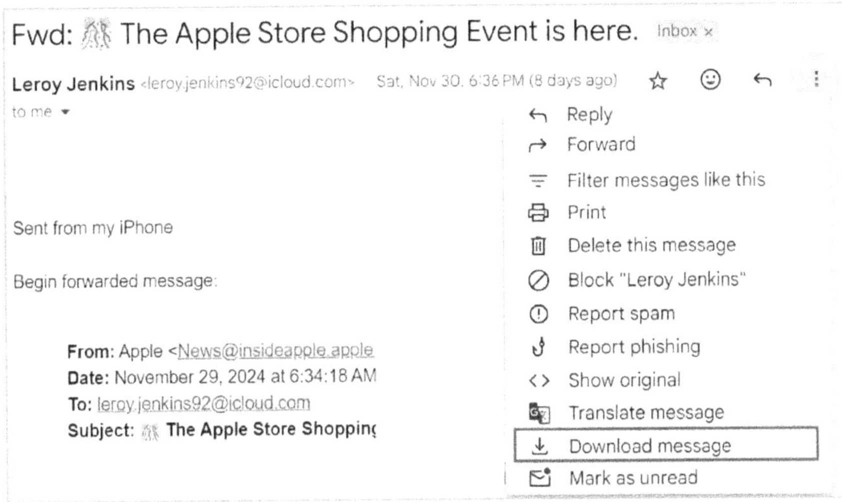

Figure 8.40 – Example of downloading an email from a Gmail account

28. The two sample emails in this dataset use the `.eml` extension because they were exported directly from a Gmail account. To review these files outside of a forensic suite, we can use a dedicated viewer. **SysTools** offers several lightweight tools for different email formats; for `.eml` files specifically, download their **EML Viewer**: `https://www.systoolsgroup.com/eml-viewer.html`.
29. Once installed, launch the application and use the left-hand navigation pane to browse to the folder containing the sample emails. Selecting the folder will display each message in the main viewing area:

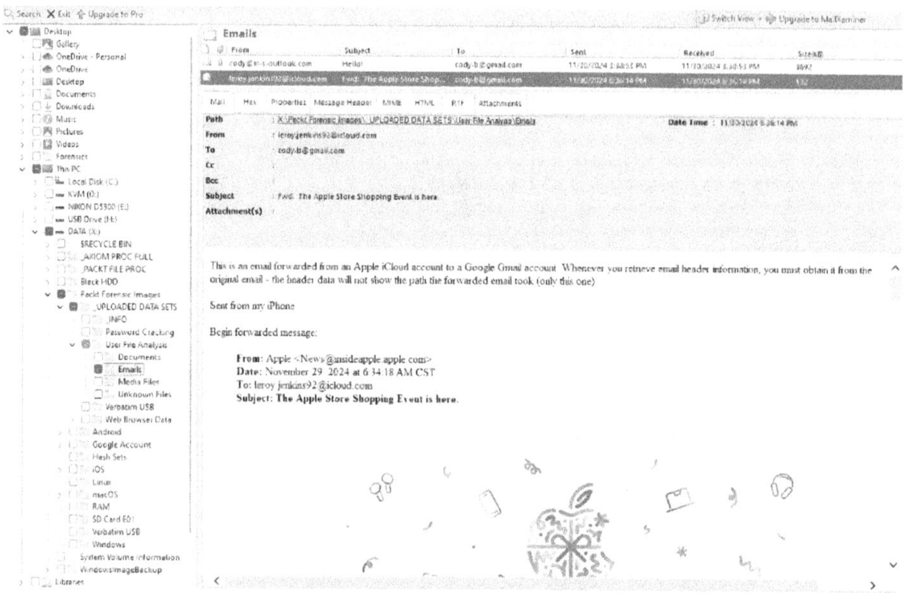

Figure 8.41 – Viewing emails with SysTools EML Viewer

30. After selecting an email, the viewer presents the message body along with a set of tabs that allow you to inspect different aspects of the file – including **hexadecimal view**, **HTML view**, **attachments**, and most importantly, **Message Header**.
The message header is one of the most valuable components of any email, as it shows the *path* the message took through mail servers, complete with timestamps, originating IP information, and detailed sender/recipient metadata.

31. Click the **Message Header** tab to view this information:

Figure 8.42 – Email message header information

Email headers can look overwhelming at first, but they simply list (from **bottom to top**) the path the message took as it moved from the sender's mail server to the recipient's inbox. A few elements in this header are especially important during forensic analysis:

- The `Message-ID` is a unique identifier generated by the *sending* mail server, consisting of random characters followed by the server's domain. In the earlier example, this appears as `B895B093-A7E0-4628-9F89-6F3F13136914@icloud.com`. This value is extremely useful when you need to correlate the email with server logs or search for other copies of the same message. A mismatch between the Message-ID domain and the email's visible **From** address may indicate **spoofing**, similar to putting a fake return address on an envelope.
- `Received` entries show the servers a message passed through, including server name, IP address, and timestamp. These hops allow you to reconstruct the email's delivery path.
- `X-Mailer` is not always present, but when included, it reveals the email client used to create the message (e.g., *iPhone Mail (21F90)*). This can help confirm which device generated the message.
- `X-Originating` entries (such as X-Originating-Email or X-Originating-IP) can expose the sender's true email address or originating IP. Modern providers rarely include the originating IP anymore because of privacy and security concerns, but you'll still encounter it in older messages or from poorly configured servers.

Like other forms of metadata embedded within user-created files, email header information can vary depending on the service and infrastructure used to send the message. Even so, headers remain one of the most valuable sources of information for identifying routing paths, confirming authenticity, and narrowing down the true origin of an email. You can review this metadata manually, but header analysis tools can present the information in a clearer and more efficient format.

32. Copy the full header from the email titled `The Apple Store Shopping Event is here.eml` (*Ctrl* + *C*), then paste it into the **Email Header Analyzer** provided by MxToolBox at `https://mxtoolbox.com/EmailHeaders.aspx`
33. Click **Analyze Header**. The tool will break down relay hops, identify delays, and present the header fields in a more readable structure:

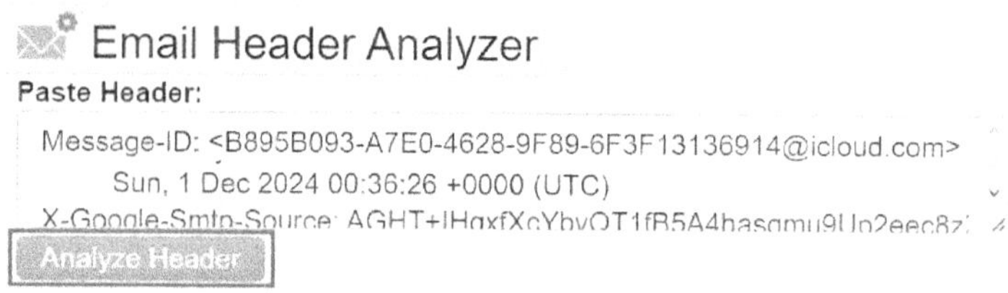

Figure 8.43 – Email message header information

> **Note**
>
> Try Not to Be So Forward
>
> I have found it rather common that investigators who do not specialize in cyber-related investigations may forward me an email that was forwarded to them from a victim. The header information in such an email is no good, as it only shows the relay and data for the email the investigator sent me—we must have the original email directly from the victim account to see the path the email took from the suspect account to the victim account. Look closely at the header for the email we are using as an example here, and you will notice it is a forwarded email, originally received as an advertisement from Apple and then sent by account `leroy.jenkins92@icloud.com` to `cody-b@gmail.com`. This means the path we are looking at shows only how the email was relayed from the `leroy.jenkins92@icloud.com` account to `cody-b@gmail.com`, and **not** the path of the original message received from Apple.

34. Within the email header, you may have noticed references to **DMARC**, **SPF**, and **DKIM**. The Email Header Analyzer tool evaluates these authentication fields and flags potential failures or inconsistencies:

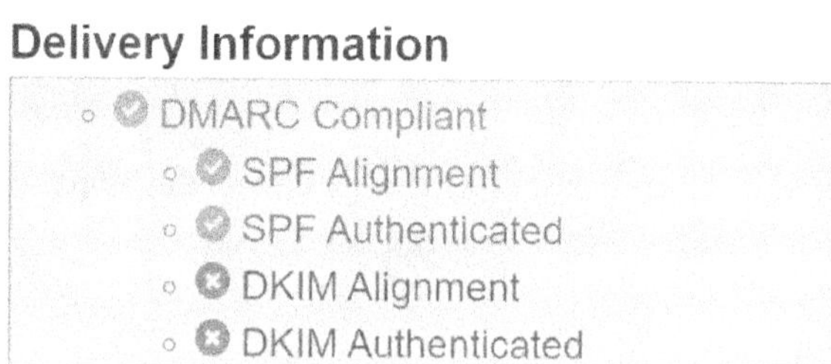

Figure 8.44 – Email authentication checks from Email Header Analyzer

These terms refer to standard email authentication protocols:

- **SPF (Sender Policy Framework)** verifies that the sending **IP address** is authorized to send email on behalf of the domain. This helps prevent spoofing, such as someone sending an email that *appears* to come from a trusted domain but originates from an unauthorized server.
- **DKIM (DomainKeys Identified Mail)** attaches a **cryptographic signature** created by the sending domain's private key. The receiving server uses the public key (published in DNS) to verify that the message hasn't been altered in transit.
- **DMARC (Domain-based Message Authentication, Reporting, and Conformance)** builds on SPF and DKIM. It tells receiving mail servers what to do if SPF and/or DKIM fail—such as allow, quarantine, or reject the message. It also provides reporting options, so the domain owner is notified when unauthorized senders try to impersonate their domain.
- **ARC (Authenticated Received Chain)** is used when email passes through multiple intermediate services (e.g., forwarding systems). ARC preserves authentication results across those hops so SPF/DKIM failures caused by forwarding do not incorrectly label legitimate emails as spoofed.

Together, these protocols help identify whether a message is authentic, altered, or spoofed – making them extremely useful during forensic email analysis.

35. Although the Email Header Analyzer displays DKIM and SPF failures for the sample emails, this occurs because the email addresses in the dataset were manually altered to simulate what spoofing or tampering evidence can look like. For example, the `Hello!` email fails *all* authentication checks:

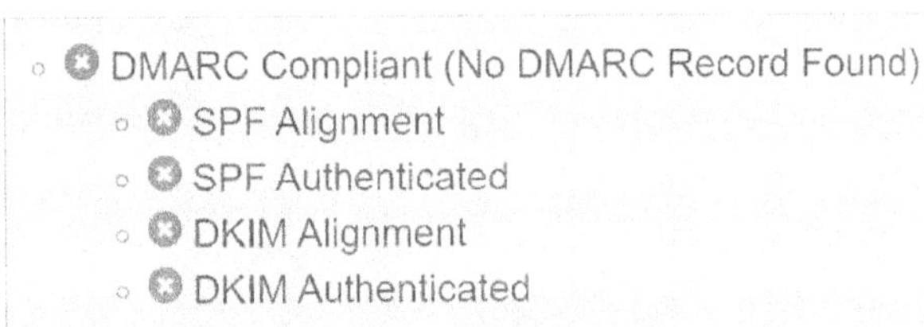

Figure 8.45 – Email authentication failures from Email Header Analyzer

It's also important to understand the **No DMARC Record Found** warning. This does **not** automatically indicate malicious activity; it simply means the domain does not publish a DMARC policy. Many small domains and older configurations lack DMARC. The practical implication is that such domains are more susceptible to spoofing, because receiving mail servers have fewer instructions to follow when SPF or DKIM fail.

If you test additional legitimate email headers from your own inbox using the MxToolbox Email Header Analyzer, you'll often see a warning that the **DKIM Signature Body Hash could not be verified**. This condition is common and typically results from the way the header was copied and pasted into the tool – not from an actual DKIM failure.

Because automated parsing tools can misread or truncate long DKIM fields, you should always confirm authentication results by manually reviewing the raw header. In most legitimate emails, you will find that DKIM validation is recorded as a *pass* within the header itself unless the message truly failed authentication:

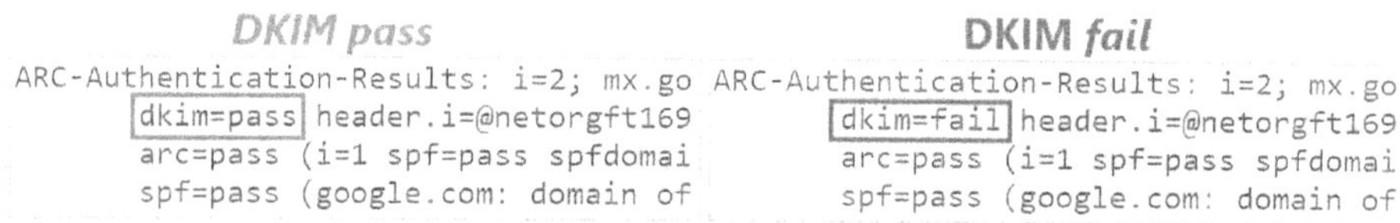

Figure 8.46 – DKIM pass/fail examples from raw email header

36. Finally, we will often encounter files whose types are not immediately identifiable. In some cases, the file simply has no extension, which is common for many system and application files that don't require one to function. In other cases, the file does have an extension, but it does not match the actual file type; for example, applications that store cached images using a `.0` extension, or a user deliberately removing or altering an extension to disguise a file.

    Regardless of the reason, unknown or mismatched file types may contain critical evidence and must be correctly identified. Most forensic suites handle this automatically by examining the file signature, also known as the *magic number*, which consists of the first several bytes of a file. Matching the file signature against the reported extension allows us to flag files with extension mismatches, many of which will simply be system artifacts – but some may be highly relevant to the investigation.

    In Autopsy, identification of unknown files and extension mismatches can be automated using the **File Type Identification** and **Extension Mismatch Detector** ingest modules. These modules classify files based on their signature rather than their extension, ensuring accurate identification even when the extension has been altered.

    Below is an example of a PNG signature, which begins with the hex sequence `89 50 4E 47`:

```
0x00000000: 89 50 4E 47  0D 0A 1A 0A
0x00000010: 00 00 00 30  00 00 00 30
0x00000020: 87 00 00 03  32 49 44 41
```

Figure 8.47 – File signature / magic number of a PNG file

37. For quick reference, commonly used file signatures can be found in a variety of trusted online tables, such as Gary Kessler's original file signatures list, which is now stored by Search.org at `https://filesig.search.org`.

    ExifTool, created by Phil Harvey, is another excellent option for viewing embedded file metadata – and it also helps identify unknown file types. Unlike many other utilities, ExifTool analyzes both the metadata and the file signature, allowing it to determine the true file format even when the extension is missing or incorrect.

38. Download ExifTool from `https://exiftool.org/index.html`, extract the archive, and locate the executable titled `exiftool(-k).exe`. To view metadata for any file, drag and drop the file onto the executable. ExifTool will open a command-line window displaying all available metadata and signature-derived identification.

    For example, the screenshot below shows ExifTool processing the `IMG_2442.HEIC` file from the User File Analysis dataset:

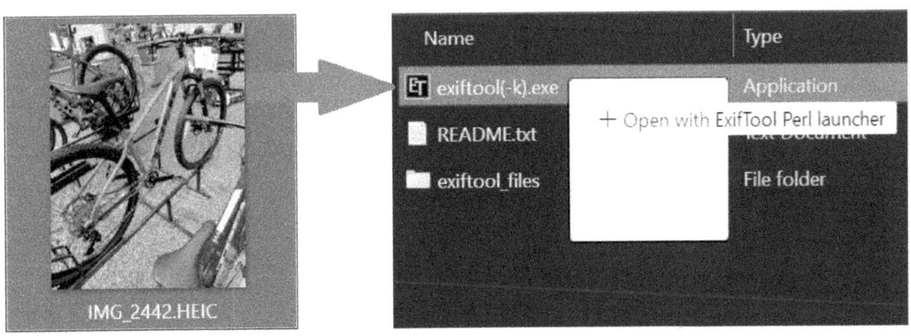

Figure 8.48 – Processing a file with ExifTool

39. Once dropped onto the ExifTool executable, a Command Prompt window will open displaying all available metadata for the selected file. Among these entries, ExifTool will also identify the detected file type, allowing you to confirm whether the file extension matches the actual signature:

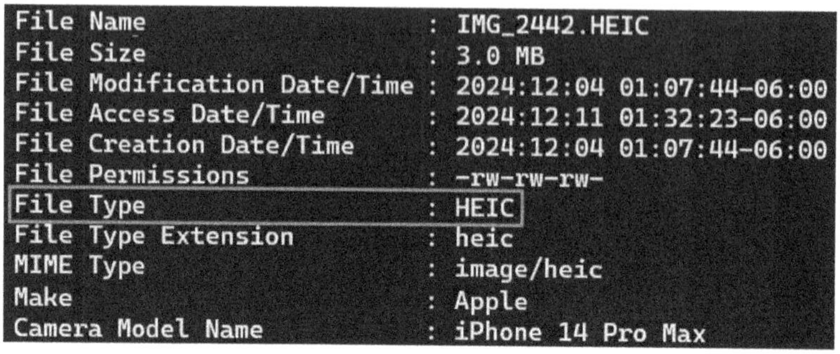

Figure 8.49 – Viewing results in ExifTool

Also included within the User File Analysis dataset are five files whose extensions have been removed or intentionally altered to obscure their true type. Using the methods demonstrated in this section (file signature review, metadata extraction, and comparison against known file signatures) try to identify each file type.

HINT: The first four files can be quickly identified using tools such as ExifTool, Autopsy, or FTK Imager. However, the file `05.exe` will likely generate an error in ExifTool because it is *not* an executable. For this file, you will need to examine its file signature manually using a hex viewer (Autopsy, FTK Imager, or HxD), then reference the appropriate signature in Gary Kessler's File Signatures Table.

Correct answers:

- `File 01.0`**:** Apple Property List (.plist)
- `File 02.txt`**:** Portable Document Format (.pdf)
- `File 03`**:** Windows Executable (.exe)
- `File 04.csv`**:** MPEG Audio Layer 3 (.mp3)
- `File 05`**:** Windows Event Log (.evtx)

How it works...

User files are generally easy to view, but it is their metadata, or *data about data*, that can truly reveal crucial information about *how*, *when*, and *where* a file was created or interacted with. Unlike file system metadata, embedded metadata is stored inside the file, meaning it can often survive transfers between devices, downloads, copying, and most routine user activity. For that reason, embedded metadata is often *far more reliable* as evidence.

However, its reliability is not absolute. Metadata is only as accurate as the device that generated it. For example, EXIF timestamps can be misleading if the camera or phone had an incorrect system clock at the time the photo was taken. Still, when intact, embedded metadata can provide one of the most direct insights into a file's origin and history.

It is also important to recognize that embedded metadata is not guaranteed to be present. Some file types contain almost nothing; others (like digital photographs) contain exceptionally rich detail.

And while embedded metadata is resistant to casual alteration, it is not immune:

- Many social media and cloud platforms automatically strip metadata to protect user privacy.
- Many editing applications regenerate metadata when a file is modified.
- Advanced users can deliberately alter metadata using dedicated tools.
- Even Apple's native Photos application allows users to edit timestamps and embedded GPS data directly.

For these reasons, metadata should be treated as a powerful evidentiary source, but one that must be validated. Comparing metadata across multiple sources (such as file system timestamps, application logs, backups, and cloud artifacts) helps confirm authenticity and identify inconsistencies.

Cloud storage and online accounts

As digital forensic professionals, we cannot afford to overlook the growing volume of data stored in online accounts and cloud services. Today, nearly every user has *something* synced to the cloud. In some cases, this is intentional, such as using social media or cloud storage to access files across devices. In others, it occurs automatically, as many modern operating systems and applications automatically sync documents, settings, photos, and backups without the user's full awareness.

Cloud-stored data introduces both challenges and opportunities. It often contains critical artifacts that never existed locally, such as version histories, deleted-but-retained cloud files, or data synchronized across multiple devices. At the same time, traditional forensic imaging will not always capture these artifacts, and they must instead be obtained through legal processes or direct credential-based access to the target account.

Because cloud accounts can mirror activity across computers, mobile devices, and even IoT hardware, they can provide additional copies of user files. These copies can include metadata not present on the local device, logs indicating access from other locations or devices, communication history, backup artifacts independent of local deletions, and more.

The key takeaway is that cloud storage and online accounts are now core components of user behavior and should be treated as first-class sources during analysis, especially when local artifacts appear incomplete or inconsistent.

> **Note**
>
> Accidental uploads
>
> Given that most online platforms take proactive measures to scan for and report users who store illicit files online, law enforcement agencies around the globe are often tasked with investigating these reports. Over the years, I have been part of numerous investigations where an illicit file was uploaded to a popular online storage platform and reported. During several of these instances, the suspect claimed they never uploaded the file. While this is often a claim made by those faced with an arrest, there were instances where the claim was truthful. While the individuals were still in possession of the illicit material, they didn't always upload it on purpose – rather, their system chose to back the files up by auto-syncing them. This can be beneficial for those who lose their data and need to retrieve it, but not such a great feature when the files are illegal.

For this recipe, we will examine cloud storage and online account artifacts using the provided datasets, focusing on how to analyze exported account data (such as Google Takeout), identify synchronized content, and correlate cloud-based activity with artifacts recovered from the local system.

Getting ready

The dataset for this section (**Google Account**) is available in this book's GitHub repo. To access the repository link, follow the steps in the *Download the example code files* section in the *Preface*.

You will also need the **Microsoft Windows** dataset from *Chapter 4*.

Unzip the Google Account archive and create two separate copies of the contained Takeout file, titled `takeout-20241201T074048Z-001.zip`. We will use these copies for two distinct purposes:

- **Copy A (for Autopsy):**
    - Add the zipped archive directly into Autopsy as a *logical evidence source*.
    - Process it using the default ingest modules: Recent Activity, Hash Lookup, File Type Identification, Extension Mismatch Detector, Embedded File Extractor,

Picture Analyzer, Keyword Search, Email Parser, Encryption Detection, and Interesting File Identifier.

- **Copy B (for manual review):**
    - Unzip this copy so we can manually browse the extracted directory structure and artifacts outside of Autopsy.

Why two copies? A Takeout ZIP archive functions as a sealed container preserving the filesystem metadata (especially timestamps) of the files inside it. Extracting that ZIP inherently alters metadata on the resulting files. Using one preserved copy for Autopsy and a second for manual inspection ensures forensic integrity while still giving us direct file access for hands-on review.

How to do it...

We will begin by examining data obtained directly from an online account, which may be obtained through user consent or legal process.

The file `takeout-20241201T074048Z-001.zip` is a Google Account export created using **Google Takeout** – a method we previously covered in *Chapter 3*. Now, refer to the following steps:

1. Using the `extracted` archive, open the file `archive_browser.html` located in the root of the `Takeout` directory. This HTML page provides a structured overview of the exported account data, showing what categories were included, how many files were recovered, and the delivered formats:

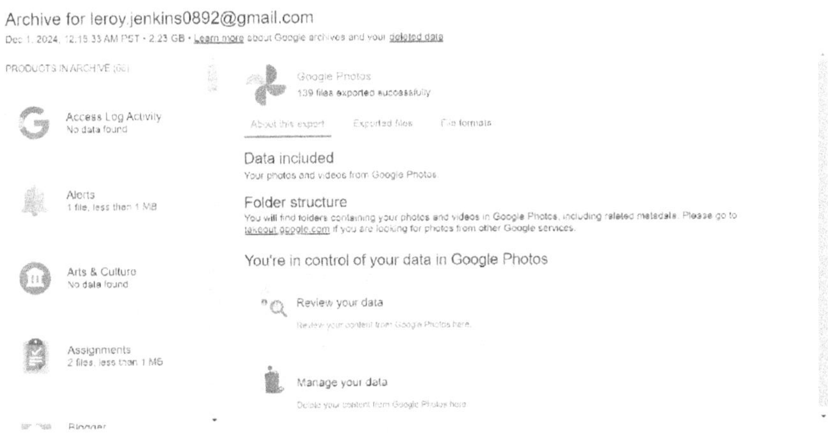

Figure 8.50 – Overview of Google account data acquired using Takeout

Within the unzipped archive you'll also find numerous subfolders (one for each Google service included in the Takeout export). Only the services the user actually interacted with will contain meaningful data.

For example, browse to the `Google Photos` directory and then into `Photos from 2017`. Each folder contains the original photo files uploaded or synced by the user and also a corresponding JSON sidecar file for each image, which duplicates the EXIF and other metadata stored inside the photo itself.

2. These JSON files make metadata review easier because they extract timestamps, device information, and location data into a simple text structure without requiring image parsing:

Figure 8.51 – User photographs stored in Google Photos online account

3. Return to the Takeout parent directory and open the `Drive` folder, then the `My Laptop` folder. Here you'll find the Microsoft Windows directories that the user configured to sync with Google Drive, along with the full contents of those folders at the time of sync. This type of dataset is extremely valuable when the original computer is unavailable—whether because it was destroyed, wiped, lost, or otherwise inaccessible. Synced Drive data often preserves user-created documents, Desktop or Downloads folder contents, working project directories, and files the user may have tried to delete locally. In many cases, Drive sync becomes a reconstruction tool for a machine you never get to examine directly:

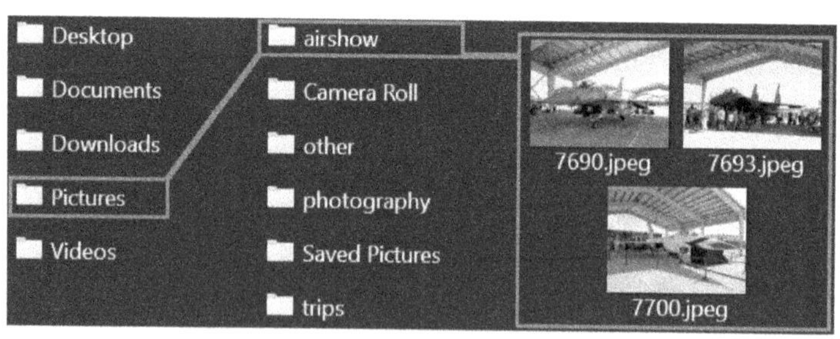

Figure 8.52 – Data synced from computer to Google Drive

4. Within the Takeout parent directory, open the `Google Account` folder and select the file named `leroy.jenkins0892.SubscriberInfo.html`. This report provides core

account-level intelligence, including the user's account name and creation details, recovery email addresses, the date and public IP address used when the account was first created, and a list of Google services associated with the account.

5. The Services section is especially important, as it highlights which Google services contain user activity. In this case, you will see the user had **Web & App Activity** enabled—one of the richest sources of behavioral evidence in Google datasets.

GOOGLE SUBSCRIBER INFORMATION

Google Account ID: 198338552529
Name: Leroy Jenkins
Given Name: Leroy
Family Name: Jenkins
e-Mail: leroy.jenkins0892@gmail.com
Alternate e-Mails:

Created on: 2024-06-19 19:46:33 Z
Terms of Service IP: 23.84.149.7
Terms of Service Language: en
Terms of Service Country: United States
Provider for Consumer Services: Google LLC
Birthday (Month Day, Year): August 23, 1992

Services: Gmail, Web & App Activity, YouTube, Google Calendar

Figure 8.53 – Google Account user details

6. Continue browsing the remaining Takeout folders. You'll notice that Google exports data in HTML, JSON, and CSV formats, depending on the service. Understanding these formats is essential, as different artifact types are easier to parse with different tools and for different investigative objectives.

7. Now review the results from processing the `takeout-20241201T074048Z-001.zip` archive in Autopsy. As you browse the parsed artifacts, you'll notice that Autopsy successfully identifies and extracts many types of user-generated content contained within the Takeout archive.

   However, you will not see web browser artifacts parsed here, even though we enabled the ingest module for browser data. This is expected. Google Takeout exports web activity in JSON, CSV, or HTML formats, not in the native browser databases used by Chrome (such as History, Cookies, and Web Data). Because there are no native browser databases present inside Takeout exports, Autopsy's browser ingest module has nothing to parse. This is a common real-world example where automated tools may not fully parse available data.

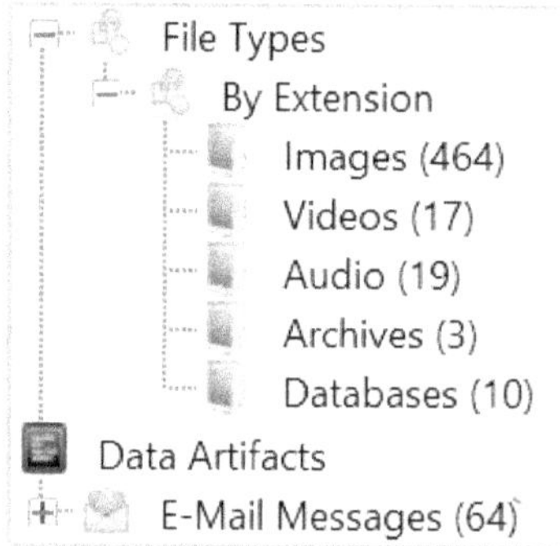

Figure 8.54 – Google account information processed in Autopsy

8. Now, compare this to the unzipped `takeout-20241201T074048Z-001.zip` data. Inside the `Takeout` parent folder, select the `Chrome` directory. Here you'll find a large volume of user web activity (including full browsing history), along with additional activity logs stored under the `My Activity` directory.

9. Even though this data clearly exists, it is saved in HTML, JSON, and CSV formats. Because Autopsy expects Chrome artifacts in their `native SQLite databases` (such as History, Web Data, and Cookies), it cannot process the Takeout versions automatically. This limitation is common, as many forensic analysis suites struggle to ingest web-activity data when it is exported in non-native formats.
For that reason, manual review is essential. Each platform structures its exports differently, and relying solely on automation risks missing key evidence:

Figure 8.55 – User web browser history stored to Google Account

10. Next, let's examine how this Google account synced data to the physical computer. Google Drive is the service responsible for syncing files between a user's device and their Google account. This syncing can occur through a web browser, but the *automatic* syncing of local folders only happens when the *Google Drive* desktop application (*DriveFS*) is installed.
Earlier, we observed that several Microsoft Windows directories had been synced to the account. This strongly suggests that the Google Drive app was installed on the system at some point because only the desktop client creates mirrored folder structures and

continuous sync behavior. On Windows, Google Drive stores cached data, synced metadata, and file-tracking information per-user at:

- \AppData\Local\Google\DriveFS\<Google Account ID>
- In our Microsoft Windows dataset, this is found under the Leroy Jenkins profile: \Users\LeroyJenkins\AppData\Local\Google\DriveFS\105752886608300313788
- Export the metadata_sqlite_db database and its supporting wal/shm files, then open the database and locate the items table:

stable_id	trashed	is_owner	mime_type	modified_date	viewed_by_me_date	local_title	subscribed
204	0	1	image/jpeg	1723354648012	1723354648012	IMG_5879.JPG	1
205	0	1	image/jpeg	1723354649867	1723354649867	IMG_5876.JPG	1
206	0	1	image/jpeg	1723354651873	1723354651873	IMG_5871.JPG	1
207	0	1	image/jpeg	1723354653741	1723354653741	IMG_5867.JPG	1
208	0	1	image/jpeg	1723354655410	1723354655410	IMG_5877.JPG	1
209	0	1	image/jpeg	1723354657165	1723354657165	IMG_5882.JPG	1
210	0	1	image/jpeg	1723354658850	1723354658850	IMG_5875.JPG	1

Figure 8.56 – Google Drive metadata_sqlite_db database

The items table contains a complete inventory of files known to the Google Drive client, whether they originated locally or from the cloud. It includes filenames, file paths, timestamps, file sizes, and indicators showing whether a file was deleted. This makes it one of the most valuable artifacts when reconstructing sync activity or usage behavior.

Files synced or placed into Google Drive are also cached locally, per user, at \AppData\Local\Google\DriveFS\<Google Account ID>\content_cache\

Google Drive renames cached files and stores them across numerous subdirectories, making it difficult to identify them by filename alone. For example, locate the d34 subdirectory and examine cached file 336. While the raw content is clearly visible, it cannot be easily correlated to the original file from within the metadata_sqlite_db database.

This is because Google Drive stores cached file metadata in BLOB fields, not as readable filenames. To properly link a cached file to its source, the BLOB data must be extracted and decoded.

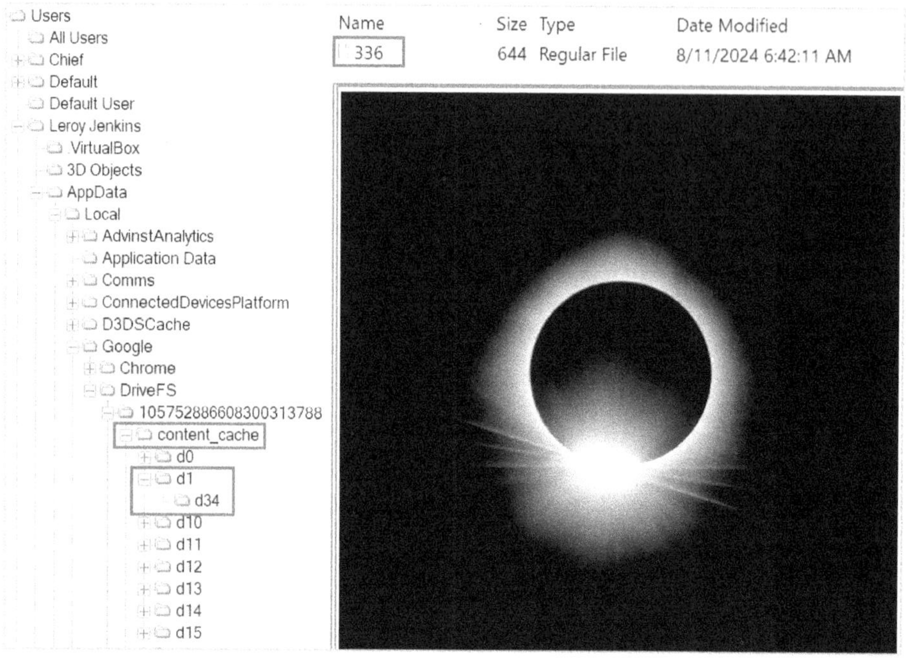

Figure 8.57 – Google Drive cached file content

Fortunately, there is a tool that can do this for us called **gMetaDataParse** which can be downloaded from: `https://github.com/00010111/gMetaDataParse`

11. Download this tool and run the executable file titled `gMetaDataParse.exe`. Export the entire `105752886608300313788` Google Drive directory. Within gMetaDataParse, open the **File** menu and click on **Open cache folder**, pointing the tool to the `content_cache` directory of the Google Drive Account.
12. Open the **File** menu again and click on **Open database**, pointing the tool to the `metadata_sqlite_db` database, then click **Reload** from the **File** menu. This will load and parse our Google Drive content. Expand the results for **My Drive**, where we can now locate the file `336` within the `Cache file name` column to easily correlate our cached file to its associated database entry. This also gives the added benefit of automatically decoding our timestamps and provides a complete file path to each cached file as decoded from the database entries:

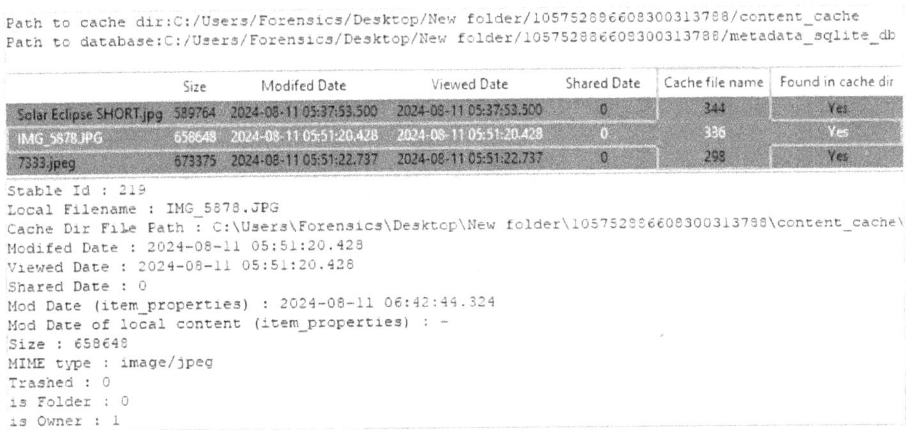

Figure 8.58 – Using gMetaDataParse to parse Google Drive data

Though we have focused on analysis of Google Drive on a Microsoft Windows system for our example, other online data storage platforms such as Microsoft OneDrive and Dropbox almost all act in a similar manner – caching files and storing information about what was uploaded to a database.

For example, Microsoft OneDrive maintains a SQLite database within each user directory at `\AppData\Local\Microsoft\OneDrive\logs\Personal\` within the `SyncEngineDatabase.db` and Dropbox uses a number of SQLite databases to store metadata within each user profile at `\AppData\Local\Dropbox\instance1\`.

How it works...

Cloud storage is now so widespread that it has to be treated as a standard evidence source, not an optional one. Data from online accounts can typically be obtained through user-provided credentials or legal process served on the provider. Once acquired, this cloud data can be compared against artifacts found on any physical devices the user accessed the account with.

This correlation is often extremely valuable: cloud-stored files and metadata can reveal what existed on a device even if the physical device is missing, destroyed, encrypted, or wiped, and local artifacts can confirm what was synced to the online account. Because services like Google, Microsoft, and Dropbox retain extensive metadata (timestamps, device identifiers, sync logs, and sometimes past versions), cloud data often becomes one of the most reliable ways to reconstruct user activity.

Even though cloud evidence comes in many formats (HTML, JSON, CSV, and service-specific structures that forensic tools may fail to parse correctly), it remains a critical component of most modern investigations. Manual review is often required, but the insight gained from these artifacts is well worth the effort.

Mass storage devices

Even with widespread cloud adoption, many users still rely on external storage devices (USB flash drives, portable hard drives, and other removable media) to store or back up data. When these devices are connected to a system, the operating system commonly records identifiers, mount points, drive labels, and associated timestamps. In some cases, the system may also write small artifacts or temporary files to the external drive itself.

These traces can be extremely useful in an investigation. System-side artifacts can reveal which storage devices were connected, when they were connected, and sometimes what activity occurred during the connection window. If the investigation begins with a standalone USB drive, artifacts stored on the drive can sometimes identify the systems it was previously connected to or the sequence of interactions.

Because removable drives can be carried, hidden, wiped, or destroyed far more easily than a full computer, they often play a role in evidence concealment. Understanding how systems track external storage (and how much information can survive even after a user attempts to erase their tracks) can provide valuable leads when other data sources are limited.

In this recipe, we will examine removable storage artifacts using the provided datasets, focusing on how to identify connected devices, interpret system-level tracking data, and correlate activity across multiple operating systems.

Getting ready

For this section, you'll be using two datasets: **Verbatim USB** and **Storage Drive OS Artifacts**, both available through this book's GitHub repository. To access the repository link, follow the steps in the *Download the example code files* section in the *Preface*.

The Storage Drive OS Artifacts set contains material collected directly from the Microsoft Windows, Apple macOS, and Linux forensic images examined earlier in Chapters 4 and 5, and already processed in Autopsy during *Chapter 7*. The Verbatim USB dataset represents a removable storage device that had been connected to each of those systems beforehand.

You'll begin by examining the USB drive itself, then pivot to the artifacts left behind on each operating system to see how they tracked the device and recorded interactions with it.

How to do it...

1. Load the **Verbatim USB** forensic image into a tool capable of browsing forensic images (FTK Imager is used in the examples shown, though you may choose to use any capable

hex viewer). You'll see three total partitions on the device. The first, `Blue1`, is formatted as NTFS. The second, `Blue2`, uses the exFAT file system. The third partition is listed as `Unrecognized`, even though its structure superficially resembles a FAT32 file system. When a forensic tool can't properly identify a file system, it usually indicates either a file-system type the tool doesn't support or the presence of encryption. In this case, the third partition displays the kind of high-entropy, randomized data pattern that strongly suggests it has been encrypted rather than corrupted or misidentified:

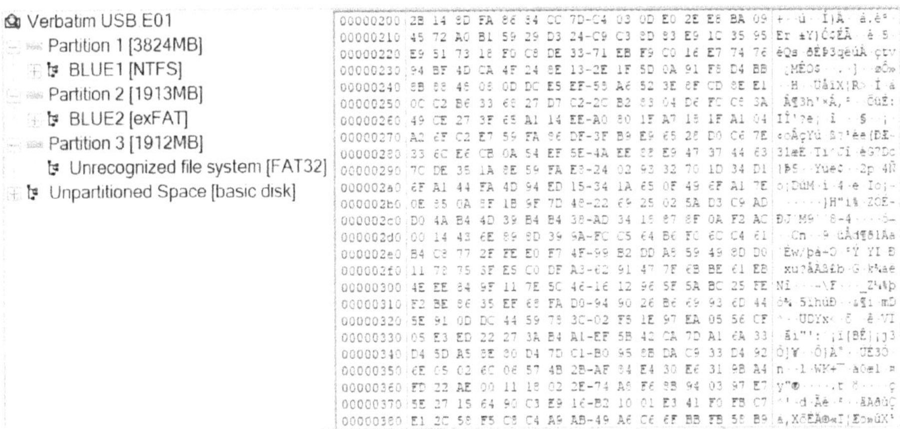

Figure 8.59 – Verbatim USB dataset partitions with third partition encrypted

2. You can select each of the two unencrypted partitions and view their corresponding volume serial numbers (VSNs). A VSN identifies the **volume**, not the physical USB device. Each serial number is generated at the moment the partition is formatted, and the timestamp used in that process introduces enough randomness that the odds of two different volumes sharing the same VSN are extraordinarily low. Realistically, identical VSNs only show up when a volume has been cloned sector-for-sector. Because of this, a VSN is reliable for tying a specific partition to activity on a system. The only caveat is that the identifier will change if the user reformats the partition; it's persistent across normal usage, but not across reformatting:

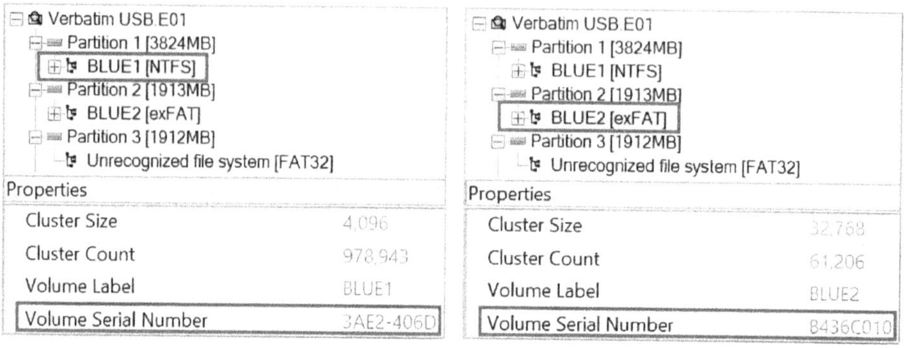

Figure 8.60 – Verbatim USB volume serial numbers

3. Because this USB device contains NTFS, exFAT, and FAT32 partitions, it already suggests the drive was originally partitioned and formatted on a Microsoft Windows system. However, once you select the **[root] of the BLUE2 partition** in FTK Imager, the picture becomes clearer.

4. Inside that partition you'll see `.fseventsd` and `.Spotlight-V100`, both of which are hidden directories automatically created when an external drive is connected to an Apple macOS machine. These folders store file system event logs and Spotlight indexing data. If the macOS user had deleted anything from the drive, you would normally also see a `.trashes` directory. Instead, this drive shows `Trash-1000`, which serves the same purpose but is created by Linux systems.
   In other words, the BLUE2 volume carries clear artifacts showing it has been plugged into both macOS and Linux systems after being formatted on Windows:

Name	Size	Type	Date Modified
.fseventsd	32	Directory	8/20/2024 10:56:36 PM
.Spotlight-V100	32	Directory	8/20/2024 10:56:35 PM
.Trash-1000	32	Directory	8/21/2024 9:55:15 AM

Figure 8.61 – Evidence of Verbatim USB being connected to a Mac system

5. When you examine `.Trash-1000`, you can actually see which files were deleted while the USB was connected to the Linux system. The `files` subdirectory contains the deleted item itself; in this case, `7700.jpg`. The `info` subdirectory holds a companion metadata file, `7700.jpeg.trashinfo`, which records when the deletion occurred. These artifacts make it possible to determine not only that the drive was used on a Linux system, but also exactly which files were removed and the timestamp of that action:

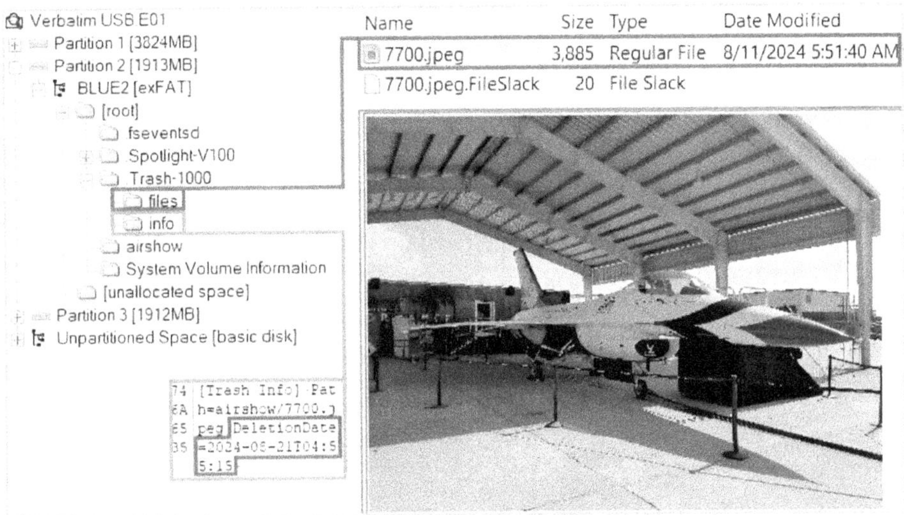

Figure 8.62 – Evidence of file deleted from Verbatim USB using Apple system

Beyond the volume serial numbers created during formatting, every physical storage device also has a hardware-level serial number, often referred to as the **iSerialNumber**. This identifier is written into the device's firmware and remains constant even if the drive is repartitioned or reformatted.

Because firmware-level properties are not captured in a forensic image, the iSerialNumber must be obtained either from the live system while the device is connected or from the acquisition log generated by the forensic imaging tool.

When using software like FTK Imager, the device's properties window will display this iSerialNumber, and the value will also be recorded automatically in the case log created during acquisition:

Information

Device USBSTOR\
\Disk&Ven_Verbatim&Prod_STORE_N GO&Rev_1100\04750701106
0079D&0 was configured.

Figure 8.63 – Serial number of Verbatim USB viewed in Microsoft Windows

Note

Serial Numbers That Aren't

The serial number of the physical device may seem like the better option to identify a connected storage drive, but this is not always true. When I was new to digital forensics, I was attempting to prove that a storage device was

> connected to a Windows system but there was a problem – the serial number of the known device did not match all the instances recorded by the system that I was so sure of. I began to believe I was making a mistake, or perhaps I was wrong in my conclusion. It turns out I was not wrong; I just did not realize at the time how unreliable this data can be, as Windows will sometimes assign arbitrary serial numbers for some devices that are different from the one embedded in firmware. Other issues for this discrepancy can be an external serial number printed on the device not matching the one embedded in firmware, a printed external serial number different from that of the storage drive inside the case, or issues with how the system records the serial number based on how the device was attached, such as devices indirectly attached via a USB hub or docking station. Be cautious here!

Let's now turn to the systems we believe this Verbatim USB drive was previously connected to and see what evidence we can find.

6. We will start with our Microsoft Windows acquisition, as Windows tends to record device connection events rather extensively. Remember, the specific data needed for this section is provided in the `Storage Drive OS Artifacts` dataset. In *Chapter 4*, we used Eric Zimmerman's Registry Explorer to familiarize ourselves with the Windows Registry. Use this tool to load the provided Registry files, then select **Common** from the **Bookmarks** menu. Click on **USB (USB Devices)**.
   This will display a table of previously connected devices, including the device serial name and first/last connected times. Notice that, at least in this case, the device serial number from *Figure 8.64* matches the device serial number shown in the Windows Registry:

Serial Number	Service	Device Desc	Device Name	First Installed	Last Connected
4&25a8364&0	usbhub	USB Root Hub		2024-06-20 02:57:45	2024-08-11 08:35:35
4&32698a7f&0&0	USBHUB3	USB Root Hub (USB 3.0)		2024-06-20 02:57:45	2024-08-11 08:35:35
NULL	usbccgp	USB Composite Device	Integrated Camera	2024-06-20 02:57:47	2024-08-12 03:27:41
6&173f8c3&0&0000	usbvideo	Integrated Camera	Integrated Camera	2024-06-20 03:04:18	2024-08-12 03:27:42
6&173F8C3&0&0002					
0360922040001393	USBSTOR	USB Mass Storage Device	Flash Drive FIT	2024-08-12 03:54:40	2024-08-12 03:54:40
047507011060079D	USBSTOR	USB Mass Storage Device	STORE N GO	2024-08-11 09:49:41	2024-08-12 03:45:17
5&23b1421d&0&7	BTHUSB	Intel(R) Wireless Bluetooth(R)		2024-06-20 03:04:18	2024-08-12 03:27:39
5&15b6459c&0&1	usbhub	Generic USB Hub		2024-06-20 02:57:46	2024-08-12 03:35:36

Figure 8.64 – Connected device artifacts located in Windows Registry

7. Registry Explorer and many other tools will attempt to centralize the most relevant data into a single view by piecing together various information located throughout the registry. The majority of this data is in the SYSTEM Registry file at `/ControlSet001/Enum/USBSTOR`, `/ControlSet001/Enum/SCSI`, and `/ControlSet001/Control/DeviceClasses` (or `/ControlSet001/Enum/HID` for other types of USB attached devices like peripherals and `/ControlSet001/Enum/USB` for MTP connections from attached mobile devices).
   These tools present related artifacts with varying levels of completion, so we should never assume that all available information is being revealed. For example, go to `/MountedDevices/` within the SYSTEM Registry file and you will find artifacts showing our Verbatim USB was last mounted as drive F:, an artifact is not presented by the summary style view in Registry Viewer:

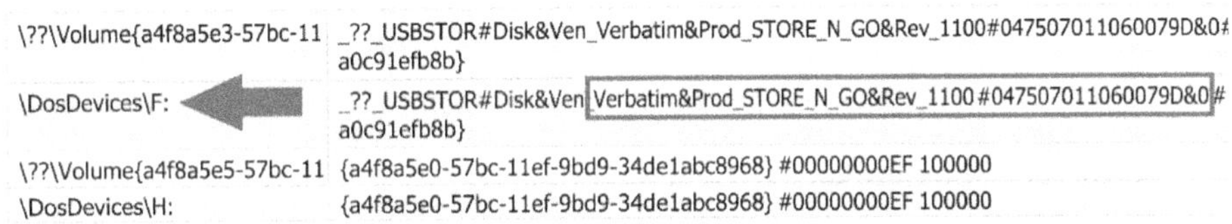

Figure 8.65 – Windows Registry artifact showing the assigned drive letter

Windows Event Logs also record a significant amount of data pertaining to connected devices. There are a number of logs that may record this, though some of the most prevalent are typically recorded by Event Log IDs `400, 410, 411, 420, 430, 440, 442, 500, 505, 507, 20001, 20003,` and `1006` (perhaps the most useful of the logs for showing devices being connected and disconnected).

In *Chapter 4*, we explored Windows Event Logs. If we examine the provided logs for evidence of USB device activity, we can identify entries associated with the Verbatim USB drive. An example is shown below from an event with ID 507:

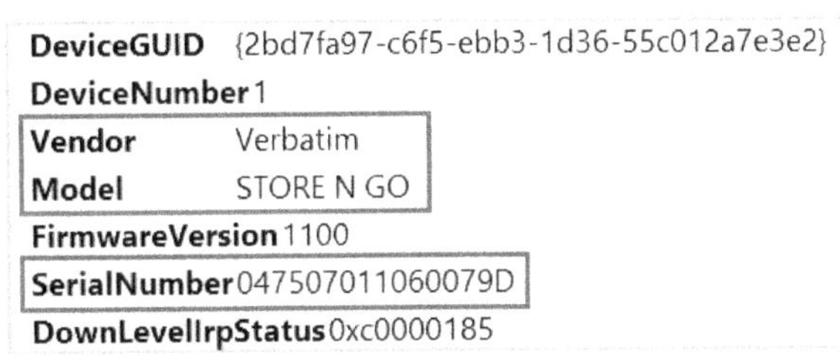

Figure 8.66 – Connected device information from Windows Event Log

8. Windows Jump Lists, LNK files, and ShellBags also tend to record useful information referencing attached mass storage devices. Use Eric Zimmerman's `JumpList Explorer`

tool from *Chapter 4* to open the jump list in the provided `Storage Drive OS Artifacts` dataset.

9. Locate the column with an Absolute Path of `My Computer \F:\airshow` and note that `F:` is the assigned drive letter we identified earlier and now we have a potential folder titled `airshow` that may exist on the previously connected drive. Double-click on this row.
10. In the new window that opens, look at the **Volume information** area where we can see the volume label and VSN from one of the USB drive partitions:

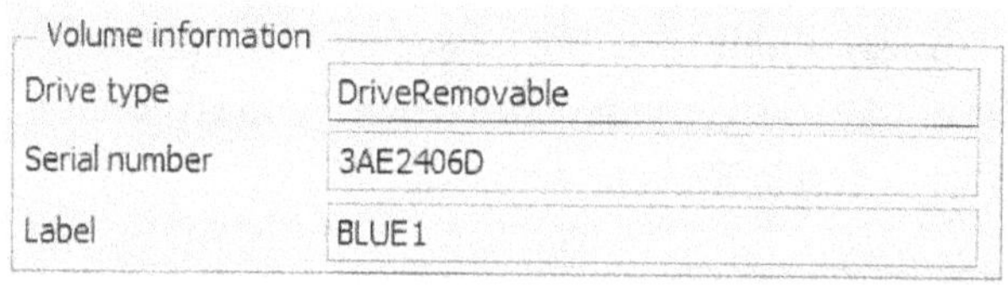

Figure 8.67 – VSN and volume label shown in Windows Jump List file

11. Using Eric Zimmerman's LECmd tool from *Chapter 4*, review the link (LNK) files in the provided `Storage Drive OS Artifacts` dataset. As a reminder, the provided link files can be loaded using the command `LECmd.exe -d <path to Link Files folder>`. Notice that the link files provided show a VSN we have not yet discovered, with a volume name of `BLUE3`. Though we cannot prove it quite yet, it appears this is likely the third partition we determined earlier was encrypted:

Figure 8.68 – Connected storage drive artifacts from Windows LNK file

Moving on to Apple macOS, artifacts detailing the connection of external drives are not as extensive as those in Windows but often exist within various unified logs. Unfortunately, there are a great number of these logs (more than 4 million within our *Apple macOS* sample dataset).

12. Unified logs can primarily be located at `/private/var/db/diagnostics/` within the subdirectories `Persist`, `Signpost`, and `Special`. Many digital forensic analysis suites will attempt to parse unified logs, presenting the most relevant information in an easily readable format. Otherwise, the best way to find relevant information for connected storage drives is to perform keyword searches for text strings within the acquired data.

13. If we use a text editor to open the unified log provided with the `Storage Drive OS Artifacts` dataset, we can find instances of keywords pertaining to `Verabtim` and `BLUE1` for our storage drive. This can be a good starting place to see if such evidence exists, but we would need to more thoroughly parse these logs to establish some context and gain more insight:

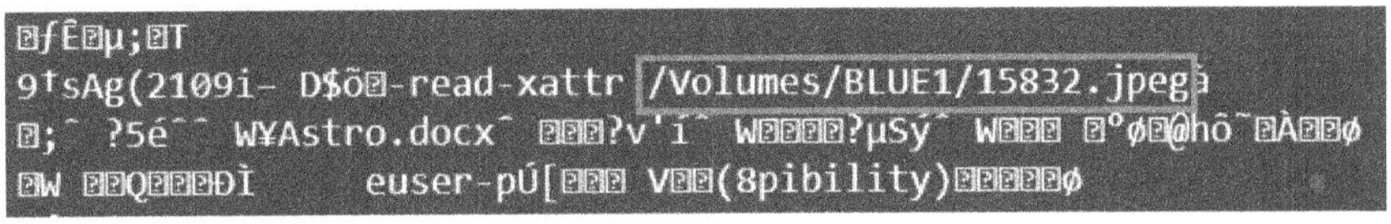

Figure 8.69 – Evidence of the BLUE1 volume in the Apple macOS unified log

14. We can also look at the `com.apple.finder.plist` file located within each macOS user account at `\Users\<user account>\Library\Preferences\`.
15. Open this property list file using the **Xplist** tool we utilized during *Chapter 5* and expand the section titled `FXDesktopVolumePositions`.
16. This lists the volume names seen by the system when an external drive has been connected. We can see both the `BLUE1` and `BLUE2` volume names were recorded. The `BLUE3` volume could not be seen when the USB drive was connected because that volume is encrypted.

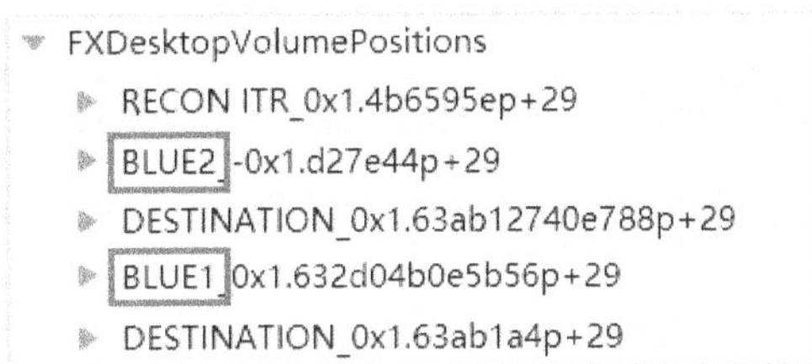

Figure 8.70 – Volumes from connected storage drive recorded by Apple macOS

Linux systems also maintain evidence of previously connected devices, but unlike macOS unified logs, Linux logs are far simpler to access and review. Most Linux logs are located in **/var/** at the root of the system, and can be examined with any standard text editor.

17. Open the syslog file from the `Storage Drive OS Artifacts` dataset and search for identifiers tied to our USB device – terms like `Verbatim`**,** `BLUE1`**,** or `BLUE2`. The syslog provides extensive detail, including the device description, serial number, and precise timestamps showing when each partition was attached (mounted) and detached.

As you continue scrolling, you'll see multiple mount/dismount events for the drive and its volumes, giving a clear timeline:

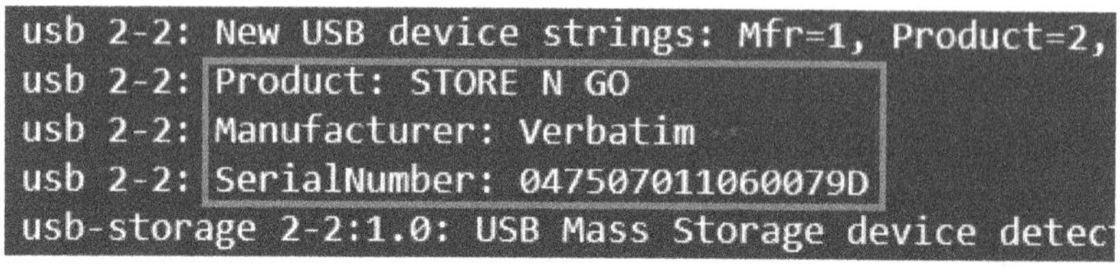

Figure 8.71 – Linux syslog showing information for an attached USB device

18. We can also sometimes determine what was accessed from the mounted storage drive by looking at recent files. Linux often keeps a log of recent files within each user account at `/home/<user>/.local/share/recently-used.xbel`. Open the provided `recently-used.xbel` file using a text editor and review the contents, which are in XML format. In Linux, attached storage drives are mounted within the `/media/` directory at the root of the system, so we can search for this directory name to find potential files accessed from an attached storage drive.
19. In doing this, you will see that the `Budget.xlsx` and `Astro.docx` files were accessed from the `BLUE1` volume of our USB drive, along with dates associated with file access. A closer look at this file will also reveal where an attached Samsung Android device was viewed by the user of our Linux system:

Figure 8.72 – Linux recently-used log showing access to an attached storage device

20. Lastly, if we look at the Autopsy case we processed during *Chapter 7* using our `Microsoft Windows, Apple macOS`, and `Linux` datasets, we will see in the artifact tree that data was parsed for attached USB devices.
21. Open the Autopsy case and click on the **USB Device Attached** artifact type. You will see Autopsy successfully parsed data pertaining to our Verbatim USB storage device, including the serial number and a single associated date; however, Autopsy missed most of the relevant artifacts and parsed nothing related to the Apple or Linux systems. While many commercial tools tend to parse these artifacts more reliably, even the best available tools often fail to locate all relevant artifacts.

Date/Time	Device Make	Device Model	Device ID
2024-08-11 22:54:41 CDT	Silicon Motion, ..	Flash Drive	0360922040001393
2024-08-11 22:45:17 CDT	Verbatim, Ltd	Flash Drive	047507011060079D
2024-08-11 22:27:42 CDT	Intel Corp.	Bluetooth wireless interface	5&23b1421d&0&7

Figure 8.73 – USB Device Attached artifacts presented by Autopsy

22. We can begin to overcome this and even find other areas we may not think to check for evidence of mass storage drive attachments by performing a keyword search once we have identified a potential device to search for. Use the **Keyword Search** feature of Autopsy to perform an **Exact Match** search across all evidence sources for the keyword `BLUE1`, which is one of the volume labels for our Verbatim USB.

    Notice the results include the `syslog` file from our Linux system, the unified log we examined from our Apple macOS system, and even a Google Drive database file from our Microsoft Windows system. This can be a great way to dig deeper during analysis and begin locating additional artifacts.

Name	Keyword Preview	Location
000000000000000c.tracev3	sAg(2109i-read-xattr /Volumes/«BLUE1«/1583	/img_Apple Macbook.dmg
syslog	/dev/sdc1 at /media/leroy/«BLUE1« on behalf	/img_Linux USB.E01
root_preference_sqlite.db	1ef-9bd9-34de1abc8968 «BLUE1« F:\ 4 7 4009	/img_Lenovo ThinkPad.E01

Figure 8.74 – Keyword search results sample from Autopsy

23. Finally, if you find yourself conducting a significant number of investigations involving the attribution of attached USB devices, specifically involving Microsoft Windows systems, then consider using **USB Detective** software to help automate the process. This software does an exceptional job at finding and presenting attached USB device artifacts throughout the Windows environment, including shell items, Registry artifacts, and Event Logs – even on live systems:

Serial/UID	Description	First Connected (UTC)	Last Connected (UTC)	Volume	Drive	VSN
0360922040001393	Samsung Flash Drive FIT USB	8/12/2024 3:54:40 AM	8/12/2024 3:54:43 AM	TRIAGE	E:	F6E93E58
047507011060079D	Verbatim STORE N GO USB	8/11/2024 9:49:41 AM	8/12/2024 3:45:17 AM	BLUE1	F:	3AE2406D
4&91408&0&010000	PLDS DVD-RW DA8A6SH	6/19/2024 1:57:59 AM			D:	
4&91408&0&000000	WDC WD5000LPLX-08ZNTT0	6/19/2024 1:57:56 AM				

Figure 8.75 – USB Detective sample analysis results

How it works...

Mass storage drives remain a common way for users to store, move, and back up data. Any time these devices intersect with an investigation, our job is to determine who connected what, when, and where – and operating systems give us plenty to work with.

When a USB device is plugged into a system, the operating system almost always leaves behind a trail: Registry entries, event logs, mount points, shortcut artifacts, recent-file logs, and sometimes even hidden metadata or support files written directly onto the external drive. By correlating these sources, we can often reconstruct not only which devices were connected, but also what activity occurred while they were mounted, and sometimes even which systems a drive has traveled between.

This data becomes crucial across case types—from criminal cases involving illicit material, to insider-threat investigations, to IP-theft scenarios where establishing file movement is essential. Understanding how storage-drive artifacts behave across Windows, macOS, and Linux gives us the ability to treat USB activity as an evidentiary timeline just like any other user behavior source to cross-validate data and uncover attempts at concealment.

Summary

User-focused forensic analysis moves beyond understanding systems and into reconstructing human behavior. By examining web activity, user-created files, embedded metadata, cloud-synchronized data, and external storage devices, investigators can identify intent, establish timelines, and correlate activity across multiple platforms. These artifacts often provide the clearest insight into what a user actually did, even when attempts have been made to delete, conceal, or obscure evidence. By combining automated parsing with manual validation and cross-artifact correlation, investigators can build more accurate and defensible conclusions about user actions.

At this point, you should be able to:

- **Identify and analyze common web browser artifacts** (history, downloads, search terms, cache, cookies, and profiles) across multiple platforms.
- Correlate browser artifacts to reconstruct user intent, activity patterns, and file acquisition.
- **Locate and interpret embedded metadata** within common user file types, including documents, images, and media files.
- Distinguish between file system metadata and embedded metadata and understand the reliability and limitations of each.
- **Extract and validate EXIF data**, including timestamps, device information, and geolocation data from image files.
- **Identify and analyze email artifacts**, including message content and header metadata used to determine origin and authenticity.

- **Recognize and analyze cloud-synchronized data** (such as Google Takeout and Drive artifacts) and correlate it with local system activity.
- **Identify artifacts related to external storage devices** and correlate them with how operating systems track device usage and interaction
- **Apply both automated tools and manual techniques** to validate findings and avoid missed or misinterpreted evidence

In the next chapter, we will take a more manual approach to analysis, where we run our own queries on SQLite databases, implement techniques involving timelining and baselining artifacts, and cross-verify our findings to reach accurate conclusions.

Get this book's PDF copy, code bundle, and more

Scan the QR code (or go to `packtpub.com/unlock`). Search for this book by name, confirm the edition, and then follow the steps on the page.

UNLOCK NOW

Note: Have your invoice handy. Purchases made directly from the Packt website don't require an invoice.

9

Manual Analysis and Techniques

Our automated tools get us through most examinations, but manual techniques tell us whether those results are complete and correct. Throughout this book, we've relied on a deliberate balance of automation and hands-on analysis because real-world cases demand both. Automation is only as reliable as the assumptions behind it, and sooner or later, every investigation reaches a point where the examiner must step outside predefined modules and interpret the raw data directly. This often happens because the output is incomplete or a detail matters more than it initially appears – and when our findings can influence life-changing decisions, we have to validate them. Failing to do so isn't just sloppy; it's unethical and undermines our credibility as forensic professionals.

This chapter turns fully toward that side of the craft, where your knowledge becomes the primary tool. When a parser fails, an artifact isn't supported, or timestamps and other evidence refuse to line up, manual analysis is what reveals the truth.

Understanding how artifacts are structured, how to pivot between sources, how to reconstruct timelines, and how to verify your conclusions is what separates a technician from an investigator, and a "push-button" operator from a digital forensic analyst. We'll also look at techniques that improve efficiency in complex examinations, helping you cut through noise and recognize relationships across scattered evidence.

In this chapter, we're going to cover the following main topics:

- SQLite databases
- Timelining
- Baselining
- Cross verification

Technical requirements

For this chapter, you will need:

- A computer running Microsoft Windows as your forensic workstation.
- 64-bit Windows 11 with an Intel i7 quad-core processor or better, and a minimum of 16 gigabytes of RAM is recommended.
- Your working installation of Autopsy (used in chapters).
- Access to the datasets we have been using throughout this book and available at the Packt Publishing GitHub repository. To access the repository link, follow the steps in the *Download the example code* files section in the *Preface*.
- FTK Imager (as used in previous chapters) or an alternative tool capable of browsing forensic images. For example, 7-Zip can be used with additional support (such as the Forensic7z plugin) to access forensic image contents, as introduced earlier in this book.
- DB Browser for SQLite (as used in previous chapters) for examining SQLite databases.

SQLite databases

SQLite is everywhere. Millions of mobile apps rely on it, and while forensic tools can parse the most common ones, those represent only a tiny fraction of what users actually install. As a result, automated tools inevitably fail to parse a large number of application databases. Even when a supported app *is* parsed, the tool frequently misses tables, columns, or records that contain meaningful evidence. Developers also routinely change database schemas, causing automated tools to skip or misinterpret data entirely.

Up to this point, we've only taken brief, surface-level looks at the SQLite databases we encountered during earlier chapters. This section now shifts toward a deeper and more systematic understanding of SQLite – one of the most pervasive data-storage formats in modern digital forensics across desktop systems, mobile devices, and countless applications.

A working knowledge of SQLite allows us to bypass these limitations. It gives us direct access to all available data, lets us interpret it on our own terms, and provides a way to validate or challenge the output of automated tools. Once you understand how to navigate these databases manually, you can analyze unsupported applications, uncover artifacts that tools overlook, and build a more accurate picture of user activity than automation alone can ever provide.

In this recipe, we'll manually analyze a SQLite database to extract, interpret, and validate user activity using targeted SQL queries.

Getting ready

For the exercises in this section, we'll rely on several well-structured databases from the **Apple iOS** dataset. iOS artifacts use **SQLite** extensively and provide a consistent, documented environment to practice manual analysis and querying.

You'll need a tool capable of browsing forensic images (such as **FTK Imager**) to export the databases from the **iOS evidence** and **DB Browser for SQLite** to open them, review their structure, and run SQL queries.

How to do it...

1. Within the **Apple iOS** dataset, navigate to the file path: `/private/var/mobile/Library/CoreDuet/knowledge/`, and export the files `knowledgeC.db`, `knowledgeC.db-wal`, and `knowledge.db-shm` to a working directory on your workstation:

Name	Size	Type	Date Modified
knowledgeC.db	1,512	Regular File	9/9/2024 6:09:04 PM
knowledgeC.db-shm	32	Regular File	9/9/2024 6:10:50 PM
knowledgeC.db-wal	3,839	Regular File	9/9/2024 6:23:50 PM

Figure 9.1 – The knowledgeC database and associated files

Up to this point we've exported and reviewed many SQLite databases, but we haven't looked closely at the companion files that appear alongside almost every SQLite database. These additional files control how data is written, cached, and recovered. Understanding them is essential for accurate analysis.

The `-shm` file (shared memory) is usually very small. It coordinates access to the database when multiple processes interact with it. It rarely contains meaningful forensic data and can generally be ignored, though it's still good practice to collect it for completeness.

The `-wal` file, however, is critically important. The `Write-Ahead` Log stores changes that have not yet been committed to the main database, making it one of the highest-value artifacts in forensic database work. The `WAL` often contains the most recent records – including data the user may not realize is still present. **SQLite** uses this mechanism to maintain stability during crashes or unexpected shutdowns, but from a forensic perspective, it provides a snapshot of "pending" activity.

Anytime you analyze a **SQLite** database, you must acquire the `WAL` file as well, or your results risk being incomplete.

2. Open `knowledgeC.db` in **DB Browser for SQLite**, making sure the `knowledgeC.db-wal` file is stored in the same directory. When both files are present, DB Browser automatically incorporates the WAL contents into the main database, allowing you to view the most current state of the data.
3. Once the database is open, select the **Edit Pragmas** tab rather than the **Browse Data** tab you've used throughout earlier chapters:

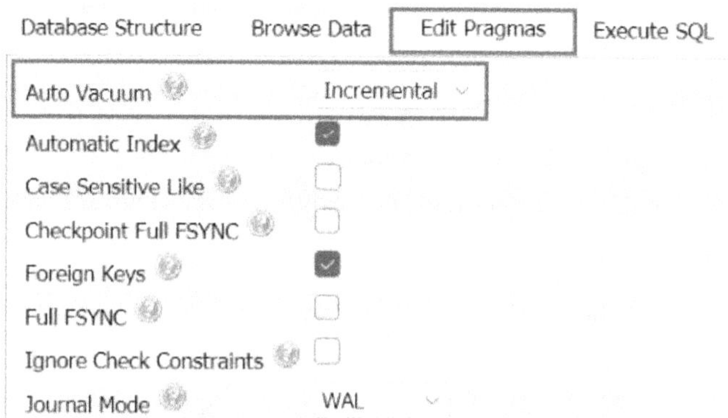

Figure 9.2 – SQLite database pragmas

The **Edit Pragmas** view exposes internal settings that govern how the database handles storage, maintenance, and deletion. One of the most important for forensic purposes is `auto_vacuum`. In this case, the **knowledgeC** database is configured for **incremental vacuuming**. This means deleted rows are not immediately removed; instead, they remain in the database until small portions of free space are reclaimed during normal operations. Because incremental vacuuming steadily overwrites older unallocated space with new entries, databases like **knowledgeC** typically retain only a few weeks of historical data when the device is used regularly.

If `auto_vacuum` is set to `full`, the database rewrites its contents into a compacted version during vacuum operations, permanently removing all deleted records to reduce file size. If it is set to `none`, no automatic cleanup occurs. However, this does not mean deleted data persists indefinitely – natural churn ensures that free pages are eventually reused and overwritten, sometimes very quickly. It simply means the database does not proactively clean itself.

Understanding these settings is crucial. The vacuum mode directly affects how far back historical activity can be recovered, and it reinforces why the timely acquisition of mobile devices is essential before volatile artifacts disappear.

4. Click the **Browse Data** tab and navigate to the **ZOBJECT** table we first examined during the Apple iOS section of this book:

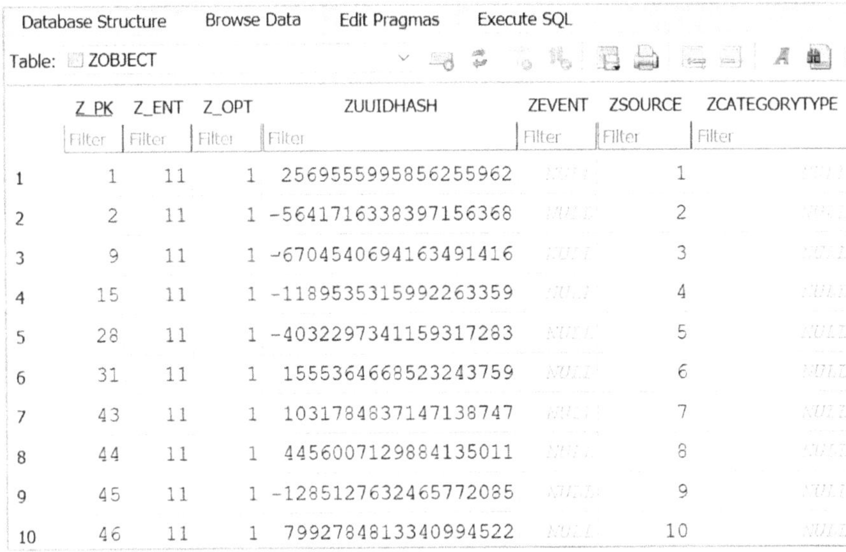

	Z_PK	Z_ENT	Z_OPT	ZUUIDHASH	ZEVENT	ZSOURCE	ZCATEGORYTYPE
1	1	11	1	2569555995856255962	NULL	1	NULL
2	2	11	1	-5641716338397156368	NULL	2	NULL
3	9	11	1	-6704540694163491416	NULL	3	NULL
4	15	11	1	-1189535315992263359	NULL	4	NULL
5	28	11	1	-4032297341159317283	NULL	5	NULL
6	31	11	1	1555364668523243759	NULL	6	NULL
7	43	11	1	1031784837147138747	NULL	7	NULL
8	44	11	1	4456007129884135011	NULL	8	NULL
9	45	11	1	-1285127632465772085	NULL	9	NULL
10	46	11	1	7992784813340994522	NULL	10	NULL

Figure 9.3 – ZOBJECT table from knowledgeC database

SQLite tables function much like spreadsheets, where rows represent individual records, and columns represent the attributes of those records. The value stored at the intersection of a row and column can take on one of several core SQLite data types:

- **INTEGER (INT)** – whole numbers (positive or negative). Commonly used as boolean flags (1 = true, 0 = false) or as numeric identifiers.
- **REAL** – floating-point numbers for values requiring decimals.
- **TEXT** – string data such as file paths, message bodies, names, and descriptors.
- **NULL** – indicates that no value is present.
- **BLOB** – Binary Large Objects used to store raw binary data. Small embedded artifacts (like thumbnails, JSON structures, or small images) often appear as BLOBs, while larger items such as full-resolution photos or videos are typically stored externally and referenced by path within the database.

These basic data types form the backbone of almost every modern application's storage structure, which is why understanding them is so important when performing manual database analysis.

SQLite tables can be extremely large, and scrolling through them manually often provides little insight without additional context. Many fields also store values that only become meaningful once interpreted in context – such as integers representing boolean settings, state flags, or categorical codes. Automated tools translate some of these values for us, but they rarely parse every column, and unsupported third-party apps are often left untouched. That means we must be able to extract and interpret the data ourselves.

Fortunately, forensic examiners do not need to become full-time database developers. In most investigations, we simply need to select the relevant fields, filter the data, convert timestamps, and add human-readable context. A small set of SQL commands will get us most of the way there:

Command	**Function**
`SELECT`	Retrieves data from a table
`FROM`	Specifies the table to query
`WHERE`	Applies conditions to narrow results
`AS`	Renames a field or value for clarity
`ORDER BY`	Sorts results (often with **ASC** or **DESC**)
`CASE`	Begins a conditional expression
`WHEN`	Used in a conditional query to describe an expression
`THEN`	Used in a conditional query to set an action to perform
`ELSE`	Performs another action if other conditions are not present
`DATETIME()`	Converts Unix epoch values into readable timestamps
`LIKE`	Pattern matching for partial strings (useful for searches)
`IN`	Filters for a list of possible values
`BETWEEN`	Filters by a ranged set of values (useful for timestamps)

Command	Function
`LIMIT`	Restricts the number of returned rows
`JOIN`	Combines related tables based on a common value

Table 9.1 - Set of SQL commands

These commands handle nearly all common forensic scenarios – extracting meaningful data, adding descriptive labels, filtering down to the relevant timeframe, and validating what our automated tools report. As we work through the following examples, you'll see how far a small, well-chosen subset of SQL can take you in real investigations.

5. Select the **Execute SQL** tab. This is where we can begin writing queries to extract and manipulate data directly from the database. For this example, we want to determine each time the iPhone was successfully unlocked and calculate how long it remained unlocked. To do this, we need three values: the start time of the event, the end time of the event, and the event's boolean value indicating whether the unlock actually occurred.
6. Enter the following SQL query:

```
SELECT
ZSTARTDATE,
ZENDDATE,
ZSTREAMNAME,
ZVALUEDOUBLE
FROM ZOBJECT
```

7. Here, `SELECT` specifies the columns we want to retrieve, and each listed field (except the last) ends with a comma. `FROM ZOBJECT` tells SQLite which table to pull the data from. The selected fields in this query help describe the event and its associated metadata:
   - `ZSTARTDATE` contains the timestamp representing when the event began.
   - `ZENDDATE` contains the timestamp representing when the event ended.
   - `ZSTREAMNAME` shows the event description.
   - `ZVALUEDOUBLE` holds the event's numeric value – in this case, whether the unlock event is true (typically 1) or false (0).

8. Click the **Play** button to execute the query. Once it completes successfully, the results will appear in the pane beneath the command window:

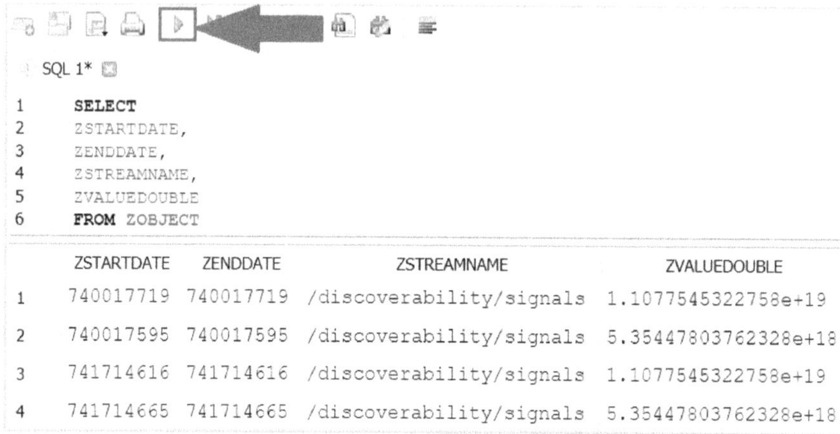

Figure 9.4 – SQLite query to select data from table

9. The results still look messy. We've returned more than 1,200 rows, and almost none of them relate to device unlock activity. To narrow the dataset to only the events that record when the phone was locked or unlocked, we can filter on the `ZSTREAMNAME` column.

10. If you browse through `ZSTREAMNAME` within the ZOBJECT table, you'll notice multiple entries labeled `/device/isLocked`. These are the events we care about – each one indicates a transition between the device being locked or unlocked.

11. Add the following line to the end of your existing query, then click **Play**:

```
WHERE ZSTREAMNAME = '/device/isLocked'
```

12. The `WHERE` clause restricts the results to only those records where the `ZSTREAMNAME` field matches the text string `/device/isLocked`. After applying this filter, the dataset is reduced substantially – down to around **68 rows**, depending on the specific acquisition:

```
SELECT
ZSTARTDATE,
ZENDDATE,
ZSTREAMNAME,
ZVALUEDOUBLE
FROM ZOBJECT
WHERE ZSTREAMNAME = "/device/isLocked"
```

	ZSTARTDATE	ZENDDATE	ZSTREAMNAME	ZVALUEDOUBLE
1	744937893	744937923	/device/isLocked	0.0
2	745104092	745104123	/device/isLocked	0.0

Figure 9.5 – SQLite query to find only lock/unlock events

13. Even with the `/device/isLocked` filter applied, we're still seeing both lock and unlock events. Since our goal is to identify each moment, the device was successfully unlocked, we can remove the redundant "locked" events.
    The `ZVALUEDOUBLE` field tells us the lock state at each event. Because the field corresponds to `isLocked`, a value of `0.0` means it *is not locked*—in other words, this is the user unlocking the phone.

14. To isolate only the unlock events, append the following condition to the end of the existing query and click **Play**:

```
AND ZVALUEDOUBLE = 0.0
```

This expands the `WHERE` clause so it now retrieves only records where

- the event type is `/device/isLocked`, **and**
- the device state recorded is `0.0` (unlocked)

With both conditions applied, the data collapses further to around **33 rows**, each representing a moment when the device was successfully unlocked:

```
SELECT
ZSTARTDATE,
ZENDDATE,
ZSTREAMNAME,
ZVALUEDOUBLE
FROM ZOBJECT
WHERE ZSTREAMNAME = "/device/isLocked" AND ZVALUEDOUBLE = "0.0"
```

	ZSTARTDATE	ZENDDATE	ZSTREAMNAME	ZVALUEDOUBLE
1	744937893	744937923	/device/isLocked	0.0
2	745104092	745104123	/device/isLocked	0.0

Figure 9.6 – SQLite query now showing only unlock events

15. Though this is starting to look better, our timestamps still need to be converted to a readable format. We can use the `DATETIME` function to change our original selection of the `ZSTARTDATE` field to the following:

```
DATETIME (ZSTARTDATE, 'unixepoch'),
```

This interprets the values in `ZSTARTDATE` as Unix epoch timestamps and converts them into a human-readable date and time:

```
SELECT
DATETIME (ZSTARTDATE, "unixepoch")
ZENDDATE,
ZSTREAMNAME,
ZVALUEDOUBLE
FROM ZOBJECT
WHERE ZSTREAMNAME = "/device/isLocked" AND ZVALUEDOUBLE = "0.0"
```

	ZENDDATE	ZSTREAMNAME	ZVALUEDOUBLE
1	1993-08-09 23:11:33	/device/isLocked	0.0
2	1993-08-11 21:21:32	/device/isLocked	0.0

Figure 9.7 – SQLite DATETIME query to convert Unix epoch timestamps

You may notice a problem here: every converted timestamp now shows the year **1993**. Since iPhones did not exist in 1993, something is clearly off. The reason is that this database doesn't use the Unix epoch – it uses **Mac Absolute Time**, which begins on **January 1, 2001 at 00:00:00 UTC**. Unix epoch time begins on **January 1, 1970 at 00:00:00 UTC**, so when we force a Mac Absolute timestamp through a Unix conversion, SQLite interprets it as occurring 31 years too early.

Fortunately, we can manually correct this in SQLite. Because these timestamps are stored in **seconds**, all we need is the exact number of seconds between the two epochs. Using an online time-duration calculator (such as the one at `www.calculator.net/time-duration-calculator.html`), we can determine that the difference between the Unix epoch and the Mac epoch is **978,307,200 seconds**:

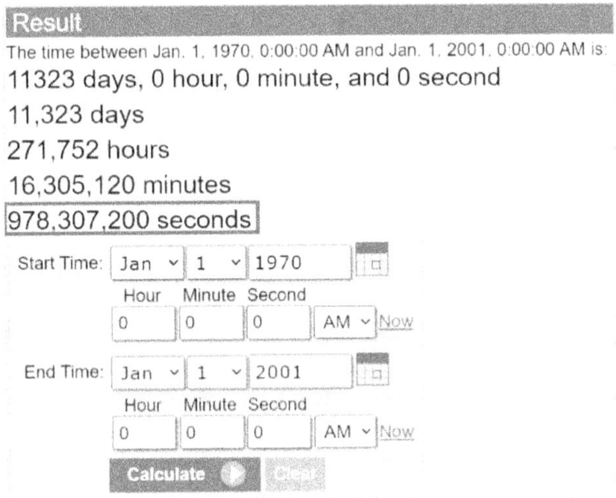

Figure 9.8 – Finding seconds between Unix and Mactime epochs

16. Now that we know the number of seconds between the Unix and Mactime epochs, we can apply a simple mathematical adjustment to correct our timestamp conversion. By adding **978,307,200 seconds** to the existing values, we shift each timestamp forward into the correct range before converting it with the Unix-based DATETIME function:

```
DATETIME (ZSTARTDATE + 978307200, 'unixepoch'),
```

17. This works because the data inside the database is stored in **Mac Absolute Time**, but SQLite's built-in DATETIME function only interprets timestamps as **Unix epoch**. Adding the offset bridges that gap and gives us accurate, human-readable results:

```
SELECT
DATETIME (ZSTARTDATE+978307200, "unixepoch")
ZENDDATE,
ZSTREAMNAME,
ZVALUEDOUBLE
FROM ZOBJECT
WHERE ZSTREAMNAME = "/device/isLocked" AND ZVALUEDOUBLE = "0.0"
```

	ZENDDATE	ZSTREAMNAME	ZVALUEDOUBLE
1	2024-08-09 23:11:33	/device/isLocked	0.0
2	2024-08-11 21:21:32	/device/isLocked	0.0

Figure 9.9 – SQLite query to accurately convert Mactime epoch timestamp

Note

Back to the Future

We can also convert these timestamps into local time rather than UTC. To do this, add an extra parameter to the DATETIME function. For example:

DATETIME(ZSTARTDATE + 978307200, 'unixepoch', 'localtime')

Be aware this will use the **local time zone of your workstation**, so make sure your analysis machine is set to the same time zone as the device being examined when you run the query.

If timestamp conversion feels messy at first, that's normal – and it's exactly why validation matters. These manual conversions are the same operations your automated tools perform behind the scenes. Understanding how they work allows you to parse unsupported databases confidently and verify the accuracy of automated parsing when a case demands it. This knowledge gives you the ability to explain what is happening, why the results are accurate, and how you know your findings can be trusted.

18. You may have noticed that the `ZENDDATE` field is still incorrect or may have even disappeared entirely. This is expected because we've only converted the start timestamp so far. The end timestamp must also be explicitly converted before our output will display it correctly.
19. Add the same `DATETIME` conversion we used earlier, applied to `ZENDDATE`, and remember to include a comma at the end of each line so the query parses properly:

```
DATETIME (ZENDDATE + 978307200, 'unixepoch'),
```

20. Run the query again, and you'll now see the corrected, readable end times appear in the results:

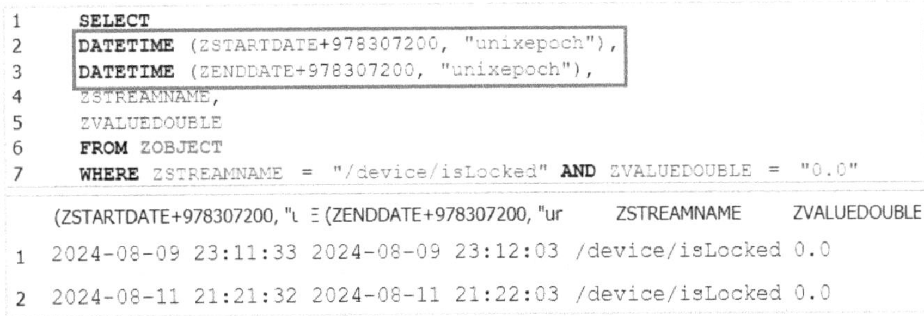

Figure 9.10 – SQLite query to accurately convert Mactime epoch timestamp

21. Our dataset is now filtered to only the events we care about, but the output still isn't very readable. If we handed this to a stakeholder, the raw field names would create unnecessary confusion. To make the results intuitive, we can rename the columns using the `AS` command.

22. Add the following labels to the end of your two `DATETIME` lines, remembering to maintain the existing commas at the *end* of each statement:

```
AS 'Start Date / Time',
AS 'End Date / Time',
```

Renaming the fields in this way gives our output clear, meaningful column headers. This dramatically improves readability without changing the underlying data.

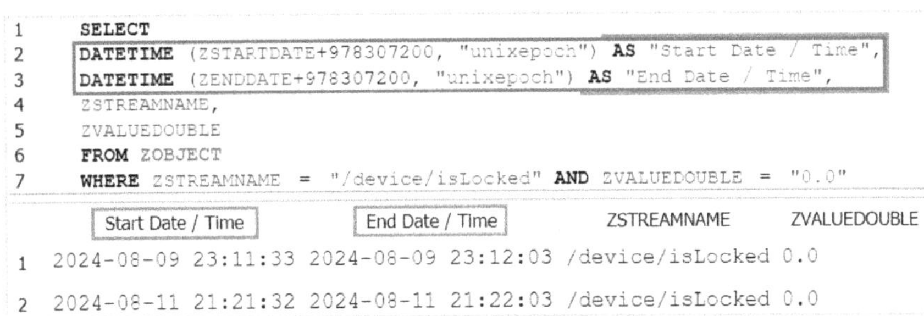

Figure 9.11 – SQLite query to change ZSTARTDATE/ZENDDATE field names

23. We can also make the values within each field more readable by translating them into human-friendly labels. The `ZVALUEDOUBLE` field is a good example, as a value of 0.0 indicates *unlocked* and a value of 1.0 indicates *locked*, but this isn't intuitive to most individuals. Using a `CASE` expression, we can map those values to clear descriptors.

24. Replace the existing `ZVALUEDOUBLE` line in your query (line 5) with the following block, then run the query:

```
CASE
WHEN ZVALUEDOUBLE = 0.0 THEN 'Unlocked'
ELSE 'Unknown'
END AS 'Lock Status'
```

This maps the values as follows:

- If `ZVALUEDOUBLE` equals `0.0`, label the event as `Unlocked`.
- If any other unexpected value appears, mark it as `Unknown` so nothing slips past unnoticed.

25. Because our event type is now fully represented through `Start Date / Time`, `End Date / Time`, and the clearer `Lock Status` field, we can remove the `ZSTREAMNAME` selection entirely. Once you do, your query should match the example shown in *Figure 9.12* and will present a clean, readable set of unlock events instead of raw fields:

```
SELECT
DATETIME (ZSTARTDATE+978307200, "unixepoch") AS "Start Date / Time",
DATETIME (ZENDDATE+978307200, "unixepoch") AS "End Date / Time",
CASE
WHEN ZVALUEDOUBLE = 0.0 THEN "Unlocked"
ELSE "Unknown"
END AS "Lock Status"
FROM ZOBJECT
WHERE ZSTREAMNAME = "/device/isLocked" AND ZVALUEDOUBLE = "0.0"
```

	Start Date / Time	End Date / Time	Lock Status
1	2024-08-09 23:11:33	2024-08-09 23:12:03	Unlocked
2	2024-08-11 21:21:32	2024-08-11 21:22:03	Unlocked

Figure 9.12 – SQLite query showing each device unlock event

26. With the field names cleaned up and the values translated into something meaningful, our query is finally readable. The last improvement we can make is to ensure the results appear in chronological order. To do that, simply add the following line to the end of the query:

```
ORDER BY ZSTARTDATE ASC
```

This tells SQLite to sort all returned records by the original start-time field in ascending order, giving us a proper timeline of unlock events instead of a jumble of rows. It also reinforces a best practice: whenever you're reconstructing user behavior from event logs, always confirm that your output is chronologically sorted so the sequence of activity is preserved.

27. Once you've built a query that extracts meaningful insight from a database, you don't want to reinvent it each time a similar case comes along. DB Browser for SQLite makes this easy by allowing you to export and import your SQL statements. The **Save SQL file** option lets you preserve any query you create, and the **Open SQL file(s)** option allows you to load those queries back in for reuse later. This is especially helpful when you've developed a reliable parsing method for an artifact you expect to encounter again – whether it's a mobile app, a system database, or a browser file that automation often overlooks:

Figure 9.13 – Saving and importing queries in DB Browser for SQLite

28. Once your query returns a clean, readable dataset, DB Browser for SQLite also allows you to save the *results* themselves – not just the query. Clicking the **Save results view** button lets you export the output as either a CSV or JSON file. This is especially useful when you're preparing exhibits, sharing findings with other examiners, or preserving the exact dataset used for a report. Exporting the results ensures that stakeholders can review the interpreted data without needing access to the full database or the SQLite tool:

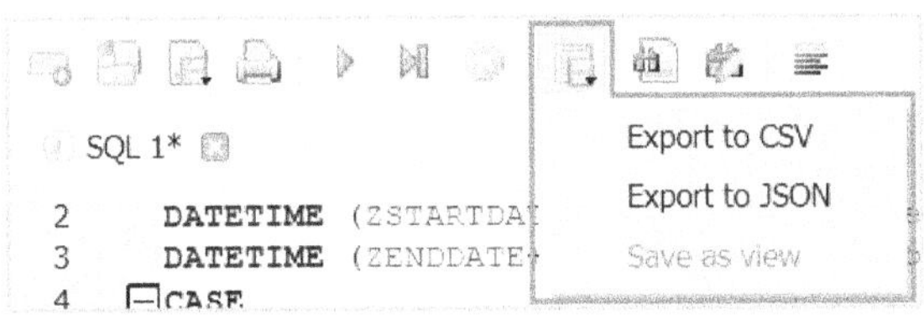

Figure 9.14 – Saving query results in DB Browser for SQLite

29. As an added challenge, modify the query we've built to include **both** lock and unlock events. The logic is identical to what we've already used – your only task is to expand the filtering and labeling so that events with a `ZVALUEDOUBLE` value of `1.0` are displayed and identified correctly.

30. This can be done by adding a second condition within the `CASE` statement to label events with a value of `1.0` as **Locked**, and by extending the `WHERE` clause with an `OR`

condition so that locked events are also included in the results. When completed, the final output should resemble the example below:

	Start Date / Time	End Date / Time	Lock Status
1	2024-08-07 20:18:26	2024-08-09 23:11:33	Locked
2	2024-08-09 23:11:33	2024-08-09 23:12:03	Unlocked
3	2024-08-09 23:12:03	2024-08-11 21:21:32	Locked
4	2024-08-11 21:21:32	2024-08-11 21:22:03	Unlocked
5	2024-08-11 21:22:03	2024-08-13 02:50:20	Locked
6	2024-08-13 02:50:20	2024-08-13 02:51:34	Unlocked
7	2024-08-13 02:51:34	2024-08-13 02:51:42	Locked
8	2024-08-13 02:51:42	2024-08-13 02:52:43	Unlocked
9	2024-08-13 02:52:43	2024-08-13 02:52:52	Locked
10	2024-08-13 02:52:52	2024-08-13 02:52:57	Unlocked
11	2024-08-13 02:52:57	2024-08-13 02:54:59	Locked
12	2024-08-13 02:54:59	2024-08-13 02:55:36	Unlocked
13	2024-08-13 02:55:36	2024-08-13 03:17:06	Locked
14	2024-08-13 03:17:06	2024-08-13 03:17:59	Unlocked
15	2024-08-13 03:17:59	2024-08-13 03:18:22	Locked

Figure 9.15 – SQLite query results showing device lock and unlock events

The full SQL query used to generate these results is displayed in ***Figure 9.16***:

```
SELECT
DATETIME (ZSTARTDATE+978307200, "unixepoch") AS "Start Date / Time",
DATETIME (ZENDDATE+978307200, "unixepoch") AS "End Date / Time",
CASE
WHEN ZVALUEDOUBLE = 0.0 THEN "Unlocked"
WHEN ZVALUEDOUBLE = 1.0 THEN "Locked"
ELSE "Unknown"
END AS "Lock Status"
FROM ZOBJECT
WHERE ZSTREAMNAME = "/device/isLocked" AND ZVALUEDOUBLE = "0.0"
OR ZSTREAMNAME = "/device/isLocked" AND ZVALUEDOUBLE = "1.0"
ORDER BY ZSTARTDATE ASC
```

Figure 9.16 – Final SQLite query to show device lock and unlock events

How it works...

Manual SQLite analysis gives us direct access to the raw data stored by thousands of mobile and desktop applications. Automated tools simplify this work, but they only interpret what they recognize, and they routinely miss fields, mislabel values, or fail to parse entire databases.

By writing our own queries, we can reconstruct events, validate tool output, and analyze unsupported apps with full control and transparency.

The process itself is straightforward: understand the schema, select the fields you need, convert timestamps, add context with conditional logic, and shape the results into something meaningful for stakeholders. This is precisely what commercial forensic tools do behind the scenes; the difference is that we can now verify their accuracy and go further when needed.

For unfamiliar or unsupported applications, the key is determining what the values actually represent. When necessary, we can build a controlled test dataset by installing the app on a test device, performing carefully documented actions, and then examining the resulting database. By comparing our interaction log to the stored records, we can map the meaning of unknown fields. Although this level of reverse-mapping is time-consuming, it's occasionally required – and knowing how to do it gives us the ability to extract evidence from *any* SQLite database we encounter.

Timelining

Timelining is where manual analysis becomes investigative reconstruction. Once we've pulled meaning from individual artifacts (whether system logs, web activity, knowledgeC entries, or application databases), the next challenge is putting those pieces in order. A single artifact rarely tells a story by itself, but a timeline *does*. It allows you to see behavior, sequence actions, identify inconsistencies, and detect both intentional manipulation and accidental anomalies.

Up to this point, we've interpreted artifacts individually, and while Autopsy can build small, automated timelines for us, those timelines are only as good as the data they parse and often miss events that fall outside their ingest modules. A true forensic timeline requires pulling from **many** systems or sources simultaneously and normalizing them into a single chronological narrative.

Creating this kind of timeline manually not only reveals relationships that automation blurs or overlooks, but also exposes gaps. In real-world cases, gaps matter just as much as events: missing logs, sudden timestamp resets, clusters of deleted entries, or periods where expected activity goes silent. These signals are often the earliest indicators of anti-forensics or user intent. They can also be critical during incident response or threat-hunting investigations where an adversary's movement must be traced across multiple systems.

In this recipe, we'll build and analyze a forensic timeline using Plaso and Timeline Explorer to reconstruct user activity across multiple artifacts.

Getting ready

For this section, we'll build a detailed forensic timeline using `log2timeline/Plaso` and review the results with *Eric Zimmerman's Timeline Explorer*, which is extremely effective at filtering and interpreting large sets of data output. To keep the processing efficient, we'll work with the **Microsoft Windows dataset** from *Chapter 4*. Plaso supports macOS, Linux, Android, and iOS as well, and you can run the same workflow later for any of those sources. Windows provides a high density of events with relatively efficient processing time, making it ideal for demonstration.

In addition to our Microsoft Windows dataset, you will need the following tools:

- **Timeline Explorer** by Eric Zimmerman. A powerful Windows-based timeline-review interface capable of opening very large CSV files and filtering events in milliseconds: `https://ericzimmerman.github.io/#!index.md`
- `log2timeline / Plaso` and `psort` (included with Plaso)
- The extraction engine that parses artifacts and normalizes timestamps from our evidence sources (with `psort` giving us the ability to filter, sort, and export the timeline to a CSV file compatible with Timeline Explorer).

Plaso can ingest E01 images, raw DD files, and directory exports. For this chapter, we'll assume an `E01` input (from our Microsoft Windows dataset) to keep the process consistent.

> Note
>
> NOTE: While Plaso used to be distributed as a native Windows executable, that is no longer the case, and Plaso is now developed exclusively for Linux workstations. So, for our Windows workstations, we will simply run Plaso through **Windows Subsystem for Linux (WSL)** using Ubuntu.

First, WSL needs to be enabled on our system so Windows can run a native Linux environment. This is done from PowerShell by entering:

```
wsl --install
```

Once WSL completes its initial setup, **install Ubuntu from the Microsoft Store** and allow it to finish its configuration. From there, Plaso installation mirrors any normal Linux deployment. After updating your package lists with sudo apt update and upgrading packages with sudo apt upgrade -y, you can add the GIFT project's stable repository and install Plaso using the following:

```
sudo add-apt-repository ppa:gift/stable
sudo apt update
sudo apt install -y plaso-tools
```

This installs all Plaso components (`log2timeline.py`, `psort.py`, `pinfo.py`, and their dependencies) without any of the compatibility issues you would encounter attempting a native Windows installation. Once installed, Plaso can be launched from within the Ubuntu terminal just like on any other Linux distribution. Output files can be written to the Windows file system by navigating to `/mnt/c/`, allowing you to seamlessly move results into your standard analysis workflow. This approach gives you a stable, fully supported environment.

Everything produced inside the Linux environment can be viewed, copied, and opened from Windows without any additional tooling. This gives us the best of both worlds: the reliability of Plaso on Linux and the convenience of working from a Windows workstation.

How to do it...

1. On your forensic workstation, create a dedicated folder to store your Plaso output and exports. Place your Microsoft Windows dataset in an easily accessible location so it can be referenced cleanly from within the WSL command line. For the examples in this section, the working directory is: `C:\Timelining\`
   Inside it, a subfolder named **Sources** contains the evidence image: `C:\Timelining\Sources\Lenovo ThinkPad.E01`

   Using a simple folder structure like this keeps paths predictable when typing commands in WSL (especially if you are new to Linux-style environments or mixing Windows and Linux paths):

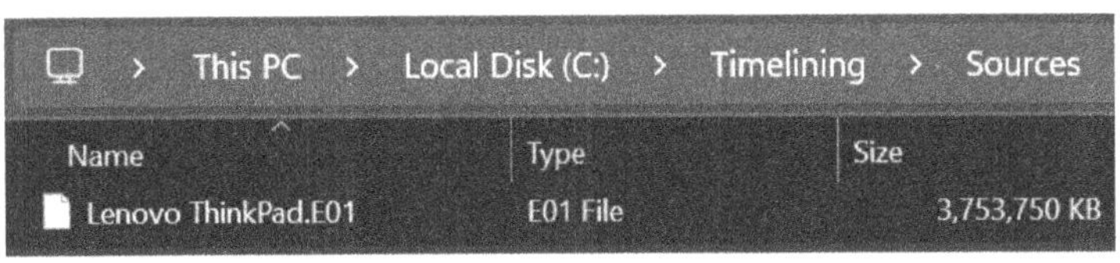

Figure 9.17 – Storage location chosen at the root of Windows workstation

2. Open your Ubuntu (WSL) terminal and navigate to your working directory on the Windows file system where your Plaso output will be stored. In WSL, the Windows `C:`

drive is mounted at `/mnt/c/`, so if you created your working directory at `C:\Timelining`, you can reach it with:

```
cd /mnt/c/Timelining
```

Next, verify that your evidence source is in the expected subfolder. Since you are already inside `/mnt/c/Timelining`, you only need to list the contents of the **Sources** directory:

```
ls Sources/
```

You should see your Windows forensic image (for example, `Lenovo ThinkPad.E01`) listed within this directory:

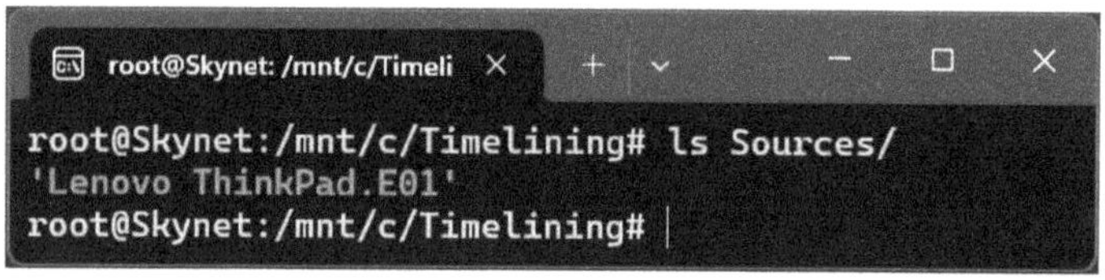

Figure 9.18 – Navigating and listing files using Terminal commands in WSL

3. From your timelining directory (`/mnt/c/Timelining`), run `log2timeline` to generate a Plaso storage file containing all extracted and normalized events:

```
log2timeline.py --status_view linear --workers 4
--timezone "UTC" --storage_file timeline.plaso "/mnt/c/Timelining/Sources/
Lenovo ThinkPad.E01"
```

Here's what each component of the command does:

- `--status_view linear` keeps console output readable by using Plaso's simpler linear status view.
- `--workers 4` specifies the number of worker processes Plaso will use. Increase this value if your system has more CPU cores.
- `--timezone` standardizes timestamps using UTC. This avoids confusion when evidence sources come from different time zones, and ensures psort exports align cleanly.
- `--storage_file` tells Plaso what to name the output file where all extracted events are stored.

The final argument specifies the full path to the evidence source (for example, `Lenovo ThinkPad.E01`), which Plaso will process recursively.

If entered correctly, Plaso will begin parsing artifacts from the image, including registry hives, event logs, browser data, and countless other sources. You should see progress output similar to *Figure 9.19* as the parser runs:

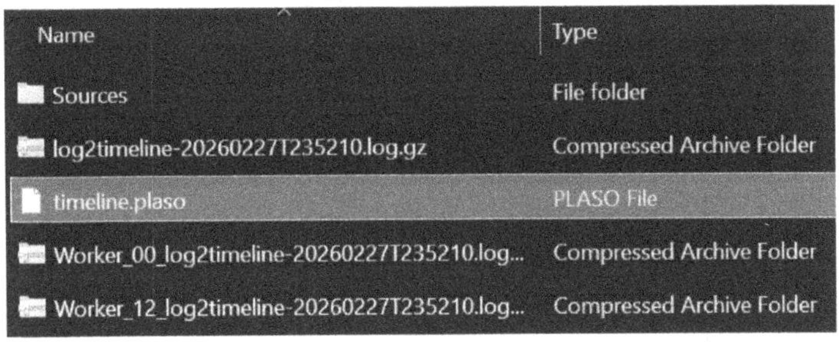

Figure 9.19 – Plaso storage file created from log2timeline

Processing time varies significantly based on CPU and worker count. With 14 workers, for example, a full Windows image may take around an hour to complete. Once finished, you will see `timeline.plaso` (along with supporting log archives) appear in your working directory. This file now contains every normalized event extracted from the evidence.

4. Now that we've generated our `timeline.plaso` storage file, we need to convert it into a CSV file that can be opened and analyzed with Timeline Explorer. From within the WSL environment, run:

```
psort.py -o l2tcsv -w windows.csv timeline.plaso
```

This command tells psort to do the following:

- `-o l2tcsv` – export the timeline using Plaso's CSV output format
- `-w windows.csv` – name our resulting CSV file (Windows is used here so the file clearly corresponds to our Windows evidence source)
- `timeline.plaso` – read from the Plaso storage file we created in the previous step

Once processing completes, you'll find `windows.csv` in your working directory. This CSV contains every normalized event Plaso extracted from the image, including timestamps, sources, paths, descriptions, and user context:

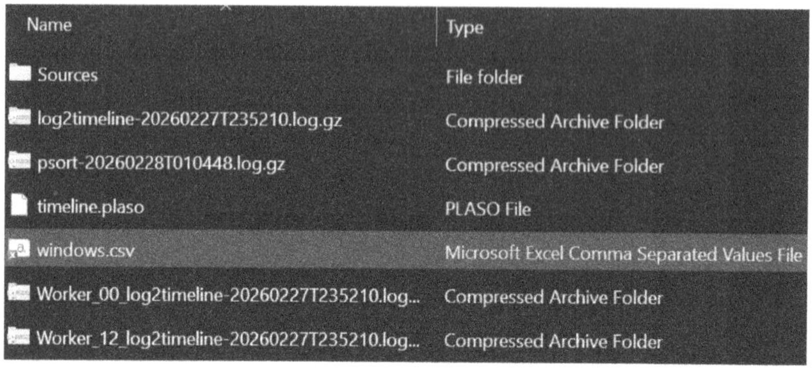

Figure 9.20 – windows.csv file generated from Plaso using psort

If your case involves multiple systems or produces hundreds of thousands of timeline events, a full export may be overwhelming. In these situations, psort can slice the timeline to a specific investigative window. To do that, append the `--slice` parameter:

```
--slice "2026-01-01T00:00:00,2026-03-01T00:00:00"
```

This example would export only events occurring between January 1, 2026, and March 1, 2026, using whichever time zone you specified earlier (UTC in our example). Time slicing is especially useful during intrusion investigations, when identifying exactly what happened within a narrow window can save you from wading through millions of irrelevant events.

5. Launch **Zimmerman's Timeline Explorer**. On first run, you may be prompted to install the **Microsoft .NET Framework** (this is required and only needs to be done once).
6. Click **File | Open**, then browse to your exported `windows.csv` file to load it into Timeline Explorer:

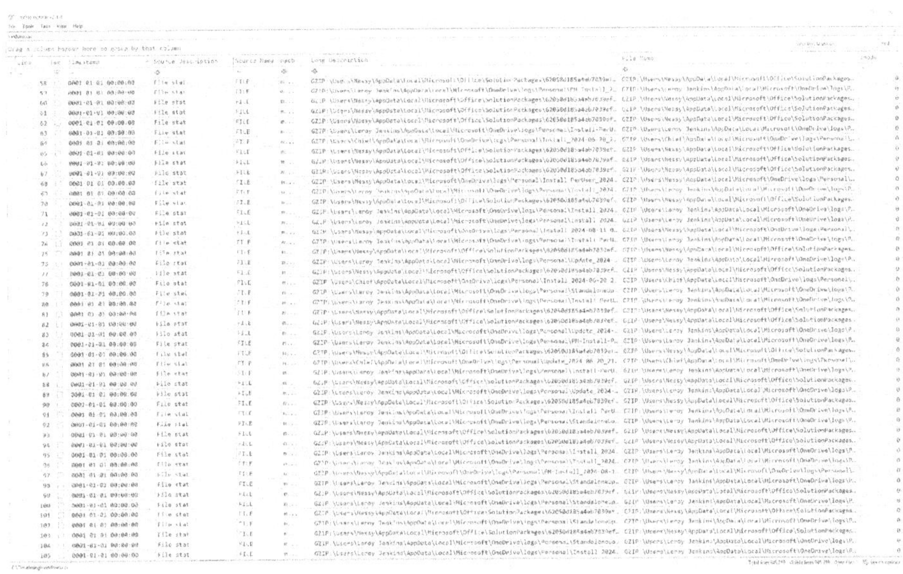

Figure 9.21 – Opening a Plaso CSV in Timeline Explorer

You'll immediately see that the dataset is enormous – nearly a million rows for a single Windows system. If your first visible timestamps all read **0001-01-01**, this is expected; Timeline Explorer sorts chronologically by default, and entries lacking timestamps or defaulting to a zero/epoch value will naturally appear at the top.

To work effectively with this volume of data, it helps to understand the key Timeline Explorer columns you'll be using most often. Many are intuitive, but several contain forensic-specific values that deserve explanation:

- **Source Description** – A short identifier for the artifact category (e.g., `FILE`, `REG`, `WEBHIST`, `EVT`).
- **Source Name** – The tool or subsystem that generated the event (e.g., **WinEVT**, **Chrome History**, **Prefetch**, **LNK Parser**).
- **Long Description** – A more complete description of the event. This is where the "story" is usually found.
- **Inode** – The internal file record number (MFT entry identifier on NTFS), critical for detecting renames, overwrites, or same-file references during reconstruction.
- **macb** – Forensic timestamp indicators describing which timestamp categories apply to each event. To better understand how MACB values are interpreted during timeline analysis, the following table summarizes each timestamp indicator and its meaning:

Letter	Designation	Meaning
m	Modified	Shows when file contents were changed
a	Accessed	Indicates user or system interaction
c	Changed	Refers to *metadata* entries being updated
b	Birth (created)	Tracks when a file or artifact first appears
.	(dot)	Timestamp not recorded or does not exist

Table 9.2 – Timestamp indicator

With this amount of data, we need a fast way to sift through it and isolate what's relevant. Timeline Explorer includes several powerful search and filtering features to help with this.

7. The simplest is the **global search bar** in the upper-right corner of the interface. This allows you to enter keywords that will be matched across *all* parsed artifacts:

Figure 9.22 – Timeline Explorer global search

8. For more control, Timeline Explorer provides additional **Search options**, accessible in the bottom-right corner. These allow you to adjust matching behavior, toggle case sensitivity, and refine how your search terms are interpreted:

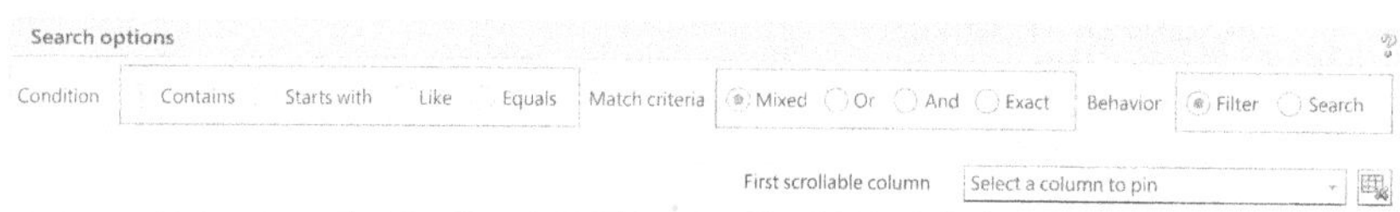

Figure 9.23 – Timeline Explorer general search options

However, the most precise and efficient search capability comes from **column-level filters**. Each column header contains two tools:

- A **search logic selector** (left side of *Figure 9.24*), which lets you define how the column interprets your query (contains, equals, etc.)
- A **filter menu** (right-side of *Figure 9.24*), which lets you include or exclude specific values within that column

This combination allows you to quickly isolate clusters of activity (USB artifacts, browser events, logon sequences, process execution, or anything else Plaso normalized) without scanning through the entire dataset:

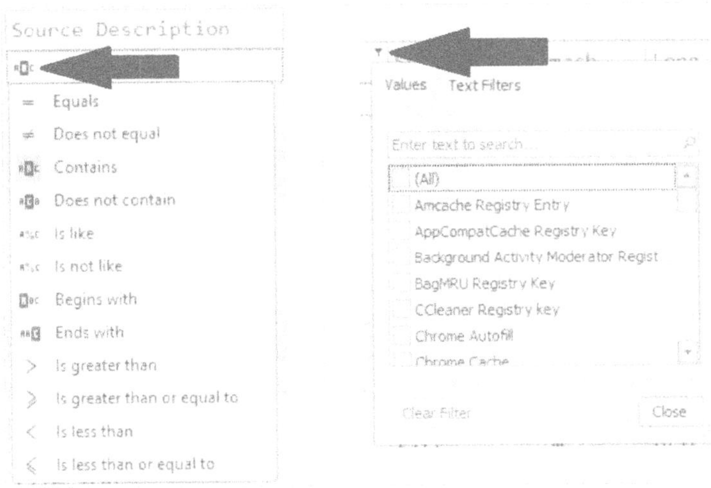

Figure 9.24 – Timeline Explorer column search and filter options

Now let's use some of these filtering features to begin exploring our timeline. Start by narrowing the results to only web-related activity:

1. Click the filter icon under the **Source Description** column and select **Chrome History**.
2. Next, click the filter icon under the **Source Name** column and choose `WEBHIST` (Plaso's designation for **web history** artifacts).

This instantly reduces the view to only events generated by Chrome web activity, making it far easier to identify user browsing patterns:

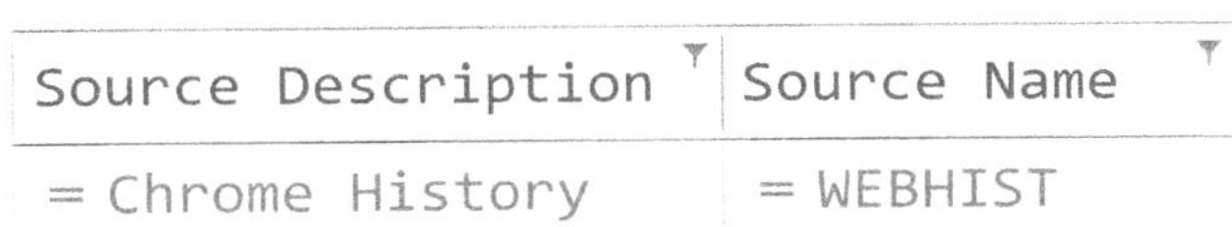

Figure 9.25 – Filtering columns for specific artifacts in Timeline Explorer

With the filters applied, begin scanning through the resulting rows for activity that stands out.

One pattern you may notice is a cluster of Chrome history entries from **August 11, 2024**, involving searches and visits related to *Unetbootin* and *Rufus*—both utilities commonly used to create bootable USB drives. Activity like this may indicate preparation for system modification, reinstallation, or the creation of external boot media:

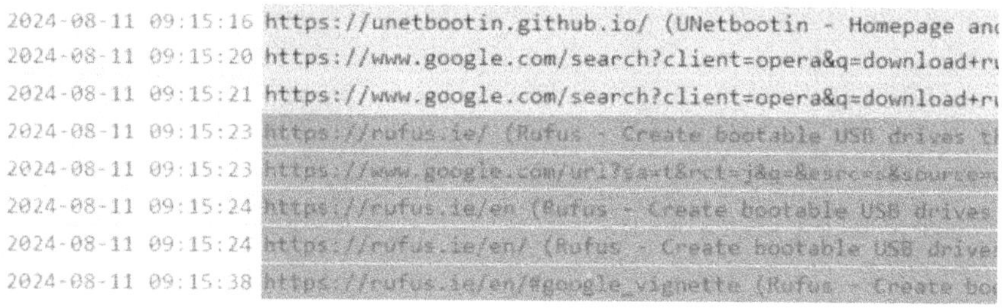

Figure 9.26 – Filtered results in Timeline Explorer

9. As you come across artifacts that appear relevant, use the checkbox in the **Tag** column to flag them. Tagged items can later be isolated with a single filter, allowing you to quickly return to every event you marked as important without having to reapply your earlier searches or filters:

Figure 9.27 – Tagging data of possible interest in Timeline Explorer

10. Continue exploring your timeline by combining different search and filter techniques to uncover additional context around the Unetbootin and Rufus activity. If you apply a global search for either term, you'll notice other artifacts from **August 11, 2024**, suggesting the utilities weren't just downloaded – they were also executed on the system.

    At this point, begin focusing on that date and pivot across artifact types (event logs, file system activity, prefetch, LNK files, browser history, etc.) to reconstruct what happened. Tag each item that appears relevant so you can return to this cluster of activity later with a single filter:

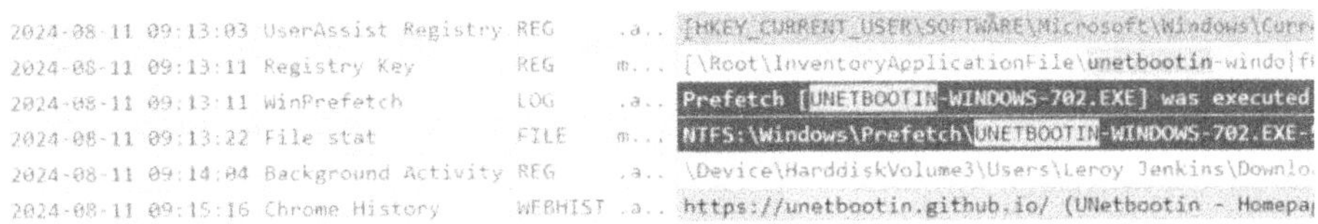

Figure 9.28 – Honing in on activity of interest in Timeline Explorer

11. Once you've identified artifacts that appear related, you can filter for only the items you tagged by selecting the checkbox filter at the top of the **Tag** column. In *Figure 9.29*, the tagged results begin forming a coherent picture of activity; web history shows the user accessing pages for Unetbootin or Rufus, Prefetch and file-access artifacts indicate those utilities were launched alongside a Linux distro ISO, and shortly afterward CCleaner appears in the timeline.
    Taken together, the tagged timeline strongly suggests the following sequence of events involving the `Leroy Jenkins` account:
    - Google Chrome was used to download Unetbootin / Rufus, both utilities capable of creating bootable USB media.
    - These utilities were executed with what appears to be a Linux ISO, as supported by Prefetch and file system activity.
    - A bootable Linux "Store N' Go" USB may have been created, supported by corresponding USBSTOR entries in Windows Event Logs.
    - CCleaner was launched soon afterward, potentially indicating an effort to remove traces of recent activity.

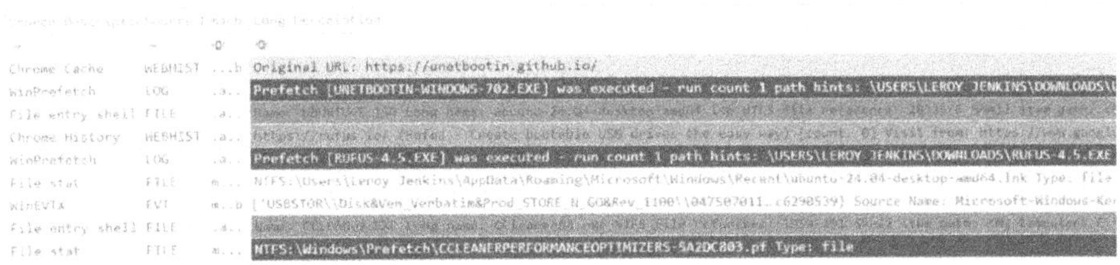

Figure 9.29 – Related events reduced in Timeline Explorer

How it works...

Timelining takes the thousands (or millions) of discrete artifacts scattered across a system and reconstructs them into a single, normalized sequence of events. Rather than reviewing each log source in isolation, Plaso brings all of these event sources into one chronological view. That unified picture allows us to recognize patterns and behaviors that would be almost impossible to identify by examining artifacts individually.

Because Plaso accepts *multiple* evidence sources, we can combine timelines from other systems in the same investigation. A Windows laptop, an employee's workstation, a domain controller, a web server, and even mobile devices or online account data can all be processed into a single .plaso store and exported as one integrated CSV. When these datasets are merged, correlations appear immediately – logons on one system coinciding with suspicious downloads on another, shared USB activity, overlapping browser behavior, or lateral movement that jumps from host to host. This is especially powerful in incident response and threat hunting, where adversaries rarely act on just one endpoint. Timelines can reveal pivot points, escalation phases, periods of reconnaissance, data staging, or exfiltration attempts across an entire environment.

Once everything is parsed, the timeline also exposes gaps (missing logs, abrupt timestamp resets, oddly silent periods, or clusters of deleted artifacts). These gaps can often highlight anti-forensics, tampering, or system misconfigurations that would otherwise go unnoticed. By layering these signals on top of normal activity, we can generate leads more quickly, begin to validate conclusions, and build a defensible narrative based on a more complete picture of activity. Ultimately, timelining is not just about ordering events – it's about transforming raw artifacts into a coherent investigative story and giving us more clarity.

Baselining

As our investigations expand across larger datasets, one of the biggest challenges isn't finding evidence – it's ignoring everything *that isn't* evidence. Modern systems generate thousands of routine files, logs, and artifacts every day, and most of them have nothing to do with the user actions we're trying to interpret. Baselining gives us a way to strip that noise away. By establishing a reference set of known-good system files, defaults, and expected behaviors, we can immediately narrow our focus to the small percentage of artifacts that truly matter.

In the public sector, this often means relying on trusted collections like the **NSRL Reference Data Set (RDS)** to eliminate standard operating system files and common application binaries. In private-sector and enterprise work, Standardized Deployment Images (SDIs) and corporate workstation builds serve the same purpose. When we can compare an examined system against a clean, known configuration, deviations begin to stick out (unauthorized tools, unexpected executables, suspicious scripts, and user-created content stand out instantly).

In this recipe, we'll create and apply a baseline hash set to reduce system noise and isolate artifacts that deviate from a known-good configuration.

Getting ready

For our baselining example, we'll use the same **Microsoft Windows dataset** you've worked with throughout this book. The goal is to extract hashes, format them into a reusable baseline, and then import that baseline back into Autopsy so it can automatically filter out routine system noise during future investigations.

You will need the following:

- **Autopsy** (use the case we already created during *Chapter 7*)
- **FTK Imager** (or a similar tool capable of exporting file hash lists)
- **A spreadsheet application** to prepare the hashes for ingest

How to do it...

1. In our example, we're using the Microsoft Windows dataset to demonstrate how a baseline hash list is created. In real investigations, however, this list should be generated from a freshly deployed **System Deployment Image (SDI)** or another known-clean reference system. The goal is to capture the hashes of files that *should* exist on a clean machine so they can be marked as "Known Good" during analysis, reducing the noise from thousands of irrelevant files.
2. Load the Windows dataset into a forensic tool capable of exporting file hash lists. For the examples shown, **FTK Imager** has been used by selecting **Export File Hash List...** from the **File** menu.
3. Choose a storage location and generate a CSV containing hash values for every file encountered. FTK Imager exports both MD5 and SHA-1 by default; SHA-256 is preferable for modern integrity work, but MD5 remains acceptable for baselines since hashes are used to suppress known files rather than verify integrity:

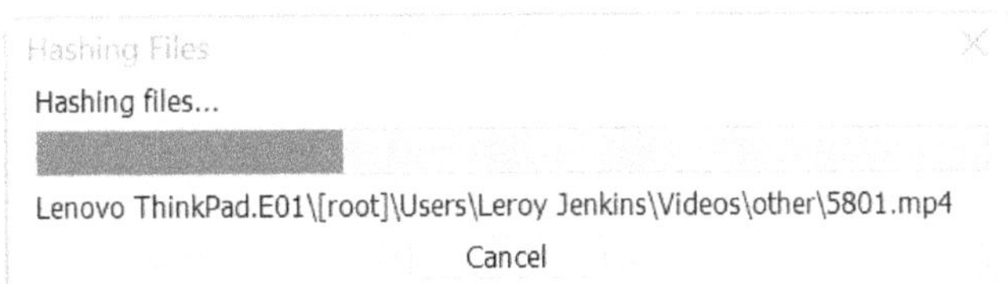

Figure 9.30 – Exporting all file hashes using FTK Imager

4. Open the exported CSV file in Microsoft Excel or LibreOffice Calc.
5. Remove the `FileNames` column, one of the `hash` columns (either `MD5` or `SHA-1`), and the `header row` so you're left with a single clean column of hash values. In this example, we'll keep MD5 for simplicity.
6. Optionally, you can remove duplicate hashes now to reduce redundancy:
   - **Microsoft Excel:** use **Data | Remove Duplicates**
   - **LibreOffice Calc**: use **Data | More Filters | Filter | Remove Duplicates**

7. Once the column is cleaned, press *Ctrl+A* to highlight all values, copy them, and paste them into a new plain text file. This will become the hash list we import into Autopsy:

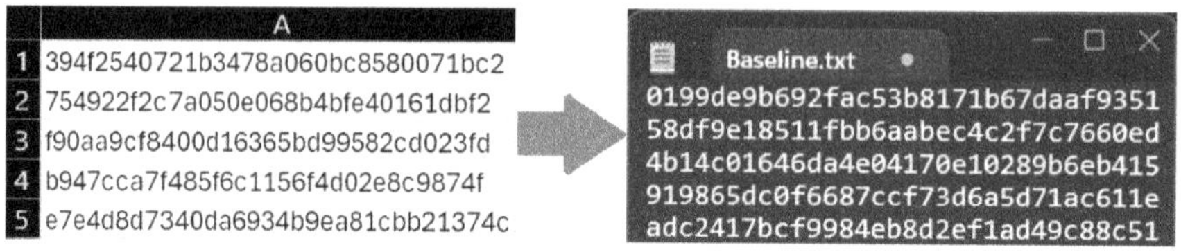

Figure 9.31 – Copying hash values from CSV file to a new text file

If you chose to remove duplicate hashes in the previous step, your text file will still contain well over 47,000 hash values. Most forensic suites, including Autopsy, can ingest a text file containing hashes as long as each value appears on its own line with no additional formatting.

8. Open your existing Autopsy case from *Chapter 7*, then navigate to **Tools** | **Options** | **Hash Lookup**. Click **Import Hash Set**.
9. In the dialog box:
   - Set **Hash Set Path** to the text file you created
   - Name the set `Baseline`
   - Select **Known (NSRL or other)** to categorize these as known-good reference hashes
10. Click **OK** to import:

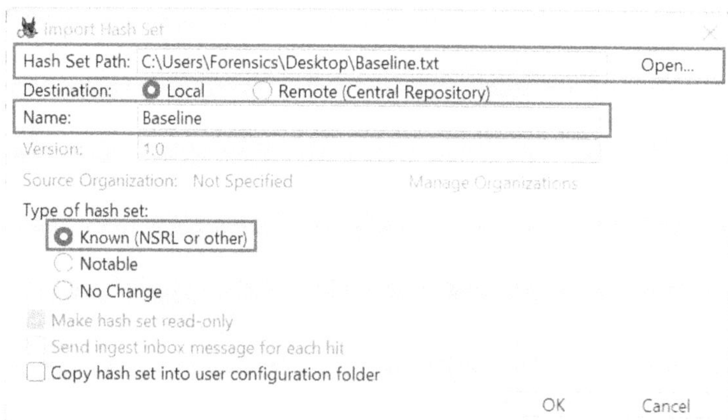

Figure 9.32 – Importing a hash set into Autopsy

11. Click the **Index** button to index your newly imported hash set. When indexing finishes, click **Apply**, then **OK**.

12. Next, return to **Tools | Run Ingest Modules** and choose the evidence source `Lenovo ThinkPad.E01`, which contains the Microsoft Windows dataset we processed earlier.
13. In the ingest configuration window:
    - Select **only** the **Hash Lookup** ingest module
    - In the module options, select the hash set **Baseline (Known)**
14. Click **OK** to begin applying the baseline to the dataset:

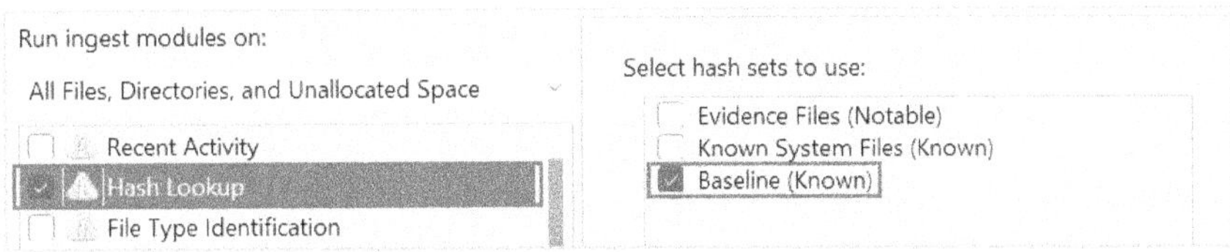

Figure 9.33 – Applying the hash set to an Autopsy case

Autopsy will now compare every file in the case against your baseline and automatically tag matching items as known good.

15. Once processing finishes, expand **File Views | By Extension | Executable** in the tree viewer pane on the left, and select `.dll`.

    The result viewer will populate with every DLL file Autopsy identified on the system, giving you a clear view of all dynamic libraries present before applying the baseline filter:

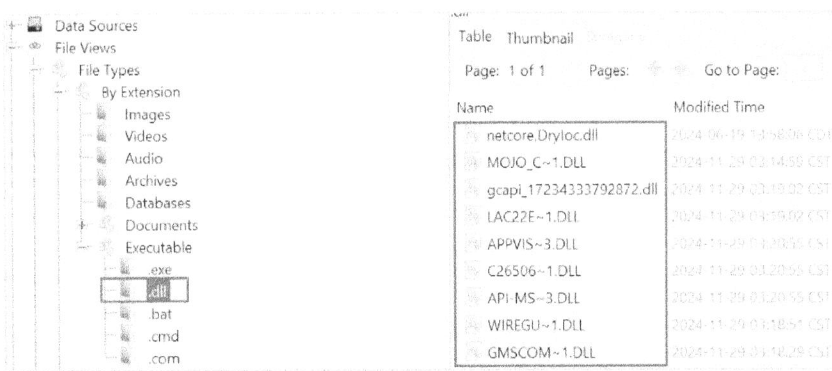

Figure 9.34 – Viewing DLL files processed using Autopsy

We can now use the baseline hash set to immediately reduce noise by hiding files that match the known-good values.

16. Click the **gear icon** above the tree viewer pane and ensure the **Views area** option is selected under **Hide known files**. This tells Autopsy to suppress any file whose hash appears in the Baseline set, leaving only items that deviate from a clean system image:

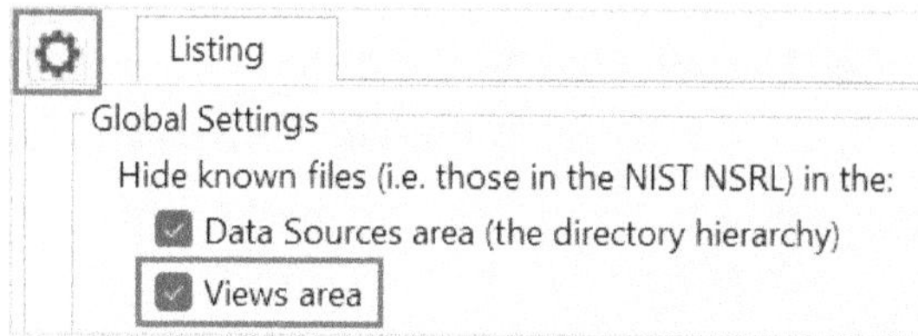

Figure 9.35 – Hiding known files from the baseline hash set in Autopsy

17. Return to the `DLL` files, and you'll notice that none appear—because Autopsy is now hiding all files that match your baseline hash set.

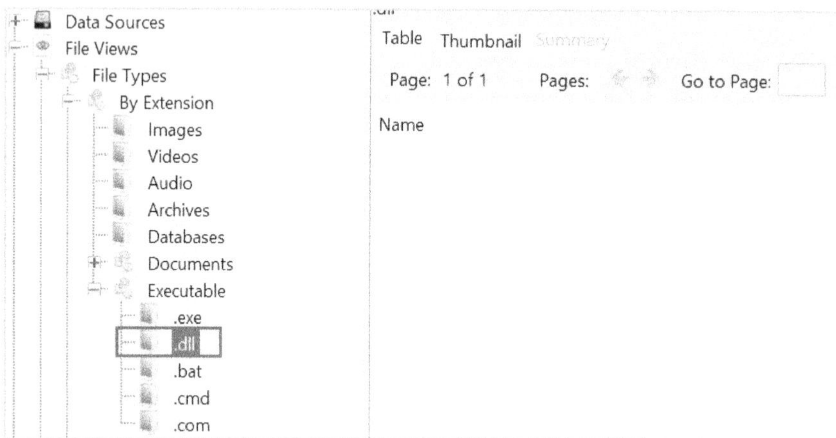

Figure 9.36 – Reducing the dataset using baseline hash values via Autopsy

In a real investigation, many files unrelated to malicious activity will still remain, such as documents the user created, legitimate application updates, newly installed software, and so on. But baselining dramatically reduces the overall noise level, allowing anomalies to stand out rather than getting buried. When applied to DLLs, this technique can help isolate suspicious or unexpected library files, highlight persistence mechanisms, or identify changes introduced by malware. The same approach can be applied to any file category as needed.

How it works...

Baselining gives us a known-good reference point—a snapshot of what a clean system looks like before a user touches it. Whether that baseline comes from a freshly deployed SDI or a trusted reference set such as NSRL RDS, the principle is the same: separate expected system noise from meaningful change.

Every operating system contains tens of thousands of files that never vary between installations. Without a baseline, those files dilute the artifacts present during an investigation. By hashing a clean system and marking those hashes as *Known*, we allow the forensic suite to automatically hide or de-prioritize anything that matches the baseline. What remains becomes drastically easier to evaluate, as items such as new executables, modified DLLs, altered configuration files, and user-created content stand out immediately instead of being lost in a sea of normal system artifacts.

This approach scales well. A single baseline can be applied across dozens or hundreds of identical systems in an enterprise, allowing investigators to rapidly isolate anomalies on each machine while ignoring the millions of unchanged files that would otherwise consume time and attention. The same method applies across platforms: Windows, macOS, Linux, Android, iOS—any environment where known-good system images can be captured and hashed.

Baselining does not replace analysis; it accelerates it. By stripping away the background noise, it lets an examiner focus on *what changed* and *when it changed*. This is a powerful technique that is often underutilized, and the clarity that baselining can provide helps us determine which artifacts need our attention the most during manual analysis.

Cross verification

Verifying our data and findings is the final safeguard between analysis and evidence. Even when our tools parse artifacts correctly, we must ensure results are accurate, reproducible, and corroborated by independent sources. In real investigations, this step is what protects you on the witness stand and prevents a single parsing error, unsupported timestamp, or mistaken assumption from undermining an entire case.

At its core, validation means three things:

- **Verify the data itself** – confirming that what we're examining hasn't changed since acquisition, typically through hashing or other integrity checks.
- **Verify the interpretation** – cross-checking a conclusion against other artifacts (for example, aligning a browser history event with system logs, prefetch records, or knowledgeC entries)
- **Verify the tool output** – reviewing raw artifacts whenever a parser fails, timestamps look off, or results appear incomplete or inconsistent.

Good validation is not complicated; it's disciplined. Strong conclusions come from artifact convergence: when multiple independent records align without contradiction. When they don't, the discrepancy *is* the finding, and often the most important one.

In this recipe, we'll validate forensic findings by verifying data integrity, cross-checking interpretations across artifacts, and confirming tool output against independent sources.

Getting ready

To work through the verification techniques in this section, you won't need any new tools—only the same core utilities used throughout this book. Verification is fundamentally about *cross-checking*, so the key requirement is simply access to multiple artifact types from the same system.

For consistency and speed, we'll continue using the Microsoft Windows dataset you processed in earlier chapters, including the Autopsy case created in *Chapter 7*. The principles demonstrated here apply equally well to any other dataset (mobile, desktop, or cloud-based), and the logic of validation remains the same regardless of platform.

How to do it...

1. To begin validating our dataset, we'll revisit the most fundamental check: **verifying the data itself**, or confirming that the data we are analyzing has not changed since acquisition. In *Chapter 3*, we demonstrated this technique using Zimmerman's Hasher utility on simple files. Here, we'll apply the same principle to a full forensic image.
2. Use Zimmerman's **Hasher** (or another binary hashing tool of your choice) to calculate a hash of the `Lenovo ThinkPad.E01` forensic image provided as the Microsoft Windows dataset. In the examples shown, the following MD5 value was calculated: `D1EA9B0F5B7C27A98B2C2C443E350417`
3. Next, load the same Lenovo ThinkPad.E01 forensic image into a forensic tool capable of validating disk images. For this example, **FTK Imager** was used by selecting **File | Verify drive/image...**.
   This time, you will notice a *different* MD5 hash: `95D0C79DD868B2B49F26403FD02F1FA9`

Figure 9.37 – Differing resultant hash values

   This discrepancy is normal, expected, and extremely important to understand. Hasher calculates the MD5 of the **E01 container file**, including compression, metadata blocks, and header information. FTK Imager and similar disk hashing utilities, on the other hand, verify the **raw disk image contained inside the E01** by hashing the 1:1 sector-level representation of the source drive. These are two different objects, so their hashes will never match.

A similar mismatch occurs with evidence acquired from **SSDs**, where wear-leveling and background firmware processes constantly move physical data blocks. In modern mobile forensics, hashing the original device is impossible because every acquisition requires the device to be powered on, meaning the source is inherently in flux.

This is why validation focuses on **hashing the acquired evidence**, not the original source. The purpose of hashing is to prove that *your evidentiary copy* remained unchanged throughout analysis – not to prove that the original device remained static. Understanding this distinction is critical for explaining hash differences in reports, testimony, or peer review, and prevents false assumptions that a mismatch implies contamination or error.

Verifying the interpretation of our data is the next phase of validation, and it is something we've been practicing throughout this book. Not every artifact carries the same evidentiary weight, and not every timestamp reflects the same level of accuracy. When an artifact contains information that may influence our investigative conclusions, we must confirm what we are seeing by comparing it to other independent sources on the same system.

As an example, when we reviewed our Plaso timeline earlier in this chapter, the Unetbootin utility appeared to have been launched on August 11, 2024, at approximately 09:13:22 (UTC). If this timestamp mattered in an investigation, we would need to verify it.

Open your Autopsy case and run a Keyword Search for **Unetbootin**. One of the first results will be a corresponding Prefetch file:

```
UNETBOOTIN-WINDOWS-702.EXE-5739F073.pf
```

This file shows a modification timestamp of **2024-08-11 09:13:22 UTC**. This aligns with Plaso's output, giving us two separate tools reporting the same event:

Figure 9.38 – View of Prefetch file in Autopsy

4. At this point, we have confirmed the file system metadata, but that alone is not sufficient. Select the Prefetch file and examine the **Data Artifacts** tab in Autopsy to compare the internal Prefetch timestamps with the file system times:

Type	Value
Program Name	UNETBOOTIN-WINDOWS-702.EXE
Path	/USERS/LEROY JENKINS/DOWNLOADS
Date/Time	2024-08-11 09:13:11 UTC

Figure 9.39 – Viewing Prefetch file contents in Autopsy

You should see that the Prefetch execution timestamp is approximately **09:13:11**, with file system metadata lagging behind at **09:13:22**. This aligns perfectly with what we covered in *Chapter 4*. Prefetch internally stores more precise execution times, and the file system timestamp typically lags by about 10 seconds. This is expected behavior, and the difference here reinforces accuracy rather than inconsistency.

5. Still, one artifact is never enough. Next, validate this finding using the **Windows AmCache**.
6. Perform a keyword search for **Amcache.hve**. Drill down into: **Root | InventoryApplicationFile | unetbootin-windo|f018dce067c9d2dc**
   Here, you will find the AmCache key with a **LastWrite** timestamp of **2024-08-11 09:13:11**, matching the Prefetch internal timestamp exactly:

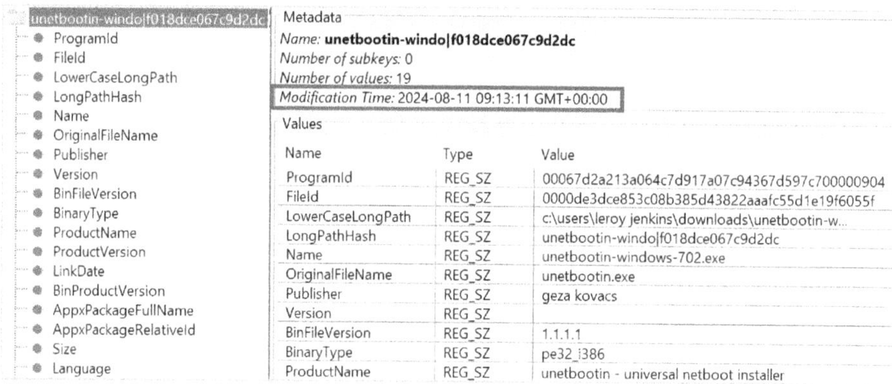

Figure 9.40 – AmCache key supporting Prefetch findings

With both Prefetch and AmCache aligned, we now have strong corroboration. To reinforce this further, let's validate using another independent artifact source: Windows Timeline (`ActivitiesCache.db`).

7. Search in Autopsy for `ActivitiesCache.db`, identify the instance tied to the `Leroy Jenkins` user profile, and extract the database and WAL file. Open it in DB Browser for SQLite and navigate to the **Activity** table.
8. Select the **Execute SQL** tab and run:

```
SELECT
AppId,
ActivityType,
DATETIME (LastModifiedTime, 'unixepoch') AS "Date"
FROM Activity
WHERE AppID LIKE '%unetbootin%';
```

This filters for Timeline entries related to Unetbootin and converts the timestamps from Unix epoch. You should see two entries, consistent with the prior artifacts:

AppId	ActivityType	Date
[{"application":"C:\\Users\\Leroy Jenkins\\Downloads\\unetbootin-…	5	2024-08-11 09:13:15
[{"application":"C:\\Users\\Leroy Jenkins\\Downloads\\unetbootin-…	6	2024-08-11 09:14:04

Figure 9.41 – Windows Timeline SQL query results for Unetbootin activity

An `ActivityType` of **5** indicates the application was active (foreground), while **6** means it transitioned to the background. From these values and timestamps, we can infer that Unetbootin was active around **09:13:15** and pushed to the background around **09:14:04**, which is entirely consistent with Prefetch and AmCache.

At this point, we have multiple independent artifact families (file system metadata, Prefetch internal execution data, registry metadata, and Timeline activity logs), all confirming the same event sequence. Additional artifacts (`Event Logs`, `SRUM`, `UserAssist`, `Jump Lists`, and more) could be checked, but the convergence already provides a solid, defensible interpretation.

This is the essence of validation: multiple artifacts, a consistent story, and no contradictions.

The final layer of verification is validating the **tool output** itself. No tool (commercial or open source) is infallible. Parsers miss fields, timestamp conversions behave differently between tools, and unsupported artifacts may be interpreted inconsistently. This is why examiners must routinely test their tools, not just trust them.

The simplest method is **tool comparison**. When an artifact carries investigative significance (such as execution history, deleted records, or evidence of external storage), run it through at least one additional tool or parser. If Autopsy, Plaso, FTK, and a manual SQLite query all tell the same story, confidence increases. If one tool disagrees, that discrepancy becomes a lead: either a parsing error or a deeper anomaly that requires manual review.

Tool validation also includes testing your tools **against known datasets**. This means periodically running parsers against images where we already know the expected results (test images, baseline installs, or datasets we have created with controlled actions) to confirm that your tools are interpreting artifacts correctly between version updates. This is how you detect parsing regressions after updates, corrupted modules, or unsupported format changes before they affect a real case.

In short: trust the evidence, not the software. Tools are accelerators, not authoritative sources. We, as the examiners (not our tools), are responsible for accuracy.

How it works...

Tool-output verification works by separating *data* from *interpretation*. Automated tools parse artifacts into readable formats, but every parsed field is ultimately just an interpretation of the underlying raw structures. When something matters to your case, you must confirm that the interpretation holds up.

This typically happens in three ways. First, you test the parser against the raw artifact—whether that's opening a database directly in a SQLite viewer, checking event logs with a hex editor, or reviewing the unparsed file system timestamps. If the raw content matches what the tool claims, confidence increases. If not, the deviation becomes an investigative clue.

Second, you verify output by cross-tool comparison. Different tools have different parsers, different assumptions, and different blind spots. When two or three independent tools all converge on the same result, the likelihood of parser error drops dramatically. When they diverge, you investigate why because both tool failures and genuine anomalies can produce mismatches.

Finally, you validate tools over time by running them against known datasets where the forensic image data is controlled and documented. This establishes whether updates, module changes, or evidence format changes have impacted parsing accuracy. A tool that performs correctly against known-good images gives you a defensible starting point when interpreting unknown evidence.

Summary

Effective digital forensic analysis depends on the ability to move beyond automated output and interpret data directly. Manual techniques allow investigators to efficiently query databases, validate tool results, reconstruct timelines across multiple artifact sources, reduce noise through baselining, and confirm findings through cross-verification.

At this point, you should be able to do the following:

- **Manually analyze SQLite databases**, extract relevant data using SQL queries, and interpret results in a forensic context
- **Build and analyze timelines** using Plaso and Timeline Explorer to reconstruct user activity across multiple artifact sources
- **Create and apply baseline hash sets** to reduce system noise and isolate artifacts that deviate from expected behavior.
- **Validate forensic findings** by verifying data integrity, cross-checking interpretations across artifacts, and confirming tool output against independent sources.
- **Correlate multiple artifact types** to identify consistent event sequences and recognize discrepancies that may indicate anti-forensics or anomalies.

In the next chapter, we shift from building and validating evidence to recognizing when that evidence has been manipulated, removed, or encrypted, exploring anti-forensic techniques and how to detect them during an investigation.

Get this book's PDF copy, code bundle, and more

10

Overcoming Anti-Forensics

Anti-forensic behavior is not always sophisticated. Sometimes it's intentional by the user, such as timestomping, selective deletion, encryption, and log tampering. Other times it's entirely unintentional, as is the case with software cleaners, routine system processes, and users who simply assume that "delete" means gone. Either way, the examiner's job remains the same: identify what should be there, determine what is actually there, and understand the gaps between the two.

Up to this point, we've learned about the common artifacts across multiple systems, built timelines, manually analyzed data, validated findings, and learned how to pivot between artifacts when things don't align. This chapter focuses on the flipside: what to do when evidence has been removed, obscured, encrypted, or manipulated. The goal is not to turn you into a data-recovery engineer or cryptanalyst, but to equip you with the practical techniques examiners use every day to recover deleted data, interpret encrypted containers, and detect when evidence has likely been altered.

Our focus here is pragmatic and efficient. You will learn how deleted data is recovered both automatically and manually, how to build high-quality wordlists from user-generated content to crack encrypted files using free tools, and how to recognize the subtle behaviors of tampering across operating systems. Anti-forensics rarely works as cleanly as intended, and with the right approach, even the "missing" evidence often leaves a trail.

In this chapter, we're going to cover the following main topics:

- Deleted data recovery
- Defeating encryption
- Data tampering indicators

Technical requirements

For this chapter, you will need the following:

- A computer running Microsoft Windows as your forensic workstation. A 64-bit Windows 11 system with an Intel i7 quad-core processor or better and a minimum of 16 gigabytes of RAM is recommended
- Your working installation of Autopsy (used in chapters)
- Datasets for analysis, as available from the Packt Publishing GitHub repository for this book. To access the repository link, follow the steps in the *Download the example code* files section in the *Preface*.
- FTK Imager (as used in previous chapters) or an alternative tool capable of browsing forensic images. For example, 7-Zip can be used with additional support (such as the Forensic7z plugin) to access forensic image contents, as introduced earlier in this book.

Deleted data recovery

Here's a reliable truth in digital forensics: when someone does something illegal using technology, they usually delete it. That's not groundbreaking, but it's accurate, and it's why deleted data recovery remains a core investigative skill. Our ability to recover a deleted artifact depends on several factors: how it was deleted, how actively the device has been used since, the file system involved, the type of storage, and the level of acquisition we were able to obtain.

> Tip
>
> It depends...
>
> An ongoing joke within the digital forensic community is our most common answer to almost every question we are asked – "it depends". This is especially true in response to questions regarding whether or not we can recover deleted data. "My suspect deleted some text messages... can you recover them?" It depends. "I have a victim that recorded a video we need, but he accidentally deleted it... can you get it back?" It depends. "I have a phone that got run over by a bulldozer, caught fire, and exploded. Is there anything you can do?" Well, probably not on that one, but you get the idea... it always depends.

We've already seen how deleted data can persist inside SQLite databases until vacuuming overwrites it. But what about deleted files, raw media, or data buried in unallocated space? This section focuses on the fundamentals of recovering deleted data from storage devices using automated forensic tools and manual techniques when deeper analysis is required.

Many forensic platforms recover deleted files using **data carving**, which typically relies on identifying a file's header and, when available, its footer (signature) within raw disk space. Some tools support a fixed set of file signatures, while others allow custom signatures for unconventional file types. The core idea is the same: locate the beginning of a file, determine where it ends, and carve out that block of bytes. Not all file types include clear trailer signatures, however, so carving tools may also rely on file structure heuristics or size estimation when a footer is not present.

Fragmented files complicate the recovery process. In those cases, the examiner (or the tool) must identify each fragment's boundaries, rebuild them in order, and accept that overwritten fragments may result in only partial data recovery. For media files, a partial recovery might still reveal meaningful content. For structured files, it may render them corrupted or unreadable. The key is understanding what can be recovered, why, and what the limitations mean for your case.

In this recipe, we'll recover deleted data using both automated carving and manual techniques to identify, extract, and validate artifacts from unallocated space.

Getting ready

We'll continue using Autopsy as our primary tool for deleted-data recovery. Autopsy includes the **PhotoRec Carver** module, which (despite its name) is not limited to photo recovery. PhotoRec supports carving for more than 300 file types, including documents, archives, media files, operating system artifacts, and even certain databases. It also allows custom file signatures, making it flexible enough for both common and unusual investigations.

We'll also continue to browse and access the file system of a forensic image file, so you will need a tool capable of doing this. In the examples shown, **FTK Imager** is used, which is capable of both browsing the forensic image and producing a hexadecimal view of content encountered. If you choose to use another utility to browse the forensic image provided, note that you will also need a hex editor for some portions of this recipe.

For this walkthrough, download the **sample SD Card acquisition image** from this book's GitHub repository.

How to do it...

1. To begin, we'll recover deleted data using the simplest method available—automation. Download the `SD Card.E01` forensic image from the book's GitHub repository and load it into a tool capable of browsing and examining forensic images (like **FTK Imager**).

Once mounted, you'll notice that no user-accessible files appear within the file system. This is expected. The SD card was intentionally reformatted, and the file system metadata no longer references any of the original files.

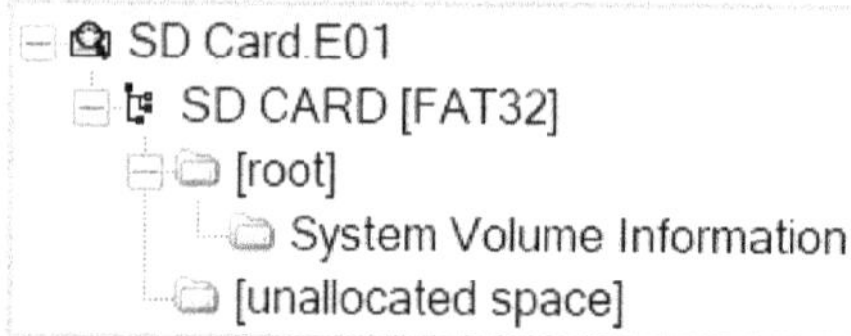

Figure 10.1 – Viewing the SD Card.E01 forensic image in FTK Imager

Despite the empty appearance, the underlying data blocks (including deleted content) still exist within the unallocated space, making this an ideal candidate for automated carving in the next steps.

2. Next, create a new case in **Autopsy** and ingest the `SD Card.E01` image as your evidence source. Make sure the setting **Ignore orphan files in FAT file systems** is **unchecked** (this allows Autopsy to surface deleted items that no longer have a parent directory). When selecting ingest modules, choose the following:

    - Recent activity
    - Hash lookup
    - File Type Identification
    - Picture Analyzer

    Once processing completes, expand the file tree. Because orphaned entries were included, Autopsy successfully identifies and presents deleted files that survived the reformatting. You should now see remnants of the card's original contents:

Source Name	File Path	Size
8CCF83~1.JPG	/img_SD Card.E01/$OrphanFiles/8CCF83~1.JPG	7364859
4111~1.JPE	/img_SD Card.E01/$OrphanFiles/4111~1.JPE	5138755
7689~1.JPE	/img_SD Card.E01/$OrphanFiles/7689~1.JPE	3230251
7691~1.JPE	/img_SD Card.E01/$OrphanFiles/7691~1.JPE	3370027
10977~1.JPE	/img_SD Card.E01/$OrphanFiles/10977~1.JPE	3996629

Figure 10.2 – Sample of deleted files recovered in Autopsy

3. The **PhotoRec Carver** module enables deeper recovery by scanning raw sectors for file signatures rather than relying on file-system metadata. To run it, go to **Tools | Run Ingest Modules** and select the `SD Card.E01` evidence source again.

In the ingest configuration window, do the following:

- Enable PhotoRec Carver.
- In its dropdown menu, choose All Files, Directories, and Unallocated Space to ensure the module examines every recoverable region.
- Leave the remaining options at their defaults unless you have a reason to carve only specific file types (PhotoRec does allow extension-based filtering if needed).

Once started, Autopsy will attempt to carve files directly from unallocated space, often recovering additional items that a simple orphan-file scan will miss:

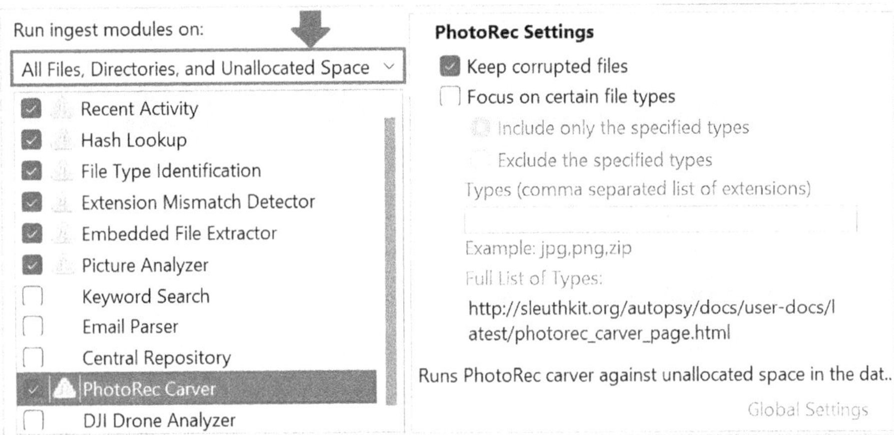

Figure 10.3 – Running the PhotoRec Carver module in Autopsy

4. After processing finishes, return to the file tree in Autopsy. You should now see additional recovered files that were not present during the initial ingest, often including items like videos, images, archives, and document fragments carved directly from unallocated space.
5. Browse the recovered items to get a sense of what was retrieved. In many cases, file carving will recover data that would otherwise appear completely lost, even on media that has been reformatted:

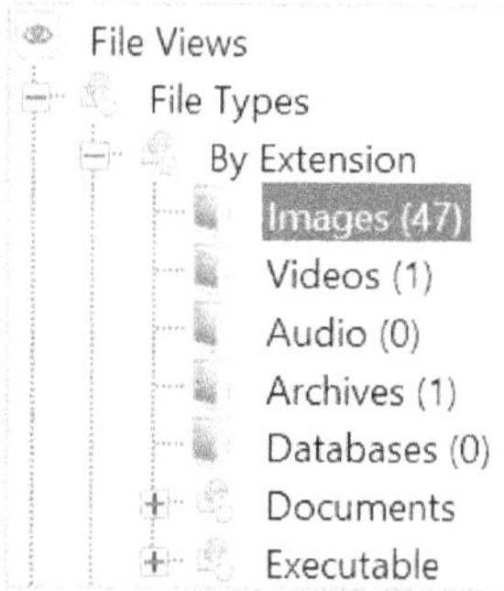

Figure 10.4 – Files recovered using PhotoRec in Autopsy

Some recovered files (especially videos and archives) may not open inside Autopsy. This is normal. Carved files often lack the full structure that Autopsy expects, even when the underlying content is still intact.

6. Right-click any recovered file and choose **Extract File(s)** to export it. Once exported, you can test it using external tools:
   - Media players (for recovered video fragments)
   - Archive utilities such as `7-Zip` or `WinRAR` (for carved ZIP/7z files)

   In many cases, the file will open normally once outside Autopsy, confirming that the recovery was successful despite appearing unreadable within the forensic suite:

Figure 10.5 – Recovered Archive.zip file exported to view contents

The **PhotoRec** Carver module supports the recovery of a wide range of file types. You can extend its capabilities by adding your own file signatures; for example, when dealing with proprietary formats or uncommon applications.

If you want to view the full list of supported file types or add custom signatures, consult the official module documentation: `https://sleuthkit.org/autopsy/docs/user-docs/4.21.0/photorec_carver_page.html`

This documentation outlines how Autopsy integrates the carving engine, details signature support, and explains how to define additional formats when deeper manual recovery control is needed.

In the previous step, we noted that non-supported file types can be added to the PhotoRec Carver by defining custom file signatures. To understand how this works and to ensure that you can recover any file type when automation fails, let's manually recover a file using the same principles that PhotoRec relies on.

Manual recovery requires only three pieces of information:

- **The file signature (header or magic number)** – This identifies where the file begins. Every carve starts here.
- **Whether the file is stored contiguously or in segments** – On our SD card (which uses the FAT32 file system), deleted files often exist as a single continuous block, making recovery straightforward. However, fragmentation is still possible, especially on more heavily used systems, and it can complicate recovery.
  On other file systems, such as NTFS, file fragmentation is even more common and typically exists across multiple clusters. In these cases, you must consult a reference structure (such as the Master File Table or $MFT) to locate each segment before carving and concatenating them. Without this, you may recover only a partial file.
- **The file's end boundary** – Either you know the original size from metadata, or you must identify the file trailer to determine where the data block ends. This tells you how much raw data to carve.

7. To begin the process, open the `SD Card.E01` forensic image and examine the `[unallocated space]` from the evidence tree, then highlight the unallocated block labeled `000006` in the file list pane:

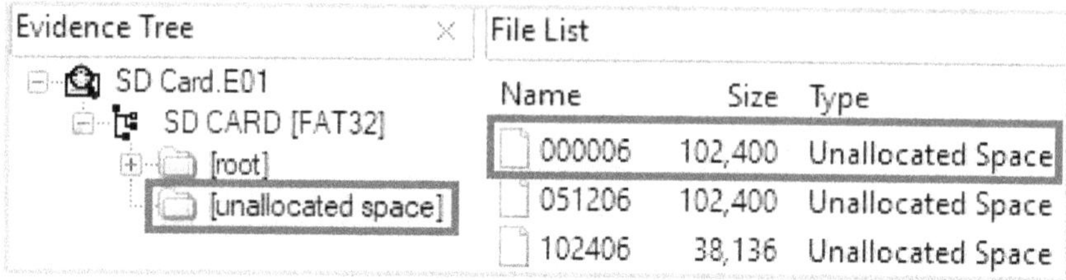

Figure 10.6 – Selecting unallocated space segment using FTK Imager

8. Within the hexadecimal view of the selected unallocated space segment, right-click and choose **Go to offset...** from the context menu. When the navigation window appears, enter a **Byte Offset** of **400e000** and ensure the **Hex** radio button is selected. This instructs FTK Imager (or similar hex viewers) to jump directly to that absolute position within the unallocated block, allowing us to examine the raw data beginning at the suspected file header location.
9. Once the offset is entered and the settings are correct, click **OK**:

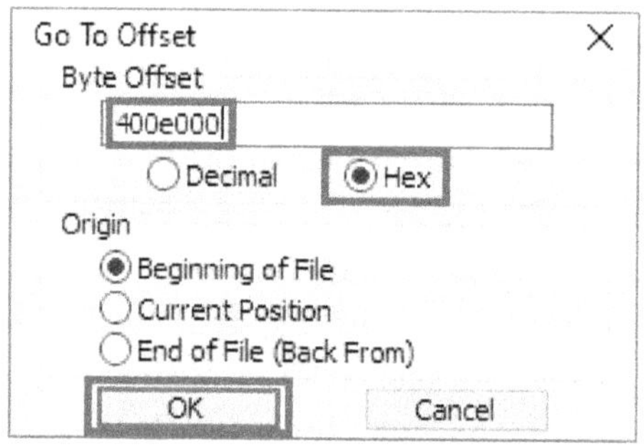

Figure 10.7 – Navigating to a specific offset in FTK Imager

This offset takes us to the beginning of the deleted JPG file we intend to carve. A standard JPEG file begins with the header signature **FF D8 FF E1**, which is clearly visible in the highlighted bytes below. If we weren't targeting a specific file, we could simply search the unallocated space for this signature to locate all potential JPG remnants.

10. Take note of the **Cursor pos** value (shown here as a decimal offset of **67166208**) because this identifies the exact starting location of the file within unallocated space. We'll use this position to determine how much data to carve:

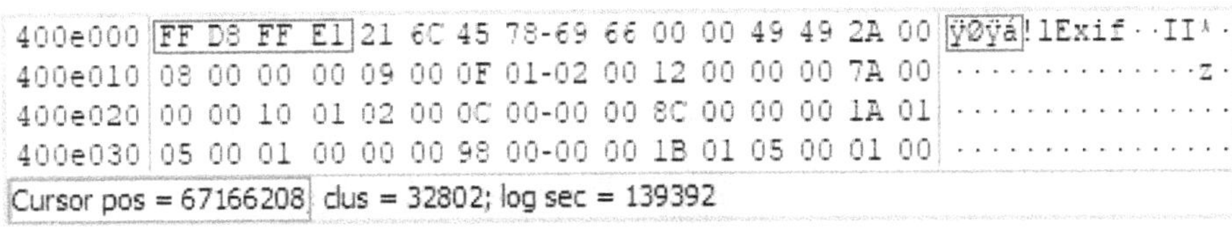

Figure 10.8 – Beginning of target file showing file signature in FTK Imager

Now that we've identified the starting point of the file, the next objective is locating its end. Because we don't have a size reference for this JPG, the most reliable method is to search for the JPEG trailer signature **FF D9**. However, these two bytes can appear inside JPG data long before the true end of the file, so we'll search for the trailer plus the padding that typically follows it in deleted FAT-based media: **FF D9 00 00 00 00 00**

This longer sequence significantly reduces false matches and helps identify the actual boundary where usable data stops.

11. Press *Ctrl+F* to open the Find window, choose **Binary (hex)** as the search type, set the direction to **Down**, and enable **Wrap**. Enter the trailer sequence above and click **Find**:

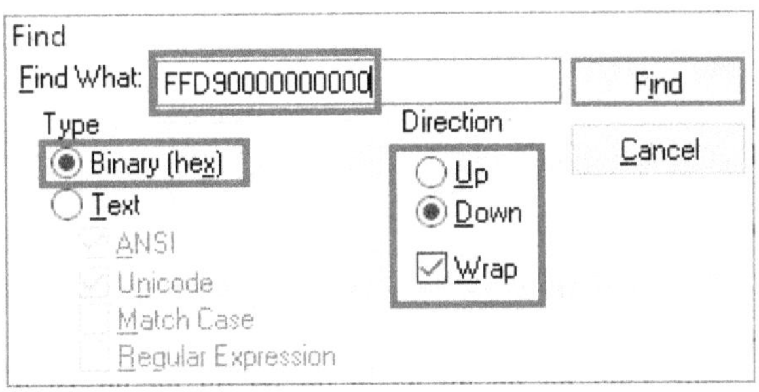

Figure 10.9 – Searching for a file trailer in FTK Imager

12. The search will jump directly to what appears to be the end of the JPG file, where the expected trailer bytes **FF D9** are located. This sequence marks the final two bytes of a valid JPEG. In the example from Figure 10.10, look at the **Sel start** offset (shown here as the decimal value **67885079**), which represents the position of the last byte belonging to this carved file:

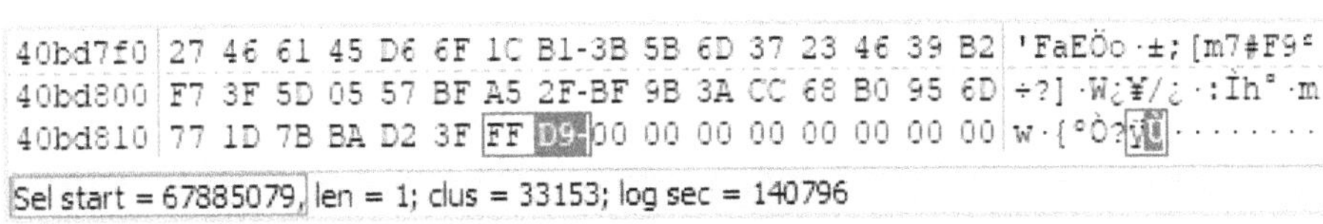

Figure 10.10 – End of target file showing file trailer in FTK Imager

13. Using the decimal offset for the **last byte** of the target JPG found in *Step 10*, subtract the decimal offset for the **first byte** of the file obtained in *Step 8*. In this example: **67885079 – 67166208 = 718871 bytes**

Figure 10.11 – Calculating file size

This gives us the **exact size** of the carved JPG file in bytes.

14. Use the shortcut keys *Ctrl+G* to open the **Go To Offset** window. Switch the radio button to **Decimal**, enter the offset **67166208**, and click **OK**.
    This takes you directly back to the **first byte** of the target JPG file so you can begin carving it out cleanly:

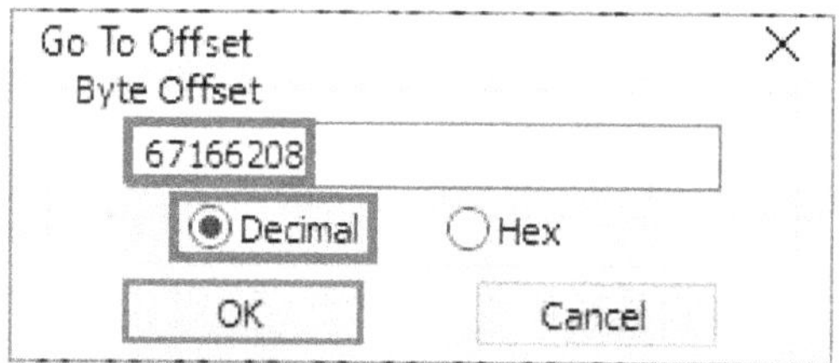

Figure 10.12 – Returning to the beginning of the target file in FTK Imager

15. Now that we're back at the beginning of our target JPG file, make sure the **first byte is selected** (Cursor pos **67166208**)
16. Right-click and choose **Set Selection Length...**, then enter the calculated file size of 718871 bytes, confirming that the **Decimal** radio button is selected.
17. Click **OK** to highlight the exact byte range representing the entire deleted JPG:

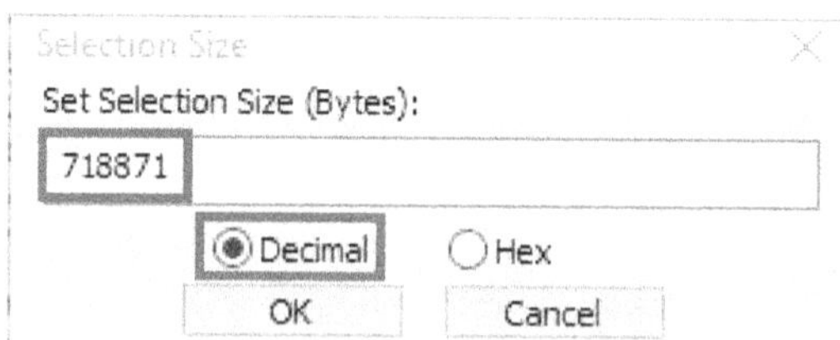

Figure 10.13 – Selecting a segment size in FTK Imager

18. The selected segment will now appear **highlighted in blue**, indicating the byte range is active. Confirm the selected length is **718,871 bytes** (in FTK Imager, you can look at the **len** value in the lower-right corner to confirm this).

    If the length matches, you've successfully isolated the full JPG file within unallocated space:

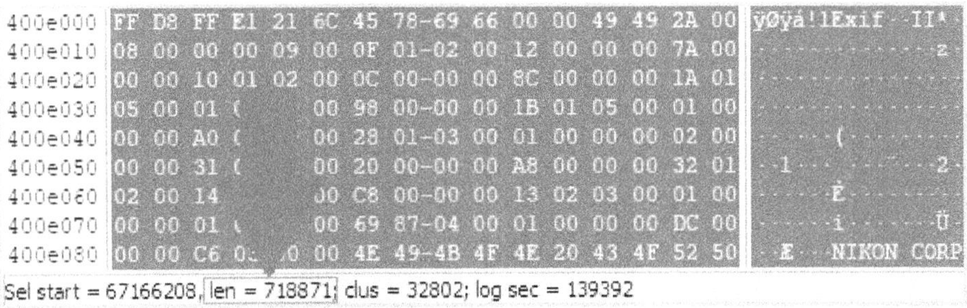

Figure 10.14 – Target file segment selected in FTK Imager

19. Right-click the highlighted data segment and choose **Save selection...**.
20. When prompted, save the carved output to your workstation as `Carved.jpg`.

    This exports the exact byte range you identified, producing a manually carved JPEG file you can examine outside of the tool:

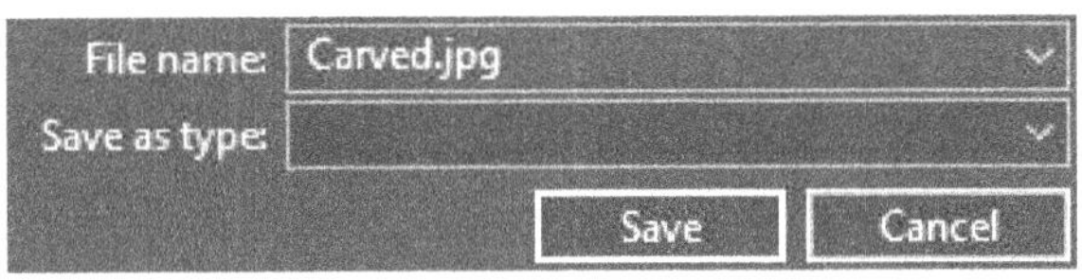

Figure 10.15 – Saving the selected segment as a JPG file

21. Navigate to the location where you saved `Carved.jpg`. If the segment boundaries were identified correctly and the carving process was successful, the file should open normally and reveal the recovered photograph; in this case, an image of a near-total solar eclipse, as shown below in *Figure 10.16*:

Figure 10.16 – Successfully carved JPG file

> **Tip**
>
> Recovering the truth
>
> A surprising number of cases are made on the strength of recovered data. I worked on a case involving a suspect who factory-reset his phone before coming in for an interview. He assumed this would destroy anything incriminating. It didn't. A factory reset wiped the internal storage, but the microSD card remained intact (just formatted – like the one we used in this section). In that case, using the same carving techniques demonstrated here, I recovered hundreds of deleted incriminatory files before he even left the interview room. His next stop was the jail.
>
> One critical thing to keep in mind during deleted data recovery is attribution: without intact file system metadata, suspects often claim "those files aren't mine... I just found the SD card and used it!" Your job is to use the numerous techniques we've covered throughout this book to tie the recovered data back to the user.

How it works...

Data carving works because most file types announce themselves with structure: a signature at the beginning, a predictable trailer at the end, and standardized patterns in between. Tools like the PhotoRec Carver automate this by scanning raw space; not just unallocated clusters, but also slack space, carved fragments inside documents, and remnants preserved inside application-specific storage. When enough of that structure survives, the tool can rebuild the original file.

The mechanics matter because you may be asked to explain your process of file recovery. Understanding basic concepts of data recovery like signatures, block boundaries, and fragmentation ensures you can defend your method and interpret the results correctly. And when a tool fails to recover a file cleanly, this knowledge gives you the ability to step in manually, validate the fragments, and reconstruct the file yourself.

Defeating encryption

Now for another quick digital-forensics truth: if a user doesn't delete something, they'll often encrypt it. A decade ago, this was relatively uncommon. Today it's standard. Modern mobile devices are encrypted by default, desktop operating systems are heading in the same direction, and many users layer additional encryption on top, such as secure folders, encrypted archives, password-locked apps, "hidden" photo vaults, and more.

There are two realities you need to understand when investigating encrypted data. First, modern encryption (when implemented correctly) is unbreakable with current computing power. A direct attack on strong encryption isn't a practical strategy; it's a thought experiment. The Sun will age out of main-sequence life before you brute-force AES-256.

Second, users rarely implement encryption correctly. That's where forensic work becomes viable. Encryption is only as strong as the password or key chosen, and most users choose passwords they can remember. When they pick something strong, they usually store it somewhere weak: reused credentials, a variation they use across accounts, a plaintext reference in notes, or even a piece of paper taped under a keyboard. Human behavior, not mathematics, is the real vulnerability.

> **Tip**
>
> Lucky guess... I guess...
>
> Half the "cracked passwords" in my career weren't cracked at all... they were simply guessed. Never underestimate light social engineering: birthdays, pet names, sports teams, hobbies, usernames reused across platforms, old Netflix passwords, etc. Nine times out of ten, the password is hiding in plain sight.

In this recipe, we'll extract password hashes and use dictionary attacks (both generic and user-derived) to recover passwords from encrypted files by leveraging human behavior.

Getting ready

For this exercise, we're focusing specifically on encrypted files. This keeps the scope tight, the workflows realistic, and the techniques immediately applicable to real cases. We also won't be using pure brute-force attacks, as those are rarely feasible and almost never necessary. Even small password spaces explode exponentially, and full brute-force is used only when all other avenues fail.

Instead, we'll rely on **dictionary attacks**, which attempt passwords from a list of likely candidates. Good dictionaries can be downloaded, but *great* dictionaries are built from the user's own data: strings extracted from documents, browser data, registry hives, configuration files, and even filenames. Because users tend to reuse memorable words, names, and numbers across accounts, custom dictionaries regularly outperform giant generic ones.

To work through the examples in this section, you'll need the following:

- **A way to browse forensic images** to explore the dataset and extract files (such as **FTK Imager** or your existing **Autopsy** case that we have built upon during previous chapters)
- **Notepad++** (as used in Chapter 8) for cleaning and curating custom dictionaries
- **Bulk Extractor** for pulling free-text strings from the dataset to help build password dictionaries. The Windows-based GUI version can be found at: `https://github.com/simsong/bulk_extractor/wiki/Installing-bulk_extractor`
- **John the Ripper (JtR)** for cracking the encrypted files. Download the *jumbo* file for your version of Windows from the official website located at: `https://www.openwall.com/john/`

We'll use encrypted files included in the **Microsoft Windows dataset** with a combination of basic dictionaries and our own dictionary sourced entirely from user-generated content. This simulates exactly how we crack encryption in real life, not by overpowering math, but by understanding human behavior.

How to do it...

1. We'll begin by attempting to recover the user password for an encrypted Microsoft Word document—a common scenario, as users frequently password-protect sensitive Office files. In our Microsoft Windows dataset, you may have already seen this document during earlier chapters. It is named `Astro.docx` and is located at: `/Users/Leroy Jenkins/Documents/Astro.docx`
2. Export the file and save it somewhere easy to access. For this walkthrough, the document has been saved to: `C:\Encryption\Files\`

3. Next, we need wordlists for our dictionary attack. A reliable, open-source collection is the **SecLists** project maintained by Daniel Miessler. It includes thousands of curated password lists commonly used in cybersecurity testing: `https://github.com/danielmiessler/SecLists/tree/master/Passwords`
4. In the repository's left navigation pane, expand **Words**, then download the file `lang-english.txt`. This will serve as a simple baseline English dictionary wordlist for our test.
5. Next, launch John the Ripper (JtR).
6. Before proceeding, ensure **Python** is installed on your workstation, as some of JtR's helper scripts require it: `https://www.python.org/downloads/`
7. Extract the JtR archive, then navigate into the **run** directory. From inside this folder, open a Command Prompt window by clicking the File Explorer address bar, typing **CMD**, then press **Enter**:

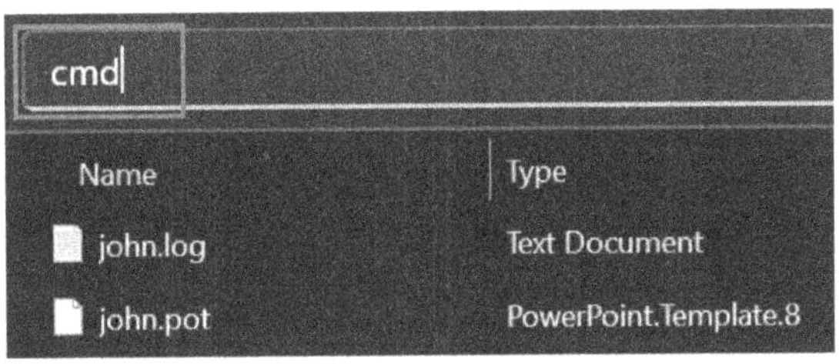

Figure 10.17 – Launching command prompt from the JtR 'run' folder

This opens a terminal session directly in the JtR run directory, ensuring all scripts and executables can be called without full path references.

8. Since John the Ripper does not attack Microsoft Word documents directly, we must first convert `Astro.docx` into its hash representation. This is accomplished by using the `office2john.py` helper script included with JtR.
9. From your command prompt (still inside the run folder), enter the following command, replacing the file path with the location where you saved `Astro.docx`:

```
python office2john.py "C:\Encryption\Files\Astro.docx" > astro_hash.txt
```

10. This generates a new file named `astro_hash.txt` in the JtR `run` directory. This file contains the extracted password hash that JtR will attempt to crack:

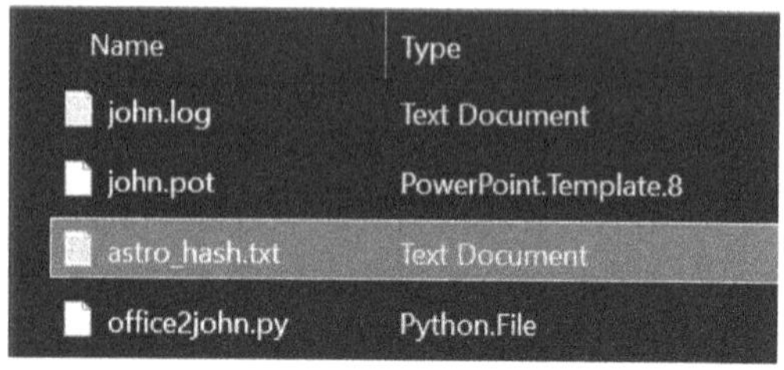

Figure 10.18 – Hash file created to attack Astro.docx

> **Note**
>
> It 'er run or else it 'er error...
>
> Sometimes half the fun of forensics is fixing errors, right? A common one at this step is that JtR produces a blank text file and throws an AttributeError in the command prompt. This is because the office2john.py script uses an outdated `getiterator()` method that was removed in newer versions of Python. To fix this, simply open the office2john.py script using a text editor, search for the word "**getiterator**", then replace that word with "**iter**". This updates the script to reflect what newer versions of Python are expecting.

Now that we have the hash file, let's attack it using our dictionary wordlist.

11. Return to your command prompt (still inside the `run` folder) and enter the following command (replacing the file path to `lang-english.txt` with the one on your system):

```
john --wordlist="C:\Encryption\Files\lang-english.txt" astro_hash.txt
```

John the Ripper will now iterate through every word in the dictionary file, testing each candidate against the password hash extracted earlier. Since our wordlist is relatively short, this process should typically take only a few minutes.

If the password is found, JtR displays it directly in the terminal. In our case, the attack is successful, and the cracked password is "**easy**":

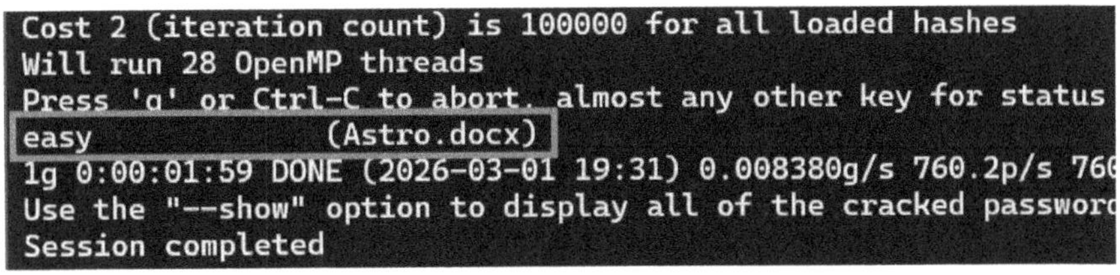

Figure 10.19 – Cracked password for Astro.docx presented by JtR

12. John the Ripper also stores cracked password results inside its persistent potfile, `john.pot`, located in the `run` directory. You can open this file to review previously cracked hashes:

Figure 10.20 – Cracked password stored in john.pot file

The simple English dictionary worked only because the password truly *was* "easy." In real cases, users often choose passwords based on personal patterns, reused credentials, or fragments of text found elsewhere on their systems. Generic wordlists rarely capture these nuances. A far more effective method is to generate a **custom dictionary** from the actual evidence.

This is where **Bulk Extractor** becomes invaluable. Bulk Extractor crawls through every byte of a dataset (allocated, unallocated, slack space, carved remnants) and extracts strings, URLs, email addresses, phone numbers, ZIP codes, usernames, and many other tokens that can often form real-world passwords.

13. Before launching it, ensure you have **Java** installed, or Bulk Extractor's viewer will fail to open (`https://www.java.com/en/download/manual.jsp`).
14. Once installed, open *Bulk Extractor* and click the **gear icon** to begin generating a new report:

Figure 10.21 – Icon to begin generating a Bulk Extractor report

15. In the **Run bulk_extractor** dialog box, change the `Scan Type` to **Image File**. Under `Image File`, browse to the `Lenovo ThinkPad.E01` forensic image. For the `Output Feature Directory`, choose a folder where your Bulk Extractor results will be stored (a clean working directory is best).
16. In the **Scanners** panel on the right, select only **wordlist**. This restricts the scan to extracting plaintext strings from the dataset, which is ideal for generating a focused, high-quality custom dictionary without the noise from other scanner types.
17. When the configuration looks correct, click **Submit Run** to begin processing:

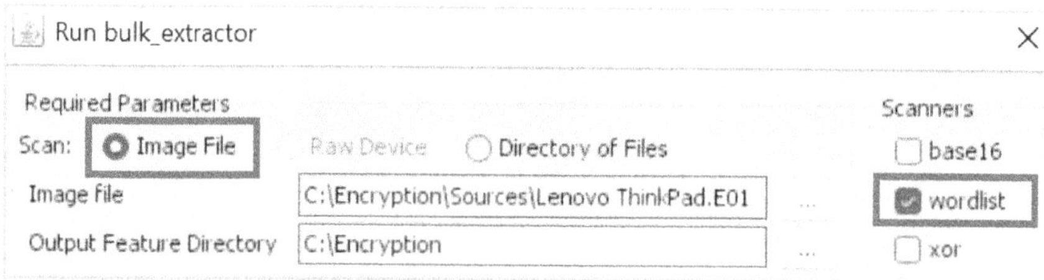

Figure 10.22 – Bulk Extractor run settings

18. Once the Bulk Extractor scan completes, navigate to the output directory you selected. You will notice that several files have been generated, each corresponding to different scanner types, even though only the `wordlist` scanner was enabled.

    The file we are most interested in is `wordlist_split_000.txt`. This file contains the extracted plaintext strings pulled from the Windows dataset and will serve as the foundation for building our custom password dictionary:

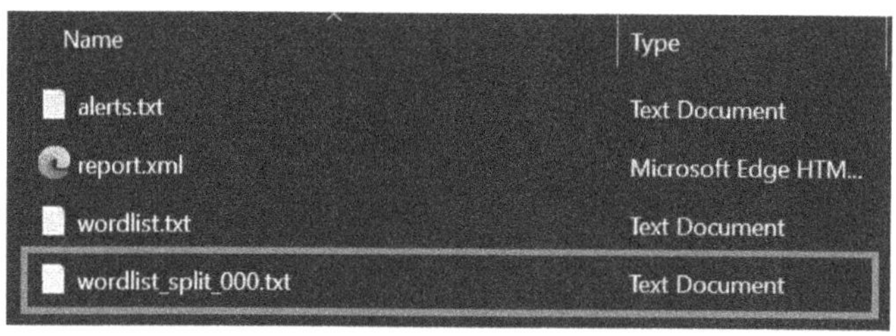

Figure 10.23 – Bulk Extractor output files

19. Open `wordlist_split_000.txt` in Notepad++. You'll immediately see that it contains over five million individual strings, each on its own line. This is exactly what we need for a usable dictionary file: large, diverse, and derived directly from the user's own file system and artifacts:

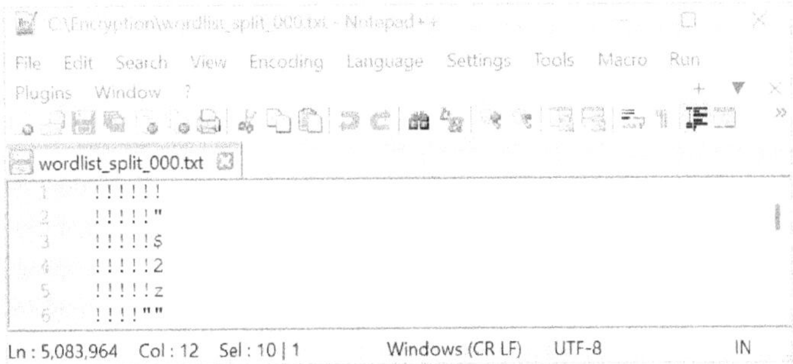

Figure 10.24 – wordlist_split_000.txt file contents

20. Bulk Extractor is incredibly powerful, but it isn't designed specifically for password-cracking workflows. As a result, many extracted strings (especially those carved out of file system structures) contain **leading backslashes** (\). If the user's real password appears in this list but begins with one of these artificial characters, John the Ripper will not recognize it. We need to clean the file before using it as a dictionary.
21. With `wordlist_split_000.txt` open in Notepad++, press *Ctrl* + *H* to open the Replace dialog. In the **Find what** field, enter: ^\\
22. Leave **Replace with** empty, then select **Search Mode** as **Regular expression**, and click **Replace All**:

Figure 10.25 – Using Notepad++ to clean Bulk Extractor output

This regular expression removes a single leading backslash from any line that begins with one – without altering the remainder of the string.

23. Press *Ctrl* + *S* to save the cleaned wordlist.
Your custom dictionary, derived entirely from content within the Microsoft Windows dataset, is now ready for use. This same workflow can be applied to any evidence source to generate highly effective user-specific wordlists.

24. Now let's examine a second encrypted file (one protected by a much stronger and more randomized password) to see whether our newly created custom dictionary can defeat it. This file is a `7-Zip archive` titled `stuff.7z`, located in the Lenovo `ThinkPad.E01` forensic image at: `/Users/Leroy Jenkins/Documents/stuff.7z`
25. Export `stuff.7z` and save it somewhere easily accessible. As with the earlier example, I've stored mine at: `C:\Encryption\Files\`

    Password-protected 7-Zip archives use AES-256 encryption with SHA-256 derived keys, which makes them effectively unbreakable through cryptographic attack. As with almost all modern encryption, the only realistically exploitable weakness is the human-chosen password – which is exactly what we're targeting again.
26. Just like before, our first step is to **extract the hash**. In the previous example (Astro.docx), we needed Python installed because office2john.py is a Python script. In this case, however, the extraction utility is written in **Perl**, so we must ensure Perl support exists on our workstation as well. If Perl is not already installed, download **Strawberry Perl** from `https://strawberryperl.com`.
27. Once ready, open a Command Prompt window from inside the JtR **run** directory (just as we did earlier), then run the following command (replacing the file path with the location where you saved stuff.7z)

```
perl 7z2john.pl "C:\Encryption\Files\stuff.7z" > 7z_hash.txt
```

28. This command generates the proper 7-Zip hash and stores it in a new file named `7z_hash.txt` inside the run folder:

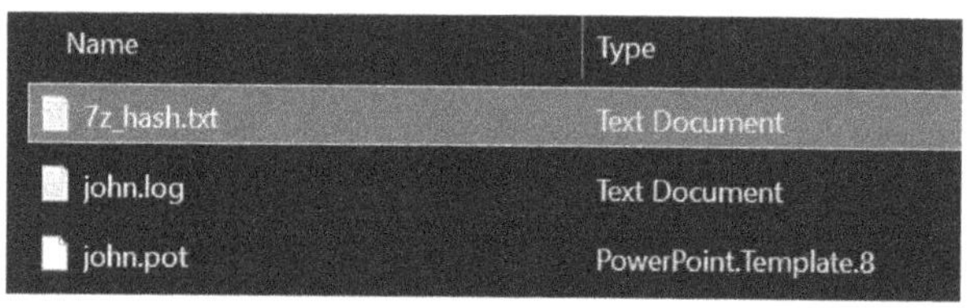

Figure 10.26 – Hash file created to attack stuff.7z

When you open this file, you'll notice the hash is significantly larger and more complex than the hash extracted from our encrypted Word document. That's expected; AES-256-protected archives require more metadata, salts, iteration counters, and configuration parameters to represent the encryption state, resulting in a much longer hash string.

29. Now we'll launch our dictionary attack against the encrypted `stuff.7z` archive using the custom wordlist created with Bulk Extractor. From the same Command Prompt window inside the JtR `run` directory, enter the following command (adjust the path to match where you saved your cleaned wordlist):

```
john --wordlist="C:\Encryption\wordlist_split_000.txt" 7z_hash.txt
```

30. Press **Enter** to begin processing. Because our custom dictionary contains `millions` of individual line entries, expect this to take some time, depending on your system's hardware. This is normal, as 7-Zip password hashes are intentionally slow to compute, and large dictionaries will take proportionally longer.

31. While the attack is running, you can press **Enter** at any time to display a status update. JtR will show progress as a percentage of the wordlist completed, along with throughput statistics and the estimated time remaining:

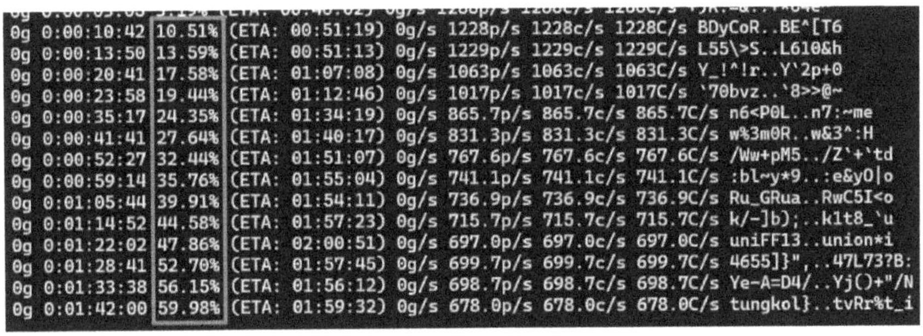

Figure 10.27 – Checking the processing status of an attack in JtR

If the attack is successful, the cracked password will be displayed in the command prompt window just like before. In this case, JtR successfully identified the password; a far more complex value this time of `89$21?AkO7`:

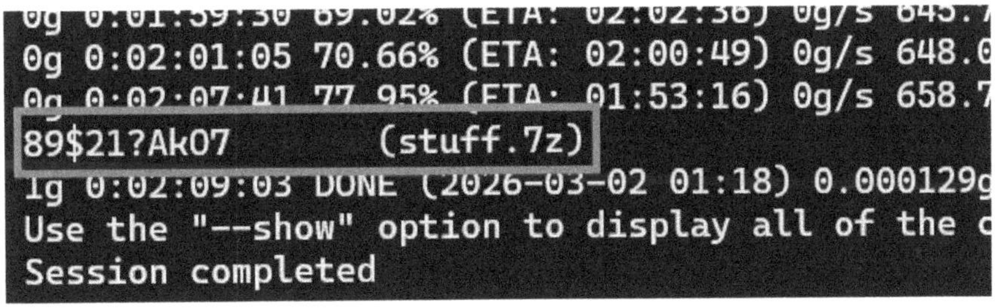

Figure 10.28 – Cracked password for stuff.7z presented by JtR

Had we not created a custom dictionary sourced from the user's own system artifacts, discovering a password with this level of complexity would have been extremely unlikely. This is exactly why user-derived dictionaries are one of the most effective strategies for defeating strong encryption in real-world investigations.

As before, the recovered password is also written to the `john.pot` file in the JtR `run` folder, preserving all previously cracked credentials for future reference and reporting.

How it works...

Encrypted files do not store the password itself. Instead, they store a **password-derived hash**, a cryptographic value created from the following:

- the user's password
- a salt (random value added before the password is hashed)
- and a key-derivation function (KDF) that intentionally performs thousands of slow computations

This means password-cracking tools do *not* try to unlock the file the way a human would. They don't "type" guesses into Word, 7-Zip, or any other application. Instead, they try to **reproduce the hash**.

This is why the first step we took was extracting the hash using tools such as `office2john.py` or `7z2john.pl`. These scripts know how to parse the encrypted file format, locate the encryption metadata, and export the hash in a format our chosen tool (John the Ripper) understands. Once you have that hash, JtR repeatedly processes candidate passwords through the same KDF and compares the result to the target hash. Once they match, it means the password has been found.

This also explains why we are not "breaking" AES-256 or modern encryption algorithms. The encryption itself is effectively unbreakable. What *is* breakable is **human behavior**: weak passwords, reused passwords, meaningful words, names, dates, patterns, and most importantly... passwords that already exist somewhere in the user's own data.

That's why creating a custom dictionary with Bulk Extractor is so powerful. It transforms the user's entire digital footprint into a targeted list of potential passwords. Rather than brute-forcing trillions of combinations, the cracking engine focuses on the far smaller (and far more realistic) set of strings the user is actually likely to have chosen.

This technique doesn't defeat encryption; it defeats the person who set the password.

Data tampering indicators

Tampering with digital evidence is more desperate than sophisticated. A user who deletes files hopes you never notice or recover them. A user who encrypts files hopes you can't break in. But a user who *modifies* evidence is silently admitting that the original data would have incriminated them.

The good news is that data tampering is extremely difficult to do without leaving faint (but often detectable) indicators. Modern operating systems (mobile and desktop alike) log user activity across dozens of independent artifacts. When someone alters or manipulates evidence, those artifacts almost never agree with one another anymore. Think back to the previous chapter when we used timelining and cross-verification: if the data hadn't lined up, it would have been obvious immediately.

We've already covered several types of tampering in previous chapters, including OS-level logging inconsistencies, file signature/extension mismatches, modified image content, anomalous baselines, and timeline conflicts.

In this recipe, we pull many of those threads together and focus on the core methods examiners use to recognize when a file has likely been manipulated, timestomped, or otherwise misrepresented, whether that's a backdated photo on an iPhone, altered document metadata, or subtle attempts to rewrite the truth.

Getting ready

At the GitHub repository for this book, download the dataset for Data Tampering. To access the repository link, follow the steps in the *Download the example code files* section in the *Preface*.

This dataset contains a single E01 forensic image of an SD card (`Tampering.E01`) that includes a mix of normal user activity and artifacts exhibiting signs of intentional manipulation.

Your task is to examine the forensic image using any of the tools we've used throughout this book (FTK Imager, Autopsy, HxD, timeline utilities, etc.). Explore the contents freely and begin separating items that appear routine from those that may indicate anti-forensic behaviors.

Once you've finished your own examination, the steps below will guide you through the key elements present in this miniature "crime scene" dataset and demonstrate how to recognize indicators of data tampering.

How to do it...

1. The examples shown will primarily use FTK Imager.
   When you first load `Tampering.E01` into FTK Imager, the file system view can look a bit overwhelming—not because there are *many* files, but because many different file types

sit directly at the root: media files, folders, apparent junk files, related slack, and orphaned content.

Sometimes the easiest way to mentally untangle this is to start by viewing the volume the same way the user would have, then pivot back to the forensic view.

In *Chapter 4*, we used **Arsenal Image Mounter** to mount forensic images. That's still a great option, but in this case, we can mount the image directly from FTK Imager since we only need a simple logical view.

With `Tampering.E01` added as an Evidence Item in FTK Imager:

- From the **File** menu, select **Image Mounting...**
- In the **Mount Image To Drive** dialog box, choose the following:
- **Mount Type:** Logical only
- Leave other options at their defaults
- Click **Mount**.

FTK Imager will assign a drive letter and mount the file system so it appears in Windows Explorer:

Figure 10.29 – Logically mounting a forensic Image using FTK Imager

Note: To unmount the image later, go back to **File | Image Mounting...**, select the mounted drive in the **Mapped Image List**, and click **Unmount**.

With the image mounted, open the new drive in Windows Explorer. From the user's perspective, there isn't much here: a handful of photos, a 7-Zip archive, and a subfolder with a few additional files.

That quick high-level pass is useful. Now, when we go back into the full forensic view (with slack, orphan files, and unallocated data), we already know what "normal" looks like on this volume. Anything outside that baseline will stand out more clearly as we hunt for signs of tampering.

2. One of the first items that stands out as potentially anomalous is a file titled `Leroy.jpg` located at the root of the drive. Its naming convention doesn't match most other files on the volume, and Windows doesn't generate a thumbnail preview for it—an immediate 'soft' indicator that something may be off.
   If you attempt to open the file in Windows, you'll see that the OS cannot display it and reports that the file format is unsupported:

Figure 10.30 – Leroy.jpg failing to open in Windows

This alone doesn't confirm tampering. Images can become corrupted for many legitimate reasons, but a *single* outlier in an otherwise uniform set of normal photos should always prompt a deeper look. In practice, indicators like these often signal one of three things:

- A mismatched file extension (e.g., renamed from another file type)
- Partial corruption or truncation
- Intentional manipulation or obfuscation by the user

3. This should become our first pivot point. The file `could` simply be corrupted, but we can test that quickly by examining its internal structure. Open `Leroy.jpg` using a hex viewer and inspect the file header. Instead of the expected JPEG signature (0x FF D8 FF), the file begins with `0x 50 4B 03 04` ("PK" in ASCII):

Figure 10.31 – Leroy.jpg file signature showing it is actually a zipped archive

This immediately confirms the file extension is misleading. As we discussed in *Chapter 8*, extension spoofing is a primitive but still very real anti-forensic tactic. Users hoping to hide something will often rename a file to make it appear harmless or uninteresting.

If we export the file and simply rename it back to `.zip`, we can open it normally. Doing so reveals the archive contains a single text file:

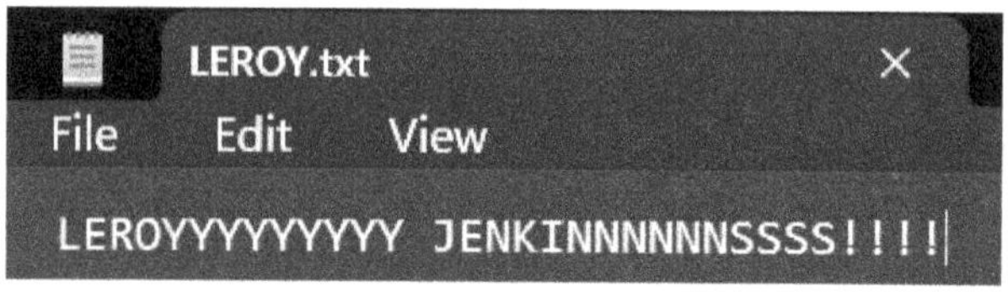

Figure 10.32 – Contents of Leroy.jpg archive file

4. This is suspicious, and seeing an oddly disguised archive immediately pushes us to examine the `other` archive sitting at the root of the drive: `Photo.7z`. Export the file and attempt to open it with 7-Zip. Instead of extracting, 7-Zip prompts for a password:

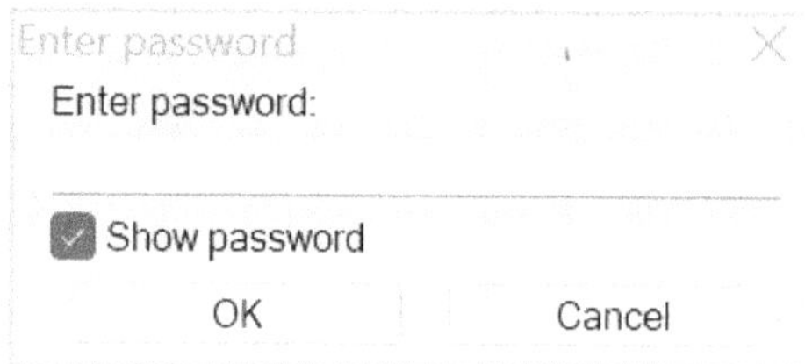

Figure 10.33 – Determining Photo.7z is encrypted

This tells us two things:

- The user intentionally protected the contents of this archive.
- Combined with the disguised Leroy.jpg archive, this increases the likelihood that the user may prefer using zipped containers as a means of deliberate concealment.

While this is definitely interesting, we're not ready to dive into it yet. For now, simply note it, preserve it, and continue examining the rest of the dataset. The context we gather next will help determine whether this encrypted archive is part of normal activity or something more.

5. Continuing our review of the files at the root of the drive, another item stands out: `MINE.JPG`. Opening the file reveals illegal contraband content, yet this file didn't appear earlier when we mounted the image and browsed it through Windows Explorer.

The reason becomes obvious once we inspect the file attributes: the **Hidden** attribute is enabled, preventing normal file browsers from showing it unless **Show hidden files** is turned on:

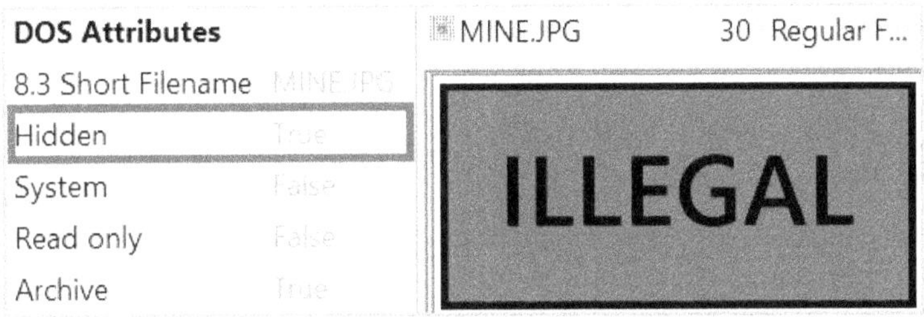

Figure 10.34 – MINE.JPG showing the 'hidden' attribute is set

Hiding files in this way is another primitive anti-forensics tactic. It doesn't modify the underlying data, but it does leave very obvious indicators of user intent. We'll often see similar strategies across multiple platforms (for example, hiding photos inside the iOS "Hidden" album or burying sensitive files deep within obscure directory paths).

While rudimentary, this type of concealment is common in real-world cases and often serves as an early signal that more sophisticated tampering may be present.

6. As we continue examining the root of the drive, another unusual item appears: a 0-byte file named `SDELTEMP`. Even without looking at its contents, the name alone should raise suspicion. This is a temporary file created by **SDelete**, a Microsoft Sysinternals tool used for secure wiping:

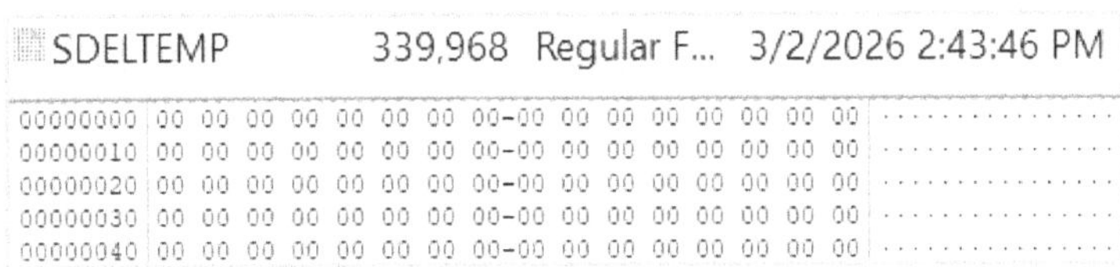

Figure 10.35 – SDelete remnant persisting after data wipe attempt

Under normal circumstances, SDelete wipes unallocated space by creating a large temporary file and overwriting it with a pattern (0x00 by default). Once the wipe finishes, the tool deletes the temporary file.

If an `SDELTEMP` file remains, it usually means one of three things occurred:

- The wipe was interrupted mid-process (e.g., system shutdown, user cancellation, crash, etc.)

- The drive ran out of space before the final cleanup pass
- A permissions or input/output error prevented proper removal

Regardless of the cause, the presence of this file strongly suggests the user attempted a wiping operation. Combined with hidden files and renamed archives seen earlier, this adds to a growing pattern of deliberate anti-forensics behavior.

7. Knowing that the user may have attempted to securely erase data, this is a good point to look for other wipe-related artifacts. Many wiping utilities exist across different OS platforms, and while most try hard to leave no trace, they often leave behind small but telling leftovers when something interrupts the process or when the underlying file system behaves in a certain way.

   In the upcoming example, FTK Imager has already flagged several deleted items within Tampering.E01 based on file system records. Deleted artifacts alone do **not** imply wrongdoing, as users delete items for normal reasons every day. However, when we combine the earlier SDelete remnant with the overall context of this SD card, certain items deserve closer inspection.

   Specifically, the orphaned folders named `!FSTMPWP` stand out:

Name	Size	Type	Date Modified
!CIM	16	Directory	11/12/2019 12:00:50 PM
!FSTMPWP	16	Directory	3/2/2026 7:31:32 PM
!FSTMPWP	16	Directory	3/2/2026 7:32:20 PM
!FSTMPWP	16	Directory	3/2/2026 7:33:06 PM
Leroy	16	Directory	3/2/2026 4:38:56 PM
Hello.docx	14	Regular File	3/2/2026 12:34:40 PM

Figure 10.36 – Evidence of deleted data identified by FTK Imager

   These folder names are a major clue pointing to the Windows **Cipher** utility.

   `Cipher.exe` is a built-in Microsoft tool used for file and folder encryption, but it also includes the `/w` option (cipher /w) that securely wipes free space by overwriting it three times:

   - First pass: 0x00
   - Second pass: 0xFF
   - Third pass: Random data

   During this process, Cipher creates temporary working directories named `EFSTMPWP` on NTFS volumes. However, we're seeing them as `!FSTMPWP` instead, and that difference tells us something important about the underlying file system.

This SD card is formatted using **FAT**, not NTFS. On FAT, deleted items have their first character replaced with 0xE5. Many forensic tools display 0xE5 as an exclamation mark (!) for readability; thus, **EFSTMPWP** becoming **!FSTMPWP** is simply the FAT deletion convention.

So, the presence of multiple `!FSTMPWP` orphaned folders strongly suggests that Cipher's free-space wipe routine was run at least once. This is yet another indicator (alongside the SDELTEMP file) that someone attempted to sanitize the contents of this drive.

8. If Cipher was used, we should expect to see its fingerprints in the **unallocated space** of the volume. Navigate to the `[unallocated space]` node, where you'll notice several numbered fragments. Opening these fragments reveals blocks of overwritten data:

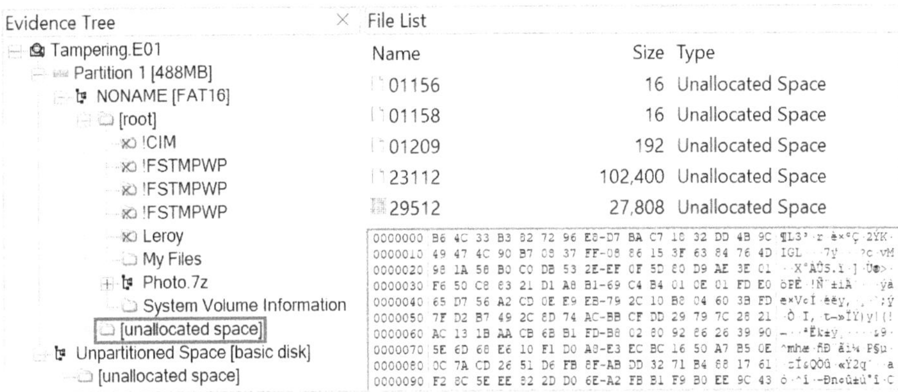

Figure 10.37 – Apparent randomized data in unallocated space

When examining this unallocated space, you may see blocks of wiped data that include 0x00 bytes, 0xFF bytes, and sometimes high-entropy data that looks "random." These patterns are consistent with the three-pass wipe performed by **cipher** `/w`, which overwrites free space with zeroes, then ones, then random bytes. However, because this drive uses the **FAT file system**, deleted directories and cluster boundaries can cause residual data that does *not* appear fully randomized. In short, the mix of zeroes, ones, and irregular high-entropy blocks *is* what a Cipher wipe looks like on FAT volumes.

So, the key point that truly matters is this: these overwritten clusters **didn't occur naturally**. They are highly consistent with free-space wiping activity.

This doesn't automatically prove the user destroyed evidence, though. Free-space wiping is extremely common even among casual users (CCleaner, for example, is popular with even inexperienced users and performs similar overwrites, often leaving behind deleted filenames rewritten as `zzzzzzzz.zzz`).

But combined with

- the hidden illicit file
- the renamed archive disguised as a JPG
- the encrypted 7-Zip file
- the SDelete remnant
- the Cipher-style !FSTMPWP orphaned folders

...the pattern strongly suggests the user was attempting to destroy or alter data in a way that would make recovery difficult or impossible.

It's also worth noting that wipe artifacts (especially those created by native system utilities like **SDelete** and **Cipher**) are regularly encountered in intrusion-response cases. Adversaries often prefer "living off the land" tools (or the use of natively installed system utilities) because they're quieter and less likely to be detected by IDS/IPS systems than installing third-party wiping tools. For examiners, seeing these artifacts together is a signal to start asking deeper questions about intent.

9. Our next logical pivot point is the lone subdirectory at the root of the drive titled **My Files**. Its existence alone is notable: in a dataset with otherwise mixed content scattered at the root level, a tidy subfolder containing only a few files often signals intentional grouping. Users rarely create isolated folders unless those files matter to them or they `want` them to stand apart from the rest.

   Opening this directory in the logical view of our mounted forensic image reveals only three items, including an Apple HEIC photo titled `IMG_4201.HEIC`:

Figure 10.38 – Viewing 'My Files' subdirectory as a mounted image

This immediately stands out. HEIC is a native iOS image format, and unlike the other media at the root of the drive (which are typical for cameras and SD cards), this file type suggests it originated from a relatively modern iPhone or iPad. When a user places such a file manually into a separate folder, it's usually deliberate, not something performed automatically by a device or operating system.

At this point, our mindset should shift from "***What** is here?*" to "***Why** is **this** here, and why is it separated from everything else?*" Anti-forensic behavior often shows itself not through a single smoking gun, but through patterned anomalies such as files placed where they normally wouldn't be, file types that stand out from their surroundings, and other contradictory signs.

This folder is small, isolated, and contains a file type that doesn't match the profile of the rest of the content, so it deserves deeper analysis.

> **Tip**
>
> One Tap Tampering: Now for Everyone!
>
> Data tampering once required a user to be moderately advanced (or at least comfortable installing third-party utilities designed to alter metadata). That is no longer true. Modern operating systems now include native tools that let users modify evidentiary metadata without any additional software.
>
> Beginning with iOS 15, Apple introduced the ability to edit photo and video EXIF timestamps directly on the device through the **Adjust Date & Time** feature. More recent versions of iOS also allow users to modify the geolocation metadata using the **Adjust Location** feature.
>
> 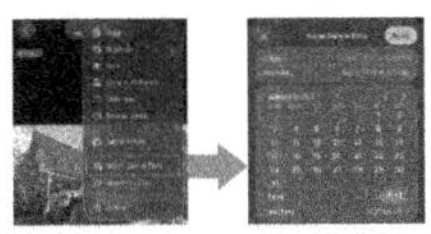
>
> *Figure 10.39 – Apple iOS native EXIF editing features*
>
> Android has followed a similar path. Many modern Android builds also allow a user to change a photo's timestamp and location metadata natively.
>
> This means a large portion of metadata tampering is now one button away for the average user. Because of this, investigators must rely less on EXIF alone and more on cross-artifact validation.

10. Export and open the `IMG_4201.HEIC` file, then review the EXIF metadata. In the example shown below, we use **IrfanView** (introduced previously in Chapter 8). Remember that EXIF data in IrfanView can be viewed by navigating to: **Image | Information | EXIF info**

    If this photograph had come directly from an iOS acquisition, we would normally expect to see a discrepancy between the **DateTimeOriginal** field (the camera-recorded timestamp) and the **DateTime** field (the 'current' or edited timestamp). iOS keeps *both* values when metadata is edited on-device so that users can later "Revert" their adjustments.

However, in this case, the image was exported from the device, and exports (especially via AirDrop, messaging apps, or cloud sync, etc.) often flatten metadata. As a result, both fields now appear identical, showing a date and time of **2025:08:17 15:14:00**:

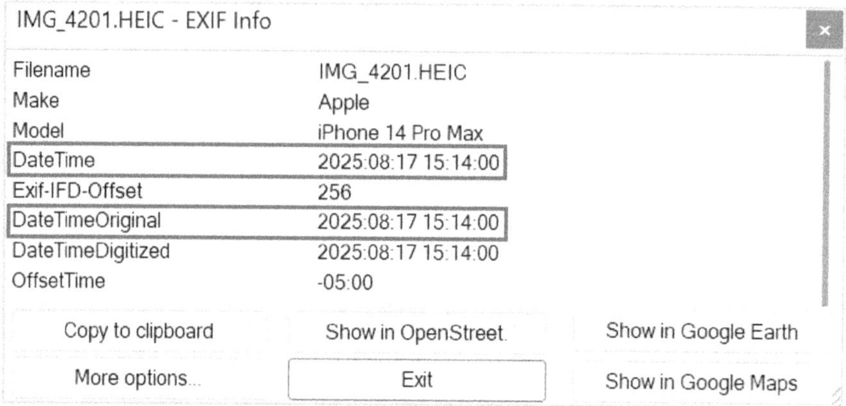

Figure 10.40 – IMG_4201.HEIC EXIF date and time fields

11. In this case, our first forensic clue is a mismatch between the edited timestamp fields and the **GPSDateStamp**, which reports a date of **2025:08:22**:

Figure 10.41 – Mismatch between EXIF date and time fields

That's **five days later** than the EXIF DateTimeOriginal and DateTime fields (2025:08:17). This discrepancy matters because the following:

- **Camera timestamps (DateTimeOriginal)** reflect when the shutter was activated.
- **GPS metadata (GPSDateStamp / GPSTimeStamp)** reflects when the device recorded location data.

Under normal conditions, these values are recorded at (or very near) the same moment. It makes little sense for a photo to be "taken" five days before it had a location. This is a huge red flag indicating the EXIF timestamp was manually edited using the iOS *Adjust Date & Time* feature (or a similar method).

12. Another indicator of tampering appears in the **sub-second fields** of the `DateTime` and `DateTimeOriginal` values; both display **2025:08:17 15:14:00** with no fractional seconds recorded:

DateTime	2025:08:17 15:14:00
DateTimeOriginal	2025:08:17 15:14:00
DateTimeDigitized	2025:08:17 15:14:00

Figure 10.42 – EXIF sub-seconds zeroed in IMG_4201.HEIC

Under normal circumstances, iPhone cameras populate **non-zero** sub-second values (e.g., 52, 87, 04) because mobile sensors capture with sub-second precision. However, when a user edits the timestamp using the iOS "*Adjust Date & Time*" feature, iOS rewrites only within a second's worth of precision and does **not** preserve the fractional second fields – instead opting to zero them out.

While it's *possible* for a photo to be taken at exactly .00 sub-seconds, the odds are extremely low, especially if the pattern occurs across multiple images. Thus, missing sub-seconds are a strong indicator that the date and time were altered.

While this nuance alone strongly suggests modification, it is not conclusive by itself. If the original device is available, additional validation could include the following:

- Original metadata from Photos.sqlite (`ZADDEDDATE`, `ZDATECREATED`)
- Filename sequence consistency within the `Apple###` folders
- Comparison to file system dates and times

This combination allows you to confirm or refute timestamp tampering with very high confidence.

> **Note**
>
> Advanced technology... average users...
>
> iOS makes it easy to edit photo timestamps, but most users don't understand the underlying metadata well enough to actually pull it off and successfully hide their tracks. In one murder case, the suspect's girlfriend altered photo iOS timestamps to give him a false alibi... but the EXIF inconsistencies shown above

> gave her away instantly. Long story short, he was convicted, and she later pled guilty to perjury. Even with modern features, tampering leaves residue. You just have to know where to look.

13. Altering date and time fields is not a new tactic in digital forensics. This is known as **timestomping**, and intentional modification of timestamps leaves patterns that rarely match organic system behavior. Beyond the iOS-specific clues we just examined, here are the broader indicators examiners rely on when evaluating potential time manipulation:
    - **Impossible timestamps** – A file showing a creation time *after* its deletion time; a photo dated *before* the device existed; system files appearing modified during periods when logs show the device was powered off or inactive.
    - **Cross-artifact inconsistencies** – File system timestamps that don't line up with related sources (logs, application databases, message records, camera roll ordering, cloud sync metadata, etc.). When timestamps disagree across independent artifacts, the manipulated field almost always stands out.
    - **Clock rollbacks or manual clock changes** – Users sometimes try to alter the system clock to disguise actions. This often produces gaps or discontinuities in operating-system logs, abrupt jumps in recorded timestamps, or event sequences that appear out of chronological order.

    Timestomping rarely succeeds when examined across multiple artifacts. Modern systems generate too many independently maintained timestamps for a user to manipulate all of them in a consistent way. At best, timestomping only disrupts a portion of your timeline, making it less *convenient*, not less *conclusive*. When the timeline stops agreeing with the rest of the evidence, the contradiction becomes its own finding.

14. At this point, you might start becoming hypersensitive to zeroed-out timestamps... and that's a good instinct. You may then notice that every file in our evidence source shows a file system **Access Time** of **00:00:00**:

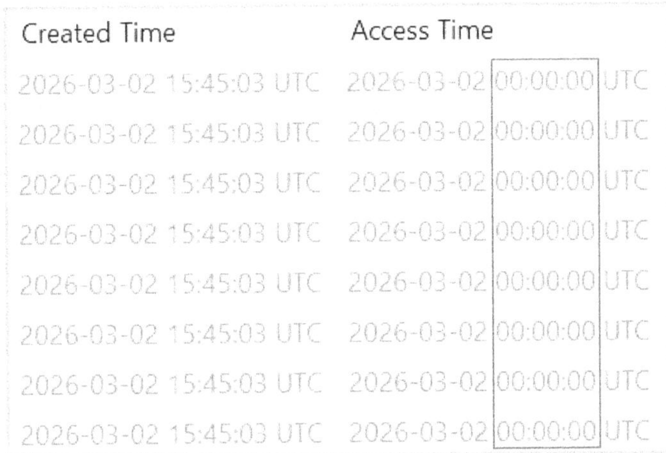

Created Time	Access Time
2026-03-02 15:45:03 UTC	2026-03-02 00:00:00 UTC
2026-03-02 15:45:03 UTC	2026-03-02 00:00:00 UTC
2026-03-02 15:45:03 UTC	2026-03-02 00:00:00 UTC
2026-03-02 15:45:03 UTC	2026-03-02 00:00:00 UTC
2026-03-02 15:45:03 UTC	2026-03-02 00:00:00 UTC
2026-03-02 15:45:03 UTC	2026-03-02 00:00:00 UTC
2026-03-02 15:45:03 UTC	2026-03-02 00:00:00 UTC
2026-03-02 15:45:03 UTC	2026-03-02 00:00:00 UTC

Figure 10.43 – File Access Times reading 00:00:00

Many timestomping techniques *do* produce zeroed-out or inconsistent timestamps. However, that is **not** what's happening here. This artifact is actually behaving *exactly* as expected for a FAT-formatted volume.

The FAT file system stores a last access ***date***, but not last access ***time***.

Because FAT does not track the time component, most forensic tools populate the missing value with 00:00:00. In other words, you're seeing a limitation of the file system, not evidence of tampering.

This is why knowing the underlying system matters. If you don't understand what a file system normally records, you won't know when something is actually abnormal and can be misled into drawing inaccurate conclusions.

15. The remaining files inside the **My Files** directory include `Hello.docx` and `Hello.docx.bak`. When we examine this folder more closely, we also see numerous apparently deleted files tied to the same document.
    At first glance, this might look suspicious, but most of what we're seeing is normal for Microsoft Word operations. Word routinely creates (and deletes) temporary files while a document is being edited, saved, and resaved. These appear as `WRL####.TMP` and `WRD####.TMP` and can accumulate quickly during normal usage.

    The part that *does* stand out is the presence of `Hello.docx.bak`:

Name	Date Modified	Size	Type
!WRD0492.TMP	3/2/2026 4:36:42 PM	14	Regular File
!WRD3064.TMP	3/2/2026 4:36:36 PM	14	Regular File
!WRL0500.TMP	3/2/2026 4:36:36 PM	14	Regular File
!WRL3123.TMP	3/2/2026 12:34:40 PM	14	Regular File
Hello.docx	3/2/2026 12:34:40 PM	14	Regular File
Hello.docx	3/2/2026 4:36:36 PM	14	Regular File
Hello.docx	3/2/2026 6:11:36 PM	14	Regular File
Hello.docx.bak	3/2/2026 4:36:42 PM	14	Regular File

Figure 10.44 – Files relating to Hello.docx

Word does **not** normally generate .bak files on its own. A `.bak` file typically means one of two things:

- The user manually created a backup by duplicating and then renaming the original file, or...
- A third-party tool or process generated a backup for some reason.

Either scenario can be benign, but in a dataset already showing multiple indicators of manipulation, a manually created `.bak` version of a file should be treated as another potential pivot point for deeper analysis.

16. Examining the metadata for Hello.docx doesn't immediately raise alarms. The timestamps appear internally consistent, and nothing in the document properties stands out as overtly manipulated. Even the content itself is minimal, containing only the phrase "**IMPORTANT. KEEP.**":

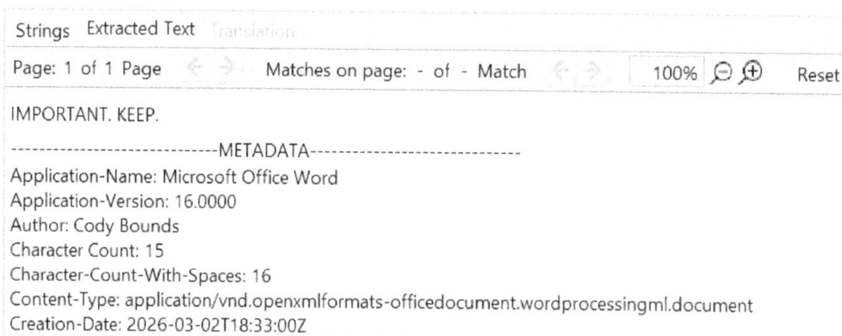

Figure 10.45 – File content and metadata of Hello.docx (viewed using Autopsy)

On its own, this tells us very little. Users create placeholder documents all the time, and the phrase could refer to almost anything. But in a dataset where we've already identified encryption, hiding, and secure-wipe attempts, a file explicitly labeled "important" with no meaningful content inside it becomes a natural point of suspicion.

17. The real clue to something `more` here is the strange companion file we noted: `Hello.docx.bak`. This is actually a backup file generated by the HxD Hex Editor, which automatically creates a `.bak` copy whenever a file is modified at the binary level. Finding an HxD backup file on a suspect device should instantly raise your suspicion. Few non-technical users install hex editors, and their presence strongly suggests intentional low-level manipulation. This leads to yet another natural pivot: *If HxD was used, what did the user change?...* and the presence of the .bak file alone indicates that Hello.docx was likely changed in some way.

    One technique employed by more advanced users is **binary steganography**, which involves embedding hidden text or data inside an otherwise normal file by writing it into unused or low-risk byte regions. Unlike normal stego methods (e.g., hiding data in image bit patterns or video frames), this method simply places concealed strings into parts of the file structure that do not affect how the file opens or behaves.

    And that's exactly what happened here.

    When we more carefully inspect *Hello.docx* in a hex viewer, we see that a password has been deliberately injected into a benign section of the DOCX file structure, invisible to the average user because it cannot be detected through normal document viewing but fully present in the binary layer:

```
2ef0  00 00 00 00 00 00 00 00-00 00 00 00 00 00 00 00  ................
2f00  00 00 00 00 00 00 00 00-00 00 00 00 00 00 00 00  ................
2f10  50 61 73 73 77 6F 72 64-3A 20 35 47 37 23 5E 68  Password: 5G7#^h
2f20  37 38 3E 26 00 00 00 00-00 00 00 00 00 00 00 00  78>&............
2f30  00 00 00 00 00 00 00 00-00 00 00 00 00 00 00 00  ................
```

Figure 10.46 – Password hidden within Hello.docx file

    This kind of tampering is extremely easy to miss unless you specifically go looking for it. Typically, you would only spot it through file system-level keyword searches or by finding and following a string of clues like the ones seen here.

    While this form of steganography is simple, it's not common in the wild. However, when it *does* appear, it's almost always deliberate. Knowing how to spot it can reveal critical evidence that would otherwise remain hidden in plain sight.

18. Now that we've identified a hidden password inside `Hello.docx`, we can return to our encrypted archive, `Photo.7z`, and test whether this password was intentionally concealed for that purpose.

Using 7-Zip, attempt to open the archive again, this time entering the password we just discovered: **5G7#^h78>&**

The archive will decrypt and reveal a single file inside, titled `IMG_7220.JPEG`:

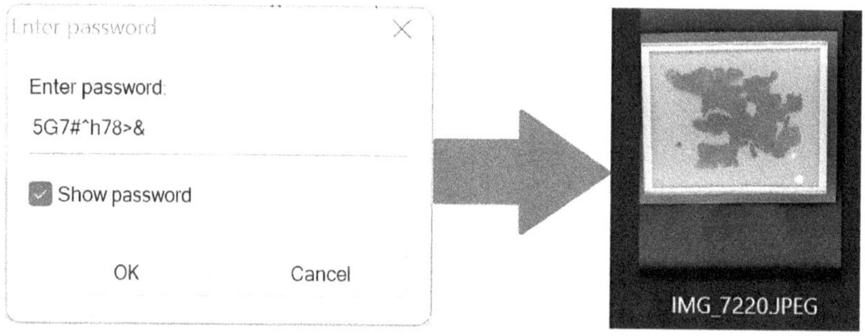

Figure 10.47 – Gaining access to encrypted Photo.7z archive

This demonstrates an important concept: while manually discovering a concealed password like this is often unlikely, our *previously demonstrated* method from the *Defeating Encryption* section would have worked here as well. If we had used Bulk Extractor to generate a wordlist from the `Tampering.E01` image, this hidden password would have appeared among the extracted strings. John the Ripper could then have cracked the 7-Zip hash naturally using that custom dictionary.

In other words, even well-hidden passwords tend to surface when you generate dictionaries from the suspect's own data.

This step ties the chapter together, showing how encryption, timestomping, steganography, and metadata manipulation often intersect, and how cross-technique analysis reveals patterns no single method could catch on its own.

How it works...

Not every discrepancy is evidence of intentional tampering. File systems, operating systems, and applications behave differently and can exhibit many quirks that are completely normal (like FAT's zeroed access times or timestamp shifts during file transfers). The examiner's job is not just to *spot* anomalies but to *explain* them accurately. That means understanding how a system records data, how related artifacts interact, and what patterns are normal for the platform you're examining.

Intentional tampering usually reveals itself when those artifact relationships break down. A user may edit EXIF timestamps, hide files, rename extensions, wipe free space, or even inject data through hex editing, but the surrounding ecosystem of artifacts rarely agrees with their edits. Modern devices often generate dozens of independent traces for a single action, and when a human alters one of them, the others remain unchanged. This produces inconsistencies that typical operating system behavior would not generate.

The human side matters as much as the technical side. The likelihood of sophisticated tampering is tied to the user's knowledge, habits, and motive. A software developer who tinkers with Raspberry Pis and commonly searches for "digital forensics" or "penetration testing" is far more capable and likely to perform advanced manipulation than a user whose web history consists of "how do I save a file." Examining behavior and skill level helps you determine whether an anomaly is a system artifact, a user mistake, or a deliberate attempt to conceal evidence.

Ultimately, detecting tampering is rarely about finding a single "smoking gun." It's about recognizing when the story told by the data no longer matches what the system itself would have produced, and understanding both the technology and the human behind it well enough to know why.

Summary

When users want to hide wrongdoing, they typically choose one of three moves: deletion, encryption, or alteration. Deleted data leaves gaps, encrypted data builds walls, and tampered data creates lies. If you can show that a user tried any of these, you're not just proving what happened... you're also showing they *knew* it was incriminating and took steps to bury it.

In this chapter, you learned how to turn those "last-ditch" efforts against the user.

At this point, you should be able to do the following:

- **Recover deleted data** using both automated carving and manual recovery from unallocated space by working with headers, footers, and byte offsets
- **Extract and attack password hashes** from common encrypted files (such as Office documents and 7-Zip archives)
- **Build high-value custom dictionaries** from a suspect's own data
- **Recognize wipe attempts and "clean-up" activity** by spotting remnants from tools like SDelete and Cipher and by identifying overwritten patterns.
- **Detect signs of metadata manipulation and timestomping** across platforms, from iOS EXIF anomalies to impossible file system sequences that break the natural story your timeline should tell
- **Catch low-level tampering and concealment** such as extension spoofing, hidden attributes, and hex-level steganography.
- **Distinguish system quirks from intent** by combining technical knowledge with behavioral assessment of the user.

The core theme of this chapter is simple: anti-forensics almost never works as cleanly as the user thinks. Deleted files, encrypted containers, and manipulated metadata all leave traces somewhere. If you understand how the system is supposed to behave and you're willing to chase down the gaps, those "hidden tracks" can end up telling the most important part of the story.

In the next chapter, we move beyond persistent storage and into memory forensics, where some of the most valuable evidence exists only temporarily. Even when data has been deleted, encrypted, or manipulated on disk, remnants may still reside in RAM, providing investigators with another powerful avenue to recover and validate critical evidence.

Get this book's PDF copy, code bundle, and more

Scan the QR code (or go to `packtpub.com/unlock`). Search for this book by name, confirm the edition, and then follow the steps on the page.

UNLOCK NOW

Note: Have your invoice handy. Purchases made directly from the Packt website don't require an invoice.

11

Memory Forensics

Investigators often rely heavily on evidence recovered from disk. However, some of the most important artifacts never exist there at all. Instead, they exist only temporarily within memory while the system is running.

In *Chapter 3*, we performed an acquisition of random access memory (RAM) from our own workstation. RAM is volatile, meaning its contents are lost when a system powers down, which is why, unlike other acquisitions, RAM must be captured on scene during evidence collection rather than later in the lab. While this makes it more challenging to preserve and analyze, it can also make memory one of the most valuable evidence sources available.

In simple terms, the purpose of RAM is to speed up system processing. When a user opens a file from disk, the operating system loads the data into RAM, which can be accessed much faster than disk storage. The central processing unit (CPU) then reads and processes that data directly from memory as the system and user interact with it. RAM therefore acts as the system's working memory between storage and the CPU:

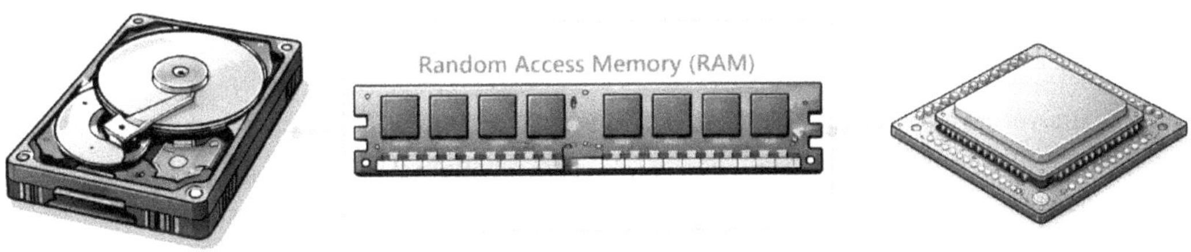

Figure 11.1 – Data flow between disk storage, RAM, and the CPU

This means that RAM contains the contents of data that was actively being used by the system and user. Some content in RAM may never be written to disk and exists only in memory. One example of this is private or incognito browsing that is never recorded in web history; the activity must still exist in order to be rendered to the user, so portions of that activity are stored temporarily within RAM while the browsing session is active. We may also find portions of data that were handled when an encrypted container or volume was being accessed, including the encryption key itself, because these keys are temporarily retained in RAM to allow the system to access the encrypted data.

Memory analysis is particularly valuable when investigating modern attacks. Sophisticated adversaries frequently attempt to operate only in memory wherever possible in order to avoid leaving evidence on disk. Techniques such as process injection, fileless malware, and in-memory payload execution are specifically designed to evade traditional forensic methods that rely on file system artifacts. By analyzing captured memory, investigators can often observe these activities directly while they are executing. In some cases, RAM may be the only place where definitive evidence of malware execution exists.

Unlike disk evidence, RAM does not contain a traditional file system. Instead, it is made up of structured operating system data (such as processes and memory regions) that are constantly changing while a system is running. This makes analysis more complex, but also uniquely valuable.

Fortunately, several powerful tools exist to help investigators analyze captured memory images. In this chapter, we will explore practical techniques for examining memory artifacts using Volatility, mounting and virtualizing memory images with MemProcFS to explore their contents interactively, extracting potential encryption keys, and identifying evidence of user activity that may exist only within RAM.

In modern investigations, memory analysis most commonly focuses on Windows systems. Many current operating systems and mobile platforms (such as macOS, iOS, and Android) implement security protections that make reliable memory acquisition difficult or impossible without specialized hardware or exploits. As a result, forensic memory analysis is most frequently performed on Windows systems, with Linux memory analysis occasionally encountered in server or cloud environments. For this reason, the examples in this chapter will focus on analyzing memory captured from a Windows system.

During analysis, we will encounter several artifacts associated with the user account `Leroy`, including evidence of external storage usage, encrypted volumes, and virtual machine activity. As we move through each technique, we will correlate these artifacts to demonstrate how memory analysis contributes to a broader forensic investigation.

In this chapter, we're going to cover the following main topics:

- Analysis
- Recovering artifacts
- Virtualization

Technical requirements

For this chapter, you will need the following:

- A computer running Microsoft Windows as your forensic workstation. 64-bit Windows 11 Professional with an Intel i7 quad-core processor or better and a minimum of 16-gigabytes of RAM is recommended.
- Your working installation of Autopsy (used in chapters).
- The **Windows_RAM.mem** dataset image, downloadable from the Packt Publishing GitHub repository. To access the repository link, follow the steps in the *Download the example code files* section in the *Preface*.
- Ensure the memory image is downloaded and extracted before beginning the following recipes.
- Optional for cross-verification and data recovery:
    - The **Microsoft Windows** dataset used throughout this book.
    - The **Verbatim USB** forensic image from *Chapter 8*.
- Volatility 3, which will be installed during the first recipe and used throughout the chapter.

Analysis

While disk artifacts tell us what happened on a system in the past, memory analysis allows us to observe what was actively occurring at the moment memory was captured. A RAM image contains a snapshot of the operating system's in-memory state, including running processes, loaded modules, active network connections, command history, injected code, and fragments of user activity that may never have been written to disk.

Unlike disk evidence, memory is not organized as a traditional file system and must instead be interpreted through operating system data structures that exist only in RAM. Because of this, analyzing memory requires specialized tools capable of identifying and reconstructing those structures directly from a captured memory image. One of the most widely used tools for this purpose is Volatility, an open-source memory forensics framework developed by the Volatility Foundation and designed to extract forensic artifacts from memory images.

Volatility works by parsing kernel and process memory structures used internally by the operating system. By identifying these structures within a captured RAM image, we can reconstruct information such as running processes, loaded drivers, open network connections, and other artifacts that existed at the time of acquisition. This makes memory analysis particularly useful for identifying malware activity, process injection, and other behaviors that may leave little or no evidence on disk. In many investigations, memory is the only place where the true runtime behavior of malware can be observed, especially when attackers rely on in-memory execution, code injection, or other techniques designed to evade traditional disk-based analysis.

In this recipe, we will use Volatility to begin examining the Windows memory image provided in the Microsoft Windows dataset used throughout this book. We will focus on several commonly used Volatility plugins that allow us to quickly understand the state of a system at the time memory was captured. These commands help establish a baseline view of system activity and verify that our memory image is being interpreted correctly.

Getting ready

Ensure that you have downloaded the `Windows_RAM.mem` dataset file from the Packt Publishing GitHub repository. To access the repository link, follow the steps in the *Download the example code files* section in the *Preface*. Store this dataset somewhere easily accessible, since we will be accessing it frequently through a command-line interface (CLI). In the examples shown throughout this chapter, the memory image is stored at: `C:\MEMORY\Source\Windows_RAM.mem`

Your directory structure may differ but ensure you know the full file path to the `Windows_RAM.mem` file before proceeding.

You may also wish to reference the `Lenovo ThinkPad.E01` image (optional), which we have used as the Microsoft Windows dataset throughout this book.

Next, download and prepare **Volatility 3**, which will be used to analyze the memory image. To download Volatility 3, open a web browser and navigate to the official Volatility Foundation GitHub repository: `https://github.com/volatilityfoundation/volatility3`

On the right-side portion of the page, locate the **Releases** section and click the **Latest release**. Then, in the **Assets** section of the page, download the `volatility-win-exes-version.zip` file. While Volatility can run on both Windows and Linux systems, this particular version is best suited for our Windows workstations and avoids the need to install Python and additional dependencies.

> Note
>
> Note that if you choose to install the non-Windows executable version, all commands shown in this section beginning with **vol.exe** will instead need to be run as `vol.py`.

Once downloaded, extract the file contents, which will include a file titled `vol.exe` along with other supporting files. Do not attempt to double-click and install this file, as Volatility is a CLI utility that must be run from the **Command Prompt**.

Open a Windows Command Prompt from the Volatility directory by typing **CMD** in the File `Explorer address bar` and pressing **Enter**.

At this point, Volatility 3 is ready to analyze memory images.

Enter the following command, where the `-f` parameter specifies the memory image file that Volatility will analyze:

```
vol.exe -f C:\MEMORY\Source\Windows_RAM.mem windows.info
```

Running the `windows.info` plugin allows us to verify that the memory image loaded correctly and provides key details about the captured system, including the Windows kernel version, build number, and system time at the moment memory was acquired, as seen in *Figure 11.2*. This command is often the first step in memory analysis because it confirms that Volatility can correctly interpret the operating system structures:

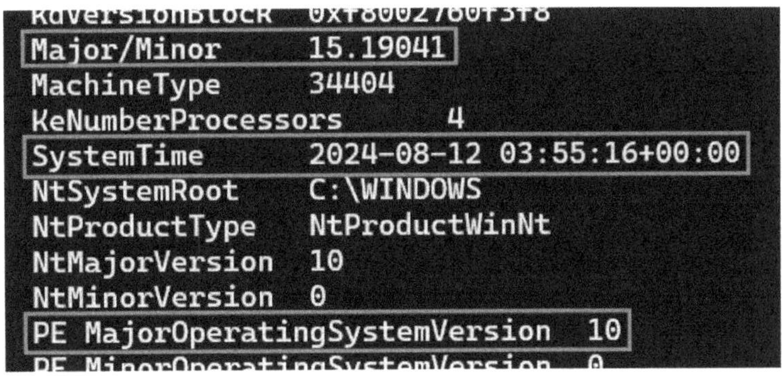

Figure 11.2 – Volatility info plugin output

Note

Early versions of Volatility (particularly **Volatility 2**) were widely used for many years, even after the release of Volatility 3. However, they relied heavily on manually created operating system profiles and became increasingly difficult to maintain as modern operating systems evolved. Volatility 3 was designed to function more efficiently by automatically identifying operating system structures within memory images, eliminating the need for manually selected profiles in most situations.

While Volatility 2 can still be useful for legacy systems (generally those older than Windows 10) and occasionally for certain plugins that were not carried over into Volatility 3, we will focus on **Volatility 3** throughout this book, as it is now the preferred framework for analyzing modern memory images.

How to do it...

1. We already used the `windows.info` plugin in the *Getting ready* section. This should often be the first command you run when beginning memory analysis, as it extracts important details about the operating system itself. The `SystemTime` field also gives us insight into which disk artifacts will likely align with what we see in the memory image. This timestamp can be particularly useful when correlating memory findings with artifacts from disk analysis, event logs, or timeline reconstruction.
   The way we ran that command will remain consistent with other basic Volatility 3 commands, where we call Volatility, use `-f` to specify the memory image file, and then specify the plugin name:

   ```
   vol.exe -f <memory image location> <plugin>
   ```

   > **Tip**
   >
   > Volatility plugins are generally organized using the following structure:
   >
   > `platform.category.plugin`
   >
   > For example, the command we used earlier:
   >
   > `windows.info` indicates that the plugin applies to **Windows memory images** and belongs to the `info` category of plugins used to retrieve basic system information.
   >
   > You may also notice that each of the plugins we run in this chapter begins with **windows**. Volatility supports analysis of multiple operating systems, including Linux and macOS. If we were examining a Linux memory acquisition instead, the equivalent command would look something like this:
   >
   > ```
   > vol.exe -f <memory image location> linux.info
   > ```
   >
   > This simply tells Volatility to use the plugin designed to interpret **Linux kernel structures** instead of Windows structures.

Note

While macOS memory analysis is still technically supported, modern versions of macOS encrypt system memory and introduce additional protections that make full memory analysis significantly more difficult. Because of this, memory analysis of Apple systems is far less common in modern forensic workflows than Windows or Linux systems.

2. Some plugins have additional capabilities that can be invoked. To see the parameters that can be added to a given plugin for additional functionality, you can add the `-h` parameter after calling the plugin, as follows:

```
vol.exe -f <memory image location> <plugin> -h
```

Tip

As we proceed, you may find that many plugins produce a large amount of output that can be difficult to read directly within Command Prompt. While increasing the window size can sometimes help, another option is to redirect the output into a saved file.

You can easily save any plugin output into a text file using the following command:

```
vol.exe -f <memory image location> <plugin> > file.txt
```

Alternatively, you can save the output to a formatted **CSV** file instead, which is particularly useful for very large data outputs and allows the results to be easily searched or sorted using tools like Excel. To do this, use the **-r csv** parameter before the plugin:

```
vol.exe -f <memory image location> -r csv <plugin> > file.csv
```

Saving plugin output can also be useful when you discover evidentiary artifacts and need to preserve your findings for later review or reporting. By default, these files are saved to the current working directory from which Volatility is being executed.

> Another helpful option when working with large outputs is to pipe the results through the Windows `more` command, which allows the output to be viewed one page at a time:
>
> ```
> vol.exe -f <memory image location> <plugin> | more
> ```
>
> This can make it easier to review results directly in the terminal without exporting them to a file.

3. Now that we understand the basic structure of Volatility commands, let's examine the processes that were active when memory was captured. Processes represent programs that were running on the system and often provide the first clues of malicious activity. Run the following command:

```
vol.exe -f C:\MEMORY\Source\Windows_RAM.mem windows.pslist
```

The `pslist` plugin lists processes identified through the Windows kernel's active process list. The output includes several important details:

PID	PPID	ImageFileName	Wow64	CreateTime
100	4	Registry	False	2024-08-11 08:35:20 UTC
408	4	smss.exe	False	2024-08-11 08:35:34 UTC
564	548	csrss.exe	False	2024-08-11 08:35:50 UTC
648	548	wininit.exe	False	2024-08-11 08:35:51 UTC
668	640	csrss.exe	False	2024-08-11 08:35:51 UTC
720	648	services.exe	False	2024-08-11 08:35:51 UTC
728	648	lsass.exe	False	2024-08-11 08:35:51 UTC

Figure 11.3 – Volatility pslist plugin output

As shown in *Figure 11.3*, some of the most useful information produced by the `windows.pslist` plugin includes:

- **PID** – The Process ID is a unique number assigned by the Windows kernel to identify each running process.
- **PPID** – This represents the Parent Process ID, showing which process created the current one. Most processes are launched by another process, so the presence of a PPID is normal. However, unexpected parent-child relationships can sometimes indicate suspicious activity.
- **ImageFileName** – The name of the executable associated with the process.

- **Wow64** – Indicates whether the process is running as a 32-bit process on a 64-bit operating system (Wow64 = **TRUE**). While many legitimate applications still run in 32-bit mode, malware is frequently compiled as 32-bit code for compatibility across systems, so unusual 32-bit processes may warrant additional attention.
- **CreateTime** – The timestamp showing when the process started. In some cases, an **ExitTime** may also be present if the process terminated before the memory image was captured.

Reviewing this list allows us to quickly identify unusual processes. For example, during a malware investigation, we often look for processes that were spawned from unexpected parent processes, since legitimate Windows programs tend to follow fairly predictable process trees, with common parent-child relationships (such as services.exe spawning svchost.exe instances or explorer.exe launching user applications). A process launched from an unusual parent process can be an early indicator of malicious activity or process injection.

Investigators will also often review the process creation timeline when examining **pslist** output. Because many legitimate system processes launch in a predictable order during system startup, processes appearing significantly later or with unusual timestamps relative to the rest of the system activity may warrant additional attention. Also, be aware that Windows may reuse PIDs after processes exit. When analyzing historical timelines, a PID alone should not be treated as a unique identifier without considering its associated timestamps.

> **Note**
>
> Make it pretty... so pretty...
>
> You may notice that Volatility output can sometimes appear compressed or difficult to read within Command Prompt. When this happens, you can clean up the formatting by invoking the **-r pretty** parameter:
>
> ```
> vol.exe -f <memory image location> -r pretty <plugin>
> ```
>
> This formats the output into a more readable layout and should be a standard part of most commands you run in Volatility. All figure images shown throughout this chapter use the **-r pretty** formatting option, even if it is not explicitly shown in the commands.

4. While `pslist` relies on the operating system's linked list of active processes, malware may attempt to hide by removing itself from that list. For this reason, we want to try to identify processes that may not appear in the standard process listing.
Run the following command:

```
vol.exe -f C:\MEMORY\Source\Windows_RAM.mem windows.psscan
```

The `psscan` plugin produces output similar to `pslist`, but instead of relying on the operating system's linked list, it scans memory directly for **process objects**. This means it searches for remnants of Windows **_EPROCESS structures** that represent processes within memory.

Because of this approach, `psscan` can identify processes that were:

- hidden from the active process list
- terminated but still present in memory
- partially unlinked from the OS's normal process tracking structures

Comparing the results of `pslist` and `psscan` can help identify anomalies that may indicate process hiding or manipulation. If a process appears in `psscan` but not in `pslist`, it may suggest that the process was intentionally removed from the kernel's active process list in an attempt to evade detection.

5. To compare those results and help visually identify which processes may exist only in `psscan` or only in `pslist`, run the following command:

```
vol.exe -f C:\MEMORY\Source\Windows_RAM.mem windows.malware.psxview
```

The `psxview` plugin correlates multiple methods of locating processes in memory. The output includes columns representing different techniques used to identify process structures. Each column will display **True** if the process was found using that technique and **False** if it was not:

Name	PID	pslist	psscan	thrdscan	csrss
RuntimeBroker.	12612	False	True	False	False
svchost.exe	1200	True	True	False	False
svchost.exe	1212	True	True	True	True
svchost.exe	1404	True	True	True	True
svchost.exe	6132	False	True	False	False
updater.exe	9408	False	True	False	False

Figure 11.4 – Volatility psxview plugin output

The first two columns correspond to the plugins we previously ran:

- **pslist** – Processes identified through the Windows kernel's active process linked list
- **psscan** – Processes discovered by scanning memory directly for process objects

The remaining columns shown in *Figure 11.4* include `thrdscan` and `csrss`, which provide additional ways to identify process activity.

Every process contains **threads**, which represent individual sequences of instructions being executed by the CPU. Because of this, thread activity can sometimes reveal processes that have been partially hidden.

To identify processes that may not appear in standard listings, the following Volatility plugins analyze thread activity and related structures to reconstruct hidden or partially concealed processes:

- **thrdscan** – Attempts to identify processes by examining thread structures in memory and reconstructing which process those threads belong to
- **csrss** – Checks whether the Windows **Client Server Runtime Subsystem (CSRSS)** still maintains thread references associated with the process

These additional checks are useful because if malware attempts to hide by unlinking itself from the operating system's active process list, other supporting structures may still exist within memory.

One of the most suspicious patterns we can look for is:

`pslist` = **False** | `psscan` = **True** | `thrdscan` = **True** | `csrss` = **True**

This combination indicates that the process is not present in the active process list, but the process structure, thread activity, and CSRSS references still exist; suggesting the process may have been deliberately removed from the linked list while still running.

This type of manipulation is commonly referred to as **Direct Kernel Object Manipulation (DKOM)**, where malware modifies kernel structures to hide its presence from standard system enumeration techniques. In this case, there are no patterns consistent with DKOM present within our dataset.

If we still suspected a malicious process might exist, we could instead focus on entries where: `pslist` = **False** but `psscan` = **True**

This alone may suggest a process was removed from the active process list. However, this scenario is also very common and usually benign. In many cases it simply indicates that a process terminated normally but remnants of its process structure were still present in memory when the acquisition occurred.

6. Another memory artifact worth reviewing is **kernel modules** loaded into memory.

> **Note**
>
> Modules are executable code designed to extend operating system functionality. These usually consist of device drivers (`.sys files`), but you will also see the kernel itself and some supporting components such as `.exe` and `.dll` files.

Malicious kernel modules can be used to maintain persistence, intercept system activity, or hide processes and files. Malware often targets drivers because they run in **kernel mode**, which provides highly privileged access to the system and allows attackers to manipulate operating system behavior at a very low level.

Run the following command:

```
vol.exe -f C:\MEMORY\Source\Windows_RAM.mem windows.modules
```

The `modules` plugin enumerates kernel modules that were loaded in memory at the time of acquisition. Reviewing this list can help identify unfamiliar drivers or modules that may warrant further investigation:

```
        Name |                                           Path | File output
ntoskrnl.exe |               \SystemRoot\system32\ntoskrnl.exe |    Disabled
     hal.dll |                    \SystemRoot\system32\hal.dll |    Disabled
   kdcom.dll |                     \SystemRoot\system32\kd.dll |    Disabled
mcupdate.dll | \SystemRoot\system32\mcupdate_GenuineIntel.dll |    Disabled
    CLFS.SYS |             \SystemRoot\System32\drivers\CLFS.SYS |    Disabled
      tm.sys |               \SystemRoot\System32\drivers\tm.sys |    Disabled
   PSHED.dll |                  \SystemRoot\system32\PSHED.dll |    Disabled
```

Figure 11.5 – Volatility modules plugin output

When reviewing kernel modules, pay close attention to module names, load order, and file paths. Malicious drivers are sometimes loaded later in the system's runtime to attach themselves to an already running system.

Look for drivers loaded from unusual locations, such as user-writable directories or temporary folders. Legitimate drivers are typically loaded from trusted locations such as: `C:\Windows\System32\drivers\`

You can also look for modules that exist in memory but do not exist on disk, which may indicate deleted driver artifacts or rootkits attempting to hide their presence.

If you encounter a suspicious module that warrants further investigation, the modules can be extracted from memory by adding the `--dump` parameter to the command. For example:

```
vol.exe -f <memory image location> windows.modules --dump
```

This will save the extracted modules to the current working directory where Volatility is being executed. Any suspicious files can then be hashed and the resulting hash value submitted to services such as VirusTotal (as discussed in the *Malware recipe* in *Chapter 2*), or the file can be provided to a reverse engineer for deeper analysis if necessary.

After exporting the modules, you will notice that the `modules` plugin will show **File output** = **Enabled** if you run it again, which helps identify which modules were successfully exported.

7. While the `modules` plugin lists drivers that Windows currently recognizes as loaded, we can also run the `modscan` plugin as an additional check:

```
vol.exe -f <memory image location> windows.modscan
```

This plugin searches memory directly for driver objects, regardless of whether Windows still lists them as active.

Because of this, `modscan` can identify the following:

- unloaded drivers that still remain in memory
- drivers that have been unlinked from the operating system's module list
- remnants of previously loaded drivers

This makes `modscan` conceptually similar to `psscan` for processes. By comparing the results of `modules` and `modscan`, we may be able to identify drivers that were hidden, manipulated, or recently unloaded.

8. If we observe a PID that warrants a deeper dive, there are several ways we can focus our analysis by specifying the PID identifier when running certain plugins using the `--pid` parameter, where #### represents the PID identifier.
First, we can examine which parent processes launched it. When we ran the `pslist` plugin earlier, usage of Google Chrome appeared to be present, indicated by an `ImageFileName` of `chrome.exe`. This process has a **PID of 1956**.

Enter the following command:

```
vol.exe -f C:\MEMORY\Source\Windows_RAM.mem windows.pstree --pid 1956
```

The `pstree` plugin displays a hierarchical view of processes, showing the parent-child relationships between processes. While this plugin can produce a very large output when listing all processes, it becomes much easier to interpret when limited to a specific PID.

The results show the process chain that launched `chrome.exe`:

```
       PID  PPID  ImageFileName              CreateTime                              ExitTime
*      8944  7968   winlogon.exe  2024-08-11 10:29:16 UTC                                 N/A
**    10000  8944   userinit.exe  2024-08-12 03:27:46 UTC  2024-08-12 03:28:03 UTC
***    8792 10000   explorer.exe  2024-08-12 03:27:46 UTC                                 N/A
****   1956  8792     chrome.exe  2024-08-12 03:36:11 UTC  2024-08-12 03:54:33 UTC
```

Figure 11.6 – Volatility pstree plugin output for PID 1956

In this case, nothing appears overtly suspicious, as chrome.exe followed a normal launch sequence:

```
winlogon.exe > userinit.exe > explorer.exe > chrome.exe
```

The `winlogon.exe` process begins the interactive user logon session. This process launches `userinit.exe`, which performs logon initialization tasks such as setting up the user environment. From there, `explorer.exe` is started to provide the Windows desktop environment, including File Explorer and the taskbar. User applications such as web browsers are typically launched from this environment.

Despite the process chain appearing normal, the **CreateTime** and **ExitTime** fields may still provide useful insight. From these timestamps, we can determine that `chrome.exe` was running for approximately **18 minutes** (between 03:36:11 and 03:54:33 UTC) on **August 12, 2024**.

This information can serve as another point of cross-verification if Chrome usage becomes relevant during the investigation, allowing us to correlate browser activity with other artifacts, such as web history, network connections, or file access timestamps.

9. We can also determine the security context under which a process was executed. This can help reveal whether a process was running under a standard user account, a privileged administrative account, or a system-level service account. We will continue examining our `chrome.exe` process for this purpose.

Enter the following command:

```
vol.exe -f C:\MEMORY\Source\Windows_RAM.mem windows.getsids --pid 1956
```

The `getsids` plugin extracts the Windows **Security Identifiers (SIDs)** contained within a process access token. This should look familiar from Chapter 4. Because Windows authorization is **group-based**, a process token typically contains multiple SIDs rather than just the user account that launched the process.

By examining these SIDs, we can determine both who launched the process and what privileges the process inherited:

Process	SID	Name
chrome.exe	S-1-5-21-3063303759-3547812523-4161226937-1001	-
chrome.exe	S-1-5-21-3063303759-3547812523-4161226937-513	Domain Users
chrome.exe	S-1-1-0	Everyone
chrome.exe	S-1-5-114	Local Account (Member of Admin)
chrome.exe	S-1-5-32-544	Administrators
chrome.exe	S-1-5-32-545	Users
chrome.exe	S-1-5-4	Interactive
chrome.exe	S-1-2-1	Console Logon
chrome.exe	S-1-5-11	Authenticated Users
chrome.exe	S-1-5-15	This Organization
chrome.exe	S-1-5-113	Local Account
chrome.exe	S-1-5-5-0-17681386	Logon Session
chrome.exe	S-1-2-0	Local
chrome.exe	S-1-5-64-10	NTLM Authentication
chrome.exe	S-1-16-8192	Medium Mandatory Level

Figure 11.7 – Volatility getsids plugin output for PID 1956

The first line in *Figure 11.7* shows the user SID associated with the `chrome.exe` process (ending in **RID 1001**), which corresponds to a normal user account. If we compared this SID to the data from our Microsoft Windows dataset from which this RAM image was acquired, we would see that it corresponds to the user account `Leroy Jenkins`.

Moving further down the list, we can see additional SIDs representing the security groups associated with that account. For example, the account is part of the **Domain Users** group and also appears in the **Administrators** group, indicating that the user has local administrative privileges.

The remaining SIDs represent common Windows authorization groups such as **Everyone**, **Authenticated Users**, and **Interactive**, which are normally present for interactive logon sessions.

The last SID shown (ending in **8192**) represents the Mandatory Integrity Level of the process. In this case, it is listed as **Medium Mandatory Level**, meaning `chrome.exe` was running under normal user privileges rather than elevated administrator or system-level privileges.

Together, these SIDs indicate that `chrome.exe` was launched by a normal interactive user session belonging to the `Leroy Jenkins` account and was running with standard user integrity levels. Nothing in this output appears suspicious.

10. If we want to explore potential user activity around this information using memory artifacts directly, we can examine the Windows logon sessions associated with running processes.
Enter the following command:

```
vol.exe -f C:\MEMORY\Source\Windows_RAM.mem windows.sessions
```

The `sessions` plugin groups processes by their associated Windows logon session and displays information about processes that belong to each session. Because these processes are listed alongside their creation timestamps, the output can also provide a useful timeline-style view of user activity within that session:

Process ID	Process	User Name	Create Time
5672	SystemSettings	-	2024-08-12 03:35:14 UTC
11696	UserOOBEBroker	DESKTOP-L83UL43/Leroy Jenkins	2024-08-12 03:35:15 UTC
1956	chrome.exe	-	2024-08-12 03:36:11 UTC
9192	ShellExperienc	DESKTOP-L83UL43/Leroy Jenkins	2024-08-12 03:36:39 UTC
5224	RuntimeBroker.	DESKTOP-L83UL43/Leroy Jenkins	2024-08-12 03:36:39 UTC
6308	SearchApp.exe	-	2024-08-12 03:39:09 UTC

Figure 11.8 – Volatility sessions plugin output for PID 1956

As shown in *Figure 11.8*, we can locate the **PID of 1956**, which corresponds to the `chrome.exe` process we examined earlier. The surrounding processes in this session appear to be associated with the `Leroy Jenkins` user account, indicating that the browser activity occurred within that user's interactive logon session.

Reviewing nearby process creation times can help investigators understand what activity was occurring around the same time as a process of interest. In this case, we can see that other processes tied to the `Leroy Jenkins` session were launched shortly before and after `chrome.exe`, further supporting the conclusion that this browser activity occurred during a normal interactive user session.

While the information we can gain about `chrome.exe` can be interesting and useful, everything we have observed so far suggests that it is a normal, non-malicious process. Because of this, there is little reason to investigate it further.

For demonstration purposes, however, let's assume that the `MsMpEng.exe` process (**PID 5296**) has caught our attention from within the available data. This process is normally associated with Microsoft Defender, but we want to verify that it has not been tampered with or abused by an attacker.

11. One useful artifact to examine is the **command-line arguments** used to launch a process. Many programs are started with additional parameters that control their behavior. These parameters may specify files to open, scripts to execute, network connections to establish, or other system actions. Because of this, examining command-line arguments can often provide valuable insight into what a process was actually doing when it started.
    Run the following command:

    ```
    vol.exe -f C:\MEMORY\Source\Windows_RAM.mem windows.cmdline --pid 5296
    ```

    The `cmdline` plugin extracts the command line used to launch a process. This allows us to see exactly how the process was started and whether any unusual arguments were supplied:

    ```
    PID     Process                                                                 Args
    5296  MsMpEng.exe "C:\ProgramData\Microsoft\Windows Defender\Platform\4.18.24070.5-0\MsMpEng.exe"
    ```

    Figure 11.9 – Volatility cmdline plugin output for PID 5296

    In this case, the command line shows that the process was launched from the Microsoft Defender platform directory, which is the expected location for Defender's scanning engine, as shown in *Figure 11.9*. There are also no additional command-line parameters present. This indicates that the process appears to have started normally and does not show signs of manipulation.

    If we had instead observed unusual parameters or an unexpected file path, this could indicate malicious activity. For example, a command such as:

    ```
    "powershell.exe -nop -w hidden -enc SQBFAFgA...AACwAxACcAKQA="
    ```

    would be highly suspicious. This command launches PowerShell in hidden mode, disables the PowerShell profile, and executes a Base64-encoded command payload. Attackers frequently use this technique to hide malicious scripts from simple detection methods.

    Command-line artifacts are often one of the fastest ways to identify attacker behavior in memory because they reveal exactly how a program was executed.

12. A **Dynamic Link Library (DLL)** is a file that contains code a program can use while it is running. Instead of every application containing all of its own functionality, most

programs rely on DLL files that provide common features, such as networking, graphics, cryptography, or system access. When a program starts, Windows loads the DLLs it needs into memory so the application can use those shared functions. **DLL sideloading** occurs when a malicious DLL is placed somewhere Windows will load it instead of the legitimate one. Windows searches for required DLL files in a specific order, and one of the first places it checks is the same directory as the program being launched. If an attacker places a malicious DLL there with the same name as the expected file, Windows may load the attacker's version first. When the program runs, the malicious code inside the DLL executes under the trust of the legitimate application.

To determine whether this process has loaded any unexpected or potentially malicious DLLs, we can examine its loaded modules in memory using Volatility.

Run the following command:

```
vol.exe -f C:\MEMORY\Source\Windows_RAM.mem windows.dlllist --pid 5296
```

The `dlllist` plugin allows us to view the DLL files that were loaded into a process at the time memory was captured. This can help reveal what capabilities a program was using and whether any unusual or malicious libraries were present. By adding the `--pid` parameter, we limit the output to only the DLLs associated with our `MsMpEng.exe` process:

PID	Process	Name	Path	LoadCount	LoadTime
5296	MsMpEng.exe	ntdll.dll	C:\WINDOWS\SYSTEM32\ntdll.dll	-1	2024-08-11 08:47:42 UTC
5296	MsMpEng.exe	KERNEL32.DLL	C:\WINDOWS\SYSTEM32\KERNEL32.DLL	-1	2024-08-11 08:47:42 UTC
5296	MsMpEng.exe	KERNELBASE.dll	C:\WINDOWS\SYSTEM32\KERNELBASE.dll	-1	2024-08-11 08:47:42 UTC
5296	MsMpEng.exe	ucrtbase.dll	C:\WINDOWS\SYSTEM32\ucrtbase.dll	6	2024-08-11 08:47:42 UTC
5296	MsMpEng.exe	ADVAPI32.dll	C:\WINDOWS\SYSTEM32\ADVAPI32.dll	6	2024-08-11 08:47:42 UTC
5296	MsMpEng.exe	CRYPT32.dll	C:\WINDOWS\SYSTEM32\CRYPT32.dll	6	2024-08-11 08:47:42 UTC
5296	MsMpEng.exe	WINTRUST.dll	C:\WINDOWS\SYSTEM32\WINTRUST.dll	6	2024-08-11 08:47:42 UTC
5296	MsMpEng.exe	msvcrt.dll	C:\WINDOWS\SYSTEM32\msvcrt.dll	6	2024-08-11 08:47:42 UTC
5296	MsMpEng.exe	sechost.dll	C:\WINDOWS\SYSTEM32\sechost.dll	6	2024-08-11 08:47:42 UTC
5296	MsMpEng.exe	RPCRT4.dll	C:\WINDOWS\SYSTEM32\RPCRT4.dll	6	2024-08-11 08:47:42 UTC
5296	MsMpEng.exe	bcrypt.dll	C:\WINDOWS\SYSTEM32\bcrypt.dll	6	2024-08-11 08:47:42 UTC
5296	MsMpEng.exe	MSASN1.dll	C:\WINDOWS\SYSTEM32\MSASN1.dll	6	2024-08-11 08:47:42 UTC
5296	MsMpEng.exe	version.dll	C:\WINDOWS\system32\version.dll	6	2024-08-11 08:47:42 UTC

Figure 11.10 – Volatility dlllist plugin output for PID 5296

From *Figure 11.10*, we can see several useful columns:

- **Path** – Shows the location on disk from which the DLL was loaded
- **LoadTime** – Indicates when the library was loaded into the process
- **LoadCount** – Shows how many times the process referenced that library (**-1** indicates the library is managed internally by the Windows loader)

When reviewing DLLs, focus primarily on where the library was loaded from. Legitimate applications typically load DLLs from trusted system directories such as `C:\Windows\`, `C:\Windows\System32\`, or `C:\Program Files\`.

If a DLL is loaded from a user-writable location (like `C:\Users\`, `C:\ProgramData\`, or `C:\Temp\`), this can be suspicious and may indicate **DLL sideloading** or **library hijacking**, where a malicious DLL is loaded in place of a legitimate dependency.

In this case, all of the DLLs shown for `MsMpEng.exe` were loaded from expected Windows system directories. Nothing in this output suggests that the process has been tampered with.

13. Similar to how we examined kernel modules earlier using the `modules` and `modscan` plugins, we can also examine the libraries loaded within a specific process to determine whether any modules may have been hidden from normal inspection. Windows maintains several internal linked lists that track which libraries are loaded into a process and how they were initialized. When a DLL is loaded normally through the Windows loader, it should appear consistently across these loader lists.
Run the following command:

```
vol.exe -f C:\MEMORY\Source\Windows_RAM.mem windows.malware.ldrmodules --
pid 5296
```

The `ldrmodules` plugin compares several loader lists maintained by Windows and reports whether each module appears where it should:

Pid	Process	InLoad	InInit	InMem	MappedPath
5296	MsMpEng.exe	False	False	False	\Windows\System32\en-US\wscapi.dll.mui
5296	MsMpEng.exe	True	True	True	\Windows\System32\mpr.dll
5296	MsMpEng.exe	True	True	True	\Windows\System32\wscapi.dll
5296	MsMpEng.exe	True	True	True	\Windows\System32\fwpolicyiomgr.dll
5296	MsMpEng.exe	True	True	True	\Windows\System32\secur32.dll
5296	MsMpEng.exe	True	True	True	\Windows\System32\FWPUCLNT.DLL
5296	MsMpEng.exe	True	True	True	\Windows\System32\rasadhlp.dll
5296	MsMpEng.exe	True	True	True	\Windows\System32\cabinet.dll
5296	MsMpEng.exe	True	True	True	\Windows\System32\srvcli.dll
5296	MsMpEng.exe	True	True	True	\Windows\System32\dhcpcsvc6.dll
5296	MsMpEng.exe	True	True	True	\Windows\System32\iertutil.dll
5296	MsMpEng.exe	True	True	True	\Windows\System32\wbemcomn.dll
5296	MsMpEng.exe	True	True	True	\Windows\System32\winhttp.dll

Figure 11.11 – Volatility ldrmodules plugin output for PID 5296

The output includes several columns that indicate whether a module appears in different loader structures maintained by Windows:

- **InLoad** – Shows whether the module appears in the **load order list**, which tracks the order in which modules were loaded into the process.

- **InInit** – Shows whether the module appears in the **initialization order list**, which tracks modules that were successfully initialized.
- **InMem** – Shows whether the module appears in the **memory order list**, which tracks modules currently mapped into process memory space.

For a normally loaded **DLL**, these values will usually all appear as **True**, indicating that the library was loaded through the standard Windows loader process.

Pay attention to entries where one or more of these values are **False**. For example, a module that appears in memory but does not appear in the loader lists may indicate that the library was manually injected or deliberately unlinked. Malware and rootkits sometimes manipulate these structures to conceal malicious libraries.

One particularly suspicious pattern would look like the following:

`InMem` = **True** | `InLoad` = **False** | `InInit` = **False**

When a module appears in memory (`InMem` = **True**) but does not appear in the loader lists (`InLoad` / `InInit` = **False**), this can indicate that the DLL was injected into the process without using the normal Windows loader. This pattern is uncommon for legitimate software and should be investigated carefully, especially if the module path or file name also appears unusual.

As with previous plugins, also pay attention to unusual file paths or library names, particularly if they appear in user-writable directories such as `C:\Users`, `C:\ProgramData`, or temporary directories.

In this case, the DLL entries for the `MsMpEng.exe` process appear consistently across the loader lists and originate from expected Windows system directories, suggesting the process has not been tampered with.

> **Tip**
>
> You may notice that some entries, such as `.mui resource` **files**, may show False values in these columns. This is normal because resource files are mapped differently than executable libraries and are not always tracked by the loader lists in the same way as DLLs. When using this plugin, focus primarily on **DLL entries** when evaluating potential injection or hiding techniques.

14. Processes interact with many system resources while they run, such as files, registry keys, network sockets, and other operating system objects. Windows manages access

to these resources through structures called **handles**, which act as references that allow a process to interact with objects managed by the operating system.

Run the following command:

```
vol.exe -f C:\MEMORY\Source\Windows_RAM.mem windows.handles --pid 5296
```

The `handles` plugin allows us to view the resources a process was actively interacting with at the time memory was captured. This can help reveal what a program was doing during execution:

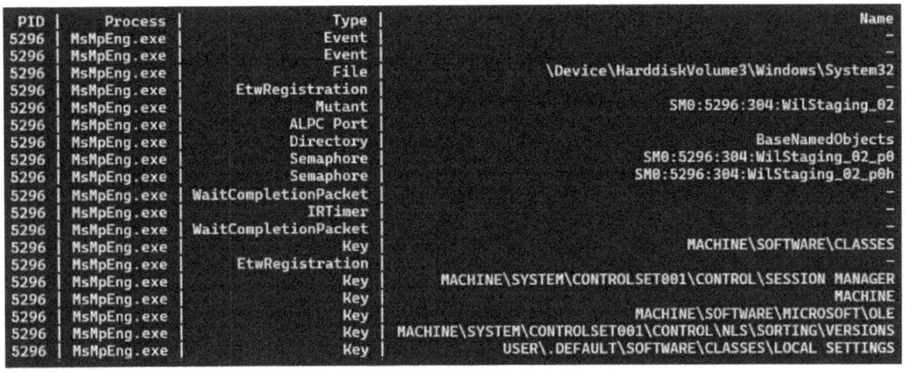

PID	Process	Type	Name
5296	MsMpEng.exe	Event	-
5296	MsMpEng.exe	Event	-
5296	MsMpEng.exe	File	\Device\HarddiskVolume3\Windows\System32
5296	MsMpEng.exe	EtwRegistration	-
5296	MsMpEng.exe	Mutant	SM0:5296:304:WilStaging_02
5296	MsMpEng.exe	ALPC Port	-
5296	MsMpEng.exe	Directory	BaseNamedObjects
5296	MsMpEng.exe	Semaphore	SM0:5296:304:WilStaging_02_p0
5296	MsMpEng.exe	Semaphore	SM0:5296:304:WilStaging_02_p0h
5296	MsMpEng.exe	WaitCompletionPacket	-
5296	MsMpEng.exe	IRTimer	-
5296	MsMpEng.exe	WaitCompletionPacket	-
5296	MsMpEng.exe	Key	MACHINE\SOFTWARE\CLASSES
5296	MsMpEng.exe	EtwRegistration	-
5296	MsMpEng.exe	Key	MACHINE\SYSTEM\CONTROLSET001\CONTROL\SESSION MANAGER
5296	MsMpEng.exe	Key	MACHINE
5296	MsMpEng.exe	Key	MACHINE\SOFTWARE\MICROSOFT\OLE
5296	MsMpEng.exe	Key	MACHINE\SYSTEM\CONTROLSET001\CONTROL\NLS\SORTING\VERSIONS
5296	MsMpEng.exe	Key	USER\.DEFAULT\SOFTWARE\CLASSES\LOCAL SETTINGS

Figure 11.12 – Volatility handles plugin output for PID 5296

The output from the `handles` plugin is particularly useful because it reveals live relationships between processes and system resources that may not be visible through disk analysis alone. By examining the objects a process was actively accessing, we can gain valuable insight into how the process was interacting with the system.

The output lists each handle along with information describing the object it references. Two of the most useful columns include:

- **Type** – The type of object the handle references, such as *File*, *Key* (registry key), *Process*, *Thread*, *Mutant* (mutex), and others.
- **Name** – The path or identifier of the handle resource (when available).

By reviewing this information, we can see what files, registry keys, or other system objects the process was interacting with. Look for file handles pointing to suspicious locations (especially user-writable areas or temporary directories) or references to unusual registry keys.

Handles can also reveal **mutex objects**, which are sometimes used by malware to ensure that only one copy of the malware runs on a system at a time. Because many malware families use distinctive mutex names, these identifiers can sometimes be searched online to quickly determine whether they are associated with known malicious software.

Reviewing the handles for our `MsMpEng.exe` process does not immediately reveal anything of particular concern.

15. Every process running on a Windows system uses portions of memory to store code, data, and other information it needs while executing. Windows organizes these memory regions using structures called **Virtual Address Descriptors (VADs)**. Each VAD describes a region of virtual memory assigned to a process, including the memory range, permissions applied to that region, and any file or resource associated with it. Run the following command:

```
vol.exe -f C:\MEMORY\Source\Windows_RAM.mem windows.vadinfo --pid 5296
```

The `vadinfo` plugin allows us to examine how a process is using memory and may help identify suspicious memory regions that could contain injected code or malicious payloads:

Protection	CommitCharge	PrivateMemory	File
PAGE_READWRITE	16	1	N/A
PAGE_READONLY	0	0	\Windows\System32\en-US\wscapi.dll.mui
PAGE_READONLY	0	0	N/A
PAGE_NOACCESS	1	1	N/A
PAGE_READONLY	0	0	\Windows\Registration\R000000000001.clb
PAGE_READWRITE	16	1	N/A
PAGE_EXECUTE_READWRITE	269	1	N/A
PAGE_READWRITE	440	1	N/A
PAGE_EXECUTE_READWRITE	269	1	N/A
PAGE_EXECUTE_READWRITE	269	1	N/A
PAGE_READWRITE	16	1	N/A
PAGE_READWRITE	440	1	N/A
PAGE_EXECUTE_READWRITE	269	1	N/A
PAGE_READWRITE	440	1	N/A
PAGE_EXECUTE_READWRITE	269	1	N/A
PAGE_READONLY	0	0	\Windows\System32\en-US\KernelBase.dll.mui
PAGE_READWRITE	16	1	N/A

Figure 11.13 – Volatility vadinfo plugin output for PID 5296

The output provides information about each memory region assigned to the process. Some of the most important fields include the following:

- **Protection** – The permissions applied to the memory region (such as read, write, or execute)
- **File** – When applicable, the file path mapped into that memory region
- **PrivateMemory** – Indicates whether the memory region is private to the process (not shared with other processes)

Most memory regions correspond to normal program components, such as executable files or DLL libraries loaded by the process. We should focus on regions that show unusual permissions or lack an associated file path.

For example, regions marked with permissions that allow both writing and execution (such as PAGE_EXECUTE_READWRITE) may indicate that code was written directly into memory and then executed. Attackers sometimes rely on these types of memory regions during techniques such as process injection, shellcode execution, or in-memory malware activity. Likewise, a VAD entry that contains executable permissions but does not reference a file on disk may warrant further investigation.

Looking at the output for our MsMpEng.exe process, we can see several PAGE_EXECUTE_READWRITE entries that do not reference a file on disk. This combination could indicate injected code or unpacked malware. However, everything else we have examined so far indicates that this process is a legitimate instance of Windows Defender.

This is often because security software such as Windows Defender performs complex memory operations while scanning files and analyzing potentially malicious behavior. These tools may dynamically allocate memory and emulate suspicious activity to analyze threats, which can produce memory regions that appear suspicious when viewed in isolation.

Also pay particular attention to executable memory regions that are both private (PrivateMemory = **1**) and lack an associated file path. While we see many of these in the vadinfo output for Windows Defender, this is not common for most software applications – but it is very common in malware.

Still, there is one more thing we can check, just to be sure.

16. To more explicitly look for indicators of code injection within our MsMpEng.exe process, run the following command:

```
vol.exe -f C:\MEMORY\Source\Windows_RAM.mem windows.malware.malfind --pid 5296
```

The malfind plugin searches for memory regions that appear suspicious based on their permissions and structure. These regions are often associated with injected code or unpacked malware. The plugin displays the first portion of the raw memory content from those regions, shown as a Hexdump, which shows the raw byte values stored in memory. These bytes represent the actual machine code that would be executed by the CPU:

```
56 57 53 55 41 54 41 55 41 56 41 57 48 83 ec 28 VWSUATAUAVAWH..(
4c 8d 3c 24 48 8b e9 48 8d b1 98 38 00 00 ff e2 L.<$H..H...8....
49 8d 67 28 41 5f 41 5e 41 5d 41 5c 5d 5b 5f 5e I.g(A_A^A]A\][_^
c3 00 00 40 00 80 00 00 00 48 89 e9 48 b8 60 52 ...@.....H..H.`R
```

Figure 11.14 – Volatility malfind plugin Hexdump output for PID 5296

Another useful indicator when reviewing `Hexdump` output is the presence of a recognizable file header within the hexdump output. For example, injected DLLs or unpacked payloads may still contain the **"MZ"** header (**0x4D5A**), which indicates the beginning of a Windows executable file. If this header appears in memory regions that are not associated with a file on disk, it can strongly suggest that a Portable Executable (PE) file was injected directly into memory.

In *Figure 11.14*, no obvious PE header (such as "MZ") is visible in the displayed memory region, which is consistent with normal process memory.

Following the `Hexdump` data is the `Disasm` column. This column translates those raw hexdump bytes into assembly instructions, which are a human-readable representation of the machine code executed by the processor. Assembly instructions such as **PUSH**, **POP**, **MOV**, **CALL**, and **JMP** are common operations used by programs to move data, manage the stack, and control execution flow:

```
0x229006b0000:  push    rsi
0x229006b0001:  push    rdi
0x229006b0002:  push    rbx
0x229006b0003:  push    rbp
0x229006b0004:  push    r12
0x229006b0006:  push    r13
0x229006b0008:  push    r14
0x229006b000a:  push    r15
0x229006b000c:  sub     rsp, 0x28
0x229006b0010:  lea     r15, [rsp]
0x229006b0014:  mov     rbp, rcx
0x229006b0017:  lea     rsi, [rcx + 0x3898]
0x229006b001e:  jmp     rdx
0x229006b0020:  lea     rsp, [r15 + 0x28]
0x229006b0024:  pop     r15
0x229006b0026:  pop     r14
0x229006b0028:  pop     r13
0x229006b002a:  pop     r12
0x229006b002c:  pop     rbp
0x229006b002d:  pop     rbx
0x229006b002e:  pop     rdi
0x229006b002f:  pop     rsi
0x229006b0030:  ret
0x229006b0031:  add     byte ptr [rax], al
0x229006b0033:  add     byte ptr [rax + 0x48000000], al
0x229006b003a:  mov     ecx, ebp
```

Figure 11.15 – Volatility malfind plugin Disasm output for PID 5296

When examining this output, investigators typically look for patterns that indicate shellcode or injected payloads, such as unusual instruction sequences, repeated jump or call instructions, or embedded memory addresses.

In this case, the instructions appear to represent normal program logic rather than an obviously malicious payload.

If the code had been injected by malware, we might expect to see behavior such as constructing a memory address and copying it into a register, for example:

```
MOV RAX, 0x64616f4c79617262
```

This type of instruction can sometimes appear when shellcode builds addresses or function pointers dynamically before transferring execution to them.

Also note that each `PAGE_EXECUTE_READWRITE` section can be mapped back to the information from the `vadinfo` plugin output by cross-referencing the **Start VPN** and **End VPN** columns, which identify the virtual memory range assigned to the process. In *Figure 11.16*, the `vadinfo` output is highlighted in white and compared to the corresponding entry from `malfind`:

Figure 11.16 – Correlating vadinfo and malfind entries in Volatility

Correlating this information can be useful when a suspicious region is identified in `vadinfo` and we want to examine the associated memory contents more closely using `malfind`.

After reviewing the `PAGE_EXECUTE_READWRITE` memory regions identified by `malfind`, we can reasonably conclude that these entries are **false positives**. The suspicious indicators we observed earlier in the `vadinfo` output are most likely the result of legitimate memory operations performed by Windows Defender.

At this point, we can feel confident that `MsMpEng.exe` is behaving as expected and does not appear to be malicious.

> **Note**
>
> While we used the `malfind` plugin here to examine a specific process by using the --pid parameter, it can also be used to scan **all processes** in a memory image for injected code. Many investigators will run `malfind` early in their workflow to quickly identify potentially compromised processes before performing deeper analysis.

17. Another sometimes underutilized method of identifying potential malware within a memory image involves extracting file artifacts directly from memory and scanning them with anti-virus software or YARA rules.
    Run the following command:

```
vol.exe -f C:\MEMORY\Source\Windows_RAM.mem windows.filescan
```

Because memory does not contain a complete file system structure like a disk image, the `filescan` plugin searches memory directly for Windows `_FILE_OBJECT` structures rather than traversing a file system. These structures represent files that were referenced by the operating system at some point while the system was running.

Output produced by this plugin includes the **Offset** value identifying the location in memory, along with a **Name** field that shows the filename and the path where the file existed on disk:

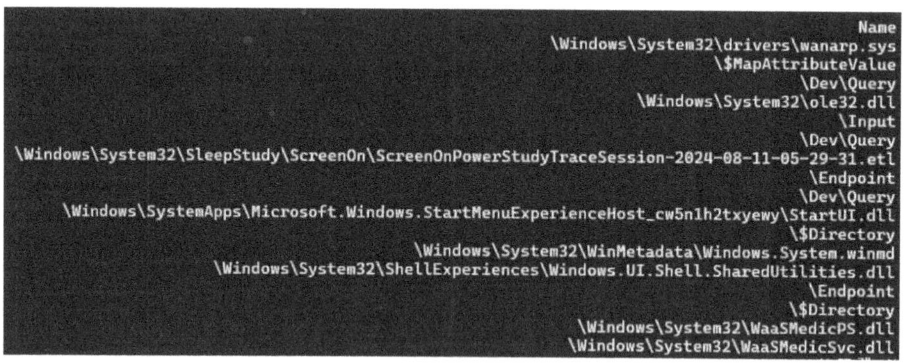

Figure 11.17 – Volatility filescan plugin output

A file listed here represents anything that was present in memory and does not necessarily mean the file was still open or actively loaded at the time of acquisition.

Closing a file does not immediately remove it from memory; the data may remain until that portion of memory is overwritten by something else.

Because of this, `filescan` can sometimes reveal files that were deleted from disk but whose metadata structures still remain in memory. Viewing this output can therefore provide a quick overview of files that existed on the system around the time the memory image was captured.

18. We can also attempt to extract the actual file contents.
    Run the following command:

```
vol.exe -f C:\MEMORY\Source\Windows_RAM.mem windows.dumpfiles
```

The `dumpfiles` plugin attempts to recover the data associated with `_FILE_OBJECT` structures and write those artifacts to disk. This process may take several minutes depending on the size of the memory image.

Once finished, any files successfully recovered will be written to the current working directory where Volatility is being executed:

Name	Type	Size
file.0xb80d4ea54990.0xb80d4ea25cd0.DataSectionObject.data_3.dat	DAT File	8 KB
file.0xb80d4ea56100.0xb80d4d73e010.SharedCacheMap.Web Data-journal.vacb	VACB File	256 KB
file.0xb80d4ea56100.0xb80d4ea1f010.DataSectionObject.Web Data-journal.dat	DAT File	8 KB
file.0xb80d4ea64520.0xb80d4ea2b810.DataSectionObject.QuotaManager.dat	DAT File	40 KB
file.0xb80d4ea64520.0xb80d4f7a96a0.SharedCacheMap.QuotaManager.vacb	VACB File	256 KB
file.0xb80d51c96470.0xb80d514d2b60.SharedCacheMap.Top Sites.vacb	VACB File	256 KB

Figure 11.18 – Files extracted from memory using dumpfiles plugin in Volatility

You may notice files with extensions such as `.vacb` among the extracted artifacts. These represent **Virtual Address Control Block (VACB)** structures used by the Windows Cache Manager to track cached file data in memory. These entries reflect cached portions of files rather than complete file contents and are normal artifacts during memory analysis.

It is also important to understand that not every potential file identified by `filescan` can be successfully extracted. The plugin may identify file references even if the file itself has already been closed, deleted, or partially overwritten in memory. In these cases, the `dumpfiles` plugin may not be able to recover usable file content.

Once files have been extracted, we can place the artifacts into a directory and run YARA rules or antivirus scanners against the recovered content to perform a quick triage scan for known malware indicators.

Keep in mind that this method should only be used as a triage technique and not as a replacement for the investigative analysis methods covered in this chapter. Antivirus engines rely heavily on known signatures and complete file structures, while many memory-based attacks use shellcode, partially unpacked payloads, or fragmented code that may not match known signatures.

> **Note**
>
> Lab leak
>
> When dealing with evidence of potential malware and exporting related files to your workstation, you should always remain mindful of the risks involved. Extracting files from memory is usually relatively safe, as the complete executable structure required to launch a program is often incomplete. However, recovered artifacts may still contain malicious scripts, macros, or fragments of executable code.
>
> Never attempt to manually execute files recovered from memory on your workstation. All extracted artifacts should be handled within an isolated analysis environment, and any attempts to run suspicious files should be performed in a properly controlled sandbox environment.

As a final note on this, if we wanted to take a more targeted approach, we could use the `filescan` plugin to locate a specific file of interest and then extract only that file rather than attempting to recover everything from memory.

To do this, note the virtual address shown in the **Offset** (virtual address) column of the `filescan` output and structure the command as follows:

```
vol.exe -f <memory image> windows.dumpfiles --virtaddr <offset>
```

For example, if `filescan` shows the following file:

`\Windows\System32\ole32.dll located at offset 0xb80d4b2cf2e0`

We could extract just that file using:

```
vol.exe -f C:\MEMORY\Source\Windows_RAM.mem windows.dumpfiles --virtaddr
0xb80d4b2cf2e0
```

This same concept can also be applied to a specific process. For example, if we wanted to extract file artifacts associated with the `MsMpEng.exe` process we examined earlier, we could run:

```
vol.exe -f C:\MEMORY\Source\Windows_RAM.mem windows.dumpfiles --pid 5296
```

This command attempts to recover files associated with that specific process.

Finally, if we wanted to extract only the memory regions previously identified as suspicious by the `malfind` plugin, we could run the following:

```
vol.exe -f C:\MEMORY\Source\Windows_RAM.mem windows.malware.malfind --pid
5296 --dump
```

This will export the contents of the suspicious memory regions directly to disk, allowing the data to be examined further or provided to a reverse engineer for deeper analysis of the assembly code.

19. After examining process activity and loaded modules, we may also be interested in determining how a program was launched in the first place. One common method attackers use to maintain access to a system is by creating or modifying a Windows service.

> Note
>
> **Services** are background programs managed by the **Windows Service Control Manager (SCM)** that can start automatically when the system boots and often run with elevated privileges.

Run the following command:

```
vol.exe -f C:\MEMORY\Source\Windows_RAM.mem windows.svcscan
```

The `svcscan` plugin scans memory for Windows service structures maintained by the OS and displays information about services that existed on the system at the time memory was captured. This allows investigators to determine whether a suspicious process is associated with a registered service.

Start	State	Type	Name	Display
SERVICE_AUTO_START	SERVICE_RUNNING	SERVICE_WIN32_OWN_PROCESS	MBAMService	Malwarebytes Service
SERVICE_BOOT_START	SERVICE_STOPPED	SERVICE_KERNEL_DRIVER	MbamElam	MbamElam
SERVICE_AUTO_START	SERVICE_RUNNING	SERVICE_FILE_SYSTEM_DRIVER	mbamchameleon	mbamchameleon
SERVICE_DEMAND_START	SERVICE_STOPPED	SERVICE_KERNEL_DRIVER	mausbip	MA-USB IP Filter Driver
SERVICE_DEMAND_START	SERVICE_STOPPED	SERVICE_KERNEL_DRIVER	mausbhost	MA-USB Host Controller Driver
SERVICE_AUTO_START	SERVICE_STOPPED	SERVICE_WIN32_OWN_PROCESS	MapsBroker	Downloaded Maps Manager
SERVICE_DEMAND_START	SERVICE_STOPPED	SERVICE_WIN32_SHARE_PROCESS	LxpSvc	Language Experience Service
SERVICE_AUTO_START	SERVICE_RUNNING	SERVICE_FILE_SYSTEM_DRIVER	luafv	UAC File Virtualization
SERVICE_DEMAND_START	SERVICE_STOPPED	SERVICE_KERNEL_DRIVER	LSI_SSS	LSI_SSS
SERVICE_DEMAND_START	SERVICE_STOPPED	SERVICE_KERNEL_DRIVER	LSI_SAS3i	LSI_SAS3i
SERVICE_DEMAND_START	SERVICE_STOPPED	SERVICE_KERNEL_DRIVER	LSI_SAS2i	LSI_SAS2i
SERVICE_DEMAND_START	SERVICE_STOPPED	SERVICE_KERNEL_DRIVER	LSI_SAS	LSI_SAS
SERVICE_DEMAND_START	SERVICE_STOPPED	SERVICE_WIN32_OWN_PROCESS	LSCWinService	LSCWinService
SERVICE_AUTO_START	SERVICE_STOPPED	SERVICE_WIN32_OWN_PROCESS	LPlatSvc	Lenovo Platform Service

Figure 11.19 – Volatility svcscan plugin output

Reviewing this output can help identify services that launch executables from unusual locations, use misleading names, or are responsible for starting suspicious processes discovered earlier in the investigation.

Some of the most important columns within the `svcscan` output and what you should look for include the following:

- **Name** – This is the internal name Windows uses to identify the service. Attackers sometimes create services with names that closely resemble legitimate services in order to avoid suspicion.
- **Display** – This is the friendly name shown in the Windows Services management console. Because this value is intended for human readability, attackers may use names that sound legitimate to disguise malicious services.
- **State** – Indicates whether the service was running or stopped at the time the memory image was captured.
- **Type** – The service type indicates how the service runs and can help clarify why multiple services may appear to share the same process. Common values include:
  - **SERVICE_WIN32_OWN_PROCESS** – The service runs within its own dedicated process
  - **SERVICE_WIN32_SHARE_PROCESS** – The service runs inside a shared Windows service host process (typically `svchost.exe`)
  - **SERVICE_KERNEL_DRIVER** – The service represents a kernel-mode driver
- **Binary** (not shown in example) – The executable file and path used to launch the service. Legitimate services typically launch executables from trusted locations such as `C:\Windows\System32\` or `C:\Program Files\`. Pay close attention to

services that launch binaries from user-writable locations or temporary directories.

- **Start** – How the service is configured to start. Common values include:
  - **AUTO_START** – the service starts automatically when the system boots; attackers frequently use this configuration to maintain persistence across system restarts
  - **BOOT_START** – the service is loaded by the system loader during boot, before most user-mode services start
  - **DEMAND_START** – the service must be manually triggered
  - **DISABLED** – the service cannot start unless it is first re-enabled

When reviewing `svcscan` output, focus on the **service name**, **binary path**, **service type**, and **start configuration**. Particular attention should be given to services that automatically launch executables from unusual locations or that have names designed to mimic legitimate Windows components.

We should also attempt to correlate suspicious services with process activity discovered earlier in the investigation. If a suspicious process identified during process analysis is associated with a service, that service configuration may reveal how the malware achieved persistence.

20. Another valuable capability of Volatility is the ability to examine network activity that existed at the time the memory image was acquired. Memory can contain information about active or recently established network connections that may not be preserved elsewhere, especially if logging is limited or disabled.
Run the following command:

```
vol.exe -f C:\MEMORY\Source\Windows_RAM.mem windows.netscan
```

The `netscan` plugin identifies network connections that existed on the system when memory was captured by scanning memory for Windows network socket structures. These structures represent network endpoints used by applications to communicate over the network.

This information is particularly powerful because it allows us to link network activity directly to the processes responsible for it.

Using this plugin, we can identify active connections, listening ports, and recently closed connections, and then attribute those connections to a specific process using the associated PID:

Proto	LocalAddr	ForeignAddr	State	PID	Owner	Created
TCPv4	0.0.0.0	0.0.0.0	LISTENING	3224	spoolsv.exe	2024-08-11 08:35:55 UTC
UDPv4	192.168.0.73	*		4	System	2024-08-12 03:28:05 UTC
UDPv4	192.168.0.73	*		4	System	2024-08-12 03:28:05 UTC
TCPv6	::1	::	LISTENING	8444	GoogleDriveFS.	2024-08-12 03:29:48 UTC
TCPv4	192.168.0.73	23.220.206.9	ESTABLISHED	1084	msedgewebview2	2024-08-12 03:57:48 UTC
UDPv4	192.168.56.1	*		4	System	2024-08-11 08:35:38 UTC
UDPv4	192.168.56.1	*		4	System	2024-08-11 08:35:38 UTC
TCPv4	0.0.0.0	0.0.0.0	LISTENING	1000	svchost.exe	2024-08-11 08:35:52 UTC
TCPv4	0.0.0.0	0.0.0.0	LISTENING	1000	svchost.exe	2024-08-11 08:35:52 UTC
TCPv6	::	::	LISTENING	1000	svchost.exe	2024-08-11 08:35:52 UTC
TCPv4	0.0.0.0	0.0.0.0	LISTENING	648	wininit.exe	2024-08-11 08:35:52 UTC
TCPv4	0.0.0.0	0.0.0.0	LISTENING	648	wininit.exe	2024-08-11 08:35:52 UTC
TCPv6	::	::	LISTENING	648	wininit.exe	2024-08-11 08:35:52 UTC
TCPv4	0.0.0.0	0.0.0.0	LISTENING	728	lsass.exe	2024-08-11 08:35:52 UTC

Figure 11.20 – Volatility netscan plugin output

Beyond the PID column, some of the most useful columns within the `netscan` output include:

- **Proto** – Shows the network protocol used by the connection. Most entries will be **TCP** or **UDP**. TCP connections are typically active sessions or listening services, while UDP entries are usually services waiting for incoming traffic without maintaining a persistent connection.
- **LocalAddr** – Displays the local IP address and port number used by the system. The port number is often the most useful artifact because certain ports are commonly associated with specific services. For example:
  - Ports **80** = HTTP
  - Port **443** = HTTPS
  - Port **3389** = Remote Desktop Protocol (RDP)
  - Port **445** = SMB file sharing
- **ForeignAddr** – Shows the remote system connected to the local host. This can reveal external servers contacted by malware or other suspicious outbound connections. Pay particular attention to unfamiliar external IP addresses or connections to unexpected systems.
- **State** – Indicates the current state of the TCP connection:
  - **LISTENING** – The system is waiting for incoming connections
  - **ESTABLISHED** – an active connection exists
  - **CLOSE_WAIT / TIME_WAIT** – connection was recently closed
- **Owner** – Displays the name of the process associated with the network connection. This field allows us to quickly determine which application initiated or received the network activity. If something appears unusual here, the PID can be used as a pivot to investigate the related process further.

When reviewing `netscan` output, look for unexpected process names, unusual ports, or suspicious external IP addresses. For example:

- An unexpected or external IP address connected over port 3389 could indicate an unauthorized remote desktop protocol (RDP) session.
- Unknown processes communicating over ports 80, 443, or 8080 may indicate malware attempting to disguise malicious traffic as normal web activity in order to blend in with legitimate network communications.

The `netscan` plugin also supports an optional parameter: `--include-corrupt`

This option performs a deeper scan of network artifacts and may recover additional socket structures that are partially corrupted or no longer actively in use. However, this deeper scan can also produce a higher number of false positives, so results should be interpreted carefully.

Lastly, if we wanted to limit output to **only active network connections** at the time memory was captured, we could use the `netstat` plugin: `windows.netstat`

There's more...

In addition to live memory acquisitions, you may also encounter portions of system memory stored on disk. These files are created automatically by the operating system and can contain valuable remnants of system memory.

On Windows systems, several files located at the root of the system drive may contain memory artifacts:

- `hiberfil.sys` – Created when a system enters **hibernation mode**, this file contains a snapshot of system memory so the system can restore its previous state when powered back on.
- `pagefile.sys` – Part of the Windows **virtual memory system**, this file is used when physical RAM becomes full. Windows may move portions of memory to this file on disk.
- `swapfile.sys` – Also part of the virtual memory system, commonly used to store memory related to **suspended applications**, particularly modern Windows applications.

Although these files are not full memory captures in the same way as a traditional RAM acquisition, they can still contain useful memory artifacts such as fragments of process memory, credentials, or other data that previously existed in RAM.

In some cases, these files must first be converted into a raw memory format before analysis. For example, `hiberfil.sys` is typically stored in a compressed format and may need to be converted using tools such as **hiber2bin** before being analyzed with Volatility.

Memory artifacts created by **virtual machines** are also sometimes located during analysis of on-disk artifacts. When a virtual machine is paused or suspended, the memory state of the VM may be written to disk in files such as:

- `VM_Name.vmem` – VMWare
- `VM_Name.sav` – VirtualBox
- `VM_Name.bin` – Hyper-V
- `VM_Name.dump` – QEMU / KVM

These files often contain the memory state of the virtual machine and can usually be analyzed directly using Volatility.

Because of this, always remember that valuable memory artifacts may exist both in live RAM captures and within on-disk memory storage files encountered during an investigation. **If** present, these artifacts can be especially useful in cases where a live memory acquisition was not possible.

How it works...

Memory analysis provides us with a detailed view into what a system was actively doing at the time evidence was captured. Unlike disk forensics, which often reveals historical artifacts, memory analysis exposes the **live system state**, including running processes, loaded modules, network connections, and open files.

It is important to remember that memory artifacts do not always disappear immediately after a process ends or even after a system reboot. Because RAM is reused gradually by the operating system, previously used memory may persist until it is overwritten by new activity. On systems with large amounts of RAM or limited usage, useful remnants of memory data may remain available long after the original activity occurred.

In this recipe, we followed a structured workflow designed to progressively narrow our focus during an investigation. We began by identifying the system profile and enumerating running processes before looking for anomalies such as hidden processes, unusual parent-child relationships, and suspicious command-line activity. From there, we expanded our analysis to include loaded DLLs, kernel modules, handles, memory regions, injected code, service persistence, file artifacts, and network connections. This mirrors how real-world investigations are often conducted: start broad, then pivot deeper into areas that appear suspicious.

When analyzing memory, many artifacts may initially appear suspicious but ultimately prove benign. Security software, system services, and normal application behavior frequently perform operations that resemble malicious activity. For this reason, avoid drawing conclusions from a single indicator and instead correlate findings across multiple artifacts; just as we would with on-disk forensic workflows.

Common indicators to investigate further include executables launched from unusual locations (such as Temp directories, user profile folders, or the Recycle Bin), processes or modules that mimic legitimate Windows names (for example `svhost.exe` instead of `svchost.exe`), suspicious services configured to start automatically, and unexpected connections to unfamiliar external systems.

Tools like Volatility are powerful, but they only surface potential evidence. It is our responsibility to interpret those artifacts, correlate them with other findings, and determine what actually occurred on the system.

Recovering artifacts

While the previous recipe focused on identifying suspicious processes and system activity, memory analysis can also reveal valuable artifacts left behind by user activity and running applications. Programs frequently load data into RAM while they execute, including fragments of web pages, file paths, usernames, chat messages, images, documents, and even encryption keys. Because memory is reused gradually by the operating system, portions of previously used memory may persist until they are overwritten by new activity.

These remnants can provide us with direct insight into what a user or program was doing on the system at the time memory was captured. By searching memory for readable strings, recognizable patterns, and fragments of binary data, we can often recover artifacts that may not exist anywhere else on disk.

In this recipe, we will demonstrate several practical techniques for recovering artifacts. These methods allow investigators to quickly surface potentially useful data from large memory images and correlate those findings with the process, network, and system activity identified earlier in our analysis.

Getting ready

Ensure that you have access to the **Windows_RAM.mem** memory image used throughout this chapter. In the examples shown, this image is stored at: `C:\MEMORY\Source\Windows_RAM.mem`

Optionally, you may also wish to have access to the **Verbatim USB forensic image** introduced in *Chapter 8*. You will need the following tools:

- **Volatility 3** as used in the previous recipe

- **Bulk Extractor** as introduced in Chapter 10 and downloadable from: `https://github.com/simsong/bulk_extractor/wiki/Installing-bulk_extractor`
- **bstrings** by Eric Zimmerman, downloadable from: `https://ericzimmerman.github.io/#!index.md`
- **Arsenal Image Mounter**, introduced in Chapter 2 and downloadable from:`https://arsenalrecon.com/downloads`

How to do it…

1. One of the simplest and most effective ways to identify artifacts within memory is to extract human-readable strings. After downloading and extracting **bstrings**, open a Windows Command Prompt from the directory containing the `bstrings.exe` file by typing **CMD** in the File Explorer address bar and pressing **Enter**.
2. From the Command Prompt, run the following command:

```
bstrings.exe -f C:\MEMORY\Source\Windows_RAM.mem > memory_strings.txt
```

This command scans the memory image directly and extracts readable ASCII and Unicode strings into a text file named `memory_strings.txt`. By default, the file will be saved to the current working directory where bstrings is being executed. The resulting file can then be opened using a text editor such as Notepad++ to search for relevant content.

> **Note**
>
> Strings extracted from memory can often include URLs and domain names, file paths, usernames, fragments of documents or chat messages, and other data that was being interacted with or was lingering in memory at the time the memory image was captured.

Searching these strings for key pieces of intelligence relevant to your investigation can quickly reveal valuable clues about activity that occurred on the system prior to the memory capture. For our memory acquisition dataset containing 8 GB of RAM, this process produced over 13 million lines of strings:

```
memory_strings.txt
dsb%22%20ForceHighConfRecipe:%22true%22&idpbck=1&form=SHTRRC
https://www.bing.com/search?q=Popular Recipes&filters=sid:%228f8db8a273
https://www.bing.com/search?q=Popular Recipes&filters=sid:%228ce22faa92
https://www.bing.com/search?q=Popular Recipes&filters=sid:%227e4ecfbbed
C:\Users\Leroy Jenkins\AppData\Local\Packages\Microsoft.Windows.Search_
C:\Users\Leroy Jenkins\AppData\Local\Packages\Microsoft.Windows.Search_
profile.default (C:\Users\Leroy Jenkins\Desktop\Tor Browser\Brows
759 (C:\Users\Leroy Jenkins\Desktop\.tmp.driveupload)
```

Figure 11.21 – Bulk strings extracted from memory using bstrings

Optionally, you can add the `--off` parameter to include the **memory offset** of where each string was extracted. This can be useful when you need to trace a particular hit back to its location in memory for deeper analysis.

3. The output from the previous step can be extremely large, so it is often helpful to narrow our results by searching for specific string types based on keywords. The `--ls` parameter tells bstrings to return only results containing a literal search term that we specify.
   For example, some of the strings recovered in the previous step appear to contain potentially interesting website URLs. If we wanted to limit our results to strings containing the HTTPS protocol, we could run the following command and redirect the results to a searchable text file:

```
bstrings.exe -f C:\MEMORY\Source\Windows_RAM.mem -m 10 --ls "https://" --off > URL_strings.txt
```

Notice in this command that we included the `--off` parameter to display the memory offset where each string was recovered. This allows us to trace a hit back to its location within the memory image if deeper analysis is required.

We also added the parameter `-m 10`. The `-m` parameter sets a **minimum string length** for output (in this case 10 characters). This reduces noise by filtering out very short or partial strings and returning only results that contain at least ten characters:

```
URL_strings.txt
https://login.windows.net/  0x1AB28EB0 (U)
https://login.microsoft.com 0x1AB28F30 (U)
https://api.intelsa.intel.com   0x1B11D204 (U)
https://www.bing.com/sa/simg/bing_p_rr_teal_min.ico 0x1B7180F0 (U)
https://duckduckgo.com/ac/?q={searchTerms}&type=list    0x1B718170 (U)
https://duckduckgo.com/ac/?q={searchTerms}&type=list    0x1B718970 (U)
```

Figure 11.22 – "https://" strings extracted from memory using bstrings

These results quickly reveal several external services the system interacted with, including Microsoft authentication services and web search queries.

Similar to the `-m` parameter, you can specify a **maximum string length** using the `-x` parameter if you want to limit results to a specific range of characters.

4. If we want to search for multiple keyword terms simultaneously, we can create a keyword search list and instruct bstrings to search for all terms contained in that file. To do this, create a text file within the `MEMORY` folder at the root of your workstation drive where the memory dataset is stored. Name the file `Search_Terms.txt`. Add the following search terms, placing each term on a separate line:

```
http://
https://
C:\Users\Leroy
```

These search terms allow us to identify website URLs using the HTTP or HTTPS protocols, as well as file paths associated with the user `Leroy`:

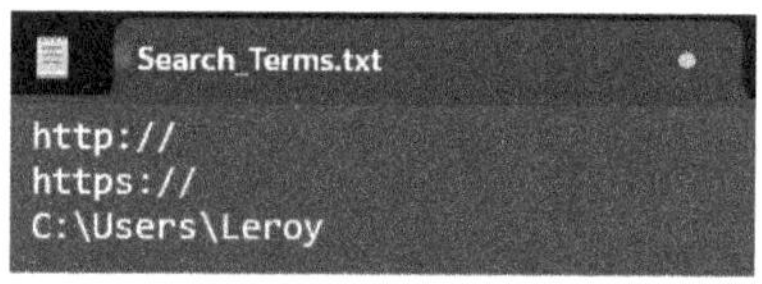

Figure 11.23 – Creating a keyword search terms list for bstrings

Next, run the following command:

```
bstrings.exe -f C:\MEMORY\Source\Windows_RAM.mem -m 10 --fs C:
\MEMORY\Search_Terms.txt > keyword_search.txt
```

The `--fs` parameter instructs bstrings to use the specified file as a list of search terms. Each line in the file is treated as an individual search pattern, allowing multiple keywords to be scanned simultaneously.

The results are written to a new file named `keyword_search.txt`:

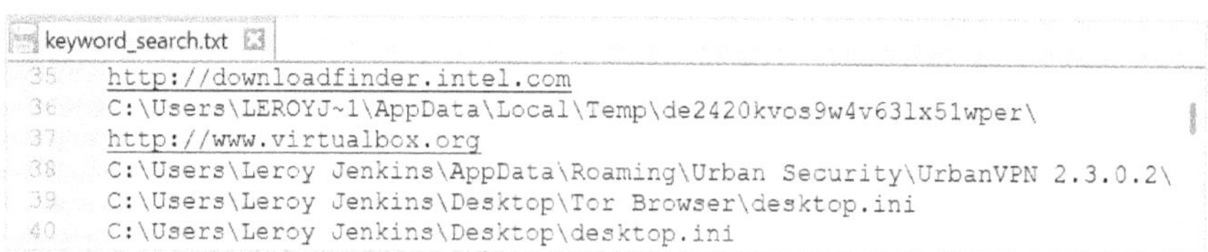

Figure 11.24 – Results from multi-keyword search using bstrings

Even with this small list of search terms, the results already reveal several interesting artifacts, including references to VirtualBox, VPN software, and Tor Browser activity, which may indicate the use of virtualization or privacy-focused tools on the system.

5. One of the most powerful features of bstrings is its ability to search using regular expressions (regex). Regular expressions allow us to search for patterns of data rather than exact strings. We previously learned about writing regex patterns during the *Applying Intelligence in Autopsy* recipe in *Chapter 7*.
   To search for a regex pattern in bstrings, we can use the following command structure:

   ```
   bstrings.exe -f <memory image location> --lr "<regex>"
   ```

   The `--lr` parameter works similarly to the `--ls` parameter we used earlier, but instead of searching for a literal string it searches for a regex pattern.

   Similarly, just like we used the `--fs` parameter in the previous step to search multiple literal strings from a file, we can also search multiple regex patterns simultaneously by using the `--fr` parameter. This allows us to specify a text file containing multiple regex patterns, with each pattern listed on its own line.

   So, `--ls` and `--fs` apply to literal string searches (either a single string or a list of strings from a file), while `--lr` and `--fr` perform the same functions for regular expression searches.

   To simplify this process even further, **bstrings includes several built-in regex patterns** that can be used without writing custom expressions. To view the available patterns, run the following command:

   ```
   bstrings.exe -p
   ```

   This command lists the available built-in regex searches included with bstrings:

```
C:\Users\Forensics\Downloads\bstrings>bstrings.exe -p
Name            Description
aeon            Finds Aeon wallet addresses
b64             Finds valid formatted base 64 strings
bitcoin         Finds BitCoin wallet addresses
bitlocker       Finds Bitlocker recovery keys
bytecoin        Finds ByteCoin wallet addresses
cc              Finds credit card numbers
dashcoin        Finds DashCoin wallet addresses (D*)
dashcoin2       Finds DashCoin wallet addresses (7|X)*
email           Finds embedded email addresses
fantomcoin      Finds Fantomcoin wallet addresses
guid            Finds GUIDs
ipv4            Finds IP version 4 addresses
ipv6            Finds IP version 6 addresses
mac             Finds MAC addresses
monero          Finds Monero wallet addresses
reg_path        Finds paths related to Registry hives
sid             Finds Microsoft Security Identifiers (SID)
ssn             Finds US Social Security Numbers
sumokoin        Finds SumoKoin wallet addresses
unc             Finds UNC paths
url3986         Finds URLs according to RFC 3986
urlUser         Finds usernames in URLs
usPhone         Finds US phone numbers
var_set         Finds environment variables being set (OS=Windows_NT)
win_path        Finds Windows style paths (C:\folder1\folder2\file.txt)
xml             Finds XML/HTML tags
zip             Finds zip codes
```

Figure 11.25 – Listing of prebuilt regex patterns available in bstrings

To use one of these built-in patterns, use the following command structure where **name** represents the pattern name listed in *Figure 11.25*:

```
bstrings.exe -f <memory image location> --lr <name>
```

For example, run the following command:

```
bstrings.exe -f C:\MEMORY\Source\Windows_RAM.mem -m 15 -x 255 --lr win_path
--sl --sa > file_paths.txt
```

In this example, we used the built-in `win_path` regex pattern to locate Windows-style file paths within memory and output the results to a file named `file_paths.txt`.

We also limited the results to strings between 15 and 255 characters by using the **-m** and `-x` parameters. Since Windows file paths typically cannot exceed 255 characters, this helps eliminate shorter, partial strings and other false positives.

The `--sl` parameter sorts results by string length, while `--sa` sorts them alphabetically. These options make the output easier to review by grouping similar artifacts together:

```
file_paths.txt
29624   C:\Users\Leroy Jenkins\Videos\gopro
29625   C:\Users\Leroy Jenkins\Videos\gopro\15917.mp4
29626   C:\Users\Leroy Jenkins\Videos\gopro\desktop.ini
29627   C:\Users\Leroy Jenkins\Videos\other
29628   C:\Users\Leroy Jenkins\Videos\other\5801.mp4
29629   C:\Users\Leroy Jenkins\Videos\other\desktop.ini
```

Figure 11.26 – Results from win_path regex search with bstrings

Organizing the results in this way also makes it easier to identify patterns within the recovered data. For example, as we review the output, we can see several file paths referencing a drive mapped as "`I:\`":

```
file_paths.txt
46363   I:\the good stuff\ILLEGAL_FILE-0890974.jpg
46364   I:\the good stuff\ILLEGAL_FILE-0984644.jpg
46365   I:\the good stuff\ILLEGAL_FILE-0987409.jpg
46366   I:\the good stuff\ILLEGAL_FILE-1
46367   I:\the good stuff\ILLEGAL_FILE-1650447.jpg
```

Figure 11.27 – Possible mapped volume file paths and data

This may indicate the presence of a removable device or mounted volume, which can provide additional investigative leads when correlated with other artifacts discovered during the analysis.

6. While we have been exporting most results to text files so far, bstrings can also display results directly in the Command Prompt window. This can be useful when the expected output is small or when we are quickly testing whether a pattern exists within memory.
   Run the following command:

```
bstrings.exe -f C:\MEMORY\Source\Windows_RAM.mem --lr bitlocker
```

This command uses the built-in `bitlocker` regex pattern included with bstrings, which searches memory for values that match the format of a BitLocker recovery key:

```
Processing strings...

598444-355498-112156-717728-512160-712580-447458-420343

Found 1 string in 102.922 seconds. Average strings/sec: 124,135
```

Figure 11.28 – Possible BitLocker recovery key recovered with bstrings

Encryption keys can often be recovered from memory because the operating system must temporarily store them in RAM while an encrypted volume is unlocked and in use. If memory is captured during this time, those keys may still exist within the memory image. In some investigations, recovering these keys can allow us to unlock encrypted volumes that would otherwise be inaccessible.

Recall from the *Mass Storage Drives* recipe in *Chapter 8* that we encountered an encrypted volume on the **Verbatim USB** forensic image. When encountering encrypted volumes during an investigation, it is important to note their presence so that we can remain aware of potential recovery keys as we perform further analysis – including memory analysis.

Since we have now recovered a possible BitLocker recovery key, we can attempt to use it to unlock the encrypted volume.

7. Mount the Verbatim USB.E01 forensic image using Arsenal Image Mounter:
    - **Mount disk image | Browse** and select **Verbatim USB.E01**
    - Choose **Disk device, read only** | Click **OK**
8. Once mounted, one of the volumes will appear encrypted and inaccessible:

Figure 11.29 – Encrypted volume mounted with Arsenal Image Mounter

9. Double-click the encrypted volume. When prompted to enter a password, select: **More options | Enter recovery key**

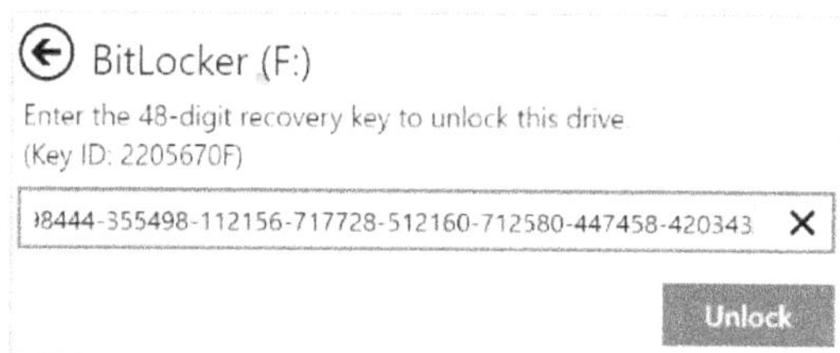

Figure 11.30 – Entering BitLocker recovery key for mounted E01 image

10. Paste the recovery key obtained from bstrings, then click **Unlock**:

Figure 11.31 – Contents of decrypted BitLocker volume

Notice that the unlocked volume contains the same suspicious file path we observed earlier in step 4 (*Figure 11.27*). The artifacts referencing the `I:\ drive` now make sense, as they correspond to the contents of this decrypted volume.

This example highlights the importance of acquiring RAM during evidence collection, as encryption keys or credentials stored only in memory may otherwise be permanently lost.

> **Note**
>
> Locked out
>
> While on-scene collecting evidence during the investigation of a serious criminal offense, I was triaging a computer and performing a RAM acquisition. The memory capture was taking a long time, and others on scene were becoming impatient. Against my better judgment, I stopped the acquisition early.
>
> Later during analysis, I encountered an encrypted volume along with ShellBag artifacts indicating suspicious file paths that likely pointed to that same volume – similar to the example shown here. Unfortunately, I was never able to recover the encryption key. While I will never know for certain whether the key was still present in memory, it very well could have been.
>
> **Never** shortcut memory acquisition. Once memory is gone, it cannot be recovered.

11. We can also use Volatility 3 to perform searches by creating **YARA rules**. YARA rules are a way of performing pattern matching to help identify text and binary data and are often used to locate suspicious indicators associated with malware. However, YARA rules can also be used to search for many other types of artifacts within memory. A YARA rule begins with the name of the rule and typically contains three main sections: an optional `meta:` section for notes, a `strings:` section that defines the search

patterns, and a `condition:` section that determines when those patterns will trigger a match:

```
rule NewRuleName
{
    meta:
        description = "What this rule does"
        author = "Your name"

    strings:
        $a = "pattern 1"
        $b = "pattern 2"
        $c = "pattern 3"

    condition:
        conditions for searching each string
}
```

The string identifiers here (`$a`, `$b`, `$c`, etc.) can be renamed to any meaningful label. Each identifier defines a search pattern that YARA will attempt to locate. These patterns typically include **text strings, hexadecimal byte patterns,** and **regular expressions**, allowing YARA to search both readable data and raw binary sequences.

The **condition** section then defines the logical rules that determine when a match should be triggered. These conditions can reference individual string identifiers along with logical operators such as **and**, **or**, or **numeric thresholds**. For example, if we wanted to search for instances where both `$a` *and* `$b` appear, we could write: **$a and $b**

Alternatively, we could search across all defined strings by specifying a single condition such as: **any of them**

To create a YARA rule to test against our memory image, open a text editor and enter the following rule (making sure each string definition appears on a single line):

```
rule MyRule
{
  meta:
    description = "Example YARA search"

  strings:
    $user_text = "Leroy Jenkins" ascii wide
    $user_path_hex = { 43 00 3A 00 5C 00 55 00 73 00
```

```
                          65 00 72 00 73 00 5C 00 4C 00
                          65 00 72 00 6F 00 79 00 }
    $url_regex = /https?:\/\/[A-Za-z0-9\-._~:\/?#\[\]
@!$&'()*+,;=%]{10,120}/ nocase

  condition:
    $user_text and 1 of ($user_path_hex, $url_regex)
}
```

Save this file as `MyRule.yar` in the root directory of your Volatility 3 application.

The identifiers within this rule perform the following searches:

- `$user_text` – searches for the literal text "`Leroy Jenkins`", matching both standard ASCII (ascii) and Unicode (wide) encodings
- `$user_path_hex` – searches for a raw byte sequence representing part of the Windows file path `C:\Users\Leroy`
- `$url_regex` – uses a regular expression to identify URLs beginning with `HTTP://` or `HTTPS://`

The **condition** section then defines when a match should be reported. In this example, a match will occur only when:

- The text string `Leroy Jenkins` is present AND
- At least **one** of the following is also found
- The Windows user path `C:\Users\Leroy` OR
- A URL using either HTTP or HTTPS

This type of logic allows us to combine related indicators rather than triggering on a single artifact.

Next, launch **Command Prompt** from the Volatility 3 application directory and run the following command:

```
vol.exe -f C:\MEMORY\Source\Windows_RAM.mem yarascan.YaraScan --yara-file
MyRule.yar | more
```

The results will show the **offset** where each match was located in memory along with the **rule name** (**Rule**) and the **string identifier** (*Component*) responsible for triggering the match. Since a single `.yar` file may contain multiple rules, this output helps identify exactly which rule and pattern produced the result:

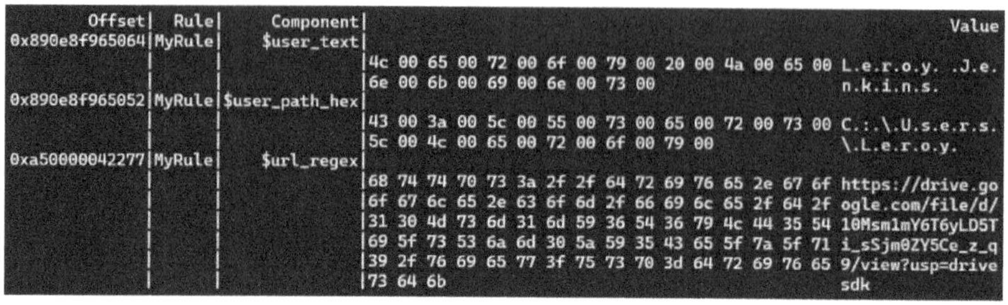

Figure 11.32 – YARA hits found using Volatility 3

YARA rules are one of the most powerful search capabilities available during memory analysis because they allow us to combine multiple related indicators rather than triggering on a single string. Since memory images often contain large amounts of unrelated data, combining conditions in this way can significantly reduce noise and improve confidence that a match is relevant.

12. In addition to text-based artifacts, memory may also contain fragments of binary data such as images or documents. These artifacts can sometimes be recovered using automated data carving tools.

    In the *Defeating Encryption* recipe of *Chapter 10*, we used Bulk Extractor to help create a custom wordlist dictionary from an E01 forensic image of the Microsoft Windows dataset.

    Launch **Bulk Extractor** and run it against our `Windows_RAM.mem` forensic image. When browsing to this image, you will need to select **All Files** from the *File of type* dropdown menu in Windows, as Bulk Extractor does not automatically recognize the `.mem` extension.

    Check all available boxes within the **Scanners** section to see what artifacts can be recovered, then click **Submit Run**. Once the scan is complete, navigate to the directory where you chose to store the output and review the results. Looking at the **Size** column of each output file can quickly help identify which scanners produced the most results:

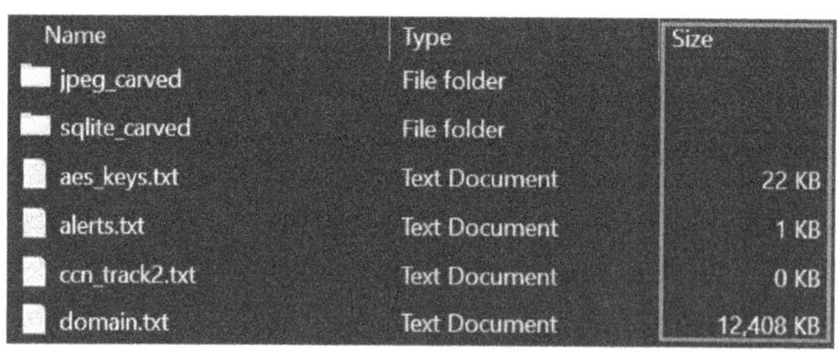

Figure 11.33 – Bulk Extractor output for Windows_RAM.mem forensic image

Bulk Extractor scans the memory image and automatically extracts many different types of artifacts. These results may include strings related to user activity, base64 encoded data, and even recovered files such as carved JPEG images and fragments of documents.

While some of the text-based output produced by Bulk Extractor may appear noisier than the string extraction methods we used earlier, it still provides another quick way to generate easily searchable artifact lists.

> **Note**
>
> One particularly interesting output file produced by the *AES scanner* (a Bulk Extractor feature that identifies high-entropy data likely associated with encryption keys) is `aes_keys.txt`, which attempts to identify blocks of data with high entropy that resemble encryption keys. This file can sometimes contain cryptographic keys associated with encrypted volumes, secure communications, or software such as VeraCrypt.
>
> Bulk Extractor also generates a wordlist file (such as `wordlist_split_000.txt`) similar to the dictionary we created in Chapter 10. This file can be cleaned and used as a custom password dictionary when attempting to defeat encryption, since memory may contain passwords or authentication material that were never written to disk.

Bulk Extractor will attempt to carve files directly from the memory image. In this case, it recovered a single JPEG file located within the `jpeg_carved` folder of the Bulk Extractor output:

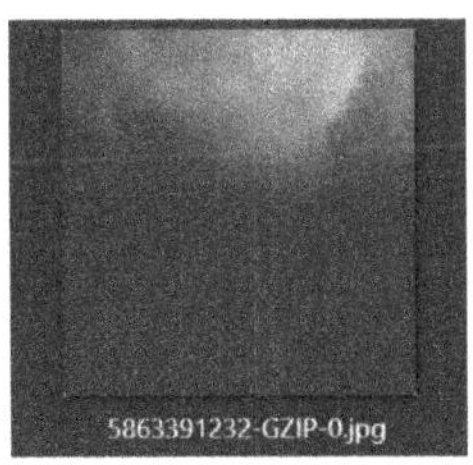

Figure 11.34 – JPEG file carved from memory using Bulk Extractor

13. Data carving methods can have varying levels of success when applied to memory images, with some tools performing better than others depending on the structure of the data being recovered. In Chapter 7, we automated analysis using the Autopsy

digital forensic analysis suite. We can apply the same approach here by running Autopsy against our memory image to attempt additional file carving.
Create a new **Autopsy** case and select **Unallocated Space Image File** as the *Data Source Type*. When configuring the ingest settings, ensure that ingest modules are configured to **Run on All Files, Directories, and Unallocated Space**, and select at least the following modules:

- PhotoRec Carver (enable Keep corrupted files)
- File Type Identification
- Picture Analyzer

Once processing is complete, review the results in the **Images/Videos** viewer:

Figure 11.35 – Images carved from memory using PhotoRec with Autopsy

Although Autopsy's PhotoRec module recovered considerably more images than Bulk Extractor did, many of the results appear partially corrupted or incomplete. This behavior is normal when carving data from memory. Because memory does not contain a traditional file system structure, portions of files may be stored across different memory regions. Without a file system or allocation table to link these segments together, carving tools often recover only partial fragments of the original files.

In many cases, images recovered from memory originate from applications that rendered them to the screen, such as web browsers or document viewers. Because these programs temporarily store decoded image buffers in memory during display, we can sometimes recover visual content that was viewed by the user even if no file was saved to disk.

Many commercial forensic tools are capable of recovering even larger quantities of file fragments from memory images, sometimes producing thousands of recovered artifacts. These fragments can occasionally include images, documents, or other content that were viewed from encrypted volumes or temporary application data and might no longer exist on disk.

How it works...

Applications frequently store temporary data in memory while they execute. This can include user input, rendered web content, decrypted files, images, network data, and encryption keys required for accessing protected resources. Because RAM is gradually reused by the operating system, portions of previously used memory may remain available until those regions are overwritten by new activity.

Forensic tools take advantage of this behavior by scanning memory images for recognizable patterns of data. Techniques such as string extraction allow us to quickly surface human-readable artifacts, including file paths, URLs, usernames, and fragments of user activity. Regular expression searches extend this capability by identifying structured data, such as registry paths, IP addresses, or encryption keys.

Pattern-matching frameworks such as YARA further enhance the process by allowing us to combine multiple indicators within a single rule, effectively creating a compound filter. This reduces noise and helps highlight artifacts that are more likely to be relevant to the investigation.

In addition to text-based artifacts, memory may also contain fragments of binary data such as images, documents, or compressed content. Because memory does not contain a traditional file system structure, these artifacts are often recovered as partial fragments rather than complete files. However, even incomplete data can provide valuable investigative insight.

Many artifacts recovered from memory originate from applications that temporarily store decoded content in RAM while rendering it to the screen. Web browsers, document viewers, and messaging applications frequently load images and media into memory buffers during display. As a result, investigators may recover visual content that was viewed by the user even if the original files were never saved to disk.

By combining string searching, pattern matching, and artifact carving techniques, we can extract meaningful evidence from large memory images and correlate those findings with process activity, network connections, and other artifacts discovered during analysis, including on-disk artifacts.

Virtualization

Unlike disk images, memory does not contain a traditional file system structure. Because of this, there is no directory hierarchy that allows us to easily browse memory contents in the same way we would examine an operating system or a removable storage device.

Some tools, however, allow us to create a virtual file system from a memory image. This approach reconstructs artifacts discovered in memory and presents them as browsable directories and files. By mounting memory in this way, investigators can explore recovered data more intuitively and quickly identify artifacts related to processes, files, registry data, and other system activity.

While tools such as Volatility rely primarily on individual plugins to extract artifacts, virtualization tools instead organize recovered data into a file system-like structure that can be explored interactively. This makes it easier to pivot between related artifacts and quickly triage large memory images during an investigation.

In this recipe, we will demonstrate how to mount a memory image using MemProcFS to create a virtual file system. This allows us to explore recovered artifacts in a more intuitive and interactive way.

Getting ready

Ensure that you have access to the `Windows_RAM.mem` memory image used throughout this chapter. In the examples shown, this image is stored at: `C:\MEMORY\Source\Windows_RAM.mem`

You will also need **MemProcFS** by Ulf Frisk, downloadable from: `https://github.com/ufrisk/MemProcFS`

How to do it...

1. Extract `MemProcFS` from within the extracted folder, open a Command Prompt by typing **CMD** in the File Explorer address bar and pressing *Enter*.
   Run the following command. If prompted about downloading symbols from the *Microsoft Internet Symbol Store*, choose **Yes**:

   ```
   MemProcFS.exe -forensic 1 -device C:\MEMORY\Source\Windows_RAM.mem
   ```

   The `-forensic 1` parameter instructs MemProcFS to start in forensic mode. In this mode, MemProcFS performs an automated scan of the memory image to identify and reconstruct artifacts such as processes, files, registry data, and other system structures. These artifacts are organized internally using a SQLite database that exists in memory during the session, although additional parameters can optionally save this database to disk.

After the scan completes, MemProcFS will display information about the mounted memory image, including the drive letter assigned as the **Mount Point**.

Note the designated mount point shown in the output:

Figure 11.36 – MemProcFS memory image mount point

2. On your workstation, browse to the mounted drive letter noted in the previous step. You will see the `Windows_RAM.mem` memory image mounted as a virtual file system:

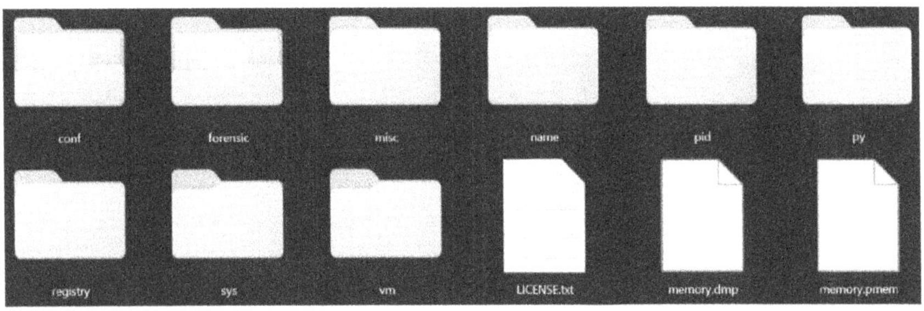

Figure 11.37 – Virtual file system structure created by MemProcFS

Explore the directory structure to see what artifacts have been reconstructed from memory. Unlike tools such as Volatility, which requires individual plugin commands to extract artifacts, MemProcFS organizes recovered data into browsable folders.

Each directory represents a different category of artifacts reconstructed from memory, allowing investigators to navigate through processes, system structures, registry data, and other recovered content in a more intuitive way.

3. Open the `forensic` folder. This contains many of the reconstructed artifacts identified during MemProcFS analysis. These artifacts can include browser history fragments, credential-related data, indicators of user activity, and recovered file metadata. This directory is particularly useful for quickly triaging the contents of a memory image.

Several directories within **forensic** attempt to reconstruct portions of the Windows file system using data discovered in memory. For example, navigating to `forensic\files\ROOT\Users\` allows us to browse recovered file paths associated with the `Leroy Jenkins` user account.

Within the `forensic\timeline\` directory, you will find several text files containing reconstructed timeline data. These files represent timeline-style output similar to what we would expect from certain Volatility 3 plugins. For example, `timeline_net.txt` contains reconstructed network connection artifacts identified in memory.

One of the more unique artifacts within this directory is the `forensic\findevil\` folder. The files in this location provide a quick triage view of potential malware-related indicators discovered in memory. These indicators are summarized in the `findevil.txt` file.

For example, the output below shows indicators related to high-entropy memory regions associated with the Malwarebytes process. High entropy can sometimes indicate encrypted or packed data often associated with malware, but in this case, the results represent expected behavior from legitimate security software and can be considered a false positive:

```
 PID Process         Type            Address          Description
---------------------------------------------------------------------
3976 MBAMService.ex HIGH_ENTROPY    0000021412af0000 Entropy:[7.63]
4216 msedgewebview2 HIGH_ENTROPY    000002b1c7570000 Entropy:[7.89]
```

Figure 11.38 – Content of findevil.txt file in MemProcFS

4. Open the `name` folder. This contains processes grouped by their executable names, while the `pid` folder organizes the same processes by their process identifier (PID). Within each process directory are additional subfolders and text files that contain artifacts associated with that specific process. These artifacts may include handles, loaded modules, memory regions, and reconstructed files related to the process.

   For example, within the `handles` subfolder, you will find the `handles.txt` file containing output similar to what we would expect from the Volatility `handles` plugin:

```
   #    PID  Handle Object Address   Access Type
------------------------------------------------------------
0000  10816       4 ffffb80d50410460 1f0003 Event
0001  10816       8 ffffb80d50410ae0 1f0003 Event
0002  10816       c ffffb80d5197d300      1 WaitCompletionPa
0003  10816      10 ffffb80d512b3f80 1f0003 IoCompletion
```

Figure 11.39 – Content of handles.txt file in MemProcFS

One of the most valuable features within these directories is the presence of reconstructed files associated with each process. Within the **files** subfolder, MemProcFS attempts to rebuild files that were mapped or loaded by the process, such as executables and DLLs. These recovered files can often be copied directly from the virtual file system and examined using traditional forensic tools for deeper analysis.

5. Open the **sys** folder. This contains low-level operating system information reconstructed from memory. This data can include kernel structures, driver information, loaded modules, and other system configuration artifacts identified during analysis.
   For example, within the `sys\sysinfo\` directory you will find a text file named `sysinfo.txt` containing various details about the system recovered from memory. This information can include system time, hardware details, counts of active and inactive processes, and recovered user accounts along with their associated security identifiers (SIDs):

```
Windows Information:
  Current Time:     2024-08-12 03:55:16 UTC
  Boot Time:        2024-08-11 08:35:20 UTC
  Version:          10.0 (build 19041)

Hardware Information:
  CPU:              Intel(R) Core(TM) i3-5005U CPU @ 2.00GHz
  MB Vendor:        LENOVO

Users:
  Leroy Jenkins   (S-1-5-21-3063303759-3547812523-4161226937-1001)

Process Information:
  Active:           185
  Inactive:         41
```

Figure 11.40 – Content of sysinfo.txt file in MemProcFS

   Artifacts such as these can help us quickly establish basic system context, including the operating system version, hardware configuration, and user accounts present on the machine at the time the memory image was captured.

6. Open the `registry` folder. This attempts to reconstruct portions of the Windows Registry using data recovered from memory. This allows us to browse registry keys in a familiar directory-style structure similar to examining registry hives on disk. Through this reconstructed view, we can identify artifacts such as autorun entries, recently accessed files, installed software, and other indicators that may reveal persistence mechanisms or system activity.

   Each recovered registry key is also saved to an individual text file, eliminating the need to load the data into separate registry viewing software. For example, navigating to `registry\HKLM\SOFTWARE\Malwarebytes\` and opening `InstallTime.txt` reveals the data stored in that registry value, showing when the software was installed on the system:

```
ffffc8055c983000:00ff8800
REG_SZ
2024-06-19T18:57:59Z
```

Figure 11.41 – Content of InstallTime.txt file in MemProcFS

Because this data is reconstructed directly from memory, it can sometimes expose registry information that is no longer available on disk or was modified shortly before memory acquisition.

7. Finally, open the `misc` folder. This contains various artifacts that do not fit cleanly into the other available categories. These can include system metadata, internal system objects, and other miscellaneous artifacts identified during analysis. While much of this data may not always be immediately useful, it is still worth reviewing during an investigation.
   For example, encryption keys may occasionally appear within this directory. If we navigate to `misc\eventlog\` we will find several recovered Windows Event Log (.evtx) files reconstructed from memory. These files can sometimes be copied out of the virtual file system and repaired using third-party forensic utilities:

Name	Type
ffffb80d4fc6e280-Microsoft-Windows-GroupPolicy%4Operational.evtx	Event Log
ffffb80d4fc57cb0-Microsoft-Windows-CodeIntegrity%4Operational.evtx	Event Log
ffffb80d4fc70b20-Microsoft-Windows-Containers-Wcifs%4Operational.evtx	Event Log
ffffb80d4fc73d20-Microsoft-Windows-Containers-BindFlt%4Operational.evtx	Event Log

Figure 11.42 – Windows Event Logs recovered in MemProcFS

Other folders such as `vm`, `py`, and `conf` primarily contain data related to internal operations performed by MemProcFS and are typically less useful during most investigations. However, the `vm` folder can sometimes display reconstructed virtual memory ranges associated with processes. This information is conceptually similar to the memory region data we examined earlier using Volatility's `vadinfo` plugin.

How it works...

Tools such as MemProcFS analyze a memory image by parsing the internal structures used by the operating system to manage processes, files, memory regions, and system objects. These structures include kernel objects, process tables, virtual address descriptors, registry structures, and other components maintained by the Windows memory manager.

Instead of simply extracting artifacts through individual commands, MemProcFS reconstructs many of these structures and organizes the results into a virtual file system. During this process, artifacts discovered in memory are indexed within an internal SQLite database and mapped to directories and files that represent different categories of system data.

For example, process structures recovered from memory are grouped into directories representing running processes, while registry structures are reconstructed into browsable registry key paths. Similarly, file objects referenced by processes may be rebuilt into directories containing executable files, DLLs, and other associated artifacts.

Because these artifacts are reconstructed directly from memory structures rather than from disk, they often represent the live state of the system at the moment memory was captured. This allows investigators to examine runtime data such as active processes, loaded modules, decrypted files, and in-memory registry information that may not exist on disk.

By presenting reconstructed artifacts through a virtual file system, tools like MemProcFS provide an alternative method for exploring memory images that complements traditional plugin-based analysis tools such as Volatility.

Summary

Memory analysis provides us with a unique view into what a system was actively doing at the moment evidence was captured. Unlike disk artifacts, which typically reflect historical activity, memory can reveal the live execution state of the operating system, including running processes, loaded modules, network connections, decrypted content, and artifacts that may never have been written to disk. Because RAM is volatile and gradually overwritten by new activity, capturing and analyzing memory can expose evidence that would otherwise be permanently lost.

In this chapter, we examined how investigators can analyze memory images using Volatility to identify system activity, detect hidden or injected processes, review command-line execution, examine DLL loading behavior, inspect memory regions, and correlate network connections with the processes responsible for them. We also explored methods for recovering artifacts directly from memory using string extraction, keyword searches, regular expressions, YARA rules, and data carving techniques.

Finally, we used MemProcFS to mount the memory image as a virtual file system, allowing reconstructed artifacts, such as processes, registry data, timelines, and recovered files, to be explored through an intuitive directory structure. At this point, you should be able to do the following:

- **Use Volatility 3 to analyze memory images** and identify running processes, system information, and suspicious activity.
- **Detect hidden processes, injected code, and unusual memory regions** using plugins such as `pslist`, `psscan`, `psxview`, `vadinfo`, and `malfind`.
- **Investigate process behavior** by examining command-line arguments, DLLs, handles, services, and network connections.
- **Recover artifacts from memory** using string extraction, keyword searches, regular expressions, and YARA rules.
- **Carve potential files and images from memory** using tools such as Bulk Extractor and Autopsy.
- **Mount and explore virtualized memory images** using MemProcFS to quickly triage reconstructed artifacts.

Together with the acquisition, triage, disk analysis, and artifact recovery techniques covered throughout this book, these methods provide us with a practical toolkit for conducting modern digital forensic investigations from collection to analysis.

Get this book's PDF copy, code bundle, and more

Scan the QR code (or go to `packtpub.com/unlock`). Search for this book by name, confirm the edition, and then follow the steps on the page.

UNLOCK NOW

Note: Have your invoice handy. Purchases made directly from the Packt website don't require an invoice.

12

Unlock Access to the Code Bundle and the PDF Version

Your copy of this book includes the following exclusive benefits:

Complete Code Bundle

Download the full source code for this book's examples and projects.

DRM-Free PDF Version

Download DRM-free PDF and ePub copies of this book.

7-Day Packt Library Access

Get 7-day unlimited access to 8,000+ books and videos. No credit card required.

Available for first-time Packt+ trial users only.

Next-Gen Reader Access

Read this book on Packt Reader with progress sync, dark mode and note-taking.

Follow this guide to unlock them. The process takes only a few minutes and only needs to be completed once.

Unlock this book's free benefits in three easy steps

Step 1

Have your purchase invoice ready for *step 3*. If you have a physical copy, scan it using your phone and save it as a PDF, JPG, or PNG.

For more help on finding your invoice, visit `https://www.packtpub.com/unlock-benefits/help`.

> Note
>
> **Note**: If you bought this book directly from the Packt website, no invoice is required. After *step 2*, you can access your exclusive content right away.

Step 2

Scan the QR code or go to `packtpub.com/unlock`.

On the page that opens (similar to *Figure 12.1* on desktop), search for this book by name and select the correct edition.

Figure 12.1: Packt unlock landing page on desktop

Step 3

After selecting the book, sign in to your Packt account or create one for free. Then, upload your invoice (PDF, PNG, or JPG, up to 10 MB). Follow the on-screen instructions to finish the process.

Need help?

If you get stuck and need help, visit `https://www.packtpub.com/unlock-benefits/help` for a detailed FAQ on how to find your invoice and more. This QR code will take you to the help page.

Note

Note: If you are still facing issues, reach out to `customercare@packt.com`.

Appendix A

Digital Forensic Fundamentals

This appendix provides a brief overview of foundational concepts referenced throughout this book. While the recipes focus on practical techniques, understanding the basic methodology behind digital forensics will help you apply those techniques more effectively.

Digital forensics is the process of identifying, preserving, acquiring, analyzing, and reporting electronic data while maintaining the integrity of the original evidence. Sometimes referred to as computer forensics, the field now encompasses a wide range of digital evidence sources, including computers, mobile devices, removable storage media, network data, cloud services, and Internet-of-Things (IoT) devices.

It combines investigative methodology with computer science principles to interpret digital evidence in a reliable and repeatable way. These methods are widely used by law enforcement, private organizations, and incident response teams to reconstruct events and identify relevant artifacts within digital systems.

The following sections introduce several core principles that support the forensic examination process and provide context for the practical workflows presented throughout this book.

The examination process

Digital forensics should be approached as a structured investigative process. Following a structured methodology helps ensure that results are accurate, repeatable, and defensible. Without that discipline, important evidence may be overlooked, evidence integrity may be compromised, and conclusions may not withstand scrutiny.

For this reason, digital forensic examinations are typically organized into four primary phases: `collection, acquisition, analysis, and reporting`, as illustrated in *Figure A.1*:

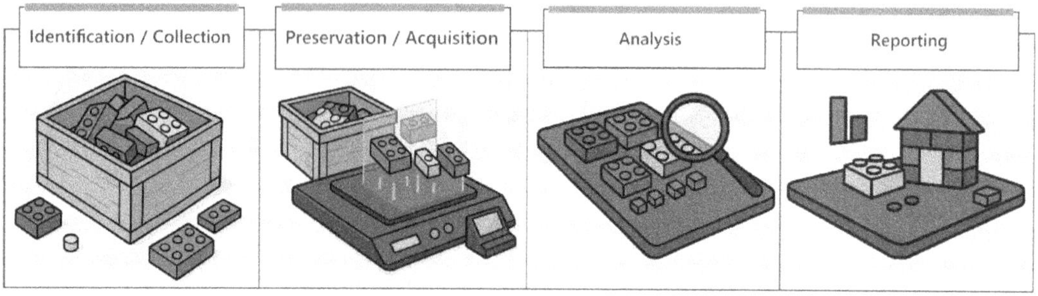

Figure A.1 – Digital forensic methodology steps

These phases form a structured workflow for identifying, preserving, analyzing, and reporting digital evidence. Each phase is outlined below.

Step 1: Collection

The collection phase involves identifying and gathering items or data that may contain evidence relevant to an investigation. In many forensic frameworks, this stage is also referred to as `identification`, as investigators must first determine which systems, devices, or data sources are likely to contain relevant evidence.

Evidence collected during an investigation may include physical devices such as computers, mobile devices, or storage media, as well as digital data obtained from external sources such as cloud services, enterprise networks, or service providers.

Proper documentation during this stage is essential. Investigators must record how evidence was identified and collected, and maintain chain-of-custody records that document who handled the evidence and when.

Step 2: Acquisition

Once evidence has been collected, the next step is the acquisition and preservation of the data. This phase involves creating a forensic image or copy of the data so it can be examined without altering the original evidence.

When devices are seized, investigators typically acquire their data using forensically sound methods designed to preserve the original state of the evidence. One common technique is the use of `write-blocking devices`, which prevent the forensic workstation from writing data to the evidence media during acquisition.

In some situations, minor changes to the original system state cannot always be avoided. For example, mobile devices may require interaction to access their data, and solid-state drives may perform internal processes when powered. When this occurs, investigators should take reasonable steps to minimize changes and document any actions taken.

Several acquisition methods are commonly used in digital forensics, including

- **Logical acquisition:** Collects active files and data accessible through the operating system. This method is typically fast and minimally intrusive, but may not capture deleted data or artifacts outside standard file structures.
- **File system acquisition:** Captures the file system structure of a device, including system directories and application databases that may not be accessible through logical acquisition alone.
- **Physical acquisition:** Creates a **bit-for-bit copy** of a storage device, including both allocated and unallocated space. Because it captures the most complete representation of the data, it is often preferred when feasible.
- **Targeted acquisition:** Collects only specific data relevant to an investigation, such as selected files, log records, or user artifacts. This approach is often used when time is limited or when a full acquisition is impractical.

More advanced techniques may also be used in specialized situations, such as hardware-level methods, including `JTAG, ISP, or chip-off` extraction.

Step 3: Analysis

The analysis or examination phase involves examining the acquired data to identify artifacts relevant to the investigation. Modern systems contain enormous amounts of data, making this phase the most time-consuming part of most investigations.

Digital forensic tools are commonly used to assist with analysis by organizing data, extracting artifacts, and allowing investigators to search and filter large datasets efficiently.

For example, media files may exist in user folders, system directories, application databases, or unallocated space. Forensic software can identify these files automatically and present them in a unified view for review. Investigators can then apply filters or searches to focus on items of interest.

While these tools greatly accelerate analysis, they are not infallible. Software updates, unsupported applications, or unusual data structures can cause artifacts to be missed or misinterpreted. For this reason, investigators should verify important findings and remain cautious about relying solely on automated output.

Step 4: Reporting

The final phase of the forensic examination process is reporting. This stage involves documenting the artifacts identified during analysis and explaining their significance within the context of the investigation. Reporting represents the final product of the forensic examination and should clearly communicate both the evidence discovered and the conclusions drawn from that evidence.

In many investigations, reporting consists of two complementary components

- **Artifact report:** A structured record of artifacts identified during analysis, sometimes referred to as a *technical report*. Many forensic tools can generate these reports automatically in formats such as PDF, CSV, or HTML, often with links to the underlying evidence.
- **Narrative report:** An explanation of how the artifacts relate to the investigation. Rather than simply listing evidence, the narrative report describes how the collected artifacts support investigative conclusions.

Together, these reports present both the technical findings and the investigative interpretation of the evidence.

In addition to reporting findings, investigators must also ensure that evidence is properly documented and preserved throughout the process.

Evidence integrity and documentation

Throughout the collection and triage phases, investigators must maintain thorough documentation describing how evidence was identified, collected, and handled. Proper documentation preserves the integrity of the evidence and ensures that investigative actions can be explained and defended if later reviewed in court.

Documentation during this stage typically includes evidence collection forms, chain-of-custody records, photographs of the scene, and a narrative report describing the actions taken during collection.

Chain of custody

Chain-of-custody documentation records each individual who has maintained possession of an evidentiary item. While this is required in criminal investigations, it should also be followed in private-sector forensic work, particularly when an investigation could lead to litigation.

Without the ability to demonstrate proper chain of custody, digital evidence may be challenged or excluded during legal proceedings.

Although documentation formats vary between organizations, chain-of-custody records typically include

- Identifying information related to the investigation, such as a case number, offense type, and any known suspect or victim names

- The name of the investigator who originally collected the evidence, along with the date and time of collection
- The location where the evidence was collected
- A unique item number and description for each item, including make, model, serial number, and physical condition
- A record of individuals who later handled the item, including dates, times, and reasons for access

The following example shows what chain-of-custody documentation typically looks like in practice:

Case Number: 26-000001 Investigation / Offense Type: Exploitation
Suspect Name: Leroy Jenkins Victim Name: Society
Evidence Collection Location: 123 Main Street, City, State
Date/Time of Collection: 03/14/26 at 11:47 hours Collected By: C. Bounds

Evidence Collected			
Item #	***Qty***	***Description***	***Location***
001	1	Apple iPhone 15 Pro (S/N: RNT435324HF) - cracked screen	Room D - Computer desk next to keyboard
002	1	Custom-built desktop PC (S/N: none) - good condition	Room D - Atop computer desk
003	2	SanDisk Cruzer Glide USB drive (S/N: none) - good condition	Room D - Clear container in top left dresser drawer
004	1	Unknown brand USB drive (S/N: none) - good condition	Room D - Clear container in top left dresser drawer
005	1	Microsoft Xbox One gaming console (S/N: 52007984) - good condition	Room A - Top shelf of entertainment center

Chain of Custody				
Item #	***Date/Time***	***Released By***	***Received By***	***Reason***
001-005	03/19/26 at 09:07	*Signature*	*Signature*	Analysis completed - returned to evidence

Figure A.2 – Example chain-of-custody form

Each item should be labeled with the corresponding evidence item number and secured in appropriate evidence packaging. Evidence bags are typically sealed and initialed by the collecting investigator, along with the date, time, and case number.

If evidence is later accessed, the item should be resealed and documented again. Maintaining this process allows investigators to demonstrate who handled the evidence, when it was accessed, and what actions were taken.

Collection documentation

Supplemental documentation should also describe the evidence collection process itself. This information is often recorded in a narrative report and may include the following:

- A description of each item collected, including make, model, serial numbers, and physical condition

- Whether devices were discovered in a powered-on or powered-off state
- Any connected peripherals such as external drives or storage media
- The date and time investigators interacted with the device and whether the system clock appeared accurate
- Actions taken during triage, such as previewing the system, acquiring data, or shutting the device down
- Any relevant artifacts observed during collection
- The reason the item was seized for further analysis

Investigators should also document the physical location where each item was found, including the room and its position within that location.

In some situations, investigators may review devices that are ultimately not seized. Documenting these decisions can demonstrate that other potential evidence sources were evaluated and determined to be unrelated to the investigation.

The collection process may also produce additional evidence, such as scene photographs or storage media used to capture acquired data. Even though these items were generated during the investigation, they must still be preserved and documented using the same evidence-handling procedures as the original seized items.

All evidence-handling actions and collection decisions should ultimately be documented within the investigative narrative.

Volatile data

Volatile data refers to information that exists only while a system remains powered. Once power is removed, this data is typically lost. In some cases, volatile data may also include information that is likely to be overwritten quickly by normal system activity and, therefore, must be captured promptly.

The most common example of volatile data is random-access memory (RAM), but volatile information may also exist on mobile devices, routers, or other network equipment.

Although not all volatile data can be easily collected (and some may not always be relevant to an investigation), it is often important to preserve it during the initial triage of a system. In many cases, this may be the only opportunity to obtain it.

To guide this process, investigators often follow the `order of volatility`, which prioritizes collecting the data that is most likely to change or disappear first.

Order of volatility

The order of volatility helps investigators collect the most fragile data first before it is altered or lost, then proceed toward more stable data sources. While the exact order may vary depending on the environment and investigation, it commonly follows the following sequence:

1. **Central Processing Unit (CPU) caches and registers:** Extremely small amounts of data are actively being processed by the CPU. Although highly volatile, this information is rarely useful in most investigations.
2. **Network activity:** Active network connections, packet data, and routing information change constantly while systems communicate.
3. **Memory (RAM):** Often one of the most valuable volatile sources. Memory may contain active processes, recent user activity, encryption keys, or malware designed to avoid leaving artifacts on disk.
4. **Temporary files:** Files created by operating systems and applications to store data temporarily before being written to permanent storage.
5. **Primary storage:** Data stored on the device's internal storage drive. Although less volatile than memory, it can still change as the system continues to run.
6. **Archived data:** Long-term storage such as optical media or other archival systems that is unlikely to change during an investigation.

This sequence is commonly visualized as a hierarchy of data volatility, as shown below:

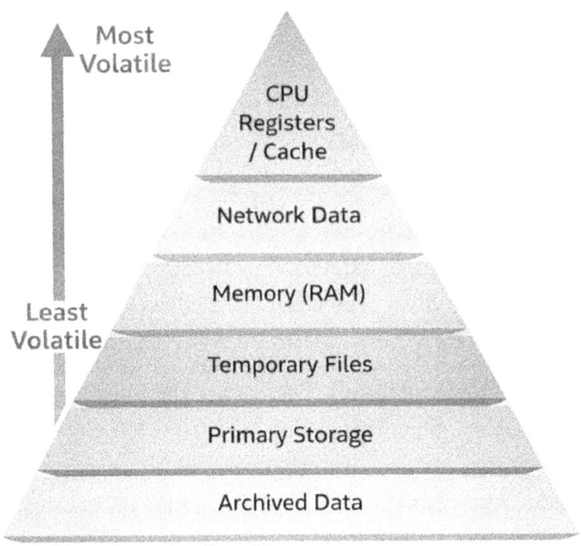

Figure A.3 – Order of volatility

The order of volatility helps guide triage decisions during evidence collection. For example, if a Windows computer is encountered in a powered-on state, investigators will often prioritize acquiring system memory before shutting the system down to preserve volatile artifacts.

Similarly, when a mobile device is found powered on and protected by a passcode, investigators typically prioritize maintaining power and isolating the device from network connectivity. Doing so may preserve volatile data associated with authentication mechanisms, such as biometric access.

Methods of collection

The method used to collect digital evidence often depends on whether a device is encountered in a powered-on or powered-off state.

Devices discovered powered off are often the simplest to collect. If investigators have reason to believe the device may contain relevant evidence, it can typically be seized and preserved for later examination without interacting with the system.

Powered-on systems require additional consideration. In these situations, investigators must evaluate how their actions may affect volatile data or system access. Powering a device off immediately may result in the loss of valuable volatile artifacts, such as system memory or active network information. In other situations, leaving a device powered on may preserve access to encrypted data that would otherwise become inaccessible.

Because of these factors, collection decisions must be made carefully and documented clearly so they can be explained if questioned later in legal proceedings.

External storage media such as USB drives or external hard drives can often be examined safely using write-blocking technology. Write blockers prevent a forensic workstation from modifying the evidence media while still allowing investigators to preview or acquire the data.

Mobile devices introduce additional challenges. Modern smartphones are typically encrypted by default and may restrict access once powered off. For this reason, investigators often attempt to preserve the current state of a device during collection. When possible, powered-on devices may be isolated from network connectivity using Faraday bags or other radio-frequency (RF) shielding methods to prevent remote access or data modification.

While computers, storage media, and mobile devices are the most common sources of digital evidence, investigators will also encounter a wide range of other electronic devices capable of storing data. As technology evolves, remaining aware of new device types and potential acquisition methods is an important part of effective forensic practice.

Artifact-based investigation

Digital forensic investigations are often described as the process of "finding evidence on a computer," but the work is rarely that simple. Rather than searching only for obvious files or documents, investigators typically rely on artifacts created by operating systems, applications, or user activity.

A `forensic artifact` is any piece of data that provides insight into how a system was used. Artifacts may reflect user actions, application behavior, system events, or communication between devices. Individually, an artifact may appear insignificant, but when multiple artifacts are correlated, they can often reveal a clear picture of what occurred on a system.

Artifacts exist throughout an operating system and within many applications. Common examples include browser history records, system event logs, application databases, configuration files, thumbnail caches, and file metadata.

These artifacts are often created automatically as systems operate and may persist even after a user attempts to delete data. For example, a user may delete a photograph from their computer, but traces of that image may still exist in thumbnail caches, application databases, system logs, or unallocated space.

Because of this, digital forensic analysis often focuses on `correlating multiple artifacts` rather than locating a single "smoking gun" file. For example, a collection of artifacts may reveal when a file was created, when it was accessed, which application opened it, where it was stored, when it was deleted, and more.

By examining these artifacts together, investigators can often reconstruct user activity even if direct evidence has been removed.

This artifact-focused approach is central to digital forensics and explains why forensic tools are designed to extract and organize artifacts from many locations across a system. The recipes throughout this book rely heavily on identifying and interpreting these artifacts during on-scene triage and analysis.

Understanding where artifacts are likely to exist is also important during triage. When multiple devices are present, investigators must prioritize the systems most likely to contain relevant artifacts, rather than attempting to collect every device encountered.

Field triage principles

Evidence triage is the process of identifying digital evidence that may be valuable to an investigation and prioritizing which items require immediate attention during collection.

Investigators often encounter many electronic devices capable of storing data, yet not all of them will be relevant to the investigation.

Triage plays a critical role in digital forensics because early decisions can determine whether important evidence is preserved or lost. Devices encountered in a powered-on state may contain volatile data or encrypted storage that could become inaccessible if handled incorrectly.

Triage also helps prevent `overcollection`, which occurs when investigators simply seize every device encountered with the intention of sorting through them later. In environments containing numerous devices, overcollection can create unnecessary analysis workload and significantly slow an investigation.

Effective triage focuses on two primary considerations:

- Which systems are most likely to contain relevant evidence
- Which systems require immediate action to preserve data

Investigators should gather as much information as possible about the case before beginning collection. Known usernames, keywords, suspected file types, device ownership, and other investigative details can help guide triage decisions.

Unlike the later stages of a forensic examination, triage may involve small elements of multiple phases of the investigative process. Investigators may perform limited acquisition, preview data, or document system conditions to quickly determine which devices should be preserved for deeper analysis.

By applying structured triage principles, investigators can focus their efforts on the systems most likely to contain useful artifacts while minimizing the risk of losing critical evidence. The techniques demonstrated throughout this book illustrate practical ways to apply triage principles during on-scene investigations.

Foundational concepts in analysis

This book is a cookbook focused on the practical application of digital forensics rather than an academic study of computer science or data structures. The goal is to demonstrate how to work through a forensic examination from start to finish and introduce techniques that investigators can apply immediately in real-world investigations.

Even so, competent analysis requires at least a basic understanding of how data is structured, how file systems organize information, and how forensic tools interpret the artifacts they identify.

Parsing the data

Data parsing is the process of organizing acquired data into a format that can be more easily reviewed and interpreted. Most of the time, this process is handled automatically by forensic tools. However, investigators occasionally need to manually examine data when tools do not support a particular artifact or when results must be validated.

At the most basic level, all digital data is stored in binary, where each bit is represented as either a 0 or a 1. When reviewing data manually, investigators typically view it in hexadecimal format because it is much easier for humans to read. Hexadecimal is a base-16 numbering system that represents values using the numbers 0 through 9 and the letters A through F.

Hexadecimal values are often prefixed with `0x` to indicate that the number is expressed in hex. For example, the ASCII letter `A` is stored in *binary* as:

```
01000001
```

The same value can be represented in *hexadecimal* as:

```
0x41
```

Forensic tools that display hexadecimal data commonly show a decoded ASCII representation alongside the raw byte values of the data to help investigators interpret the content.

You will also encounter the term `offset`, which refers to the position of bytes within a file or data structure. In the example shown in *Figure A.4*, the offset is shown in decimal format, though offsets can also be shown as hexadecimal:

Offset(h)	00	01	02	03	04	05	06	07	08	09	0A	0B	0C	0D	0E	0F	Decoded text
00000000	54	68	69	73	20	69	73	20	74	68	65	20	63	6F	6E	74	This is the cont
00000010	65	6E	74	20	6F	66	20	61	20	74	65	78	74	20	64	6F	ent of a text do
00000020	63	75	6D	65	6E	74	2E	20	57	68	61	74	20	79	6F	75	cument. What you
00000030	20	61	72	65	20	72	65	61	64	69	6E	67	20	69	73	20	are reading is
00000040	74	68	65	20	41	53	43	49	49	20	63	6F	6E	76	65	72	the ASCII conver
00000050	73	69	6F	6E	20	6F	66	20	74	68	65	20	68	65	78	2E	sion of the hex.

Figure A.4 – Viewing the content of a text file at the hexadecimal level

Viewing data at this level allows investigators to inspect raw content directly, including data that may not have been interpreted correctly by automated tools. Hexadecimal views are also useful when examining file system structures, decoding timestamps, identifying partitions, or performing manual data recovery.

File type can also be identified through hexadecimal analysis. Most files begin with a sequence of bytes known as a `file signature`, sometimes referred to as a `magic number`. File signatures help applications determine how a file should be interpreted.

For example, a PNG image begins with the file signature **0x89 50 4E 47 0D 0A 1A 0A**:

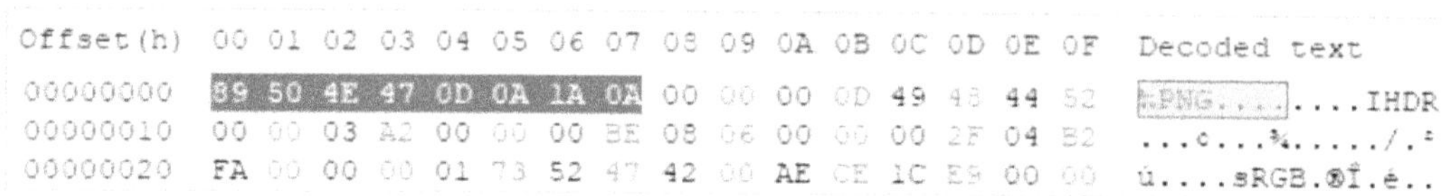

Figure A.5 – File signature of a PNG (Portable Network Graphics) image file

Forensic tools may identify file types by scanning for these signatures when locating files or carving data from unallocated space.

Understanding how data is parsed also explains why forensic tools can sometimes fail or misinterpret artifacts. If a tool expects a specific structure and an application update changes that structure, the parser may no longer interpret the artifact correctly. For example, if a SQLite database field previously named *UID* is later renamed *UserID*, an outdated parser may fail to recognize the data correctly.

For this reason, investigators should avoid relying solely on automated output and should understand at least the basic logic behind how forensic tools interpret data.

File systems

Before files can be stored on a storage device, the device must contain a `file system`. The file system organizes files and directories into a structure that allows the operating system to store, locate, and retrieve data.

When a drive is formatted, a file system is created on the partition, transforming it into a usable volume. Without a file system, the operating system would have no organized method of interacting with the storage media.

Many file systems exist, but some of the ones most commonly encountered during forensic investigations include the following:

- **FAT / exFAT**: Common on removable media such as SD cards, microSD cards, USB drives, and some external storage devices
- **NTFS**: The primary file system used by modern versions of Microsoft Windows
- **APFS**: The file system used by modern Apple systems and devices
- **ext4**: A common file system used by Linux systems and earlier Android devices
- **F2FS**: A flash-optimized file system commonly used on modern Android devices

Each file system stores and manages data differently, directly affecting how artifacts are interpreted during analysis.

For example, timestamp information in NTFS is typically stored in the `Master File Table` (`$MFT`), while similar metadata in ext4 systems is stored within `inode tables`. Understanding these structural differences helps to interpret artifacts correctly.

When reviewing raw file system structures in hexadecimal, investigators may also encounter differences in byte order, known as `endianness`:

- **Little Endian** systems store values beginning with the least significant byte
- **Big Endian** systems store values beginning with the most significant byte

Understanding endianness is important when manually interpreting values within raw data structures or when validating artifacts displayed by forensic tools.

Operating systems

While file systems organize how data is stored, the `operating system (OS)` controls how users interact with the computer and how hardware and software function together. Operating systems manage processes, memory, device communication, and system resources.

For forensic investigations, operating systems are particularly important because they generate many of the artifacts that investigators rely on during analysis. These artifacts may include system logs, application data, cached files, and other records of user activity.

The most common operating systems encountered during digital forensic investigations include Microsoft Windows, Apple macOS, Linux, Apple iOS, and Android.

Each operating system handles artifacts, logging, and system behavior differently, which is why a basic understanding of operating system functionality is valuable when interpreting forensic evidence. The recipes throughout this book demonstrate practical techniques for identifying and analyzing artifacts across these environments.

Common operating system directory structures

Understanding common operating system directory structures helps investigators quickly locate user data, application artifacts, and system files during an examination. This section provides a high-level reference to key directories across major operating systems and highlights where relevant forensic artifacts are commonly found.

Microsoft Windows

At the root of a Windows system (typically C:\) are several key directories used to store system files, applications, and user data:

- `\Windows` – Core operating system files
- `\Program Files / Program Files (x86)` – Installed applications (64-bit / 32-bit)

- `\ProgramData` – Application data shared across users
- `\Users` – User account directories

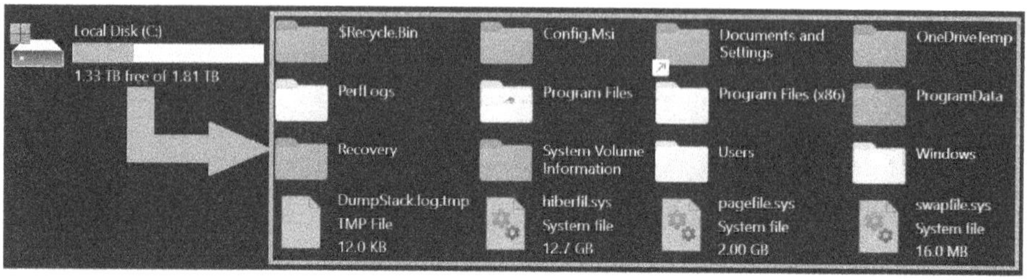

Figure A.6 – Microsoft Windows root directory contents

Within the `\Users` directory are subdirectories for each user account on the system:

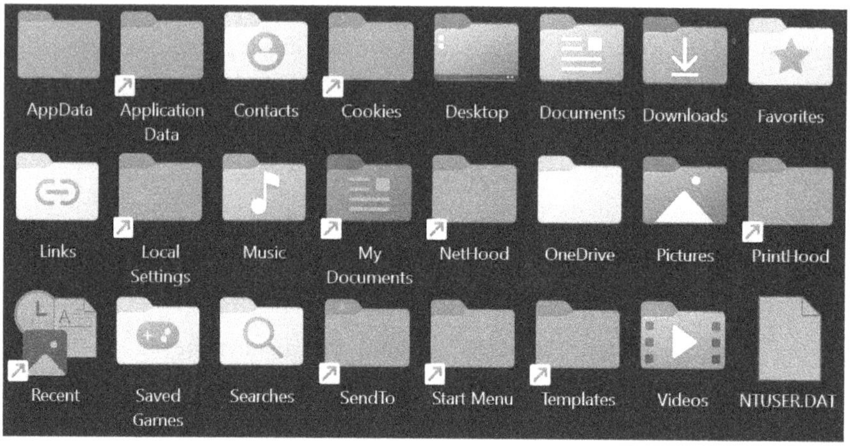

Figure A.7 – Microsoft Windows user account contents

Common user directories such as Desktop, Documents, Downloads, Pictures, and Videos store user-generated content and often contain valuable evidence of user activity. Third-party applications may create additional folders within user profiles.

Each user profile contains a hidden `AppData` directory:

- `\AppData\Local` – System-specific application data
- `\AppData\LocalLow` – Low-integrity applications
- `\AppData\Roaming` – User-specific data that may persist across systems

Figure A.8 – Microsoft Windows AppData contents

Windows uses a `Security Identifier (SID)` to uniquely identify a system and associated user accounts. It follows the format:

Figure A.9 – Microsoft Windows SID architecture

Key components include:

- **Authority** – Identifies the issuing authority (commonly 5 for NT Authority)
- **Domain Identifier** – Unique to the system or domain and can be used to distinguish systems within a network
- **Relative ID (RID)** – Identifies the specific user or group

Common RID values include:

- **500** – Local Administrator account
- **1001+** – Standard user accounts (incremented for each new user)
- **544** – Domain Administrators group

In forensic analysis, SIDs are frequently used to map artifacts to specific user accounts, identify user activity across systems, and correlate accounts in multi-user environments.

Apple macOS

At the root of a macOS volume are several key directories used to store system files, applications, and user data:

- `/System` – Core operating system files
- `/Applications` – Installed applications
- `/Library` – System-wide application support and configuration
- `/Users` – User account directories
- `/private` – Contains system data, including `/private/var` and `/private/etc`

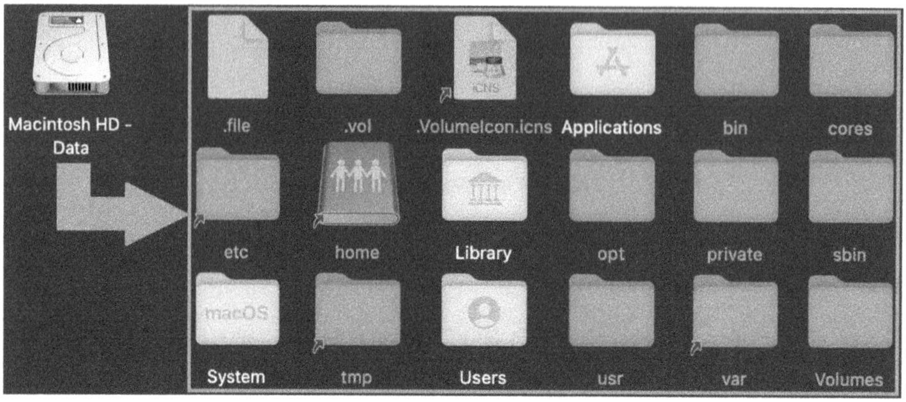

Figure A.10 – Apple macOS root directory contents

Within the `/Users` directory are subdirectories for each user account

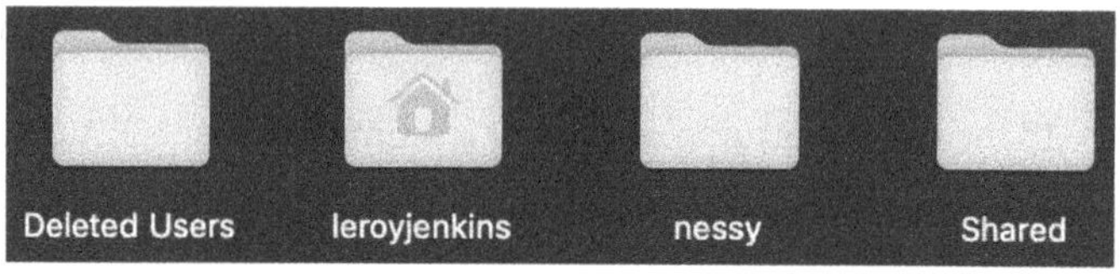

Figure A.11 – Apple macOS user subdirectories

Deleted user home directories may be preserved as .dmg images within a `Deleted Users` directory depending on system configuration.

macOS restricts access between user accounts by default, and accessing another user's home directory without proper permissions will result in access errors:

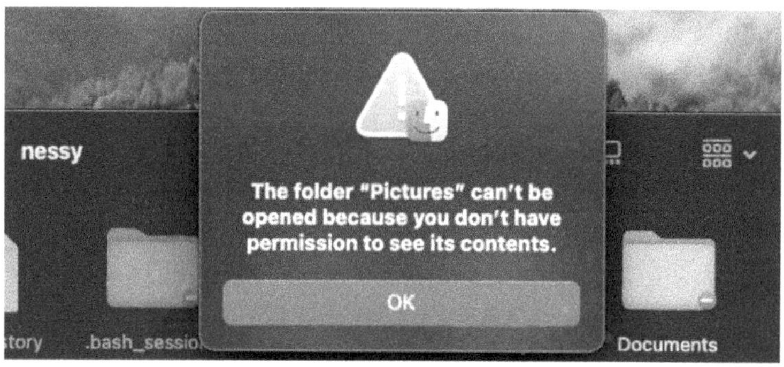

Figure A.12 – Error message from attempting to access a user account in macOS

Instead, if one user wishes to share files with another user on the system, they can do so using the *Shared* folder within the *Users* directory (*/Users/Shared*). Files stored here can be accessed by other users but are typically modifiable only by the owning user.

Each user profile also contains a hidden `Library` directory:

Figure A.13 – User account subfolders in macOS

Common user directories such as Desktop, Documents, Downloads, Movies, Music, and Pictures store user-generated content and frequently contain artifacts relevant to user activity.

Additionally, these locations frequently contain application artifacts, user preferences, and cached data:

- `/Library/Application` Support – Application data
- `/Library/Preferences` – Configuration files

Linux

The root of a Linux file system contains directories used for system binaries, configuration files, logs, and user data:

- `/bin` and `/sbin` – System binaries
- `/etc` – System configuration files
- `/var` – Logs and variable data
- `/usr` – Installed applications
- `/tmp` – Temporary files
- `/home` – User account directories

Figure A.14 – Linux root directory contents

Within the /home directory are subdirectories for each user account.

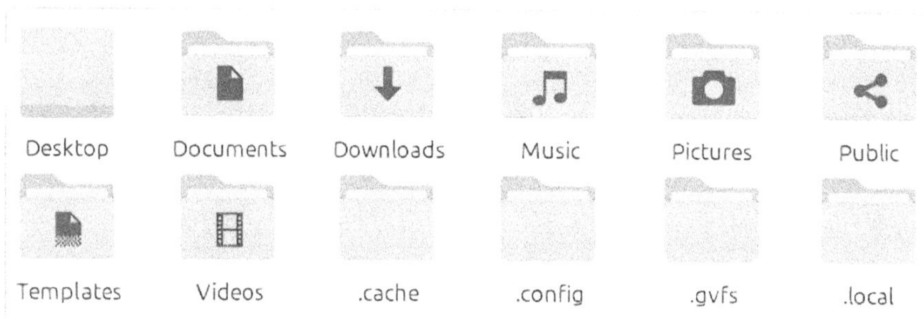

Figure A.15 – Linux user account directories

Like Windows and macOS, common user directories such as Desktop, Documents, Downloads, Music, Pictures, and Videos store user-generated content and frequently contain artifacts of user activity.

Several key per-user locations that often contain forensically relevant artifacts include:

- `~/.config` – User configuration files
- `~/.local` – Application data
- `~/.cache` – Cached files (thumbnails, activity artifacts)

These locations frequently contain application artifacts, user activity traces, and cached content.

Linux also provides users with the following shared directories:

- ~/Public – Shared files accessible to other users
- ~/Templates – User-created file templates

Apple iOS

iOS uses a sandboxed file system structure where application data is stored within isolated containers. Most relevant data resides within the */private/var/* directory:

- /private/var/mobile/ – Primary user data location
- /private/var/mobile/Containers/ – Application sandbox directories

Common artifact locations include the following:

- Library/Application Support – Application databases and user data
- Library/Preferences – Application settings (plist files)
- Library/Caches – Cached data and temporary files

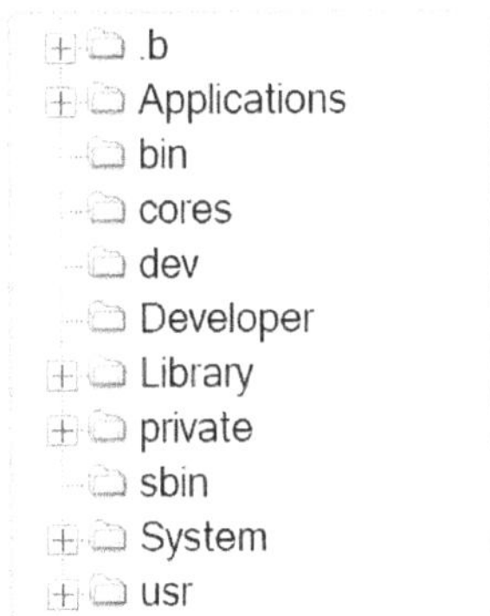

Figure A.16 – Apple iOS directories from full file system acquisition

In the iOS environment, application container names are completely randomized (UUIDs) and must be mapped to applications. These UUIDs are therefore different on every device. Data is also app-isolated by design, requiring investigators to perform analysis on a per-application basis.

Android

Android uses a Linux-based file system structure, with most application and user data stored within the */data/* directory:

- /data/data/<application_id>/ – Primary application data

- /data/user/<user>/<application_id>/ – Same as above (primary user)
- /data/media/<user>/ – User-accessible storage (photos, downloads, etc.)

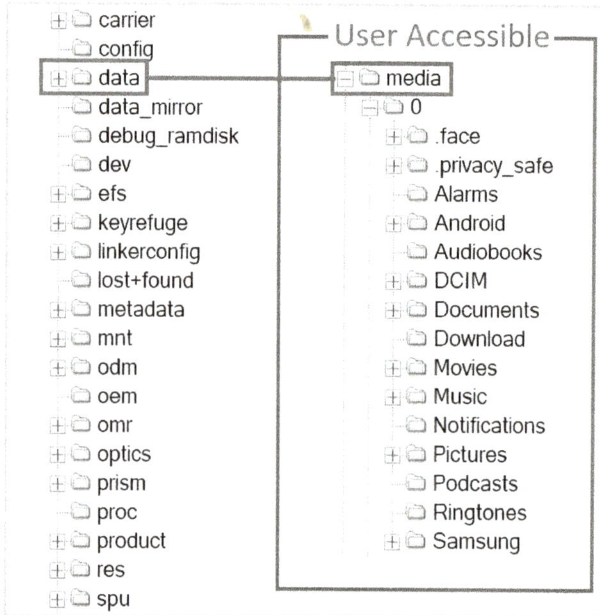

Figure A.17 – Android directory structure showing the user data directory

Android also supports multiple user profiles, which are reflected in the directory structure. Multiple user accounts may exist, though the most commonly encountered include:

- /data/media/0/ – Primary user
- /data/media/10/ – Secondary user
- /data/media/11/ – Third user (or Private Space for Google Pixel devices)
- /data/media/12/ – Fourth user
- /data/media/95/ – Dual-apps enabled to run two instances of the same app
- /data/media/150/ – Secure Folder (Samsung devices)

Figure A.18 – Android account 150 enabled for Samsung Secure Folder

The presence of additional user IDs (especially `150`) may indicate Secure Folder usage or attempts to separate or conceal data.

Key digital forensic terms

Clear and well-defined terminology is essential when describing digital forensic artifacts or evidence discovered during an investigation. Ambiguous language can easily lead to confusion or misinterpretation when explaining findings to investigators, attorneys, or a court.

For example, what does it mean when we say a file is "*deleted*" or "*active*"? Many computer users would consider a file placed in the Microsoft Windows Recycle Bin or macOS Trash to be deleted. However, the file is still allocated by the file system and can be restored by the user without specialized software. Is the file truly deleted, or is it still active and easily accessible?

Situations like this demonstrate why forensic terminology must be precise and consistently applied. Without consistent definitions, simple terms can become subjective and lead to inaccurate conclusions when describing digital evidence.

Just as following a recipe requires understanding key ingredients, digital forensic investigations require clear and consistent terminology. The following definitions establish consistent terminology used throughout this book and reflect how these terms are applied in real investigations:

- **Active File** - A file that remains allocated by the file system and is accessible to the operating system. Active files are sometimes referred to as *live files*.
- **Allocated Space** - The portion of storage that contains active files and is tracked by the file system.
- **Binary Copy** - Two files that are identical at the bit-for-bit level, meaning every byte of data is exactly the same
- **Cached** - Data temporarily stored by the operating system or an application to improve performance or reduce load times. Cached files are often stored in hidden system locations and may remain on a system even after the original file is deleted.
- **Carving** - The process of recovering data by identifying file signatures and reconstructing file content based on known data structures
- **Deleted File** - A file that has been removed from the file system's active directory structure. Although the file is no longer easily accessible to the user, the data may still exist within unallocated space until it is overwritten
- **Directory** - Often referred to as a *folder*, a directory is a container used to organize files within a hierarchical structure.

- **Easily Accessible Data -** Data that an average user can locate and access without specialized tools or advanced technical knowledge.
- **EXIF Data -** Metadata embedded within digital photographs and some video files. EXIF (Exchangeable Image Format) data may include camera settings, device information, timestamps, and sometimes geographic location data.
- **File Attributes -** Properties associated with a file or directory, such as creation time, modification time, access time, hidden status, compression status, or encryption flags. These values should be interpreted carefully because different operating systems update them in different ways.
- **File Signature -** The identifying sequence of bytes located at the beginning of a file. File signatures (sometimes called *magic numbers*) help determine file type regardless of the file extension.
- **File System -** The structure used to organize and manage files on a storage device. The file system defines how files are stored, indexed, and retrieved by the operating system. Common file systems include NTFS, APFS, ext4, and FAT/exFAT.
- **Hashing -** A mathematical process used to generate a unique value from data. In digital forensics, hash values help verify evidence integrity and identify known files using hash databases. Common algorithms include MD5 and members of the SHA-1 and SHA-2 families.
- **Logical Drive -** A virtual storage volume presented to the operating system. Multiple logical drives can exist on a single physical disk.
- **Metadata -** Data that describes other data. For example, a document may contain text as its primary content, while metadata may record the author, timestamps, or the application used to create the file.
- **Operating System (OS) -** Software responsible for managing hardware, system resources, and user interaction with the computer. Common operating systems include Microsoft Windows, macOS, Linux, Android, and iOS.
- **Partition -** A defined section of a physical storage device used to organize data. A single disk may contain multiple partitions.
- **Physical Drive -** The actual hardware storage device, such as a hard disk drive (HDD) or solid state drive (SSD).
- **Slack Space -** Unused space within a storage cluster that may contain remnants of previously stored data.
- **Thumbnail -** A small cached image generated by the OS or applications to preview media files. Thumbnails often remain on a system even after the original file is deleted.

- **Unallocated Space -** Areas of storage not currently assigned to active files. Unallocated space often contains remnants of deleted data that may be recoverable.
- **Wiping -** A process where data is intentionally overwritten to prevent recovery. Wiping is commonly used to sanitize storage devices but may also be used as an anti-forensic technique.

> Note
>
> Active, Deleted, Cached, or Easily Accessible?
>
> Some of these terms may appear similar, but it is important to distinguish among them.
>
> For example, **cached files are technically active files**, but they are not always easily accessible to an average user because they are stored automatically by the system in hidden directories or application databases.
>
> Similarly, a file placed in the *Recycle Bin* or *Trash* is not truly deleted. The file remains allocated and can be restored by the user without special tools. Because of this, it is more accurate to describe such files as **active and easily accessible** rather than deleted.
>
> Maintaining consistent terminology helps ensure that investigators clearly communicate their findings and avoid misunderstandings when explaining digital evidence.

The concepts in this appendix provide foundational context for the practical techniques presented throughout this book. The chapters in the book move away from theory and focus on applying these principles in real-world digital forensic scenarios.

Appendix B

Digital Forensic Analysis Field Guide

This appendix serves as a quick-reference field guide for commonly encountered digital forensic artifacts across multiple operating systems. It is designed to support investigators during analysis by providing concise locations and context for key artifacts without interrupting workflow.

How to Use This Field Guide

Throughout this book, the operating system chapters focused on demonstrating practical investigative techniques using a selection of common forensic artifacts. These artifacts were chosen to illustrate how investigators locate, interpret, and validate digital evidence during an examination.

In real investigations, however, examiners often need a broader reference to help locate additional artifacts across a system. This appendix serves as a practical field guide that consolidates common artifact locations and investigative workflows for the platforms covered in this book:

- Microsoft Windows
- Apple macOS
- Linux
- Apple iOS
- Android
- Memory (RAM)

Each section highlights commonly encountered artifacts, where they are typically located, and how they can help answer investigative questions. These sections are intended as quick reference material that investigators can consult when navigating large datasets or when working with unfamiliar operating systems.

While individual artifacts rarely tell the entire story on their own, correlating evidence across multiple artifact sources often allows investigators to reconstruct user activity and system behavior with a high degree of confidence.

Use this guide alongside automated forensic tools to quickly reference artifact locations, perform deeper analysis, and validate investigative findings.

Microsoft Windows

The following steps outline a practical approach to analyzing Microsoft Windows systems by focusing on common artifacts that help establish user activity, system configuration, and investigative context.

Step 1: Identify the users and basic system context

These artifacts help determine what user accounts existed on the system, which profiles were active, the system name and OS configuration, the correct time zone for timeline analysis, and which user-specific artifacts belong to which user.

Establishing this context prevents misattribution of activity to the wrong user account.

- User profile directories
  `C:\Users\`
- System Registry hives
  `C:\Windows\System32\Config\`
- Per-user Registry hives
  `C:\Users\<User>\NTUSER.DAT`

  `C:\Users\<User>\AppData\Local\Microsoft\Windows\UsrClass.dat`
- Most useful hives
  - **SAM** – user account information
  - **SYSTEM** – system configuration, time zone, device history
  - **SOFTWARE** – installed applications and OS settings
  - **SECURITY** – local security settings and policies

  - **NTUSER.DAT** – per-user settings and activity artifacts
  - **UsrClass.dat** – per-user shell and folder interaction artifacts

Step 2: Determine what programs were executed

These artifacts help determine whether a program was executed, approximately when it was first or last run, how many times it was run, whether persistence mechanisms were configured, and whether execution appears normal or suspicious.

Together, these artifacts provide strong evidence that a program executed on a system, even if the original executable has been removed. These artifacts can be further cross-verified with Windows Event Logs.

- Windows Prefetch
  `C:\Windows\Prefetch\`
- ShimCache (Application Compatibility Cache)
  `SYSTEM\CurrentControlSet\Control\Session Manager\AppCompatCache`

  *Registry value within SYSTEM hive
- Amcache
  `C:\Windows\AppCompat\Programs\Amcache.hve`
- Scheduled Tasks
  `C:\Windows\System32\Tasks`
- Service-related artifacts
  `SYSTEM\CurrentControlSet\Services`

Step 3: Determine what files existed and what happened to them

These artifacts help determine whether a file existed on the system, whether it was renamed, moved, modified, or deleted, the original path of deleted files, whether a file was opened by a user, and whether a file may have existed on removable media.

Compare findings with user activity artifacts to determine intent.

- Master File Table
  `Root of NTFS volume: \$MFT`
- USN Change Journal
  `Root of NTFS volume: \$Extend\$UsnJrnl:$J`
- Recycle Bin

C:\$Recycle.Bin

- Recent files / LNK files
  C:\Users\<User>\AppData\Roaming\Microsoft\Windows\Recent

  C:\Users\<User>\AppData\Roaming\Microsoft\Office\Recent

Step 4: Reconstruct user activity in Windows Explorer

These artifacts help determine which files and folders a user accessed, whether removable drives or network shares were browsed, what files were opened or saved, and which documents or applications were frequently accessed.

Explorer artifacts often provide direct insight into user interaction with files and storage locations, even if the files themselves are no longer present.

- RecentDocs
  NTUSER.DAT\SOFTWARE\Microsoft\Windows\CurrentVersion\Explorer\RecentDocs
- Open/Save dialog MRUs
  NTUSER.DAT\SOFTWARE\Microsoft\Windows\CurrentVersion\Explorer\ComDlg32\OpenSavePidlMRU
- ShellBags
  UsrClass.dat\Local Settings\Software\Microsoft\Windows\Shell\BagMRU

  UsrClass.dat\Local Settings\Software\Microsoft\Windows\Shell\Bags
- Jump Lists
  C:
  \Users\<User>\AppData\Roaming\Microsoft\Windows\Recent\AutomaticDestinations

  C:
  \Users\<User>\AppData\Roaming\Microsoft\Windows\Recent\CustomDestinations
- Shortcut files
  C:\Users\<User>\AppData\Roaming\Microsoft\Windows\Recent

Step 5: Determine web activity and downloads

These artifacts help determine websites visited, search terms used by the user, files downloaded from the internet, whether accounts were used or authenticated, and whether browser profiles synchronized with cloud services.

Browser artifacts often provide the clearest evidence of user intent and online activity.

Common browser user data locations:

- Microsoft Edge
  C:\Users\<User>\AppData\Local\Microsoft\Edge\User Data\Default\
- Google Chrome
  C:\Users\<User>\AppData\Local\Google\Chrome\User Data\Default\
- Firefox
  C:\Users\<User>\AppData\Roaming\Mozilla\Firefox\Profiles\

Step 6: Determine whether external devices were connected

These artifacts help determine which USB devices were connected, device manufacturer and serial numbers, drive-letter assignments, when devices were first installed or mounted, and whether files or folders on those devices were accessed.

USB artifacts can often link a specific removable device to a system, and sometimes to specific user activity.

- USB device history
  SYSTEM\CurrentControlSet\Enum\USBSTOR

  SYSTEM\CurrentControlSet\Enum\USB
- Mounted devices
  SYSTEM\MountedDevices
- SetupAPI device logs
  C:\Windows\inf\setupapi.dev.log

Additional corroborating artifacts for removable-media interaction include:

- LNK Files
  C:\Users\<User>\AppData\Roaming\Microsoft\Windows\Recent\

  C:\Users\<User>\AppData\Roaming\Microsoft\Office\Recent\

  C:\ProgramData\Microsoft\Windows\Start Menu\Programs\
- Jump Lists
  C:
  \Users\<User>\AppData\Roaming\Microsoft\Windows\Recent\AutomaticDestinations\

```
C:
\Users\<User>\AppData\Roaming\Microsoft\Windows\Recent\CustomDestinations\
```

- ShellBags
```
UsrClass.dat\Local Settings\Software\Microsoft\Windows\Shell\BagMRU
UsrClass.dat\Local Settings\Software\Microsoft\Windows\Shell\Bags
```

Step 7: Determine what happened on the system

Event logs help determine who logged onto the system and when, failed authentication attempts, system startup and shutdown events, account creation or modification, remote access activity, and attempts to clear or tamper with the logs.

Event logs are often the most reliable chronological record of system activity.

- Location
`C:\Windows\System32\winevt\Logs\`
    - **4624** – Successful logon
    - **4625** – Failed logon
    - **4634** / **4647** – Logoff
    - **4720** / **4726** – User created / deleted
    - **4723** – Password change
    - **1074** – Restart/shutdown
    - **6013** – System uptime
    - **4616** – System time changed
    - **4778** / **4779** – Remote session connect/disconnect
    - **1102** / **104** – Logs cleared

Step 8: Determine network and application usage

These artifacts help determine which applications used network resources, which networks the system connected to, historical network activity patterns, and whether suspicious applications communicated externally.

- SRUM
`C:\Windows\System32\sru\SRUDB.dat`
- Network profile registry data
`SOFTWARE\Microsoft\Windows NT\CurrentVersion\NetworkList`
- Firewall logs

```
C:\Windows\System32\LogFiles\Firewall\
```

Apple macOS

The following steps outline a practical approach to analyzing macOS systems by focusing on common artifacts that help establish user activity, system configuration, and investigative context.

Step 1: Identify users and system context

These artifacts help determine what user accounts exist on the system, which users may have logged in, the system hostname and configuration, time zone settings, and user-specific application settings.

Establishing this context first is critical because most later artifacts are stored on a per-user basis and must be correctly attributed.

- User home directories
  `/Users/`
- System configuration files
  `/Library/Preferences/`
- User preference files
  `/Users/<User>/Library/Preferences/`
- User account database
  `/var/db/dslocal/nodes/Default/users/`

Step 2: Determine what applications were executed

These artifacts help determine what applications were installed, whether applications were launched or associated with files, whether files were downloaded from the internet, and which application opened a file or handled downloaded content.

Application execution on macOS is often reconstructed by combining logs, quarantine metadata, Launch Services data, and file artifacts, rather than relying on a single execution artifact.

- Unified logs
  `/private/var/db/diagnostics/`

  **Modern macOS systems use a centralized unified logging system*

  **These logs often require specialized tooling or parsing to interpret effectively*
- Launch Services artifacts

`/Users/<User>/Library/Preferences/com.apple.LaunchServices/`

- Quarantine database (SQLite)
  `/Users/<User>/Library/Preferences/`
  `com.apple.LaunchServices.QuarantineEventsV2`
- Application installation locations
  `/Applications/`
  `/Users/<User>/Applications/`

Step 3: Determine file activity

These artifacts help determine when files were created or modified, where files were located on disk, whether files were indexed by the system, and the file paths associated with user activity.

On macOS, Spotlight and APFS metadata often provide valuable context when direct user artifacts are incomplete.

- File timestamps
  APFS commonly records Created/Modified/Accessed/Metadata modified timestamps. These timestamps are usually examined through forensic tools capable of parsing APFS volumes or through timelining techniques.
- Spotlight index
  `/System/Volumes/Data/.Spotlight-V100/`
- Spotlight metadata database
  Stored within .Spotlight-V100/ and parsed through forensic tools

Step 4: Reconstruct user file interaction

These artifacts help determine which files were recently opened, which folders or locations were accessed, whether documents were edited or revised, and which applications interacted with those files.

These are some of the most useful macOS artifacts for reconstructing user-driven file interaction rather than just file existence.

- Shared file lists / Recent Items
  `/Users/<User>/Library/Application Support/com.apple.sharedfilelist/`
- Finder preferences
  `/Users/<User>/Library/Preferences/com.apple.finder.plist`
- Document revision storage

/Users/<User>/.DocumentRevisions-V100/

Step 5: Determine whether files were deleted

These artifacts help determine which files were deleted, original file names and paths, when files were removed, and whether previous versions of files still exist.

On macOS, deleted-file investigations frequently depend on Trash artifacts and APFS snapshot analysis, especially when local file-system metadata is limited.

- User Trash
  /Users/<User>/.Trash/

  Note: External volumes may also contain .Trashes directories.

- APFS snapshots
  APFS supports snapshots that may preserve prior states of files and folders. These are typically examined using forensic tools capable of parsing APFS snapshots.

Step 6: Determine web browsing activity

These artifacts help determine websites visited, searches performed, files downloaded, user login sessions, and cached web content viewed by the user.

Browser artifacts often provide the clearest evidence of intent, online activity, and account usage on macOS systems.

- Safari history
  /Users/<User>/Library/Safari/History.db

- Safari downloads
  /Users/<User>/Library/Safari/Downloads.plist

- Safari cookies
  /Users/<User>/Library/Cookies/Cookies.binarycookies

- Chromium-based browser locations
  /Users/<User>/Library/Application Support/<Browser>/

Step 7: Determine whether external devices were connected

These artifacts help determine when external drives were connected, volume names and identifiers, mount and unmount activity, and whether removable media was accessed by the user.

On macOS, device attribution often depends on combining system logs, mount information, Finder artifacts, and per-volume metadata.

- System logs
  `/private/var/log/`
- Traditional system log
  `/private/var/log/system.log`
- System configuration
  `/Library/Preferences/SystemConfiguration/`
- Mounted volumes
  `/Volumes/`
- Finder preferences
  `/Users/<User>/Library/Preferences/com.apple.finder.plist`

Step 8: Examine system and application logs

These logs help determine login and authentication activity, system boot and shutdown behavior, software installation events, and application errors or crashes.

Unified logs are among the most valuable macOS evidence sources, but they often require filtering and targeted parsing because of their volume.

- Unified logging system
  `/private/var/db/diagnostics/`
- Traditional logs
  `/private/var/log/`
    - system.log
    - install.log

Step 9: Identify network and system usage

These artifacts help determine networks the system connected to, previously known wireless networks, network interface configuration, and possible location or environmental context.

These artifacts can be especially useful for placing a device in a specific physical or network environment.

- Network configuration
  `/Library/Preferences/SystemConfiguration/`

  `com.apple.airport.preferences.plist`

- NetworkInterfaces.plist
  `preferences.plist`
- Wi-Fi network history
  `/Library/Preferences/SystemConfiguration/`
  `com.apple.airport.preferences.plist`

Linux

The following steps outline a practical approach to analyzing Linux systems by focusing on common artifacts that help establish user activity, system configuration, and investigative context.

Step 1: Identify system configuration and users

These artifacts help determine which user accounts exist, which users may have administrative privileges, the system hostname and distribution/version, default user environments and login shells, and whether service accounts or unusual users were present.

- User account database
  `/etc/passwd`
- Encrypted password file
  `/etc/shadow`
- Group membership
  `/etc/group`
- Hostname and host configuration
  `/etc/hostname`

  `/etc/hosts`
- Distribution / OS identification
  `/etc/os-release`

Step 2: Identify user logins and authentication activity

These artifacts help determine successful logins, failed login attempts, SSH access activity, session durations, and possible brute-force or unauthorized access attempts.

- Authentication logs (Debian/Ubuntu)
  `/var/log/auth.log`
- Authentication logs (Red Hat / CentOS / Fedora)
  `/var/log/secure`

- Login session history
  /var/log/wtmp
- Failed login attempts
  /var/log/btmp
- Last login information
  /var/log/lastlog

Step 3: Determine command execution history

These artifacts help determine commands executed by users, file access attempts, network utilities used, administrative activity, and possible attacker actions or tradecraft.

- Bash history
  /home/<user>/.bash_history
- Root shell history
  /root/.bash_history
- Other shell histories
  /home/<user>/.zsh_history

  /home/<user>/.history

Step 4: Determine program execution and persistence

These artifacts help determine what programs were configured to run automatically, whether persistence mechanisms were set up, whether suspicious scripts were scheduled or launched at login, and whether malware or attackers established recurring execution.

- Cron job configuration
  /etc/crontab

  /etc/cron.d/

  /var/spool/cron/

  /var/spool/cron/crontabs/
- Systemd services
  /etc/systemd/system/

  /lib/systemd/system/

  /usr/lib/systemd/system/
- Legacy startup scripts

/etc/init.d/

- User login / shell startup files
  /home/<user>/.bashrc

  /home/<user>/.profile

  /home/<user>/.bash_profile

Step 5: Examine file system activity

These artifacts help determine file creation and modification activity, temporary file usage, possible staging of tools or stolen data, and suspicious file placement in writable directories.

- Common file system types
  Linux systems commonly use ext4, XFS, or Btrfs.
- Typical file timestamps
  Linux files commonly record: Access time (atime), Modification time (mtime), and Metadata change time (ctime)
- Locations to focus on first
  /home/

  /tmp/

  /var/tmp/

  /var/log/

  /opt/

  /usr/local/bin/

Step 6: Review system and application logs

These logs help determine system startup and shutdown events, software installation activity, hardware and device events, service errors and failures, and suspicious system behavior.

- General system logs
  /var/log/syslog

  or

  /var/log/messages
- Boot logs
  /var/log/boot.log

- Kernel logs
  `/var/log/kern.log`
- Package installation logs
  `/var/log/dpkg.log`

  or

  `/var/log/yum.log`
- System journal
  `/var/log/journal/`

Step 7: Determine network configuration and remote access

These artifacts help determine interface configuration, remote access methods used, SSH key-based access, firewall rules and exposure, and possible backdoor access mechanisms.

- Network configuration
  `/etc/network/`

  `/etc/netplan/`

  `/etc/sysconfig/network-scripts/`
- Firewall configuration
  `/etc/iptables/`

  `/etc/firewalld/`
- SSH server configuration
  `/etc/ssh/sshd_config`
- Authorized SSH keys
  `/home/<user>/.ssh/authorized_keys`

  `/root/.ssh/authorized_keys`

Step 8: Examine package management artifacts

These artifacts help determine software installed on the system, approximate installation times, update activity, and whether suspicious packages were installed normally or bypassed the package manager entirely.

- Debian-based systems
  `/var/log/dpkg.log`

`/var/lib/dpkg/`

- Red Hat-based systems

  `/var/log/yum.log`

  or

  `/var/log/dnf.log`

  `/var/lib/rpm/`

Step 9: Examine running services, processes, and exposed functionality

These artifacts help determine active services on the system, network ports exposed by those services, possible unauthorized services, and relationships between configuration and runtime behavior.

- Process information

  `/proc/`

  Runtime process and network context

  `/proc/net/`

- Service definitions

  `/etc/services`

  `/etc/systemd/system/`

  `/lib/systemd/system/`

Apple iOS

The following steps outline a practical approach to analyzing iOS devices by focusing on application data and system artifacts that help reconstruct user activity.

Step 1: Identify the device and user context

These artifacts help determine the probable device owner or primary user, the Apple ID associated with the device, the device name/model, and iOS version, time zone settings, phone number, ICCID, IMEI, MEID, and whether the device was set up fresh or restored from backup.

- Device preference files

  `/private/var/mobile/Library/Preferences/`

  `/private/var/root/Library/Lockdown/`

- Common examples include:
  `/private/var/mobile/Library/Preferences/com.apple.preferences.plist`

  `/private/var/root/Library/Lockdown/data_ark.plist`

  `/private/var/mobile/Library/Preferences/com.apple.homesharing.plist`

  `/private/var/mobile/Library/Preferences/com.apple.purplebuddy.plist`

- Telephony and device identifiers
  `/private/var/wireless/Library/Preferences/com.apple.commcenter.plist`

  `/private/var/wireless/Library/Preferences/`
  `com.apple.commcenter.device_specific_nobackup.plist`

  `/private/var/wireless/Library/Databases/CellularUsage.db`

- System / support logs
  `/private/var/logs/AppleSupport/`

Step 2: Determine installed applications and app ownership

These artifacts help determine what applications were installed, which were native vs. third-party, which container belongs to which app, when an app was acquired, which account acquired it, and what permissions the user granted to the app.

- Application state / installed apps
  `/private/var/mobile/Library/FrontBoard/applicationState.db`

- App bundle containers
  `/private/var/containers/Bundle/Application/<UUID>/`

- App data containers
  `/private/var/mobile/Containers/Data/Application/<UUID>/`

- Shared app-group containers
  `/private/var/mobile/Containers/Shared/AppGroup/<UUID>/`

- App metadata files
  Common examples include:

  `Info.plist`

  `iTunesMetadata.plist`

  `.com.apple.mobile_container_manager.metadata.plist`

- App permission database

`/private/var/mobile/Library/TCC/TCC.db`

Step 3: Reconstruct communications activity

These artifacts help determine messages sent and received, timestamps of communications, phone numbers, names and contact relationships, incoming, outgoing, and missed calls, voicemail activity, and whether third-party communication apps were used.

- SMS / iMessage
  `/private/var/mobile/Library/SMS/sms.db`
- Call history
  `/private/var/mobile/Library/CallHistoryDB/CallHistory.storedata`
- Contacts
  `/private/var/mobile/Library/AddressBook/AddressBook.sqlitedb`
- Voicemail
  `/private/var/mobile/Library/Voicemail/voicemail.db`
- Third-party messaging apps
  Typically within the app's Data container

  `/private/var/mobile/Containers/Data/Application/<UUID>/`

Step 4: Determine browser and internet activity

These artifacts help determine websites visited, browsing timestamps, user-created bookmarks, authenticated sessions preserved in cookies, and browser-related downloads or saved web content.

- Safari artifacts
  `/private/var/mobile/Library/Safari/History.db`

  `/private/var/mobile/Library/Safari/Bookmarks.db`

  `/private/var/mobile/Library/Cookies/Cookies.binarycookies`
- Third-party browsers
  Usually within each browser's app data container:

  `/private/var/mobile/Containers/Data/Application/<UUID>/`

Step 5: Identify photos, videos, and user files

These artifacts help determine what photos and videos were stored on the device, when media was created, imported, or deleted, whether content was local, synced, or cloud-only, whether a file was marked as trashed, and whether iCloud-stored files existed on or beyond the device.

- User media storage
  `/private/var/mobile/Media/DCIM/`
- Photos metadata
  `/private/var/mobile/Media/PhotoData/Photos.sqlite`
- Thumbnails
  `/private/var/mobile/Media/PhotoData/Thumbnails/`
- Files / iCloud file storage
  `/private/var/mobile/Library/MobileDocuments/`
- CloudDocs sync databases
  `/private/var/mobile/Library/ApplicationSupport/CloudDocs/session/db/client.db`

  `/private/var/mobile/Library/ApplicationSupport/CloudDocs/session/db/server.db`

Step 6: Determine location history and movement

These artifacts help determine where the device traveled, approximate movement patterns, geographic locations associated with user activity, whether photos were taken at specific places, and whether the device itself was at a location or merely received data from that location.

- Routined / cached location data
  `/private/var/mobile/Library/Caches/com.apple.routined/cache.db`
- Other location-related caches
  `/private/var/mobile/Library/Caches/locationd/`
- Photo GPS data
  Embedded within media EXIF and correlated through

  `/private/var/mobile/Media/PhotoData/Photos.sqlite`

Step 7: Examine user interactions and runtime behavior

These artifacts help determine lock and unlock states, screen and backlight activity, app usage and focus changes, battery level and charging events, flashlight use, power-on and power-off behavior, and more.

- PowerLog
  `/private/var/containers/Shared/SystemGroup/<GUID>/Library/BatteryLife/CurrentPowerlog.PLSQL`
- KnowledgeC
  `/private/var/mobile/Library/CoreDuet/knowledge/knowledgeC.db`
- Biomes
  `/private/var/mobile/Library/Biome/streams/restricted/`
- Power-related logs
  `/private/var/mobile/Library/Logs/mobileactivationd/`

  `/private/var/db/diagnostics/`

Step 8: Examine system, diagnostics, and wireless artifacts

These artifacts help determine what Wi-Fi networks the device knew or connected to, Bluetooth pairings and nearby-device relationships, support and diagnostic context, and possible device location context through known SSIDs.

- Wi-Fi artifacts
  Common examples include

  `/private/var/preferences/com.apple.wifi.known-networks.plist`
- Bluetooth artifacts
  Common examples include

  `/Library/Preferences/com.apple.Bluetooth.plist`

  `/Library/Preferences/com.apple.MobileBluetooth.devices.plist`
- Diagnostics / support logs
  `/private/var/log/`

  `/private/var/mobile/Library/Logs/`

  `/private/var/logs/AppleSupport/`

Step 9: Examine backups and synced-device data

These backups and sync sources may contain message databases, call history, contacts, application data, photos and metadata, and prior versions of artifacts that are no longer obvious on the device.

- macOS backup location
  `~/Library/Application Support/MobileSync/Backup/`
- Windows backup location
  `C:\Users\<User>\AppData\Roaming\Apple Computer\MobileSync\Backup\`
- On-device synced/cloud artifacts
  `/private/var/mobile/Library/MobileDocuments/`

  `/private/var/mobile/Library/ApplicationSupport/CloudDocs/`

Android

The following steps outline a practical approach to analyzing Android devices by focusing on application data and system artifacts that help reconstruct user activity.

Step 1: Identify the device, users, and system context

These artifacts help determine device manufacturer and model, Android OS version, device phone number, ICCID and SIM details, configured user accounts and user IDs, whether secondary profiles or Secure Folder exist, and Google account attribution or owner and account context.

- Android system properties
  `/system/build.prop`
- User / system configuration
  `/data/system/`

  `/data/system/users/`
- Samsung / vendor-specific account and device data
  Examples may include:

  `/data/user_de/0/com.samsung.android.fmm/shared_prefs/`

  `com.sec.pcw.device.xml`

  `/data/system/SimCard.dat`
- Telephony / SIM databases

/data/user_de/0/com.android.providers.telephony/databases/telephony.db

- Account-related artifacts
  Examples may include:

  /data/data/com.google.android.apps.photos/shared_prefs/accounts.xml

Step 2: Determine installed applications and app ownership

These artifacts help determine what applications were installed, how those applications were named and identified, which apps may contain communications, media, or behavioral evidence, which Google account downloaded or purchased an app, and what permissions an app was granted.

- Installed application packages
  /data/app/
- Private application data
  /data/data/<Application ID>/

  /data/user/<#>/<Application ID>/

  /data/user_de/<#>/<Application ID>/
- Examples:
  /data/data/com.whatsapp/

  /data/data/com.facebook.katana/

  /data/data/com.tinder/
- External / shared app storage
  /data/media/<user>/Android/data/
- Package-management records
  /data/system/packages.xml
- Google Play metadata
  /data/data/com.android.vending/databases/localappstate.db

Step 3: Reconstruct communications activity

These artifacts help determine messages sent and received, timestamps of communications, contacts and relationships between users, incoming, outgoing, and missed calls, and whether third-party communication apps were used.

- SMS / MMS messages

/data/data/com.android.providers.telephony/databases/mmssms.db

- Telephony provider data
  /data/data/com.android.providers.telephony/databases/
- Contacts and call logs
  /data/data/com.android.providers.contacts/databases/contacts2.db

  /data/data/com.android.providers.contacts/databases/calllog.db
- Third-party messaging apps
  Typically within the app's private data directory:

  /data/data/<Application ID>/
- Examples:
  /data/data/com.whatsapp/

  /data/data/org.thoughtcrime.securesms/

  /data/data/org.telegram.messenger/

Step 4: Examine browser and internet activity

These artifacts help determine websites visited, searches performed, downloaded files, browser-related timestamps, and authenticated sessions or retained cookies.

- Chrome browser artifacts
  /data/data/com.android.chrome/app_chrome/Default/History

  /data/data/com.android.chrome/app_chrome/Default/Cookies
- Samsung Internet or other browsers
  Typically under their app-specific directories, for example:

  /data/data/com.sec.android.app.sbrowser/

  /data/data/org.mozilla.firefox/
- Download manager
  /data/data/com.android.providers.downloads/databases/downloads.db

Step 5: Identify photos, videos, screenshots, and user files

These artifacts help determine when photos or videos were created, whether an image was a camera photo, screenshot, or app-saved file, what files were downloaded or stored on the device, what media content was viewed (even if later deleted), and possible EXIF timestamps and GPS coordinates.

- Camera / screenshot / media directories
  /data/media/<user>/DCIM/

  /data/media/<user>/Pictures/

  /data/media/<user>/Movies/

  /data/media/<user>/Download/

  Common subdirectories include:

  /data/media/0/DCIM/Camera/

  /data/media/0/DCIM/Screenshots/

- Android media database
  /data/data/com.android.providers.media/databases/external.db

- Gallery / media caches
  Examples include:

  /data/media/0/Pictures/.thumbnails/

  /data/data/com.sec.android.gallery3d/cache/

- App-specific image caches
  Common Glide cache pattern:

  /data/data/<App ID>/cache/image_manager_disk_cache/

Step 6: Determine location activity and movement

These artifacts help determine likely device movement patterns, app-related location activity, where photos were taken, and whether the device was associated with specific places or routes.

- Google Play Services / location-related artifacts
  /data/data/com.google.android.gms/

- Mapping and app-based location artifacts
  Within specific app directories, depending on the apps installed

- Media EXIF location data
  Embedded within photos stored at:

  /data/media/0/DCIM/

`/data/media/0/Pictures/`

Step 7: Examine wireless and network artifacts

These artifacts help determine what Wi-Fi networks the device connected to, network names and possible location context, wireless network credentials in some cases, Bluetooth-paired devices and their identifiers, and carrier and SIM/network context.

- Wi-Fi configuration
  `/data/misc/wifi/WifiConfigStore.xml`

  `/data/misc/wifi/wpa_supplicant.conf`

  `/data/misc/apexdata/com.android.wifi/`
- Bluetooth artifacts
  `/data/misc/bluedroid/bt_config.conf`

  `/data/misc/bluedroid/bt_config.bak`
- Telephony/carrier context
  `/data/user_de/0/com.android.providers.telephony/databases/telephony.db`

Step 8: Examine system, usage, and diagnostic artifacts

These artifacts help determine app usage and interaction patterns, timestamps associated with app foreground and background changes, crash and error context, and unusual device behavior or instability.

- System logs / dropbox
  `/data/system/dropbox/`
- Digital Wellbeing
  Common Google version:

  `/data/data/com.google.android.apps.wellbeing/databases/`
- Samsung example:
  `/data/data/com.samsung.android.forest/databases/dwbCommon.db`

Step 9: Examine downloads, documents, and transferred files

These artifacts help determine what files were downloaded, download timestamps, possible source URLs, and whether a file originated from a browser, an app, or a transfer event.

- Downloads directory

/data/media/0/Download/

- Download manager database
  /data/data/com.android.providers.downloads/databases/downloads.db

- Shared app storage
  /data/media/0/Android/data/

Memory (RAM)

The following steps outline a practical approach to analyzing system memory by focusing on volatile artifacts that can reveal active processes, user activity, and signs of malicious behavior at the time of capture (based on Volatility 3 commands).

Step 1: Identify the operating system and memory-image context

These artifacts help determine whether the memory image loaded correctly, which operating system the image represents, the kernel or build context needed for later parsing, the system time at acquisition for timeline correlation, and whether findings should align with known disk artifacts from the same host.

- Windows memory
  windows.info

- Linux memory
  linux.info

Step 2: Identify running processes and process relationships

These artifacts help determine what processes were active at capture time, which process launched another process, whether hidden or unlinked processes may exist, whether process timing aligns with user or attacker activity, and whether suspicious process trees or naming patterns exist.

- Windows memory
  windows.pslist

  windows.psscan

  windows.pstree

  windows.malware.psxview

- Linux memory
  linux.pslist

```
linux.pstree
```

Step 3: Determine user context and execution identity

These artifacts help determine which user account launched a process, whether a process was interactive, service-based, or system-level, whether the activity belongs to a normal user, admin, or privileged daemon, and whether a suspicious process ran under expected or unexpected credentials.

- Windows memory

  ```
  windows.getsids
  windows.sessions
  ```

- Linux memory

  ```
  linux.pslist
  linux.pstree
  ```

Step 4: Determine how a process was launched

These artifacts help determine whether a process was launched with suspicious flags, whether it was started by a service or background mechanism, whether encoded or hidden command execution occurred, and whether shell-based attacker activity occurred.

- Windows memory

  ```
  windows.cmdline
  windows.svcscan
  ```

- Linux memory

  ```
  linux.pslist
  linux.pstree
  ```

Step 5: Examine loaded modules, DLLs, and libraries

These artifacts help determine what drivers or kernel modules were loaded, whether suspicious DLLs or drivers were present, whether libraries were loaded from unusual paths, whether a DLL or module may have been injected or unlinked, and whether rootkit-like behavior is present.

- Windows memory

  ```
  windows.modules
  windows.modscan
  ```

`windows.dlllist`

`windows.malware.ldrmodules`

- Linux memory
  `linux.lsmod`

Step 6: Examine memory regions and look for injected code

These artifacts help determine whether executable code exists only in memory, whether a process contains suspicious private executable regions, whether injected code is present, and whether malware unpacked itself into memory rather than disk.

- Windows memory
  `windows.vadinfo`

  `windows.malware.malfind`

- Linux memory
  Useful analysis areas include suspicious mapped memory regions, executable anonymous mappings, and memory maps associated with suspicious processes

Step 7: Examine file handles, open objects, and in-memory file references

These artifacts help determine what files a process was interacting with, whether suspicious files were open or recently referenced, whether deleted or transient files may still be recoverable from memory, and whether mutex objects linked to malware families were present.

- Windows memory
  `windows.handles`

  `windows.filescan`

  `windows.dumpfiles`

- Linux memory
  Useful pivots include open-file references, process-associated file paths, and recovered strings showing temp paths/scripts/user files

Step 8: Examine network connections and listening services

These artifacts help determine what network connections existed at capture time, which processes owned those connections, whether suspicious remote systems were contacted, whether the system was listening on unexpected ports, and whether remote access or command-and-control traffic may have occurred.

- Windows memory
  `windows.netscan`

  `windows.netstat`
- Linux memory
  Useful plugins may include Linux socket/network scans depending on the framework version and support, along with process correlation

Step 9: Recover user artifacts from memory

These artifacts help determine what the user may have been viewing or typing, what files or paths were in use, whether browser or document activity existed only in memory, whether encryption keys or credentials were present, and whether mounted removable media or decrypted volumes were in use.

- Common tools
  - bstrings
  - Bulk Extractor
  - YARA
  - Volatility string/file extraction methods
- Windows and Linux memory
  Search for URLs, usernames, home/profile paths, mounted-volume paths, browser activity remnants, and encryption-related patterns

Other Books You May Enjoy

If you enjoyed this book, you may be interested in these other books by Packt:

SOC Analyst Career Guide

Kyler Kent

ISBN: 9781835467466

- Explore security operations and see how it fits into an overall business
- Discover the key functions and real-world duties of a SOC analyst
- Understand and master the tools of the trade, including SIEM
- Develop a home lab with an operational SIEM and EDR solution
- Create a compelling portfolio to impress prospective employers
- Perfect your interviewing skills and land a SOC analyst job

Cybersecurity Strategy for the AI-Driven Era

Tim Rains

ISBN: 9781806028573

- Identify common enterprise intrusion paths and reduce initial compromise
- Distinguish credible threat intelligence from industry noise
- Improve vulnerability management while reducing risk and cost
- Assess malware, ransomware, and internet-based attack techniques
- Secure APIs and reduce exposure from trusted enterprise tools
- Evaluate Zero Trust and attack-centric security strategies
- Apply cloud, resilience, and AI capabilities to improve security outcomes
- How governments request data and how enterprises manage access, risk, and oversight

Packt is searching for authors like you

If you're interested in becoming an author for Packt, please visit `authors.packtpub.com` and apply today. We have worked with thousands of developers and tech professionals, just like you, to help them share their insight with the global tech community. You can make a general application, apply for a specific hot topic that we are recruiting an author for, or submit your own idea.

Share your thoughts

Now you've finished *Digital Forensics Cookbook*, we'd love to hear your thoughts! Scan the QR code below to go straight to the Amazon review page for this book and share your feedback or leave a review on the site that you purchased it from.

https://packt.link/r/1805127551

Your review is important to us and the tech community and will help us make sure we're delivering excellent quality content.

Index

Symbols

J

K

L

M

N

O

P

R

S

www.ingramcontent.com/pod-product-compliance
Lightning Source LLC
Chambersburg PA
CBHW080611090426
42761CB00011B/111
9781805127550